W9-AGZ-639

PSYCHOLINGUISTICS

PSYCHOLINGUISTICS

Jean Berko Gleason
Boston University

Nan Bernstein Ratner
University of Maryland

HARCOURT BRACE COLLEGE PUBLISHERS

Fort Worth   Philadelphia   San Diego   New York   Orlando   Austin   San Antonio
Toronto   Montreal   London   Sydney   Tokyo

Editor in Chief	Ted Buchholz
Acquisitions Editor	Christina N. Oldham
Senior Project Editor	Steve Welch
Senior Production Manager	Kathleen Ferguson
Book Designer	Melinda Huff
Photo Editor	Steven Lunetta/Greg Meadors

We dedicate this book to our husbands, our children, and our teachers.

Requests for permission to make copies of any part of this work should be mailed to: Permissions Department, Harcourt Brace & Company, 8th Floor, Orlando, Florida 32887.

Address for Editorial Correspondence: Harcourt Brace College Publishers, 301 Commerce Street, Suite 3700, Fort Worth, TX 76102.

Address for Orders: Harcourt Brace & Company, 6277 Sea Harbor Drive, Orlando, FL 32887. 1-800-782-4479, or 1-800-433-0001 (in Florida).

Printed in the United States of America

Library of Congress Catalog Card Number: 92-81851

ISBN: 0-03-055964-2

3 4 5 6 7 8 9 0 1 2   039   9 8 7 6 5 4 3 2

Preface

In preparing this book, our aim has been to create a current and introductory level text to acquaint readers with the core concepts and range of topics that constitute the discipline of psycholinguistics. Coursework in the psychology of language has historically been an upper-level or graduate school undertaking, but there are now increasing enrollments by undergraduates at earlier points in their curriculum. Textbooks written specifically for this group of students are, unfortunately, uncommon.

As a young field undergoing dynamic and rapid growth and subspecialization, psycholinguistics has become a formidable topic area for only one or two authors to cover in a timely and authoritative fashion. We were fortunate to be able to enlist researchers with expertise in the topics chosen for inclusion in this text to write chapters in their own specialties. Each author was challenged to provide a contemporary chapter that would introduce students without prior background in linguistics or cognitive psychology to the basic issues of concern to psycholinguists working in that subdiscipline. Each chapter provides a historical perspective on the major questions that confront researchers working in the area, and carefully explains the research methodology used to obtain answers to such questions. Each chapter also contains models that have been developed to explain such major psycholinguistic functions as speech perception, lexical processing, sentence processing, spoken discourse processing, speech production, first language acquisition, second language acquisition, and reading.

The scope of chapters was chosen to reflect the wide range of topics considered as domains within psycholinguistic inquiry, including some topics often given little or no coverage in introductory texts; these include neurolinguistics, speech perception, reading, and second language acquisition. Within chapters, our intent was to develop an understanding of the major issues confronting researchers in the field, rather than an exhaustive summary of work to date. Thus, the text is introductory in intent and is meant to begin—rather than end—a student's study of the psychology of language.

The text is accompanied by an instructor's manual and stimulus tape with examples of some of the phenomena and research paradigms discussed in the chapters.

In the course of editing this book, we have become indebted to a very large number of people. Our first thanks go to the colleagues who contributed chapters to this volume. Active researchers with many competing time demands, each provided us with an excellent and up-to-date manuscript. We are also very grateful to the staff at Harcourt Brace Jovanovich, particularly to Christina Oldham, Carol Jaramillo, Steve Welch, Kathleen Ferguson, and Melinda Huff.

We thank also Mary Perry at Boston University and Mary Donaldson and Beth Coon at the University of Maryland, who have consistently helped us in myriad ways, large and small, as did Song Zhao and Matt Piermarini of the University of Maryland BSOS computer lab.

For helpful comments and suggestions for improvement, we thank John Bonvillian, University of Virginia, Martha Burton, The Pennsylvania State University, Gail McKoon, Northwestern University, Ken Kallio, The State University of New York at Geneseo, Morton Ann Gernsbacher, University of Oregon, Shari R. Speer, Northeastern University, Susan Garnsey, University of Illinois at Urbana-Champaign, Janet Nicol, University of Arizona, Chuck Clifton, University of Massachusetts at Amherst, Pat Carroll, University of Texas at Austin, and Sarah Wayland, Northeastern University.

Contents

CHAPTER 4

WORDS AND MEANING: FROM PRIMITIVES
TO COMPLEX ORGANIZATION

Kathy Hirsh-Pasek   Lauretta M. Reeves   Roberta Golinkoff

CHAPTER 5

SENTENCE PROCESSING

Arthur Wingfield

————

CHAPTER 8

LANGUAGE DEVELOPMENT IN CHILDREN

Jean Berko Gleason   Nan Bernstein Ratner

An Introduction to Psycholinguistics: What do Language Users Know?

Nan Bernstein Ratner
University of Maryland at College Park

Jean Berko Gleason
Boston University

> *L*anguage is the extended arm . . . by which our race has managed nature
> and built cooperative societies. It is material as well as instrument, a vicarious
> world in which anything can be arranged through verbal plans, then
> transferred to reality.
>
> (Bolinger, 1980; 188)

Introduction

Language is the thread that connects the experiences of our lives, giving us access to the society of others, and allowing others to understand our thoughts, needs, and desires. Communication is so basic to our existence that life without words is difficult to envision.

Because speaking, listening, reading, and writing are such fundamental aspects of our daily lives, they sometimes seem to be mundane skills. Accomplished easily and effortlessly, language use guides us through our day. It facilitates our relationships with others and helps us appreciate world events and the arts and sciences. However, as this book will demonstrate, even the simplest forms of language use are based on very complicated processes. When we thank a friend by saying, "I really appreciate your help on this project," what processes underlie our choice of words and the way we combine them? How does our thought—in this case, a sense of gratitude—become encoded into a message? Similarly, when we hear the words, "Be careful, that chair is a little wobbly," how do we determine what the message means and what it implies about the safety of sitting in that particular spot? From the speaker's thought to her message, from her words to her listener's understanding, the communicative function entails multiple stages of formulation, execution, and decoding. It is an easy and natural skill, but one that is very difficult to explain fully or to describe.

In this chapter, we begin by outlining the domain of psycholinguistic inquiry. What is the discipline known as psycholinguistics? What do psycholinguists study? Our brief introductory descriptions will preview the more detailed coverage given to major issues in psycholinguistics found in Chapters 2 through 10.

We will next establish what we mean when we talk about the use, comprehension, or learning of language. What exactly is a language? All human languages share important formal properties: they are structured, symbolic systems that distinguish them from animal communication systems. Further, every human language has arbitrary conventions that govern proper use of its sound system (**phonology**), rules of word formation and interpretation (**morphology and semantics**), sentence formation (**syntax**), and socially appropriate linguistic behavior (**pragmatics**).

After drawing a sketch of the typical language user's knowledge, we will discuss why psycholinguists must often resort to complex experimental designs to understand how people process and produce language. Our own **metalinguistic** abilities, the ability to reflect on what we know about language, and how we accomplish its use successfully, are extremely limited.

This text is written in English, and most of our tangible discussions about language processing will use examples that illustrate how English is understood and produced. But clearly, English is just one of the world's many languages, and there are many important variations among languages that should be accommodated within general models of language processing. We will briefly address this issue and explore its ramifications both in this chapter as well as in later ones. The differences, for example, between oral and gestural (or signed) languages have extremely important implications for theories of language processing, production, and acquisition. In the same vein, differences between oral language processing and the acts of reading or writing must be accommodated within models of language use and production.

Finally, we will review psycholinguistics' recent evolution as a discipline. Although many of the questions posed by psycholinguists have concerned scientists and philosophers for almost as long as people have been talking and listening, the field of inquiry that we call psycholinguistics is of very recent origin. We will trace its roots in psychology and linguistics, as well as its early development.

What is psycholinguistics?

The domain of psycholinguistic inquiry

Linguistics is the discipline that describes the structure of language, including its grammar, sound system, and vocabulary. The field of **psycholinguistics**, or the **psychology of language**, is concerned with discovering the psychological processes that make it possible for humans to acquire and use language. Conventionally, psycholinguistics addresses three major concerns (Clark & Clark, 1977; Tannenhaus, 1989):

> *How people understand spoken and written language* This is a broad area of investigation involving scrutiny of the **comprehension process** at many levels, including investigation of how speech signals are interpreted by listeners (**speech perception**, discussed in Chapter 3), how the meanings of words are determined (**lexical access**, Chapter 4), how the grammatical structure of sentences is analyzed to obtain larger units of meaning (**sentence processing**, Chapter 5), and how longer conversations or text are appropriately evaluated (**discourse**, Chapter 6). Concerns specifically relevant to how written language is processed are also part of this domain, and are discussed in Chapter 9.

> *How people produce language (speech production)* The chapters that follow suggest that it is somewhat easier to evaluate the comprehension process than the production process. We can analyze patterns of accuracy and error, response time, and other behaviors to arrive at a rough estimate of how listeners evaluate certain controlled language stimuli. However, it is more difficult to gain insight into how concepts are put into linguistic

form; the process is largely hidden from observation, and a speaker's verbal expressions, even when confronted with rather controlled eliciting stimuli, vary considerably. As Chapter 7 will indicate, the major sources of information regarding the probable nature of the speech production process are garnered from speakers' mistakes (**speech errors** or **false starts**) and from breaks in the ongoing rhythm of connected speech (**hesitation** and **pausal phenomena**, or speech **disfluencies**).

How language is acquired The major focus in this domain has been on the acquisition of a first language by children (**developmental psycholinguistics**), which is covered in detail in Chapter 8 of this volume, although Chapter 10 surveys what is known about the process of acquiring subsequent languages (foreign language learning). Developmental psycholinguistics has become, by itself, a formidably large discipline, with a wide array of journals, texts, and monographs specifically addressed to this issue.

In addition to these areas of inquiry, the search for the neurological bases of human language functioning continues. Where do language formulation and under-standing reside in the brain? What anatomical structures underlie normal develop-ment and use of the full range of language skills? **Neurolinguistics** addresses the **anatomical** and **physiological correlates** of language behaviors. As Chapter 2 demonstrates, great strides have been made in identifying particular areas of the human brain that are associated with specific linguistic abilities.

The ultimate goal of psycholinguistic inquiry is of course to develop an inte-grated account of how competent language understanding and use occur and how they are acquired so rapidly by young children. However, as we shall see, under-standing this process is a formidable goal that has not yet been met. There are many reasons for this. Language is a complex system of behavior, as the next sections describe. Additionally, the research tools and techniques best used to study particu-lar language skills do not lend themselves readily to the full array of skills found in communicative interactions. For example, methods used to investigate the compre-hension of certain syntactic structures by mature adult listeners are likely to be inap-propriate for the study of language understanding in very young children, or for the process of speech production by either adults or children. The best models of human language capacity make use of converging evidence from adult comprehension and production and from child language acquisition.

Language

. . . *the structure of language has aroused man's curiosity for all recorded time. The reason?—because it is not obvious. Meeting a stranger, one can make a fair guess at the meanings of his gestures and facial expressions. . . . But the codification of language creates a sort of mystery where guessing is of little use.*
(Bolinger, 1981; 17)

What is language?

A baby cries because she is hungry. A bee performs its "waggle dance" to inform the others from the hive that nectar can be found in a particular location. A dog barks to be let out. A parakeet says, "Pretty bird!" as he views himself in the mirror. A child says, "I hate broccoli, and I won't eat it."

Which of these represents the use of language? Certainly each example communicates a message to those who receive it. But most of us would agree that only the last example truly exemplifies the use of language. What distinguishes language from these other communicative acts?

First, language is **hierarchically structured**. By this, we mean that the message is divisible into smaller units of analysis. The child's utterance is a sentence that contains smaller discrete elements such as words and sounds, and these can be **recombined** to make other utterances (e.g., "I won't eat broccoli. I hate it.") All languages are characterized by such structural properties. Conversely, it is difficult to analyze the "substructure" of infant or animal cries.

While some substructure may appear to exist in the bee's dance and the bird's replication of human speech, such messages lack the **infinite creativity** of human

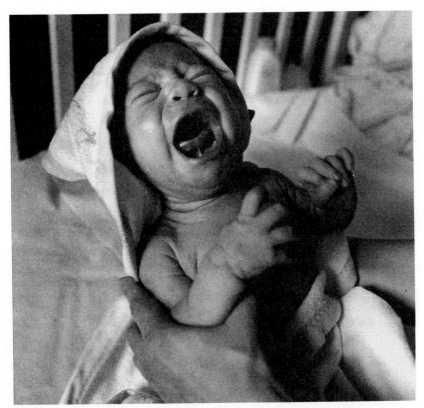

Crying precedes intentional communication and sends general messages that the listener may have trouble interpreting.

Bees can tell one another the direction of a nectar source, but their repertoire of messages is limited.

language. Competent language users are able to produce and understand a virtually unlimited number of well-formed sentences in their language. Such is not the case (as far as we can tell) with animal languages. The parakeet is not free to discuss the weather with you, nor can he even paraphrase his message and say, "I'm a pretty bird," "You're not a bird," etc. While the bee is very good at directing its fellow bees to nectar, it is incapable of warning them that an irate homeowner is coming after them with a can of insecticide. While it may (or may not) possess such knowledge, it lacks a sufficiently rich system of symbols and rules for their combination to allow transmission of a large variety of concepts.

The structural properties of any language include rules for using it properly; thus we call language a **rule-governed** system of behavior. There is no right or wrong way to bark or cry (though some versions may be more annoying than others). Conversely, the rules of English specify that the child in our example may *not* say, "Broccoli I like not, eat and it won't I." English (like other languages) has conventions for knowing what words must be included and for ordering those words in sentences. These rules are quite **arbitrary** in nature; there is no real reason why English should require the particular grammatical conventions it does. For example, English is considered to have a basic word order in which subjects precede verbs, and objects follow verbs (what is typically called S-V-O word order), although not all English sentences conform to this ordering. However, the tendency to put nouns before verbs in English sentences is no more "logical" than an insistence that it should be the verb that comes first, followed by the noun, as happens to be the case in Arabic. Furthermore, the words used to describe items, actions, and attributes in any language are

A bark can mean "I'm hungry" or "Let me out," depending on the context.

also arbitrary. There is no good reason why a *tree* should be called "tree," and of course in languages other than English, it is not. The words of a language are **symbols**, substituting one thing (in this case, the string of sounds in the word "tree") for another (the concept of a tall plant with branches, bark, and leaves). Both the grammar and vocabulary of any language represent arbitrary conventions that the users of a language agree to abide by, although languages do not vary infinitely; there appear to be constraints on the nature of possible linguistic rules that reflect the properties of the human mind (Chomsky, 1981). Likewise, all languages possess syntactic categories, such as *noun* and *verb* (Greenberg, 1963). Properties shared by all languages are called linguistic **universals**.

These characteristics of language give it many other properties not shared by animal communication or infant cries. When both speaker and hearer (or writer and reader) share the same rule system, message transmission can be not only creative, but usually **unambiguous**, its meaning clear. What the child is telling his parents is quite explicit; there is not much doubt about the meaning of his utterance, though his parents may attempt to change his mind. But an infant's parents will say, "I wonder what's wrong with the baby?" and try checking her diaper, burping her, or offering a bottle until they determine the meaning of her message, or at least until she

Some birds can mimic human speech, but they cannot generate novel utterances.

Even very young children can use language to express their desires and opinions effectively.

stops crying. The same is true for the dog, whose bark may not clearly inform its owner whether he needs to go out, needs more water, or sees a squirrel in the backyard. Language also allows us to talk about **displaced**, or absent, concepts. We can converse about the upcoming election without having the candidates present; we can discuss purchasing a new sofa without physically looking at one. In this regard, human language is quite different from animal communication systems, whose communicative behaviors require elicitation by environmental stimuli.

Is language species-specific?

No matter how eloquently a dog may bark, he cannot tell you that his parents were poor but honest.

(Bertrand Russell)

These (primate) studies have produced an uproar in intellectual and linguistic circles. They seem to call into question our long-held faith that language is a distinctly human function.

(*New York Times* Book Review of Ann Premack's *Why chimps can read* [1976])

In some ill-considered popularizations of interesting current research, it is virtually argued that higher apes have the capacity for language, but have never put it to use—a remarkable biological miracle . . . , rather like discovering that some animal has wings but has never thought to fly.

(Noam Chomsky, 1975; 40)

One of the other properties attributed to language is that it is uniquely a human behavior. Virtually all human beings spontaneously acquire a language, without overt instruction, and in a relatively short period of time during childhood, unless they possess handicapping conditions. Researchers have not yet isolated any natural form of animal communication that embodies all of the features of language we have discussed. They have probed the communicative systems of many animals, searching for the linguistic properties that define human language. While bees, birds, whales, dolphins, and nonhuman primates are capable of fairly sophisticated message exchanges (Akmajian, Demers & Harnish, 1984; Demers, 1989), their capacities fall short of those of young children.

There have been attempts to teach human language to animals, particularly primates. It is true that some of the signing apes (Terrace, 1979; Rumbaugh, 1977) are able to produce brief utterances that relate to their current intents (e.g., "Tickle Nim"), but, as Demers (1989) notes, it is the unbounded productivity of new and varying messages so characteristic of human language activity that is missing from all known animal communication systems. Animal communication is also very context or stimulus dependent; vocalizations are likely to be elicited under very narrowly specified conditions. Though not a focus of this text, much remains to be learned from the study of animal languages and attempts to teach human language to primates

(Scanlon, Savage-Rumbaugh, & Rumbaugh, 1982). However, Bolinger and Sears (1981) note, "No one knows yet how far the great apes may progress in communicating . . . using human sign language, but for all their skill in using it, they did not invent it." Language in all its variety and creativity is a uniquely human phenomenon.

Distinguishing between language and speech

Although some authors say that "language is sound" (Dinneen, 1967) or that "the medium of language is sound" (Bolinger & Sears, 1981), this is not necessarily true. Most of the world's languages *are* spoken or oral, and for most individuals speaking precedes and is of greater importance than reading or writing. However, there are a number of human languages that are **signed** or gestural. These languages, of which **American Sign Language (ASL)** is an example, have the same basic linguistic features found in oral human languages. Thus, like spoken languages, they are *rule-governed, arbitrary systems of communication*, with *hierarchical substructuring*, capable of *infinite creativity*, and *spontaneously acquired* by infants exposed to them.

For many discussions in this book, it will be extremely important to distinguish **language** from **speech**, its spoken form. In some chapters we will specifically be concerned with how people decode the sounds of language; in others we will investigate how people respond to written language. In many cases, we will draw parallels

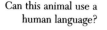
Can this animal use a human language?

between what is known about oral language comprehension and production, and the processing of sign languages.

What speakers and listeners know: A brief survey of linguistics

Linguistics . . . is or are the scientific study of language. . . .
(Waugh, cited in Smith, 1989)

Linguistics is the study of language. As a discipline, its primary concern is the **structure** of a particular language, or of languages in general. By structure, we mean the rules for the formation of acceptable utterances of the language. Linguists take as their data what people say and what people find acceptable in language use. They work from actual language examples and individual intuitions about whether such examples are well formed to develop general accounts of the grammar of a language. In this sense, linguistics is **descriptive**, rather than **prescriptive**. That is, linguists attempt to account for what we actually say, and what we find acceptable or poorly formed, rather than formulate language rules that we all must live by. When we say "acceptable" or "well formed" here we mean that speakers agree that a particular utterance can indeed be said in a particular language, and we make no judgment about whether or not it *should* be said. Many of our experiences in English grammar classes were of the prescriptive sort, in which we were cautioned about "dangling participles"; the goal of linguistics is not to ensure that people follow a standard set of rules in speaking, but rather to develop rational models to explain the language that people actually use and appreciate as well formed.

In the next sections, we will briefly survey the structural properties of human languages, properties that must be accounted for in eventually understanding how language is used and acquired. No prior exposure to linguistic terminology will be assumed. Additionally, we will concentrate on describing the properties of language, rather than enumerating specific linguistic theories that have been developed to most efficiently capture why sentences in any given language look the way they do. The role of linguistic theories in psycholinguistic research will be discussed in later sections of this chapter and text.

Levels of language analysis

If a psycholinguist wishes to understand how a sentence such as *"How do people communicate with one another?"* is processed, he or she must first acknowledge that understanding it is dependent upon a number of smaller tasks. The **sounds** of the message must be isolated and labeled. The **words** must be identified and associated with their meanings. The **grammatical structure** of the message must be analyzed sufficiently to determine the roles played by each word. The resulting **interpretation** of the message must be evaluated in light of past discussion and the current context. Only then can the utterance be considered "understood."

Linguists, philosophers, and psychologists have long appreciated that language is a complex system that can be considered at multiple levels of analysis. Every human language may be analyzed in terms of its **phonology** (sound system), **morphology** (rules for word formation), **lexicon** (vocabulary), **syntax** (rules for combining words into grammatically acceptable sequences), **semantics** (conventions for deriving the meanings of words and sentences), and **pragmatics** (rules for appropriate social use and interpretation of language in context). The goal of linguists is to develop descriptions of a language that capture its characteristics at each of these levels. Psycholinguists, in turn, seek to determine whether these levels or units of analysis are represented in the actual process of producing or understanding various forms of language. Some call this endeavor the search for the **psychological reality** of linguistic descriptions.

One may more readily appreciate the complex interaction of these systems by considering efforts to "get by" in a language we do not know. Anyone who has attempted to function in a foreign culture using an English–foreign language dictionary can appreciate how little is possible when all that is available is a list of words and their meanings. Below we shall examine some of the many specific abilities that underlie competent use of language. As we do, it may become evident that, while using and understanding language is a relatively quick and easy task for most of us, many aspects of our linguistic knowledge are subconscious in nature.

Phonology

The words of a language are divisible into sound sequences, and part of language knowledge is an understanding of the particular sounds used in a language, as well as the rules for their combination. There are a great number of speech sounds available to the world's languages. Any single language employs a subset of these sounds, usually around 23 consonants and 9 vowels, though there is substantial diversity in the world's languages, with numbers of consonants in a given language ranging between 6 and 95 and numbers of vowels ranging between 3 and 46 (Maddieson, 1984). The distinctive sounds used by a language are its **phonemes**. Phonemes are contrastive; changing from one to another within a word produces either a change in meaning or a non-word. For example, the /p/ in *pit* serves to contrast *pit* from other English words, such as *bit, sit,* and *kit,* which are similar in all respects except that they begin with different English phonemes. Most of us are familiar with the experience of trying to learn a second language whose **phonemic inventory** (sounds used by the language) differs from our own. For example, pronunciation of the French word *rue* ("street"), or German name *Bach* confronts English speakers with the need to produce phonemes that do not exist in their language. Thus, a speaker of a language needs to be able to produce all the meaningful sound contrasts of that language. The phonemic inventory of English is provided in Figure 1.1, while Figure 1.2 also provides the respective inventories of Hindi and Hawaiian for your comparison. English makes use of more phonemic contrasts than Hawaiian, but fewer than Hindi.

English									
Consonants **Place of articulation**	Bilabial	Labio-dental	Dental	Dental/alveolar	Alveolar	Palatal	Velar	Glottal	Labio-velar
Voiceless (vl) plosive	P			t			k		
Voiced (vd) plosive	b			d			g		
vl. sibilent affricate						tʃ			
vd. sibilent affricate						d₃			
vl. nonsibilent fricative		f	θ					h	
vd. nonsibilent fricative		v	ð						
vl. sibilent fricative					s	ʃ			
vd. sibilent fricative					z	3			
Voiced nasal	m			n			ŋ		
vd. lateral approximant				l,r					
vd. central approximant							j		w

Manner of articulation (vertical label on left side of table)

Vowels	Front		Back
high	i		u
	I		U
mid	e	ə	o
low	ɛ æ	ʌ	ɔ a

Figure 1.1

The phonemic inventory of English

The study of how the sounds of a language are physically articulated is known as **articulatory phonetics** and will be explored in some detail in Chapter 3. However, there is more to understanding the sound system of a language than knowing how to produce and recognize individual sounds. The process of learning which sounds can be used to signal changes of meaning in a given language also implies at some level learning which sound contrasts are *not* meaningful. For example, English contains the phoneme /p/, which contrasts meaningfully with other English sounds. Thus, words such as *pit* and *bit* demonstrate that /p/ functions to differentiate minimally different sound sequences from one another. But consider the English words *pot* and

Hawaiian Consonants

	Bilabial	Dental/alveolar	Velar	Glottal	Variable place	Labial-velar
Voiceless plosive	p		k	ʔ		
Vl. nonsibilant fric.					h	
Voiced nasal	m	"n"				
Vd. lateral approx.		"l"				
Vd. central approx.						w

Vowels

High	i		u
Higher mid			"o"
Lower mid	ε		
Low		a	

Hindi-Urdu Consonants

	Bilabial	Labio-dental	Dental	Dental/alveolar	Palato-alveolar	Retroflex	Palatal	Velar	Uvular	Glottal	Variable place
Voiceless plosive	p		t̪			ʈ		k	q²	ʔ²	
Vl. aspirated plosive	pʰ		t̪ʰ			ʈʰ		kʰ			
Voiced plosive	b		d̪			ɖ		g			
Breathy vd. plosive	b:		d̪:			ɖ:		g:			
Vl. sibilant affricate					tʃ						
Vl. asp. sib. affricate					tʃʰ						
Vd. sibilant affricate					dʒ						
Breathy vd. sib. affricate					d:ʒ						
Vl. nonsib. fricative		f²							χ²		
Vd. nonsib. fricative									ʁ²	ɦ	
Vl. sibilant fricative				"s"	ʃ²						
Vd. sibilant fricative				"z"²	ʒ²						
Voiced nasal	m					ɳ					
Breathy vd. nasal	m:					ɳ:					
Voiced trill				"r"							
Voiced flap						ɽ²					
Vd. lateral approximant				"l"							
Breathy vd. lat. approximant				"l":							
Vd. central approximant	β						j				

Vowels

	Long oral		Short oral		
High	i:	u:	ɪ	ʊ	ɑ
Higher mid	e:	o:	ə		
Lower mid			ɜ		
Low	a:		a		

	Long nasalized		Short nasalized		
High	ĩ:	ũ:	ĩ	ũ	ɑ̃
Higher mid	ẽ:	õ:	ə̃		
Lower mid			ɜ̃		
Low	ã:		ã		

Diphthongs

əe
oɪ
ə̃ẽ
õɪ

Figure 1.2

spot. Although it is not obvious to English speakers, the /p/ sounds in these two words are not produced in a similar way. More force is used and there is a resulting puff of air (**aspiration**) when we say *pot*. The /p/ of *spot* is produced without aspiration—it is **unaspirated**. Yet this articulatory difference does not lead to a phonemic contrast. To a speaker of English, "a /p/ is a /p/", even though, as Chapter 3 illustrates, there are very real **acoustical** (sound) differences between different versions. However, it is important to note that some languages create a meaningful contrast out of such differences in articulation. Hindi treats sounds similar to these two variants ([p] and [pʰ]) as two distinct phonemes, and there are words in Hindi such as *phalam* "fruit" and *palam* "bridge."[1] Most English speakers would find it difficult to hear (and perhaps produce) this distinction; their experience with English has taught them to ignore variations in production of /p/, as long as such variations do not cross a perceptual boundary and sound like other phonemes of English.

Next, consider the dilemma of a Chinese speaker learning English. English contains the phonemes /r/ and /l/, which share certain acoustic properties; Chinese has only /l/. The Chinese speaker may find it difficult both to distinguish and produce /r/, and use the well-learned native /l/ for both sounds. The French, Spanish, or Italian speaker whose language contains /i/ as in *heat*, but not /I/ as in *hit* may find production of these different words of English difficult, saying /hit/ for both words (usually written "I heet him" for "I hit him.")

As a final example, we might assume that we are trying to instruct a computer to recognize speech, so that we might talk to it, rather than type our communications. Consider the case of the common English phoneme /t/. What does it sound like? Most of us have a canonical or idealized notion of what /t/ sounds like. But consider the sentence "Tom Burton tried to steal a butter plate." There are a number of /t/ variants in this phrase, and they are not produced in an identical fashion at all. The **allophones** (pronunciation variants) of /t/ include the **aspirated** initial /t/ of *Tom*. They also include the **glottalized stop** usually found when /t/ lies between /ər/ and syllabic /n/ as in *Burton*, and the **palatalized** /t/ that usually results when /t/ precedes /r/ (as in *tried*). The words *tried to* illustrate the elongated single phoneme that may occur when /t/ is next to another /t/ or to /d/. In *steal* we find the unaspirated /t/ that occurs when /t/ is preceded by other sounds, rather than in initial position. The /t/ in *butter* is characterized by the quick, "flapped" production that tends to occur when /t/ lies between a vowel and /ər/. Finally, as the last sound in *plate*, we come to the **unreleased** or **checked** version of /t/ that typically is found when /t/ is the final sound in an utterance. Note how the sound seems to be only partially pronounced as the sentence ends. These numerous variants of /t/ cause the competent speaker or listener of English little trouble. However, the computer has every reason to assume that they represent seven distinct phonemes, since they differ acoustically, sometimes in fairly major ways. The competent user of English has learned to collapse these distinctions into one phonemic class, and does not randomly produce the

---

[1]Non-phonemic aspects of the pronunciation of sounds are conventionally enclosed in brackets ([ ]) when performing phonetic transcription. Aspiration is non-phonemic in English. Therefore, /pɛt/ is a phonemic description of the word *pet*, while [pʰɛt] is its phonetic description.

allophones in inappropriate contexts (for instance, does not attempt *Tom* with a glottal stop, flap, or unaspirated /t/). A computer must be explicitly instructed in such details of phonological knowledge, a nontrivial task, as Chapter 3 notes.

If we consider the phonemic profiles of the three languages in Figures 1.1 & 1.2, it becomes evident that a speaker of Hindi learning English must, among other things, learn to ignore certain phonemic contrasts found in Hindi but not English, such as the presence or absence of aspiration, while the Hawaiian speaker learning English will have to learn to produce and distinguish a number of phonemes not present in his native language. The processes of acquiring meaningful phonemic contrasts and learning to ignore nonmeaningful contrasts are both essential to the successful use of a language.

Sequences of sounds (phonotactics)

Phonology is more than the repertoire of sounds in a language; it includes rules for their lawful combination into words. Consider the predicament of a contestant on the popular television show *Wheel of Fortune*, who must guess a letter when the following sequence is revealed:

— T R — N —

Some guesses are more likely to be successful than others. Many readers will suggest an S for the first slot, unconsciously mindful that no other initial consonant would be permitted to precede T and R in English, though other languages might permit this. The most common guesses for final position are G, K, and D and E (T is also possible but has already been "guessed"). A common strategy for the middle slot is to see what belongs in the initial and final position and to consider what vowels (note that a vowel is assumed in this case) would result in an English word. Thus, if S is correct in the first slot, and G is the right answer for the last slot, then good guesses for the vowel are I, O, or U; A and E result in a permissible sequence of sounds in English, but not a lexically meaningful solution. Note that a guess of E for the last slot in our example leads to the same dilemma: the sequences *strane, strene, strine, strone,* and *strune* do not mean anything in everyday English, although the phonotactics of English do not prevent these sequences. The rules of English definitely prohibit K from both the initial and medial slots of our example.

The importance of knowing the rules for the combination of sounds (which exist in all languages) extends well beyond ensuring successful competition on game shows or accurate completion of crossword puzzles. As Chapter 3 demonstrates, in ordinary conversation the identity of individual speech sounds is often unclear. Experimental research indicates that listeners are often confronted with the auditory equivalent of our game show example; they hear some of the sounds, but not all, and must "fill in the blanks." The usually effortless and accurate solution to such puzzles is mediated by the listener's knowledge of his phonemic inventory, phonotactic constraints, and lexicon (vocabulary) as well as the context. Chapter 3 explores the complex deployment of these systems in the process of speech perception.

The phonological system of a language also includes rules for the interpretation of **prosody**, or intonation and stress patterns. In English, **prosodic cues** can

Solving this puzzle
requires linguistic
knowledge.

distinguish between grammatical contrasts, such as the difference between statements and questions ("You're going," vs. "You're going?"), and mark emotional content and emphasis upon particular lexical items in speech. The role of prosody in language comprehension is touched upon in Chapters 3 and 5.

The lexicon

When many people contemplate communication in a foreign language, they reach for a dictionary. Dictionaries provide meanings for the words of a given language, and provide labels for concepts that speakers wish to discuss. A more technical term for a dictionary is a **lexicon**. A capable speaker-hearer of a language possesses a vast and complicated mental lexicon whose nature is of great interest to psycholinguists. Most adults know the meanings of tens of thousands of words in their native language, and can readily comprehend or access them for communicative purposes.

What a word "means" is not simply explained. How is it that one identifies certain objects as *chairs*, no matter how they may vary in construction (Bernstein, 1983)? When does an object deserve the label *cup*, rather than *glass* (Labov, 1973)? The difficult problem of explaining how people readily label **concrete**, easily perceived concepts from "dog" to "furniture" is addressed in Chapter 4. We can also contrast the knowledge of such words with **abstract** notions such as *friendship* or *patriotism*, and **relative** words such as *good* or *short*.

Although it is not easy to account for the process of associating meaning with such words, one can define them, and dictionaries routinely do. For example, *frustrate* means, among other things, "to baffle." Some English words, however, do not easily lend themselves to definition: In the sentence "John is frustrated by calculus," what does *by* mean? In "I really love to sleep late," what does *to* mean? Somehow, the term "mean" seems inappropriate in these contexts. Most people believe that these words make the sentence grammatical, and they are right. Linguists categorize words such as *table, penguin,* and *ecstatic* differently from words like *the, for,* and *is.* The first group of words are **content words** and the second group are **function words.** Content words have "content" or external referential meaning in the usual sense; function words serve particular functions within the sentence by making the relations between the content words clearer. The distinction between content and function words is psychologically meaningful, as Chapters 2, 4, and 7 show. It is, among other things, possible to distinguish between the processes used to retrieve these two types of words in comprehension and production.

Some words also have more than one meaning. Consider this joke about a dimwitted farmer who developed two new breeds of cattle. The first breed had shorter right legs than left legs, and the second had no legs at all. Why? He wanted to raise *lean beef* and *ground beef.* Words such as *lean* and *ground* can mean a number of things. Various meanings are what makes puns, riddles, and other types of humor work. But what happens to the language comprehension process when it encounters a word with multiple entries in the lexicon? The consequences of such ambiguity are addressed in Chapter 4.

Other properties of words appear to be psychologically meaningful as well. For example, words such as *car* and *altruism* are both considered nouns in English. But the first is *concrete,* referring to a class of tangible items, while the second is *abstract,* denoting a concept which cannot be seen, tasted, or felt. Though linguistically equivalent, they seem to be learned and used differently, and may be affected in the language of language-impaired individuals differentially. The frequency with which a word is usually encountered in the language also appears to be a nonlinguistic but psychologically meaningful notion. Terms such as *traveling* and *itinerant* are roughly synonymous, but the first is more commonly used in English than the second. Chapter 4 explores frequency effects on lexical processing.

Many other normal conversational phenomena provide insight into the possible nature of our mental dictionary. Why is it that we sometimes cannot recall a word, but know what its beginning sound is? What would lead a person to say *slickery* when she means to say *slippery*? Such "performance errors" actually provide some evidence for possible models of the way in which we use our mental lexicon in constructing messages, as Chapter 7 shows.

Morphology: The study of word formation

In many languages, we can readily identify meaningful items that appear to be separable "parts" of words. In English, for example, if one is asked to arbitrarily divide the word *cats* into two units, most people will peel off the final *-s.* We readily recognize that it signifies the notion of "plurality," and can be appended to many other words we wish to pluralize. Other similar word endings in English are *-ing* as in *jumping, 's* as in *the boy's,* and *-ed* as in *dropped.* Such suffixes are **grammatical morphemes.** A morpheme, for a linguist, is the smallest unit of a language that carries definable meaning or grammatical function.

Certainly, in English, some morphemes are words. You can't divide *table* into smaller units that make sense; neither can you chop up *the.* Examples such as *cats*

This is a Wug.

Now there is another one.
There are two of them.
There are two _ _ _ _.

This is a man who knows how to Naz.
He is Nazzing. He does it every day.
Every day he _ _ _ _ _ _.

This is a man who knows how to Rick.
He is Ricking. He did the same thing
yesterday. What did he do yesterday?
Yesterday he _ _ _ _ _ _.

Figure 1.3

Your knowledge of morphology enables you to complete these phrases.

are different; it is comprised of two separable notions. *Cats* is **multimorphemic**, a word that contains more than a single morpheme. However, we can note that the parts of *cats* are in a sense unequal. *Cat* can stand by itself in a sentence; *-s* cannot. In English we recognize this difference by calling a morpheme that can stand by itself **free** and one that cannot **bound**. Another name for a bound morpheme is an **affix**. In English, we have two types of affixes, those found at the beginnings of words (prefixes), and those found at the ends of words (suffixes).

Affixes serve two distinct functions. When we attach some affixes to words, we change their meaning, or their part of speech. Consider the *7-Up* advertising campaign that called the bottled beverage the *uncola*. Its effect was the creation of a new word in English, with the meaning "not cola." Another example is when the scarecrow in the *Wizard of Oz* was awarded a degree of *thinkology*. This combination of morphemes takes the English verb *think* and turns it into a noun. Morphemes that change the meaning or grammatical function of a word are called **derivational morphemes**: They can be used to derive a new word. The word *uncola* is also attention getting because it violates the typical usage of *un-* in English, which allows *un-* to be used before verbs, adjectives, and adverbs, but not nouns (can something be an *undog*?). "Thinkology" is amusing for a similar reason—*ology* is not typically added to verbs.

A second type of bound morpheme provides additional information about a word or its grammatical function. These **inflectional morphemes** are used in English to indicate number in nouns (*cat* vs. *cats*), possession (*Harrison* vs. *Harrison's*), verb tense (*jog/jogging; study/studied*), and subject-verb agreement (*I/you/we/they understand* vs. *he/she/it understands*). Comparatives, such as *smarter*, and superlatives, such as *smartest*, are also created from the root form, *smart*, by the application of inflectional morphemes.

The distinctions between content and function words and between free and bound morphemes appear to be psychologically significant when you examine language understanding and production, as Chapters 4, 5, and 7 illustrate. Describing the root and bound morphemes that combine to create a word such as *unwaveringly* might seem to be merely an academic exercise, but there is evidence that the language comprehension process must include such a level of analysis to permit successful understanding of the word, as Chapter 4 shows. Additionally, Chapter 7 includes "slips of the tongue," or speech errors, to demonstrate how we retrieve these different classes of morphemes at different stages of the sentence formulation process during speech.

Syntax—Combining words to form meaningful propositions

> *Take a sentence of a dozen words, and take twelve men and tell to each one word. Then stand the men in a row or jam them in a bunch, and let each think of his word as intently as he will; nowhere will there be a consciousness of the whole sentence.*
>
> (William James, quoted in Clark & Clark, 1977)

Let us return to the example of a traveler who attempts to get by in an unknown language—Hungarian, for example—by using an English–Hungarian dictionary. Learning a new vocabulary and pronunciation is certainly a challenge, but our traveler would find that learning to place the new words within the framework of a new grammar is even more difficult. Not only is it important to learn how to combine words into acceptable sequences to convey propositional meaning, it is also necessary to understand the grammar of the language addressed to us. For example, if we are in Budapest and all we can understand when someone talks to us is *kocsi* (car), we won't know if they are trying to tell us that our vehicle is impressive, parked illegally, or rolling down the driveway unattended.

It is probably most natural to begin a discussion of the role syntax plays in understanding language by using simple English sentences rather than Hungarian. Consider a sentence such as: "*John loves Mary.*" This is a straightforward proposition. However, note that the utterance "*John loves Mary*" does *not* mean that "*Mary loves John.*" Many novels and movies are based upon this simple inequity in meaning. Although the words are the same, the word order differs, as does its meaning. The utterance "*Loves Mary John*" differs from our initial example in another important way: It violates conventions that govern the order in which words may appear in sentences, and this is unacceptable, or ill formed. In English, word order is extremely important to determine meaning. We typically expect the first noun in a sentence to

If you don't know the syntax of a language, communicating can be very difficult.

be the subject, and the next to be its object. We also expect subject nouns to be followed rather closely by verbs. For these reasons, English is sometimes called an S–V–O (Subject–Verb–Object) language, even though in English, as in other "word order" languages, a large number of sentences are not actually ordered this way. Crystal (1987) notes that 75 percent of the world's languages are primarily S–V–O languages (French, German, and Hebrew) or S–O–V languages (Tibetan, Japanese, and Korean). Less common primary sentence ordering patterns are V–S–O (Arabic and Welsh) and V–O–S (Malagasy). For some reason, languages that prefer word order to begin with objects are quite rare (Crystal, 1987).

Some languages of the world allow fairly variable word order, though certain orderings are more common than others. That is, words may be combined in many permissible sequences, which in English might resemble "John loves Mary," "Loves Mary John," "Mary John loves," and even "Loves John Mary." This would certainly be confusing to those of us who expect subjects and verbs to be identifiable by their positions in sentences. However, languages that permit a broad variety of orderings usually mark grammatical role in other ways. Thus, they may append suffixes to the ends of words, which essentially say: "This word is the subject, this is the object, and this is the verb." Consider the following example from Japanese (Clancy, 1985):

Taroo	ga	Hanako	ni	hon	o	age	-ta
Taroo	SUBJ	Hanako	IO	book	DO	give	PAST

In this example, *ga* indicates that Taroo is the subject (SUBJ), *o* signifies that the book is the direct object (DO), and that Hanako is the recipient, or indirect object (IO). When labeled in such a fashion, subjects, verbs, and objects may be ordered flexibly, without listener confusion. If you studied Latin, you will recall a system much like this: "Agricola amat puellam" and "Puellam amat agricola" both mean, "The farmer loves the girl."

Word order in English aids us in interpreting the relationships among words in a sentence, but not all sentences of English are arranged in S–V–O order. For example, the sentences "Mary is loved by John," "Mary showed John the old man," and "The man who lives next to my sister collects antique cars" violate the typical S–V–O order in English. The first, which is called the **passive**, is logically O–V–S. The second, which is called the **dative** construction, is S–V–IO (indirect object)–O. The third, which is a **center-embedded relative clause**, interposes a descriptive phrase between the subject and the verb and object. The embedded clause produces discontinuity in the S–V–O pattern.

As we see in Chapter 5, the implicit expectation that words follow a conventional order in English aids a listener immensely in arriving at a rapid and accurate interpretation of many sentences. We use typical word order patterns as a comprehension strategy in English (Clark & Clark, 1977). But if word order deviates from the norm, problems in interpretation can arise. For example, the active sentence, "The invasion surprised many people," is easier to process than its synonymous passive, "Many people were surprised by the invasion." In later chapters we survey some of these problems, and how the listener most efficiently resolves these problems.

There are many types of sentences in English, including those that question, command, negate, and use the passive focus. Additionally, some sentences appear to be built from a combination of smaller sentences. These are *compound* sentences "Jake swims and Sue sails," and *complex* sentences "This is the house that Jack built." If you decide to construct "sentence equations" by labeling the sequences of words that occur in all the sentences in this chapter, you would have numerous different equations. How do we know how to use a broad variety of permissible sequences while still avoiding mistakes such as *"It like I do?"* And how are a large number of possible orderings rapidly decoded to assign appropriate grammatical identity to individual words? Efforts have been made by linguists and psycholinguists to develop explanations of how declaratives, negatives, imperatives, compound and complex sentences are created by particular interrelated rules. These rules are a *parsimonious* way to describe the grammar of a language (as a grammarian might), and they also seem to be psychologically valid in some way.

> *When a thought takes one's breath away, a lesson on grammar seems an impertinence.*
> (Thomas Wentworth Higgenson, in the Preface to Emily Dickinson's *Poems*, 1890)

Grammars. As a minor example of the way you might search for rules in language, we might attempt to create a grammar of the cardinal numbering system in English. By careful intuition and observation we would discover that spoken English uses a small number of basic units: The words *zero* through *nineteen*, plus separate words for *twenty*, *thirty*, and so forth; the terms *hundred, thousand, million*, and so forth. English employs a limited number of rules for combining these terms to represent all possible numbers. Limitless new numbers can be formed by using the rule that allows a new number simply to be called a given number plus one. Therefore, thanks to linguistics, the U.S. debt can rise to a hundred trillion and one dollars! In such ways, an infinite system could be described using a finite number of rules that seem to be intuitively natural. Over the years, linguists and psychologists have explored the possible rules that might govern aspects of sentence understanding and formation. In all cases, the goal is similar to that posed for creating an infinite numbering system. We would like to explain the boundless creativity of human language by developing confined sets of rules that can convert a small number of basic linguistic forms into all possible sentences a speaker/hearer might need to say or understand.

One approach to such a grammatical description of English was developed by linguist Noam Chomsky (1957; 1965). **Transformational generative (TG) grammar** revolutionized linguistic theory and provided the impetus for much early psycholinguistic research. Although many of its specific tenets have undergone radical revision in the ensuing years, a review of the original version of TG grammar, now called the Standard Theory, provides an excellent example of how a linguistic description can be tested for its psychological validity. In the next section, we briefly outline the theory, its possible psychological implications, and some of the psycholinguistic evidence which evaluated its adequacy in describing the process of language comprehension. Then we will address more current approaches to grammatical theory.

Syntactic theory in the 1960s: Transformational grammars.   Following principles discussed in Chomsky (1957), linguists began to distinguish among three conceptual levels of language description. Using ambiguous sentence examples such as "Visiting relatives can be a nuisance," Chomsky and others illustrated that a single well-formed sentence could have more than one meaning. Further, by using virtually synonymous paraphrases such as the active-passive pairs, "Hope kissed Michael" and "Michael was kissed by Hope," linguists were able to demonstrate that a single meaning could be conveyed by more than one given sentence. These two phenomena contributed to the linguistic distinction between **deep structures** and **surface structures**. The underlying grammatical concepts which the speaker wishes to convey is considered a deep structure; the concept's final grammatical goal is the surface structure. These two levels of grammar were linked by transformations, which systematically derived surface structures from deep structures.

To more efficiently describe the derivation of large numbers of differing sentence types in English, it was usually assumed that deep structures were limited in number, and most closely resembled the simplest and most basic types of English sentences, such as simple, active, affirmative declaratives. Thus, it was proposed that from a base form describing the notions

> *Sue + admire (present tense) + Jonathan*

surface structure sentences such as "*Sue admires Jonathan,*" and "*Does Sue admire Jonathan?*" and "*Jonathan is admired by Sue*" could be formed, using transformations that changed word order and inserted mandatory grammatical elements. Specific movement transformations related simple active forms and their corresponding question and passive versions. Other types of transformations combined deep structures or eliminated deep structure elements in the eventual surface structure expression. For example, a sentence such as *"Tim and Chris like to hike and climb"* could be viewed as the surface structure representation of four deep structure concepts, which roughly correspond to *"Tim likes to hike,"* *"Tim likes to climb,"* *"Chris likes to hike,"* and *"Chris likes to climb."* Transformations combine these meanings, and delete redundant identical elements so that each is expressed only once. Readable introductions to the principles of the Standard Theory of TG grammar can be found in Akmajian and Heny (1975) and Baker (1978).

Such a description of language is potentially a description of how speakers and listeners actually produce and understand sentences—it has potential psychological reality. For example, transformational grammar, by claiming that passives are derived from underlyingly active forms, predicted that they might take longer to process than an active affirmative declarative sentence, because listeners would have to "undo" their transformational derivation in order to appreciate their deep structure meanings. As we shall note later in the chapter, many of the first modern psycholinguistic studies addressed this hypothesis, which was called the **Derivational Theory of Complexity (DTC)**.

While early results were somewhat supportive of the Derivational Theory of Complexity, more rigorous tests of the predictions made by the Standard Theory did not suggest that the comprehension process reflected the proposed linguistic derivation of sentences. Additionally, many of the rules used by the Standard Theory to account for the broad variety of syntactic constructions found in any language were seen as too numerous and cumbersome actually to be used by speakers, hearers, and learners of the language. Winograd (1973) suggested that, while early transformational grammar was adequate in its ability to reflect the logical structure of language, it implied the need for "astronomically large amounts of processing." The DTC was also critically based on the assumption that structures that were more complex derivationally took more time to process, a hypothesis that may or may not be true. Berwick & Weinberg (1984) propose that more complex structures may simply tax the language processing system more, without taking longer to comprehend. Addidtionally, it may be possible for more than one operation to be carried out simultaneously by the language processing system, a concept known as **parallel processing**. Both of these notions complicate evaluation of the DTC.

Changes in grammatical theory.   The Standard Theory of transformational grammar underwent substantial revision during the 1970s and 1980s. Though many competing theories of syntax emerged (McCloskey, 1988), a major successor was what has come to be called **Government and Binding (GB)** theory (Chomsky, 1981; 1986). A readable description of the principles of GB is provided by Cook (1988); a briefer discussion can be found in Leonard and Loeb (1988). The broad array of transformations posited by TG grammar have been eliminated, leaving only the possibility of movement of certain elements. The role of the lexicon has been expanded. Linguists now suggest that the lexical entry for a verb such as *greet*, for example, not only includes information about what *greet* "means," but also specifies the requirement that it be followed by a noun phrase in a sentence, so that *"Joe greeted his opponent,"* is permissible in English, but *"Joe greeted"* is not. Thus, the lexicon "projects onto" the syntax, blurring previous distinctions between these two aspects of linguistic knowledge.

Efforts to evaluate the psychological reality of GB theory have been carried out mainly by linguists (Berwick & Weinberg, 1984; Frazier, 1988), who are often able to reconcile problematic results from older experimental evaluations of TG grammar with changes to the grammatical theory. However, as Miller (1990) and Tannenhaus (1989) note, efforts by psychologists to use theories of grammar as input to study the adult sentence comprehension process declined as early versions of transformational grammar underwent dynamic reconfiguration during the mid-1970s and 1980s. There have been far greater efforts to evaluate claims made by current grammatical theory to the process of language acquisition by children, which will be discussed in greater detail in Chapter 8. Additionally, there have been some attempts to reconcile the performance patterns of adults whose language function has been impaired by brain damage (**aphasics**, Chapter 2), and children who are language-learning disabled, with the principles and predictions made by GB grammar (Bates, Friederici & Wulfeck, 1987; Leonard, Sabbadini, Leonard & Volterra, 1987). We will return to the role of grammatical theory in the history of psycholinguistic research in the final sections of this chapter.

Discourse and the pragmatics of language usage

There is a weird power in the spoken word.

(Conrad, *Lord Jim*)

Beyond the level of understanding single words or sentences, we more typically need to evaluate things we hear or read within a larger framework. When someone says, "Professor Murk doesn't give make-up exams," the message is typically taken as more than a simple comment. It may be viewed as a *warning* or a *threat*. Language is clearly more than collections of grammatical utterances. Language is what it *does*. We use language to inform, to promise, to request, to query. *How to do things with words* (Austin, 1962) is the domain of **pragmatic inquiry**. Pragmatics determine our choice of wording and our interpretation of language within the social context. Just as there are rules for creating grammatical sentences, there are also linguistic conventions for the appropriate use of language in various contexts.

The situational setting or context of spoken messages is often crucial to their successful interpretation. "Success," in this sense, is taken as the hearer's full appreciation of the speaker's intent. The simple comment, "It's 8:15" assumes new dimensions if both speaker and hearer are sitting in traffic on the way to the airport to catch a plane scheduled to leave at 8:30 a.m.

We often encounter sentences that do not seem to "mean what they say." A woman who informs her friend standing near the window that, "It's hot in here," is probably asking her to open it. A parent who complains, "Your room is a total mess," usually views such a statement as an order to clean it up. Such indirect statements contrast with the more direct, "Open the window," and "Clean up your room."

Although it may appear to complicate conversation, indirect phrasing is often used to make requests of others, because it is usually viewed as more deferential or polite. Such conversational modifications can occasionally lead to communicative breakdowns, in which the speaker's intent does not match the listener's interpretation (Tannen, 1990). Successful use of language within society also demands awareness of how conversation needs to be modified when addressing different types of listeners. A comment such as, "If it's not too much trouble, may I have a word with you about a personal problem I'm having?" is more likely to be uttered to a clergyman than to a teenaged younger sibling. Speech styles can vary with the context, the characteristics of the addressee, or the characteristics of the speaker, as well as with the medium of discourse (written or spoken, telephoned or face-to-face, etc.). These specially marked ways of speaking are called **registers**. Babytalk, foreigner talk, and the style used by some nurses talking to patients are but a few examples of different registers. Some registers typify casual interaction, while others are more appropriate to formal events. The language used to talk about chores around the house is usually distinct from that used in religious or legal settings. Conventions for the use of language with varying addressees include constraints on what is said, and how it is phrased, as Chapter 6 demonstrates.

The situational and world knowledge that conversational participants share determines the form and content of their utterances. Usually it is necessary to specify a noun first, before a pronoun can be used. Thus, the sentence, "Did you get it?" makes a poor opening gambit in conversation with a stranger on a bus, but makes perfectly good sense if it is said to a child you just sent to the store to buy a loaf of bread. As a further example, pronouns commonly replace proper names in conversational interactions. The comment, "She's late again" is well-formed and understood by students gazing at the empty podium where their instructor should be standing, but it is meaningless when the antecedent or reference for the pronoun cannot be determined.

Much of our language use involves verbal or written interactions longer than single utterances. Conversation and written text are governed by **discourse** conventions that determine the appropriateness of content, structure, and turn-taking behaviors.

Metalinguistic capacity: The ability to analyze our own language competence

Metalinguistics refers, literally, to "language about language," and to our capacity to reflect upon our own language. It is often difficult to explain our own language knowledge. Consider the following two examples. In English, we can produce sentences such as a) and b), that appear to be well formed and synonymous:

a) Bill threw out the garbage.
b) Bill threw the garbage out.

Next, consider the following:

c) Bill looked out the window.
d) *Bill looked the window out.

(Linguists use *'s to indicate that a sentence is ungrammatical or unacceptable.) Why then is it that we can create a grammatical sentence such as c), but not one such as d)? (If you are stumped for a quick answer to such a question, you are not alone. The answer is provided at the end of the chapter.) Most of us quickly judge a), b), c) to be correct, and d) as ungrammatical, and conventionally produce sentences such as a), b), c), but not d). That seems to be the easy part of our language knowledge. It is explaining how and why we know that the first three sentences are well formed, while the last is not that lies at the heart of much psycholinguistic research. Our talent for speaking well and understanding competently are aspects of our linguistic knowledge, whereas our ability to reflect upon our language, our understanding of how we do these things represents an aspect of our metalinguistic knowledge. This book is primarily an exercise in metalinguistics. In it, we ask not, "What are the words of English?" but rather, "How do I understand the meaning of a word?"; "How do I find words when I want to talk about things?" and "Are some words easier or harder for people to understand?"

A linguistics text might simply note that English allows sentences such as, "The guy who sits next to Susan is a geology major," "I know a guy who is a geology major," and "That John is a geology major surprises me." This text is more concerned with exploring what procedures a listener or reader might use in understanding what these sentences mean, generating comparable sentences on his or her own, and whether the sentences differ in their processing demands.

As you read through this text, consider how effortlessly you understand the examples. Language use is a rapidly paced phenomenon. The task for the psycholinguist is to account for the discrepency that often arises between the time required to produce or understand an utterance, and the time required to explain how this was accomplished! As an example of this, we can consider a very simple sentence construction in English, the **tag question** (Akmajian & Heny, 1975). Tag questions have the general form provided below:

a) It's raining, *isn't it*?
b) He isn't going, *is he*?

If you are provided with additional starting points, you can easily provide the little "tags" that end them:

c) She doesn't like ice cream, _____ ?
d) They are expensive, _____ ?

But how do you know what to do? Try to form a rule that will generate the right answers to c) and d) above. Time yourself. Next consider whether or not your rule will "work" for the following:

e) Your little sister likes ice cream, _____ ?
f) The new people who moved in next door most certainly will want to be invited, _____ ?

Estimate roughly how much time it takes you to revise your rule to account for the right answers to e) and f), if your first account was lacking in some way. And if you find it difficult and time consuming, don't despair. It is very difficult to develop succinct and accurate answers to such questions, even for linguists. A suggested answer is provided at the end of the chapter. The major point we would like to make here is that saying and understanding such sentences is rather trivial; it is figuring out our subconscious strategies for doing such things that tantalizes the psycholinguist.

Linguistic exercises like the ones in this chapter demonstrate that much of our knowledge of the language is implicit and not easily available for self-examination. We can perform the task, but we cannot peer into the process and understand how it occurs. This distinction between linguistic and metalinguistic ability is both frustrating and fascinating to the psycholinguist, and often requires us to develop special experimental techniques for indirectly measuring and describing the ways people generate and understand language.

We should note before concluding this topic that even when people think they know how they perform a linguistic task, they may not be correct. It is possible that you developed a rule for one of our examples that differed from our answer, or that was incomplete. The process of "being metalinguistic" also seems more cumbersome than the process of speaking or listening. This dichotomy has its parallels in many other human endeavors. For example, one of us is a terrible tennis player. When an instructor finally dispaired of improving our actual ability to play, she offered this advice: "Tell your opponent you really admire her serve. Then ask her whether she throws the ball up before or after she steps toward the line. Her serve won't be that great for the next few minutes while she thinks about it!"

Language diversity and language universals

Language use is so important to our everyday life and such a comfortable aspect of our behavior that it is tempting to view it rather narrowly, within the confines of our own particular language. Because this book is written in English and because most of our readers will be most comfortable with English, we will concentrate heavily on research into the processes that underlie speaking and listening in English. However, in the broader perspective of human communicative behavior, this may provide an incomplete picture. As we noted earlier, languages differ markedly in their construction: Their sound systems may vary widely, their word formation rules and lexical inventories differ, and rules for ordering elements within sentences may differ from English. When possible we will attempt to note how the processing strategies used by speakers of different languages tell us more about either universal tendencies in linguistic processing, or specific strategies that may be limited to a particular language. In general, more cross-linguistic research has been carried out in developmental psycholinguistics (cf. Slobin, 1985, and in press) than in the study of adult language comprehension and production, though effort is increasing in these areas (cf. MacWhinney & Bates, 1989).

The great variability found in human languages has prompted the search for linguistic universals or constant features that might characterize languages, their use, and their acquisition. A **universal grammar (UG)** is a "system of principles, conditions, and rules that are elements or properties of all human languages . . . the essence of human language" (Chomsky, 1976; 29). UG is not merely a collection of absolute regularities across languages. It also specifies principles that may have differing realizations from language to language. A given language uses just one of the finite number of options (or parameters) specified by the principle. For example, a single parameter may distinguish between languages which demand that sentences express subjects (as in English, which is typified by sentences such as "I am hungry") and languages which permit subjects to be omitted (so-called "pro-drop" languages like Spanish and Italian, which allow speakers to say, "Tengo hambre" [literally, "am hungry"]). The ordering of elements within noun phrases, verb phrases, and so forth, across languages may be determined by a binary choice between competing realizations of a different, single parameter.

Linguists continue to search for candidate rules for the universal grammar (Chomsky, 1986). Recently, child language acquisition and second language research have both become increasingly concerned with testing theories about the nature of the universal grammar (Hyams, 1986; Cook, 1988), thus attempting to link hypothetical linguistic universals with strategies seen in language learning.

There has been similar interest in what a psycholinguistic universal might look like. This notion has been pursued more intensely in the developmental domain than in study of adult language processing. A psycholinguistic universal might be based on cognitive and perceptual factors, as well as linguistic factors. Slobin (1973; 1985) proposed universal operating principles that govern the course of child language development. For example, he suggests that language learners *pay attention to the ends of words*, thus accounting for the usually early acquisition of inflectional morphemes in a wide variety of highly inflected languages. Another principle would lead children to *avoid discontinuous elements* in their speech, such as embedded clauses, "*The man who lives next to my sister is a doctor*," or discontinuous constructions such as the English present progressive, "*Jimmy is going*," and the French "*je ne suis pas*," where the *ne* and *pas* together signal negation. Thus, appropriate usage of these forms would occur later in language development, regardless of the language being learned.

Oral and signed language

One major way languages can differ is in whether they are spoken/heard (oral/aural) or encoded manually, as in sign language. Oral languages are more numerous, but there are also many signed languages in the world, all of which differ crucially in their phonology (which in this case includes permissible handshapes, movement patterns, and placement of signs in space or in contact with the body), lexicon, and syntax (Bellugi & Klima, 1979; Wilbur, 1989). The signed language that has been studied most extensively is **American Sign Language (ASL)**. As some of the chapters to follow will indicate, there are basic similarities in processing, whether language is signed or spoken. Brain damage often impairs spoken and signed communication in similar ways, suggesting a common neurological representation for the two types of language. "Slips of the tongue" and "slips of the hand" as well as

Figure 1.4

The sign for 'cat' in four of the world's sign languages. The many sign languages of the world have differing phonologies, lexicons, and grammars.

"WHISKERS"

American   Brazilian

"SCRATCH/PET"

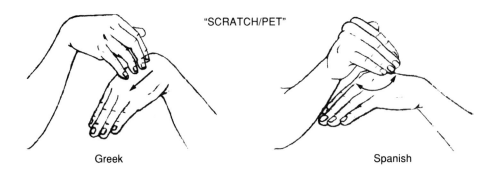

Greek   Spanish

verbal recall errors made by speakers and signers tend to be similar, thus bolstering our confidence in some accounts of language processing that were originally developed to account only for oral language. However, we can also ask whether the differing demands of gestural and oral language also require some different psycholinguistic strategies. While this issue will be discussed briefly, it is an area of great interest and importance in fully understanding the human capacity to learn, understand, and produce the full array of languages used by diverse communities (Wilbur, 1989; Poizner, Klima & Bellugi, 1987). Similarities between signed and spoken languages are an important area of inquiry for many psycholinguists.

Written language

. . . writing is nothing more than a variety of speech which endures after it is spoken—what we may call the soul *of the words.*
                        (Castiglione, in Hayden, Alworth, & Tate, 1967)

Writing, when properly managed (as you may be sure I think mine is) is but a different name for conversation.
                        (Lawrence Sterne, *Tristram Shandy*, 1760/1964)

All human cultures possess either spoken or manual languages (or both). However, not all languages have an associated writing system, and it is evident that writing is a more recent talent in the history of human development than is speech. Written languages vary widely in their characteristics, though some broad categories of writing systems can be described (Crystal, 1987; Garman, 1990; Sampson, 1985).

The minimal unit, or building block, of any written system is the **grapheme**. Many writing systems reflect the phonological properties of the oral language they encode, and are thus sound based. A sound based writing system that uses individual symbols, or letters, to represent the phonemes of a language is considered alphabetic. Written English is primarily a system of this sort, though it is not completely regular in its representations, as anyone who has suffered through spelling tests or used a word processing spelling checker will readily agree. A sound such as /f/ may be written as *f, ph, -gh,* or *ff.* An unstressed spoken vowel, as in *bottom,* could conceivably be represented by an *a, e, i,* or *u.* George Bernard Shaw once complained that the word *fish* could just as easily be spelled *ghoti* (*gh* as in enou*gh*, *o* as in w*o*men, *ti* as in na*ti*on)! This is not really true (an initial *gh* is always pronounced as [g], the pronunciation in *women* is truly exceptional, and *ti* is only pronounced as [š] when it appears between two syllables in a word). It is clear, however, that the English writing system, though imperfect, is alphabetic in principle. Other languages, such as Spanish, have more regular phoneme-grapheme correspondences.

The writing systems of some languages represent syllables, rather than individual phonemes. Such systems (as seen in the Indian language Kannada) are called **syllabaries**. As Chapter 9 shows, there is evidence that readers of sound-based written material make grapheme-phoneme correspondences (associate graphemes or grapheme sequences with their appropriate pronunciation) during certain reading activities. Very frequently encountered or very irregularly spelled words may be processed differently.

Many of the world's languages possess writing systems that are not sound based. Such systems link linguistic concepts (lexical and grammatical) with written symbols, and are considered ideographic or logographic. Written Chinese is an example of such a system. Ideographic writing systems use **ideograms** to symbolize an idea rather than a particular word, and logographic systems use **logograms** to represent whole words. We also use a few logograms in our writing system—for instance $ stands for *dollar.*

Figure 1.5

The early literary efforts of this 6-year-old reflect attempts to master English phoneme-grapheme correspondences.

my Bast ♥
Dremes

I coD Dreme
av laly pops
I coD Dreme
av a far
I coD Dreme
av aneThing

I coD Dreme
av BaD gies
I coD. Dreme
av wichis.

I COD Dreme
av farys I coo
Dreme av Love
I coo Dreme
av maricls
I coD Dreme
av aneThing.

The End

By Jamie

The evolution of psycholinguistic inquiry

Why study language? . . . language is a mirror of the mind in a deep and significant sense. It is a product of human intelligence, created anew in each individual by operations that lie far beyond the reach of will or consciousness.
(Chomsky, *Reflections on language,* 1975)

Many of the questions that spur current psycholinguistic inquiry have been of enduring interest to philosophers, linguists, and scientists. Plato's *Cratylus* dialogue considers at length the relationships between words and the concepts they encode. The participants in his dialogues disagree; one argues that the names of objects are of divine origin, while another suggests that words are merely societal conventions that arbitrarily link concepts and language. Pursuing this second view, Aristotle sought to determine the formal properties that define a particular word's meaning.

Chapter 2 explains in some detail how the role of the brain in language functioning has been explored since the days of the Egyptian pharoahs. The writings of Herodotus in the fifth century B.C. also suggest that at least one pharoah, Psammetichus, was also fascinated by the origins of human language. Chapter 8 recounts how he isolated two infants with a mute caretaker in an attempt to attribute their first eventual vocalizations to humanity's first language.

Some view psychologist Wilhelm Wundt (1832–1920) as the founder of modern psycholinguistics. He developed the earliest theory of speech production, and piloted the use of many experimental measures considered basic to psycholinguistic research, such as **reaction time (RT)**. Reaction time studies will be covered in detail in some of the other chapters. The premise which underlies the measurement of reaction time is that the time taken to process different experimental tasks reflects the degree of mental complexity involved in the task.

However deep its historical roots, however, the field of psycholinguistics is relatively young. Some researchers date its birth to the early 1950s (Brown, 1970; Tannenhaus, 1989; and Miller, 1990), when psychologists and linguists met to discuss whether advances in experimental psychology could be applied to the study of language performance and comprehension. Psychology during the 1950s was strongly governed by behaviorist, or learning theory, principles which emphasized serial patterning in behavior. Though psychologists such as Hull, Watson, and Skinner differed in their specific accounts, all viewed learning as the outcome of successive stimulus-response-reinforcement chains. Behaviorist accounts of syntactic functioning based upon transitional probabilities (or the statistical likelihood that one word is likely to follow another) were advanced by Osgood (1963), Jenkins and Palermo (1964), and Staats (1964). Skinner (1957) formulated a behavioral model of language functioning that became particularly controversial. Its major focus was in predicting the conditions which elicit the use of a given word. As Fodor, Bever, and Garrett (1974) review in great detail, such theories faced many difficulties in explaining the complex nature of language production and understanding, as the following examples will show.

Learning theories were especially limited when attempting to account for the processing of phrases that contain discontinuous elements. (For instance, an embedded relative clause interrupts the main clause in, "The rider who fell off the horse broke a leg.") It is unclear in a sentence such as this how *rider* can condition the word *broke*, which is five words away from it. Behavioristic theories were also inadequate to account for elements early in a phrase whose specification was clearly determined by later, nonadjacent elements. For example, it was difficult to account for the generation of questions like, "Are all the registered voters in this county Democrats?" where the number agreement on the fronted auxiliary verb is clearly motivated by the speaker's use of a plural subject yet to come.

Finally, as Bever, Fodor, and Weksel (1965) noted, theories based upon either association or upon transitional probabilities do not predict the initial stages of language learning by children. For example, although *article + noun* sequences are extremely common in English, children's earliest utterances do not contain articles. More importantly, early child language often contains utterances that do not replicate anything the child has heard from adults: It is difficult to account for an utterance such as, "I do it Jamieself" by appealing to the learning of sequences of frequently associated items in the language. Nor is it readily apparent how children would achieve the ability to pluralize and otherwise inflect nonsense words (*a wug/two wugs;* Berko, 1958) by mere observation of regularly observed patterns of adult language, although the learning principle of generalization has been invoked to do this.

However provocative, early behaviorally oriented psycholinguistic models were quickly undermined by rapid changes in linguistic theory. The emergence of the transformational generative grammatical framework (Chomsky, 1957; 1965) dramatically altered the study of language structure and its mental representation (Fodor, Bever & Garrett, 1974; Newmeyer, 1986; Tannenhaus, 1989).

Linguist Noam Chomsky's (1957) *Syntactic Structures* and (1958) critique of Skinner's (1957) *Verbal Behavior* caused both linguists and psychologists to view language in new ways. Linguists were challenged to enlarge the goals of linguistic inquiry beyond the description of structural regularities in a given language. Generative grammarians sought to include speakers' intuitions about grammatical and ungrammatical utterances, relationships that seem to exist between types of sentences in a language (such as between actives and their corresponding passives), and the problem of language acquisition by children.

The new transformational framework that guided much of linguistic theory for the next two decades was immediately pursued by psychologists, who attempted to determine whether the new approaches to describing the utterances of a language mirrored the mental operations required by speakers and hearers when they used the language. As mentioned earlier in our discussion of syntax, some initial findings suggested that listeners might mentally "undo" the grammatical transformations that linguists used to derive interrogative, passive, and negative sentences from simple active affirmative sentences (Miller & McKean, 1964; Clifton & Odom, 1966). Child language researchers such as Menyuk (1968) and Brown and Hanlon (1970) explored the possibility that language development was dependent upon the acquisition of transformations that operated upon early acquired simple active declarative sentences to create more complex linguistic forms.

Research on transformations, while partially supportive of the psychological reality of transformational generative theory, did not fully substantiate its mental representation. That is, the linguistic theory did not always accurately predict subjects' experimental behaviors, or children's observed patterns of language development, as Fodor, Bever & Garrett (1974) explain in detail. Moreover, linguistic theory began to evolve extremely rapidly, changing both in detail and in major focus, making it difficult for psychologists to keep pace with new developments. As Miller (1990) and Tannenhaus (1989) note, the brief, close working relationship between linguistic theorists and psychologists began to erode by the early 1970s when their respective goals began to diverge markedly, and their orientations toward human language became more distinct. Miller (1990; 321) simplifies what appear to be their current respective biases when he observes that, "linguists and psychologists talk about different things . . . grammarians are more interested in what could be said than in what people actually say, which irritates psychologists, and psychologists insist on supplementing intuition with objective evidence, which irritates linguists."

During the 1970s, psychologists also discovered interactions between the various levels of linguistic analysis and situational context in language processing, and in large part explored the nature of comprehension without explicit reference to a particular theory of grammar. Work that examined the role of context in interpreting ambiguous speech signals (Garnes & Bond, 1976), and in making unstated inferences, or logical assumptions, from experimental sentences (Bransford & Franks, 1972) suggested that many kinds of information serve as input to the process of language understanding. Not all of these sources of information were adequately described by linguistic theory. While the bulk of psycholinguistic work done in the 1960s had investigated syntactic processing, much of the work done in the 1970s concentrated on the mental organization of the lexicon, and on the processing of text or discourse. Unlike syntax, these other areas of inquiry were less dependent upon the vagaries of current linguistic theory.

More recently, there have been increasing attempts to relate the principles of newer transformational grammars, such as Government and Binding theory, to adult sentence processing, child language acquisition, and language disorder. These attempts will be evaluated most extensively in the chapter on child language acquisition (Chapter 8), where they have been most vigorously pursued.

The acquisition of language by children

The Seventh Wonder of our modern world is a human child, any child . . .
Why didn't our evolution . . . allow . . . us to jump catlike from our juvenile to
our adult (and, as I thought) productive stage of life? I had forgotten about
language, the single human trait that marks us out as specifically human . . .
the most compulsively, biologically, obsessively social of all creatures on earth
. . . I had forgotten that, and forgotten that children do that in childhood.
Language is what childhood is for.

(Lewis Thomas, 1983; 61)

The rapidity with which children acquire language competence has fascinated scholars (and many parents) for thousands of years. Though the methods and lines of argumentation that explore the nature of child language learning have varied, there are many recurring themes. As Chapter 8 notes, there has been enduring argumentation over the respective roles of the environment and innate (or inborn) abilities in helping the child master language. Do adults gently "teach" language to children by using special kinds of language with them, and providing them with feedback when they have used the language well or poorly? Or do children come into this world possessed with a special, unique human talent that can extrapolate the grammar of a language without overt instruction or correction?

What role do adults play
in children's language
development?

An important component of Chomsky's early writings (1957; 1965) was its emphasis on the role of linguistic theory, and the limits of behavioralist psychology (detailed in the following section) in explaining the acquisition of language by children. He argued pursuasively that behaviorist learning principles could not account for the rapid acquisition of an infinitely productive language faculty. A series of studies of young children's language learning (Berko, 1958; Brown, 1965; and Braine, 1965) did, in fact, strongly suggest that children were active language learners, whose grammatical systems, while quite systematic, reflected the use of nonadult-like rules.

Additionally, Chomsky first addressed two problems which have spurred enduring controversy in the field of child language development. The first is what has become known as the degeneracy problem (Berwick & Weinberg, 1984). Simply put, Chomsky and others contended that the language overheard by young children contains many incomplete and ungrammatical sentences, as well as limited exposure to the full range of structures used by the language. Thus, there may not be sufficient positive evidence available to the child to permit adequate, competent language development. Further, a second problem was noted. The **negative evidence problem** argued that children are not overtly instructed that some structures are not permissible in the language, either by parental correction of their errors (Brown & Hanlon, 1970) or by literal instruction (e.g., "You can say X in English, but you can't say Y"). As Chapter 8 explores in great detail, both the validity and interpretation of such claims are a matter of spirited inquiry and debate within the field of child language acquisition. Numbers of child-language researchers have proposed that environmental influences play a substantive role in the acquisition of language by children.

Summary

Language is an integral aspect of our human existance. While the ability to formulate and understand language underlies almost every activity, the mental operations which enable language use are still poorly understood. Psycholinguistics explores the processes of language understanding, language production, and language acquisition.

In this chapter, we have briefly surveyed the broad domain of human language ability, which includes knowledge of the sound system of a language (its phonology), the vocabulary (its lexicon), rules for creating words (morphology), rules for including and sequencing words within sentences (syntax), and rules for using language appropriately within the social context (pragmatics).

The principles that govern appropriate use of each of these components of language are largely implicit, and most speaker-hearers have difficulty describing why they make certain judgments about good and poor examples of language use, or how they generate or understand particular sentences. Our metalinguistic ability is usually quite poor, forcing psycholinguists to develop experimental strategies for better describing the mental operations which underlie language use.

Relatively recent changes in linguistic theory which occurred in the late 1950s spurred the cross-disciplinary evolution of psycholinguistic inquiry. During the ensuing years, linguists and psychologists have attempted to apply developments in grammatical theory to models of language use and learning. Psychologists have additionally been concerned with issues in the use of language which are not generally addressed by linguistic theory, such as the role of context or experience in language processing.

The chapters which follow introduce the new student of psycholinguistics to the major questions that have been asked about how competent speaker-hearers of a language understand and produce sentences, the process of child language development, and the biological foundations which underlie language learning and use. We will additionally explore what is currently known about the processes of reading and second language learning.

References

Akmajian, A., Demers, R., & Harnish, R. (1984). *Linguistics: An introduction to language and communication* (2nd ed.). Cambridge, MA: MIT Press.

Akmajian, A., & Heny, F. (1975). *An introduction to the principles of transformational syntax.* Cambridge, MA: MIT Press.

Austin, J. (1962). *How to do things with words.* Cambridge, MA: Harvard University Press.

Baker, C. L. (1978). *Introduction to generative-transformational syntax.* Englewood Cliffs, NJ: Prentice-Hall.

Bates, E., Friederici, A., & Wulfeck, B. (1987). Grammatical morphology in aphasia: evidence from three languages. *Cortex, 23,* 545–574.

Bellugi, U., & E. Klima (1979). *The signs of language.* Cambridge, MA: Harvard University Press.

Berko, J. (1958). The child's learning of English morphology. *Word, 14,* 150–177.

Bernstein, M. (1983). Formation of internal structure in a lexical category. *Journal of Child Language, 10*(2), 381–400.

Berwick, R., & Weinberg, A. (1984). *The grammatical basis of linguistic performance.* Cambridge, MA: MIT Press.

Bever, T., Fodor, J., & Weksel, W. (1965). Theoretical notes on the acquisition of syntax: A critique of "contextual generalization." *Psychological Review, 72,* 467–482.

Bolinger, D. (1980). *Language: The loaded weapon.* London: Longman.

Bolinger, D., & Sears, D. (1981). *Aspects of language* (3rd ed.). New York: Harcourt Brace Jovanovich.

Braine, M. (1965). On the basis of phrase structure. *Psychological Review, 72*(6), 483–492.

Bransford, J., Barclay, J., & Franks, J. (1972). Sentence memory: A constructive vs. interpretive approach. *Cognitive Psychology, 3,* 193–209.

Brown, R. (1970). *Psycholinguistics.* New York: Free Press.

Brown, R., Cazden, C., & Bellugi, U. (1969). The child's grammar from I to III. In Hill, J., (Ed.), *Minnesota Symposia on Child Psychology,* Vol. II. Minneapolis: University of Minnesota Press.

Brown, R., & Hanlon, C. (1970). Derivational complexity and order of acquisition in child language. In Hayes, J., (Ed.), *Cognition and the development of language.* New York: Wiley.

Castiglione, B. (1561). *The book of the courtier.* Reprinted in D. Hayden, E. Alworth & G. Tate (1967), *Classics in linguistics.* New York: Philosophical Library.

Chomsky, N. (1986a). *Knowledge of language: Its nature, origin and use.* New York: Praeger.

Chomsky, N. (1986b). *Barriers.* Cambridge, MA: MIT Press.

Chomsky, N. (1975). *Reflections on language.* London: Temple-Smith.

Chomsky, N. (1965). *Aspects of the theory of syntax.* Cambridge, MA: MIT Press.

Chomsky, N. (1957). *Syntactic structures.* The Hague: Mouton.

Chomsky, N. (1981). *Lectures on government and binding.* Dordrecht, Holland: D. Reidel Publishers.

Clancy, P. (1985). The acquisition of Japanese. In D. Slobin (Ed.), *The crosslinguistic study of language acquisition. Volume 1: The data.* Hillsdale, NJ: Erlbaum.

Clark, H., & Clark, E. (1977). *Psychology and language: An introduction to psycholinguistics.* New York: Harcourt Brace Jovanovich.

Clifton, C., & Odom, P. (1966). Similarity relations among certain English sentence constructions. *Psychological Monographs, 80.*

Cook, V. J. (1988). *Chomsky's universal grammar: An introduction.* Cambridge, MA: Basil Blackwell.

Crystal, D. (1987). *The Cambridge encyclopedia of language.* Cambridge, MA: Cambridge University Press.

Demers, R. (1989). Linguistics and animal communication. In F. Newmeyer (Ed.), *Linguistics: The Cambridge survey. III. Language: Psychological and biological aspects.* Cambridge, MA: Cambridge University Press.

Dinneen, F. (1967). *An introduction to general linguistics.* New York: Holt, Rinehart & Winston.

Fodor, J., Bever, T., & Garrett, M. (1974). *The psychology of language: An introduction to psycholinguistics.* New York: McGraw-Hill.

Frazier, L. (1988). Grammar and language processing. In F. Newmeyer (Ed.) *Linguistics: The Cambridge survey. II. Linguistic theory: Extensions and implications.* Cambridge: Cambridge University Press.

Garman, M. (1990). *Psycholinguistics*. Cambridge: Cambridge University Press.

Garnes, S., & Bond, Z. (1980). A slip of the ear: A snip of the ear? A slip of the year? In V. Fromkin (Ed.), *Errors in linguistic performance: Slips of the tongue, ear, pen and hand*. New York: Academic Press.

Hyams, N. (1986). *Language acquisition and the theory of parameters*. Dordrecht, Holland: Reidel.

Jenkins, J., & Polermo, D. (1964). Mediation processes and the acquisition of linguistic structure. In U. Bellugi & R. Brown (Eds.), *The acquisition of language*. Chicago: University of Chicago Press.

Labove, W. (1973). The boundaries of words and their meanings. In C. J. Bailey & R. Shuy (Eds.), *New ways of analyzing variation in English*. Washington, DC: Georgetown University Press, 340–373.

Leonard, L., & Loeb, D. F. (1988). Government-binding theory and some of its applications: A tutorial. *Journal of Speech and Hearing Research, 31* (4), 515–524.

MacWhinney, B., & Bates, E. (1989). *The cross-linguistic study of sentence processing*. Cambridge: Cambridge University Press.

Maddieson, I. (1984). *Patterns of sounds*. Cambridge: Cambridge University Press.

McCloskey, J. (1988). Syntactic theory. In F. Newmeyer (Ed.), *Linguistics: The Cambridge Survey. I. Linguistic theory: Foundations*. Cambridge: Cambridge University Press.

Menyuk, P. (1968). *Sentences children use*. Cambridge, MA: MIT Press.

Miller, G. (1990). Linguists, psychologists, and the cognitive sciences. *Language, 66*, 317–322.

Miller, G., & McKean, K. (1964). A chronometric study of some relations between sentences. *Quarterly Journal of Experimental Psychology, 16*, 297–308.

Newmeyer, F. (1986). *Linguistic theory in America* (2nd ed.). Orlando: Academic Press.

Osgood, C. (1963). On understanding and creating sentences. *American Psychologist, 18*, 735–751.

Poizner, H., Klima, E., & Bellugi, U. (1987). *What the hands reveal about the brain*. Cambridge, MA: MIT Press.

Premack, A. (1976) *Why chimps can read*. New York: Harper Colophon.

Rumbaugh, D. (Ed). (1977). *Language learning by a chimpanzee*. New York: Academic Press.

Sampson, G. (1985). *Writing systems*. London: Hutchinson Press.

Skinner, B. F. (1957). *Verbal behavior*. New York: Appleton-Century.

Slobin, D. (1985). *The crosslinguistic study of language acquisition. Volume 1: The data. Volume 2: Theoretical issues*. Hillsdale, NJ: Erlbaum.

Smith, N. (1989). *The twitter machine: Reflections on language*. Oxford: Basil Blackwell.

Staats, A. (1971). Linguistic-mentalistic theory vs. an explanatory S-R learning theory of language development. In D. Slobin (Ed.), *The ontogenesis of grammar*. New York: Academic Press.

Sterne, Laurence (1760; 1964). *The life and opinions of Tristram Shandy, gentleman*. New York: Dell.

Tannen, D. (1990). *But you just don't understand*. New York: Morrow.

Tannenhaus, M. (1989). Psycholinguistics: An overview. In F. Newmeyer (Ed.), *Linguistics: The Cambridge survey, Volume III*. Cambridge: Cambridge University Press.

Terrace, H. (1979). *Nim*. New York: Knopf.

Thomas, L. (1983). *Late night thoughts on listening to Mahler's Ninth Symphony*. New York: Viking.

Wilbur, R. (1989). *American Sign Language: Linguistic and applied dimensions*. Boston: College-Hill Press.

Answers to problems:

1. The difference between the two sets of sentences lies in the two differing functions of the word *out*. In a) and b), *out* is not a preposition, as most students assume it is. It is what is called a verb particle, a portion of a two-part verb. English has many two-part verbs, such as *throw out, call up, look up,* and *give back*. (Consider the difference in meaning between the sentences, *"He threw out the ball,"* and *"He threw the ball."*) English permits the placement of verb particles, in most circumstances, either next to the verb, or after the object, as in a) and b). In c), however, *out* functions as a preposition, which must always remain at the beginning of a prepositional phrase. Children seem to inherently know this and do not attempt to say d). However, they are often unaware that verb particles must be moved away from their verbs when the object is a pronoun as in **"I called up her," "I called her up,"* or the child who says, *"Blow up this"* when offering a balloon. This exception to the generally free placement of verb particles is often a later acquisition.

2. A usual starting place is to note that the tag portion of the sentence reuses (or copies) parts of the original declarative. While one could simply say that the pronoun and its verb are to be copied, and their order inverted, this is insufficient to yield the results in e) and f). Rather, you must locate the subject and derive an appropriate corresponding pronoun for it (one which is matched to the subject in person, number, and case); that is, you do not see either direct copying of the subject **"The boy isn't happy, is the boy?"* or mismatched pronouns **"The boy isn't happy, is me?"* Next, while it would be easy and sufficient for examples a)–d) to say that the verb is copied, in fact only part of the verb is replicated in the tag. Note that the auxiliary (or helping verb) in a) and b) is the only part of the verb used; in f), only the modal form *will* is used. In general, only the first part of the verb phrase is used to build the tag. Example e) is problematic. In sentences where the verb is not the copula (verb *to be*) or has no auxiliary or modal elements, a helping verb (always derived from the verb *do*) must be "manufactured" to complete the tag; thus, we get *"Your sister likes ice cream, doesn't she?"* rather than **"Your sister likes ice cream, likesn't she?"* Akmajian and Heny (1976) provide detailed analysis of this and other common sentence forms of English, albeit within the framework of transformational generative grammar. Our point in this book is merely to illustrate the immense difference between uttering or comprehending such sentences, and knowing what implicit rules we use, or what processes are involved.

The Biological Bases of Human Communicative Behavior

WILLIAM ORR DINGWALL

The University of Maryland at College Park

Introduction

This chapter explores the anatomical and physiological bases of speech and language behavior. In other chapters, we are most concerned with asking *how* people understand spoken and written language, and how they produce it. Here we ask *where* such talents lie within the brain. Can given communicative abilities be attributed to particular areas of the cerebral cortex? How does one determine where in the brain a particular function is encoded? Are particular speech and language abilities represented in a single discrete area, or multiple areas? What happens to communicative ability in the presence of brain damage? These and other questions will be addressed as we survey historical and current **neurolinguistic** inquiry.

In the first section of this chapter, we note how early researchers first discovered and investigated the relation between brain and language. This section will also acquaint you with some of the basic "geography" of the human nervous system. Section two details the anatomy and physiology of the brain and describes some speech and language consequences of brain damage, which have the potential to allow us to see the role which particular parts of the brain apparently play in language production and understanding. This section will also examine the question of whether we can assign the various components of language (articulation, naming, grammatical formulation, comprehension, etc.) to specific areas or interconnected combinations of areas within the human nervous system, using the consequences of brain damage as a guide. Section three examines the relative contributions made by the two cerebral hemispheres to speech and language function, a concept termed **lateralization of function**. Section four explores the recent experimental techniques that have been developed to allow researchers to more precisely localize particular speech and language functions to specific areas within each hemisphere using subject responses during actual language tasks. Our final section explores the efforts of linguists, neurologists, and psychologists to integrate findings from both normal and language-impaired individuals to construct a rational model of the neurological bases of speech and language function.

Language and the brain: A historical perspective

He is speechless, it means he is silent in sadness, without speaking.
(Case 22, The Edwin Smith Surgical Papyrus of 3000 B.C.)

The long history of the study of the relationship between language functioning and the brain (cf. Young, 1974; Clarke & O'Malley [Eds.], 1968) is peopled with a cast of unforgettable characters of great intellectual insight. This section provides you with a brief overview of some of these individuals and their accomplishments.

It was unfortunately violence which provided us with our first insights into how the brain controls behavior. Starting with stones, and "progressing" to more advanced technology, humans have managed to inflict a wide variety of head injuries upon one another. From such injuries as well as the results of various diseases particular patterns of behavior following brain damage were noted even in early times.

Early neurolinguistic observations

Edwin Smith, an American, acquired a papyrus scroll in 1862 which many believe contains the first mention of the consequences of brain injury. Parts of this scroll have been dated to 3000 B.C. Forty-eight cases were discussed in this papyrus. Case 22 (quoted above) notes that the loss of speech skills was possible following head trauma. Many have regarded it as the first mention of **aphasia** (loss of language abilities due to brain damage). To this day, trauma (injury to the brain produced by external force) continues to provide us with insights into brain function.

The ancient Greeks, when speculating about brain function, offered little insight, despite their contributions in many other areas of inquiry. For example, Aristotle (384–322 B.C.) said that the heart performed what we know to be brain functions and that the brain was just a cooling system, a radiator. This theory led Shakespeare, centuries later, to query in the *Merchant of Venice*: "Tell me where is fancy bred, or in the heart or in the head?"

Hippocratic scholars (460–370 B.C.) correctly observed that brain injury often produced contralateral (opposite sided) paresis (semiparalysis). They also noted that speech disturbances commonly accompanied left-sided brain injury and right-sided paresis. However, they never related these two crucial observations.

Herophilus and Galen, in the second century, developed the Ventricle or Cell Theory of brain function, which localized brain activity to its cavities, the ventricles, where cerebral spinal fluid (CSF) production takes place. It was Leonardo da Vinci (1452–1519) who disproved the Greek theory that the ventricles played a major role in brain functioning. Leonardo demonstrated this through animal dissections proving that the nerve tracts traveling from the retina of the eyes (the optic nerves) go nowhere near the ventricles.

By the eighteenth century almost all known language and speech disorders had already been described (Benton & Joynt, 1960). In the sixteenth century, a prominent medical scholar, Johann Schenk Von Grafenberg (1530–1598) was probably the first to point out that language disturbances due to brain damage (aphasia) were not due to paralysis of the tongue, thus distinguishing between aphasia and the neuromotor speech disorder we now call **dysarthria**, in which the ability to articulate speech sounds has been impaired.

At about the same time, G. Mercuriale (1588) first described what is now known as **pure alexia** or **alexia without agraphia**. He was astonished that his patient ". . . could write but could not read what he has written." In an age when scholars spoke Latin as well as their local language, the first cases of **bilingual aphasia** (aphasia affecting the use of two languages) were documented (Gesner, 1770). This same scholar provided us with the first descriptions of **jargon aphasia** and **jargon agraphia**, in which the affected patient's speech and writing was filled with seemingly meaningless nonsense words. The retained ability to recite overlearned materials such as prayers in the presence of severe aphasia was also noted by Peter Rommel in 1683. This retention of **automatic speech** has been documented countless times since then.

The view that language might be localized to a particular part of the brain, in particular the frontal lobes, was advanced in 1819, by Franz Josef Gall (1758–1828). This distinguished neuroanatomist, who was the first to point out the difference between white and gray matter in the brain, was also the founder of **cranioscopy** (better known today as **phrenology**). Gall felt that those particularly gifted in the memorization of verbal materials could be distinguished by prominent, even bulging eyes. His explanation for this "fact," years later, was **hypertrophy** (excessive growth) of the brain tissue in back of the eyes. Gall went on to postulate some 27 mental "organs" encompassing such traits as vanity, friendship, wisdom, and religion, which by hypertrophy or atrophy could affect the behavioral make-up of individuals.

As extraordinary as this view appears, it may well be correct in its basic outline. As Jerison (1977) has observed, the concept of localization of function in the brain still has validity. What is evidently incorrect is the type of mental faculties that Gall chose to localize. Language is undoubtedly localized in the brain in some complex manner but not, as we shall see, as a unitary phenomenon. However, Gall was able to document cases of trauma and stroke in the frontal cortex resulting in loss of what he termed "verbal memory," thus providing much stronger evidence for the role of that portion of the brain in language functioning.

Localization of function (nineteenth and twentieth century neurology)

It was during the nineteenth century, however, that the first concentrated attempts were made to understand how language was organized within the brain through the study of aphasic patients. The first behavior of any type to be localized within the human brain was articulate (spoken) language (Young, 1974).

The French surgeon Pierre Paul Broca (1824–1880), who made this remarkable discovery, is portrayed in Figure 2.1 in a manner that would have undoubtedly pleased him. This statue, which unfortunately no longer exists, shows Broca measuring a human skull with a sliding caliper, one of the many instruments which he invented for *craniometry* (measurement of skulls and/or brains).

As a founding father of what we now call physical anthropology, Broca was greatly intrigued with brain size and its relationship to age, sex, intelligence, race, and environment. This area of study is extremely controversial (see M. Hahn et al. [Eds.], 1979; Passingham, 1982, for recent overviews). Broca belonged to an anthropological society whose members examined human skulls and occasionally conducted research on the brains of deceased medical patients. Through such research they sought to attribute various behaviors to either the shape or size of the cranium

Figure 2.1

The statue of Broca, Place de l'École de Médecine (1887–1942), Boulevard St. Germain, by Choppin. The inscription reads: Paul Broca, Fondateur de la Société d'Anthropologie, Professeur à la Faculté de Médecine de Paris, Sénateur, 1824–1880. (Courtesy Viollet, 6 Rue de Seine, Paris.) (from Schiller, 1979)

or to sites of damage in the brain. It was during the meetings of this society in 1861 that another member, Dr. Ernest Aubertin, mentioned a patient of his who had a traumatic frontal cranial defect. When Aubertin applied light pressure to the frontal area while the patient was speaking, he would stop in midword, only to begin speaking again once the compression ceased.

Shortly thereafter, Broca encountered a patient in Paris by the name of Leborgne. He had been a patient in a nursing home for some 21 years, and thus Broca was able to obtain an overview of the progression of his illness. The patient had been admitted at the age of 31 years because he had lost the ability to speak. He seemed to understand what was said to him but answered queries with the single syllable *tan* accompanied by gestures. If sufficiently provoked, he was also capable of producing a few swear words.

Broca invited Dr. Aubertin to examine Leborgne in order to compare this patient's language deficit with the type that his fellow physician would expect to follow from a frontal lobe lesion. After his examination, Aubertin affirmed this diagnosis. When Leborgne died, Broca performed the autopsy and confirmed a striking frontal lobe lesion in the area of the third frontal convolution (**gyrus**) in the left hemisphere.

By 1868, Broca had studied 20 cases like that of Leborgne. In 19 of these, the lesion occupied the posterior part of the left third frontal convolution (Broca, 1868). A speech sample from what has come to be called a **Broca's aphasic** is provided in Table 2.1, together with other samples of disordered communication which we will discuss in the next section.

Note that the speech of the patient in Sample A appears halting, sparse, and devoid of recognizable sentence structure. This nonfluent, agrammatic type of output is characteristic of Broca's aphasia. By 1885, Broca felt that he had amassed enough evidence to proclaim that for the vast majority of people "nous parlons avec l'hémisphère gauche," (we speak with the left hemisphere), (Broca, 1865, p. 384).

Gall had not lateralized language to either frontal lobe. Broca made it clear that we are usually left-lateralized for articulate language (la faculté du langage articulé), but not for the motor act of articulation, which he correctly stated depended to an equal degree on both hemispheres (Broca, 1865, p. 384).

Broca was also one of the first to relate lateralization of language to handedness. He did not do so in the simplistic manner of Dax (1836), who said that language was always left-lateralized. Nor did he assume that right-handers are left-lateralized and left-handers are right-lateralized—a view that has unfortunately been repeatedly attributed to Broca as well. Rather, Broca related both handedness and lateralization of language to the precocious development of the left hemisphere. He also advanced the possibility of **plasticity** of brain function, stating:

> . . . *a lesion of the left third frontal convolution, apt to produce lasting aphemia (Broca's term for aphasia) in an adult, will not prevent a small child from learning to talk.* . . .

(Broca, 1865; 392)

Table 2.1	
Four Examples of Communicative Disorders in Speakers of English	A. ***Broca's Aphasia.*** Yes . . . ah . . . Monday . . . er . . . Dad and Peter H . . . (his own name), and Dad . . . er . . . hospital . . . and ah . . . Wednesday . . . Wednesday, nine o'clock, ah doctors . . . two . . . an' doctors . . . and er . . . teeth . . . yah. (Patient's effort to explain that he came into the hospital for dental surgery.)
	B. ***Wernicke's Aphasia.*** Well this is . . . mother is away here working her work out here to get her better, but when she's looking, the two boys looking in the other part. One their small tile into her time here. She's working another time because she's getting, too . . . (Patient's description of a scene in which two children are stealing cookies while the mother's back is turned.)
	C. ***Jargon Aphasia.*** All right. Azzuh bezzuh dee pasty hass rih tau dul too. Aulaz foley ass in duh porler dermass died duh paulmasty kide the, the, baidy pahsty bide uh . . . laidy faid uh . . . tiny bride. Uh . . . uh . . . orlihmin fee in a do . . . but uh, ordimis fihd and it was ahrdimidehsty by uhbuhtray dis (unintelligible) you do you know. (In answer to the question: What kind of work did you do?)
	D. ***Dementia.*** Well, it's about half and half. It's a marble and it's half and half. Uhm, that uhm, I'm trying to think what the and ya know and I've been doing all this color work and uhm. I'm trying to think. There's a white and there's a black and there's a, uhm, uhm, I'm trying to think, uh, it, it's, like uhm, oh, what that called? Ym, more of a, oh damn, in the colors that I have in my book is uhm more vivid, and this is a little darker, and I'm trying to think, what's it called purple, more on the purple order this is. (In answer to the question: Tell me about this marble.)

In the years since then, we have come to see additional examples of the flexibility of the young brain in responding to brain damage. Lenneberg (1968) went so far as to posit that there was a critical period for language acquisition, during which language learning occurred readily, and brain damage did not produce lasting communicative disorder. As we shall see later in the chapter, children do appear to make remarkable recovery from brain injury, although subtle changes in linguistic ability may be detectable.

Some support for the notion of a critical period beyond which language learning or recovery might be difficult was provided by the discovery, in 1970, of a young girl who had been brought up under conditions of extreme neglect and abuse. Between the ages of 2 and 13½, this child, Genie, was kept confined and was provided with little or no verbal interaction. Genie was unable to speak or understand language when removed from the home by social welfare workers. Although she was provided with intensive language stimulation and instruction following her rescue by authorities, she experienced great difficulty in learning expressive grammar, despite rather good progress in language comprehension and vocabulary development. A full discussion of this unfortunate but remarkable case is provided by Curtiss (1977) and Rymer (1992).

We have already said that even in ancient Greece, there was enough evidence to establish lateralization of function. Why was this association not made? Perhaps for the same reason that Broca's views were resisted when he announced them. For example, in discussing these views in 1865, Laborde (quoted in Berker et al., 1968) stated that he found it difficult to admit that "two parts of the same organ, whose situation, size, and detailed anatomical structures were absolutely identical and symmetrical, could have different functions."

The premise that the hemispheres are anatomically identical turns out to be false, and it was Broca himself who first demonstrated that this was so. He completed analysis on 37 brains and found that the mean weight of the right hemispheres was slightly greater than that of the left; however, the mean weight of the left frontal lobe was greater than the right (Broca, 1875). Both of these findings are supported by current research.

It is interesting to note that Leborgne's preserved brain has actually been analyzed by a neuroimaging technique known as a CT scan or **computerized transaxial tomography**. Figure 2.2 displays a horizontal section showing a massive lesion of the left frontal convolution (F_3), which has come to be known as **Broca's area**, as well as the precentral gyrus and the insula.

This modern CT scan analysis also shows another, intact, area of the brain, implicated in language and speech processing by a neurologist contemporaneous with Broca. This area is now named after Carl Wernicke (1848–1904). Wernicke, a German, studied along with Sigmund Freud (1856–1939) and Theodor Meynert

Figure 2.2

A horizontal section obtained via CT scan through the brain of Broca's patient, Leborgne, demonstrating involvement of the left third frontal convolution, precentral and postcentral gyri with sparing of Wernicke's area in the left first temporal gyrus (from Signoret et al., 1984).

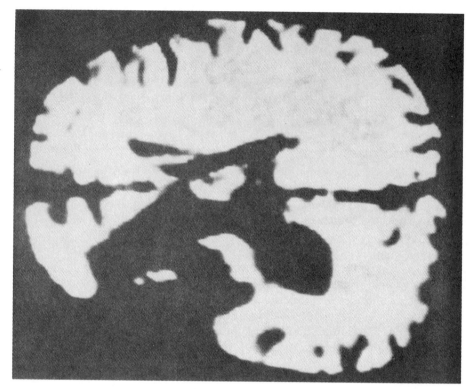

(1833–1892), a neurologist who traced the elusive and most complex cranial nerve, the auditory nerve, which reaches from the ear to the cortex. The highest (most **rostral**) area of hearing is known as **Heschl's gyrus**, and is buried deep within the Sylvian fissure. The area of interest to Wernicke was contiguous with this cortical area for hearing. Damage to this area resulted in a complex of symptoms very different from those which Broca had observed.

A typical example of Wernicke's aphasia is illustrated in Sample B in Table 2.1. Unlike Broca's aphasics, these patients are fluent—so garrulous in fact that they have been termed **logorrheic**. For the most part, this patient's speech has discernible grammatical structure. However, it doesn't appear to make much sense; consider the somewhat random array of words in the phrase, "one their small tile into her time here." While Broca's aphasics are acutely aware of their language problems, Wernicke's aphasics often are not and may even deny that they are ill **(anosognosia)**. Both Broca's and Wernicke's aphasics have comprehension problems, but they are much more severe in Wernicke's aphasia, although many Wernicke's patients appear to understand at least some of what is addressed to them, but wander further and further astray as they respond. Some patients produce jargon, as in Sample C, using "Jabberwocky" words that do not exist in English, such as *porler, demass,* and *ahrdimidehsty*. Even when such jargon is absent, their speech rapidly becomes meaningless and filled with inappropriate words.

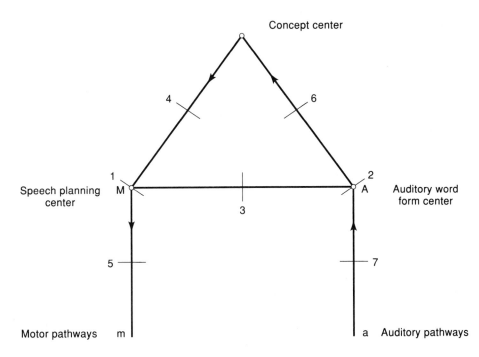

Concept center

Speech planning center

Auditory word form center

Motor pathways

Auditory pathways

Figure 2.3

The Wernicke–Lichtheim Model of the Aphasias

1. Cortical Motor Aphasia (= Broca's aphasia)
2. Cortical Sensory Aphasia (= Wernicke's aphasia)
3. Conduction Aphasia
4. Transcortical Motor Aphasia
5. Subcortical Motor Aphasia (= pure word mutism)
6. Transcortical Sensory Aphasia
7. Subcortical Sensory Aphasia (= pure word deafness)
(Adapted from Lichtheim, 1885)

As the speech samples and our discussions illustrate, Broca's and Wernicke's aphasia differ strikingly. The Broca's aphasic is nonfluent, using language which seems sparse, labored, and **agrammatic** (missing important grammatical morphemes), although his or her comprehension appears reasonable. The Wernicke's aphasic appears fluent, using long complicated utterances which unfortunately do not make much sense. Their speech is apt to be full of **neologisms** or nonsense words. Finally, they appear quite disordered in their ability to understand both the speech of others and their own output.

Later, Wernicke, working with the neurologist Ludwig Lichtheim (1885), was able to provide a classification of the observed aphasias as well as those logically possible, though not yet described (Wernicke, 1906). This classification is shown in Figure 2.3.

The Wernicke-Lichtheim model is based on neuroanatomical considerations, and predicts the communicative consequences of injury to various parts of the brain. It has become the "classical model" of the aphasias within neurology and has been elaborated by the great American neurologist, Norman Geschwind (Geschwind, 1974). From its inception, it was not without detractors (Goldstein, 1948; Head, 1963; Cole & Cole, 1971) and, as you shall see, it is being attacked once again today. Although admittedly simplistic, the model has proved remarkably resilient (Goodglass, 1988). This may be because this model makes good neurological sense. It constitutes a first approximation to the final goal of localizing speech and language functions within the brain. The next section will survey the anatomical considerations which contribute to the development of such a model of the aphasias. In it, we will examine the anatomy of the brain and central nervous system, and more closely ana-lyze the behaviors which result from damage to various portions of this system.

Functional neuroanatomy and neuropathology

> . . . an enchanted loom where millions of flashing shuttles weave a dissolving pattern, always a meaningful pattern though never an abiding one; a shifting harmony of subpatterns.
>
> (Sherrington, *Gifford Lectures*, 1937–8)

The student who seeks to explore brain/behavior relationships should first under-stand the anatomy and physiology of the nervous system. Having gained a fairly detailed idea of how the human nervous system functions in the healthy individual, the next topic to approach is **neuropathology**, the study of what can go wrong with the system. It is from the study of such "experiments of nature" that much of our knowledge of the human nervous system stems. Finally, an acquaintance with the available research techniques is useful. These range from detailed single case studies through highly sophisticated neuropsychological experimentation to the use of advanced instrumentation employed in neurological diagnosis. A guide to the litera-ture in these areas is provided in Dingwall (1981).

Neuroanatomical structures involved in speech and language

Figure 2.4 depicts the central nervous system (CNS)—that part of the nervous sys-tem housed within the bony structures of the skull (**cranium**) and vertebral column. Not only is it protected by these bony coverings, it is wrapped in three layers of membranes, the **meninges**, and floats in **cerebral spinal fluid (CSF)** produced in the four ventricles of the brain. Despite its minuscule weight, averaging about 3.5 pounds, the brain utilizes one-fifth of the body's blood supply.

The most rostral (from the Latin "toward the beak") structure, the cerebral cor-tex, is depicted at the very top of Figure 2.4. ("Cortex" is Latin for "bark," as in bark of a tree.) Its general appearance characterized by hills (gyri) and valleys (sulci or fissures) may have influenced its naming by medieval anatomists. (In fact, most of the basic structures of the central nervous system have names with very down-to-earth meanings in Greek or Latin. I find that learning these meanings helps me remember the names.) Actually, the reason for the barklike appearance of the cortex, which is roughly 2.5 square feet in area, is dictated by folding a sheet of this size into the confines of the cranium.

The cortex, like almost every structure in the brain (and in the body), is paired (e.g., it has a left and right part). These two parts are the cerebral hemispheres,

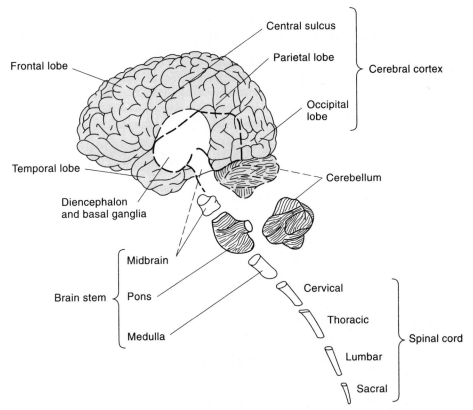

Figure 2.4

The parts of the central
nervous system (from
Kandel and Schwartz,
1981)

which are connected by a number of fiber tracts (commissures) the most massive of which is known as the **corpus callosum** (calloused body) shown in Figure 2.5.

We have already learned that although the two hemispheres appear identical, in fact, they are not. There are morphological (form) differences between them, which have now been extensively catalogued. While language, in the vast majority of individuals, is lateralized to the left hemisphere, this is not true for articulation, which is subserved by both hemispheres. It is evident that handedness appears to be correlated in some manner with "brainedness." Language behavior is subserved by different cortical areas or loci located within different lobes of the cortex.

When Gall introduced the distinction between white and gray matter within the brain, he was referring to the nerve fibers and groups of nerve cells (neurons) respectively. Grossly, the brain resembles a layer cake with alternating layers of these two types of matter. As can be seen in Figure 2.4, and in more detail in Figure 2.6, at the very center of the brain is a mass of neurons, the **diencephalon** (between brain). This may be regarded as the first layer of gray matter. This paired structure is made up of a number of components which, among many other functions, serves as a way station for all incoming sensations (with the exception of smell [olfaction]) before they travel on to the cortex. It also plays a major role in providing motor feedback to

Corpus
callosum

Figure 2.5

Is Your Left
Hemisphere Different
from Your Right?

Photo of human brain as
seen from above, looking
down on partially split
corpus callosum.

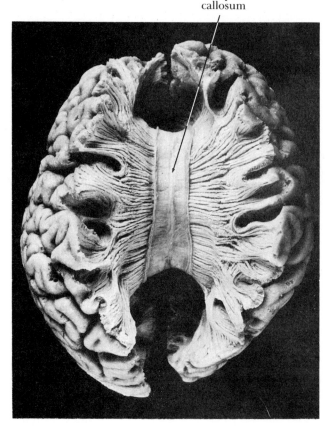

the cortex. The **dorsal thalamus**, one of the components of the diencephalon, has been shown to be lateralized like the overlying cortex. Damage to the left side can produce both aphasia and **dysarthria**, an articulation disorder (Kennedy & Murdoch, 1989). The white matter layers of the brain are made up of ascending and descending fibers to and from the cortex. Those surrounding the diencephalon are known as the **internal capsule**.

The next layer of gray matter that we encounter is made up of the **basal ganglia**. This complex structure not only plays a major role in the control of movement but also appears to be involved in cognitive functioning. Damage to the basal ganglia can result in poverty of movement (**hypokinesia**), as in Parkinson's disease, or too much movement (**hyperkinesia**), as in Huntington's chorea (dance), as well as tremor at rest. It is also known now that damage here can result not only in dysarthria but also aphasia.

Surrounding the basal ganglia is another white matter layer, the external capsule, beyond which lies the cortical mantle, the cerebral cortex. Below the cerebral hemispheres lies the cerebellum (little brain). (See Figures 2.4 and 2.7.) This structure is known to play a major role in motor control in conjunction with the basal ganglia, diencephalon, and the cortex itself. Damage to the cerebellum results in a

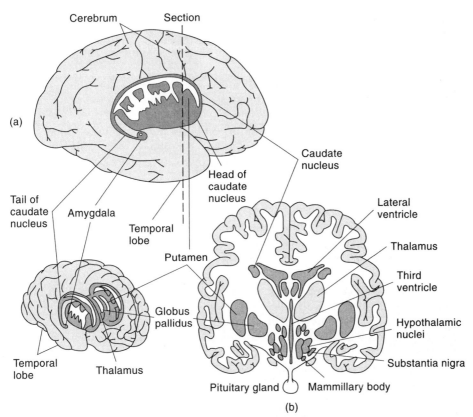

Figure 2.6

(a) Lateral view of the basal ganglia and thalamus. (b) Frontal section through the brain at the plane shown in (a).

breakdown in movement coordination (**ataxia**) as well as tremor in voluntary movements. Dysarthria can result from damage to the cerebellum. Currently no language deficits have been reported from damage to this area.

At the very base of the brain is the **brain stem**, composed of the **midbrain**, **pons** (bridge), and **medulla** (marrow). In some sense, this could be regarded as the most important part of the brain, as it controls the functioning of the heart and lungs.

The remainder of the central nervous system consists of the **spinal cord** housed within the vertebral column. It directly controls motor and sensory functions of the entire body with the exception of the face area. The human spinal cord is unfortunately **non-autonomous**. By this we mean that ultimately all functions of the body are controlled from the brain via the spinal cord. The spinal cord in humans cannot function independently of the brain. This is why a broken neck can lead to paralysis of the entire body below the neck.

The **peripheral nervous system (PNS)** encompasses those components of the nervous system that lie outside of the bony coverings of the central nervous system. This includes the **cranial nerves** that issue directly from the cranium and the **spinal nerves** that issue from the vertebral column. The cranial nerves are important in controlling such functions as vision, smell, hearing, and facial sensation. Specific cranial nerves play crucial roles in **phonation** (laryngeal or voice activity) and tongue movement necessary for articulation.

How speech is controlled by the brain

Language is not the only species-specific aspect of human communicative behavior; speech is, as well (Dingwall, 1975). Darley et al. (1975) have estimated that speech involves at least 100 muscles, each controlled by perhaps as many motoneurons. At a normal speech rate of about 14 sounds per second, this would mean that 140,000 neuromuscular events per second are required for speaking.

Research suggests (Kuypers, 1981) that there are at least three distinct motor systems in all primates, including humans. One system controls individual movements of the fingers (digits); a second system controls independent movements of the hands and arms; and the third controls posture and bilateral trunk and limb movements.

A striking dissociation of these motor control systems is often seen in global aphasia, where a patient with little evidence of speech, language, or the ability to carry out individual limb movements to command (ideomotor praxis) can nevertheless respond to complex axial commands, such as "stand up, turn around, go to the door, bow, etc."

The best candidate for the motor control system of speech appears to be the first "finger" system. It is most highly developed in primates, particularly the chimpanzee

Figure 2.7

Sagittal section of the human brain showing the medial aspect of the left hemisphere.

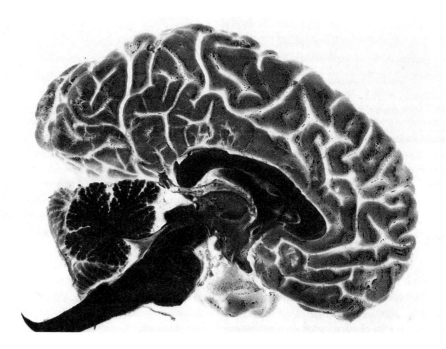

and humans. It corresponds to the fibers of the pyramidal tract that cross over either in the brain stem or in the spinal cord in Figure 2.8. The fibers we are interested in are not only those that cross, but that also make direct contact on motoneurons either in the brain stem or spinal cord.

Let us examine this tract briefly. Note, first of all, the odd-looking creature perched at the top of the figure. This is the famous motor homunculus (little man) schema of motor organization suggested by neurosurgeon Wilder Penfield (1891–1976), who mapped functional areas in the brain by electrically stimulating them. Since the brain itself is without pain receptors, such stimulation can be carried out on conscious patients under local anesthesia prior to medically necessary removal (ablation) of diseased neuronal tissue. Neurosurgeons must obviously try to avoid damaging the speech and language areas of the cortex we have discussed, and one way to locate these areas is via **electrical stimulation of the brain (ESB)**. Penfield was a pioneer in this area, and his book *Speech and Brain-Mechanisms*, which summarizes some of his findings, is well known (Penfield & Roberts, 1959). In it, the awkward little homunculus "lies across" areas of the cortex which appear to control the function of his various body parts. Note how large his head and tongue appear in relation to his trunk, for example; this is because proportionately more cortical area appears to be devoted to head and tongue functioning than the torso. We may also note that while many areas adjacent to one another cortically subserve adjacent body parts (hip to knee to ankle to toes), the homunculus is not an exact photocopy of an actual person (consider the proximity of the neck and thumb to one another in their cortical representation, for example).

The aspect of the pyramidal tract which interests us in this discussion arises in part from the motor strip (Brodmann area 4) along which the homunculus lies, and in particular from that lower portion where the face and some of the speech organs are represented. Fibers from this area travel downward and cross at the level of the brain stem making contact with (synapsing) nerves (in this case, cranial nerves), that exit directly from the skull to control, among other things, the speech musculature. There are 12 pairs of cranial nerves in humans (other animals have more). Some are sensory; some, motor; some, both. In a tangential way, all could be said to be involved in some aspect of human communication. But we are only interested here in those involved in speech production. For example, the fifth cranial nerve (trigeminal) handles both motor function and sensation for portions of the jaw and face. The seventh (facial) nerve controls motor and sensory functioning of most of the facial musculature, enabling aspects of articulation and facial expression. The tenth (vagus) controls aspects of laryngeal function necessary for voicing, and the twelfth (hypoglossal) controls tongue movement necessary for articulation. The eighth cranial nerve is the auditory nerve, which has been discussed earlier. Still other cranial nerves are responsible for aspects of vision, eye movement, and olfaction (smell), which will not be described in detail.

While some of the cranial nerves clearly must play some role in vocalization and articulation, they have not yet been studied in sufficient detail in humans or nonhuman primates to allow us to determine their precise role in speech production. The Czech physiologist J. Krmpotić (1959) noted that both the length of these nerves and their diameters vary greatly, two factors involved in speed of conduction of neural

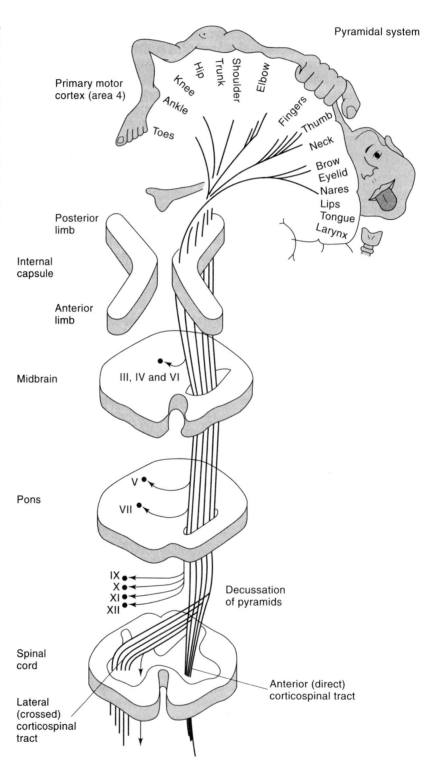

Figure 2.8

The Pyramidal Tract

The portion of this tract that decussates in the brain stem or spinal cord with direct synapse on lower motoneurons is that motor system controlling fine movements in the digits as well as the speech mechanism in humans (from Netter, 1983). CIBA West Caldwell, N.J.

Pyramidal system

Primary motor cortex (area 4)

Hip
Knee
Ankle
Toes
Trunk
Shoulder
Elbow
Fingers
Thumb
Neck
Brow
Eyelid
Nares
Lips
Tongue
Larynx

Posterior limb

Internal capsule

Anterior limb

Midbrain — III, IV and VI

Pons — V, VII

IX
X
XI
XII

Decussation of pyramids

Spinal cord

Anterior (direct) corticospinal tract

Lateral (crossed) corticospinal tract

impulses. This raises the totally unresolved issue as to how the various aspects of the vocal tract are coordinated in the production of speech.

The evolution of human communicative ability

 Another approach which may provide us with insight into how human communicative ability is mediated by the brain is to study communicative behavior in closely related species. It is unlikely that speech and language arose as a single genetic mutation; rather, it is much more likely that such a complex behavior developed gradually over time. Toulmin (1971) has offered the opinion that certain physiological behaviors, once used for nonlinguistic purposes, eventually became associated behaviorally with language functions.

Recent research using squirrel monkeys has identified areas which, when damaged, result in the disturbance or elimination of vocalization. Similar vocalization areas exist in man, and their damage results in similar consequences. The monkey's cingulate cortex and supplementary motor area (roughly equivalent to the human Brodmann area 6) appear to be necessary for the initiation of conditioned vocalization, but not for the production of innate calls.

It appears that control of nonhuman primate vocalization terminates at subcortical levels, unlike human cortical representation of language abilities. Unilateral or bilateral destruction of areas of the monkey cortex comparable to the human language areas does not produce appreciable effects on their vocalizations (Steklis & Raleigh, 1979; Passingham, 1982; Dingwall, 1988).

Neural cells and their connections: The ultimate basis of all behavior

This section was titled *functional neuroanatomy*, rather than neuroanatomy and neurophysiology, as this latter term has come to refer to function at a much more microscopic or cellular level. The brain is composed of but two types of cells: nerve cells, **neurons**, and **glia** (glue cells). We do not win a prize for the largest number of these cells—there are animals larger than us in body size and brain weight. All these cells could be wired together, but they are not. Instead, a gap (the synapse) of minuscule proportion exists between one nerve cell and its processes (axons and dendrites) and the cells (often large in number) that are in contact with it. Across this gap, transmission occurs via chemical rather than electrophysiologic means. The chemical agents involved in this transmission are naturally known as **neurotransmitters**. It is in this microscopic world of cells, their membranes and neurochemistry that the true nature of our being may lie. Sherrington's comment at the beginning of this section mirrors the wonder he felt for the events transpiring in this realm.

One way of analyzing areas of the brain is in terms of **cytoarchitecture** (the organization of cells, their morphology and layering). One of the most often referenced "maps" of this type was produced by the German anatomist Korbinian Brodmann in 1909 (Figure 2.9). The numbers on this map (52 areas in all) are often utilized to this day as reference points. The table accompanying this figure may aid you in gaining an initial understanding for the location and function of some of the areas Brodmann designated in the cerebral cortex.

What can go wrong with the brain: Neuropathology

Unfortunately, many things can go wrong with a system this complex. Table 2.2 lists some common types of neuropathology and the communication disorders with which they are associated.

Cerebrovascular diseases kill neurons by cutting off their blood supply, thus depriving them of glucose and oxygen. Other pathologies such as trauma, tumors, and **hydrocephalus** destroy neuronal tissue by producing space-occupying masses consisting of blood, glial cells, or cerebrospinal fluid within the cranium. Such masses can even result in herniation of neural tissue around the meninges or through the **foramen magnum** (the hole in the base of the skull through which the spinal cord connects with the brain stem). Some diseases, such as **multiple sclerosis**, affect conduction of nerve impulses by eating away at the **myelin** (composed of oligodendroglial cells in the CNS and Schwann cells in the PNS) coverings of axons. Parkinsonism and Huntington's chorea result from neurotransmitter imbalances affecting the functions of the basal ganglia. Still other diseases such as **myasthenia gravis** come about from a decrease in neurotransmitter receptor sites on muscles. Thus, as you can see, if something can malfunction it will (see Gilroy & Holliday, 1982, for a concise and relatively comprehensive guide to neuropathology).

Examining the consequences of cortical damage

We have already discussed Broca's aphasia (labeled *cortical motor aphasia* in Figure 2.3). Other common terms for this condition include **expressive** or **nonfluent** aphasia. Broca said that this condition resulted from a lesion of the third frontal convolution. This region lies directly in front of the face area of the motor strip, and is labeled *Broca's area* on Figure 2.10. A lesion to the motor strip itself can produce a neuromotor disorder of speech called **dysarthria**. Dysarthric patients have laborious and inaccurate articulation, though their ability to formulate language is intact.

The area which Wernicke said produced **cortical sensory aphasia** (synonyms: **receptive** or **fluent** aphasia), which we have discussed, is located in the posterior third of the first temporal gyrus. This area, which has been shown to extend into the deep valley called the Sylvian fissure, lies behind the cortical area for audition (Heschl's gyrus), and has become known as **Wernicke's area** in his honor. Slightly

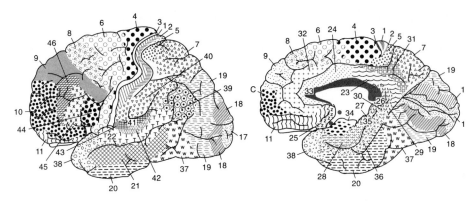

Figure 2.9

The cytoarchitectural maps of the lateral and medial surfaces of the human brain developed by Korbinian Brodmann (1909). The accompanying table provides information concerning the anatomical sites and functions of some of the fifty-two areas involved directly or indirectly with HCB.

BRODMANN AREA	ANATOMICAL LOCATION	FUNCTION
1, 2, 3	Postcentral gyrus	Primary sensori-motor area (Sm I)
4	Precentral gyrus	Primary motor-sensory area (Ms I)
6	Premotor cortex	Premotor area supplementary motor area (on medial surface) (Ms II)
8	Caudal part of middle frontal gyrus	Frontal eye field
9, 10, 11	Superior, middle and inferior frontal gyri	Judgment, foresight, mood
17	Walls of calcarine sulcus	Primary visual area
18, 19	Occipital lobe	Visual association areas
39	Angular gyrus	Reading and writing (dominant hemisphere)
40	Supramarginal gyrus	Repetition (possibly due to disruption of arcuate fasciculus) (dominant hemisphere)
41	Heschl's gyrus	Primary auditory area
42	Belt of cortex surrounding Heschl's gyrus	Auditory association area
22	Superior temporal gyrus	Posterior third = Wernicke's area (dominant hemisphere)
44, 45	Third frontal gyrus (pars opercularis and triangularis)	Broca's area (dominant hemisphere)

Table 2.2

Types of
Neuropathology and
Their Associated
Communicative
Disorders

TYPES OF NEUROPATHOLOGY	TYPES OF COMMUNICATION DISORDERS
Cerebrovascular Disease (hemorrhage, aneurysm, atherosclerosis, arteriovenous malformation (AVM)	Aphasia, dysarthria, dementia[1]
Degenerative Disease (e.g., Alzheimer's, Pick's Disease)	Dementia
Trauma (penetrating and closed head injury [CHI])	Aphasia, dysarthria, language of confusion
Parkinsonism	Dementia and dysarthria
Multiple Sclerosis	Dysarthria
Hydrocephalus	Aphasia
Tumor (neoplasm) (benign or malignant)	Aphasia and/or dysarthria
Huntington's chorea	Dementia and dysarthria
Hereditary ataxias	Dysarthria
Amyotrophic lateral sclerosis (ALS)	Dysarthria
Myasthenia gravis	Dysarthria

[1]The communicative disorder associated with dementia is often referred to by the rather cumbersome term: *language of generalized intellectual impairment.*

behind Wernicke's area lies the **angular gyrus**. The angular gyrus apparently plays a large role in the process of lexical access, or word retrieval, which is discussed in greater detail in Chapter 4. Damage to this area can produce a disorder known as **anomia**, in which the patient experiences difficulty in naming items, even though he or she can comprehend vocabulary reasonably well.

Given these two very different types of aphasias and the neuroanatomic sites associated with them, what other types of speech and language disorders might be possible?

Let us suppose that Wernicke's area and Heschl's gyrus are intact, but that the two are disconnected by some sort of lesion produced perhaps by a stroke or gunshot wound. Would the patient be able to hear? Yes. Heschl's gyrus is intact. Would he be able to understand what was said to him? No, because auditory signals are prevented from arriving at Wernicke's area by the lesion. This disorder is termed **subcortical sensory aphasia** in Figure 2.3 and is known as *pure word deafness* today. Patients with this disorder have been known to state: "I can hear what you say, but it just doesn't compute." Such patients can speak, write, and read normally. They may be able to distinguish nonspeech sounds but unable to interpret their own speech.

What might happen, on the motor (output) side, if Broca's area were disconnected from the face area of the motor strip or if the link between Wernicke's and

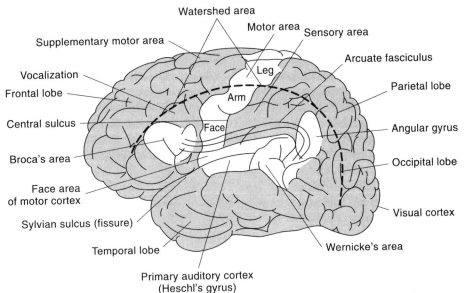

Watershed area
Motor area Sensory area
Supplementary motor area
Arcuate fasciculus
Leg
Vocalization
Parietal lobe
Frontal lobe
Arm
Central sulcus
Face
Angular gyrus
Broca's area
Occipital lobe
Face area
of motor cortex
Visual cortex
Sylvian sulcus (fissure)
Temporal lobe
Wernicke's area
Primary auditory cortex
(Heschl's gyrus)

Figure 2.10

Lateral view of the cerebral cortex of the left hemisphere showing the areas involved in language (Adapted from Kandel and Schwartz, 1981)

Broca's areas were disrupted? In the first case, patients should have preserved comprehension of what is said to them, as Wernicke's area is intact; however, they should be incapable of volitional speech as well as repetition, because Broca's area can no longer control the motor output to the vocal tract. This is true because Broca's area is no longer connected with the motor strip. Lichtheim (1885; pp. 449–453) documents a number of such cases of subcortical motor aphasia.

In the second case, conduction aphasia, a quite different picture emerges. Because the speech production and auditory comprehension areas are intact, the output of such patients is reasonably well formed, and they understand most of what they hear. However, because messages cannot travel via the **arcuate fasciculus** between the auditory and speech production areas, they are basically unable to repeat what they hear, though they may understand the message.

Wernicke and Lichtheim also proposed a concept center which when damaged produces **dementia** or **agnosia**. A conversational sample from a patient with dementia is provided in Table 2.1, Sample D, along with our examples of aphasic output. Note that what appears to be lacking in this patient's language is conceptual, rather than linguistic. Thus, while the ability to produce language has been spared, the process of thought, or ideation, appears to have been disrupted.

We have already observed that brain damage can dissociate speech from language (dysarthria) and language from speech (jargon aphasia). Can you imagine speech and language without ideation or the converse? Such dissociations do occur.

Suppose an individual suffered damage to the vast majority of the region below the dashed line in Figure 2.10. This **perisylvian area** (the area surrounding the Sylvian fissure) contains most of the cortex exclusively devoted to language. Now also suppose that this damage is reversible. What might this disorder look like? Well, the patient has damage to Broca's area and Wernicke's area as well as everything in between. He should thus lose all speech and language abilities. This type of aphasia (which Wernicke did not postulate) occurs, and is known as **global aphasia**.

A patient with an unusual reversible aphasia of this type due to epilepsy, **paroxysmal aphasia**, has been documented by Lecours and Joanette (1980). Their case provides insight into not only the consequences of such an aphasia, but also into the separability of thought and language processes. Brother John, a Catholic monk, periodically experiences "spells" which do not render him unconscious but rather globally aphasic. Lecours and Joanette describe one such spell during a train trip from Italy to Switzerland. Despite the loss of speech production, comprehension, and reading ability, Brother John was able to get off the train at the appropriate stop, find his hotel, find yet another place to stay when informed by gestures that his hotel is full, and order supper in a restaurant by pointing to items on the menu and hoping to get something he will like! By the next morning, all of his language skills returned to normal. This case offers striking support, as do other documented cases of global aphasia (cf. Gordon, 1990), for the retention of ideation or thought precesses in the absence of language, and for the separability of linguistic and cognitive competence. Possible dissociations between cognitive and linguistic capacity are also discussed in Chapter 8, where we describe language acquisition in children.

The converse dissociation, retention of language abilities with little evidence of intact thought processes, has also been observed. The lesion in this case is above the dashed line in Figure 2.10 and has thus been termed isolation of the speech area or **mixed transcortical aphasia**. The most detailed description of such a case is found in Whitaker (1976). The patient, HCEM, who was found upon autopsy to have suffered from Pick's disease, was totally noncommunicative with no spontaneous speech and little evidence of language comprehension. She spent most of her days quietly watching T.V. in the lounge of her nursing home.

One could demonstrate, however, that HCEM had not lost all aspects of communicative behavior. If one approached her and spoke to her directly, HCEM was **echolalic** (that is, she echoed or repeated what was said to her). The ability to repeat is the hallmark of all transcortical aphasias and was first suggested by Lichtheim (1885). In Table 2.3, you are presented with some of Dr. Whitaker's conversational exchanges with the patient.

In Sample A, you can see how adept HCEM is at repetition. In fact, she could even repeat foreign words but with an American accent! As Samples B and C demonstrate even more clearly, HCEM does not just echo. She repeats, applying the rules of her dialect of English. HCEM is not a parrot, but a human being who, although she has not lost the complex rule system of her native language, appears to be unable to use this linguistic "competence" to communicate.

HCEM's disorder, mixed transcortical aphasia, involves a combination of both transcortical motor aphasia and transcortical sensory aphasia. What distinguishes the transcortical aphasias from other types of aphasia is the preservation of the ability to repeat. Thus, transcortical motor aphasia is like Broca's aphasia, and transcortical sensory aphasia is like Wernicke's aphasia in terms of the patients' communicative abilities, save for the transcortical patients' ability to repeat what is said to them. As

	Table 2.3
A. HW: What's your name? 　　HCEM: What's your name? 　　HW: The car was bought by John. 　　HCEM: The car was bought by John. B. HW: °This is a yellow tencil. 　　HCEM: yellow pencil 　　HW: °That's a piece of dandy. 　　HCEM: That's a piece of candy. C. HW: °I talk to her yesterday. 　　HCEM: I talked to her yesterday. 　　HW: °She had four childs. 　　HCEM: She had four children.	Examples of Conversational Exchanges With a Patient (HCEM) Suffering From Mixed Transcortical Aphasia

the examples above show, HCEM can neither produce nor comprehend language; all she is capable of is repetition.

Lateralization of function

Nous parlons avec l'hémisphère gauche.

(Broca, 1865; 384)

As discussed earlier, Broca and Dax both introduced the idea that the two cerebral hemispheres, despite their apparent symmetry, might differ in function. In fact, Broca provided evidence for an anatomical asymmetry and furthermore noted the relationship between handedness and "brainedness."

Over the years, researchers have tried to relate "brainedness" not only to "handedness" and hand posture but also to age variances, gender, race (Tsunoda, 1985), and education differences (Bogen et al., 1972), human versus nonhuman and so forth. Additionally, researchers have more closely examined the specific functions which the two hemispheres appear to be specialized for. Some communicative functions, as we shall see, do appear to reside in the nondominant (usually right) hemisphere.

Current evidence does suggest that the left and right hemispheres differ in some way in their function. This difference is clearly not dichotomous but ranges along a continuum. It does relate in some manner to some of the variables mentioned in the previous paragraph, but this correlation is far from completely clear.

It seems evident at this point that in the normal human brain both hemispheres are involved, perhaps to differing degrees, in language function. But it is also clear that such bihemispheric involvement may not be necessary for reasonably normal functioning. In the next section, we survey some of the experimental findings which lead to these conclusions.

Putting one half of the brain to sleep: The Wada test

Accurate knowledge of lateralization of language is crucial prior to surgery that may intrude upon the classical language areas. In 1949, the Japanese neurosurgeon, Juhn Wada, developed a test for language dominance involving injection of the drug sodium amytol (Wada, 1949). Originally, the injection was made in the **internal** or **common carotid arteries** in the neck. But now it is more common to inject the drug via a catheter threaded up into the internal carotid from a femoral artery in the thigh. The injection results in deactivation of the hemisphere **ipsilateral** (on the same side) to the side of injection.

The patient, who lies on the operating table with his legs drawn up, his forearms raised, and his fingers moving, is asked to count backwards. The injection generally produces immediate contralateral **hemiplegia** (paralysis of one side). The forearm and leg on the side opposite to the injection fall. In all instances, counting is momentarily interrupted, but with nondominant deactivation, it resumes within 5 to 20 seconds. Yet if the dominant hemisphere is involved, dysphasic responses may persist for as long as 1–3 minutes. One common method of testing language functioning is by having the patient name objects projected on an overhead screen.

The results of such testing on two groups of patients studied by Rasmussen and Milner (1977) in Montreal is presented in Table 2.4 One group had no evidence of early left cerebral damage, while the other did. The proportions of patients with left, right, and bilateral (both hemispheres) language representation are compared.

This table provides clear evidence of the relationship between two variables and language lateralization: handedness and age. On the basis of these results, it is clear that the vast majority of right-handed individuals display left lateralization for language. While the majority of left-handed individuals and ambidextrous individuals without early brain damage are left-lateralized as well, there is a large proportion with right as well as bilateral representation. A history of early left hemisphere damage increases the possibility of bilateral or right hemispheric lateralization for language functions.

A recent study by Loring et al. (1990), using tasks involving counting, comprehension, naming, and repetition, found that out of 103 patients, 79 had exclusive left hemisphere language representation, 2 had exclusive right hemisphere language representation, and 22 had bilateral representation. Bilateral representation was much higher in left-handed individuals (nondextrals, 41.7 percent) than in right-handed individuals (dextrals, 18.7 percent).

The dramatic shift in dominance in nondextrals with early brain damage appears to support Broca's early view that the right hemisphere can assume many language functions if damage is early enough. How early is early enough? Rasmussen and

Speech Lateralization as Related to Handedness in 262 Patients Without Clinical Evidence of Early Damage to the Left Cerebral Hemisphere					
		SPEECH REPRESENTATION			
HANDEDNESS	NO. OF CASES	LEFT	BILATERAL		RIGHT
Right	140	134	0		6
		96%	0%		4%
Left or mixed	122	86	18		18
		70%	15%		15%

Speech Lateralization as Related to Handedness in 134 Patients Patients With Definite Clinical Evidence of an Early Left-Hemisphere Lesion					
		SPEECH REPRESENTATION			
HANDEDNESS	NO. OF CASES	LEFT	BILATERAL		RIGHT
Right	42	34	3		5
		81%	7%		12%
Left or mixed	92	26	17		49
		28%	19%		53%
(from Rasmussen and Milner, 1977)					

Table 2.4

The results of sodium amytol testing (The WADA Test) in populations differing in handedness and evidence of early left hemisphere damage

Milner (1977) found that damage after five years of age rarely results in shift of laterality. Not only does age seem important but also site of lesion is important. According to their findings, only lesions within the perisylvian language and speech region result in shift of laterality. If damage to this region occurs before five years of age, then the originally damaged perisylvian region may be surgically removed, if required, without producing aphasic disturbance.

Splitting apart the hemispheres: Commissurotomy

One neurosurgical procedure that has captured widespread public attention is known as **commissurotomy**. It was introduced in 1940 by the neurosurgeon Van Wagenen (1940) as a treatment to prevent the spread of the electrical discharges from one hemisphere to another associated with epilepsy. By destroying the major commissures between the two hemispheres, including the **corpus callosum**, it was hoped that the spread of impulses, and thus the severity of the epileptic condition, could be contained.

The aim of this surgery was to disconnect the two cerebral hemispheres. Yet, after examining the first series of patients, Akelaitis, a psychologist, failed to find any major effects involving language (Akelaitis, 1964). At this point, some respected individuals in academe suggested that perhaps the only function the corpus callosum served was to hold the two hemispheres together!

It was actually Ronald Myers (1955) who first discovered that the estimated 200 million fibers of the corpus callosum don't just bind the hemispheres together. Take a look at Figure 2.11. Section the corpus callosum at the midline. Suppose you now present the subject with a picture of a common object as was done in the Wada Test. What do you think the subject will do? He should name it correctly, because, although the corpus callosum is sectioned, he can still scan the picture with his eyes. The optic tract decussates and thus the image of the picture goes to both hemispheres.

Myers sectioned both the corpus callosum and the optic chiasm in a group of laboratory animals. Let's assume we are dealing with a monkey. We've done this surgery, and we cover one eye and present the monkey with a discrimination task. He has to distinguish between a triangle and a square, and if he can do this, he will receive a reward—say, a candy. After a large number of trials, he learns this task. Suppose we now cover the eye through which he learned this discrimination and allow him to perform the task using the opposite, unpatched eye. What do you suppose will happen? With the other eye, the monkey now performs as if he had never

Figure 2.11

Visual pathways are completely crossed, so that when the eyes are fixated on a point, all of the field to the left of the fixation point excites the visual cortex in the right hemisphere and stimuli from the right visual field excite the left visual cortex. The visual cortexes can communicate via the corpus callosum, which connects the two hemispheres. (from Kimura, 1973). A. From *"The Asymmetry of the Human Brain,"* by Doreen Kimura (91). Copyright © 1973 *Scientific American*, Inc. All rights reserved. B. Graphic representation of A.

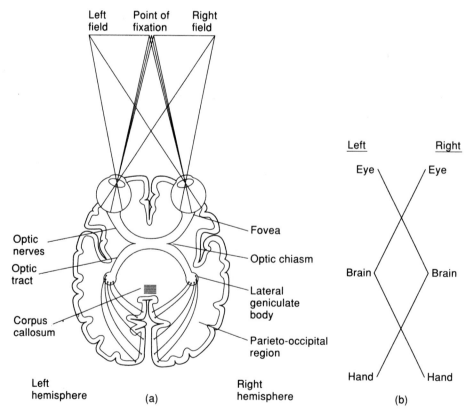

been exposed to the task. Learning in one hemisphere fails totally to transfer to the other hemisphere.

We cannot ethically transect the optic chiasm in a human being, but we can accomplish the same effect by having the subject fixate on a midpoint as shown in Figure 2.11. All the information presented to the right visual field is then projected to the left (generally language dominant) hemisphere and all the information flashed in the left visual field is projected to the right (usually nondominant) hemisphere. Information must be presented at a rapid rate (generally around 50 milliseconds per stimulus), before the eyes have a chance to move from the fixation point. The device used to present stimuli in this manner is known as a **tachistoscope** or T-scope. The major paths of information flow under these conditions, from hand and eye to the brain, for example, are presented schematically in part B of Figure 2.11. There has been a vast amount of research on callosally sectioned (split-brained) patients employing this type of task (cf. Springer & Deutsch, 1989).

A few examples may describe the general findings of such research. Suppose the word HE | ART is flashed on the screen with the midpoint dividing the word as indicated. Can you already predict what the "split-brain" patients will say they have seen? Asked this question, they will *say* ART and nothing more. Asked to point out with the *left* hand which word they have seen, subjects invariably point to HE rather than ART. Subjects cannot write words or the names of objects flashed to the nondominant hemisphere. However, the dominant hemisphere has no difficulty with these tasks.

Are we to assume from these results that no language abilities reside in the nondominant hemispheres of these patients? Not at all. Such patients can locate a requested object with the left hand when requested verbally even when the items are described in a circumlocutory manner. Thus, when requested to find the thing that monkeys eat, subjects are able to locate a banana with the left hand behind a screen. Later, when the same piece of fruit is placed in this hand, it cannot be named. The nondominant hemisphere is capable of finding an item presented to it visually or tactually from among a list of words. This item cannot be named, however, until it is located on the list.

It thus appears that in the vast majority of these patients (there are exceptions) only the dominant hemisphere can produce verbal output, but the nondominant hemisphere is not without language abilities.

Taking out half the brain: Hemispherectomy

It is difficult to imagine a more radical surgery on the brain than that of disconnecting the two cerebral hemispheres. But in 1927, the Johns Hopkins neurosurgeon Walter Dandy introduced a procedure involving the total removal of an entire hemisphere (**hemispherectomy**) for the treatment of intractable epilepsy which appeared to originate from large areas of diseased tissue in one of the two hemispheres (Dandy, 1928). Upon hearing of this extraordinary operation, Dr. W. W. Keen, a fellow neurosurgeon, wrote him:

Figure 2.12

How The Split Brain Integrates Input

Information was presented simultaneously to the left and right visual fields of a split brain patient. When focusing on the dot in the midline, all information on the left goes to the right hemisphere and vice versa. The split brain subject is asked to point to the card that is most related to the picture. The left hand should point to what is being processed in the right hemisphere and vice versa because of contralateral control of motor function. All subjects did extremely well on such a task. What was of interest was how the subjects interpreted their choices. Asked why they picked a shovel and a chicken, the subjects answered: "You have to clean out the chicken shed with a shovel." What is going on here? What does this tell us about how the human brain operates?

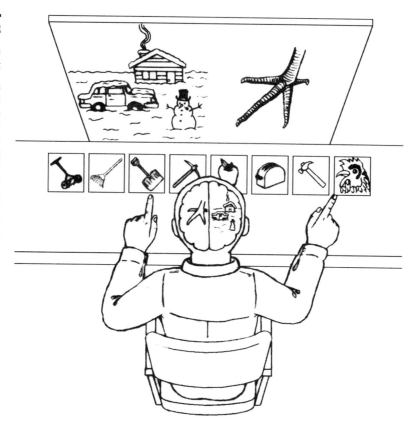

March 21, 1928

My dear Dandy:
    As I have told you before, you are rightly named. Here you are removing half of a fellow's brains and letting him go around just as usual. Whenever you get to the point when you can take out all the brains, I may consult you.

Sincerely yours,
W. W. Keen
(quoted in Fox, 1984)

Since that time, hundreds of such operations have been performed on children, as well as adults, for treatment of various neuropathologies.

In all cases of dominant hemispherectomy in adults, verbal output, while not totally obliterated, was very severely affected. The same was true of writing. Comprehension appeared to be much less involved. However, gradual recovery of language abilities appeared to be almost complete if the surgery was performed early enough in the child's development, as was often the case, (Smith, 1966). Such findings are consistent with the critical period hypothesis discussed earlier.

What is your reaction to such findings? Virtually, half of the **telencephalon** (far brain) has been removed, but there are no lasting effects on speech and language, and it doesn't appear to matter which hemisphere is removed as long as such surgery is performed early enough—before five years of age. I raise this question with you, because it seems reasonable that we have roughly the right amount of brain tissue to survive as a species, rather than twice as much as we need. Removing a massive amount of this tissue has got to have an effect on a behavior as complex as communicative behavior—and, as is usually the case, with careful testing, it does. It is now evident that removal of the dominant hemisphere, no matter how early, does exact a toll.

Dennis and Whitaker (1976) studied language abilities in three 9- and 10-year-old children, employing a wide variety of both standardized and specially developed tests of speech and language functioning. In one of these children, the right hemisphere had been removed; in two others, the left hemisphere. In each case the operation had occurred before five months of age. It was found that all children did equally well on tasks involving phonological and semantic abilities. In the two patients whose left hemisphere had been removed, however, it was discovered that the right hemisphere did poorly on tasks involving any degree of syntactic complexity. One of the tasks involved detection of semantic and syntactic anomalies. All three subjects did well at correcting semantic anomalies such as: "My favorite breakfast is radios with cream," but only the left **hemidecorticates** demonstrated problems in detecting syntactic anomalies. Presented with the anomalous sentence: "The best cars in Canada is a Ford and some Datsun," one subject responded: "Wrong, it's a Mercury." These results seem to suggest that the right hemisphere is incapable of acquiring all aspects of language even when the left hemisphere is removed at a very early age. However, as Broca postulated, the brain does demonstrate a great deal of plasticity in regard to language functions. The one exception appears to be syntax, that aspect of communicative behavior which many linguists regard as unique to our species.

All of the evidence relating to the organization of speech and language within the brain we have presented so far stems from individuals whose brains are damaged. In 1878, the British neurologist Hughlings-Jackson issued a dictum that is probably the most frequently cited and frequently ignored in this field: "To locate the damage that destroys speech and to localize speech are two different things," (Jackson, 1878). In fact we are now in a position to directly investigate Hughlings-Jackson's caution through the use of neuroimaging techniques which compare the effects of lesions in one part of the brain with metabolic activity at other loci. Preliminary findings do indicate metabolic abnormalities in presumably healthy tissue located at a distance from the lesion site (**diaschesis**). Thus, brain damage in one area may have consequences for brain functioning in another.

Listening with both ears: The dichotic listening technique

Thus, what we need is evidence from normal individuals that will allow us to understand more fully what we see in cases of brain pathology. Luckily a number of techniques exist that are capable of providing us with such information.

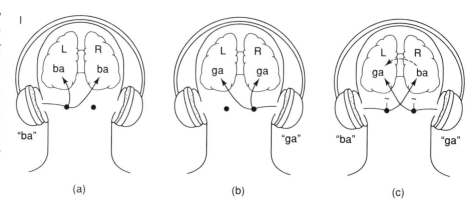

(a)   (b)   (c)

Figure 2.13a

Kimura's model of dichotic listening in normal subjects. A. Monaural presentation to the left ear is sent to the right hemisphere by way of contralateral pathways and to the left hemisphere by way of ipsilateral pathways. The subject reports the syllable ("ba") accurately. B. Monaural presentation to the right ear is sent to the left hemisphere by way of contralateral pathways and to the right hemisphere by way of ipsilateral pathways. The subject reports the syllable ("ga") accurately. C. In dichotic presentation, ipsilateral pathways are suppressed, so "ga" goes only to the left (speech) hemisphere and "ba" to the right hemisphere. The syllable "ba" is accessible to the left (speech) hemisphere only through the commissures. As a consequence, "ga" is usually reported more accurately than "ba" (a right-ear advantage).

One such technique is **dichotic listening**. The basic paradigm for this approach was created by the British psychologist Donald Broadbent (1954) in connection with his studies of attention. Broadbent presented subjects with a sequence of three digits to one ear, while simultaneously presenting another sequence to the opposite ear. Thus, one ear might be presented with a sequence such as 1-7-6 while the other ear received another sequence such as 8-5-2. Figure 2.13a shows a schematic diagram of this experimental procedure.

In administering this test to patients at the Montreal Neurological Institute, Kimura (1961) discovered that digits presented to the ear contralateral (opposite) to the dominant hemisphere were reported more accurately. This same effect was later observed in normal subjects.

Kimura attributed this effect to cerebral dominance, coupled with the greater strength of the contralateral pathways over the ipsilateral ones. When stimuli were presented monaurally, however, the right ear advantage was not observed. Kimura hypothesized that this occurred because the ipsilateral pathways are inhibited only under dichotic presentation. Strong support for this explanation is provided by studies of dichotic listening in commissurotomy (Sparks & Geschwind, 1968) and hemispherectomized patients (Curry, 1968). Such studies show a drastic decline in accuracy for the left ear. These results can only be attributed to inhibition at a peripheral level, as all other pathways from the ear ipsilateral to the dominant hemisphere do not exist in these patients (see Krashen, 1972, for a complete discussion of this topic). See Figure 2.13b.

Combined results from the dichotic listening paradigm, tachistoscopic presentations, tests of observed hand movements, and tactile sensitivity of the two hands are presented in Table 2.5, which is adapted from Kimura (1973). The left hemisphere, as one might expect, more quickly and accurately processes words, whether presented aurally, or in writing. It also does better at identifying letters. Perhaps surprisingly, the left hemisphere also seems to have an advantage when processing nonsense syllables and backwards speech, or when performing manual tasks while speaking. The right hemisphere appears to do better when asked to process musical stimuli, or human nonspeech stimuli (such as a cough). It also seems to show an advantage during visual-spatial processing tasks.

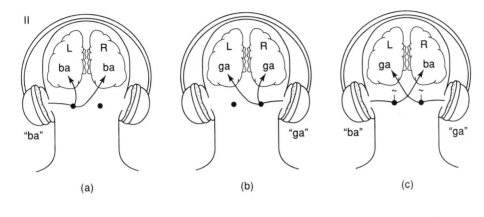

(a)   (b)   (c)

Figure 2.13b

Dichotic listening in split brain subjects. A., B. Monaural presentations operate as they do with normal subjects. Because both ipsilateral and contralateral pathways are unaffected by commissurotomy, the patient can accurately report a signal to either ear. C. In dichotic presentation, the ipsilateral pathways are suppressed (as in normal subjects), but "ba" is not accessible to the left (speech) hemisphere because the commissures are cut. Only "ga" is reported in complete right-ear advantage. (Springer & Deutsch)

Some researchers have proposed a **functionalist hypothesis** to explain laterality. They suggest that the function served by a stimulus, rather than the physical characteristics of the stimulus, determines laterality of processing. This hypothesis suggests, for example, that only if tone is used to signal meaning differences in a language will it be lateralized to the dominant hemisphere. This is exactly what has been found in dichotic listening experiments comparing English and Thai speakers. Only in the Thai group was a right ear advantage for tonal contrasts demonstrated (Van Lancker & Fromkin, 1978). However, Shipley-Brown et al. (1988) demonstrated a left ear advantage not only for affective prosody (happy, angry, and sad readings of simple sentences such as: "The cat slept by the fire"), but also for linguistic prosody (declarative, question and continuation-type intonations of the same sentences).

What functions reside in the nondominant hemisphere?

As we have already seen in our study of commissurotomy and hemispherectomy patients, it is clear that linguistic processing is not entirely confined to the dominant hemisphere. Metabolic neuroimaging techniques, as we shall see, strongly support the view that both hemispheres are active during linguistic processing. Thus, laterality appears to be continuous rather than dichotomous.

While aphasia is extremely rare from right hemisphere lesions in right-handed individuals (approximately 4 percent of such individuals evince so-called "crossed aphasia"), such lesions do affect communication. There are a number of language functions which are disturbed following damage to the right hemisphere. Many of these problems relate to less "structural" aspects of linguistic functioning. That is, patients with right hemisphere lesions do not appear to have problems with phonology, lexicon, or syntax, but often seem to confuse the order of events in a story, are unable to formulate a moral for a story, and are impaired in their ability to draw inferences from a story. They also experience problems with ambiguous, metaphorical and figurative terms, and tend to interpret them narrowly and literally. Thus, a

Table 2.5

Summary of
Left/Right
Hemisphere Test
Scores in Normal,
Right-Handed
Subjects in Three
Modalities

MODALITY	LEFT/RIGHT HEMISPHERE TEST SCORE RATIO
AUDITORY	
words	1.88:1
nonsense syllables	1.73:1
backward speech	1.66:1
melodic pattern	1:1.19
human nonspeech sounds	1:1.08
VISUAL	
letters	1.23:1
words	1.47:1
two-dimensional point location	1:1.18
dot and form enumeration	1:1.20
matching of slanted lines	1:1.05
stereoscopic depth perception	1:1.28
MANUAL	
skilled movements	1.13:1
free movements during speech	3.10:1
tactile dot patterns (Braille)	Right advantage (initial findings)
nonvisual location	1:1.12

(from Kimura,. 1973)

"broken heart" may be understood as a cardiac condition! Finally, they experience difficulty in using and interpreting prosodic cues in conversation. Intonation may be impaired, and use of stress and intonation to understand both the meaning and intent of utterances may be disordered. This may lead the patient with right hemisphere damage to misinterpret sarcasm, for example. Problems with this paralinguistic domain of emotional expression may extend to difficulties in reading facial expression or gestural cues which accompany conversation (Code, 1987; Pimental & Kingsbury, 1989; Myers, 1986; and Perecman, 1983).

The literature dealing with possible functions of the two hemispheres now is so vast that we can provide only a few findings here to initiate discussion. We have talked about some of the variables relating to laterality, such as handedness and age, but with great oversimplification. Broca's finding of morphological differences between the two hemispheres has been demonstrated for other language-related areas, in particular, the **planum temporale** which, buried in the Sylvian fissure, lies behind Heschl's gyrus (Geschwind & Levitsky, 1968). Strangely enough, if bigger means better, then the right (nondominant) hemisphere wins! Broca, as usual, was correct in his observation that the right hemisphere is generally heavier. It also often has two Heschl's gyri, a larger superior temporal gyrus and parietal lobe as well as a greater volume of blood flow. It also matures earlier (Chi et al., 1977). However, none of these morphological differences has been directly related to function.

Many of the variables mentioned above, as well as others, may aid us in understanding "brainedness" in our species. One variable currently of some interest is gender. Do men and women differ in their lateralization patterns? There is evidence for hemispheric differences related to this variable in animals (Nottebohm & Arnold, 1976). Whether such differences exist in humans is, at present, unclear (Kolb & Whishaw, 1990). Possible differences are suggested by the following facts:

Aphasia is more common after left hemisphere damage in males than it is in females, suggesting that language functions may be more diffusely organized in women. The corpus callosum is also larger in females. In general, recovery from aphasia is better for women than for men. These and other observations about brain and language functioning in men and women continue to spur further research into gender differences (Kimura, 1992).

When sign language users become aphasic

In all of our discussions, we have confined ourselves to the analysis of the consequences of brain damage on the production and comprehension of spoken language. What happens when a deaf sign language user suffers damage to the areas of the brain normally associated with language processing in oral language users? Poizner, Klima & Bellugi (1987) have investigated this question. The deaf signers they followed showed left hemispheric specialization for language, just as right-handed oral language users. Moreover, because many syntactic functions are coded using spatial cues in ASL, it might have been reasonable to suspect that they would be preserved if the right hemisphere, normally attributed with spatial processing, was spared. This, however, was not the case. Left hemisphere damage had the potential to disrupt the use of space to convey syntactic information in deaf signers.

Intrahemispheric localization of function

> . . . he (Gall) . . . developed a correct theoretical framework, which is his enduring contribution to the neurosciences: the concept of localized functional areas in the brain, including the cerebral cortex.
>
> (Jerison, 1977)

To lateralize a function is to attribute it to a given hemisphere. To localize a function is to specify exactly where within the brain a function appears to reside. There is no doubt that many functions can be localized within the human brain and, for that matter, within all other vertebrate brains that have been studied.

Figure 2.14

The following is a sample of Gail D.'s interchanges with the examiner, all in ASL. The examiner's probes are given in English translation; Gail D.'s signing is in English gloss for signs. The first drawing shows Gail D.'s awkward rendition and effortful articulation of the sign BROTHER, taken from her description of the picture.

EXAMINER: What's that? [Pointing to the picture.]
GAIL D.: THREE.
EXAMINER: Who is that? [Pointing to the woman in the picture.]
GAIL D.: MOTHER.
EXAMINER: Who is that? [Pointing to the boy.]
GAIL D.: BROTHER...BROTHER...

Correct form   Gail D.'s form

Brother   Brother

Effortful production typical of Gail D.'s signing.

Correct form   Gail D.'s form

Girl   Girl

Articulatory difficulty characteristic of Gail D.'s signing. In the example, Gail D. searches for the Hand Configuration and Movement of the sign, although on occasion she produces the sign smoothly.

EXAMINER: What else happened?
GAIL D.: CAR...DRIVE...BROTHER...DRIVE...I...
S-T-A-D. [Attempts to gesture "stand up."]
EXAMINER: You stood up?
GAIL D.: YES...I...DRIVE... [Attempts to gesture "wave goodbye."]
EXAMINER: Wave goodbye?
GAIL D.: YES...BROTHER...DRIVE...DUNNO... [Attempts to gesture "wave goodbye."]
EXAMINER: Your brother was driving?
GAIL D.: YES...BACK...DRIVE...BROTHER...MAN... MAMA...STAY...BROTHER...DRIVE.
EXAMINER: Were you in the car?
GAIL D.: YES.
EXAMINER: Or outside?
GAIL D.: NO.
EXAMINER: In the car.
GAIL D.: YES.
EXAMINER: You were standing up with your mother?
GAIL D.: NO...BROTHER...DRIVE...[Points in back.]... DEAF BROTHER...I...
EXAMINER: Your brother didn't know you were in the car?
GAIL D.: YES.
EXAMINER: Your brother was driving and saw you in the back seat?
GAIL D.: YES, YES. [Laughs.]
EXAMINER: Oh, I see.

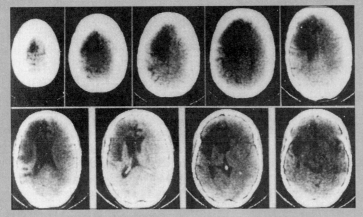

Gail D.

Lateral reconstruction of lesion and CT scan of left = lesioned patient Gail D.

However, even in functions which seem relatively "simple" when compared to speech and language use, localization to one single area of the brain has not been possible. Vision, for example, involves the entire occipital lobe, inferior portions of the temporal lobe, the frontal eye fields (Brodmann area 8), the cranial nerves for eye movement and other aspects of ocular motor function, the optic tectum, as well as parts of the parietal lobe, and the lateral geniculate nucleus of the metathalamus. Vision is by no means a "simple" function, but compared to human communicative behavior, it is indeed. Remember that vision constitutes but one of the input modalities involved in our complex form of communication. The specific localization of many speech and language functions has proven to be a formidable task.

Measuring blood flow in the brain

We have utilized Broca's remarkably insightful research in the nineteenth century as a kind of leitmotif in this chapter. In 1879, shortly before his death, he devised an instrument which he dubbed a **thermometric crown**, composed of six symmetrically arranged thermometers shielded with cotton, for precisely identifying functional as well as diseased areas of the brain. Broca proposed to measure increases or decreases in **regional cerebral blood flow (rCBF)** with this device; thus, we may regard his research as the first step in developing modern techniques for measuring this indicator of metabolic activity within the brain.

The blood flow of the brain is ultimately controlled by the metabolic activity of neuronal tissue. A number of techniques are currently available for measuring regional cerebral blood flow to study functional changes within discrete areas of the brain during various behaviors. One method involves the injection of xenon[133], a radioactive isotope, dissolved in a saline solution, into the internal carotid artery. The Swedish group of Lassen, Ingvour and Skinhj (1978) utilized an array of detectors to monitor gamma ray emission produced by the isotope. They worked under the assumption that the faster tissue clears (the steeper the decay curve), the faster the blood flow in a region.

How might you test the validity of such a procedure? We could first ask a subject to perform a relatively simple behavior, the localization of which within the cortex is presumed to be well established. Suppose we have him simply wiggle the fingers of his right hand. Where in the cortex would you expect an increase in blood flow? There should be an increase in the hand area of the motor and perhaps sensory strip of the contralateral hemisphere. This is exactly what happens. The supplementary motor area also "lights up." In fact, this area appears to be involved bilaterally in all complex movements, whether of the foot, hand, mouth, or eyes (Orgogozo & Larsen, 1979). Lassen et al., (1978) postulate that this area may control the programming of complex movements, while the sensory cortex is the controller and the primary motor cortex is the executor of such movements.

These same investigators found that listening to simple words produces involvement of the auditory cortex in both hemispheres, while speaking aloud adds three more areas: the face areas of the sensorimotor strips, the supplementary motor areas, and Broca's area in both hemispheres. Reading aloud adds the visual association cortex in the occipital lobes, as well as the frontal eye fields (Brodmann area 8) bilaterally.

This bilateral pattern of activation has also been demonstrated in a more recent study which, unlike the Lassen et al., study, examined rCBF in both hemispheres simultaneously during humming and automatic speech (repetition of the days of the week) (Ryding et al., 1987). While both tasks activated the brain bilaterally, there were differences in the regions of activation. An area that the investigators believed corresponded to Broca's area was activated in both tasks only on the left. In speech, the left hemisphere was most extensively activated in precentral (motor) regions, while the right hemisphere showed predominant activation of postcentral (sensory) regions.

Let us examine the results of one final study which employed an even more sophisticated method of monitoring cerebral blood flow. This method employs a scanning technique known as **positron emission tomography (PET)**, which provides a three-dimensional representation of blood flow within the brain and allows monitoring of subcortical structures (Petersen et al., 1989). Studies of the processing of single words presented aurally and visually were carried out in a hierarchical manner allowing for computer-assisted subtraction of what was hypothesized as simpler processing from more complex processing. Four tasks of increasing complexity were utilized: a) fixation on a crosshair on a screen, b) presentation of a noun either visually below the crosshair or aurally, c) pronouncing aloud the visually or aurally presented noun, and d) production orally of a semantically appropriate verb for each noun presented (thus, given "cake," "eat" might be produced by the subject). Figure 2.15 presents the lexical processing model that Petersen et al. propose to account for their findings. In it, different portions of the cortex are assumed to take primary responsibility for different speech and language tasks. If the task is to take auditory input and do something with it, such as tasks b) through d), then the primary auditory cortex first receives and processes the input, passing it next to the temporoparietal cortex, which analyzes its phonological structure. Its semantic interpretation is apparently derived in the anterior inferior left frontal cortex, while the commands necessary to pronounce the word or its associate are generated first in the supplementary motor area, and next in the motor cortex. Visually presented input follows a somewhat different route: early visual processing of the material is accomplished in the striate cortex, which sends its results to the extrastriate cortex for coding and further analysis by the semantic association areas mentioned earlier. We can also note from this model that information may flow in both directions from "level" to "level" of processing, allowing the system to check itself for possible analytical errors.

What do these results tell us about the role of the lateral surface of the cortex in speech and language functions? First it appears that both hemispheres are involved, though in differing degrees, in speech and language. We would expect this to be the case for early auditory and visual processing as well as for motor (articulatory) output. We have also noted that the **supplementary motor area (SMA)** appears to be activated in a variety of complex motor tasks including speech. Previous rCBF studies had shown bilateral activation of the temporoparietal cortex (Wernicke's area) while

Figure 2.15

The Petersen et al.
model of different levels
of lexical processing
based on their rCBF
study. (from Petersen et
al., 1989)

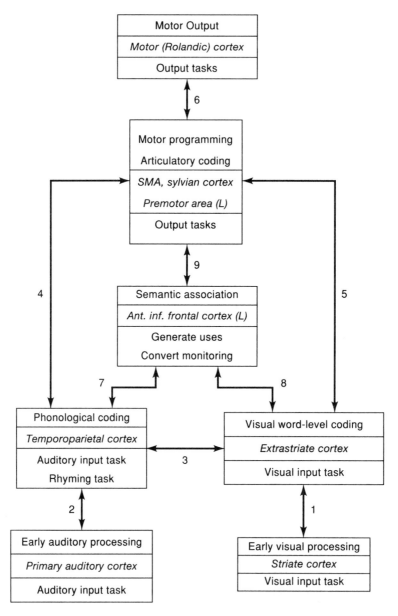

listening to speech, as well as visual association areas (**extrastriate cortex**) while reading words. The earliest blood flow studies failed to detect metabolic changes in Broca's area; however, both the Ryding et al. and Petersen et al. studies note activation of this area in the left hemisphere. In addition, Petersen et al. observed left activation of the inferior prefrontal as well as anterior cingulate cortex during a task involving generating verbs compatible with nouns.

The role of subcortical structures in speech and language

In addition to the areas on the lateral and medial surfaces of the cerebral hemispheres, it is now also evident that subcortical structures are in some manner involved not only in speech but language functions as well. Dysarthrias resulting from damage to the basal ganglia (hypokinetic and hyperkinetic dysarthria) and the cerebellum (ataxic dysarthria) have long been documented (Darley et al., 1975). It is now evident that dysarthria can also follow from thalamic hemorrhages and infarctions (Cappa & Vignolo, 1979). Articulation in such disorders may be slow, laborious, and inaccurate.

In addition to neuromotor speech disorders, it has recently been discovered that damage to the basal ganglia, thalamus, and surrounding white matter (internal capsule) may produce aphasic disturbances unlike those from purely cortical damage. (Damasio et al., 1981; Naeser et al., 1982; and Metter et al., 1983). Lesions of the thalamus result in preserved ability to repeat and relatively good auditory comprehension. However, spontaneous speech is of diminished quantity and characterized by word selection errors. Patients tend to avoid speaking unless it is absolutely necessary, and they produce semantic paraphasias, substituting inappropriate words for their intended targets when speaking. Lesions of the globus pallidus (part of the basal ganglia) also result in speech characterized by semantic paraphasias. Lesions involving other subcortical structures such as the internal capsule and caudate nucleus may result in dysarthria, suggesting that these structures may play some role in motor speech planning and execution. How these structures participate in language formulation is at present poorly understood. It is clear that both the basal ganglia and thalamus are lateralized in function. Whether their role in language functions is a distinct one or is involved with disruption of cortical functioning in general is not clear (Crossen, 1985; Murdoch, 1990).

Ways of viewing the relationship between brain and language

> . . . *modern linguistic aphasiology has been developed by psychologists and linguists whose interests are in how language breaks down, and in what the pattern of breakdown reveals about normal language and its processing. Much work has gone on in this area without concern for the details of the correlation between symptoms and neural lesions.*
>
> (Caplan, 1987; XI)

There are a number of approaches to the study of behavior in general and to speech and language functioning in particular. Of the approaches that focus not only on external, observable behaviors but also allow for the investigation of the hidden, internal processes which produce such behaviors, one may note a dichotomy, as old as time, between mind and brain. Disciplines such as psycholinguistics typically attempt to provide explanations of behaviors in terms of information-processing descriptions, while neurolinguistics seeks explanations for the same behaviors in terms of neurological processes. The approach exemplified in this chapter is most akin to neurolinguistics.

Linguistic aphasiology

In the 1980s a quite different approach developed within psychology from a blending of **cognitive psychology** and **neuropsychology**. This new subdiscipline, **cognitive neuropsychology**, has two basic aims: (1) to explain the patterns of impaired and intact cognitive performance seen in brain-injured patients in terms of damage to one or more of the components of a theory or model of normal cognitive functioning, and (2) to draw conclusions about normal, intact cognitive processes from the patterns of impaired and intact capabilities seen in brain-injured patients (Ellis & Young, 1988; p. 4). The study of language functions is but a part of this broader endeavor. The study of language within this approach has recently been termed **linguistic aphasiology** (Caplan, 1987).

Note while reading in later chapters that psycholinguists generally construct their models of language processing from the study of normal populations. Linguistic aphasiologists seek to accomplish the same end by studying brain-damaged populations. A basic tenet of their approach is that the mind is composed of a set of processing elements, **modules**, which are dissociable. This view, which is reminiscent of Franz Josef Gall's study of craniology discussed earlier in this chapter, has recently been revived in several versions by Chomsky (1980), Gardner (1983), and Fodor (1983).

These modules are held to be related to distinct areas of the brain. If we are to assume that brain damage can provide us with insight as to how complex cognitive processes such as language operate in normals, then as Caramazza (1984) makes clear, it must be that neural modules can be differentially damaged, (**fractionation**) and that, given such damage, we can ascertain what very specific linguistic ability has been lost (**transparency**). This is a tall order, and it is not at all certain that such an approach can accomplish its goals.

The models that result from this approach are generally not related to neurological structures at all, as was the case in the famous Wernicke-Lichtheim model. Researchers within this paradigm rightfully point out that these earlier diagram makers were overly simplistic in their analysis of language processes. Some say that what we need first is a better and more complete understanding of the processes involved in language production and comprehension (psycholinguistic findings) before they can be related successfully to neural structures (neurolinguistic findings). Research on both oral and sign language users, however, does suggest that differing aspects of language, such as lexical retrieval and grammatical encoding, can be dissociated and differentially impaired following brain damage.

Linguistic aphasiologists also critique the terminology of traditional aphasic syndromes on a number of grounds: (1) they are not fine-grained enough in their analysis of the language dysfunctions under consideration, (2) many components of the syndrome need not be present for a patient to be placed within a category (e.g., agrammatism is not a necessary feature of Broca's aphasia), (3) many components are shared by different syndromes (e.g., anomia), and finally (4) many, perhaps even the majority of patients, perhaps given the inherent nature of diffuse brain damage itself, cannot neatly be classified under the criteria for any given syndrome. These critiques are well founded and have led many investigators to return to a detailed study of individual cases of brain damage, as opposed to group studies (Caramazza, 1984).

Consider the syndrome of Broca's aphasia. It often includes apraxia of speech, anarthria, dysarthria, and agrammatism, as well as disturbances of repetition, reading, and writing. Can such associated characteristics be decomposed in terms of differential lesion sites which make sense neurologically? The answer is "yes" in many instances. Thus, apraxia of speech appears to be associated with a lesion confined to Broca's area alone (e.g., the left third frontal convolution). Although apraxia of speech usually co-occurs with aphasia, it can appear in isolation (Wertz et al., 1970). Broca's aphasics are often dysarthric but need not be. Finally, it is now clear that Broca's aphasia need not be characterized by agrammatism; in some cases, the speech errors of such patients involve major content items rather than grammatical elements. We thus need to investigate the lesion sites that result in this syndrome with and without agrammatism. Mohr (1976), in a review of autopsy records at the Massachusetts General Hospital, found that in order to produce a persistent Broca's aphasia with all of the elements usually included in the syndrome, a lesion confined to Broca's area is insufficient: rather, a much more widespread infarct is required encompassing, in addition to Broca's area, the insula and often the region underlying it, both pre- and post-central gyri as well as often anterior parietal cortex. (For an excellent introduction to cognitive neuropsychology including how this approach is applied to language, see Ellis & Young, 1988; for a more detailed discussion of this approach devoted solely to language, see Caplan, 1987; 1992. For examples of many of the techniques employed in the localization of functions mapped onto such models, see Kertesz, 1983).

Summary

What are we? What are we not? The dream of a shadow is man.

Pindaros

As noted at the beginning of this chapter, the brain may well be so complex as to defy its comprehension of itself. It is a complex physical structure composed of billions of cells, with a connectivity per cell that often exceeds many thousands of synapses complicated by differential chemical means of transmission. We must relate this structure to what is probably the most complex form of human behavior known. Understanding this relationship in all its facets may well prove to be immensely difficult if not impossible—not only because of the awe-inspiring complexities involved, but also because the brain, like most natural phenomena, is characterized by a great deal of individual variation.

However, we do understand something about how speech and language ability is instantiated in our nervous system. We shall probably never understand this relationship totally, but we must try not only because it tells us something we want to know about ourselves, but also because what we learn may help to mend dysfunctions due to brain damage. What we have learned so far points to a complex and interconnected set of cortical and subcortical areas, each of which appears to subserve different aspects of the communicative process. Thus, discrete areas of the brain have been identified which play a major role in articulation, grammatical formulation, word finding and speech comprehension. Additional areas may have special responsibility for tasks such as reading, writing, and the ability to repeat utterances.

The two sides of the brain, while fairly comparable in size and form, appear to specialize in handling various language and nonlinguistic tasks. For most individuals, language appears to reside in the left hemisphere, although some linguistic skills, such as interpretation of discourse and figurative or humorous language appear to be mediated by the right hemisphere. If the left hemisphere is damaged early enough in development, the right hemisphere is capable of assuming many, though not all, language functions which usually reside in the left side of the cortex.

Although the earliest evidence concerning lateralization and localization of language functions utilized analysis of brain damaged individuals, new procedures have been developed which allow us to study cortical activity in normal subjects during specific linguistic and nonlinguistic tasks. From dichotic listening, tachistoscopic, and cerebral blood flow studies, we obtain greater information about the neurological bases of normal language processing.

As linguistic theory continues to evolve, it will hopefully provide us with new theories to explore. New experimental techniques will undoubtedly be developed within psychology. There will be advances in statistical procedures which will allow us to better interpret our data. Computer modeling of neural processes may provide us with new insights into how human beings accomplish similar tasks. One of the most exciting developments within neuroscience has been the proliferation of many new forms of neuroimaging. Just as we have become ever more adept at probing the universe around us, so we have advanced greatly in our investigation of the universe within us. There will be increased study of old and newly discovered disease processes affecting the brain which, as in the past, will undoubtedly provide new perspectives on brain function. There is increased interest in the study of those with exceptional language abilities and individuals with dissociated cognitive and linguistic abilities (Obler & Fein, 1988) as well as individuals who use a variety of different languages, including signed language (Poizner et al., 1987). The list of topics for study is only constrained by our own creativity. In regard to every aspect of brain and language functioning that is studied, it is important to utilize all available approaches—theoretical as well as experimental—whether from linguistics, psychology, or neuroscience.

The two universes mentioned above, one surrounding us, one within us, are both being actively explored today as never before. In the exploration of both these new frontiers, we may come closer than ever before to interpreting "the dream of a shadow" that we are.

References

Akelaitis, A. J. (1964). Study of gnosis, praxis, and language following section of corpus callosum and anterior commissure. *Journal of Neurosurgery, 1,* 94–102.

Bayles, K., & Kaszniak, A. (1987). *Communication and cognition in normal aging and dementia.* Boston: College-Hill.

Benton, A. (1981). Aphasia: Historical perspectives. In M. Sarno (Ed.) *Acquired aphasia.* New York: Academic Press.

Benton, A. & Joynt, R. (1960). Early descriptions of aphasia. *Archives of Neurology, 3,* 205–222.

Berker, E., Berker, A., & Smith, A. (1986). Translation of Broca's 1865 Report. Localization of speech in the third left frontal convolution. *Archives of Neurology, 43,* 1065–1072.

Bihrle, A., Brownell, H., & Gardner, H. (1988). Humor and the right hemisphere: A narrative perspective. In H. Whitaker (Ed.) *Contemporary reviews in neuropsychology.* New York: Springer-Verlag.

Bogen, J., Dezure, R., Tenhouten, W. D., & Marsh, J. (1972). The other side of the brain IV. The A/P ratio. *Bulletin of the Los Angeles Neurological Societies, 37,* 49–61.

Botez, M., & Barbeau, A. (1971). Role of subcortical structures, and particularly the thalamus in the mechanisms in speech and language. *International Journal of Neurology, 8,* 300–320.

Brazier, M. (1959). The historical development of neurophysiology. In H. Magoun (Ed.), *Handbook of physiology, Vol. I, Section 1,* 1–58. Washington, DC: American Physiology Society.

Broadbent, D. (1954). The role of auditory localization in attention and memory span. *Journal of Experimental Psychology, 47,* 191–96.

Broca, P. (1861a). Sur le volume et la forme du cerveau suivant les individus et suivant les races. *Bulletins de la Société d'Anthropologie de Paris, 2,* 139–204.

Broca, P. (1861b). Remarques sur le siege de la faculté du langage articulé suivés d'une observation d'aphémie. *Bulletins de la Société d'Anthropologie de Paris, 6,* 330–357.

Broca, P. (1868). *Recherches sur la localization de la faculté du langage articulé.*

Broca, P. (1875). Sur le poids relatif des deux hémisphères cérébraux et leur lobes frontaux. *Bulletins de la Société d'Anthropologie de Paris, 10,* 534–536.

Broca, P. (1885). Du siège de la faculté du langage articulé dans l'hémisphère gauche du cerveau. *Bulletins de la Société d'Anthropologie de Paris, 6,* 377–393.

Brodmann, K. (1909). *Vergleichende Lokalisationslehre der Grosshirnrinde in ihren Prinzipien dargestellt auf Grund des Zellenbaues.* Leipzig: J.A. Barth.

Brown, J., & Perecman, E. (1985). Neurological basis of language processing. In J. Darby (Ed.), *Speech and language evaluation in neurology: Adult disorders.* Orlando: Grune and Stratton.

Caplan, D. (1987). *Neurolinguistics and linguistic aphasiology. An introduction.* New York: Cambridge University Press.

Caplan, D. (1992). *Language: Structure processing and disorders.* Cambridge, MA: MIT Press.

Cappa, S. & Vignolo, L. (1979). Transcortical features of aphasia following left thalamic hemorrhage. *Cortex, 15,* 121–130.

Caramazza, A. (1984). The logic of neuropsychological research and the problem of patient classification in aphasia. *Brain and Language, 21,* 9–20.

Caramazza, A. (Ed.). (1990). *Cognitive neuropsychology and neurolinguistics.* Hillsdale, NJ: L. Erlbaum.

Chi, J., Dooling, E., & Gilles, F. (1977). Gyral development of the human brain. *Annals of Neurology, 1,* 86–93.

Chomsky, N. (1959). Review of Skinner's *Verbal behavior. Language, 35,* 26–58.

Chomsky, N. (1980). Rules and representations. *The Behavioral and Brain Sciences, 3,* 1–61.

Clarke, E., & O'Malley, C. D. (Eds.). (1968). *The human brain and spinal cord: A historical study illustrated by writing from antiquity to the twentieth century.* Berkeley: University of California Press.

Code, C. (1987). *Language, aphasia, and the right hemisphere.* New York: John Wiley and Sons.

Cole, M., & Cole, M. (Eds.). (1971). *Pierre Marie's papers on speech disorders.* New York: Hafner.

Crossen, B. (1985). Subcortical functions in language: A working model. *Brain and Language, 25,* 257–292.

Curry, F. (1968). A comparison of the performance of a right hemispherectomized subject and 25 normals on 4 dichotic listening tasks. *Cortex, 4,* 144–153.

Curtis, S. (1977). *Genie. A psycholinguistic study of a modern-day "wild child."* New York: Academic Press.

Cutting, J. (1972). A parallel between encodedness and the magnitude of the right ear effect. Status Report on *Speech Res.* (Haskins Labs.) 29/30. 61–68.

Damasio, A., Damasio, H., Gush, F., Varney, N., & Rizzo, M. (1981). Atypical aphasia following lesions of the dominant striatum and internal capsule. *Neurology, 31,* 82.

Dandy, W. (1928). Removal of right cerebral hemisphere for certain tumors with hemiplegia: Preliminary report. *Journal of the American Medical Association, 90,* 823–825.

Darley, F., Aronson, A., & Brown, J. (1975). *Audio seminars in speech pathology: Motor speech disorders.* Philadelphia: W. B. Saunders.

Darley, F., Aronson, A., & Brown, J. (1975). *Motor speech disorders.* Philadelphia: W. B. Saunders.

Dennis, M., & Whitaker, H. (1976). Language acquisition following hemidecortication: Linguistic superiority of the left over the right hemisphere. *Brain and Language, 3,* 404–433.

Diamond, M., Scheibel, A., & Elson, L. (1985). *The human brain coloring book.* New York: Barnes and Noble.

Dingwall, W. (1975). The species-specificity of speech. In D. Dato (Ed.), *Developmental psycholinguistics: Theory and applications,* (17–62). Georgetown University Press.

Dingwall, W. (1975). Broca's contributions to physical anthropology relating to the brain and its functions. *Working Papers in Biocommunication, 1,* 1–28.

Dingwall, W. (1981). *Language and the brain: A bibliography and guide.* New York: Garland publishers.

Dingwall, W. (1988). The evolution of human communicative behavior. In F. Newmeyer, (Ed.). *Linguistics: The Cambridge Survey, Volume III: Language: Psychosocial and biological aspects.* New York: Cambridge University Press.

Eccles, J., & Gibson, W. (1979). *Sherrington: His life and thought.* Heidelberg: Springer-Verlag.

Eggert, G. (1977). *Wernicke's works on aphasia: A sourcebook and review.* The Hague: Mouton.

Ellis, A., & Young, A. (1988). *Human cognitive neuropsychology.* Hillsdale, New Jersey: L. Erlbaum.

Fodor, J. (1983). *The modularity of mind.* Cambridge, MA: The MIT Press.

Fodor, J., Bever, T. & Garrett, M. (1974). *The psychology of language.* New York: McGraw-Hill.

Fox, W. (1984). *Dandy of Johns Hopkins.* Baltimore: Williams and Wilkins.

Galaburda, A., Sauides, F., & Geschwind, N. (1978). Human brain: Cytoarchitectonic left-right asymmetries in the temporal speech region. *Archives of Neurology, 35,* 812–817.

Gardner, H. (1983). *Frames of mind: The theory of multiple intelligences.* New York: Basic Books.

Gazzaniga, M. (1970). *The bisected brain.* New York: Appleton-Century-Crofts.

Gazzaniga, M. & LeDoux, J. (1978). *The integrated mind.* New York: Plenum Press.

Geschwind, N. (1974). *Selected papers on language and the brain.* Dordrecht, Holland: D. Reidel.

Geschwind, N., & Levitsky, W. (1969). Human brain: Left-right asymmetries in temporal speech area. *Science, 161,* 186–187.

Gilroy, J., & Holliday, P. (1982). *Basic neurology.* New York: Macmillan Publishers.

Glick, S. (Ed.). (1985). *Cerebral lateralization in nonhuman species.* New York: Academic Press.

Goldstein, K. (1948). *Language and language disturbances.* New York: Grune and Stratton.

Goodglass, H. (1988). Historical perspectives on concepts of aphasia. In F. Boller & J. Grafman (Eds.), *Handbook of neuropsychology, Vol. 1,* (pp. 249–265). New York: Elsevier.

Gordon, B. (1990). Human Language. In R. Kessner & D. Olton (Eds.), *Neurology of comparative cognition,* (pp. 21–49). Hillsdale, NJ: L. Erlbaum.

Haggard, M. (1971). Encoding and the REA for speech signals. *Quarterly Journal of Experimental Psychology, 23,* 34–45.

Hahn, M., Jensen, C., & Budelk, B. (Eds.). (1979). *Development and evolution of brain size.* New York: Academic Press.

Head, H. (1963). *Aphasia and kindred disorders of speech.* New York: Hafner.

Hendersen, V. (1986). Paul Broca's less heralded contributions to aphasia research. *Archives of Neurology, 43,* 609–612.

Itoh, M., & Sawanawa, S. (1984). Articulation movements in apraxia of speech. In J. Rosenbek, M. McNeil, & A. Aronson (Eds.). *Apraxia of speech.* San Diego: College-Hill Press.

Jerison, H. (1977). Should phrenology be rediscovered? *Current Anthropology, 18,* 744–746.

Juegens, U. (1976). Reinforcing concomitants of electrically elicited vocalizations. *Experimental Brain Research, 26,* 203–214.

Juegens, U. (1990). Vocal communication in primates. In R. Kessner & D. Olton (Eds.) *Neurobiology of comparative cognition,* (pp. 51–76.) Hillsdale, New Jersey: L. Erlbaum.

Juegens, U. & Ploog, D. (1976). Zur Evolution der Stimme. *Archiv für Psychiatrie und Nervenkrankheiten, 222,* 117–137.

Kandel, E., & Schwartz, J. (1981). *Principles of neural science.* New York: Elsevier/North-Holland.

Kennedy, M., & Murdoch, B. (1989). Speech and language disorders subsequent to subcortical vascular lesions. *Aphasiology, 3,* 221–247.

Kertesz, A. (Ed.). (1983). *Localization in neuropsychology.* New York: Academic Press.

Kimura, D. (1961). Cerebral dominance and the perception of verbal stimuli. *Canadian Journal of Psychology, 15,* 166–171.

Kimura, D. (1973). The asymmetry of the human brain. *Scientific American, 228,* 70–78.

Kimura, D. (1992). Sex differences in the brain. *Scientific American, 267,* 118–125.

Klor, B. (1984). *Speech and language profiles of aphasic adults.* Tigard, OR: C.C. Publications.

Kolb, B., & Whishaw, I. (1990). *Fundamentals of human neuropsychology.* New York: W. H. Freeman.

Krashen, S. (1972). Language and the left hemisphere. UCLA Work Pap. Phonetics 24.

Krmpotic, J. (1959). Donnees anatomiques et histologiques relative aux effecteurs laryngo-pharyngo-buccaux. *Rev. Laryngol., 11,* 829–848.

Kuehn, D., Lemms, M., & Baumgartner, J. (Eds.). (1989). *Neural Bases of speech, hearing, and language.* Boston: College-Hill Pub.

Kuypers, H. (1981). Anatomy of the descending pathways. In V. Brooks (Ed.) *Handbook of physiology, Vol. II, Part I,* (pp. 597–666). Bethesda, MD: American Physiology Society.

Larson, C. (1985). The midbrain periacqueductal gray: a brainstem structure involved in vocalization. *Journal of Speech and Hearing Research, 28,* 241–249.

Lassen, N., Ingvour, D., & Skinhj, E. (1978). Brain function and blood flow. *Scientific Am., 239,* 62–72.

Lecours, A., & Joanette, Y. (1980). Linguistic and other psychological aspects of paroxysmal aphasia. *Brain and Language, 10,* 1–23.

Lichtheim, L. (1885). On aphasia. *Brain, 7,* 433–484.

Loring, D. W., Meador, K., Lee, G., Murro, A., Smith, J., Flanigan, H., Gallagher, B., & King, D. (1990). Cerebral language lateralization: Evidence from intra-carotid amobarbital testing. *Neuropsychologia, 28,* 831–838.

Marie, P. (1906). La troisième circonvolution frontale gauche ne joue aucun role special dans la fonction du langage. *Semaine medicale, 26,* 241–247.

Metter, E., Riege, W., Hanson, W., Kuhl, D., Phelps, M., Squire, L., Wasterlain, D., & Benson, D. (1983). Comparison of metabolic rates, language, and memory in sub-cortical aphasias. *Brain and Language, 19,* 33–47.

Mohr, J. (1976). Broca's area and Broca's aphasia. In H. Whitaker and H. A. Whitaker (Eds.), *Studies in neurolinguistics, Volume I.* New York: Academic Press.

Murdoch, B. E. (1990). *Acquired speech and language disorders.* New York: Chapman and Hall.

Myers, P. (1986). Right hemisphere communication impairment. In Chapey, R. (Ed.) *Language intervention strategies in adult aphasia.* Baltimore: Williams and Wilkins.

Myers, R. (1955). Interocular transfer of pattern discrimination in cats following section of crossed optic fibers. *Journal of Comparative and Physiological Psychology, 48,* 470–473.

Naeser, M., Alexander, M., Helm-Estabrooks, N., Levine, H., Laughlin, S., & Geschwind, N. (1982). Aphasia with predominantly subcortical lesion sites. *Archives of Neurology, 39,* 2–14.

Netter, F. (1983). *The nervous system.* The CIBA collection of medical illustrations. West Caldwell, New Jersey: CIBA.

Newmeyer, F. (Ed.). (1988). *Linguistics: The Cambridge survey.* New York: Cambridge University Press.

Nolte, J. (1988). *The human brain: An introduction to its functional anatomy.* St. Louis: C.V. Mosby.

Nottebohm, F., & Arnold, A. (1976). Sexual dimorphism in vocal control areas of the songbird brain. *Science, 194,* 211–213.

Obler, L., & Fein, D. (1988). *The exceptional brain.* New York: The Guilford Press.

Orgogozo, J. & Larsen, B. (1979). Activation of the supplementary motor area during voluntary movements in man suggests it works as a supramotor area. *Science, 206,* 847–850.

Papez, J. (1953). Theodor Meynert (1833–1892). In W. Haymaker and F. Schiller, (Eds.) *The founders of neurology* (pp. 57–62). Springfield, IL: C. C. Thomas.

Passingham, R. E. (1982). *The human primate.* San Francisco: W. H. Thomas.

Penfield, W. & Roberts, L. (1959). *Speech and brain-mechanisms.* Princeton, NJ: Princeton University Press.

Perecman, E. (Ed.). (1983). *Cognitive processing in the right hemisphere.* New York: Academic Press.

Petersen, S., Fox, P., Posner, M., Mintern, M., & Raichle, M. (1989). Positron emission tomographic studies of the processing of single words. *Journal of Cognitive Neuroscience, 1,* 153–170.

Pimental, P., & Kingsbury, N. (1989). *Neuropsychological aspects of right brain injury.* Austin, TX: Pro-Ed.

Pinel, J. (1990). *Biopsychology.* Boston: Allyn and Bacon.

Poizner, H., Klima, E., & Bellugi, U. (1987). *What the hands reveal about the brain.* Cambridge, MA: The MIT Press.

Rasmussen, T., & Milner, B. (1977). The role of early left-brain injury in determining lateralization of cerebral speech functions. *Annals of the New York Academy of Sciences, 299,* 355–369.

Robins, R. (1967). *A short history of linguistics.* Bloomington, IN: Indiana University Press.

Rumelhart, D., McClelland, J., & the PDP Research Group. (1986). *Parallel distributed processing.* Cambridge, MA: The MIT Press.

Ryding, E., Bradvik, B., & Ingvar, D. (1987). Changes of regional cerebral blood flow measured simultaneously in the right and left hemisphere during automatic speech and humming. *Brain, 110,* 1345–1358.

Rymer, R. (1992). A silent childhood–I The New Yorker, April 13 (41–81); April 20 (43–77).

Sacks, O. (1985). *The man who mistook his wife for a hat and other clinical tales.* New York: Summit Books.

Schiller, F. (1979). *Paul Broca.* Berkeley: University of California Press.

Sherrington, C. (1951). *Man on his nature.* Cambridge: Cambridge University Press.

Shipley-Brown, F., Dingwall, W., Berlin, C., Yeni-Komshian, G., & Gordon-Salant, S. (1988). Hemispheric processing of affective and linguistic intonation contours in normal subjects. *Brain and Language, 33,* 16–26.

Signoret, J. L., Castaigne, P., Lhermitte, F., Abelavet, R., & Lavorel P. (1984). Rediscovery of Leborgne's brain: anatomical description with CT scan. *Brain and Language, 22,* 303–319.

Smith, A. (1966). Speech and other function after left (dominant) hemispherectomy. *Journal of Neurology, Neurosurgery and Psychiatry, 29,* 467–471.

Sparks, R., & Geschwind, N. (1968). Dichotic listening in man after section of neocortical commissures. *Cortex, 4,* 3–16.

Springer, S., & Deutsch, G. (1989). *Left brain, right brain.* New York: W. H. Freeman.

Steklis, H., & Raleigh, M. (Eds.). (1979). *Neurobiology of social communication in primates. An evolutionary perspective.* New York: Academic Press.

Studdert-Kennedy, M., & Shankweiler, D. (1970). Hemispheric specialization for speech perception. *Journal of the Acoustical Society of America, 48,* 579–94.

Toulmin, S. (1971). Brain and language: A commentary. *Synthese, 22,* 369–95.

Tsunoda, T. (1985). *The Japanese brain.* Tokyo: Taishukan Publishers.

Van Lancker, D., & Fromkin, V. (1978). Cerebral lateralization of pitch contrasts in tone language speakers and in musically trained and untrained English speakers. *Journal of Phonetics, 6,* 19–23.

Van Wagenen, W. P., & Herren, P. Y. (1940). Surgical division of commissural pathways in the corpus callosum: Relation to spread of epileptic attack. *AMA Archives of Neurology and Psychiatry, 44,* 740–775.

Wada, J. (1949). A new method for the determination of the side of cerebral speech dominance. *Igaka to Seibutsugaku, 24,* 221–222.

Wernicke, C. (1906). Der aphasische Symptomenkomplex. Berlin: Deutsche Klinik am Eingange des 20. Jahrhunderts, Bd. 6, Abt. 1, Ed. by V. Leyden et al., 487–556.

Wertz, R., Rosenbek, J., & Deal, J. (1970). *A review of 228 cases of apraxia of speech: Classification, etiology, and localization.* Presented at the American Speech and Hearing Association Convention, New York, New York.

Whitaker, H. (1976). A case of the isolation of the language function. In H. Whitaker and H. A. Whitaker (Eds.), *Studies in neurolinguistics, Vol. II,* New York: Academic Press.

Young, R. (1974). *Mind, brain and adaptation in the 19th century.* Oxford: Clarendon Press.

Speech Perception

GRACE H. YENI-KOMSHIAN
The University of Maryland at College Park

Introduction

In this chapter, we explore the processes by which people decode spoken messages. When we listen to a lecture, view a movie or participate in a conversation, we must attach meaning to the sounds we hear. In later chapters, we examine how the meanings of words are accessed, and how the grammar of sentences is analyzed to get the full sense of a message. But before these stages of language understanding can occur, we must first determine what sounds we have heard. Thus, in order to appreciate the advice, *"Don't slip on that banana peel!"* we need to realize that we have heard a sequence of speech sounds. Next, we may need to label these sounds as particular sounds of English. At some point, we must decide when a string of sounds has become a recognizable and meaningful word or sentence.

Although the process of decoding speech occurs rapidly, understanding how we accomplish the task is quite complex. In this chapter, we survey what is known about the process by which listeners assign identity to speech sounds. This basic stage in communication is complicated by the fact that the sounds of a language do not have constant, unvarying acoustic characteristics. A sound such as the English phoneme /t/ will sound different, for example, when spoken by different speakers, and when it appears in different words. We examine this problem of variation within the speech signal, as well as other problems which make the understanding of speech by people or machines such a prodigious feat. Additionally, we discuss a number of theories which have been developed to explain the process of speech perception in syllables and words and the potential contribution of these theories to the full task of understanding language.

The historical roots of speech perception research

When compared with many other areas of inquiry in psycholinguistics, speech perception research is extremely recent in origin. Study of the physical properties of sound was conducted by Willis (1829) and Helmholtz (1859) in the nineteenth century. However, specific research into the way we perceive speech emerged just prior to and during the Second World War. Much of the pioneering work in speech perception depended on the development of equipment for speech analysis and **synthesis** (computer simulation of speech). The technology required for the development of such devices was not available until the middle of the twentieth century, and the primary motivation for developing them was commercial. The first such machine was developed by Homer Dudley of Bell Telephone Laboratories, who called it a *vocoder*, a term derived from the words *vo*ice and *coder* (Dudley, 1936, 1939). Originally, the vocoder was designed to provide a means for the efficient transmission of speech signals over long and expensive telephone circuits. It accomplished this task by analyzing and recoding the speech into a simpler signal which contained less information to be transmitted. Dudley and others quickly came to appreciate that natural speech contains **redundant** (multiply specified) information. This means that many factors may contribute to our recognition of a speech sound; all of them do not need to be present for speech to be interpreted, either in laboratory experiments, or over the telephone. Dudley and his coworkers also discovered that they could use the vocoder to generate synthetic speech (Dudley, Reisz, & Watkins, 1939). This early attempt produced speech that had an unpleasant "electrical accent," and was not very easy to understand (Schroeder, 1966). The principles used to design the vocoder advanced the development of the **sound spectrograph**. This instrument analyzes audio signals according to the distribution of sound frequencies (spectrum) contained in the signal. In analyzing speech, the spectrograph displays *frequency* on the ordinate (y-axis), *time* on the abscissa (x-axis), and *amplitude* by the darkness of the markings. Speech analysis through the use of sound spectrography existed during the Second World War, but was kept a military secret, eventually becoming available to the public only after the war. An early model was built at the Bell Telephone Laboratories and it could produce an instantaneous visible record of running speech. At that time the output was called *visible speech* (Potter, Kopp, & Green, 1947). It soon became clear that the moving visible pattern of speech sounds was impossible to "read," so the spectrograph was modified to produce a printout capable of displaying about two seconds of speech. The picture generated by a spectrograph is called a sound **spectrogram**. An example of a spectrographic display is provided in Figure 3.1. Spectrograms provide us with a stationary display of the speech signal which permits us to evaluate which aspects of the signal might be important for the perception of speech segments.

   Thus, the roots of speech perception research lie in commercial and military interest in developing better communication systems. Over the years, as society has increased its use of audio equipment for work and leisure, many strides have been made in developing machinery which can better analyze and recreate the speech signal. Much of this work is now done by specialized computers. Commercial interest in speech perception continues because of the strong desire to develop computers that can understand speech, and perhaps even identify speakers from their speech patterns. Current machine speech recognition capacity is very limited. At present, no machines exist that can recognize speech that is spoken in a normal conversational manner.

Major questions in speech perception

How do we identify and label phonetic segments?

In terms of its **acoustical** (or sound) properties, human speech is a very complex signal, containing many kinds of information at any single moment, and varying

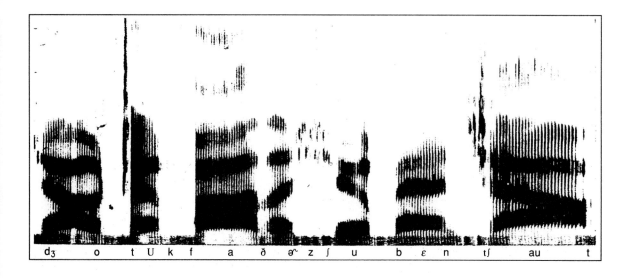

Figure 3.1

Spectrogram of the sentence "Joe took father's shoe bench out." Note that the pauses (the absence of energy) are not between words. (from Tartter, V. C. [1986], *Language Processes*, NY: Holt, Rinehart and Winston, Figure 7.1 page 210.)

continuously over time. Conversational speech in any language tends to be paced at between 125–180 words per minute. This rate of speech can be translated to mean that we probably process approximately 25–30 phonetic segments per second (Liberman, 1970). To add to the problems inherent in decoding such a rapid and complex signal, conversational speech is a continuous signal. Let us return to Figure 3.1 for a moment. You will note that while there are a number of breaks in the visual pattern, individual sounds and words flow together in the spectrogram without easily identifiable boundary markers. The apparent gaps seen in Figure 3.1 are caused by specific articulatory movements associated with certain speech sounds, and are not determined by the beginnings and ends of individual words. Articulatory movements for certain speech sounds require periods of silence, and these are the visible breaks seen in the figure.

Finding out how we manage to decode speech signals into phonetic units and derive meaningful words is a problem of great interest for speech perception research. Although the speech signal that reaches our ears varies more or less continuously over time, we perceive utterances as made up of discrete segments. We do not seem to have a major problem in segmenting speech into units of consonants and vowels, nor in identifying phonetic segments wherever they may appear in an utterance.

As a concrete example, let us consider the case of a student taking lecture notes. To do that, one needs to segment a continuous signal into the units that correspond to the English alphabet. The concern here is not how to spell the words, but how it is that one is able to hear a flowing, continuous signal and then transform it into a *sequence of different speech segments*. Unlike print, speech does not contain cues for the beginning and end of words or of individual speech units, which we will call *phonetic segments*. When we speak, our articulatory gestures are smooth and continuous. If we were to write speech as it actually sounds, we might transcribe our lecture notes as follows: *Spokenwordsarenotseparatedbyspaceslikewordsareinprint*. Notice that it is difficult to read such a sentence because it is less obvious when words end and new words begin.

Even though it is relatively easy for us to segment speech, we should remember that phonetic segments are not like beads strung on a string, one segment after another. Rather, it is better to compare speech to a braid, in which the properties which help us identify phonetic segments are tightly intertwined and overlap greatly. One of the greatest challenges for speech perception researchers is to determine how individual sounds are isolated (segmented) from the complex speech signal, and how they are identified appropriately.

The "lack of invariance" problem

It would be relatively easy to develop models of the speech perception process if each distinctive sound in a language was associated with a standard acoustic pattern. Unfortunately, neither speech nor its acoustic characteristics are that simple. Rather than displaying **invariant** (standard, unvarying) patterns, speech sounds vary considerably in their acoustic characteristics, for a number of reasons. There is no simple one-to-one correspondence between the phonemes of a language and their acoustic realization. One very important reason for this variation is that the production, and hence the acoustics, of the same phonetic segment varies depending on the context in which the segment is produced. There are many other factors which contribute to the absence of invariance. Both what we have pronounced before and after a given segment affect the actual articulatory movements we make for the production of that segment. For example, in Chapter 1, we considered the example of the words *key* and *koala*, in which the place of articulation for [k] varies as a function of the following vowels. These context effects, which result in overlapping movements for speech, are called **coarticulation**. In Chapter One we have already explored the **allophonic variation** that occurs when speech sounds are embedded in certain contexts, such as initiating words, ending utterances, or when they are the neighbors of other specific sounds. The example given for this variability in phoneme realization was the sentence, "Tom Burton tried to steal a butter plate," with its many varieties of [t].

Next, the physical properties of speech sounds, especially vowels, vary according to whether they have been produced by either men, women, or children, whose vocal tracts differ in size and configuration. It is thus somewhat surprising that we do not have problems in understanding speech produced by such diverse speakers, and speech perception researchers must account for our relative ease in processing these varying speech signals.

Another factor leading to variation in the acoustic properties of speech sounds is that we do not pronounce the same utterance in exactly the same way twice. This tendency makes speech sound natural and we seem to have no problem in dealing with this type of variation.

Yet another factor leading to variation in the speech signal stems from the properties of rapidly articulated conversational speech. There is a great difference between saying single words slowly and carefully and the way we actually pronounce words when we speak fluently. The acoustic characteristics of speech segments are reduced and much more variable in fluent speech than in careful enunciation of words. Speech perception research must explain how such "messy" samples of speech are processed by listeners.

Solving the invariance problem can also lead to the development of machines that can process spoken, rather than typed input. Consequently, solving the invariance problem is of great commercial interest. Attempts to get computers to recognize speech segments or words have not been tremendously successful because segments and words do not exist as stable acoustic patterns in fluent speech and cannot be easily recognized using pattern-matching techniques. Research has shown that segments that are clearly visible when words are spoken one at a time, may be shortened, altered, deleted, or combined with other segments when the same words are produced in conversation (Klatt & Stevens, 1973; Reddy, 1976; Klatt, 1977). Thus, a machine cannot be programmed to search through a large but limited number of stored patterns and convert the patterns to phonetic segments and ultimately to words and sentences. The variations seen in conversational speech are so complex and diverse that at present there is no system available that allows machines to recognize speech as you and I are able to do. Currently, such "intelligent" machines can only process a limited repertoire of words spoken one at a time using template-matching programs. A few systems can recognize a larger vocabulary, but they can process speech only from a single speaker who must first provide samples of his or her own speech. Such a system is called **speaker-dependent**. A system which can recognize more than a single speaker is said to be **speaker-independent**; at present these systems can process only a very limited vocabulary, such as numbers. Some readers may have experienced telephone services which use a speaker-independent system. (For a survey of research into this problem, see Schwab & Nusbaum, 1986; Zue, 1985, 1991.)

We should not end this section without pointing out that recent work appears to be pointing to invariant cues to identify stop consonants under specific conditions (Blumstein & Stevens, 1979, 1980; Stevens & Blumstein, 1981; Kewley-Port, 1982, 1983; Sussman, McCaffrey, & Matthews, 1991). Our ears may be using invariant cues for the identification of sounds; however, it could be that new techniques are needed to isolate and describe them.

How is speech perceived under less than ideal conditions?

We have just indicated that conversational speech is quite variable in its acoustic characteristics. Sometimes speakers **underarticulate** (miss articulatory targets) when talking, so much so that the words lose much of their identifying information. Yet, listeners do not usually have trouble understanding such speech samples. We will show how lexical, syntactic, and contextual information are used to interpret **ambiguous** (unclear speech) signals. Models of speech perception will need to explain how these other levels of processing contribute to the process of speech understanding.

In summary, the major research issues in speech perception research have to do with delineation of the mechanisms we use in segmenting and recognizing speech. These mechanisms are the basis for speech perception. Although the ultimate goal for some is to explain not only how we perceive, but also how we understand spoken language signals, most of the available research has focused on investigating the perception of well defined samples of speech that are restricted as far as other aspects of language, such as meaning and syntax. Typically, studies have used syllables or single words as the experimental stimuli to be processed. The field has progressed enough to set the stage for a move toward using larger and meaningful units of speech in perceptual studies (Cole, 1980; Spoehr, 1981; Pisoni & Luce, 1987). Some of these studies will be discussed later on in the chapter. Before we can discuss the nature of speech perception, however, it is important to be familiar with the way in which speech sounds are produced, and the way that they are classified. We will also briefly explain the acoustical properties of the speech signal.

The speech signal

How speech is produced

In this section, we briefly survey the process by which speech sounds are produced. How and where sounds are produced within our **vocal tracts** determines the acoustic properties of those sounds. Because of this, sometimes we can also work backwards, and identify where and how a particular sound was articulated from its acoustic image on a spectrogram.

Let us first identify the body parts that are involved in speech production. Figure 3.2 is a diagram of most of the organs used in speech production. The places of articulation for English consonants are noted on it. Starting at the bottom of Figure 3.2, you can see the **glottis**, which is part of the **larynx**. The larynx contains the **vocal folds** and the glottis is the opening between the vocal folds where the folds meet when they vibrate to produce voice or **phonation**. You can also see the **pharynx**, the **nasal cavity**, and the various parts of the **oral cavity**. These include the **uvula**, the **velum** (or soft palate), the **hard palate**, the **alveolar ridge, tongue, teeth** and **lips**. The area from the larynx to the lips is called the **vocal tract**, and as can be seen in Figure 3.2, it has the appearance of a tube.

There are three major systems for speech production: (1) the vocal tract, (2) the larynx, and (3) the **subglottal system**, which includes the lungs, and associated muscles needed for inhalation and exhalation, and the trachea or the windpipe. The subglottal system provides the air support for speech, which is produced on exhalation. Movements in these three systems are coordinated during the production of speech sounds.

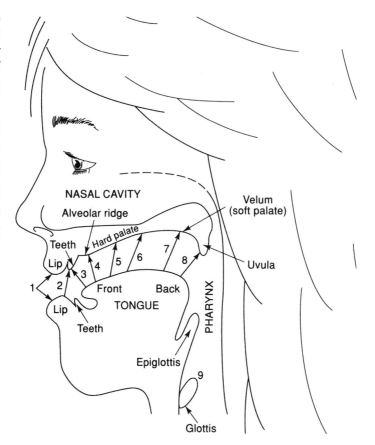

There are two classes of speech sounds: vowels and consonants. These two types of sounds are produced differently. The major difference is that consonants are produced with more articulatory movement and more constriction (narrowing in a location in the vocal tract) than are vowels.

Consonants and vowels have also been further classified by linguists according to different categories. One of the most common and basic systems is to classify sounds by where in the vocal tract they are made, and how they are made. Table 3.1 lists most of the English consonants according to such a system.

Place of articulation

The numbers along the vocal tract in Figure 3.2 refer to the various places where constriction for different English consonants takes place. We call each of these locations *place of articulation*. Common places of articulation for English consonants are **bilabial** (closing the lips to create [p], [b], and [m]), **labiodental** (with the top teeth against the bottom lip, as in [f] and [v]), **interdental** (with the tongue protruding between the lips, as in the production of [θ] and [ð], as in to*th* and *th*e), **alveolar** (with the tongue placed behind the upper teeth, as in [t], [d], [n], [s], [z], [l], and [r]), **palatal** (with the tongue against the palate, as in [ʃ] hu*sh*, [ʒ] lei*s*ure, [tʃ] *ch*ur*ch*, [dʒ] *j*u*dg*e, and [j] *y*es), and **velar** (with the body of the tongue contacting the velum or soft palate, as in [k], [g], and [ŋ] as in si*ng*).

Manner of production

The source of acoustic energy for speech sound production comes from modulations in the air flowing from the lungs to the lips. The production of any sound involves the movement of air molecules. To be able to speak we need to have air in our lungs that will serve as the power supply for the production of speech. The air flowing from the lungs to the lips is called the *airstream*. During regular quiet breathing, the vocal tract is open and the air flows out freely, either through the nose or mouth. During speech production, however, some part (or parts) of the vocal tract constricts to a degree that is enough to impede the air flow. The manner in which the constrictions

Table 3.1

English consonants classified according to place of articulation and manner of production

Manner of production	Bilabial	Labiodental	Interdental	Alveolar	Palatal	Velar
	Place of articulation					
Oral stop voiceless / voiced	p (pin) b (bin)			t (tin) d (din)		k (kin) g (get)
Nasal stop voiced	m (map)			n (nap)		ŋ (sing)
Fricative voiceless / voiced		f (fin) v (van)	θ (thin) ð (than)	s (sin) z (zone)	ʃ (shin) ʒ (leisure)	
Affricate voiceless / voiced					tʃ (chin) dʒ (gin)	
Liquid voiced				l (law) r (raw)		
Glides voiced					j (yes)	w (we)

are made in the vocal tract affects the air stream, and results in different ways in which speech sounds can be produced (See Table 3.1, "Manner of Production").

Some sounds are produced by modulating the airstream by the periodic opening and closing of the vocal folds at the glottis, also called *glottal pulsing*. As the vocal folds open and close, puffs of air are generated and flow through the *oral cavity*. These airflow pulses are *periodic* (occurring at regular intervals), rapid, and produce a sound which has a buzz-like quality. Sounds produced by the action of vocal fold vibration are called **voiced** or **phonated**. In English, all vowel sounds and the consonants in Table 3.1 which are classified as voiced make use of the voiced sound source in their production. You can feel the vibration of your vocal folds (by placing your fingers on your throat) when you produce a sustained [z]. You can also feel the absence of vibration when you produce a sustained [s]. Try this procedure with the other pairs of voiced and voiceless fricatives, stops, and affricates. Also note that nasal stops, glides, and liquids are voiced; you can feel your vocal folds vibrate when you produce these consonants.

The rate at which the glottal pulsing occurs during sound generation (phonation) is called the **fundamental frequency (F0)**. It is about 125 glottal pulses per second for adult males, about 200 pulses per second for adult females, and about 300 pulses per second for children. The perceived difference between the pitch of men, women, and children is based on the rate of glottal pulsing.

A second type of sound source is achieved when air is forced through a narrow constriction in the oral cavity. For example, in the production of [s], a narrow slit is formed between the tip of the tongue and the alveolar ridge. Air rushes through this slit. The flow of air creates a *turbulent* speech sound. The turbulence produces friction noise that has a hissing quality. The same thing happens if you blow air through a narrow constriction, such as a slit through a grass blade or two sheets of paper. The turbulent airstream does not pulse periodically, but has random variations in airflow. This **aperiodic** (turbulent) sound source is the basis for the production of consonants called *fricatives* and *affricates*. Voicing and turbulence may be combined in the case of voiced fricatives and affricates, as Table 3.1 indicates.

In English, a number of speech sounds are made by stopping the airflow completely for a short period of time and then abruptly releasing it. This describes a third type of sound source, called a *transient sound source*, which is used in the production of oral stop consonants, shown in Table 3.1. The production of these consonants requires a complete closure of the oral cavity, which in effect stops the airflow for a short period and increases air pressure. These movements are then followed by an abrupt release of the airstream, which creates the sound (burst). If we make similar articulatory movements for oral stop consonants, but allow air to flow from the nasal cavity, we produce the nasal stops shown in Table 3.1.

Speech sounds that combine the gestures for stop consonants and fricatives are called affricates (in English *ch* in and *j* am). Speech sounds classified as liquids (*l* aw and *r* aw) have a voiced sound source and air flow is minimally constricted. Sounds classified as glides (*y* es and *w* e) are the consonants that are the closest to vowels because they allow the air to flow freely. However, the articulators move faster than they do for the vowels. All these consonants are listed in Table 3.1. In contrast, in the production of vowels, air flow from the lungs is unobstructed.

Distinctive features

Linguists have used concepts such as voicing or place of articulation to develop a system of **distinctive features** for describing speech sounds. For example, all sounds are characterized either by the feature +*voice* (voiced) or −*voice* (voiceless). Sounds are additionally described by other features, such as whether the air stream exits the mouth as opposed to the nose. This produces the feature contrast +*oral/*−*oral*. Sounds classified as −*oral* would be the English nasal stops [m], [n], and [ŋ].

Sounds made with continuous air flow, such as vowels, fricatives, glides, and liquids, are noted by the feature +**continuant**. The stops, which require an abrupt stoppage of air flow in generating the transient sound source, receive the feature −**continuant**.

Place of articulation can also be captured by feature notation. Sounds made at the front of the mouth, such as [p], [b], and [m] are noted as +**anterior**. Sounds made by placing the tongue in contact with the palate [t], [d], and [n] are considered +**coronal**. By combining these features, we can arrive at a complete feature specification for a given English sound. For example, [b] could be described as:

$$
\begin{bmatrix}
+ \text{oral} \\
- \text{continuant} \\
+ \text{voice} \\
+ \text{anterior}
\end{bmatrix}
$$

We will not exhaustively survey the full range of distinctive features which have been developed to describe the sounds of English and other languages. However, it is interesting and important to note that common misperceptions of speech appear to reflect a change in the value of a single feature. That is, when we misperceive we are frequently off by only one distinctive feature. The results of many experiments, using single syllables as stimuli, have demonstrated this phenomenon and have also delineated the order in which confusions between features are likely to occur (Miller & Nicely, 1955; Wang & Bilger, 1973). Later in the chapter we will see how misperceptions occur in fluent speech. Additionally, as Chapter 7 shows, some speech errors suggest that distinctive features may be real "building blocks" in the speech production process. It is possible to find examples of speech errors in which a given feature, such as voicing, is misplaced, producing the unintended output, "Ball and Peth" for the intended sequence, "Paul and Beth."

Acoustical properties of speech sounds

Vowels: The simplest case

It is easiest to demonstrate the acoustical properties of speech sounds by describing single vowels. All speech sounds are composed of complex sound waves; that is, they contain many different frequencies simultaneously, like a musical chord that contains many notes. The vowels we hear are based on a modification of the sound source in a manner that is determined by the **resonant characteristics** of the oral cavity or vocal tract during the production of that sound.

What are resonant characteristics? When air flows through any bounded area we hear sound. The specific sound we hear is composed of the resonance frequencies associated with the size and shape of the space through which air is flowing. We have heard the sounds made while filling a bottle with water. Actually the change in the sound while filling the bottle with water indicates to us that it is time to turn off the tap. That is, we have learned to assign some meaning to the changes in sound. The changes in the sound are created by the change in the size and shape of the space through which the air is flowing out of the bottle. When the bottle is empty, the air in it is contained in a relatively large space. As you fill the bottle with water the air space gets smaller; therefore, the resonance characteristics of the smaller space will be different from those of the larger space. The resonance of a relatively empty bottle is low pitched and the resonance of a bottle that is about to overflow is high pitched.

Let us now take the case of the voiced sound source, which is used in the production of all vowels. The frequency components, **spectrum**, of this sound source at the glottis include the fundamental frequency (F0) and even multiples of the fundamental frequency. The multiples of the F0 are called **harmonics**. Thus, if the F0 is at 100Hz, the harmonics would be at 200Hz, 300Hz, 400Hz, 500Hz, and so on up to and beyond 8,000Hz. The unmodified spectrum at the sound source would have frequency components that are even multiples of 100Hz, though some of these frequencies would be of higher or lower **amplitude** (loudness). In the production of a vowel sound, for example [u] as in the vowel of the word *boot*, the shape of the oral cavity for producing [u] will determine the frequency components that will be prominent (resonate) when the airstream flows through that particular oral cavity shape. The oral cavity shape for [u] is such that bands of low frequency components will resonate. The bands of *resonant frequencies* for speech change in relation to the movement of our articulators while producing speech. These bands of resonant frequencies are called **formants**. The shape of the oral cavity is changed when we pronounce [i], or [a], or any other speech sound. Figure 3.3 displays spectrograms of English vowels. Spectrograms display frequency on the vertical axis, time on the horizontal axis, and amplitude in the darkness of the markings. Formants (bands of resonant frequencies) are easily visible on the sound spectrograms.

The single vowels and diphthongs displayed in Figure 3.3 are organized according to their place or production. Figure 3.3(A) lists the front vowels, Figure 3.3(B) the back vowels, Figure 3.3(C) the central vowels, and Figure 3.3(D) the diphthongs. These vowels were produced by a male speaker. Even though these samples are not typical of conversational speech style, certain concepts are easier to illustrate using such simple examples. The most noticeable aspect of the individual patterns shown in Figure 3.3 is that each vowel appears to be characterized by at least three broad, dark, horizontal stripes. These stripes are the **vowel formants**. On the figure, each formant is marked with a small line to help you locate them. Formants are numbered from low to high frequency such that the first formant (F1) is associated with the lowest frequency resonance band, the second formant (F2) with the next band of frequencies and so on up to five or more formants.

Vowels are differentiated by the relative position of the first two formants, which appear to be sufficient for their identification. Thus, it is the pattern of a low

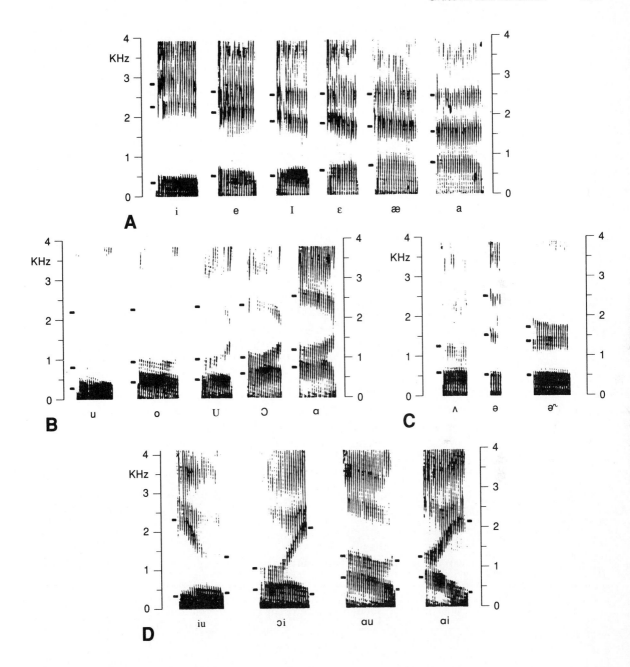

Figure 3.3

Spectrograms of examples of the vowels and diphthongs of American English. The approximate midvowel locations of the first three formants are indicated by the bars beside each spectrogram. (from Pickett, J. M. [1980] *The Sounds of Speech Communication*, Baltimore, University Park Press Figure 30, pages 74–75.)

frequency F1 and a very high frequency F2 which appears to be characteristic of [i], shown in Figure 3.3(A), while the pattern which identifies [u] consists of two very low frequency formants, as in Figure 3.3(B). It is important to note that the frequency components of formants are affected by the size and shape of the vocal tract and to some degree by the fundamental frequency. Because of this, men, women, and children have different absolute values for the formants of given vowels. The fact that listeners can process vowels from men, women, and child speakers, whose vowels vary in absolute frequency, implies that a pattern recognition system is in operation, rather than reference to absolute values. We call the ability of listeners to use pattern recognition to identify vowels spoken by different speakers *speaker normalization*.

Changes in the oral cavity for the production of different vowels in isolation are simple in comparison to the changes that take place in diphthongs, syllables, and conversational speech. Diphthongs, which are two vowels produced in a smooth glide, have formants moving from one vowel to another, as shown in Figure 3.3(D). These movements are called *formant transitions*. For example for [au], the formants begin in a pattern similar to that for [a] and move to end like the pattern for [u]. Formant transitions reflect the movements of the articulators and are faster and sharper in consonants than in vowels. In fact, single vowels produced in isolation, such as those in Figure 3.3 (A), (B), and (C), do not have formant transitions. These relatively flat formant patterns are called *steady states*. In fluent conversational speech, however, we hardly ever see vowels produced in steady state, and vowel formants have fairly sharp transitions going in and out of adjacent consonants. If you compare Figures 3.3 and 3.4, the differences in vowel formant patterns are evident.

Acoustic characteristics of consonants

Consonants are characterized by an array of different patterns on a sound spectrogram. Once more, we will start with more easily identifiable patterns. If you examine Figure 3.4, in which the speaker is saying, "*She sells sea shells*," the turbulence associated with the fricatives [s] and [ʃ] is visible as thick columns of aperiodic energy interspersed among the vowel formants. The difference between [s] and [ʃ] is signalled by the range of frequencies included in the columns. You will note that [ʃ] is lower in frequency than [s]. As fricatives vary in their place of articulation, these differences are reflected in changes in the range of frequencies seen in their spectrographic displays.

The most visible feature of oral stop consonant displays is the thin vertical line associated with the sudden release of air pressure (the burst). The burst is a very rapid acoustic event, and may be of low intensity (e.g., it is not readily visible in *Bab*). For this reason, the various stop consonants are more readily distinguished on the spectrogram in Figure 3.5 by the distinctive formant transitions to their adjacent vowel sounds. In the sentence, "Bab gagged Dad," the formants appear to rise upward from the release of the consonant to the vowel in *Bab*, they fall in *gag*, and stay relatively level in *Dad*. It is these formant movements, or formant transitions, which appear to play a large role in deciding which stop consonant has been heard. For additional information on the acoustic characteristics of speech sounds see Pickett (1980), and Borden and Harris (1984).

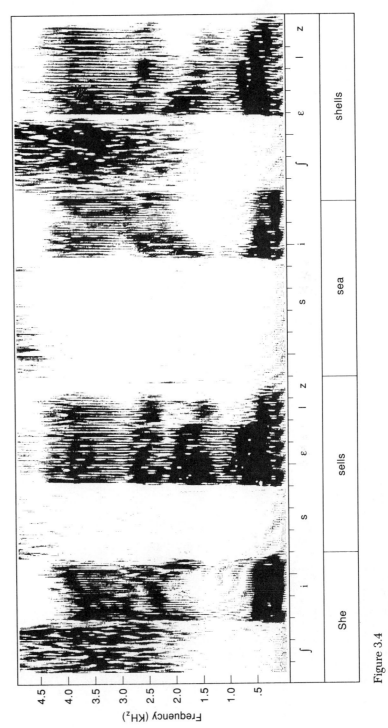

Figure 3.4
Spectrogram of the phrase "She sells sea shells"

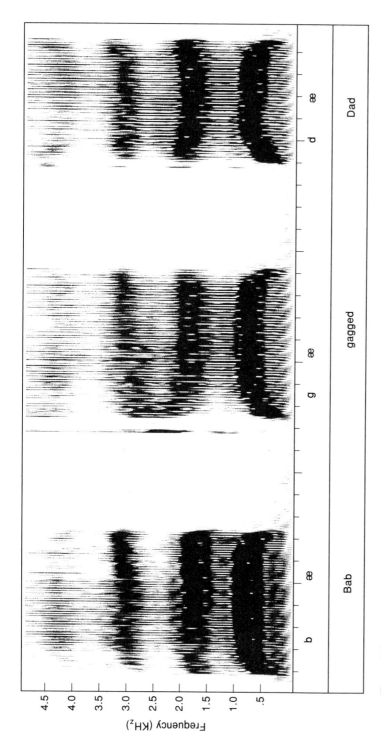

Figure 3.5

Spectrogram of the sentence "Bad gagged Dad"

Perception of phonetic segments

In this section our concern is with the perception of phonetic segments. As we have seen, the speech signal is complex and contains a lot of information in the time, frequency, and amplitude domains. We have also seen that even though we can psychologically and linguistically identify segments or phonemes in fluent speech, the acoustic signal does not contain visible markers that correspond to the segments. Furthermore, when we listen to someone, we not only hear the linguistic message, we also hear the special characteristics of the speaker's voice and emotional state, though they are not necessary for determining the identity of the phonetic segments (phonemes) contained in the linguistic message.

One of the most important goals of research in this area has been a search for specific aspects of the complex sound pattern that would be necessary for the identity of a given phoneme. These critical parts of the complex sound pattern are called *acoustic cues*. Certain equipment had to be available before researchers could begin to work in this area. They had to make use of speech analysis machines like the sound spectrograph and also had to have the capacity to synthesize speech according to precise specifications. The aim was to create speech stimuli that could be used to evaluate the perceptual relevance of acoustic cues.

The role of speech synthesis in perceptual research

The collaboration of three pioneers in speech perception research at Haskins Laboratories signaled the start of research on the perceptual evaluation of acoustic cues. In the early 1950s, Franklin Cooper, an engineer, Alvin Liberman, a psychologist, and Pierre Delattre, a linguist, joined forces to study the perception of speech. It was true then and also true now that progress in speech perception relies on interdisciplinary cooperation.

They utilized a speech synthesizer called the Pattern Playback, constructed by Cooper and his colleagues (Cooper, Delattre, Liberman, Borst, & Gerstman, 1952). This machine was designed to synthesize speech sounds by converting visual patterns to complex sound waves. The pattern playback device could synthesize speech from the formant patterns displayed on a spectrogram; it could also generate the sound associated with any pattern that one painted on its cellulose acetate belt. The researcher would paint a pattern on the belt and the machine would play the pattern back. Figure 3.6 is a picture of the Pattern Playback Synthesizer.

One of the first things discovered using this machine was that intelligible speech could be obtained from highly simplified spectrograms. For example, synthesis of the first two vowel formants and an appropriate transition were enough to produce intelligible CV (consonant-vowel) syllables. This finding, like earlier observations about telephone transmission (Dudley, 1936, 1939) demonstrated that speech was highly redundant.

Early observations and experiments with the pattern playback made use of only
two formant stimuli and were concerned with delineating the acoustic cues necessary
to identify stop consonants synthesized with different vowels in the shape of CV syllables (Cooper et al., 1952; Liberman, Delattre, & Cooper, 1952). The researchers
would paint a pattern and play it back to see if it produced the desired sound; if not,
they would modify the pattern and play it again, until they got the desired sound. In
this process, they discovered the acoustic cues necessary for the identity of that particular speech sound. The resulting report by Liberman et al., (1952) anticipated and
described many ideas that have become the foundation of research in speech perception. This initial work set the stage for charting the acoustic cues that perceptually
differentiate one phoneme from another.

Ways in which speech perception is tested

Many experiments in speech perception that we will discuss in the following sections
have made use of two tasks: discrimination and identification. In **discrimination**,
the listener is asked to indicate whether two stimuli are the same or different. There
are several methods for obtaining this type of information, which may differ in the
amount of memory required by the task. In discrimination, the listener can decide

whether two stimuli are same or different without having to identify, label, or determine the meaning of the stimuli. In **identification**, the task is to label or determine the identity of the stimulus. Thus, in identification the listener has to provide or select a label and may require input from the lexicon for the decision. For example, listeners may be asked, "Write the word that you hear." In other situations, they may be provided with a fixed number of alternatives and asked to choose the alternative that best matches the label or identity of the stimulus. This type of task is similar to a "multiple choice" exam.

In the following sections, we describe certain illustrative speech perception studies in detail, so that the reader can better appreciate the complex procedures used in evaluating how listeners perceive speech.

Perception of vowels

What is the most important part of the vowel signal for its identity? The early studies made use of extended **steady state** vowels as stimuli. One experiment made use of the pattern playback to synthesize stimuli to investigate how listeners respond to one and two formant steady state stimuli (Delattre, Liberman, Cooper, & Gerstman, 1952). Listeners were able to perceive some vowels created with only a single formant. Low frequency single formants were generally associated with back vowels, for example [u], [a], and higher frequency single formants with front vowels, for example [i], [e]. This finding suggests that the frequency information contained in one formant is enough to provide the listener with the percept of a vowel. When stimuli which contained two formants were presented, however, agreement across listeners was high in identifying the stimuli as that particular vowel whose natural formant patterns had served as the model for the synthesis. This study and others that followed suggested that the steady state portion of the first two formants of a vowel are the necessary and sufficient acoustic cues to determine its identity. As we shall see, this view was later modified as the perception of more natural speech samples was investigated.

Steady states versus formant transitions in vowel identification: An illustrative study

Recall that vowels contained in regular words are produced in the context of consonants. Acoustically this means that vowels are marked by formant transitions going in and out of the adjacent consonants and contain steady state segments that are either very short or not present at all. The next logical question, which compared the perceptual saliency of vowel steady states and formant transitions, was not investigated for three decades (Jenkins, Strange, & Edman, 1983). We will describe this study in some detail, not only because its findings are interesting, but also because it shows that controlled and precise stimuli can be created with real speech stimuli. In fact, at present both speech synthesis and computer control of real speech are common techniques for producing stimuli for speech perception research.

As test stimuli, Jenkins et al. (1983) used CVC syllables which began and ended with [b], but contained nine different vowels (*beeb, bib, bab, bob,* etc.). A male speaker produced these nine syllables. With the use of a computer, the syllables were digitized and edited. Each syllable was then divided into three components: (a) the formant transitions from the initial consonant to the vowel, (b) the central vocalic (vowel) portion, and (c) the transition from the vowel to the final consonant. These segments will be referred to as (a), (b), and (c). Listeners evaluated the following types of stimuli:

(1) The unmodified original syllable, called *control syllables*, composed of segments (a) + (b) + (c);

(2) *Silent center syllables*, which consisted of segments (a) + silent gap + (c). The silent gap was as long as segment (b) for that syllable. This type of stimulus preserved the formant transitions and the actual duration of the vowel but did not contain the steady state information;

(3) *Variable center syllables*, which consisted of only the (b) portion of each syllable. These stimuli preserved the steady state portion of the target vowel and its inherent duration;

(4) *Fixed center* stimuli were constructed by trimming segment (b) in each syllable to match the duration of the shortest target vowel. These stimuli preserved the steady state portion of the vowels, but did not contain durational information;

(5) Finally, listeners evaluated *abutted syllables*, which were composed of segments (a) + (c). These stimuli did not contain any information concerning segment (b). That is, they did not contain a steady state portion at all.

Groups of subjects were asked to identify the vowels within each type of stimulus and the unmodified original control syllables. The results showed that silent center stimuli were identified as accurately as the original control syllables. Listeners made significantly more errors in identifying the variable center (steady state and temporal information) and abutted syllables. The lowest accuracy level was for the fixed center (steady state only) stimuli. The authors interpreted their results to indicate that formant transitions and vowel duration are more important cues to the identity of vowels than a fixed sample of the steady state information. This finding has been replicated and extended in other studies. A more detailed account of more recent studies and a model of vowel perception can be found in Strange (1989a, 1989b).

This and other research on vowel perception suggest that perception of isolated sounds and continuous speech differ. What appeared to be an important acoustic cue for vowel identity (its steady state) in an isolated and extended segment of synthetic speech does not appear to be the most important acoustic cue in natural speech. Acoustic cues thought to be important when evaluating simplified speech (two formants only) may not be as important when natural speech is considered (many formants). Thus, the history of research on vowel perception demonstrates that our understanding of how we process speech is bound to change as we improve and diversify our methods of investigation.

Current research seeks to approach the characteristics of actual conversational speech sounds by utilizing modern computer techniques which edit natural speech to generate stimuli that are controlled and at the same time reflect the characteristics of normal conversation.

Perception of consonants

In both conversational speech and laboratory studies, vowels are perceived more accurately than consonants. The intensity of the signal may play a role in the advantage seen in vowel identification. The acoustic energy associated with vowels is stronger by about six decibels (dB) than for consonants. In addition, most consonants are shorter in duration than vowels. Thus the short duration and lower amplitude of consonants makes them harder to perceive than vowels.

Stop consonants have been studied extensively in speech perception research. We have already noted that in English, the stops [b,d,g] are +*voice*, and [p,t,k] −*voice*. All languages have oral stop consonants represented in their phonological system. Unlike other consonants, stops lose their identity when presented in isolation. For example, in a syllable such as [ba], it is impossible to separate the [b] portion from the [a] portion of the syllable. If one removes the entire vowel (transition plus steady state) from the syllable, the resultant segment sounds like a 'chirp' rather than the phoneme [b]. Stop consonants in syllable initial position must contain a small piece of the transition segment in order to be perceived accurately. In other words, the acoustic signal from the articulation of the stop consonant *plus* the formant transitions into the adjacent vowel are needed before we can hear the consonant. It is as if the consonant and the vowel information are merged together in the syllable, somewhat like the analogy of the braid mentioned earlier in this chapter. When the acoustic information of adjacent phonetic segments are merged, the phonetic segment is described as being **encoded**. In our example, [b] would be considered encoded, since there is no single acoustic segment that we can isolate that would sound like [b]. We can only extract the identity of [b] from the merged consonantal and vowel information. This means that the information about the consonant and the vowel is transmitted in parallel to the listener. This type of **parallel transmission** is most dramatically evident in highly encoded phonetic segments such as oral stop consonants. The formant transitions between the consonant and vowel appear to play a large role in deciding the identity of the stop consonant and the vowel.

Stop consonants are highly encoded; other consonants are not as encoded. Even when isolated segments retain their phonetic identity, the acoustic signals of all consonants and vowels are affected by the characteristics of their adjacent phonemes. That is, all speech sounds change character as a function of the sounds with which they are produced, the phenomenon we have already called **coarticulation**.

Phoneme identity is context dependent

Since the late 1950s, a great deal of research has been devoted to other types of perceptual studies that were primarily concerned with determining the acoustic cues for all the phonetic contrasts in English and other languages. A lot of empirical information has been accumulated on this subject matter. In this chapter we highlight two major general findings that have been repeatedly observed across different stimulus conditions and experimental techniques. The first finding is that acoustic cues are highly dependent on context effects. That is, there is not a single acoustic cue that is present in all instances of a given phoneme. The acoustic cue for a phoneme changes as that phoneme is paired with other phonemes. In addition, research has shown that context dependent variations are most pronounced in highly encoded speech sounds like the stop consonants. For example, as illustrated in Figure 3.7, the acoustic patterns of the second formant transitions from the consonant into the vowel of [di] and [du] differ dramatically, yet listeners will agree that the consonant in these two syllables is the same [d]. This illustrates the effects of coarticulation and the "lack of invariance" problem described earlier in the chapter.

Another important general finding is that there is more than one acoustic cue for differentiating a phonetic contrast. This is true even when context effects are accounted for. As we shall see, **voice-onset-time (VOT)** will be identified as the best single measure for signalling the difference between voiced and voiceless stop consonants in syllables such as [ba] versus [pa]. There are, however, additional cues such as the amount of energy in the burst, onset frequency of the first formant, and rate of first formant transition that also contribute to the perception of voicing distinction in syllables (Lisker & Abramson, 1964; Summerfield & Haggard, 1974). This multiplicity of acoustic cues, which contributes to redundancy in the speech signal, is evident in many phonetic contrasts and appears to be the rule rather than the exception. Theoretical accounts of speech perception have not as yet taken this empirical finding into consideration.

Voice-onset-time: An important acoustic cue

Researchers have extensively evaluated the perception of stop consonants. One of the aims of their research was to determine the perceptual salience (importance) of specific acoustic cues used to distinguish among the various English stops. As we noted earlier, one way in which stops differ from one another is in whether they are voiced (+ voice, accompanied by vocal fold vibration) or voiceless (− voice, without vocal fold vibration). In English, three pairs of stop consonants are identical except for the voicing feature. That is, [b] and [p], [d] and [t], and [k] and [g] are pairs of phonemes distinguished only by the feature (voice). In each pair, the first sound is produced with accompanying vocal fold vibration, [+ voice], while the second is not, [− voice].

While it might appear that the presence or absence of voicing during stop production is a rather easy cue to the discrimination of sounds, describing listeners' actual discrimination between voiced/voiceless stop *cognates* (sounds differing only in one feature, in this case the voicing feature) turns out to be more complex than anticipated. Researchers had already noted from spectrograms of speech samples that voicing distinctions were associated with different acoustic patterns depending on the phoneme and where in the word the contrast occurred. In the case of word initial contrasts, what really appeared to be important for distinguishing between pairs such as [ba] and [pa], for instance, was a parameter called voice-onset-time (VOT). In a stop-initial CV syllable, VOT represents the time between the release of

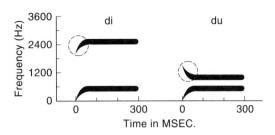

Figure 3.7

Two formant syllables produced on the Pattern Playback synthesizer identified as [di] and [du]. Notice the difference in the beginning of the second formant of each syllable. (from Borden, G. J., and Harris, K. S. [1984] *Speech Science Primer* [second edition], Baltimore, Williams and Wilkins, Figure 5.31, page 213) Original figure from A. M. Liberman (1970) The grammars of speech language. *Cognitive Psychology, 1,* 301–323.

air pressure (the burst) and the onset of vocal fold vibration (voicing) for the adjacent vowel (Lisker & Abramson, 1964). On a spectrogram this is seen as the time between a sharp onset of broadband energy (the burst) and the onset of the formant transition (onset of vocal fold vibration). Figure 3.8 displays two spectrograms to illustrate this point. In both spectrograms, the initial consonant is an alveolar stop and the vowel is [i]. Which will be heard as [d] and which as [t]? Figure 3.8(A) demonstrates a VOT of about 10 milliseconds: there is a 10 milliseconds gap between the stop burst and the onset of the following vowel's first formant. As we shall see, such a pattern is heard as [di]. In 3.8(B), there is a VOT of approximately 60 milliseconds duration, meaning that 60 milliseconds have elapsed between the stop burst and the onset of voicing for the following vowel; it is heard as [ti]. The horizontal bracket marks the VOT region. VOT has been demonstrated to be the best single acoustic cue that differentiates between syllable initial voiced and voiceless stop consonants [b,d,g vs. p,t,k] (Lisker & Abramson, 1964).

If all voiced stops had VOTs of zero, and all voiceless ones were characterized by VOTs of 60 milliseconds, explaining the discrimination of voicing would be relatively simple. However, the actual VOTs seen in stop production vary widely. Sometimes vocal fold vibration (voicing) is actually initiated before the release of the burst in a "voiced" stop such as [d], and at other times voicing is initiated up to 30 milliseconds later. On the other hand, "voiceless" stops such as [t] are characterized by VOTs that range between 40 to 100 milliseconds. Do listeners hear these sounds as different types of [d]s and [t]s? The answer turns out to be *no*. In order to explain how listeners evaluate the acoustic cue for voiced or voiceless initial stops, we shall discuss the findings of studies in which VOT values for stops were varied systematically such that the only difference among the stimuli was in VOT. The systematic variations, in the VOT of each stimulus in the series, form a continuum that is anchored by a voiced and a voiceless stop at either end of the series. Stimuli forming a continuum are synthesized and not based on natural speech, because we cannot control our articulators to produce the required systematic changes while keeping everything else constant. The listeners described in the experiments below were asked to both identify the test stimuli and to discriminate between pairs of stimuli.

Categorical perception of the voicing contrast

Many researchers have evaluated the perception of voicing in initial stop consonants (Liberman, Harris, Kinney, & Lane, 1961; Liberman, Harris, Eimas, Lisker, & Bastion, 1961; Liberman, Cooper, Shankweiler & Studdert-Kennedy, 1967; Abramson

Figure 3.8

Spectrograms of the
syllables [di] and [ti] to
illustrate
voice-onset-time (VOT).
In each syllable the
burst is seen as the dark
vertical line to the left.
The onset of voicing is
indicated by the
formants (start of the
segments that have
regular striations). VOT
is the distance between
the burst and the onset
of voicing, horizontal
bracket to the left of
each syllable.

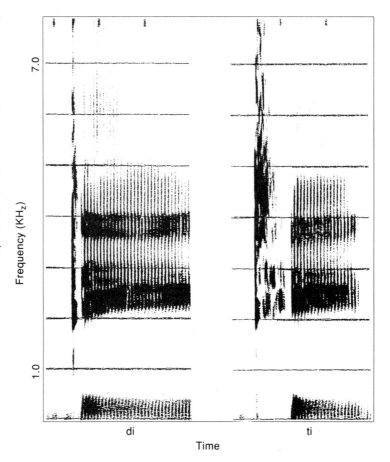

& Lisker, 1970). In these studies, a synthesized continuum of 10–15 different VOT values was used as stimuli. For illustrative purposes, we will describe a simpler study, based on the design of an experiment carried out by Yeni-Komshian and LaFontaine (1983), which used seven stimuli.

To establish the perceptual relevance of VOT as an important acoustic cue, seven stimuli along a continuum were constructed. In each case, the experimental syllable started with a burst and formant transitions which would normally elicit perception of an alveolar stop (either [d] or [t]) by the listener. The first syllable was characterized by zero milliseconds, VOT. That is, voicing for the following vowel was simultaneous with articulation of the stop consonant. The second through seventh stimuli were constructed to be identical to the first stimulus, except that the VOT in each was 10 milliseconds longer for each subsequent stimulus. The result was a seven-stimuli continuum, varying only in VOT in 10 millisecond steps. These stimuli were then used to construct identification and discrimination tasks.

In a typical identification task involving a continuum such as this, the seven different stimuli in the continuum are presented in random order at least 10 times, creating an identification test that contains 70 trials. The subjects are usually given two alternatives, for example *da* or *ta*, to choose from, and are asked to indicate which they have heard.

In the discrimination test, the subject has to indicate whether a pair of stimuli are identical (same) or differ in any way (different). Some trials will contain identical stimuli and others will be composed of two different stimuli. The "different" trials may consist of pairs of stimuli varying by one-step along the continuum (e.g., stimuli no. 1 and no. 2) or two-steps (e.g., stimuli no. 1 and no. 3). The "different" and "same" trials would then be presented in random order at least 10 times. In this particular example we will include the two-step trials only. Even with this reduced number of pairings, the minimum number of trials would be 170, (100 "different" trials and 70 "same" trials). Thus, a discrimination test is much more time consuming to administer than an identification test.

The idealized results of such an experiment are shown in Figure 3.9. The identification scores (bars) are plotted in terms of percent [da] responses. We can see that stimuli no. 1, no. 2, and no. 3 were consistently identified as [da] and were never labeled as [ta]. On the other hand, stimuli no. 5, no. 6, and no. 7 were always labeled [ta] and never as [da]. In the case of stimulus no. 4 the results are mixed: in 50 percent of the trials, it was heard [da], but the rest were heard as [ta]. In experiments such as this, it is not the case that the subject hears an in-between kind of speech sound. Rather, the perception of the stimulus is unstable; it is sometimes heard as [da] and at other times heard as [ta]. This perceptually unstable stimulus (no. 4 in our example) is called the **cross-over stimulus**, meaning it is the one that separates one phoneme category, [d], from the other phoneme category, [t]. Thus these results indicate that the listener classified stimuli no. 1, no. 2, and no. 3 in one phoneme category, [d]; and stimuli no. 5, no. 6, and no. 7 in a different phoneme category, [t]. The individual members within each phoneme category are physically different and each one is an **allophone** of that phoneme category. Thus, one of the things that this type of an identification test would tell us is the range and boundary of each *phoneme category*. The identification test also demonstrates that for the listener, a group of physically different stimuli are consistently judged to be the same phoneme. Then, rather suddenly, the next stimulus in the continuum is perceived as a different phoneme. This sharp shift in perception is suggestive of a *perceptual discontinuity* across a continuously varying physical dimension. This response is characteristic of a perceptual phenomenon called **categorical perception**.

A reader might say that there is nothing special in the identification results. The listeners were given two options. They just divided the stimuli in the continuum into two piles in a manner that validates VOT as an acoustic cue for the voicing contrast in stops. One might suggest that, had the listeners been given the opportunity to describe the differences they heard among some of the stimuli, the results might be different. Such comments are well taken as long as the results are limited to the identification test. To be able to establish whether stimuli in a continuum are perceived categorically, discrimination responses are necessary and these should fit a specific pattern. The results shown in Figure 3.9 (line graph) demonstrate the discrimination pattern typical of categorically perceived stimuli.

Figure 3.9

Identification (bars) and Discrimination (line) functions for alveolar stop consonants varying on voice-onset-time (VOT). The illustration is for a 7-step continuum, varying from [da] to [ta].
The horizontal axis contains the number and VOT value (in brackets) of each stimulus in the continuum. The left vertical axis is for the identification results and is expressed in % identified as "da." The right vertical axis is for the discrimination results and is expressed in % correct.

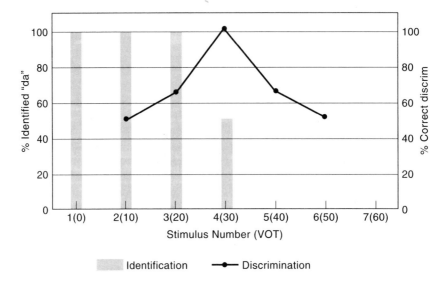

Idealized Results

The line graph shown in Figure 3.10 is based on the results of the "different" trials. All subjects were highly accurate in indicating *same* when in fact the pair of stimuli were identical. This is what we would expect. All trials that contained physically different stimuli that had been judged on the identification task to fall within the same phoneme category (e.g., the pairs of stimuli heard as [da]: no. 1–no. 3 and as [ta]: no. 5–no. 7) were discriminated at a chance level of accuracy. That is, about half the time they were judged to be the same, and the rest of the time, they were heard as differing.

Trials that contained the cross-over stimulus (e.g., no. 2–no. 4, no. 4–no. 6) show a better than chance level accuracy (65 percent). The highest level of accuracy, called the **discrimination peak**, is for trials that contain a pair of stimuli from two different phoneme categories. In our example, it is the pair no. 3–no. 5. This demonstrates that the discrimination peak is situated at the boundary between the two phoneme
categories.

While the stimuli in pair no. 3–no. 5 are discriminated highly accurately, it is somewhat surprising that a difference of the same magnitude (pairs no. 1–no. 3 and no. 5–no. 7) is not discriminated as accurately. In other words, perceptual discontinuity is demonstrated because the same amount of physical difference (in our example it is 20 milliseconds) does not have the same perceptual impact at all locations along the continuum. The listeners' ability to discriminate is not better than their ability to identify. What this means is that their discrimination of acoustic differences could be predicted from their performance on the identification test. A hallmark of categorical perception is that discrimination is not any better than identification.

In many perceptual domains, discrimination is better than identification. We usually can discriminate between two different stimuli much better than we can label or identify two different stimuli. Consider the following example from the visual domain. Let us imagine a series of photographs of two individuals who look somewhat alike. We could photograph each standing up with arms pressed against his sides. We could then take a second, third, and fourth photograph of each individual, asking each of them to raise his arms about 20 degrees for each photograph. The discrimination task would be to ask the viewer whether a pair of photographs were identical or not. In identification the task would be to label the identity of the person in the picture. In this example you would not find it difficult to tell whether any two photographs of the *same* individual were identical or not (discrimination). In contrast, with speech stimuli such as [da] and [ta] your ability to tell whether two stimuli that you have already labeled [da] are the same or different is at chance level at best.

To summarize, the identification results establish the boundaries of the two phoneme categories ([d] and [t]) and confirm the validity of VOT as a relevant perceptual cue. The discrimination results, when viewed in relation to identification results, determine whether a phonetic contrast is perceived categorically.

Other categorical perception studies

Over the years a large number of studies have been administered using test procedures similar to those described above to examine the perception of other acoustic cues and to determine whether they are perceived categorically. The experiment that discovered categorical perception and inspired the large number of studies that followed was published by Liberman, Harris, Hoffman, & Griffith (1957). It investigated the perceptual consequences of second formant transitions, rather than VOT. In the experiment, 14 two formant CV syllables were synthesized on the pattern playback. These 14 stimuli differed only in the onset frequency and direction of the second formant transitions. The vowel for all the stimuli was [a]. A schematic representation of the continuum is shown in Figure 3.10. Note that the continuum spans three phoneme categories that differ in place of articulation. These stimuli were identified as [ba], [da], or [ga]. Figure 3.10 shows the range and boundary of each phoneme category (the divisions marked by arrows at the bottom of the figure). The results of the discrimination test showed two discrimination peaks that coincided with the two phoneme boundaries. The combined patterns of the identification and discrimination results indicated that speech sounds representing these three phoneme categories were perceived categorically.

The categorical perception studies that followed the original Liberman et al. (1957) study were only limited by the speech synthesis capabilities of the time. At one time the quality of synthesized stop consonants was much better than fricatives, liquids, and affricates. In time, just about all consonantal contrasts were investigated and found to be perceived categorically (for a recent review, see Repp, 1984). With vowels, the results were complicated. In research using vowel stimuli, isolated and extended vowels were not perceived categorically. However, vowels of short duration (Pisoni, 1975) or in the context of consonants (Stevens & Ohman, 1969) were perceived categorically.

Table 3.2 lists the major acoustic cues for selected phonetic contrasts that have been studied and found to be perceived categorically. It is important to understand

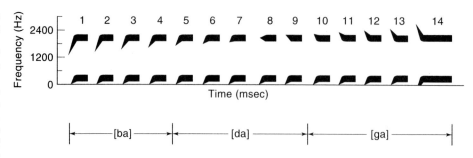

Figure 3.10

Two formant syllables produced on the Pattern Playback synthesizer. The illustration is for a 14-step continuum. Each stimulus is numbered. The stimuli vary in the onset and direction of the second formant transition. This acoustic cue signals place of articulation for the stop consonants, [ba], [da] and [ga]. The divisions marked by arrows at the bottom of the figure mark the phoneme boundaries. (from Handel, S., [1989] *Listening*, An Introduction to the perception of auditory events. Cambridge, MA, A Bradford book, The MIT Press. Figure 9.3, page 275.)

that these major acoustic cues are subject to context effects and other effects of coarticulation. The distinctions listed are based on pairs of single syllables that differ by one distinctive feature. Table 3.2 also demonstrates that the acoustic cues for voicing vary depending on the type of speech sounds (stops vs. fricatives) and whether the contrast is word initial or word final.

Categorical perception: Specific to speech perception?

The initial interpretation of categorical perception was that it was a phenomenon that was limited to the perception of speech sounds. It was argued that speech is perceived in a special mode, the *speech mode*, in which we automatically compute a phonetic label and discard the acoustic information. Thus, once physically different stimuli are given the same phonetic label, they are no longer distinguishable from each other. The Motor Theory of Speech Perception (Liberman, Cooper, Shankweiler, & Studdert-Kennedy, 1967), to be discussed later, relied heavily on this line of reasoning.

There have been, however, other studies indicating that categorical perception is not a phenomenon that is only demonstrated with speech sounds. For example, categorical perception has been reported for complex tones that vary in sharpness of onset (Cutting & Rosner, 1974), for noise buzz sequences that vary on noise lead time (Miller, Weir, Pastore, Kelly, & Dooling, 1976), and for tones that vary on relative onset time (Pisoni, 1977). These and other studies that have addressed the question of whether categorical perception is special to speech and limited to humans (Kuhl & Miller, 1975) have emphasized the functioning of a general auditory component in speech perception. Handel (1989) provides an extensive evaluation of the available research on auditory perception of speech and non-speech stimuli.

Other applications of the categorical perception test paradigm

Other research questions have been investigated successfully with the use of speech stimuli forming various continua in identification and discrimination tests. Investigations of phoneme boundaries for contrasts in languages other than English constitute one example. Abramson and Lisker (1970) compared the perception of the same set of stimuli that spanned a voicing contrast, by Thai and American English monolinguals. The subjects were given the same identification and discrimination tasks. They

CONTRAST	MAJOR ACOUSTIC CUE
Word initial voicing in oral stops [ba-pa]	Voice Onset Time
Word final voicing in oral stops [ab-ap]	Duration of preceding vowel
Place in oral stops [ba-da-ga]	Start and direction of the second formant
Place in nasal stops [ma-na]	Start and direction of the second formant
Voicing in final fricatives [as-az]	Duration of preceding vowel
Place in fricatives [sa-ʃa]	Frequency of the turbulent noise
Liquids [la-ra]	Frequency of the third formant

Table 3.2

Major acoustic cues for selected voicing and place contrasts that are perceived categorically.

The syllables listed in the brackets are just one example for each of the contrasts.

found that Thai speakers identified and discriminated the test stimuli according to the phonology of the Thai language, which is very different from English. The phonetic boundaries for the Thai listeners were different from those of English listeners. In other words, the same set of stimuli were perceived differently by the speakers of these two languages, and the differences were directly related to the phonological differences found between the two languages. Other studies have been conducted to compare bilingual with monolingual listeners. These include an investigation of the perception of stop consonant voicing in Canadian French-English bilinguals (Caramazza, Yeni-Komshian, Zurif, & Carbone, 1973) and Spanish-English bilinguals (Williams, 1977, 1980). One of the questions here is whether bilinguals identify stimuli differently according to their two languages. The studies with bilinguals generally show that they have a single perceptual system rather than two separate language-bound systems. The bilinguals' perceptual categories appear to be situated at a midpoint between the two categories set by the monolingual speakers of their two languages. Other studies have been concerned with the perception of [r] and [l] by Japanese-English bilinguals (Strange & Jenkins, 1978; MacKain, Best, & Strange, 1981; Strange & Dittman, 1984). In such studies, the test stimuli consisted of continua spanning the [r] and [l] phonetic contrast. The results of these studies reveal the extent of the difficulties that Japanese listeners have in discriminating these speech sounds. The effect of special training on discrimination ability was also assessed by using these research paradigms. These studies show fairly clearly the nature of the effects of linguistic experience on speech perception. They demonstrate that our perceptual capabilities are directly related to the phonology of the languages we speak.

Another set of research issues that can be profitably investigated with the use of stimuli along a continuum have to do with charting the extent of loss of normal speech perception by aphasics (Blumstein, Cooper, Zurif, & Caramazza, 1977; Yeni-Komshian & Lafontaine, 1983). Identification and discrimination test results demonstrate the degree to which phonetic boundaries are altered among aphasics. A typical result is that aphasics differ greatly in their perceptual responses. Many aphasics tend to have unstable responses for several stimuli in the phonetic boundary area. That is, their phonetic boundaries are not set as clearly as normal listeners.

Speech perception beyond a single segment

This section reviews the perception of speech signals which are longer than a single phoneme. We start with studies of the perception of two adjacent phonetic segments, and conclude with studies of fluent speech. Almost all the experiments reported in this section point to the role that our expectations play in speech perception. In our perception of normal conversational speech, we weigh our knowledge of phonological sequences in English, the topics relevant to the context (semantic factors), and our expectations of appropriate syntactic structure to arrive at an image of what we have "heard."

The perceptual outcome of coarticulation

As described earlier in this chapter, articulatory movements for different sounds within a word do not move in a series of separate gestures. Instead, there is temporal overlap of articulatory movements in producing a sequence of phonetic segments. This temporal overlap of articulatory movements is called coarticulation. For a definition and detailed discussion of different types of coarticulation see Daniloff and Hammarberg (1973). The type of coarticulation discussed in this section is exemplified by the way we produce the [s] in the words *see* and *Sue*. Try to say these two words in front of a mirror and pay attention to your lips while you produce the [s] portion of the syllable. You will see that your lips are in the position of a smile for the word *see* and puckered for the word *Sue*. These different articulatory gestures mean that the [s] in these two words is produced in two different ways. An experimental question is whether any information concerning the vowel in *Sue* is contained in the consonant that preceded it.

Several researchers have investigated issues related to the perception of coarticulated segments (Kuehn & Moll, 1972; LaRiviere, Winitz, & Herriman 1975; Mann & Repp, 1980). The general technique for generating stimuli for such experiments is to start with samples of natural speech, for example the word *see*, [si], then to remove the vowel and leave the [s] segment as the stimulus. The listeners' task is to indicate whether they can hear the *excised* (removed) vowel from the consonant segment. Studies have demonstrated that listeners can identify the excised vowels in certain CV combinations, but not in others.

One investigation of this sort was carried out by Yeni-Komshian and Soli (1981). The stimuli were 12 CV syllables composed of four fricatives produced in three different vowel contexts, (e.g., [si, zu, ʃa]). Computer editing procedures were used to generate the stimuli. All of the vowels were removed and 150 millisecond segments of just the fricative portions of the syllables were used as stimuli. One of the tasks in the experiment was to identify the excised vowel by listening to the fricative portion only. Results indicated that the vowels [i] and [u] were identified reliably in the fricative segments, but not the vowel [a]. This demonstrated that the fricative portion not only contained information about the consonant but also contained information about the identity of the following vowel. That is, information about the fricative and vowel is available simultaneously in the same acoustic segment. Here is another example of **parallel transmission** of information, a term used to describe the perceptual outcome of coarticulation.

Even though parallel transmission of information is very common in speech, it appears that this additional source of perceptual information is available when articulatory compatibility exists between segments. When two adjacent segments can be produced with noncontradictory tongue movements, they are compatible. For example, the tongue is raised for both consonant and vowel in the production of [si]. However, when adjacent segments require contradictory tongue movements, they are incompatible and are not coarticulated. In our example, contradictory tongue movements are involved in the production of [sa] and [ʃa]. For example in [sa], the tongue is raised for [s] and has to be lowered for [a].

To summarize, coarticulatory effects do not exist uniformly across all adjacent segments, and do not uniformly distribute perceptual information throughout the speech signal. Instead, when articulatory compatibility is possible, speakers naturally engage in coarticulation and this may provide an additional source of perceptual information to the listener.

Perceptual effects of speaking rate

The effects of speaking rate on segmental distinctions has been investigated and reviewed by Miller (1981). The acoustic characteristics of sounds are altered as speaking rate increases. Changes from **citation form** (the way sounds are produced carefully in isolation) are more evident in vowels than in consonants. Nevertheless, all phonetic segments undergo modification. The general findings in perceptual studies of speaking rate indicate that listeners make perceptual adjustments for speeded speech. The typical research paradigm is to place a target stimulus (for example, a word) in a **carrier phrase** (standard, unvarying sentence) that is either fast or slow and instruct the listener to identify the target stimulus. Listeners apparently form certain expectations on the basis of the rate of the carrier phrase. Consequently, the same target stimulus may be identified as two different words or sound sequences depending on the rate of the carrier phrase. The shift in the perceptual response is directly related to the changes we make when we alter the rate of our speaking.

Lexical and syntactic factors in word perception

Unlike perception of meaningless isolated phonetic segments, perception of meaningful words in connected fluent speech is influenced by higher level knowledge of semantics and syntax. Very early work in this area indicated that single words presented in noise are recognized more accurately in a sentence context than when spoken in isolation (Miller, Heise, & Lichten, 1951). In another study, words embedded in sentences were perceived more accurately than when the same words were excised from their sentences and presented in isolation (Pollack & Pickett, 1964). The researchers recorded conversations, and excised individual words from the taped material. They then presented these isolated words to listeners for identification. Only about half of the excised words were recognized correctly. When the words were presented along with one or two neighboring words from the original conversational sentences, successful identification of the target words increased dramatically.

Words produced in conversational speech are less intelligible than isolated words because in fluent speech we pronounce words less precisely than in citation form. It is also clear from results such as these that in a sentence context, semantics and syntax help the listener decode individual words in fluent speech. This means that what is called **top-down processing** (the use of semantic and syntactic information) as well as phonological **bottom-up processing** (using only acoustic information to decode the speech signal) operate jointly in everyday perception of conversation. Later in this chapter there will be brief discussions of several models that attempt to account for the joint action of bottom-up and top-down processing of speech.

A classic demonstration of the effect of context on speech perception is a phenomenon called **phonemic restoration** (Warren, 1970). In this study, Warren replaced a phonetic segment (for example, the [s] in *legislature*) with a coughing sound of about the same intensity as the excised segment. The word was then presented in a sentence context and the subjects were asked to indicate where in the sentence the cough occurred. Surprisingly, subjects were not accurate in locating the cough. Their typical response was that they heard the full word *legislature*; the cough was heard as background noise. Thus, the subjects generated or *restored* a phoneme that was not part of the signal. The results were interpreted to suggest that when we listen to words, our expectations affect what we perceive. If most of the information necessary to specify a word is available, we mentally "smooth over" minor discrepancies in the speech signal.

The question then is, under what circumstances do we detect irregularities in words or sentences that we hear? Cole and his colleagues devised an ingenious method and carried out studies aimed at answering this question (Cole, 1973; Cole, Jakimik, & Cooper, 1978; Cole & Jakimik, 1980). The *listening for mispronunciation (LM)* detection task is an interesting way to examine the stimulus characteristics we pay attention to in recognizing words in the context of running speech. The subjects' main task was to listen for mispronunciations. This technique has been used to ask questions such as: Which part of a word or a syllable do we pay attention to while listening to connected speech? (Answer: the initial part). Do we detect mispronunciations in predictable sequences better than in unpredictable sequences? (Answer: yes).

Cole (1980) reports various examples of the uses of the LM procedure. The part that we will concentrate on is the one that has to do with inferring the relative perceptibility of different distinctive features in naturally produced fluent speech (Cole,

Jakimik, & Cooper, 1978). This was done by examining the results of different feature changes in target words in short stories. For example, to examine the perceptibility of the stop consonant voicing feature, the target word, *broom*, was systematically mispronounced. All mispronunciations resulted in phonologically permissible nonwords. That is, *b*room could be changed to *t*room, *d*room, or *f*room, but not to *s*room or *n*room, because *sr-* and *nr-* sequences are not acceptable in English. The mispronunciations were embedded in a story that was about 20 minutes long. The subject's task was to listen to the story and to push a button as soon as possible whenever they heard a mispronunciation.

The first experiment dealt with voicing in word initial stops, fricatives, and affricates. Results suggested that voicing changes were detected most accurately for stops (*b*oot to *p*oot) (70 percent), followed by affricates (*ch*ance to *j*ance) (64 percent), and least accurately for fricatives (*f*in to *v*in) (38 percent). The reduced ability to detect mispronunciations in fricatives may be due to their relatively weak acoustic signals. It is also true that there are few English words which contrast minimally in the voicing characteristics of initial fricatives. It is suggested that since this contrast is rare in the language, listeners pay little attention to it.

In further experiments, place, voicing, and manner changes in initial consonants were investigated. In general, subjects were fairly accurate in detecting the mispronunciations based on place (80 percent–90 percent). Changes based on place differences (*t*ake to *p*ake) were more perceptible than those based on voicing (*t*ake to *d*ake). In addition, mispronunciations based on both place and voicing (*t*ake to *g*ake) were not detected any better than place changes alone. These findings elaborate and extend earlier research on perception of distinctive features (Miller & Nicely, 1955; Wang & Bilger, 1973) to the conversational speech level.

A final experiment in this series compared the perception of changes in word-initial and word-final consonants. The changes sampled involved place in nasals (*m*ake to *n*ake; dru*m* to dru*n*) and voicing in stops (*d*ish to *t*ish; spli*t* to spli*d*). The results indicated that for all comparisons, over twice as many detections were made for word initial (72 percent) mispronunciations than for word final (33 percent). The poor detection of word final consonant mispronunciation may be partially explained on acoustic grounds for oral stops but not for the nasal stops. These results appear to indicate that listeners pay more attention to beginnings of words rather than ends of words. It is suggested that the listener accesses a word candidate soon after hearing the beginning of the word and "fills in" for the end of the word.

Following a review of their research using the LM technique Cole and Jakimik (1980) conclude that words are recognized through the interaction of sound and knowledge. Sounds in the beginning of a word are used to access word candidates, sounds in a word are recognized sequentially, and once recognized, words provide semantic and syntactic constraints used to recognize the rest of the message (Cole & Jakimik, 1980, p. 161). These studies and others conducted by this team of researchers clearly demonstrate the joint influence of bottom-up and top-down processes operating when we listen to conversational speech.

We will end this section by describing an experiment to illustrate another interesting method for investigating the influences of bottom-up and top-down processing. This study was designed to examine the role of semantic influences in word identification. The test stimuli in Garnes and Bond (1976) were tokens in a 16-step continuum spanning the sequence *bait-date-gate*. The test stimuli were identical except for the starting frequency of the second formant, which was changed systematically in equal steps to signal place of articulation differences. These single word stimuli were used in an identification test to define the boundaries for the three phoneme categories. These same 16 stimuli were also used as the last word in the following three carrier sentences:

1. Here's the fishing gear and the _____.
2. Check the time and the _____.
3. Paint the fence and the _____.

Subjects were asked to indicate which of the three words they thought they heard at the end of each sentence. The results indicate that the unambiguous stimuli (those that were consistently identified as either *bait*, *date*, or *gate*) were perceived accurately regardless of the carrier sentence. That is, subjects reported hearing semantically implausible sentences (e.g., "*Paint the fence and bait.*") as long as the stimuli were unambiguous. Perception of the ambiguous stimuli (stimuli near the phoneme boundary or at the crossover), however, was influenced by the semantic message of the carrier sentence. Thus, for phonetically ambiguous stimuli, the semantic content of the carrier sentence affected the listener's perceptual judgment. This study shows that listeners use semantic information to aid in final decoding of the lexical message. It also demonstrates the importance of semantic input in processing speech when the signal is not acoustically optimal, a condition that is common in regular conversational speech. Other studies on the role of the lexicon in speech perception are reviewed in Samuel (1986).

Models of speech perception

In this section we describe several models that have been advanced to explain some of the mechanisms involved in speech perception. To date, none of the models is developed enough to explain the basic problems in speech perception or to account for the accumulated empirical information. Two early models will be described first, because they inspired and guided much of the research carried out up until the early 1980s. These are the *Motor Theory of Speech Perception* and *Analysis-by-Synthesis*. These two models and a more recent model called the *Fuzzy Logical Model* view the process of perception going through stages from the auditory input, to a phonological level, and up to word identification. This view is called **bottom-up**, and does not incorporate the effects of lexical and other "higher level" cognitive knowledge into the process of speech perception. Another view, called **top-down,** proposes that higher levels of knowledge play a significant role in speech perception. Models that incorporate the joint operation of multiple sources of information, including both bottom-up and top-down information, are called *interactive*. The main concern of interactive models is word recognition, whereas for bottom-up models, perception of phonetic segments is a major goal in itself. Most of the recent models incorporate an interactive approach. Two interactive models are summarized briefly. These are: the *cohort theory* and *TRACE model*. There are other models in the literature and reviews of various speech perception models can be found in collections edited by Schwab & Nusbaum (1986) and Perkell & Klatt (1986). The brief review of models in this chapter has relied primarily on the following sources: Pisoni, 1978; Pisoni & Luce, 1986, 1987.

The Motor Theory of Speech Perception

The main thesis of the motor theory is that, at some point in the speech perception process, speech signals are interpreted by reference to motor speech movements. This theory directly links the processes of speech production with speech perception, since it states that we perceive in terms of how we produce speech sounds. This theory was advanced by Liberman and his colleagues at Haskins Laboratories (Liberman, Cooper, Shankweiler, & Studdert-Kennedy, 1967; Liberman, 1970). The theory was developed to deal with the absence of invariance between the acoustic signal and its phonemic representation, a problem we have already discussed. In Liberman et al. (1967), differences in the acoustic signals of the same phoneme in various contexts are emphasized. As discussed earlier, the acoustic patterns associated with [d] in the syllables [du] and [di] differ, yet all listeners agree that the initial portion of the two syllables contains the same phoneme. If you pronounce these two syllables and pay attention to the movements of your tongue, you can feel a similarity in the motor movements of your tongue at the beginnings of the two syllables. This apparent similarity in motor gestures could then be used to counter the acoustic variance. Thus, the early form of the theory hypothesized invariance at the motor articulatory level of speech production. However, research in search of motor invariance did not produce the desired results. Later versions of the model hypothesized that the invariance most probably exists at an earlier neuromotor level, not at the actual stage of articulation, where motor commands to the articulators are made.

Another important assumption of the motor theory is that speech perception is phonetic and is different from auditory perception. According to the theory, speech is a special type of auditory stimulus for human beings; when we are exposed to it, we shift automatically to the *speech mode*, which uses different processes and criteria to evaluate speech, as opposed to music or other nonspeech sounds. Perceiving in the speech mode is innate and species specific, that is, it is a uniquely human property that we are born with. It enables us to link articulatory gestures involved in the production of a heard sound with the intended phonetic segment. The interpretation of categorical perception also relied on this special way human beings react to speech sounds. The motor theory motivated an extensive body of research on speech perception. The evidence accumulated from such research, however, has not provided strong support for the position that it is necessary to engage in some form of articulatory knowledge during perceptual processing of speech. Furthermore, arguments based on the special status of categorical perception, as discussed earlier, have not been upheld. More recent accounts of the motor theory, incorporating the idea of modularity, are presented in Liberman & Mattingly (1985, 1989).

Analysis-by-Synthesis

The basic assumptions of the Analysis-by-Synthesis model proposed by Stevens (1960) and Stevens & Halle (1967) are similar to the motor theory in that speech perception and production are closely tied. This model assumes that we make use of an abstract distinctive features matrix in a system of matching which is crucial to the speech perception process. The major claim of the theory is that listeners perceive (analyze) speech by implicitly generating (synthesis) speech from what they have heard and then compare the "synthesized" speech with the auditory stimulus. According to this model, the perceptual process begins with analysis of auditory features of the speech signal to yield a description in terms of auditory patterns. A hypothesis concerning the representation of the utterance in terms of distinctive features is constructed. In cases where phonetic features are not strongly influenced by context, and thus contain an invariant attribute, the auditory patterns are tentatively decoded into phonemes. When there are no invariant attributes to identify a phonetic feature, additional processing is required. A hypothesis concerning the distinctive feature representation of the utterance is formed. This message forms the input to a set of generative rules that synthesize candidate patterns, which are subsequently compared with the patterns of the original utterance at a neuroacoustical level, rather than an articulatory level, as in motor theory. The results of this match are sent to a control component that transfers the phonetic description to higher stages of linguistic analysis.

Analysis-by-Synthesis is an abstract model of the speech perception process, and little direct empirical evidence has been found to support it. It is vague in its evaluation of speech perception as special and different from auditory perception. More recent versions of the theory hypothesize that the properties of speech can be uniquely and invariantly specified from the acoustic signal itself (Stevens & Blumstein, 1978; Blumstein & Stevens, 1979). Research continues into the problem of invariance, and there have been several reports showing evidence of invariance in stop consonant characteristics (Blumstein & Stevens, 1979, 1980; Stevens and Blumstein, 1981; Kewley-Port, 1982; Sussman, McCaffrey, & Matthews, 1991). More work in this area will provide information regarding our ability to extract the identity of a given phonetic segment from apparently diverse acoustic signals related to that segment.

The Fuzzy Logical Model

Speech perception, according to this model, is viewed as a prime example of pattern recognition (Massaro, 1987, 1989; Massaro & Oden, 1980). The model assumes three operations in speech perception: *feature evaluation*, *integration*, and *decision*.

Prototypes, which are summary descriptions of the perceptual units of language, contain a conjunction of various distinctive features. The features of the prototype correspond to the *ideal values* that a token should have if it is a member of that category. Continuously fed information is evaluated, integrated, and matched against prototype descriptions in memory, and an identification decision is made on the basis of the relative goodness of match of the stimulus information with the relevant prototype descriptions. The role of prototypes in determining the meanings of words is discussed in Chapter 4. According to this theory, to recognize the syllable [ba], for example, the perceiver must be able to relate the information provided by the syllable itself to some memory of the category [ba], which is represented by a prototypical or idealized version of the syllable. *Feature evaluation* provides the degree to which each feature in the syllable matches the corresponding feature found in the prototype in memory. The outcome of *feature integration* consists of the degree to which each prototype matches the syllable. During *feature decision*, a relative "goodness of match" is made and the proportion of times the syllable is identified as an instance of the prototype is computed.

The model hypothesizes that multiple features corresponding to a given phonetic contrast are extracted independently from the waveform and then combined according to logical integration rules. These rules operate on *fuzzy truth values* so that information regarding a given feature may be represented in *degree of match*, rather than absolute identical form. This model stresses continuous rather than all-or-none information. Massaro's model thus attempts to account for the difficulties of mapping acoustic attributes onto higher level representations by viewing phonetic perception as a probabilistic process of matching features to prototype representations in memory.

The three models just described are primarily concerned with perception of phonetic segments. Each model attempts to devise a means of correspondence between the acoustic speech signals and phonetic segments. In these models, the end results of phonetic segment identification is achieved without reference to meaning or syntax. The following two models to be described are concerned with auditory word recognition. For these models the end result is a meaningful utterance, rather than a meaningless syllable, for example. These models aim to describe the interaction between the processes of phoneme recognition and word recognition.

Cohort Theory

This theory of word recognition was developed by Marslen-Wilson and his colleagues (Marslen-Wilson & Welsh, 1978; Marslen-Wilson, 1987), and consists of two stages. In the first stage of word recognition, the acoustic-phonetic information at the beginning of a target word activates all words in memory that resemble it. For example, if the word is *drive*, then words beginning with [d] are activated (*dive, drink, date, dunk,* etc.). These activated words make up the "cohort." The activation of the cohort words is achieved on the basis of the acoustic information in the target word and is *not* influenced by other levels of analysis. The second stage of word recognition begins once a cohort structure is activated. In this second stage, all possible sources of information may influence the selection of the target word from the cohort. These interactive sources of information work toward *eliminating* words that don't resemble the cohort. For example, further acoustic-phonetic information may eliminate some of the cohort words (*date* and *dunk*); and higher-level sources of information may appear and eliminate other members of the cohort that might not fit with the available semantic or syntactic information (*dive* and *drink*). Finally word recognition is achieved when a single candidate remains in the cohort.

Marslen-Wilson has used his own and others' research on fluent speech perception, similar to the material presented earlier in this chapter (e.g., Cole & Jakimik, 1980), in developing his theory. The theory has been revised and extended to take into account other sources of information, such as word frequency effects, which impinge on the word recognition process (Marslen-Wilson, 1987).

TRACE Theory

This is a neural network model developed by Elman and McClelland (1984, 1986). It is based on a system of processing units called *nodes*. Phonetic or distinctive features, phonemes, and words constitute nodes that represent different levels. Each node has a resting level, a threshold, and an activation level that signifies the degree to which the input is consistent with the unit that the node represents. In the presence of confirmatory evidence (input appropriate to the node), the activation level of a node rises towards its threshold; in the absence of such evidence, activation decays toward the resting level of the node.

Nodes within this system are highly interconnected and when a given node reaches threshold, it may influence other nodes to which it is connected. Thus, a node that has reached threshold may raise the activation of some of the nodes to which it is connected, while lowering the activation of others. Connections between levels are excitatory and bidirectional. Thus, phoneme nodes may excite word nodes and word nodes may excite phoneme nodes. For example, excitation of nodes representing the phonemes [b] and [o] would conceivably lead to excitation of word nodes containing candidates whose first two sounds are [bo], such as *boat* and *bone*. Connections within levels, however, are inhibitory and bidirectional. Thus, the probability that a sound has been identified as a particular phoneme, such as [b], presumably lowers the activation levels of other nodes representing competing sounds, such as [d] or [p]. This theory is still actively undergoing development, refinement, and evaluation (McClelland & Elman, 1986; Elman & McClelland, 1988; Massaro, 1989).

Summary

Human speech processing is a rapidly paced phenomenon which requires the listener to impose a phonemic identity on incoming sounds. As the sound sequences are identified, it then becomes possible to decide which words are represented in the signal. This process is complicated because the speech typically shared between conversational participants is rapidly articulated, with great variation in the acoustic realization of phonemes.

Variation is induced by differences between speakers, by degree of care taken in articulation, and most importantly, by the many changes in acoustic characteristics which occur when target sounds are coarticulated with other sounds in running speech. Models of speech perception must recognize and deal with the lack of invariance characteristic of spoken segments. Some have done this by suggesting that resemblance to a prototypical segment is sufficient for identification. Other researchers continue to search for invariant cues which may exist in the signal, but which have not yet been described.

Research also suggests that there is lexical, syntactic, and contextual input to the speech perception process which operate in cases of unclear or unresolved acoustic information. Thus, what listeners expect to hear in a particular context is likely to affect what they think they actually heard. It is this flexible trading relationship among domains of linguistic knowledge that make machine speech processing particularly formidable.

References

Abramson, A. S., & Lisker, L. (1970). Discriminability along the voicing continuum: Cross-language test. *Proceedings of the Sixth International Congress of Phonetic Science*, 569–573. Prague: Academia.

Blumstein, S., Cooper, W., Zurif, E., & Caramazza, A. (1977). The perception and production of voice onset time in aphasia. *Neuropsycholgia, 15*, 371–383

Blumstein, S. E., & Stevens, K. N. (1979). Acoustic invariance in speech production: Evidence from measurements of the spectral characteristics of stop consonants. *Journal of the Acoustical Society of America, 66*, 1001–1017

Blumstein, S. E., & Stevens, K. N. (1980). Perceptual invariance and onset spectra for stop consonants in different vowel environments. *Journal of the Acoustical Society of America, 67*, 648–662

Borden, G. J., & Harris, K. S. (1984). *Speech Science Primer: Physiology, Acoustics and Perception of Speech*. Baltimore, MD: Williams and Wilkins

Caramazza, A., Yeni-Komshian, G. H., Zurif, E. B., & Carbone, E. (1973). The acquisition of a new phonological contrast: The case of stop consonants in French-English bilinguals. *Journal of the Acoustical Society of America, 54*, 421–428.

Cole, R. A. (1973). Listening for mispronunciations: A measure of what we hear during speech. *Perception and Psychophysics, 13*, 153–156.

Cole, R. A. (Ed.). (1980). *Perception and production of fluent speech*, Hillsdale, NJ: Lawrence Erlbaum.

Cole, R. A., & Jakimik, J. (1980). A model of speech perception. In R. A. Cole (Ed.), *Perception and Production of Fluent Speech* (pp. 133–163). Hillsdale, NJ: Lawrence Erlbaum.

Cole, R. A., Jakimik, J., & Cooper, W. E. (1978). Perceptibility of phonetic features in fluent speech. *Journal of the Acoustical Society of America, 64*, 44–56.

Cooper, F. S., Delattre, P. C., Liberman, A. M., Borst, J. M., & Gerstman, L. J. (1952). Some experiments on the perception of synthetic speech sounds. *Journal of the Acoustical Society of America, 24* (6), 597–606.

Cutting, J. E., & Rosner, B. S. (1974). Categories and boundaries in speech and music. *Perception and Psychophysics, 16,* 564–570.

Daniloff, R., & Hammarberg, R. (1973). On defining coarticulation. *Journal of Phonetics, 1,* 185–194.

Delattre, P., Liberman, A. M., Cooper, F. S., & Gerstman, L. J. (1952). An experimental study of the acoustic determinants of vowel color; observations on one- and two-formant vowels synthesized from spectrographic patterns. *Word, 8,* 195–210.

Dudley, H. (1936). Synthesizing speech. *Bell Laboratories Record, 15,* 98–102.

Dudley, H. (1939). Remaking speech. *Journal of the Acoustical Society of America, 11,* 169–177.

Dudley, H., Reisz, R. R., & Watkins, S. S. A. (1939). A synthetic speaker. *Journal of the Franklin Institute, 227,* 739–764.

Eimas, P. D., & Miller, J. L. (Eds.). (1981). *Perspectives on the Study of Speech.* Hillsdale, NJ: Lawrence Erlbaum.

Elman, J. L., & McClelland, J. L. (1984). The interactive activation model of speech perception. In N. Lass (Ed.), *Language and Speech,* (pp. 337–374). New York: Academic Press.

Elman, J. L., & McClelland, J. L. (1986). Exploiting lawful variability in the speech wave. In J. S. Perkell, & D. H. Klatt (Eds.), *Invariance and Variability in Speech Processes* (pp. 360–380). Hillsdale, NJ: Lawrence Erlbaum.

Elman, J. L., & McClelland, J. L. (1988). Cognitive penetration of the mechanisms of perception: Compensation for coarticulation of lexically restored phonemes. *Journal of Memory & Language, 27,* 143–165.

Garnes, S., & Bond, Z. S. (1976). The relationship between semantic expectation and acoustic information. In W. Dressler & O. Pfeiffer (Eds.) *Proceedings of The Third International Phonology Meeting.* Innsbruck: Phonologische Tagung.

Handel, S. (1989). *Listening: An introduction to the perception of auditory events.* Cambridge, MA: The MIT Press.

Helmholtz, H. (1859). Ueber die Klangfarbe der Vocale [On the quality of vowels]. *Ann. Phys. Chem., 108,* 280–290. See also Boring, E. G. (1942). *Sensation and Perception in the History of Experimental Psychology.* New York: Appleton Century Crofts.

Jenkins, J. J., Strange, W., & Edman, T. R. (1983). Identification of vowels in "vowelless" syllables. *Perception & Psychophysics, 34* (5), 441–450.

Kewley-Port, D. (1982). Measurements of formant transitions in naturally produced stop consonant-vowel syllables. *Journal of the Acoustical Society of America, 72,* 379–389.

Kewley-Port, D. (1983). Time-varying features as correlates of place of articulation in stop consonants. *Journal of the Acoustical Society of America, 73,* 322–335.

Klatt, D. H. (1977). Review of the ARPA speech understanding project. *Journal of the Acoustical Society of America, 62,* 1343–1366.

Klatt, D. H., & Stevens, K. N. (1973). On the automatic recognition of continuous speech: Implications of a spectrogram-reading experiment. *IEEE Transactions. Audio Electroacoustics, AU-21,* 210–217.

Kuehn, D. P., & Moll, K. L. (1972). Perceptual effects of forward coarticulation. *Journal of Speech and Hearing Disorders, 15,* 654–664.

Kuhl, P. K., & Miller, J. D. (1978). Speech perception by the chinchilla: Voiced-voiceless distinction in alveolar plosive consonants. *Science, 190,* pp. 69–72.

LaRiviere, C. J., Winitz, H., & Herriman, E. (1975). The distribution of perceptual cues in English prevocalic fricatives. *Journal of Speech and Hearing Disorders, 18,* 613–622.

Liberman, A. M. (1970). The grammars of speech and language. *Cognitive Psychology, 1*, 301–323.

Liberman, A. M., Delattre, P. C., & Cooper, F. S. (1952). The role of selected stimulus-variables in the perception of the unvoiced stop consonants. *American Journal of Psychology, 65*, 497–516.

Liberman, A. M., Harris, K. S., Hoffman, H. S., & Griffith, B. C. (1957). The discrimination of speech sounds within and across phoneme boundaries. *Journal of Experimental Psychology, 54*, 358–368.

Liberman, A. M., Harris, K. S., Eimas, P. D., Lisker, L., & Bastian, J. (1961). An effect of learning on speech perception: The discrimination of durations of silence with and without phonetic significance. *Language and Speech, 4*, 175–195.

Liberman, A. M., Harris, K. S., Kinney, J. A., & Lane, H. (1961). The discrimination of relative onset time of the components of certain speech and nonspeech patterns. *Journal of Experimental Psychology, 61*, 379–388.

Liberman, A. M., Cooper, F. S., Shankweiler, D. P., & Studdert-Kennedy, M. (1967). Perception of the speech code. *Psychological Review, 74*, 431–461.

Liberman, A. M., & Mattingly, I. G. (1985). The motor theory of speech perception revised. *Cognition, 21*, 1–36.

Liberman, A. M., & Mattingly, I. G. (1989). A specialization for speech perception. *Science, 243*, 489–494.

Lisker, L., & Abramson, A. S. (1964). A cross-language study of voicing in initial stops: Acoustical measurements. *Word, 20*, 384–422.

MacKain, K., Best, C., & Strange, W. (1981). Categorical perception of English /r/ and /l/ by Japanese Bilinguals. *Applied Psycholinguistics, 2*, 369–390.

Mann, V. A., & Repp, B. H. (1980). Influence of vocalic context on perception of the [ ] - [s] distinction. *Perception and Psychophysics, 28*, 213–228.

Marslen-Wilson, W. D. (1987). Functional parallelism in spoken word recognition. *Cognition, 25*, 71–102.

Marslen-Wilson, W. D., & Welsh, A. (1978). Processing interactions and lexical access during word recognition in continuous speech. *Cognitive Psychology, 10*, 29–63.

Massaro, D. W. (1987). *Speech perception by ear and eye: A paradigm for psychological inquiry.* Hillsdale, NJ: Lawrence Erlbaum.

Massaro, D. W. (1989). Testing between the TRACE Model and the fuzzy logical model of speech perception. *Cognitive Psychology, 21*, 398–421.

Massaro, D. W., & Oden, G. C. (1980). Speech Perception: A framework for research and theory. In N. J. Lass (Ed.), *Speech and language; Advances in basic research and practice Vol. 3*, (pp. 129–165). New York: Academic Press.

McClelland, J. L., & Elman, J. L. (1986). The TRACE model of speech perception. *Cognitive Psychology, 18*, 1–86.

Miller, G. A., & Nicely, P. (1955). An analysis of perceptual confusions among some English consonants. *Journal of the Acoustical Society of America, 27*, 338–352.

Miller, J. L. (1981). Effects of speaking rate on segmental distinctions. In P. D. Eimas & J. L. Miller (Eds.), *Perspectives on the study of speech.* Hillsdale, NJ: Lawrence Erlbaum.

Miller, G. A., Heise, G. A., & Lichten, W. (1951). The intelligibility of speech as a function of the context of the test materials. *Journal of Experimental Psychology, 41*, 329–335.

Miller, J. D., Weir, C. C., Pastore, R., Kelly, W. J., & Dooling, R. J. (1976). Discrimination and labeling of noise-buzz sequences with varying noise-lead times: An example of categorical perception. *Journal of the Acoustical Society of America, 60*, 410–417.

Perkell, J. S., & Klatt, D. H. (Eds.). (1986). *Invariance and variability in speech processes.* Hillsdale, NJ: Lawrence Erlbaum.

Pickett, J. M. (1980). *The sounds of speech communication: A primer of acoustic phonetics and speech perception*. Baltimore, University Park Press.

Pisoni, D. B. (1975). Auditory short-term memory and vowel perception. *Memory and Cognition, 3*, 7–18.

Pisoni, D. B. (1977). Identification and discrimination of the relative onset time of two component tones: Implications for voicing perception in stops. *Journal of the Acoustical Society of America, 61*, 1352–1361.

Pisoni, D. B. (1978). Speech Perception. In W. K. Estes (Ed.), *Handbook of learning and Cognitive Processes. Vol. 6* (pp. 167–233). Hillsdale, NJ: Lawrence Erlbaum Associates.

Pisoni, D. B., Nusbaum, H. C., Luce, P. A., & Slowiaczek, L. M. (1985). Speech perception, word recognition and the structure of the lexicon. *Speech Communication, 4*, 75–95.

Pisoni, D. B., & Luce, P. A. (1986). Speech perception: Research, theory, and the principal issues. In E. C. Schwab & H. C. Nusbàum (Eds.), *Pattern recognition by humans and machines: Vol. 1* (pp. 1–50). Orlando, FL: Academic Press, Inc.

Pisoni, D. B., & Luce, P. A. (1987). Acoustic-phonetic representations in word recognition. *Cognition, 25*, 21–52.

Pollack, I., & Pickett, J. M. (1964). The intelligibility of excerpts from conversation. *Language and Speech, 6*, 165–171.

Potter, R., Kopp, G., & Green, H. (1947). *Visible speech*. New York: Van Nostrand Reinhold Co. (Reprinted in 1966 by Dover Press.)

Reddy, R. (1976). Speech recognition by machine: A review. *Proceedings of the IEEE, 64*, 501–531.

Repp, B. H. (1984). Categorical perception: Issues, methods, findings. In N. J. Lass (Ed.), *Speech and language: Advances in basic research and practice, 10*, 243–335, New York: Academic Press.

Samuel, A. G. (1986). The role of the lexicon in speech perception. In E. C. Schwab & H. C. Nusbaum (Eds.), *Pattern recognition by humans and machines: Vol. 1.* (pp. 89–111). Orlando, FL: Academic Press, Inc.

Schroeder, M. R. (1966). Vocoders: Analysis and synthesis of speech. *Proceedings of the IEEE, 54*(5), 720–734.

Schwab, E. C., & Nusbaum, H. C. (Eds.). (1986). *Pattern recognition by humans and machines: Vol. 1. Speech Perception*, Orlando, FL: Academic Press Series in Cognition and Perception.

Spoehr, K. T. (1981). Word recognition in speech and reading: Toward a single theory of language processing. In P. D. Eimas & J. L. Miller (Eds.), *Perspectives on the study of speech* (pp. 239–282). Hillsdale, NJ: Lawrence Erlbaum.

Stevens, K. N. (1960). Towards a model for speech recognition. *Journal of the Acoustical Society of America, 32*, 47–55.

Stevens, K. N., & Halle, M. (1967). Remarks on analysis by synthesis and distinctive features. In W. Wathen-Dunn (Ed.), *Models for the perception of speech and visual form* (pp. 88–102). Cambridge, MA: MIT Press.

Stevens, K. N., & Blumstein, S. E. (1978). Invariant cues for place of articulation in stop consonants. *Journal of the Acoustical Society of America, 64*, 1358–1368.

Stevens, K. N., & Blumstein, S. E. (1981). The search for invariant acoustic correlates of phonetic features. In P. D. Eiman & J. L. Miller (Eds.), *Perspectives on the study of speech* (pp. 1–38). Hillsdale, NJ: Lawrence Erlbaum.

Stevens, K. N., & Ohman, S. E. G. (1969). Crosslanguage study of vowel perception. *Language and Speech, 12*, 1–23.

Strange, W. (1989a) Evolving theories of vowel perception. *Journal of the Acoustical Society of America, 85*, 2081–2087.

Strange, W. (1989b) Dynamic specification of coarticulated vowels spoken in sentence context. *Journal of the Acoustical Society of America, 85,* 2135–2153.

Strange, W., Verbrugge, D., Shankweiler, D., & Erdman, T. (1976). Consonantal environment specifies vowel identity. *Journal of the Acoustical Society of America., 60,* 213–224.

Strange, W., & Jenkins, J. J. (1978). Role of linguistic experience in the perception of speech. In D. Walk & H. J. Pick, Jr. (Eds.), *Perception and experience* (pp. 125–169). New York: Plenum.

Strange, W., & Dittman, S. (1984). Effects of discrimination training on the perception of /r-l/ by Japanese adults learning English. *Perception and Psychophysics, 36,* 131–145.

Summerfield, Q., & Haggard, M. P. (1974). Perceptual processing of multiple cues and contexts: Effects of following vowel upon stop consonant voicing. *Journal of Phonetics, 2,* 279–295.

Sussman, H. M., McCaffrey, H. A., & Matthews, S. A. (1991). An investigation of locus equations as a source of relational invariance for stop place categorization. *Journal of the Acoustical Society of America, 90,* 1309–1325.

Wang, M. D. & Bilger, R. C. (1973). Consonant confusion in noise: A study of perceptual features. *Journal of the Acoustical Society of America, 54,* 1248–1266.

Warren, R. M. (1970). Perceptual restoration of missing speech sounds. *Science, 167,* 392–395.

Williams, L. (1977). The perception of stop consonant voicing by Spanish-English bilinguals. *Perception & Psychophysics, 21* (4), 289–297.

Williams, L. (1980). Phonetic variation as a function of second-language learning. In G. H. Yeni-Komshian, J. F. Kavanagh, & C. A. Ferguson (Eds.), *Child Phonology, Perception: Vol. 2* (pp. 185–215). New York, NY: Academic Press.

Willis, R. (1829). On vowel sounds and on reed organ pipes. *Trans. Cambridge Philosoph. Soc., 3,* 231–268.

Yeni-Komshian, G. H., & Soli, S. D. (1981). Recognition of vowels from information in fricatives: Perceptual evidence of fricative-vowel coarticulation. *Journal of the Acoustical Society of America, 70,* 966–975.

Yeni-Komshian, G. H., & Lafontaine, L. (1983). Discrimination and identification of voicing and place contrasts in aphasic patients. *Canadian Journal of Psychology, 37,* 107–131.

Zue, V. W. (1985). The use of speech knowledge in automatic speech recognition. *Proceedings of the IEEE, 73,* 1602–1615.

Zue, V. W. (1991). From signals to symbols to meaning: On machine understanding of spoken language. *Proceedings of the 12th International Congress of Phonetic Sciences, 1,* 74–83.

Words and Meaning: From Primitives to Complex Organization

KATHY HIRSH-PASEK & LAURETTA M. REEVES
Temple University

ROBERTA GOLINKOFF
University of Delaware

*T*was brillig, and the slithy toves
Did gyre and gimble in the wabe;
All mimsy were the borogoves,
And the mome raths outgrabe.
(Carroll, 1862; 176)

Introduction

You see the words, but what do they mean? Despite the fact that most educated adults probably know between 75,000 (Oldfield, 1963) and 150,000 words (Seashore & Eckerson, 1940), few of the words above look familiar. In this chapter, we discuss the organization and processing of words and meanings.

Many consider words to be the building blocks of language, for it is words and combinations of words that come to symbolize the objects and the events in the world around us. The study of words and meaning (often called semantics) has a long and rich history, dating back at least to 420 B.C. when Democritus wrote his book entitled, *On Words*. In that book and in Plato's *Cratylus* that followed, philosophers addressed the question of the origins of words.

Are words naturally bound to their meanings in the same way that the word "swish" is to the sound of water, or are they arbitrary (but socially agreed upon) labels for things such "that which we call a rose, By any other name would smell as sweet" (Shakespeare, *Romeo and Juliet*, 1975, 1020), and would still be a rose? Throughout the years, philosophers, linguists, and psychologists have puzzled over the ways in which words relate to meanings. In this chapter, we ask you to think about words. Where do we store words? How are they organized in our minds, and how do we recognize words that we see or hear? What is meaning? And how are words related to meanings? The last two decades of research and writing on these topics have been particularly productive, and have offered partial answers to these questions.

In the first section of the chapter, we begin our journey by separating words from their meanings, and by learning to treat each as a separate domain of inquiry. In the next section, we dissect each discrete space to show how philosophers and psycholinguists study words and meaning, and how we think people organize and process them. Finally, in the last section, we align the two topics again to demonstrate how the organization and positioning of words influences meaning and how different meanings and events affect word organization. In the end, we hope to show that even Jabberwocky can convey meaning.

Words and meanings: Separate but linked domains

A number of findings, some anecdotal and some empirical, can be used to convince you that words and meanings are related but separate entities. Three lines of argument will be used to make this point. The first, the *translation* argument, suggests that for any given language, there are some words that are not dependent on meaning for their existence, and some meanings for which there are no single words. If meanings and words were tightly yoked all of the time, this could not be true. The second argument for a separation of the two subjects comes from the *imperfect mapping* illustration, suggesting that for any given language there can be many meanings for a specific word, and many different words for a given meaning. Finally, the third argument for treating words and meanings as separate comes from the *elasticity* demonstration, illustrating that a word meaning can change when it is found in different contexts. Let us briefly examine each of these arguments.

Most of us have experienced the *translation* argument. For example, the Yiddish word, "schlep," requires a long-winded explanation in English: "To move a heavy and usually bulky item from place to place." Those who have incorporated this Yiddish term into their vocabularies can talk about "schlepping" a load of books from class to class. Here we have a good *meaning* for which there is no single *word* in English. Similarly, there are any number of words that one could create that would have little meaning to us. In the poem cited above, "borogove" offers one example (which does have a meaning, according to "Humpty Dumpty," but you'll have to wait until the end of the chapter to find out what it is). All of us have had the experience of knowing something is a word without knowing what it means. Thus, we can know words for which there are no meanings stored in our brain. For example, many people are uncertain of the meaning of "churlish" (COARSE, RUDE AND VULGAR). And many nonmusicians know that "adagio" is a word without knowing that it means SLOWLY.

Empirically, there have also been demonstrations of the translation problem. Two are particularly well known. The first comes from a study by Heider, now Rosch, (1972) in which she investigated the language of the Dani, a Modern-era Stone Age tribe who live in Indonesian New Guinea. In their language, there were only two color terms, "mola," designating bright, warm hues, and "mili," designating dark, cold hues. Does this lack of differentiation in the word domain indicate a similar restriction in their conceptual world? That is, do the Dani people only perceive or recognize two colors? No, it appears that the Dani can perceive more than just how dark or bright colors are. In fact, Heider's (1972) research on the topic suggested that the Dani people see the color spectrum in exactly the same way that we do. A second celebrated example shows the impoverished English vocabulary for different kinds of snow. Whereas Eskimos have four different root words for snow, "aput" (SNOW ON THE GROUND), "quana" (FALLING SNOW), "pigsirpog" (DRIFTING SNOW), and "qimuqsuq" (A SNOW DRIFT), English speakers have only the lonely word "snow" (Boas, 1911; Pullum, 1990). In short then, the translation argument demonstrates the distinction between words and meanings because, while they are closely related, each can exist without the other.

The *imperfect mapping* illustration also shows that there is no one-to-one mapping of words and meanings. Here we see many different meanings for a single word (ambiguity) and many words for a single meaning (synonymy). Thus, meaning can be marked in any number of different ways with language. One of the best illustrations of word ambiguity comes from the study of jokes and riddles. The success of some jokes hinges on setting up one meaning of a word when another is actually required

(Fowles & Glanz, 1977; Hirsh-Pasek, Gleitman, & Gleitman, 1978; Shultz & Horibe, 1974). The following, admittedly bad, joke makes the point clear:

Doctor: Eyes checked?
Patient: No, they're blue.

The humor (such that it is) derives from the word "checked," which has two meanings, one referring to the act of looking or examining, and the other referring to a perceptual pattern. A number of experiments on word ambiguity demonstrate that people have multiple meanings available for words at any given time in processing. For example, Simpson (1981) found that in processing ambiguous sentences such as, "We had trouble keeping track of the *count,*" both meanings of the word—number of items and European nobleman—were called up from subjects' mental dictionary (although this need not be conscious, and is demonstrable only through experimental techniques).

The other half of the imperfect mapping illustration turns on the availability of two or more words for a single meaning, or synonymy. Although some argue that there are no true synonyms (Clark, 1987), for many of us, the words "sofa" and "couch" mean the same thing; so do the words "pail" and "bucket."[1]

Finally, there is the *elasticity* argument, the demonstration that words can have varied meanings depending on the contexts in which they are found. Some clear examples are adjectives that modify different properties of the words they serve in different contexts. A "tall flea" is surely not as tall as a "tall building." A "light elephant," but not a "light feather," could still crush your toe (for further discussion see Katz & Fodor, 1963). Meanings of words are therefore context-dependent to some extent. Thus, meanings and words are not unequivocally yoked.

Taken together, these three arguments suggest that words and their meanings, while closely related, are not identical. Having driven the wedge between these two types of psychological entities, it becomes possible to examine each domain separately. Indeed, within the field of psychology, these two topics have been treated very differently. Words have typically been studied through how they are accessed or recognized in speech or reading, whereas the study of meaning has concentrated on how these meanings are stored. In the discussion that follows, we look at the organization and processing of words in the mental *lexicon* (Greek for "dictionary"), and then ask about the representation of meaning within the mind. For notational clarity, whenever we are referring to specific words, we will enclose that particular word in quotation marks, for example, "chicken." Whenever we are referring to the meaning designated by a particular word, we will capitalize it, for example, CHICKEN. Thus "chicken" refers to the name or word that we use. Presumably, if the English

---

[1]However, some words are more suited to certain contexts, and synonyms alter the meaning of the sentence itself (even if the words are identical in meaning). For example, "name" and "nomenclature" have identical meanings. However, Shakespeare's romantic quip, "A rose by any other name would smell as sweetly," loses some of its poetic charge in, "A rose by any other nomenclature would smell as sweetly." Again, the fact that meanings and words are not exclusively yoked to one another leaves room for a separate examination of each domain.

speaking community decided *en masse* to change the name to "bukbuk," no one would be deeply offended. However, changing the name would not change the meaning to which we are referring, it would still be a CHICKEN, defined as "a galvanatious bird," or offspring that has chickens as parents. No worldwide council could arbitrarily change these facts of definition, for once a chicken ceases to have parents who are chickens, its very essence is altered. Given that we can now talk separately about words and meanings, let's discuss what philosophers and psychologists say about "words" and their MEANINGS.

The study of words

In this section on words, we address three major issues: What is a word, and what methods do psychologists and psycholinguists use to study the storage and organization of words? In what form is information stored in the lexicon? And according to what principles are words accessed or retrieved from this lexicon (as these principles may provide some clues as to how the lexicon is organized)? A mini-experiment may help to illustrate some of the points covered in this section.

Experiment 1: Morphology (adapted from Freyd, 1981). Let's start with the root word "snark." The following words can be generated from this root: "snarkment, snarkify, snarkest, snarkfully." Which of the words created above would you use to complete each of the following sentences?

1. Everyone agreed she was the _____ woman on the volleyball team.
2. At the conference, he delivered the opening speech _____.
3. His stock broker pleaded with him to _____ his investments.
4. She referred to the _____ to write her report.

"Snark" is a nonsense word. Yet, you can confidently fill-in the blanks according to the required grammatical class. It seems as though you have implicit knowledge not only of what words are legal words (you knew "snark" was a nonsense word), but also of how words can be changed via prefixes or suffixes to modify their meaning and grammatical class.

Let us now discuss some of the other experimental techniques used by cognitive psychologists to answer these questions.

Methods of studying lexical organization and meaning

In participating in the mini-experiment above, you have already experienced a task in which you were asked to make decisions about lexical items. If a friend had been watching as you participated in the mini-experiment, what could he or she have concluded about your internal cognitive and linguistic processes? In all likelihood, nothing, because very little in your overt behavior sheds any light on what is taking place inside your mind. For this reason, psychologists interested in language processes have been forced to devise clever experimental methods to determine the way in which individual words, or their parts, are stored in memory, and how these words are organized into related sets within memory.

Another example may help to illustrate how psychologists must devise experiments to get at unobservable processes related to words and meanings.

Experiment 2: Lexical Decision and Access. Below are two lists of letter strings. Some are words, some are nonwords, or arbitrary strings of letters. As you read each word to yourself, say aloud, "yes" if the string is a word, "no" if the string is a nonword. Using a stopwatch with a second hand, time yourself on how long it takes you to complete each list.

List 1: gambasty, revery, voitle, chard, wefe, cratily, decoy, puldow, raflot, oriole, voluble, boovle, chalt, awry, signet, trave, crock, cryptic, ewe, himpola

List 2: mulvow, governor, bless, tuglety, gare, relief, ruftily, history, pindle, develop, gardot, norve, busy, effort, garvola, match, sard, pleasant, coin, maisle

Reaction time experiments

You have just participated in what is known as a **reaction time experiment**, one of three major techniques psychologists often use to study cognitive processes. In an actual experiment, the stimuli above would have been presented on either a computer or a **tachistoscope** (an apparatus which allows the experimenter to strictly control the duration of a stimulus), and your response would have been measured in milliseconds (one millisecond = one-thousandth of a second).

It should have taken you several seconds longer to complete list 1 than list 2 because the words in list 1 are less frequently used in English than the words in list 2 (words from Zechmeister & Nyberg, 1982). For example, "awry" in list 1 is less common in either spoken or written speech than is "busy" in list 2. Because words which are less common are probably harder to retrieve, you have to search your internal dictionary more carefully to respond "yes" or "no" to rare words. That is, it takes more cognitive energy to search through your lexicon and to decide whether the low frequency words in list 1 are words. The cumulative effect is that the list as a whole is more difficult to process than list 2, the assumption being that cognitive processes which require more work will also take longer. Hence, the list containing rare words is slower to process, which lengthens the reaction time.

The logic behind reaction time tests is illustrated by the following example. Visualize starting to leave your house and realizing that you have forgotten your keys. You believe they are either in the living room nearby, or upstairs on the table in your bedroom. If you went from the front door to each of the locations and back again, the trip to your bedroom should take longer. Likewise, in the experiment in which you just participated, it may take longer to respond to a list of low frequency words than to high frequency words, because the low frequency words are not as available in memory. In this case, however, what is being measured is *psychological* rather than physical or actual distance (and may not be distance at all).[2] The important point is that because the brain mediates cognitive processes very quickly, differences in reaction times between conditions in an experiment are often very small. If time differences between two kinds of words are both statistically significant, and consistently in the same direction in several experiments (e.g., it always takes longer to judge low frequency than high frequency words), then the research claims can be taken as valid. Thus the first way in which reaction time experiments are used is to determine the accessibility of words.

A second way reaction times are valuable is in determining the amount of processing different subprocesses take. For example, if you are seated in front of a computer and asked to press a button to indicate if the strings of letters you see are words or nonwords, part of your response time includes pressing the button (Task B) and part includes actually deciding whether the stimuli are words or not—word recognition (Task A). This whole process takes, on average, 550 milliseconds (Forster, 1990); thus, time (Task A) + time (Task B) = 550 milliseconds. If I am only interested in the amount of time it takes for word recognition (Task A), I could find out how long it takes you on average to push the button, and can subsequently subtract this time from the 550 milliseconds.

Several methods take advantage of the assumptions and technique of reaction time experiments. We discuss just four of these methods below.

Lexical decision tasks.   Lexical decision tasks, developed by Herbert Rubenstein in 1970, are one variant of reaction time experiments. In such experiments, subjects are presented with either a word ("table") or a nonword ("vanue"), and are asked to press a button to indicate whether the stimulus they see is a word (yes response) or not (no response).

In one example of a lexical decision task, much like Experiment 2, in which you participated just minutes ago, Rubenstein, Garfield, & Millikan (1970) presented strings of letters which were either words or nonwords to subjects, and timed their responses. As in our earlier demonstration, they found that subjects responded more quickly to commonly used words than to rarely used words, and faster to words than to nonwords.

Semantic verification tasks.   A second type of reaction time experiment requires that subjects judge whether a statement about category membership is true or false; then their response times are measured. For example, "A robin is a bird" is true; "An acorn is a bird" is false. These are known as semantic verification tasks, and can be used both to determine how words are stored in semantic memory (e.g., memory about meaning, in this case of words and concepts), and how meaning is represented for those words.

---

[2]We use the concept of semantic distance here only as an analogy, and do not propose that associated words are stored close together in the brain. As will be evident later in the chapter (see section on the Models of Lexical Access), theories treat the concept of semantic relatedless and frequency in very different ways, which often have nothing to do with distance or space at all.

Rips, Shoben, and Smith (1973) and Rosch (1973), for example, varied semantic verification statements to include members of a category that were considered typical of that category (a robin is a very typical kind of bird) and members not so typical (a penguin is an atypical bird). They found that statements about typical category members were verified more rapidly (lower RT) than statements about atypical category members. For example, it would take subjects a shorter period of time to respond to the statement, "A robin is a bird," than to, "A penguin is a bird," even though the words "robin" and "penguin" are of equal frequency in the language. It thus appears that typical members of a category are more easily accessible than atypical members, according to the logic of reaction time experiments.

Priming tasks.   A third example of how reaction time methods are used to study the composition and organization of words is through priming experiments. The concept of priming is analogous to that of warming up your car during the winter months. The car engine may take a long while to start at first, but if you turn it off and restart the engine, the second start-up is much quicker. We could say that the car had been warmed up or "primed" by the initial start. Likewise, a word is responded to more rapidly the second time it is presented than the first. In fact, Scarborough, Cortese, and Scarborough (1977) showed evidence for a repetition effect in lexical decision tasks; repeating words in an experiment led to faster reaction times the second (and third, etc.) time the word occurred. This technique is also interesting because we can use it to determine how related words are connected, and how these related words may prime each other. For example, will a word be responded to more quickly when presented after a related word (e.g., table—chair) than after an unrelated word (e.g., zebra—chair)? If so, the first word would be said to *facilitate*, or prime, recognition of the second.

In a classic semantic priming experiment, Meyer & Schvaneveldt (1971) presented subjects with pairs of words, nonwords (strings of letters), or a word-nonword combination. Subjects were to respond whether both strings of letters were words or not (thus it was simultaneously a lexical decision task). Of key interest was the reaction time for the second word in each pair, in which the pairs were either semantically associated (e.g., bread—butter) or not (e.g., bread—doctor). Response times to the second word in the associated word pairs were significantly faster than response times to the second word of the nonassociated pairs, suggesting that the initial word in the associated pairs primed other semantically related words. This implies that one way in which words might be organized in the lexicon is based on their semantic relatedness. Priming, however, can also be negative in that one word can *inhibit* the recognition of a word. For example, subjects trained to expect the second word in a pair to be the category name of the first (e.g., apple—fruit) were slower to recognize the second word when it was the wrong category name (e.g., apple—bird) (Antos, 1979).

Phoneme monitoring.   A fourth and final example of a reaction time experiment is that of phoneme monitoring. In phoneme monitoring tasks, subjects are asked to respond every time they hear a particular phoneme, such as /b/, in a word or sentence. Read the following sentence aloud, and tap your finger on the desk every time you hear the phoneme /b/ in the following sentences:

(1)   "The men started to drill before they were ordered to do so."
(2)   "The men started to march before they were ordered to do so."

In both sentences, you should have tapped your finger once, when "before" occurred. Although you did not test your reaction time, if you were like the subjects in an experiment by Foss (1970), your response time to the /b/ in sentence (1) would have been 50 milliseconds longer than to the /b/ in sentence (2). This is because phonemes that appear after ambiguous words such as "drill" (which can refer either to soldiers marching or to boring a hole in an object), have greater processing demands than nonambiguous words, because at least two meanings have been activated. These greater processing demands prevent subjects from responding as quickly to phonemes after ambiguous words. We may not be *conscious* that two meanings are being "lit up" (or "activated" in psychological jargon), but must rely on differences in response times to phonemes after ambiguous and nonambiguous words to infer that multiple meanings of ambiguous words are triggered upon presentation. Experimental techniques, such as reaction time methods, can yield information that could not be obtained by asking subjects about their mental processes; much cognitive activity takes place at a preconscious or unconscious level.

Thus, researchers use a variety of reaction time techniques, such as lexical decision tasks, semantic verification, priming tasks, and phoneme monitoring, to determine how words and meanings might be stored, how words are recognized, and how words might be organized in the lexicon. Though all of the techniques differ in what they require of subjects, they are based on the same logic: Processing with more effort takes greater lengths of time. Much of the research we discuss throughout this chapter utilizes reaction time measures. Psychologists, however, do not rely on only one method for studying linguistic and conceptual phenomena. In the next section we will cover experimental techniques related to word access or retrieval.

Naming/word access

A second major way psychologists measure the availability of words and hypothesize about how they may be organized is with naming or lexical access methods. "Lexical access" refers to the task of recognizing a word we either see or hear by appealing to the information stored in our mental lexicons. We can then respond by deciding that a stimulus is either a word or a nonword, or by pronouncing it. As will be seen, some of these techniques use the logic and method of reaction time experiments as well.

Naming.   In lexical decision tasks, not only does the reaction time include lexical access time and motor response time (e.g., time to press the response button), but also decision time, that is, the milliseconds needed to decide, "yes, this is a word," or "no, this isn't." Some experimenters (e.g., Forster, 1990) have claimed that a purer measure of lexical access is a naming task, where subjects are presented with a series of words and nonwords, and asked to pronounce them aloud as quickly as possible. Response times can be measured in this type of task to gauge the accessibility of words over nonwords because words are speeded by lexical access while nonwords have no lexical entries. Naming can also be used to test the availability of frequent words over rare words. Reaction times are measured from presentation of the stimulus to the beginning, or onset, of the subject's vocal response (a voice operated relay is used). Errors in naming can also be judged to test for lexical access. Many English words have irregular pronunciations, such as "bough," "cough," "dough," and "rough." Without pulling up information about each word from the lexicon, these words are likely to be read incorrectly. This is one way to test whether subjects are using a strategy to sound out the stimuli, or actually using stored lexical information.

Forster and Chambers (1973, see also Frederickson & Kroll, 1978) found that words were named faster than nonwords, and that high frequency words were named more rapidly than rare words. This suggests that the reading of letter strings is facilitated by lexical access, and also suggests greatest availability for common words in comparison to rare words.

Word association.   To illustrate the method of word association, read each of the following words (or read them to a friend), and say aloud the first word that comes to mind:

    1–wet
    2–swift
    3–petal
    4–apple
    5–shoot

You may have said, "dry; fast; flower; fruit; gun" in response to the words. If so, in each case you named a related or associated term, even though "wet" and "dry" are related in a different way than "apple" and "fruit." The first relation is based on opposites in meaning; the second one is based on category membership (see Miller, 1951, for a more detailed classification). Similar in logic to priming experiments, discussed above, free association experiments are designed to assess which words are related and the *way* in which words are related. For example, are the associates of target words more likely to be semantically related (as "salt"—"pepper"), or are they more likely to be phonologically related (as "chill"—"pill," or "fish"—"fissure")?

Numerous experimenters have conducted word association experiments, where sometimes thousands of subjects, either adults (e.g., Jenkins, 1970) or children (e.g., Palermo, 1963), are presented with a word, and asked to respond with the first word that pops into mind. Analysis of these word norms reveals three major findings. The first is that subjects are most likely to respond with a semantically similar word (Ervin, 1957). For example, subjects are more likely to respond "thread," "pin/s," and "sew" to "needle," rather than "nail" or "poker," which are also long, pointed objects (Aitchison, 1987), or rather than "wheedle" or "nettle," which sound like "needle." A second finding is that, if the target word is a member of a pair, such as "king," subjects are most likely to free associate the other item in the pair, such as "queen." The third finding is that adults (but not necessarily children) are most likely to associate a word of the same grammatical class as the target, noun with noun ("hammer"—"nail"), verb with verb (e.g., "run"—"jump"), adjective with adjective ("dark"—"light"), and so forth (Brown & Berko, 1960). These findings again lend credence to the notion that two main principles of word organization in the lexicon are meaning and grammatical class.

Cued lexical access.   In memory experiments, cues or hints about the stimuli to be remembered often improve subjects' recall. Likewise, certain cues or hints may help people retrieve certain words. If some cues are more effective than others, we can assume that the cues which most facilitate lexical access do so because they are based on the principles of word organization used by the mind. Cued lexical access is similar to semantic priming in that response times for word retrieval are often measured.

An experimental example may help demonstrate this technique and its import in studying the lexicon. Freedman & Loftus (1971) asked subjects to name a member of a category which either began with a certain letter (e.g., "Name a fruit beginning with 'p.'") or had a certain property (e.g., "Name a fruit which is red."). In half the trials, the category name was presented first (as in the examples); in the other half of the trials, the letter or adjective was presented first (e.g., "Name a red member of the fruit category."). Thus, either the category name served as a prime for the target letter or property, or the letter/property served as a prime for the target category name. Reaction times to name an appropriate object were significantly lower (e.g., faster) when the category membership was given first, leading Freedman and Loftus to conclude that category names primed the individual members of the category. Putting the letter or adjective first in the sentence did not facilitate lexical retrieval, and they were thus ineffective as primes. These findings suggest that hints about a word's semantic nature get us closer to the lexical entry for that word than do hints about its initial letter or the item's properties, and thus priming with category names leads to faster access times. These results confirm what we have already suggested—that meaning is a central principle of organization within the lexicon, and helps to determine connections between words stored therein.

We have now examined two important methods, reaction time and lexical access experiments, that psychologists use to better understand the human linguistic system. The third and last method takes advantage of mistakes in speech which occur naturally. Analysis of speech errors can yield important findings as to word and meaning storage and organization.

Speech error analyses

As was already mentioned with regard to the experimental technique of phoneme monitoring, noting people's errors in lexical access and spontaneous speech can provide insight into word units in the lexicon, and potentially word organization. Two methods for analyzing speech errors are discussed below.

Tip-of-the-tongue phenomena.   Have you ever had the experience of knowing part of a word that you wanted to say (e.g., the first letter), but were unable to retrieve the whole word? This is known as the "tip-of-the-tongue" phenomenon. The guesses subjects make when they are unable to access the desired word often provide information about the possible structure of our mental dictionary.

The guesses made by people suffering from the tip-of-the-tongue phenomenon tend to be substitutions that respect word type boundaries; nouns are substituted for nouns, verbs for verbs, and so forth. This suggests that words of the same grammatical class are stored together, which is consistent with the word association data mentioned earlier (Jenkins, 1970). Aitchinson (1987) notes that tip-of-the-tongue states are subject to the "bathtub effect," the first and last parts of words are best remembered, in the same way that the head and feet of a person in a bathtub may be visible, but not his or her middle. For example, Brown & McNeill (1966) found that subjects were most likely to mistakenly say that a word was the target word when the first and last parts were similar to the correct or intended term. For example, if the target word in a tip-of-the-tongue state was "sextant" (a navigational instrument used to measure angular distances, such as the altitude of the moon and stars), "sextet" was more likely to be mistakenly "recognized" by subjects than "compass," which is semantically similar. In fact, while 70 percent of the tip-of-the-tongue errors were similar in sound to the target, only 30 percent were similar in meaning. This suggests that once subjects have in mind a certain word based on its meaning, they can be tricked into accepting a phonological relative of the intended word. Thus, both meaning and phonology play a part in accessing and producing lexical items. Knowing the meaning may lead subjects to the right lexical entry, but if the phonology is not completely specified, phonological neighbors of the target word may be inaccurately produced or "recognized." This research also suggests that the beginnings and endings of words are prominent in the lexical store (Brown & McNeill, 1966).

Speech errors.   As with tip-of-the-tongue phenomena, the speech errors of normal and brain damaged subjects can be analyzed for clues into lexical units and organization. For example, we all make mistakes when speaking, such as saying, "she sore" for "seashore," or "thermometer" for "barometer." Spoken speech errors are often known as "spoonerisms" after the Rev. William A. Spooner, who became famous for his amusing (and possibly deliberate) speech errors, such as "He dealt a blushing crow" (for "He dealt a crushing blow."), or, "You have hissed all my mystery lectures" (for "You have missed all my history lectures."). Even more humorous than spoonerisms are some of the speech (or perhaps hearing) errors of the late Gilda Radner's character from *Saturday Night Live*, "Emily Litella." She was puzzled about "What's all this talk about sax and violins on TV? What do people have against musical instruments?" Fromkin (1971, 1973) and others (Bock, 1990; Dell, 1986) have convincingly argued that speech errors show a regularity which portrays the underlying representations and principles of organization used by the linguistic system.

Speech errors can be classified in a number of ways. Sometimes the correct words are chosen, but come out sounding the wrong way, as in the "she sore/seashore" example. More interesting are selection errors, in which the wrong word is chosen. These substitutions can be based on meaning, as the substitution of "horse" for "camel"; sound, as when "list" is substituted for "lisp"; or a combination of meaning and sound, as in the mistake one of us heard on the radio—"Tandem commuters" for "Tandem computers," both terms evoking images of the business world. Blends are cases where two intended words get combined into a single word or pseudo-word, such as "Plastic bags are *dispendable*," a combination of "disposable" and "expendable" (Aitchison, 1984).

Brain-damaged patients often provide the most fruitful and most plentiful speech errors. As Chapter 2 notes, patients with aphasia often develop a syndrome known as *anomia*. Anomic patients have difficulty in retrieving words, and thus often retrieve approximations of the target word. Their difficulties are even evident when an object, or a picture of the object, is right in front of them. For example, a patient studied by Gardner (1974) said "knee" for elbow, "hair" for comb, "chair" for table, and "ankely" for ankle. You'll notice that these errors tend to be close approximations to the target word, either in meaning ("knee" for "elbow") or sound ("ankely" for "ankle"). From slips of the tongue like this, we can infer that words in the lexicon may be connected on the basis of semantic and phonological similarity. Analysis of such results is complex, and it may be that lexical access and production can be thwarted at any stage, leading to either phonological errors or semantic errors, depending on what stage is interrupted.

Although speech errors might seem to be a strange way to study language skills, the systematic characteristics of slips of the tongue can provide convincing evidence about the design of the cognitive system. By noting the regularity and patterns of speech errors, we can discern the principles by which language normally operates. Their value in proposing a model of speech production is discussed in great detail in Chapter 7.

You have now reviewed the three major techniques used by psychologists in the study of language and meaning. Reaction time experiments, lexical access tasks, and speech errors have provided a corpus of data that researchers have used to devise hypotheses about our linguistic system, and the principles by which it may be structured. These are reviewed in Table 4.1.

The most convincing evidence is when all three methods yield similar results (known as *converging evidence*), such as the findings that semantic meaning plays a large part in lexical organization, as seen in priming and word association experiments, and in data on speech errors. Thus, below we will discuss how these methods have been used to suggest the building blocks from which words are built, how words are accessed, and the organization of the words in the lexicon.

I.   REACTION TIME EXPERIMENTS
    a. Lexical Decision Tasks
    b. Semantic Verification Tasks
    c. Priming Tasks
    d. Phoneme Monitoring
 	
II. NAMING/WORD ACCESS
    a. Naming
    b. Free Association
    c. Cued Lexical Access
 	
III. SPEECH ERROR ANALYSES
    a. Tip of the Tongue Phenomena
    b. Speech Errors
	Table 4.1
	
	Methods of Studying Lexical Organization and Meaning

Word primitives

Let us begin by dissecting the sentence, "The impartial judge ruled the defendants guilty." What do we know about the sentence? First, we know that it describes something that happened in the past because "rul*ed*" indicates past tense in English. Second, we know that there was more than one defendant because of the "-s" on the end of the word "defendant." From our ability to analyze and to produce such multimorphemic words easily, we can make inferences about how words are stored in the lexicon. These words, prefixes (e.g., "im-"), and suffixes (e.g., "-s") constitute what are known as "word primitives."

There are two hypotheses as to exactly what linguistic unit functions as a word primitive. The first hypothesis is that each word has a separate entry in the lexicon, and is its own primitive, without being broken down any further. For example, in the sentence above, "ruled," "defendants," and "guilty" would all be stored as wholes. A second, more widely accepted hypothesis is that words are stored as morphemes, which were defined in Chapter 1 as the smallest meaningful units of speech.

Words as word primitives

The first of these views is that words (or at least some multimorphemic words) are stored as wholes in the lexicon, so that each word is its own primitive (Aitchison, 1987; Aronoff, 1976; Monsell, 1985; Sandra, 1990). Under this hypothesis, each individual word has its own lexical entry, sometimes called a **lexeme** (Monsell, 1985), so that there would be one representation for "book," another for its plural "books," and a third for the adjective, "bookish." Likewise, there would be separate entries for "bookmark" and "bookshelf." The word primitive view states that when we read or hear a word, we access that word directly within the lexicon.

Almost no one believes that all multimorphemic words are stored as whole words in the lexicon; this, after all would not be very economical. If all words were stored independently, there would be much duplication or redundancy in the lexicon, and unnecessary space will be used up by copies of words which are very much alike. Researchers who support the existence of lexemes as word primitives do so for either frequently occurring words, or for some compound words, such as "buttercup" (Monsell, 1985; Osgood & Hoosain, 1974; Sandra, 1990).

Morphemes as word primitives

The more common theoretical viewpoint is that words, which we know to be composed of smaller parts, are represented in the lexicon by their constituent morphemes (MacKay, 1979; Murrell & Morton, 1974; Taft & Forster, 1975, 1976; Taft, 1981; Smith & Sterling, 1982). When we listen to someone speaking, we *decompose* the words into morphemes, which allows us to comprehend spoken language. From this point of view, we "strip" words of all their affixes, suffixes, and so forth, and access the roots in our lexicon, as in the example of "book" + "-s" above. When we produce speech, the decompositional view states that we access morphemes, and combine these word primitives to make up whole words, and then sentences. Thus, the root word "rule" plus the morpheme "-ed" would be combined to produce "ruled."

From a logical standpoint, one advantage of the morpheme view is its emphasis on *cognitive economy*. That is, fewer lexical units need be stored because the same morphemes can be combined to form an infinite number of words. In the word-as-word-primitive view, all possible variations and combinations of a word would need to be stored in the lexicon separately, which would take up much more room. Think back to the "snark" experiment at the beginning of this chapter. You easily combined "snark" with bound morphemes to create new words, perhaps because this is a common occurrence in language.

Evidence about word primitives

You now have two theories of what constitutes a word primitive. What methods could be used to test whether people store whole words or morphemes in their lexicon? One way to do this is through a lexical decision task, in which subjects are presented with words composed of just one morpheme, and very similar words composed of multiple morphemes. "Corner" and "hunter," for example, are similar in their structure, have the same number of letters and syllables, and are equally frequent in usage. However, "hunter" is a multimorphemic word composed of the root, "hunt" and the suffix, "-er"; "corner," on the other hand, is a monomorphemic word which cannot be further broken down (although "corn" is a word/morpheme, it has an independent meaning quite different from "corner"). If it takes significantly longer to process multimorphemic words than similar monomorphemic words, then words may be stored as morphemes which need to be pieced together or broken apart during language production/recognition.

The existing data often support the morpheme-as-sublexical unit hypothesis. Speech error experiments reveal substitutions of morphemes, such as, "It waits to pay," (for "It pays to wait") (Garrett, 1976, 1980), and perseverations of affixes, such as "Minister in the church*es*," (for "Minister*s* in the church") are quite common (Shattuck-Hufnagel, 1979). It thus looks as if individual morphemes are mobile and can float away from their root morphemes without complications. The example, "She wash upped the dishes," (Aitchison, 1987) seems to show that root and bound morphemes are independently retrieved and combined later in the speech production process. MacKay (1978) presented subjects with root morphemes (e.g., "decide"), and asked them to respond with a variation of that word (e.g., "decision"). The more morphologically complex the response (e.g., the more morphemes added to the root), the longer the response times. This suggests that subjects had to piece together more lexical units in the more complex words, not just simply to retrieve another word whole from the lexicon.

The experiments just cited rely on cases where people produced speech. Findings from comprehension experiments also support a decompositional view of word storage. For example, subjects take longer in lexical decision tasks to recognize pseudo-prefixed words such as "result" or "interest" (each looks like it has a prefix but does not) than either prefixed (e.g., "recall," "interstate") or unprefixed words

(Taft, 1981). The search process takes longer, Taft argues, because subjects try to strip away the "re-" or "inter-" and look for "sult" or "est," respectively, which of course are not root morphemes. Tyler, Behrens, Cobb, and Marslen-Wilson (1990), testing speech comprehension, found that Broca's aphasics represent root and bound morphemes separately. Trouble integrating several morphemes may lead to comprehension (and also production) impairments in these patients.

Although the bulk of the evidence from reaction time and speech error research suggests that people store multimorphemic words economically as morphemes, some have found evidence against a "morpheme-stripping" view. In speech errors, for example, the suffixes are usually maintained, as in "provisional" for "provincial" (Aitchison & Straf, 1982). It also does not take any longer to recognize a suffixed word, such as "dust-y," than a similar pseudosuffixed word, such as "fancy" (Manelis & Tharp, 1977). Rubin, Becker, and Freeman (1979) found differences in lexical processing time between suffixed (e.g., sender) and pseudosuffixed words (e.g., sister) *only* when at least 50 percent of the experimental list was composed of suffixed words. This suggests that decomposition of words into morphemes may have been a strategy that subjects used after noticing differences in the types of words in the list.

One way to reconcile the findings with those which support the morpheme-as-word-primitive view is to claim that frequently encountered affixes and/or words are treated differently. For example, "impossible" may be stored whole, whereas less frequent affixed words, such as "imperceptible," are stored as separate morphemes (Carroll, 1986). Furthermore, Sandra, 1990; Monsell, 1985; Osgood & Hoosain, 1974 determined that some compound words (e.g., "butterfly") may have independent lexical entries, even though there are also entries for their morphemic constituents ("butter" and "fly"). It depends on whether the meaning of the compounds can be determined from their constituents or not. For example, "buttonhole" is composed of "button" and "hole," which makes it easy to gauge its meaning from the two words which compose it. Thus, "buttonhole," as well as "teaspoon" and "beanpole," are semantically *transparent*. It is, however, unclear how "butter" and "fly" combine to get the meaning of "butterfly." Thus terms like "butterfly" and "buttercup" are semantically *opaque*. In priming experiments, transparent compounds are primed by words semantically related to only one of their morphemes (e.g., "pea"–"beanpole"), but opaque compounds were not (e.g., "bread"–"butterfly") (Monsell, 1985; Osgood & Hoosain, 1974; Sandra, 1990). This suggests that semantically opaque compound words are not decomposed into their constituent morphemes, and have their own lexical entries.

From all of the data discussed above, then, we can see that the basic tendency of the lexical system is toward morphemic storage. However, some multimorphemic words—opaque compound words, and frequently occurring words (e.g., "gooseberry," "ruler")—serve as their own lexemes. While this violates the concept of cognitive economy, it may have its own benefits. Economy in storage may detract from economy in processing times because units (e.g., morphemes) are more embedded in the system and must be pieced together or broken down for production or comprehension. The cognitive system must thus balance between thrift in space and thrift in processing.

Factors influencing word access and organization

Once we discover how individual words are represented in memory, the next issue is the organization and access of words within the lexicon. It seems useful at the onset to merely list the kinds of word properties or factors that have been known to influence either word access, lexical organization, or both. How and why these factors influence lexical access and organization varies with the theory that one is discussing, as we shall see in the section on models of lexical access. For now, we will simply present factors and research findings that these models must take into account.

If given the task of simulating a single person's lexicon with a computer program, how would you do it? What principles might be used to sort words into separate files so that they could be retrieved when necessary? Would you first separate the words into files based on their initial phoneme or sound (e.g., all the /s/ words would be stored together, or rhyming words like "name" and "same")? Would you separate words into files according to semantic category (e.g., FRUITS, ANIMALS), or semantic opposites (e.g., salt-pepper)? Maybe you would attend to the frequency of words, so that the most commonly used words would be stored in their own file so that they would be easily accessible? What about dividing words into verbs, nouns, and adjectives, so that "jump," "tree," and "sweet" would be in separate files within the computer program? Yet another alternative would be by syllables—either that words with the same number of syllables, "napkin" and "puddle," would be stored together, or with the same initial syllables, "retrieve" and "return."

Of course, it is possible that all these principles may determine how easily words get accessed and their organization within the lexicon, but that some are more important than others. It may also be the case that one can choose the strategy by which one accesses words, depending on the task demands. That is, when you are writing poetry, you may access words by phonology or syllable or accent structure so that you may construct rhymes and rhythms, but in delivering a speech, you may retrieve words based on the meaning you want to convey. Many of the experimental techniques already discussed have been used to discover factors which operate in lexical access.

Frequency

Which word is more common—"predict" or "villify?"—"Angry" or "puddle?" As we have already seen from several studies, high frequency words tend to be responded to more quickly in lexical decision tasks (Rubenstein et al., 1970) and in naming tasks (Forster & Chambers, 1973). The effect of frequency on lexical processing is a robust experimental finding: While reading, or listening to someone speak, high frequency words tend to be accessed or recognized more quickly and easily. Because of the consistency of these findings, frequency has played a major role in the development of models of lexical access (discussed in the next section). However, the presence of the frequency effect, and the degree to which it affects lexical processing, may depend on the type of task being studied. For example, Balota and Chumbley (1984) found large effects of frequency on lexical decision tasks when people were asked to respond whether a tachistoscopically presented letter string was a word or not. However, the researchers found only a moderate frequency effect in naming tasks, and only a very small effect in category verification (where subjects respond "true" or "false" to statements like, "A canary is a bird"). Since all three tasks involve lexical access, frequency should have affected all three to at least a moderate extent, argued Balota and Chumbley (1984). They thus concluded processes which occur after lexical access, such as decision processes or pronunciation, are responsible for frequency effects. The evidence taken as a whole suggests that frequency plays a role in lexical access, but the effects can be attenuated by subsequent lexical processing.

Imageability and concreteness/abstractness

As you read each of the following words, close your eyes and try to picture the object or idea portrayed by the words: *umbrella; lantern; freedom; apple; knowledge; evil*. Were some words, such as *umbrella, lantern,* and *apple* easier to image? Did you have difficulty coming up with internal pictures for *freedom, knowledge,* and *evil*? If not, you probably imaged a symbol for the concept portrayed, such as the Liberty Bell for "freedom," rather than generate an image of the word meaning per se. This issue is sometimes divided into one of concreteness and abstractness; concrete words such as "apple" are more imageable. Paivio (1969) found that high imagery words were more easily recalled in a memory test than low imagery words. Bleasdale (1987) also found that, in a lexical decision task, words primed other words only when both words were of the same type, for example, concrete-concrete or abstract-abstract, but not concrete-abstract or vice versa. From this, he concluded that the lexicon is organized separately for concrete and abstract words.

The principle of imageability also interacts with the principle of frequency in word access; high frequency–high imagery words (such as "student") are best accessed and recalled; low frequency–low imagery words (such as "excuse") are least easily accessed, with high frequency–low imagery words (such as "justice") and low frequency–high imagery words (such as "elbow") somewhere in the middle (Paivio, 1969).

Semantics/meaning

Some brain-damaged patients have trouble accessing certain semantic categories of words. Hart, Berndt, and Caramazza (1985) found that some patients were better at identifying inanimate objects (e.g., chair) than at identifying living things or foods. This suggests that the lexicon may also be organized according to semantic characteristics of words. Likewise, Meyer & Ellis (1970) asked subjects to respond yes or no as to whether a word was a member of a semantic category. The smaller the category (e.g., BIRDS has fewer members than ANIMALS because all BIRDS are ANIMALS, but not all ANIMALS are BIRDS), the faster the reaction times, as though subjects had to search through less cognitive "space" to determine whether the word belonged in that category. Recall also the priming study discussed earlier in the chapter; Meyer & Schvaneveldt (1971) found that semantically related words (e.g., butter-bread) could facilitate access to a target word, and unrelated words could inhibit access in a lexical decision task. Canas (1990) also found that the strength of semantic association exists between prime and target influenced reaction times in a lexical decision task. Thus, "nurse-doctor" would be responded to faster than "office-doctor" at short exposure times because "nurse" is more semantically related to "doctor" than is "office."

Like frequency and imageability, word meaning seems to be an important principle of word storage and organization, as supported in a variety of studies.

Lexical ambiguity and context effects

As we know, sometimes a single word can have multiple meanings, such as "letter" (postal or alphabetical letter), "right" (correct or opposite of left), "drill" (the power tool or military practice), and so forth. Oftentimes the context a word appears in will resolve which meaning is meant, as in, "Albert drove in the righthand lane." What happens during word access when two different meanings are associated with a single word? Do they both get activated? Evidence suggests they do. Swinney (1979) had subjects listen to sentences containing ambiguous words such as "bugs" (meaning either insects or spy equipment), while simultaneously participating in a lexical decision task. Although the passage clearly referred to the insect sense, immediately after hearing "bugs," subjects responded as quickly to "spy" as to "ant," and both were significantly faster than response to an unrelated word such as "sew." Thus, it seems as if presentation of ambiguous words activates both or all meanings, and that resolution of which meaning is intended is resolved *after* lexical access, by taking into account sentence context.

Grammatical class

Words also seem to be organized based on their grammatical class, such as whether they are nouns, verbs, or adjectives. Evidence for grammatical class as a lexical organizing principle comes from speech errors. Nouns tend to be substituted for nouns, as in, "She was my strongest *propellor* (proponent) during the campaign"; verbs for verbs, as in, "The nation's dictator has been *exposed* (deposed)"; and adjectives for adjectives as in, "His mother is too *progressive* (possessive)." In word association tasks, adults most commonly respond to the stimulus word with a word of the same grammatical class (Ervin, 1957; Jenkins, 1970).

Again, the evidence from several experimental techniques converges to suggest that the grammatical category of a word may determine how it is stored and organized in relation to other words.

Open/closed class

Related to the principle of grammatical class, words could be stored based on whether they were open or closed class. **Open class** words are the basic content words in the language expressed as nouns, verbs, adjectives, and adverbs. There could be an infinite number of these types of words, as new words get invented to explain new objects or concepts (e.g., the words "computer" or "corporation" would have been of little use in ancient Greece). As Aitchison (1987) analogizes, open class words are the bricks of our sentences, closed class words are the mortar. **Closed class** words are function words that traditionally do not bear content, but do provide the architecture for our sentences, words such as "the," "and," "from," and so forth. They are so called because the set of words is "closed" in that it rarely admits new members. For example, when was the last time you learned a new preposition? Content words can be invented as the need arises. We had to invent the term "computer" to deal with modern technology, but the number of function words has not changed much through time.

Support for a lexicon organized according to closed/open class words comes from Broca's aphasics, who are selectively impaired predominantly in their production of closed class words. For example, Gardner (1974) relates a speech sample from an aphasic patient trying to describe going home from the hospital on weekends, ". . . Thursday, er, er, er, no, er, Friday . . . Bar-ba-ra . . . wife . . . and, oh, car . . . drive . . . purnpike . . . you know . . . rest and . . . tee-vee." Notice that the sentence is like a telegram in that it contains content words, or bricks, but very little mortar. Bradley (1983) and colleagues (Bradley, Garrett, & Zurif, 1980) also did not find frequency effects for closed class words in a lexical decision task, despite the fact that frequency effects for *open* classed words are a robust phenomenon (Forster & Chambers, 1973). This finding, along with the evidence from Broca's aphasics suggests separate storage and access routes for open and closed class words.

Syllables

Just as words can be said to be structured from morphemes, syllables, or phonemes, syllables can be said to have their own structure. Initial syllables may be one basis for organization within the lexicon. MacKay (1972), for instance, noted that word blend speech errors, where two words get combined, such as "be-hortment" for "behavior" + "deportment" (Wells, 1951), often respect syllable boundaries.

There is some evidence, however, that speech errors in which whole syllables are substituted are very rare (Shattuck-Hufnagel, 1979; Dell, 1986). Syllables are composed of two parts. The first consonant phoneme in a syllable is known as its **onset**, the vowel and any following consonants its **rime**. Work by Treiman (1988; Treiman & Chafetz, 1987) suggests that people may be more apt to break syllables into their constituent phonemes. In a lexical decision task, subjects responded more quickly to words separated after their initial consonant or consonant cluster (CR// ISP) than to words with slashes after the vowel (CRI//SP) (Treiman, 1988). Thus, speech errors that preserved syllable boundaries may simply mean that onset and rime travelled together after first being combined from the smaller syllable units.

Although there is some evidence for syllabic storage, most of the evidence from reaction time and speech error studies points to a finer breakdown of syllables into their constituent onset and rime.

Phonology

It may be that words which sound alike, even though their first syllables are not identical, might also be connected or stored close together in the lexicon. Recall from the earlier discussion that by inducing tip-of-the-tongue phenomena in the lab, Brown and McNeill (1966) found that subjects were more likely to approximate the target words with similar sounding words than with similar meaning words. For example, "sarong" would be more likely to be mentioned by subjects as a possible response for "sampan" than would "houseboat" or "junk."

In speech errors, substitutions of similar sounding words are quite common, as in "medication" for "meditation," "cylinders" for "syllables," "goof" for "golf," "psychotic" for "psychological" (Tweney, Tkacz, & Zaruba, 1975). This is especially true when the beginnings and endings of words are similar, as though phonological cues are preserved as access routes within the lexicon (recall the "bathtub effect" mentioned earlier). What may happen is that similar sounding words are clustered together, and attempts to retrieve one may also activate its phonological neighbors. This follows not only for words that start with the same sound, but also for words that sound alike but have different meanings called **homophones** (e.g. sale, sail).

What we can thus see is that access to the lexicon may be very flexible, and that activation of lexical entries can occur using multiple criteria (although some principles of access may be more prevalent than others). Some principles, like frequency and meaning, seem to permeate all the other principles. In this respect they are more global aspects of the lexical system. Multiple principles of organization and access may be necessary to accomplish all the jobs the lexicon is called on to perform. In modeling a computer simulation of a person's lexicon, one goal is for the program to be able to provide information based on request. Words will need to be accessed through multiple means, depending on the task demands, and sometimes a request may require the use of several channels or principles at once. It is as though the human mind supplies us with a dictionary, thesaurus, grammar book, and poet's rhyming book all in one, reflecting the different lexical access routes of form/definition, semantic relatedness, grammatical class, and phonology, respectively. We can now move on to see how different theoretical models account for how all these principles can operate within a single cognitive system.

What we can thus see is that access to the lexicon may be very flexible, and that activation of lexical entries can occur using multiple criteria (although some principles of access may be more prevalent than others).

Models of lexical access

What is meant by a model of lexical access? How could anyone possibly sort out all the different principles which operate in word access and organization, and then combine them into a coherent whole? How, for example, do we determine when the mind prefers to act like a dictionary rather than a thesaurus? A thesaurus rather than a grammar book? There are two major classes of models which detail how words get accessed (or recognized) during reading or listening. These models also implicitly provide us with some hypotheses as to how the lexicon might be organized.

The first type of theory is typically referred to as a **serial search model**. It claims that when we encounter a word, while reading, for example, we look through a lexical list to determine whether the item is a word or not, and to retrieve the necessary information about the word (such as its meaning). Serial search means that the process takes place by scanning one lexical entry at a time, sequentially. The best known serial search model is Forster's (1976) autonomous search model. The second type of model is known as a **parallel access model**. It proposes that perceptual input about a word can activate a lexical item directly, and that multiple lexical entries are activated in parallel. That is, a number of potential candidates are activated simultaneously, and the stored word which shares the most features with the inputted word wins. Most models then propose some kind of decision stage, during which the accessed word is checked against the input. There are three major versions of direct access models, the earliest version being John Morton's **logogen model**. Two other direct access models, connectionist models (e.g., McClelland & Rumelhart, 1981), and cohort models (Marslen-Wilson, 1987), are adaptations of the basic premises of the logogen model.

It should be noted that both types of theories, serial search and parallel access, consider word recognition to be an automatic process, not subject to conscious examination. That is, we are not cognizant of "searching" through a lexical list or of "activating" numerous stored words during lexical access. At best, we are conscious only of the end result of these processes—when we realize that we "know" what the word is and what it means. Each of the various serial search and direct access models attempts to account for some the effects we have already discussed—mainly word frequency effects, why words are recognized faster than nonwords, and context and priming effects. Thus each of these models draws on some of the principles of organization we mentioned earlier. The two types of models, serial and parallel (also called indirect and direct access), account for these lexical effects in different ways. Let us compare the ways these two types of theories explain research findings about lexical access, and how successful each is in accounting for the data.

Serial search models

Forster's (1976) *autonomous search* of lexical access is best illustrated by comparing the lexicon to a library. A word, just like a book, can only be in one place in the lexicon/library, but its location can be determined from several card catalog entries (e.g., card catalogs for author, for title, or for subject matter). In the autonomous search model, these card catalogs are known as "access files." Forster (1976) posited three major access files—orthographic, through which words are accessed by their visual features; phonological, through which words are accessed by how they sound; and semantic/syntactic, through which words can be retrieved according to their meaning. Given these three access files, lexical entries can be accessed during reading, listening, and speaking. These access routes can be utilized only one at a time (just as you can't look up books in more than one card-catalog at a time). That is, input from only one modality (visual or auditory) can only be used one at a time; it will not speed access time if you hear a word at the same time you read it.

When a word is presented (either visually or phonologically), a complete perceptual representation of the word is constructed, and then, is activated in the access file, based on its initial letters or sounds. Once you have derived the location of a word based on its access code (or its index in the file drawer, to carry out the library analogy), a search for the word entry in the master lexicon must still be conducted. Thus, Forster's model posits a two-stage process. Just as a person can determine which section of the library a book is in, but still has to search on the specific shelf, we can find the general location of a lexical entry, but still have to search for its unique location. It is this entry (not the partial entries in the access files) which contains *all* linguistic information about the word (e.g., its meaning, spelling, pronunciation, part of speech).

The master lexicon is assumed to be organized into "bins" or storage units, with the most frequent entries in that bin on the top. This is analogous to putting your books in stacks, with the most frequently used books on the top, and accounts for why high frequency words are accessed more quickly than low frequency words. Once an access file directs the search to the appropriate lexical bin, entries are searched one by one until an exact match to the perceptual representation is found. Figure 4.1 depicts how this process takes place. The sequential search proposed by the autonomous search model is very different from parallel search models, such as the logogen model, which will be examined presently.

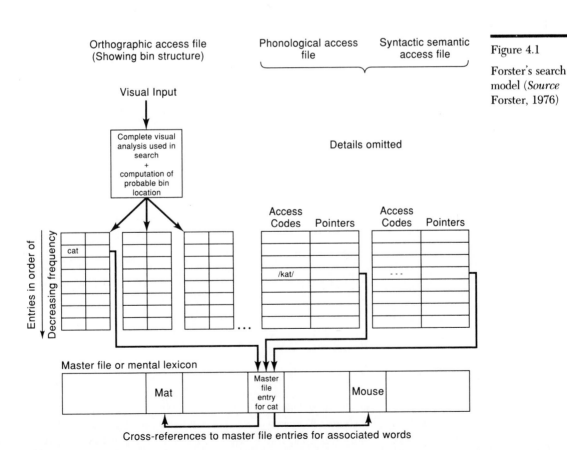

Figure 4.1

Forster's search model (*Source* Forster, 1976)

When the relevant lexical entry in this serial model is retrieved, it is checked against the input (e.g., the written word), known as a "post-access check." If correct, the search is discontinued. If incorrect, such as when a string of letters (nonword) resembles a word, as "rceord" resembles "record," the search either begins again, or the perceptual input is recognized as an illegal word. Legal nonwords typically take longer to respond to than real words, as they do in reaction time experiments, because a more exhaustive search must be conducted. According to the autonomous search model, the search for a word stops once its lexical entry is located, but all possible entries must be scanned in the case of nonwords, thereby delaying response time. Nonwords which are similar to real words, such as "coffei" may mistakenly activate the lexical entry for "coffee," and then prolong response time as the system conducts its post-access check to assure identity between input and lexical item. Letter strings which do not resemble words at all, like "psbtu," are not subject to the extra time needed for the post-access check.

Forster's (1976) model did not initially account well for priming and context effects. However, modifications proposed by Becker (1979) aided the explanatory power of serial-search models. Becker stated that a semantically defined search can be conducted, aided by connections between associated words (e.g., "doctor" and "nurse") within the master lexicon. Once one word is accessed, the system generates a list of potential words that *may* come next. This newly generated list is bound to be shorter than the list from a bin, thereby leading to quicker recognition of the second word in a priming pair ("doctor-nurse") or to words suggested by the context of a sentence.

Forster's (1976, 1989) autonomous search model is not the only serial search proposal; Becker's (1979) *verification model* is of the same flavor, as is that of Glanzer and Ehrenreich (1979). The latter accounts for frequency effects by positing that we have both a large, unabridged dictionary composed of all words known to a person, and then a smaller pocket dictionary composed of high frequency words. When confronted with a high frequency word, only the pocket dictionary need be used, decreasing search time. While the number of alternative models continues to expand, Forster's autonomous search model has been the most influential. Most of the serial models use Forster's approach as a prototype, but greatly expand its tenets to account for more data, such as the ability to pronounce nonwords (e.g., see Henderson, 1982).

Next we turn our attention to parallel access models. As we shall see, these models use explanations for the various factors which influence lexical access that are very different from those proposed by serial search models.

Parallel access models

Logogen model.   Morton (1969, 1979) proposed that words are not accessed by determining their locations in the lexicon, but by being activated to a certain threshold. Thus, a space analogy of lexical access such as we saw in Forster (1976) is replaced with a more electrical analogy—a word will "light up" once its activation is sufficient, in the same way that a lamp lights up when the electrical current is

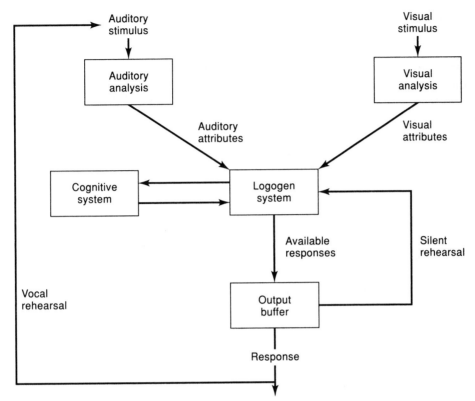

Figure 4.2

The logogen model (*Source* Morton, 1970)

The concept of direct access The most well-known model of this class is John Morton's (1969, 1979) *logogen* model. It is called a *direct access* model.

sufficiently strong. How does this activation occur, and what determines the threshold of a certain word?

Morton (1969) claimed that each word (or morpheme) has its own "logogen," which functions like a scoreboard, tabulating the number of features that a lexical entry shares with a perceptual stimulus. They sum all available input—orthographic, phonological—to determine which lexical entry should be accessed. In Forster's autonomous search theory (1976) access routes could be used only one at a time, whereas Morton's model initially permitted summation of input from multiple modalities. These various sources of perceptual input, however, operated in parallel in the race to the finish—accessing the correct word. The logogen system tabulates the relative probability of lexical candidates based on their shared features with the inputted word. Any logogen for whom the total activation reaches a predesignated threshold, based on sufficient similarity to the stimulus word, is accessed. If several entries are activated to threshold, the one with the highest count wins, and is "recognized." It then returns to a zero feature count, known as its resting level.

Thus, in the logogen model, depicted in Figure 4.2, there are no separate access routes by which to search a master list of lexical items. Rather, subjects make use of all available data—the context of a sentence suggests some meanings over others, the letters used in the orthographic representation of a word activate logogens with those same letter features. And all this information adds up to converge on (usually) a single candidate in the lexicon.

Why, then, are high frequency words easier to access than low frequency words? Under the logogen model, frequency effects are due to the lowering of the threshold of the stored representation of a word that is used frequently. That is, it takes less activation to fire a high frequency word than a low frequency word. Such a lowering of the threshold takes place over a long period of time.

Priming, on the other hand, is accomplished by a quick and temporary lowering of the threshold of the logogens related to a prime. The logogen system itself does not contain semantic or associative data about words; rather, the cognitive system does (pictured as a separate "box" in Figure 4.2). However, once a word is accessed, the cognitive system receives this information, and feeds information back to the linguistic system. Logogens which are associatively or semantically related to the prime receive increments to their logogens, and thus less perceptual input will be needed to achieve threshold. This results in quicker access times for primed words. Contextual effects are achieved the same way.

Morton's logogen was the most influential of the parallel word access models and served as the basis for all of the parallel models that followed. As with any model, however, modifications were made to perfect the system. To show you how scientific progress forced changes in the model, consider the following example. The prediction of the original model that auditory presentation of a word would prime subsequent visual presentation of the same or related words turned out not to be the case, so the logogen model was revised in 1979 (Morton, 1979; Morton & Patterson, 1980) to constrain priming across modalities. Thus, while the model is good at explaining frequency and priming effects, its assumption that perceptual input is summed across modalities to achieve lexical access has been toned down, as suggested by new data. The newest version, depicted in Figure 4.3, posits separate input paths and logogens for words presented in visual channels versus auditory channels.

The initial logogen model also had difficulty accounting for how the linguistic system responds to nonwords. This required a further modification in the model. To ameliorate this problem, Coltheart, Davelaar, Jonasson, & Besner (1977) suggested that there must be a deadline within which words are recognized within the logogen system. If a stimulus word is not recognized within this deadline, it is rejected as a legal word. Nonword letter strings which most resemble words, such as "coffei" above, will cause more general activation in the logogen system and thus will be rejected later and will take even longer to reject than will nonwords such as "hmrfi," which do not resemble real words at all.

Connectionist models.   A contemporary cousin of the logogen model comes from what is known as **connectionism**. Advocates of this position in psychology, philosophy, computer science, and other fields, known as connectionists, use the analogy of the brain and neurons to develop models of cognition. Their computer models of cognitive processes (such as lexical access) are instituted in "neural nets," composed of nodes and connections between these nodes. There are three types of nodes: input nodes, which process the auditory or visual stimuli; output nodes, which determine responses; and hidden nodes, which perform the internal processing

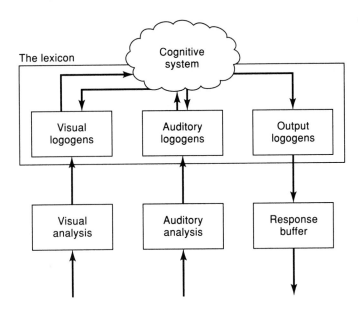

Figure 4.3

The later version of the logogen model (A, corresponding to the layout of the original; B, an alternative, equivalent layout; C, a further equivalent layout. Non-lexical routes from input to response are not shown. *(Based on Morton and Patterson 1980)*

between when we hear/see a word and when we respond to it. The hidden nodes do the lion's share of lexical processing as depicted (in simplified form) in Figure 4.4.

Connectionist models (e.g., that of McClelland & Rumelhart, 1981) share many tenets of the logogen model, such as direct access to lexical entries, that multiple candidates are activated simultaneously, and that many types of information can be used to access a target word. However, connectionists are more explicit in defining exactly what the cognitive and linguistic architecture looks like—that is, how words are represented. Each functional level of the hidden nodes represents different aspects of words—for example, their visual, orthographic, phonological, and semantic natures, and so forth. Processing proceeds from input to deciphering the raw perceptual input at a featural level (e.g., does a written letter have a curved section); nodes activated here then activate letter units which share those features (e.g. P, R, B, G, etc.), which then activate words which share those letters. Figure 4.5 shows how the word "time" might be recognized in a connectionist model. Connections between layers are assumed to be excitatory, while connections within layers are inhibitory. This allows lower units to feed into higher level units (e.g., letter features must be activated before word units can fire), but units within a layer compete with each other for activation during recognition of a given stimulus. Once one representation achieves threshold, it inhibits the firing of similar units with regard to a specific stimulus.

Connectionist models deal with frequency effects in the same way as the logogen model—more frequently used word units will have lower firing thresholds. Priming and context effects are also explained the same way: When a node or connection is activated, a spread of activation occurs in all directions, incrementing representations which are similar to the target visually, phonologically, semantically, and so forth.

Figure 4.4

Connectionist network for word recognition. Units at each level have inhibitory connections (not shown here), which vary in strength. Connections between levels are excitatory. Initially every unit is connected to every unit at the next level, but as a function of experience some of these connections are weakened and others are strengthened.

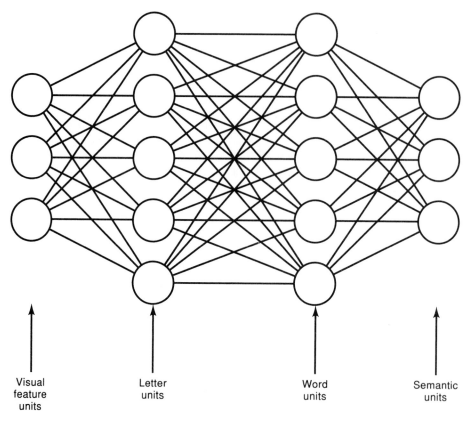

Visual feature units

Letter units

Word units

Semantic units

Connectionist models are also the only lexical access theory to, albeit implicitly, supply a theory of word organization: Organization is nothing more than the strength of connections between nodes (either word-word nodes, or word-feature nodes), based on past association.

Cohort model.   The cohort model shares basic assumptions about lexical access with the logogen model, but was designed to account only for auditory word recognition. Marslen-Wilson et al. (Marslen-Wilson & Welsh, 1978; Marslen-Wilson & Tyler, 1980, 1981) proposed that when we hear a word, all of its phonological neighbors get activated as well. Thus, upon hearing the sentence, "Paul got a job at the ca-. . . ," "candy," "cash," "candle," "cashier," "camp," and many others would be available for selection. This set of words is known as the "word initial cohort," (though *cohort*'s original meaning was a division of the Roman Army, here it refers to a "division" of words). Thus, as in the logogen model, many more words are activated than need to be, and the original activation of word is based on direct communication between the perceptual input and the lexical system.

Whereas activation in the logogen system can be piecemeal, with some words' logogens only partially lighted, words in the cohort model are either fully activated or not at all. Rather than the summing of partial inputs to logogens, all potential candidates for lexical access are fully activated by the perceptual input, and then progressively eliminated. This elimination takes place in one of two ways—either the context of a spoken sentence narrows the initial cohort, or candidates are discarded as more phonological information comes in. In the latter case, as more of the spoken word is recognized, the cohort narrows down to only one, or several possible choices. For example, if the phoneme /n/ was heard after the "ca-," "candy" and "candle" (plus any other "can-" words) would be the only lexical items still possible from the initial cohort. The field of candidates is narrowed as more stimulus information is received. Eventually, only one candidate will remain. Figure 4.6 depicts the lexical elimination and access process for what might happen if one heard the sentence, "John was trying to get some bottles down from the top shelf. To reach them he had to "sta-". . . ;" the words preceding "sta-" would result in stage 3, where "stack" and "stand" are the only available remaining options.

Initially, the cohort model was very dependent on an exact match between a spoken word and its phonological representation in the lexicon. However, it was then determined that people could recognize aurally presented words even if mispronounced, or if a sound (like a cough) blocked out part of the stimulus. The theory was

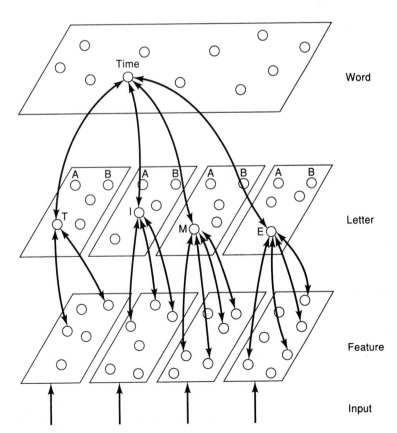

Figure 4.5

A sketch of the interactive activation model of word perception. Units within the same rectangle stand for incompatible alternative hypotheses about an input pattern, and are all mutually inhibitory. The bidirectional excitatory connections between levels are indicated for one word and its constituents. (*From "Putting Knowledge in its Place: A Scheme for Programming Parallel Processing Structures on the Fly" by J. L. McClelland, 1985,* Cognitive Science, 9, *p. 115.* Copyright 1985 by Ablex Publishing. Reprinted by permission.)

Figure 4.6

The cohort model

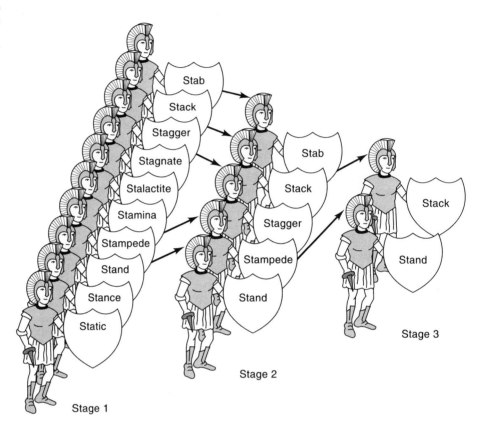

Stab
Stack
Stagger
Stagnate
Stalactite
Stamina
Stampede
Stand
Stance
Static

Stage 1

Stab
Stack
Stagger
Stampede
Stand

Stage 2

Stack
Stand

Stage 3

revised recently (Marslen-Wilson, 1987) so that the system chooses the best match to fit an incoming word. This also makes the lexical access system less reliant on the word initial cohort. Under the original model, if a word did not make it into the first cohort, it had little chance of being chosen; now, as long as it shares enough features with the auditory stimulus, it can be selected for recognition.

Thus, like the logogen model and the connectionist model, the cohort model of lexical access posits that multiple candidates are activated in parallel. Unlike its cousins, the cohort model states that the list of word candidates is narrowed as the auditory input proceeds serially. It explains frequency and nonword effects in much the same way as the logogen theory. Context or priming is assumed to narrow the original set of candidates, and this shorter initial cohort leads to quicker recognition of a target word.

We have thus completed our discussion of words, and the methods that psychologists use to study the lexicon and its organization. From available research, it can be seen that most words are stored decomposed into their constituent morphemes, except when it makes processing more economical to store certain words as wholes, as in frequently occurring multimorphemic words. We have also suggested that the linguistic system is very flexible with regard to word storage and use. Factors such as frequency, imageability, word class, and phonology, among others, can determine how words are stored and retrieved. And to paraphrase a song, "No word is an island, no word stands alone." Each word is functionally connected to other words similar in semantic meaning, sound, grammatical class, and so forth, which provides the scaffolding for an organization of the lexical system. It also provides numerous pathways to access words under different task demands. The serial search and parallel access models coalesce some of these principles and experimental findings into theories of lexical access.

The task now remaining is to analyze meaning separately from the words we use to convey meaning. Of course at this point, it may seem to you as though words are integrally bound with meaning, because words without meaning are called pseudowords (or nonwords). However, let us reiterate that the two are not identical. Language may be heavily dependent on meaning, but meaning is not as dependent on words or language. Drawing a distinction between signs and symbols may further illustrate the point. Think of animal communication. A honeybee, through its dance, communicates the meaning that there is honey in a given direction. A deer running through the woods with his tail up communicates that there is a hunter or some other danger nearby. Both the honeybee and the deer do not need words to convey meaning. Likewise, nature provides its own instances of meaning without words. For example, bird tracks in the snow mean that birds have traveled that terrain; black clouds mean that a storm is coming. These examples of meaning are often known as natural *signs*. Such signs have meaning intrinsically, and can't help but convey the meanings that they do. Words, on the other hand, do not achieve their meaning naturally. Assignment of words to world objects (or events) started out as arbitrary (even though we may now agree on the association between a word and its meaning). That is, there is no reason why the first person to apply the word "cat" to a furry creature with four legs that catches mice, should not have originally called it a "table" or "snowflake." For this reason, words are known as *symbols* rather than signs.

Because of the separate but integral relations between words and meanings, the study of meaning is, in its own right, very important to the study of words and language. We have already seen that much psychological evidence points to semantic meaning and semantic relatedness as major factors in word organization. Now we shall attempt to determine on the basis of what features words, sentences, or larger linguistic units *mean* what they do. Then we shall describe psychological theories of how meaning is stored in our minds. Recall that we will use capital letters to express concepts or meanings, GIRAFFE, and quotation marks to express the words that are associated with these concepts, "giraffe."

Meaning

What is it that a person knows when he or she knows the meaning of a word? Take, for example, the term, "bachelor?" What do I mean when I say that, "Pierre is a bachelor?" One might easily respond that it means that Pierre is an unmarried male.

Thus, UNMARRIED MALE is the meaning of "bachelor." But what about the Pope? Is he a bachelor, despite the fact that he has taken a vow never to get married? We could modify our definition to include ELIGIBLE, UNMARRIED MALE. The Pope is not eligible, therefore he is not a bachelor. What about a divorced man? He is ELIGIBLE *and* UNMARRIED, but we typically don't think about people who have been married already (even though they no longer are) as bachelors. Social trends also complicate efforts to isolate the meaning of bachelor. Men and women may live together as partners without being married. Technically and legally, the men in these relationships are still eligible for marriage. Is it then accurate to portray them as "bachelors?" Isn't it misleading to state, "Despite having a lifelong relationship with Simone deBeauvoir, Jean Paul Sartre died a bachelor?"[3]

You begin to get a sense of how difficult it is to define even simple concepts like BACHELOR. Every time we think we have the ultimate definition, we can think of an example that the definition doesn't cover. Determining what constitutes meaning and formulating accurate definitions which cover all possible instances of a concept, has been the difficult job of philosophers for centuries, and psychologists for the twentieth century.

Before moving on to a philosophical and psychological analysis of meaning, an explanation may be useful about the association between words and concepts, and about the difference (and similarity) between concepts and categories. The meaning of a term is referred to as its **intension**. For example, there are two intensions of the concept CHAIR—an object upon which we sit, and a person who heads a meeting or organization. The set of things in the world to which a word applies is known as its **extension**. To continue our example, the extension of the first meaning of CHAIR would be all the things you could point to and label "chair." The same general idea carries for the second meaning of CHAIR.

Often, empirical evidence about the *ex*tension of a term is used to justify one or another theory of intension. That is, knowing how people apply concept words to objects can tell us about the meaning of concepts, and how they might be structured cognitively. Accordingly, any theory about word meaning, or intension, should be able to accurately predict what things in the world will, and will not, be labeled with that term (Malt, in press). This means that our theories of intension are often based on research about extension. For example, if removing the back from a chair causes it to be labeled a "stool," but sawing off one of its legs does not, then we can assume that the characteristic "having a back" is critical to the conceptual structure of CHAIR, but "having four legs" is not. Although we will try to bifurcate language and meaning to discuss meaning (intension), we will be forced to rely on evidence of word application (extension) and categorization to illustrate and support semantic viewpoints.

Again, although it seems that words and meaning are inextricably bound, there is a difference between a category or set of birds, and the essence of BIRDness which all birds share. Perhaps a better illustration would be the concept of RED. RED

---

[3]We are indebted to Robert Weisberg and Michael Tye for a discussion on defining features of "bachelor" that yielded many of our counterexamples.

defines a perceptual characteristic which can apply to apples, Valentine's Day cards, blood, velvet cloth, and so forth. Thus there is a category of RED *things*, but only a concept of RED.

Because philosophers were the first to start thinking about theories of meaning, we will begin our discussion with a presentation of the major philosophical accounts of meaning.

Philosophical theories of meaning

As we noted earlier, the study of meaning in the philosophy of language is known as semantics. While linguists and psychologists have been interested in the processes by which people learn and use language, philosophers have been interested in *how* it is that a word or sentence has meaning. As psychologists, our main question here will be how we learn and use linguistic terms to converse about what is not linguistic—the world, real or imagined.

Reference theory

If a friend asks you a question, such as, "What is the meaning of the word *house*?" you may simply turn around and point to the nearest family-type dwelling. If so, you would be demonstrating a view which was prevalent in the early part of the century, known as the *reference theory of meaning*. This theory postulates that the meaning of a term is the object which that term refers to in the real world (e.g., its "referent"). For example, "the Liberty Bell" and "Abraham Lincoln" point to or *denote* a specific object and person, respectively, whereas "geraniums" and "firefighters" point to or denote a class of things or people, respectively. Likewise, terms such as "red," "round," and "ripening" refer to actual properties of an object (or objects), such as a garden tomato. The theory thus draws a distinction between proper names referring to a specific person or thing, category names, and property names.

If reference theory completely explained meaning, it would make the study of semantics rather concrete and easy: The meaning of a word is the object or property it denotes.

According to this view, terms which stand for the same object have the same meaning. Both the proper name "Mick Jagger" and the descriptions "lead singer of the Rolling Stones" and "husband of model Jerry Hall" point to or denote the same man. According to the reference view (as originally conceived), these two sets of words have identical meaning, and we should be able to substitute one term for the other without changing the meaning of the sentence. Of course, the situation is not that easy. "Mick Jagger is the lead singer of the Rolling Stones," does not have the same meaning as "Mick Jagger is the husband of model Jerry Hall," nor conveys the same information as "Mick Jagger is Mick Jagger." Thus, one problem with a strict reference view is that it does not explain how two terms can have the same referent (e.g., the person Mick Jagger) and yet have different meanings (or "senses" in philosophical parlance).

There are other problems with the reference view. One objection to this theory is that not all words *name* things—think of "and," "not," and "or." Yet these words have meaning as used in ordinary speaking—"Frank is going to the charity ball" means something very different than "Frank is *not* going to the charity ball."

A second objection to this theory is that we can talk about things for which there are no real "objects" existing in the world, such as "freedom." Although we can picture signs/symbols of freedom, such as the Liberty Bell, or a raised flag, those images are not really the "thing" denoted by the word *freedom*. We also have discussions about objects that we infer to exist (such as quarks, or black holes), but for which there may be no real objects *per se*. Thomas Hobbes, an early proponent of the referent theory, claimed that all terms that refer to nonreal objects (such as "angels") are meaning*less* (Hobbes, 1651/1958). Under such a view, any discussions we would have about Hamlet, or unicorns, or Athena—the Greek goddess of wisdom and arts— would of necessity be meaningless. We, however, agree with the King of Hearts in *Alice's Adventures in Wonderland*, who exclaimed, "If there's no meaning in it, . . . that saves a world of trouble, you know as we needn't try to find any. And yet I don't know, . . . I seem to see some meaning in them afterall" (Carroll, 1862/1990, p. 148). Clearly we can discuss the character of Hamlet, and be able to communicate our opinion to another person, so that the discussion, and the term "Hamlet," as well as "angel" and "unicorn," have meaning. Such problems with the reference theory led philosophers to posit alternative views.

Ideational theory

One remedy is to claim that what words actually denote are *ideas* rather than objects. According to the British philosopher John Locke (1690/1967, p. 225), "Words in their primary and immediate signification stand for nothing *but the ideas in the mind of him that uses them*." Thus, the terms "Hamlet" and "unicorn" have meaning by virtue of our mental ideas about them, even if the objects themselves do not exist. This view is known as the *ideational theory of meaning*. Although it is a tempting alternative because it can take into account the imagined world, it is not itself without problems. If meaning is always in the head, how am I to know that we both mean the same thing when we use a hand gesture like waving, or when we speak words or sentences? The ideational theory makes meaning, and the language used to convey meaning, private, so that we can never be entirely certain that other people mean what we interpret. After all, language is often a public endeavor, and as in the examples of signs cited earlier in this chapter, some meanings are found in the real world, not just in one's head.

Alternative theories: Meaning is in the public domain

Both reference and ideational theories of meaning have been criticized for treating all meaningful terms and expressions as names. There are other words besides those that refer to properties or nouns, such as words that have meaning because of their role or function within language (e.g., "not," "the," "a," "and," "because"). Perhaps then, the meaning of names and properties derives from their participation in language as well. What gives words their meaning is often how they are used in conjunction with other words in the language.

This view is supported by philosophers such as Quine (1960), who postulates that the meaning of individual words can never be strictly derived. Under his view, words, and even sentences, have no meaning independently, but are based on their connection to other words and sentences within the language. Wittgenstein (1953) helped bridge philosophy and psychology in the study of semantics by claiming that meaning should be determined by how language terms are used by ordinary speakers. All competent speakers are assumed to use words in the same way. This concept is known as *conventionality*, the tendency for linguistic usage to be agreed upon by members of a community. Quine and Wittgenstein's views have become very influential in current psychological theorizing about semantics, as we shall see.

The reference and ideational theories have intrinsic appeal because we tend to think of the meaning of terms as objects or concepts we can point to or describe. Both, however, have their failings. Any philosophical theory of meaning must ultimately account for how word meanings are interconnected within a larger semantic and linguistic theory. For this reason, philosophers need psychologists, and vice versa, for adequate theorizing. Both armchair and empirical experiments are necessary.

As we did with words, let's now look at the building blocks (or primitives) of meaning, principles of meaning, and finally theoretical models which describe how concepts and meaning may be organized cognitively.

Conceptual primitives

In our earlier discussion of word primitives, we saw that: (1) Words are constituted of morphemes, which are considered word primitives; (2) that the lexicon stores most words as broken down into their constituent parts; and (3) that the combination of these parts or morphemes can yield new words, and change the meaning and grammatical class of their roots (e.g., "fish" to "fisher"). These points are analogous to points that can be made about meaning, as we shall see.

Holistic versus feature views

There are three major issues involved in determining meaning primitives. The first issue is, what are the smallest units of meaning? Are they the definitions of single concepts, such as TREE, which then have interconnections to other concepts such as FOREST? The view that the definition of concepts or terms cannot be broken down any further is labeled the **holistic view** (Armstrong, Gleitman, & Gleitman, 1983). Or are primitives the features that make up the concept TREE, such as having branches, having grown from tree seeds, having leaves or needles and roots, and so forth? This is the hypothesis that characterizes the **feature view**, which states that meaning primitives are the features that formulate concepts. As in the morpheme as word primitive view, most researchers believe in a decompositional view of meaning such that concepts are composed of bundles of smaller units called features. These features are the attributes, characteristics, and properties of a concept. Some of the characteristics that count as features can be designated as either perceptual (e.g., GREY, LARGE, like an elephant), functional (USED TO TRANSPORT PEOPLE, of vehicles), microstructural (COMPOSED OF HYDROGEN AND OXYGEN MOLECULES, of water), or societal/conventional (SUPREME RULER OF A COUNTRY, of a king or queen). Features can also be considered meaningful units themselves (e.g., RED could be both a feature of blood and a concept itself), just as morphemes can be meaningful units themselves, and the primitives of words. In the same way that words can be broken down into the linguistic units of morphemes, syllables, and phonemes, concepts can be broken down into their constituent units, and features.

A second issue concerns whether concepts have clear conceptual boundaries. That is, are concepts structured so that it is very clear what CUPS are and are not, so all items imbued with the meaning of CUP share a common set of features?

The third issue for a theory of meaning to address is whether or not there is a single mental representation for a broad category. That is, when people store information about the meaning of a category term, is there a single description or list of features, which they store as the meaning of that category? Does only one mental representation serve as the basis for the meaning of a concept, and for categorizing items in the real world?

These issues will become clearer as we portray the differences between various feature theories.

Variations of feature theories

Although most philosophers and psychologists agree that concepts are themselves composites of features that serve to define each concept, there are disagreements about what features are necessary in defining each concept, and about the structure of meaning in the mind. Three main views can be discerned among the theories committed to a feature definition of concepts—the classical view, the prototype view, and the exemplar view. In addition, in recent years a new class of theories has developed that are less feature based and which argue that we know more about concepts than what features are associated with them. According to this new breed of theory, we typically have additional information that causes us to weigh some features more than others, to know which features tend to co-occur (e.g., laying eggs and having feathers). This new approach is termed knowledge-based theory of conceptual coherence.

Despite widespread agreement on a featural account of meaning, philosophers and psychologists diverge in their pursuit of what a theory of meaning must explain. Most philosophers are interested in determining what constitutes the *essence* of a concept. That is, what features distinguish one concept from another, and what conditions must be met for an object to be considered an instance of that concept. Thus, any definition of a concept must be true in all possible circumstances and in all possible cases. Psychologists, on the other hand, are more interested in explaining how

1. What are the smallest units of meaning? 2. Are concepts defined in a rulelike fashion, with clear conceptual boundaries? 3. Does a single representation serve as the basis of meaning of a concept?	Table 4.2 Questions About Meaning: Conceptual Theories

humans represent meaning in the mind, and how they use and apply meaningful concepts. This has sometimes led to differences in the bases of philosophical and psychological theories of meaning, although philosophers and psychologists have begun to cooperate and to influence each other's views on meanings, as we shall see.

Before we begin discussion of the variations in feature theories, let us start with an exercise that will help describe some of the differences in feature views.

Experiment 3: On a sheet of paper, list all the characteristics or properties of the concept BIRD you can think of (and hold onto your list, it will be important later).

Did your list include features and attributes such as: can fly, lays eggs, has feathers, builds nests, is small, has bones, has skin, among others? A feature-based view states that these features are listed with the concept BIRD in memory, and serve to define what is meant when we use the term "bird." Yet each of the feature theories treats the importance of these features differently.

The classical view.   The classical view states that, for any given concept, there are features that all instances of that concept share, and that these features are necessary and sufficient to claim that something is an instance of that concept. Take, for example, the concept TRIANGLE. All triangles (instances of the concept TRIANGLE) are (1) closed figures, (2) have three sides, and (3) angles that add up to 180 degrees. They *must* have these three features to be triangles (thus these features are singly *necessary* for something to be a TRIANGLE), and all objects which have these features must be triangles (thus they are jointly *sufficient* for considering something to be a TRIANGLE).

Beyond the existence of necessary features for each concept, the classical view makes some other strong claims. By way of example, all triangles are considered to be equally good triangles; no figure is considered to be a better instance of the concept TRIANGLE than any other. Thus, equilateral triangles are no better triangles than nonequilateral triangles because they all fulfill the necessary and sufficient conditions. Some figures, such as equilateral triangles, may be more common in a person's experience, and equal sides and angles may be more *characteristic* of triangles, but this does not make them *better* triangles than others without these features. The distinction between necessary (or defining) and characteristic features is an important one, especially if we want to talk about how people process concepts.

The classical view dates back at least to Aristotle, and is still the prevalent view held by many philosophers (e.g., Katz & Fodor, 1963) and some psychologists (e.g., Glass & Holyoak, 1976). It has, however, been challenged by Wittgenstein (1953) and his supporters, and by the empirical data which seem to suggest that people do not use necessary and sufficient features in categorization tasks (Rosch, 1975).[4]

Thus, proponents of the classical view consider features to be the smallest units of meaning. They also contend that concepts are defined in a rule like fashion, with clear boundaries. The classical view states that there are definitely discrete boundaries to concepts; an item either has the necessary and sufficient features or it does not. If so, it is an instance of the concept; if not, it is not an instance of the concept. The classical view also postulates that a single representation characterizes a concept. After all, there is only a single list of necessary and sufficient conditions, and this list is stored cognitively to depict the meaning of a conceptual term. It is also used to determine category membership.

The prototype view.   Before going on, let's expand Experiment 3 from the beginning of this section. Take a minute to list all possible instances of BIRDS you can think of. Number your entries in the order in which you produced them.

Did birds such as robins, sparrows, crows, bluejays pop into your head first as you tried to think of all the members of the bird category? Do odd birds such as penguins, flamingos, and toucans appear toward the end of your list? If so, you are like most other people who participate in this task (Battig & Montague, 1969). Sometimes people even include bats, which are not birds at all, but are birdlike in certain ways.

Now get your list of BIRD features, and check off the characteristics a bird *must* have in order to be considered a bird. Did you think it was necessary for birds to fly to fit the concept of BIRD? But ostriches and penguins don't fly. What about the feature of having feathers? Yet isn't the Thanksgiving turkey on your table in November still a bird? You may have thought that it was mandatory for a bird to both fly and have feathers in order to be considered a bird. However, animals which we definitely consider to be birds don't fit these conditions. Looking at your list of kinds of birds, it appears that it is certainly *characteristic* of birds to fly and lay eggs, but not mandatory.

Many psychologists (e.g., Lakoff, 1987; Rosch, 1973) do not think the world, nor the world as represented in our minds, is as clear-cut as the classical view of meaning would have us believe. If you listed all the features of all the birds on your list, there are no features common to *all* instances of the concept BIRD. This, argues Rosch (1973, 1975), demonstrates that there are no necessary and sufficient conditions for BIRD, nor indeed, for any concept. Rather, instances of a concept are sets of features related to the overall category/concept only probabilistically. "Having feathers" is probabilistically correlated with BIRD in that it is characteristic of birds to have feathers, and if something is a bird, it has a high probability of having feathers. In

---

[4]One reason that philosophers have traditionally been on the side of the classical view and psychologists on the side of the prototype view is a difference in academic missions. Philosophers are interested in the *essence* by which something gets its meaning, psychologists in how people *use* and *store* representations of meaning. Thus it is possible that both views are correct—there *may* be necessary and sufficient conditions for concepts, but people may only focus on characteristic features.

Rosch's view, then, we think of meaning as a set of weighted features such that some are more probable and others less so within the set of each features for a given concept. The prototype view also emphasizes features that are easily accessible to people when they make category and concept judgments. These will most often be perceptual features (e.g., "has feathers") and readily available facts (e.g., "lays eggs").

Rosch's theory is based on the philosophical position of Wittgenstein (1953). Wittgenstein's most famous example of a concept with no defining or sufficient features is that of the concept GAME. The word "game" is applied to a variety of instances, from board games, to soccer games, to war games. Not every instance of a game shares a single feature or set of features. For example, you can think of counter examples to every possible criterion of the concept GAME. Not all games are played on boards (e.g., tennis), nor involve two or more people (e.g., solitaire), nor are all games competitive (e.g., ring around the rosie).

This brings us to the second premise of the prototype theory; that of *family resemblance* (Rosch, 1973, 1975; Rosch & Mervis, 1975). Rather than share a set of necessary and sufficient conditions, instances of a concept may overlap in some traits, not so in others. The objects to which a single term, such as "game," refers are similar to each other in the same way that members of a family are similar to each other in a photograph. That is, they share a family resemblance to each other, in the same way you can have your mother's eyes, your father's mouth, and ears like your uncle, and you thus resemble each of them without them resembling each other. And in Figure 4.7, you can see that the Smith brothers resemble each other, even though no two brothers share common features. Rosch and Mervis (1975) asked subjects to list all the attributes of twenty kinds of fruits, and found that there were no features common to all. No single instance of a category has all the attributes of the concept, although all instances have *some* characteristic attributes.

A third tenet of the prototype view, from which the theory derives its name, is that some instances of a category or concept are more representative than others. The best example of a concept or category is known as the **prototype**. Rosch & Mervis (1975) found that prototypes of a concept tended to share more features with the other instances of that concept, and fewer features with related categories. Thus, APPLE, which is considered a very typical fruit (Armstrong, Gleitman, & Gleitman, 1983; Battig & Montague, 1969), is very similar in features to many other exemplars of FRUIT, and very dissimilar to exemplars of other categories, such as VEGETABLE. However, TOMATO, which is a more peripheral instance of FRUIT (indeed we sometimes mistake it for a VEGETABLE), shares featural similarity with both concepts. This is an example of "fuzzy boundaries" (Lakoff, 1987), also a tenet of prototype theory. That is, some instances of one category can overlap significantly with other categories, in the way that TOMATO, CUCUMBER, and OLIVE are all FRUIT concepts that seem to be equally well qualified for VEGETABLE status.

An experiment by Armstrong, Gleitman, & Gleitman (Experiment 1, 1983) illustrates the typicality effects of the prototype theory. They asked people to rate the typicality of exemplars from categories such as FRUIT, in which a family resemblance explanation is appropriate, and for ODD NUMBER and FEMALE, categories we think of as having defining features. Thus, while we expect people to rate *apple* as a "better" exemplar of the category fruit than STRAWBERRY, APRICOT,

Figure 4.7

The Smith brothers and their family resemblance

The Smith brothers are related through family resemblance, though no two brothers share all features. The one who has the greatest number of the family attributes is the most prototypical. In the example, it is Brother 9, who has all the family features: brown hair, large ears, large nose, moustache, and eyeglasses. (Courtesy Sharon Armstrong)

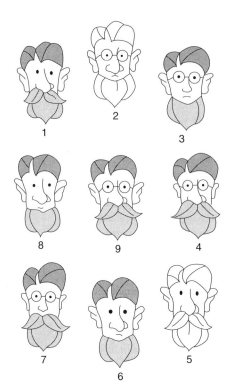

PINEAPPLE, FIG, or OLIVE, we would expect all odd numbers to be rated as equal members of that category because all of them have a remainder of one if divided by the number two. However, people actually responded that "13" is a better odd number than "23," "57," and "501" (Armstrong et al., 1983)! The same subjects also rated a MOTHER as a better example of FEMALE than WAITRESS or COMEDIENNE. How can one odd number be more odd than another, or one woman more female than another? This suggests that we get a prototypicality effect even for well defined categories with necessary and sufficient conditions, such as ODD NUMBER and FEMALE, which should show no typicality effects. Moreover, these results were also reflected in reaction times during a semantic verification task, using stimuli such as, "57 is an odd number."

When making category judgments, the prototype of the category is, according to the theory, used as a reference point (Rosch, 1975). That is, the best instance of a concept is used to stand for that concept. Thus, in deciding whether a FLAMINGO is a BIRD, we would compare FLAMINGO to our mental representation of ROBIN (the prototype). In this respect, the prototype of a concept serves as the representation for the whole concept.

We can now return to our three initial issues to discern how the prototype theory differs from the classical view. Both the classical and prototype views agree on the answer to question one—that the primitive building blocks of concepts are features. However, the two disagree on the answer to question two, about whether concepts are structured in a rulelike fashion, and whether conceptual boundaries are well defined. While the classical view argues for strict boundaries and concepts defined by necessary and sufficient features, the prototype view states that emphasis on characteristic features makes concept boundaries fuzzy. Concepts are graded as to typicality within a category. On the third issue, about whether there is a single mental representation stored at the concept level, the prototype theory, says "yes—the best example or prototype." It is on the issue of whether there is one representation that stands for a category that the prototype theory differs from the exemplar view, to which we now turn our attention.

The exemplar view.   A third feature theory, the exemplar view, posits that concepts and categories are not represented by necessary and sufficient features, nor by prototypical instances. Rather, concepts are represented by all the particular items to which the concept label extends (Medin & Schaffer, 1978).

The exemplar theory denies that just one representation can serve as the model for a whole category. Most newer computer models of the exemplar view (e.g., Hintzman, 1986; Nosofsky, 1988) store each specific encounter with a category member in an individual memory trace. The trace would include all features of that category instance. Thus under the rubric of the concept BIRD, exemplars of specific ostriches, bluejays, and penguins you had encountered (and their features), would be stored in memory. A novel bird would get matched to the most similar exemplar retrieved. If the new bird shared more features with an exemplar from the BIRD category than to exemplars from other categories, it would get classified as such. A unique aspect of this theory is that it regards semantic memory (about meaning) as a consequence of episodic memory (individual events or encounters in your life, for example, not only viewing a robin, but viewing *that* robin in your backyard at 10:00 Sunday morning).

An example may illustrate the point. Suppose you had never seen a flamingo, but had seen both standard birds (like robins and sparrows) and less common birds (ostriches). Under the prototype view, you would compare the features of the flamingo to the prototypical instance of the category BIRD (in this case ROBIN). But under the exemplar view, you would recognize the flamingo as a BIRD because of its similarity to OSTRICH, with which it shares more features.

At the category level, a concept is defined not by a prototype, but by a **disjunctive** set of exemplars: either X or Y, or Z. Each exemplar is comprised of its own bundle of features which may or may not overlap with other instances of the category. This being the case, it will be nearly impossible to come up with a set of necessary or jointly sufficient features that all exemplars of a single concept share (the same claim made by the prototype view). However, the category is not defined by its most typical member; the concept of BIRD does not contain only the feature information for ROBIN, but is defined as either ROBIN or OWL or CARDINAL or PENGUIN, and so forth.

How does the exemplar view account for typicality effects in semantic verification tasks? Some exemplar theorists believe that we implicitly calculate similarity ratios when making conceptual judgments (Medin & Schaffer, 1978). Items are recognized as members of a category based on the ratio of how similar they are to any exemplars of that category, *relative* to their similarity to other categories. Thus, less typical members of a concept (think back to the TOMATO, CUCUMBER, and OLIVE examples of FRUIT, referred to earlier) are likely to share more features with other concepts (such as VEGETABLE) than are more central members (e.g., APPLE). These peripheral members may thus take longer to classify.

Hintzman's (1986) exemplar model of categorization also posits an abstractor mechanism whereby a prototypical representation composed of the most common features of exemplars in that category can be retrieved from memory. When a novel instance of a concept is encountered, all exemplars that share some features with that instance are activated. The simultaneous activation of these stored exemplars can leave an "echo" in which the most strongly activated individual *features* from the exemplars stand out. This echo, then, will be composed of the most frequent features of the concept from which the exemplars are activated, and is likely to resemble the central member of that concept, for example, the prototype. Thus it is possible to compare new instances of a category to that concept's prototype, but even this avenue is based on mass retrieval of specific exemplars.

A comparison of the three feature theories we have just presented highlights these points: The classical view states that an item must have all the necessary and sufficient features (F1, F2, and F3) to be an instance of a concept, and thus is a conjunctive theory. The prototype theory proposes that an item must overlap in its characteristic features with the prototype for the concept to be considered a category member. The exemplar view states that a new item must overlap with *any* stored representation of that concept, either X (with Features 1–10) or Y (with Features 6–15), or Z (with F1, F2, and F9–12).

Regarding issue one, about meaning primitives, the exemplar theory, like the classical and prototype views, states that concepts can be broken down into bundles of features. Like proponents of the prototype view, exemplar theorists believe there are no rules for concept inclusion, nor any clear cut boundaries to concepts. However, unlike prototype theorists, adherents of an exemplar view do not believe that a single instance of a concept is stored at the category level. Not only a prototype, but all particular items belonging to a category are stored. This requires less abstraction than the prototype theory because one need not calculate probabilities of features, but only need to store incoming information as is.

Thus far, then, we have discussed three theories of concept structure and category organization. Common to each of these approaches is the claim that features are central to the definition of concepts. To represent the units of meaning, we must first abstract the relevant bundles of features. Concepts are judged as similar to one another to the extent that they share the same features, and categories are formed from sets of similar concepts.

Knowledge-based approaches

The feature-based view has been the cornerstone for research in concepts and categorization for the past 15 years. Recently, however, the very foundation for these views has been shaken. Led largely by Medin and his colleagues (Murphy & Medin, 1985; Medin & Wattenmaker, 1987; Medin, 1989), a revolution is underway in our understanding of the nature of concepts. This revolution questions the centrality of features in defining similarity and category membership and posits in its stead what has been called a knowledge-based or theory-based view of conceptual coherence. To gain some appreciation for this new movement in the field, it is important to first provide some criticism of the feature view and then to demonstrate how our inherent general knowledge about biology and our environment may supplement the feature approaches in explaining our conceptual judgments.

Several arguments make clear the problems with feature theories. The first addressed by philosophers and psychologists alike, concerns the question, "What counts as a feature?" The most parsimonious explanation of concepts for the feature theorist would be that humans are equipped with a kind of finite alphabet of conceptual features that combine in any number of ways to yield all of the concepts that we could conceivably think about. Unfortunately, however, no such alphabet of meaning primitives has been discovered. Take the BACHELOR example as a case in point. Above it was suggested that BACHELOR can be decomposed into more primitive concepts UNMARRIED and MAN. Is UNMARRIED a primitive? Do we help the situation greatly by saying that UNMARRIED is decomposable into NOT and MARRIED? Where do we go from here? The problem of basic feature analysis becomes one of infinite regress.

A second problem that arises for the feature theorists is evident in the question, "Which of the available features should be chosen when representing a concept?" As with lexical access, conceptual judgments often depend on the type of task a subject participates in, and on the context in which an item is presented. For example, Barsalou (1982, 1987) argues that features and types of information about concepts may be differentially available depending upon the presentation context. We may not consider "floats" as a feature of the concept BASKETBALL unless we are told someone used a basketball as a life preserver. Likewise, subjects presented with the sentence, "The man lifted the heavy piano," were likely to respond more quickly to "piano-heavy" in a priming/lexical decision task than those presented with "The man tuned the piano" (Barclay, Bransford, Franks, McCarrell, & Nitsch, 1974). You can see some of the problems if you take just a moment to jot down all of the features that you can think of for the category VEGETABLE. Were the characteristics "green, grows in my garden, and sweet" among your choices? These are excellent choices if your category of comparison is FURNITURE. They are, however, less good choices if the comparison category is FRUIT, for apples are sweet and can be green, and tomatoes can grow in your garden. The context of comparison in this task alters the features that we choose as representative of a particular concept.

The issues of task and context dependency also arise in a third example that damages the reputation of feature theories. In fact, you are already equipped with the relevant data. In the experiment mentioned above by Armstrong, Gleitman, & Gleitman (1983), subjects were willing to claim that 13 was a prototypical odd number and that housewives were "better" females that were comediennes. Something is surely wrong when feature assignment is so slippery that we are willing to impose weights on characteristics that should be very clear cut.

Finally, to borrow yet one more example, from Barsalou & Medin (1986), see if you can determine what features the following examples share: children, jewelry, portable television sets, photograph albums, manuscripts, and oil paintings. None? Without sharing features, these concepts should not form a coherent category. Yet, when placed in the context, "things to take out of the home during a fire," they cohere quite naturally—with no featural similarities at all.

The point to be made with these examples is that any theory of meaning based upon concepts and categories that are bound only by featural definition and similarity will be insufficient. First, features themselves are not well specified. Second, the choice and weighting of features is context- and task-dependent, and third, and most importantly, something more significant than feature extraction and feature matching is at work when we think about conceptual coherence and organization.

These concerns about features, and hence about feature theories, have led to the revolutionary idea that concepts must be represented and organized according to peoples' theories about the world. It is not a bundle of independent features that creates the concept BIRD, but rather a *theory* about bird structure that makes the features relevant. Features are mere surface cues to underlying knowledge, such that when we see an older woman with gray hair making chicken soup, we assume that she is a grandmother, even though the essential characteristics of grandmother are that she be a mother of a mother. Quite often, though not always, the features lead us to the correct inductions.

This shift in perspective, from feature theories to knowledge-based or theory-based theories sets a new agenda for those studying conceptual coherence and category organization. What counts as a "theory" about a concept? How fully formed must our theories be before we can abstract the relevant features? Is there a time in development when we rely more crucially on the surface properties of objects only later to rely on the deeper theoretical relations behind these surface cues? While these questions are being hotly debated, two types of theories are being discussed in the literature: *psychological essentialism*, and what we will call *psychological contextualism*. Let us briefly review each now.

Psychological essentialism.   Psychological essentialism is the position advocated by Medin (Medin & Ortony, 1989; Murphy & Medin, 1985), that "people act as if things (e.g., objects) have essences or underlying natures that make them the thing that they are" (Medin 1989, p.1476). It seems that people want to have a reason or an explanation for the ways they categorize the world. There should be a reason why birds have wings, live in trees, and have beaks. For example, they are genetically endowed with a means for flying away from their predators. Indeed, even if people don't know the theory behind the features, they are committed to the notion that such a theory exists (or essence) and that it is discoverable (at least by scientists). Thus, people have a way of making sense out of the collection of features that they see and of using these features when they encounter them again as signposts for the theory.

To demonstrate the theory/feature divide here, Medin and Shoben (1988) conducted an experiment in which they asked subjects to judge which terms were more similar: white hair and gray hair or white clouds and gray clouds. The subjects claimed, despite the similarity in features across the two conditions, that white and gray hair were more similar—a finding that the authors interpret to be a consequence of a theory of aging. In short, then, relations among features are the byproducts of theory and theory forms the essence of concepts.

This position on psychological essentialism is actually derived from work by philosophers like Quine (1977), Putnam (1973, 1975), and J.S. Mill (1843), who argue that extensional labels are applied according to essential features, even if those features are not readily apparent. Someone may call a tomato a vegetable only until they are reminded that it is a fruit. To use one of Putnam's famous examples (Putnam 1973, 1975), people may believe that gold has a particular microstructure by virtue of which it is gold. Any substance which is not known to have that structure (e.g., brass) will not be called "gold." It is not that people necessarily know what the microstructure of gold is; they rely on scientific experts to know that. It is enough to know that the microstructure *is* an essential feature. The belief in essential properties acts as a theory by which people label and categorize items, and these theories constrain and have causal links to more superficial or characteristic properties. That is, the characteristic yellow color of gold is dictated by its molecular structure. The molecular structure both defines the concept GOLD, and is the basis for the characteristic features associated with it (e.g., its color, ability to be forged, etc.).

Much of the research on psychological essentialism comes from the developmental literature (Keil, 1989; Carey, 1985; Gelman & Markman 1986, 1987; Murphy & Medin 1985; and Gelman & Coley, in press). To illustrate the force of psychological essentialism, let's engage in another thought experiment paraphrased from work by Keil (1989). Think of all the features associated with RACCOON. Now consider an actual raccoon; if I dye its fur so that it is black with a white stripe down its back, is it still a raccoon or has it become a skunk? What if I sew a smelly sack inside it and teach it to spray the contents of the sack during times of danger? Has it remained a raccoon then? Now let's change our creature so that it no longer washes its food before it eats. At what point is the creature no longer a raccoon, but something else, such as a skunk? You might argue that it is a raccoon until you change its DNA, or the fact that it was born of raccoon parents. If so, you would be arguing that there are essential features of any instance of a concept which necessarily define that concept.

Keil (1987, 1989) actually posed the raccoon experiment to children, and argued that the results, as well as evidence about conceptual development in children, suggest that children have theories from a very early age. In the beginning, these theories are more crudely developed, leaving children more reliant on external features (e.g., like prototypes). With development, and by the age of 8 years, their theories are already sophisticated enough to suggest that a skunk by any other appearance is still a skunk. Thus, for example, very young children (kindergarteners and younger) may not know enough about DNA and genetic endowments, and are thus more likely to say that the deformed raccoon we discussed above was no longer a raccoon once all its characteristic features were changed (Keil, 1987, 1989). Once this information is acquired, children develop a *theory* about a given domain (e.g., ANIMALS), rather than simply noting what features correlate with other features, and that these theories often contain information about the necessary or essential features of concepts. We can then use these theories to change how we break up the world into categories, and to decide on the meaning of concepts. We don't wait to attain theories to begin categorizing, we just have different kinds of categories before this, often based only

Figure 4.8

Examples of drawings that accompanied descriptions used in the second discoveries study.

Natural kind

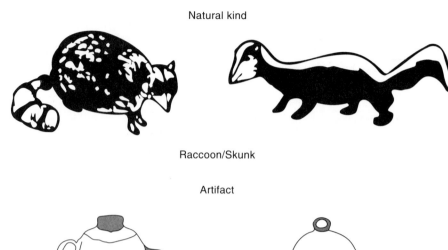

Raccoon/Skunk

Artifact

Coffeepot/Birdfeeder

on characteristic features. As our internal theories get tested in the world, and new information arrives, the theories get modified.

A belief in biological essence may prove to be a guiding factor in defining what Keil called *natural kinds terms*, things found naturally in the world, like ANIMALS. In contrast, with *nominal terms*, which refer to objects invented by humans, such as COFFEEPOTS, a different picture emerges. Using a story analogous to the raccoon story, Keil tells children that a coffeepot is melted down and turned into a birdfeeder. Here children of all ages show no resistance to the change from one human-made artifact to another. The biological essence or theory for natural kind terms is the glue that holds the features together. A surface change in biological features does not indicate (at least to children age 8 and older) a shift in biological essence. However, a shift in the external features for an artifact or nominal term may indeed indicate a shift in kind. Once you change the function of a human-made object, you have changed its essence, and thus the object itself. We would expect, then, theories about artifacts to be different from theories about biological things.

In summary, then, psychological essentialism is the modern extension of feature theories. Features are embedded within richer mental constructs—theories—that organize meaning. Concepts are thus represented at many levels in the system, as correlated bundles of features *and* through an internal essence or theory of which these features are a part. Theories constrain the features; features do not construct the theories.

The work on psychological essentialism is largely being conducted with special attention to natural kind terms (Gelman & Coley, in press), naive theories of biology and naive theories of physics. There is one other class of theories that is also gaining attention. These knowledge-based theories, what we have termed psychological contextualism, also go beyond individual feature analysis to ask how the context in which we find objects and events influences our meaning representations of those objects and events.

Psychological contextualism.   Psychological contextualism refers to the idea that certain contexts, either defined by goal or by culture, can provide the bond between features in a concept and concepts in a category. Here we note but two examples to make the point. The first is the already mentioned example of Barsalou's, "things to take out of a burning house." Barsalou's point is that the objects in the collection, "children, portable television sets, and jewelry," do not cohere into a group until there is some contextual goal that links them. All concepts (e.g., the basketball example) have both a set of context-independent features (e.g., "bounces" and "round" for basketball) that are inextricably linked to the object, and a set of context-dependent features (e.g. "floats") that can be called upon as needed. It is our knowledge of goals and past events that allows us to link these unusual features into a concept and the unusual set of concepts into a category. Hence, higher-order knowledge constrains the features that we choose and yokes them together with an underlying purpose (as in the fire example).

Not only can contextual goals and memory serve as the knowledge base upon which conceptual relations are formed, so too can cultural goals. In a now classically cited example by Lakoff (1987), the Dyirbal language spoken in parts of Australia treats "women, fire, and dangerous things" as a coherent category, each preceded in the language by a unitary marker "balan." While this categorization makes little sense to the Western mind, at least one writer, Dixon (1986) demonstrates that underlying this classification system there is a principled, though culturally constructed, way to classify things. (Those tempted should see Lakoff, 1987, pp. 92–102, for the anthropological hypotheses as to why these members are related.)[5]

These last two examples highlight the enormous flexibility and complexity inherent in the human conceptual system. They also demonstrate how our overall knowledge base interacts with conceptual features to create any number of viable categorization systems, from the biological to the sociological. To refer back to our initial questions in Table 4.2, the two knowledge-based theories claim that concepts have relevant features, but that these features are not defining of the category. As to

---

[5]We realize that classifying the conceptual theories of Barsalou (1989) and Lakoff (1987) together under the heading of "psychological contextualism" blurs some essential distinctions between them. However, at the most general level, both of these theories can be used to demonstrate the ways in which contextual knowledge influences our construction of categories.

question 2, Barsalou and Lakoff emphatically deny that concepts are defined in a rulelike way, with clear conceptual boundaries. Rather, concepts are constructed as needed for different contexts or goals (in Barsalou's theory), or on the basis of cultural criteria which may or may not be immediately evident (in Lakoff's theory). Neither knowledge-based theory is committed to a single representation for an entire concept, nor do they think that any exemplar of a category is a "better" example of that category than any other.

What we have seen in these newer versions of conceptual theory is a shift away from the more surface view that concepts are defined by independent bundles of features. In its place, the newer theories suggest that correlated sets of features that we observe in concepts are the product of our underlying knowledge and/or theories. By way of example, psychological essentialism, particularly from the research on natural kind concepts, demonstrates how biological theories can form the basis for some of our conceptual knowledge. As Ghiselin (1969, p. 83) summarizes, "Instead of finding patterns in nature and deciding that because of their conspicuousness they seem important, we discover the underlying mechanisms that impose order on natural phenomena, . . . then derive the structure of our classification systems for this understanding" (in Gelman & Coley, in press). For ad hoc concepts like those proposed by Barsalou or Lakoff, the slippery slope of category membership may still be the rule.

Summarizing the theories presented in this section, we find that there are two broad classes of theories of conceptual structure. Some are feature-based approaches (e.g., the classical view, prototype view, and the exemplar view) in which the features provide the basis of the theory of meaning. Others are theory-based or knowledge-based approaches (psychological essentialism and psychological contextualism) in which features play a more ancillary role. In the former case, features are defining of the concept. In the latter case, features can be used to identify members of a category but do not define concepts. Features in these theory- or knowledge-based approaches don't point to the essence of the concept. They assist us in finding gray-haired old women, but cannot assure us that those women will be grandmothers.

Whichever view we adopt, one point is clear from this discussion: If we are to understand conceptual structure, we must understand more than the concept alone. We must understand the relationship between concepts and how they are organized—into models (in the feature-based views) and into theories (in theory-based views). It is to the question of conceptual organization that we now turn.

Conceptual organization

How are our concepts organized? Most of the models that we are about to look at use features as their building blocks, in part because they all preceded the more contemporary theory- and knowledge-based theories. Thus, we will only discuss the classical findings to give you the flavor of this literature. Refer to Chang (1986) for a more thorough analysis of theories of semantic memory and their relative success in explaining the data. The most common methods of study have been semantic verification and priming tasks, one of the reaction time methods discussed earlier in this chapter. The models of semantic organization to be discussed are largely based on the findings of such experiments.

Models of semantic representation

Hierarchical network.   The first cognitive model of semantic representation, by Collins and Quillian, appeared in 1969. Individual concepts such as ANIMAL and FISH, are represented as "nodes," with the properties specific to each concept stored at the same level, and connections between associated concepts. This model proposed that concepts are organized in our minds as "pyramids" of concepts, with broader, superordinate concepts at the top of the pyramid (such as ANIMAL), and more specific, subordinate concepts at the bottom (such as CHIHUAHUA) (Collins & Quillian, 1969, 1970; Quillian & Collins, 1972). In the middle are basic level categories (such as BIRD, DOG, ELEPHANT, and FISH). Figure 4.9 gives you a pictorial representation of how meaningful information is presumed to be stored in a hierarchical network.

One important aspect of this model is its emphasis on cognitive economy, defined earlier. Obviously, any member of a superordinate category such as ANIMAL will have all the features attributed to ANIMAL, plus its own features. However, in Collins & Quillian's semantic network, the features would only be stored at the higher level concept in order to save space. For example, (refer to the diagram for clarification): BIRDS and FISH, in virtue of being ANIMALS, have all the features attributed to animals—having skin, being able to move, eat, and breathe. However, you do not see these features duplicated at the BIRDS and FISH nodes, because this would violate the concept of cognitive economy. In a now classic experiment, Collins and Quillian (1969) presented subjects with one of two types of semantic verification tasks. In the first, subjects were asked to judge category membership with statements such as, "A canary is a bird," or "A canary is an animal." In the second, subjects were asked to judge *feature attributes* of given concepts in property verification statements such as, "An ostrich has skin," or "An ostrich has feathers." Which of the two sentences in these experiments do you think would be responded to more quickly (e.g., have a lower reaction time)? Why? What would the hierarchical network model predict?

Collins and Quillian were interested in judging "semantic distance effects." That is, looking at Figure 4.9 again, CANARY is further away from ANIMALS than it is from BIRDS. Thus, according to the model, "A canary is an animal" should take longer to verify than, "A canary is a bird," because in the former, two nodes must be traversed instead of just one. In property verification statements, it is necessary to go to the appropriate node before the features at that level can be retrieved. As with category statements, the number of nodes which must be traversed to determine feature attributes will determine reaction times. To verify, "An ostrich has skin," one must traverse two nodes up (BIRDS, ANIMALS), and then note that "has skin" is an attribute of ANIMALS. With the statement, "An ostrich has feathers," one only need go up one node, to BIRDS, and note the features there. It should thus take longer to

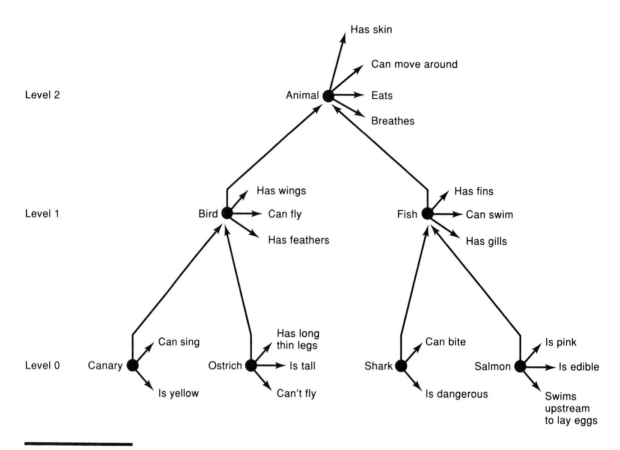

Level 2

Level 1

Level 0

Figure 4.9

Example of a hierarchically organized memory structure. *(From "Retrieval Time from Semantic Memory," by A. M. Collins and M. R. Quillian. In* Journal of Verbal Learning and Verbal Behavior, *1969, 8, 240–248. Copyright 1969 by Academic Press, Inc. Reprinted by permission.)*

verify that an ostrich has skin than that it has feathers. It should also take longer to verify features than to verify category membership because not only must one move from node to node, but one must also retrieve features stored at that node. All these assumptions were found to be the case across a number of experiments (Collins & Quillian, 1969, 1970): The further the semantic distance between two concepts, the longer the reaction times in the semantic verification tasks. Additionally, property verification statements take longer to respond to than category membership statements.

A second finding of interest in these experiments was the "category size effect." That is, the larger the category, the longer time was required for search. For example, because the concept ANIMAL embodies *all* instances of BIRDS, as well as all instances of FISH, DOGS, HORSES, and so forth, it is of necessity a larger category than any of its member categories. Presumably, larger categories force us to muddle through more information before retrieving the relevant facts.

There are several logical and empirical criticisms of the hierarchical network model of conceptual organization. These criticisms were responsible for modifying the views of the experimenters, and for the creation of subsequent semantic network models which could better explain the data. One problem with the hierarchical network model is that it is too hierarchical, and may only work for taxonomic categories such as ANIMALS, DWELLINGS, and FURNITURE, and so forth, but not for more obtuse concepts such as VIRTUE, GOOD, and EMOTION.

An important study by Conrad (1972) revealed a number of other empirical and theoretical criticisms of the hierarchical network view. Conrad found that semantic distance effects were confounded by frequency effects of features. For example, subjects list the feature, "moves," as a feature of ANIMALS more frequently than, "has ears," even though both are assumed to be stored at the ANIMALS node. Likewise, Conrad argued that the semantic distance effects found by Collins & Quillian (1969) need not be explained by semantic distance at all, but by the strength of association between two concepts, or between a concept and a feature. For example, the reason "sings" may be verified as a property of CANARY more rapidly than "has skin" is because singing is more frequently associated with CANARY.

Rips, Shoben, and Smith (1973; also Rosch, 1973) note that the hierarchical network model treats all members of a category as equal members of that category. Yet it seems clear that a GERMAN SHEPHERD is a better instance of DOG than is a CHIHUAHUA; a COLLIE a more typical member than an AFGHAN. Rips et al. (1973) argued that more typical members of a category should be verified more quickly than less typical members in semantic verification tasks. They did indeed find typicality effects, which were reflected in the reaction times of subjects who performed semantic verification tasks.

A third criticism of the hierarchical network theory is that it cannot account for *reverse* category effects which turned up later (Smith, Shoben, & Rips, 1974). In some cases, it takes longer for subjects to verify that an item is an instance of a super-ordinate categories than it does to verify that it is an instance of a lower level category. For example, it took less time for subjects to respond to, "A chimpanzee is a primate," than it did to, "A chimpanzee is an animal," even though ANIMAL would be stored at a higher category level than PRIMATE (Smith et al., 1974).

The problems with the hierarchical network model led some to postulate other models that had more explanatory power than a strict hierarchy could provide. The next major model to be developed was that of Smith, Shoben, and Rips (1974).

Feature comparison model.   Smith et al. (1974) also took a feature-oriented view of meaning. Instead of nodes, however, they postulated that concepts are represented as lists of features of two types, both (1) *defining* features which are critical for inclusion in a category and (2) *characteristic* features, which members of a category usually but do not necessarily have. For example, it is a defining feature of a PROFESSOR to have an academic appointment, and characteristic but not necessary that he or she wear tweed. Likewise, it is necessary for BIRDS to have skin and bones but not that they fly (think of chickens and penguins). In contrast to the hierarchical network theory, all features are assumed to be stored under all relevant concepts. Although this violates the assumption of cognitive economy, it renders the feature comparison model better able to account for some of the empirical findings.

According to Smith et al. (1974), semantic verification tasks are performed by comparing the number of overlapping features of two or more concepts. Feature comparison in semantic decision tasks is assumed to be a two-stage process. In the first stage, all the features, defining and characteristic, of two concepts are compared in a global comparison. If a sufficient level of similarity is attained, a "yes" response would result. If the degree of similarity is too close to call, a second comparison step is instituted in which only the defining features of the two concepts are compared. Thus this second stage would be slower and more evaluative than the first more global comparison. For example, refer to Figure 4.10 to see how a ROBIN would be verified as a category member of BIRD, relative to how it would be verified in the hierarchical network model.

Since comparisons are based on similarity rather than category size, the feature comparison model can account for both category size effects, and reverse category effects, because its predictions are based on number of overlapping features between two concepts rather than distance. The model also predicts semantic distance effects; COLLIE should be classified as a DOG more quickly than an ANIMAL because more features overlap with the concept DOG. The effects of typicality can also be explained; more typical members of a category would be verified more quickly because the number of overlapping features would be larger than for less typical members. For example, the concept of ROBIN should share more features with BIRD than does FLAMINGO.

Feature comparison theory is not without its share of problems. Most critical is an issue with which you are already familiar—whether there really are defining features of concepts. It is not always clear that humans rely on defining features to make category judgments, and sometimes the distinction between defining and characteristic features is not clear.

Second, why couldn't we store category membership directly, as one of the features under a concept? That is, why couldn't we store "is a fish" as a feature under the concept SALMON? That way, to decide that a SALMON is a FISH, we need only scan the list of SALMON features rather than compare the feature lists from both concepts.

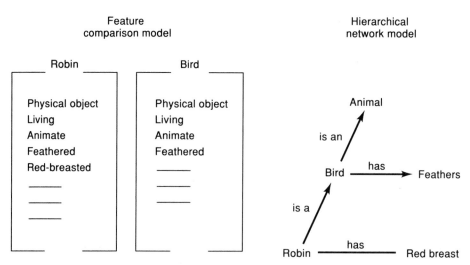

Figure 4.10

Distinction between the feature comparison model and the hierarchical network model. *(From "Theories of Semantic Memory," by E. E. Smith. In W. K. Estes (Ed.),* Handbook of Learning and Cognitive Processes *(Vol. 6). Copyright 1978 by Lawrence Erlbaum Associates, Inc., Publishers. Reprinted by permission.)*

Another criticism of this model is that feature *lists* cannot account for all that people know about concepts; they also know that some features are more highly correlated with others. Features are linked, not independent units. For example, the features of "small" and "sings" are highly correlated for birds. Likewise, despite the fact that small spoons are considered more typical than large spoons, small *wooden* spoons are considered *less* typical than large wooden spoons (Rumelhart & Ortony, 1977). A theory such as the feature comparison view, which posits lists of independent features cannot account for Rumelhart and Ortony's findings (Medin, 1989).

Spreading activation network.   In order to better account for the empirical findings which challenged his first semantic model, Collins, of Collins & Quillian (1969, 1970), developed a spreading activation model of semantic representation (Collins & Loftus, 1975). Like the earlier hierarchical network, concepts are represented as nodes, and associated concepts are connected, as in Figure 4.11. However, now properties such as RED or LARGE, or TRANSPORTS PEOPLE are also nodes within this model, and in this way are treated as concepts in their own right. Relations between concepts (including concepts and feature concepts) are represented via connecting nodes, not number of overlapping features as in the feature comparison view. The length of each line between nodes represents the degree of association between the two concepts—shorter lines mean stronger associations. Again, this distance is only metaphorical, and does not necessarily represent how far apart concepts are stored in the brain.

Like the hierarchical model, the spreading activations is still an associated network. However, the structure is not that of a strict hierarchy, but a more complex web of concepts and relations between concepts. Note its resemblance to connectionist models of cognition, such as the connectionist model of lexical access discussed earlier in the chapter. For example, the concept FLOWERS is linked not only to VIOLETS and ROSES, but indirectly to FIRETRUCK via the RED concept node. With regard to concepts, no distinction is made between defining and characteristic features; some connections are simply seen to be stronger than others. The degree of association between nodes is represented by distance, with highly associated concepts, such as CANARY and SINGS, closer than more weakly associated concepts, such as CANARY and SKIN.

An important aspect of this model is the principle of spreading activation, from which it gets its name. Think of the model as a large electrical network. When a single concept is activated, the "electricity" spreads to connected concepts, decreasing in strength as it emanates outward. Assume that you are participating in a lexical access task. Through stimulus input the concept of SALMON is activated. Like the electricity in a circuit, all nodes connected to the concept SALMON, such as FISH, ANIMAL, STREAM, PINK, EDIBLE, and GILLS, would be activated to a certain degree as well. Thus, if you are asked to verify the sentence, "A salmon has gills," it should be quicker to verify than "A salmon has feathers." Why? Because once SALMON is activated, GILLS will also receive some activation, whereas FEATHERS will not. Likewise, "A salmon has gills," should be verified more quickly than "A salmon has skin," because GILLS are more highly associated with SALMON, and thus "closer" together in the network. Likewise, CHERRY would be confirmed more

Figure 4.11

Example of a spreading
activation model in
which the length of each
line (link) represents the
degree of association
between two concepts.
*(From "A Spreading
Activation Theory of
Semantic Processing," by
A. M. Collins and E. F.
Loftus. In* Psychological
Review, *1975, 82,
407–428. Copyright
1975 by the American
Psychological
Association. Reprinted
by permission.)*

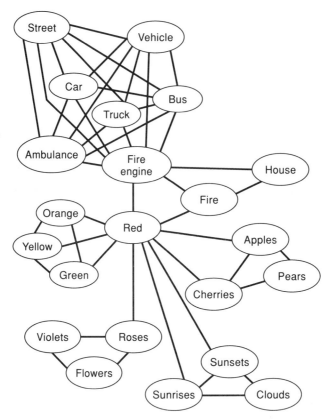

quickly than FIG as FRUIT because CHERRY is closer to the subordinate category (FRUIT), because of its higher frequency and stronger association.

The strength of association between concepts (including property concepts), represented via degree of distance in the model, can explain category effects, reverse category effects, and typicality effects in categorization and semantic verification tasks. Notice that the spreading activation network can also be used to explain priming effects. In lexical decision tasks, it should take a shorter time period to recognize the word "nurse" if it follows the term "doctor," than if it follows "bread," because the concept node for NURSE would have already been somewhat activated from DOCTOR. Similar to the logogen and connectionist models of lexical access, semantic priming in the spreading activation model is accomplished via the lowering of thresholds.

You can see that a major advantage of such a model is its explanatory power in accounting for a wide variety of experimental findings. The spreading activation model is flexible enough to account for multiple access routes to concepts and their features, and to explain many of the empirical findings related to lexical and conceptual research.

One gets a sense that meanings may not only be related through rigid taxonomic structures, but also that the best theories are ones flexible enough to account for all aspects of human performance. There are many criteria which can be imposed on the organization of concepts, in the same way that many criteria can be imposed on the organization of the lexicon. Task demands, contextual cues, and other factors can all influence what information is accessed, and how. Theories that posit different points of access, association, and activation, as spreading activation models do, are bound to have more explanatory power than more rigidly designed models.

As you have seen, each problem space—language and meaning—raises a vast number of questions ripe for research effort. Having dissociated meaning and lexical symbols, let us discuss some final issues related to their reassociation.

Summary

In the earlier sections of this chapter, we asked you to think separately about words and meaning, about language and the thoughts it represents. As you probably noticed, complete separation of these domains is almost impossible. Even our discussion of the lexicon suggested that word organization is permeated by discussions of meaning. One of the many ways in which we organize the internal lexicon is through our built-in thesaurus. Having attempted the exercise of splitting words and meanings, however, we can now demonstrate that putting them together again poses its own set of difficulties. In this section we attempt to show that the mapping between words and meanings, and more generally between language and thoughts, while inexorably linked, is nonobvious.

The illustration that makes this point most clearly comes from an example with words offered by the philosopher Quine (1960) in his book *Word and Object*. To paraphrase his example, we ask you to imagine that you are a linguist in a foreign land, Kalaba, trying to decode a language about which you known nothing (Kalaban). Your job is a simple one (or so it seems). You need only link the sounds that you hear with the objects and events that you see. Suddenly, a rabbit hops by and the native speaker near you says, "Gavagai." "Aha," you think, "perhaps 'gavagai' means RABBIT." Shortly thereafter, another rabbit scurries by and again you hear, "gavagai." Now you feel certain and write the word in your vocabulary notebook.

While you feel certain as a linguist and a reader, Quine rightly casts doubt on your conclusion. The word "gavagai" could mean any number of things because the label-to-word mapping is an ambiguous one. There are any number of things or properties of the scene with which the term "gavagai" could be associated. For example, could it not refer to rabbit ears, or legs, or fur? Couldn't it also refer to the act of hopping that you saw both times? Even less likely, but possible, "gavagai" could refer to the movement of the rabbit relative to the background, or to the way the sun reflected off the rabbit fur in the two cases. These and many other referents could be valid meanings for the term "gavagai." How, then, did you arrive so swiftly at a definite conclusion?

A recent body of work, mostly on the learning of object names, suggests that the very use of words and language constrains or limits the possibility for word-meaning mappings (Clark, 1983, 1987; Golinkoff, Mervis, & Hirsh-Pasek, submitted; Keil, 1989, 1990; Markman, 1989; and Merriman & Bowman, 1989, for reviews). The point of this research is that once a word is used, certain meanings or mappings become more probable than others. Golinkoff et al. (submitted) have reviewed this research, and have assembled a list of prominent assumptions that word learners seem to use in learning new terms: (1) The reference assumption leads learners to assume that a word refers to something. This is why you would assume that "gavagai" refers to something in the environment. (2) The whole object assumption leads learners to look for a whole object rather than object parts as the referent (Markman & Wachtel, 1988). Thus you are more likely to see the rabbit as the referent in Quine's example above rather than the rabbit's ears or paws, or fur. (3) The extend-ability assumption posits that a child is directed to assume that a word refers not to a single object, action, or event, but to a class of objects, actions, and events. These classes can be defined in a number of ways, as thematic associations (e.g., pen-paper) or taxonomically defined associations (e.g., teaspoon-tablespoon). (4) The taxonomic assumption leads learners to focus on extensions that are *taxonomic* (Markman & Hutchinson, 1984; Waxman & Gelman, 1986). For example, you would be most likely to associate "gavagai" with rabbits as a taxonomic class, rather than things asso-ciated by theme (e.g., rabbits and carrots), or by event (e.g., rabbits, roads, and tribesmen). (5) The new word/new object assumption leads learners to assume that a new word refers to a new object in the environment rather than to an object that already has a name (Clarke, 1987; Markman, 1989; Merriman & Bowman, 1989). Hence the assumption is that the new term refers to the new object in the scene, the rabbit, rather than to the trees on the other side of the road. Taken together this body of research suggests that there is something about language that directs atten-tion to some meanings over others.

Recent research on primates underscores this finding. Working with chim-panzees, Premack and Premack (1983) presented evidence that language trained chimpanzees classify objects differently than do nonlanguage trained chimps. Trained and untrained chimpanzees learned what is called a *match-to-sample* task, such as the one you see in Figure 4.12a. That is, when shown an apple as target, and then an apple and a banana as selections, the chimps were rewarded for choosing the apple because it matches the target apple. However, when shown a match-to-sample as in Figure 4.12b, where the match is to "half," only the language trained primate was able to group the half glass of water and the half cut apple together. Thus the mere presence of language seems to guide assumptions about meaning.

The studies presented above focus on ways in which word use and word knowl-edge might prime certain mappings between words and their meanings. Yet, these findings can be viewed within an even larger arena of relations between language and thought. In one case, the use of language can change or determine how one thinks, as in the case of Premack's language trained chimpanzees. Based on recent findings, Waxman and Gelman (1986) reported that the use of an adjective with a noun—even a novel adjective with a novel noun—leads children to look for subordinate classifica-tions. The word "rose," for example, refers to a taxonomic class that includes red roses, pink roses, and yellow roses, as well as climbing roses. Once an adjective is used, however, the field is narrowed to a particular type of rose as in the example of the climbing rose. Not only does the inclusion of adjectival markers therefore direct

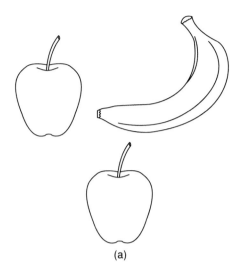
(a)

(b)

Figure 4.12

Match-to-sample task

attention to certain meanings, but certain patterns of grammatical use lead to assumptions about meanings. Without knowing any of the words, to use a further example, you know that "X blixes Y" suggests some causal action with X as the actor and Y as the recipient of the action. Similarly, you know that "X and Y are blixing," and that "X blixes with Y," do not lead you to make causal assumptions. In fact, in the latter cases, you assume that X and Y are simply doing something (here *blixing*) together (See Hirsh-Pasek, Golinkoff, Gleitman, Gleitman, & Naigles, 1989, for a more detailed discussion). The syntactic frames in which words are found reveal aspects of their meaning. According to Fischer, Gleitman, and Gleitman (in press; see also Gleitman, 1990), using these syntactic cues will allow us to be accurate in our attribution of meaning most of the time.

Just as language can direct us to particular meanings and thoughts, the very makeup of our conceptual system works—in reverse—to influence the creation of words and language structures. Talmy (1975, 1985) noted that certain semantic properties are universally signalled by verbs. Verb systems of languages around the world specify MOTION, MANNER, LOCATION, and CAUSE in various combinations. For example, some English verbs use a combination of MOTION and CAUSE, as in the verbs, "blew," "pulled," or "kicked." Others use MOTION and MANNER, or the way in which the motion occurs as in, "slid," "swung," and "swirled." The conceptual structure embedded in the verb meaning serves to determine the propositional structure. This, in turn, determines the required syntax. By way of example, you can't think of BLOWING without thinking of an *agent* (e.g., person or fan) who does the blowing and an *object* (e.g., feather or dress) that is blown. Given this semantic base, any sentence or syntactic representation is bound to have a *subject noun* (the blower), a *verb* (the act of blowing), and a *direct object* (the thing being blown).

A number of psycholinguists are investigating these correlations between meaning and words and between meaning and syntax (Fischer, Gleitman, & Gleitman, in press; Grimshaw, 1985; Pinker, 1989) in an effort to see how young learners might use their early knowledge of meaning and semantic structure to bootstrap their way into a knowledge of grammatical structure. Again, the point is that just as language directs thought, properties of thought direct the composition of language.

In summary, while we try to separately think of words and meanings for the purpose of research, they are tightly wed. Words and concepts, and language and meanings, are tied together in a fluid dialectic such that words and word patterns direct our attention to particular meanings, and concepts and propositions guide in the construction of language and language structure. Each informs the other. Thus, any account of word access and organization must include entries not only for frequency, recency, syllable structure, and phonemes, but also for information about the meaning structure and the kinds of meaning propositions into which the word will fit. It is clear that the lexicon is organized simultaneously along a number of dimensions, which allow rapid retrieval of words in comprehension and speech production. Evidence from reaction time and priming studies, as well as speech errors and the speech of brain-damaged patients all contribute to our understanding of this rapid and flexible word search capacity.

Evidence suggests that words must be analyzed in terms of smaller units that underlie both word retrieval and how meaning is associated with words. Thus, it appears probable that we decompose words into morphemes in understanding and formulating language; we also appear to represent the meaning of a concept by considering features either necessary or typical of category members.

There is, of course, much more to learn about the ways in which we represent words, about the nature of meanings, and about the connections between words, meaning and language, meaning and thought. Yet, the past two decades of psycholinguistic research have taken us a long way toward formulating some tentative answers to the questions that philosophers posed long ago.

In closing, let us return to our opening example and reexamine whether this passage in Jabberwocky *really* has no meaning. You probably know what we are about to say: You know a great deal about the meanings of these sentences, even before hearing our explanation (and Humpty Dumpty's):

> 'Twas brillig, and the slithy toves
> Did gyre and gimble in the wabe:
> All mimsy were the borogroves,
> And the mome raths outgrabe.

Just to get you started, you know that "gyre" and "gimble" are verbs, and actions that must be able to be performed at the same time. You know this even before Humpty Dumpty informs Alice that they mean, "to go round and round like a gyroscope," and "to make holes like a gimlet," respectively. Furthermore, you know that "slithy" and "mimsy" are adjectives modifying the nouns "toves" and "borogroves." How? Adjectives in English often take the morpheme "-y," and the plural "-s" typically indicates the word is a noun. For further elucidation, "slithy" means both "lithe and slimy," "mimsy" is "flimsy and miserable." And according to Humpty Dumpty, a "borogrove" is a thin, shabby-looking bird with its feathers splaying out all over, while a "tove" is something like a badger, something like a lizard, and something like a corkscrew, that makes its nest under a sundial and lives on cheese. You get the picture. The rest of the interpretation we leave to the reader's devices (or refer you to *Through the*

Looking Glass for further exposition). Now, however, you see the words, and not only have some idea about what they mean, but how they are stored and accessed.

References

Aitchison, J. (1984). The mental representation of prefixes. *Osmania papers in linguistics, 9–10* (Nirmala Memorial Volume), 61–72.

Aitchison, J. (1987). *Words in the mind: An introduction to the mental lexicon.* Oxford: Basil Blackwell.

Aitchison, J., & Straf, M. (1982). Lexical storage and retrieval: A developing skill. In A. Cutler (Ed.), *Slips of the Tongue and Language Production.* Berlin: Mouton.

Antos, S. J. (1979). Processing facilitation in a lexical decision task. *Journal of Experimental Psychology: Human Perception and Performance, 5*, 527–545.

Armstrong, S., Gleitman, L., & Gleitman, H. (1983). What some concepts might not be. *Cognition, 13*, 263–74.

Aronoff, M. (1976). *Word formation in generative grammar.* Linguistic Inquiry Monograph 1. Cambridge, MA: MIT Press.

Ashcraft, M. H. (1989). *Human memory and cognition.* Boston, MA: Scott, Foresman, and Company.

Balota, D. A., & Chumbley, J. I. (1984). Are lexical decisions a good measure of lexical access? The role of word frequency in the neglected decision stage. *Journal of Experimental Psychology, 10*, 340–357.

Barclay, J. R., Bransford, J. D., Franks, J. J., McCarrell, N. S., & Nitsch, K. (1974). Comprehension and semantic flexibility. *Journal of Verbal Learning and Verbal Behavior, 13*, 471–481.

Barsalou, L. W. (1982). Context-independent and context-dependent information in concepts. *Memory & Cognition, 10*, 82–93.

Barsalou, L. W. (1987). The instability of graded structure: Implications for the nature of concepts. In U. Neisser (Ed.), *Concepts and Conceptual Development: Ecological and Intellectual Factors in Categorization.* New York: Cambridge University Press.

Barsalou, L., & Medin, D. (1986). Concepts: fixed definitions or context-dependent representations? *Cahiers de Psychologie Cognitive, 6*, 187–202.

Battig, W. F., & Montague, W. E. (1969). Category norms for verbal items in 56 categories: A replication and extension of the Connecticut category norms. *Journal of Experimental Psychology Monograph, 80*, 1–46.

Bleasdale, F. A. (1987). Concreteness-dependent associative priming: Separate lexical organization for concrete and abstract words. *Journal of Experimental Psychology: Learning, Memory and Cognition, 13*, 582–594.

Boas, F. (1911). *The handbook of North American Indians.*

Bock, K. (1982). Toward a cognitive psychology of syntax: Information processing contributions to sentence formation. *Psychological Review, 89*, 1–47.

Bock, K. (1990). Structure in language: Creating form in talk. *American Psychologist, 45*, 1221–1236.

Bradley, D. C. (1983). *Computational Distinctions of Vocabulary Type.* Bloomington, Indiana: Indiana University Linguistics Club.

Bradley, D. C., Garrett, M. F., & Zurif, E. B. (1980). Syntactic deficits in Broca's aphasia. In D. Caplan (Ed.), *Biological Studies of Mental Processes.* Cambridge, MA: MIT Press.

Brown, R. (1986). *Social Psychology* (2nd edition). New York: Free Press.

Brown, R. & Berko, J. (1967). Word association and the acquisition of grammar. In L. Jakobovits & M. Miron (Eds.) *Readings in the Psychology of Language.* Englewood Cliffs, NJ: Prentice-Hall.

Brown, R., & McNeill, D. (1966). The "tip of the tongue" phenomenon. *Journal of Verbal Learning and Verbal Behavior, 5,* 325–537.

Cairns, H. & Kamerman, J. (1976). Lexical information processing during sentence comprehension. *Journal of Verbal Learning and Verbal Behavior, 14,* 170–179.

Canas, J. J. (1990). Associative strength effects in the lexical decision task. *The Quarterly Journal of Experimental Psychology, 42A,* 121–145.

Carey, S. (1985). *Conceptual Change in Childhood.* Cambridge, MA: MIT Press.

Carroll, D. W. (1986). *Psychology of Language.* Monterey, CA: Brooks/Cole Publishing Co.

Carroll, L. (1862/1990). *Alice's Adventures in Wonderland,* and *Through the Looking Glass.* In M. Gardner (Ed.), *More Annotated Alice.* New York: Random House.

Chang, T. M. (1986). Semantic memory: Facts and models. *Psychological Bulletin, 99,* 199–220.

Clark, E. (1983). Meanings and concepts. In J. H. Flavell & E. Markman (Eds.) *Handbook of Child Psychology, Vol. 3: Cognitive Development.* New York: John Wiley & Sons, p. 787–840.

Clark, E. (1987). The principle of contrast: A constraint on language acquisition. In B. MacWhinney (Ed.), *Mechanisms of Language Acquisition.* Hillsdale, NJ: Lawrence Erlbaum.

Collins, A. M., & Loftus, E. F. (1975). A spreading activation theory of semantic processing. *Psychological Review, 82,* 407–428.

Collins, A. M., & Quillian, M. R. (1969). Retrieval time from semantic memory. *Journal of Verbal Learning and Verbal Behavior, 8,* 240–248.

Collins, A. M., & Quillian, M. R. (1970). Facilitating retrieval from semantic memory: The effect of repeating part of an inference. *Acta Psychologia, 33,* 304–314.

Coltheart, M., Davelaar, E., Jonasson, J., & Besner, D. (1976). Access to the internal lexicon. In S. Dornic (Ed.) *Attention and performance. Volume VI.* Hillsdale, NJ: Erlbaum.

Conrad, C. (1972). Cognitive economy in semantic memory. *Journal of Experimental Psychology, 92,* 149–154.

Dell, G. (1986). A spreading activation theory of retrieval in sentence production. *Psychological Review, 93,* 283–321.

Dixon, R. M. (1982). *Where have all the adjectives gone?* Berlin: Walter de Gruyter.

Ervin, S. M. (1957). Grammar and Classification. Paper presented at American Psychological Association annual meeting, New York, September.

Fischer, C., Gleitman, L., & Gleitman, H. (in press). On the semantic content of subcategorization frames. *Cognitive Psychology.*

Forster, K. I. (1976). Accessing the mental lexicon. In F. J. Wales, & E. Walker (Eds.), *New Approaches to Language Mechanisms* (pp. 257–287). Amsterdam: North-Holland Publishing.

Forster, K. I. (1990). Lexical processing. In D. Osherson and H. Lasnik (Eds.), *Language.* Cambridge, MA: MIT Press.

Forster, K. I., & Chambers, S. M. (1973). Lexical access and naming time. *Journal of Verbal Learning and Verbal Behavior, 12,* 627–635.

Foss, D. J., & Hakes, D. T. (1978). *Psycholinguistics: An introduction to the psychology of language.* Englewood Cliffs, NJ: Prentice-Hall, Inc.

Foss, D. J. (1969). Decision processes during sentence comprehension: Effects of lexical item difficulty and position upon decision times. *Journal of Verbal Learning and Verbal Behavior, 8,* 457–462.

Foss, D. J. (1970). Some effects of ambiguity upon sentence comprehension. *Journal of Verbal Learning and Verbal Behavior, 9,* 699–706.

Fowles, B., & Glanz, E. (1977). Competence and talent in verbal riddle comprehension. *Journal of Child Language, 4,* 433–452.

Frederiksen, J. R., & Kroll, J. F. (1976). Spelling and sound: Approaches to the internal lexicon. *Journal of Experimental Psychology: Human Perception and Performance, 2,* 361–379.

Freedman, & Loftus, E. (1971). Retrieval of words from long-term memory. *Journal of Verbal Learning and Verbal Behavior, 10,* 107–115.

Freyd, R. (1981). *Individual differences in the acquisition and use of English derivational morphology.* Unpublished doctoral dissertation, University of Pennsylvania.

Fromkin, V. (1971). The non-anomalous nature of anomalous utterances. *Language, 47,* 27–52.

Fromkin, V. (1973). *Speech errors as linguistic evidence.* The Hague: Mouton.

Gardner, H. (1974). *The shattered mind.* New York: Random House.

Garrett, M. F. (1976). Syntactic processes in sentence production. In R. J. Wales & E. Walker (Eds.), *New approaches to language mechanisms.* Amsterdam: North-Holland.

Garrett, M. F. (1980). Levels of processing in sentence production. In B. Butterworth (Ed.), *Speech production (Vol. 1).* New York: Academic Press.

Gelman, S. A., & Coley, J. D. (in press). Language and categorization: The acquisition of natural kind terms. In S. A. Gelman & J. P. Byrnes (Eds.), *Perspectives on Language and Thought: Interrelations in Development.* Cambridge: Cambridge University Press.

Gelman, S. A., & Markman, E. M. (1986). Categories and induction in young children. *Cognition, 23,* 183–208.

Gelman, S. A., & Markman, E. M. (1987). Young children's inductions from natural kinds: The role of categories and appearances. *Child Development, 58,* 1532–1541.

Ghiselin, M. (1969). *The triumph of the Darwinian method.* Chicago: University of Chicago Press.

Glanzer, M., & Erhenreich, S. (1979). Structure and search of the internal lexicon. *Journal of Verbal Learning and Verbal Behavior, 18,* 381–398.

Glass, A. L., & Holyoak, K. J. (1975). Alternative conceptions of semantic memory. *Cognition, 3,* 313–333.

Gleitman, H. (1991). *Psychology.* New York: Norton.

Gleitman, L. (1990). The structural sources of verb meanings. *Language Acquisition, 1,* 3–55.

Golinkoff, R., Mervis, C., & Hirsh-Pasek, K. (submitted). Early object labels: The case for lexical principles.

Gould, S. J. (1983). What, if anything, is a zebra? *Hen's teeth and horses' toes.* New York: W. W. Norton and Company.

Grimshaw, J. (1985). Form, function and the language acquisition device. In C. L. Baker & J. McCarthy (Eds.), *The logical problem of language acquisition.* (pp. 165–183) Cambridge, MA: MIT Press.

Grimshaw, J. (1986). Form, function and the language acquisition device. In C. L. Baker & J. J. McCarthy (Eds.), *The logical problem of language acquisition.* Cambridge, MA: MIT Press.

Hart, J., Berndt, R. S., & Caramazza, A. (1985). Category-specific naming deficit following cerebral-infarction. *Nature, 316,* 439–440.

Heider, E. R. (1972). Universals in color naming and memory. *Journal of Experimental Psychology, 93,* 10–20.

Henderson, L. (1982). *Orthography and word recognition in reading.* London: Academic Press.

Hintzman, D. L. (1986). "Schema abstraction" in a multiple-trace memory model. *Psychological Review, 93,* 411–428.

Hirsh-Pasek, K., Gleitman, L., & Gleitman, H. (1978). What did the brain say to the mind? In A. Sinclair, R. J. Jarvella, & W. J. M. Levelt (Eds.), *The child's conception of language.* Berlin: Springer-Verlag.

Hirsh-Pasek, K., Golinkoff, R., Gleitman, L., Gleitman, H., & Naigles, L. (in preparation). Syntactic bootstrapping: Evidence from comprehension.

Hobbes, T. (1651/1958). *Leviathan.* H. W. Schneider (Ed.). New York: Bobbs-Merrill Co.

Hogaboam, T., & Perfetti, C. (1975). Lexical ambiguity and sentence comprehension. *Journal of Verbal Learning and Verbal Behavior, 14,* 265–274.

Jenkins, J. J. (1970). The 1952 Minnesota word association norms. In L. Postman & G. Keppel (Eds.), *Norms of word association.* New York: Academic Press.

Katz, J., & Fodor, J. A. (1963). The structure of a semantic theory, *Language, 39,* 170–210.

Keil, F. C. (1987). Conceptual development and category structure. In U. Neisser (Ed.), *Concepts and conceptual development: Ecological and intellectual factors in categorization.* New York: Cambridge University Press.

Keil, F. C. (1989). *Concepts, kinds, and cognitive development.* Cambridge, MA: The MIT Press.

Lakoff, G. (1987). *Women, fire and dangerous things: What categories reveal about the mind.* Chicago: University of Chicago Press.

Locke, J. (1690/1967). *An essay concerning human understanding.* A. S. Pringle-Pattison (Ed.). London: Oxford University Press.

MacKay, D. (1966). To end ambiguous sentences. *Perception and Psychophysics, 1,* 426–436.

MacKay, D. (1972). The structure of words and syllables: Evidence from errors in speech. *Cognitive Psychology, 3,* 210–227.

MacKay, D. (1978). Derivational rules and the internal lexicon. *Journal of Verbal Learning and Verbal Behavior, 17,* 61–71.

MacKay, D. (1979). Lexical insertion, inflection, and derivation: Creative processes in word production. *Journal of Psycholinguistic Research, 8,* 477–498.

Malt, B. C. (1990). Features and beliefs in the mental representations of categories. *Journal of Memory and Language, 29,* 289–315.

Malt, B. C. (in press). Word meaning and word use. In P. Schwanenflugel (Ed.), *The psychology of word meaning.* Hillsdale, NJ: Lawrence Erlbaum Associates.

Manelis, L., & Tharp, D. A. (1977). The processing of affixed words. *Memory & Cognition, 5,* 690–695.

Markman, E. (1989). *Categorization and naming in children.* Cambridge, MA: The MIT Press.

Markman, E., & Hutchinson, J. E. (1984). Children's sensitivity to constraints on word meaning: Taxonomic vs. thematic relations. *Cognitive Psychology, 16,* 1–27.

Markman, E., & Wachtel, G. F. (1988). Children's use of mutual exclusivity to constrain the meanings of words. *Cognitive Psychology, 20,* 121–157.

Marslen-Wilson, W. D. (1987). Functional parallelism in spoken word-recognition. *Cognition, 25,* 71–102.

Marslen-Wilson, W. D., & Tyler, L. K. (1980). The temporal structure of spoken language understanding. *Cognition, 8,* 1–71.

Marslen-Wilson, W. D., & Tyler, L. K. (1981). Central processes in speech understanding. *Philosophical Transactions of the Royal Society of London, B 295,* 317–332.

Marslen-Wilson, W. D., & Welsh, A. (1978). Processing interactions and lexical access during word recognition in continuous speech. *Cognitive Psychology, 10,* 29–63.

McClelland, J. L. (1985). Putting knowledge in its place: A scheme for programming parallel processing structures on the fly. *Cognitive Science, 9,* 113–146.

McClelland, J., & Rumelhart, D. (1981). An interactive activation model of context effects in letter perception. Part 1: An account of basic findings. *Psychological Review, 88,* 60–94.

McClelland, J. L., & Rumelhart, D. E. and the PDP Research Group (1986). *Parallel distributed processing: Explorations in the microstructure of cognition (Vol. 1 & 2).* Cambridge, MA: MIT Press.

Medin, D. L. (1989). Concepts and category structure. *American Psychologist, 44,* 1469–1481.

Medin, D. L., & Ortony, A. (1989). Psychological essentialism. In S. Vosniadou and A. Ortony (Eds.), *Similarity and analogical reasoning.* New York: Cambridge University Press.

Medin, D. L., & Schaffer, M. M. (1978). Context theory of classification learning. *Psychological Review, 85,* 207–238.

Medin, D., & Shoben, E. (1988). Context and structure in conceptual combination. *Cognitive Psychology, 20,* 158–190.

Medin, D. L., & Wattenmaker, W. D. (1987). Category cohesiveness, theories and cognitive archeology. In U. Neisser (Ed.), *Concepts and Conceptual Development.* Cambridge: Cambridge University Press.

Merriman, W. E., & Bowman, L. L. (1989). The mutual exclusivity bias in children's word learning. *Monographs of the Society for Research in Child Development, Serial No. 220, 54* (3–4), 1–123.

Meyer, D. E., & Schvaneveldt, R. W. (1971). Facilitation in recognizing pairs of words: Evidence of a dependence between retrieval operations. *Journal of Experimental Psychology, 90,* 227–234.

Meyer, D. E., & Ellis, G. B. (1970, November). *Parallel processes in word recognition.* Paper presented at the meeting of the Psychonomic Society, San Antonio, TX.

Mill, J. S. (1843). *A system of logic.* London: Longmans.

Miller, G. A. (1951). *Language and communication.* New York: McGraw-Hill.

Monsell, S. (1985). Repetition and the lexicon. In A. W. Ellis (Ed.), *Progress in the psychology of language (Vol. 1).* Hove and London: Lawrence Erlbaum Associates.

Morton, J. (1969). Interaction of information in word recognition. *Psychological Review, 76,* 165–178.

Morton, J. (1970). A functional model of human memory. In D. A. Norman (Ed.), *Models of human memory.* New York: Academic Press.

Morton, J. (1979). Facilitation in word recognition: Experiments causing change in the logogen model. In P. A. Kolers, M. E. Wrolstad, & H. Bouma (Eds.), *Processing of visual language.* New York: Plenum Press.

Morton, J., & Patterson, K. (1980). A new attempt at an interpretation, or, an attempt at a new interpretation. In M. K. Coltheart, K. Patterson, & J. C. Marshall (Eds.), *Deep dyslexia.* London: Routledge and Kegan Paul.

Murphy, G. L., & Medin, D. L. (1985). The role of theories in conceptual coherence. *Psychological Review, 92,* 289–316.

Murrell, G. A., & Morton, J. (1974). Word recognition and morphemic structure. *Journal of Experimental Psychology, 102,* 963–968.

Nosofsky, R. M. (1988). Exemplar-based accounts of relations between classification, recognition, and typicality. *Journal of Experimental Psychology: Learning, Memory, and Cognition, 14,* 700–708.

Oldfield, C. R. (1963). Individual vocabulary and semantic currency. *British Journal of Social and Clinical Psychology, 2,* 122–130.

Osgood, C. E., & Hoosain, R. (1974). Salience of the word as a unit in the perception of language. *Perception and Psychophysics, 15,* 168–192.

Paivio, A. (1969). Mental imagery in associative learning and memory. *Psychological Review,* *76,* 241–263.

Palermo, D. S. (1963). Word associations and children's verbal behavior. In L. P. Lipsitt & C. C. Spiker (Eds.), *Advances in child development and behavior (Vol. 1).* New York: Academic Press.

Pinker, S. (1989). *Learnability and cognition.* Cambridge, MA: MIT Press.

Premack, D., & Premack, A. J. (1983). *The mind of an ape.* New York: W. W. Norton & Co.

Pullum, G. (1990, June). The great Eskimo vocabulary hoax. *Lingua Franca,* 28–29.

Putnum, H. (1973). Meaning and reference. *Journal of Philosophy, 70,* 699–711.

Putnum, H. (1975). The meaning of "meaning." In H. Putnum, *Mind, language, and reality: Philosophical papers (Vol. 2).* Cambridge, England: Cambridge University Press.

Quillian, M. R. (1969). The teachable language comprehender: A simulation program and theory of language. *Communications of the ACM, 12,* 459–476.

Quine, W. V. O. (1960). *Word and object.* Cambridge, MA: MIT Press.

Quine, W. V. O. (1977). Natural kinds. In S. P. Schwartz (Ed.), *Naming, necessity, and natural kinds.* Ithaca, NY: Cornell University Press.

Rips, L. J., Shoben, E. J., & Smith, E. E. (1973). Semantic distance and the verification of semantic relationships. *Journal of Verbal Learning and Verbal Behavior, 12,* 1–20.

Root, M. (1979). Quine's thought experiment. In P. A. French, T. E. Euhling, Jr., & H. K. Wettstein (Eds.), *Contemporary perspectives in the philosophy of language* (pp. 275–289). Minneapolis, MN: University of Minnesota Press.

Rosch, E. H. (1973). On the internal structure of perceptual and semantic categories. In T. E. Moore (Ed.), *Cognitive development and the acquisition of language.* (pp. 111–144). New York: Academic Press.

Rosch, E. H. (1975). Cognitive representations of semantic categories. *Journal of Experimental Psychology: General, 104,* 192–233.

Rosch, E. H., & Mervis, C. B. (1975). Family resemblances: Studies in the internal structure of categories. *Cognitive Psychology, 7,* 573–605.

Rubenstein, H., Garfield, L., & Millikan, J. A. (1970). Homographic entries in the internal lexicon. *Journal of Verbal Learning and Verbal Behavior, 9,* 487–494.

Rubin, G. S., Becker, C. A., & Freeman, R. H. (1979). Morphological structure and its effect on visual word recognition. *Journal of Verbal Learning and Verbal Behavior, 18,* 757–767.

Rumelhart, D. E., & Ortony, A. (1977). The representation of knowledge in memory. In R. C. Anderson, R. J. Spiro, & W. E. Montague (Eds.), *Schooling and the acquisition of knowledge* (pp. 99–135). Hillsdale, NJ: Lawrence Erlbaum Associates.

Ryle, G. (1949). *The concept of mind.* New York: Barnes and Noble.

Sandra, D. (1990). On the representation and processing of compound words: Automatic access to constituent morphemes does not occur. *The Quarterly Journal of Experimental Psychology, 42A,* 529–567.

Scarborough, D. L., Cortese, C., & Scarborough, H. (1977). Frequency and repetition effects in lexical memory. *Journal of Experimental Psychology: Human Perception and Performance, 7,* 3–12.

Schank, R., & Abelson, R. (1977). *Scripts, plans, goals, and understanding.* Hillsdale, NJ: Lawrence Erlbaum Associates.

Seashore, R. H., & Eckerson, L. D. (1940). The measurement of individual differences in general English vocabularies. *Journal of Educational Psychology, 31,* 14–38.

Shakespeare, W. (1975). Romeo and Juliet. In *The complete works of William Shakespeare.* Minneapolis, MN: The Amaranth Press.

Shattuck-Hufnagel, S. (1979). Speech errors as evidence for a serial-ordering mechanism in sentence production. In W. Cooper & E. C. T. Walker (Eds.), *Sentence processing*. Hillsdale, NJ: Lawrence Erlbaum.

Shultz, T., & Horibe, F. (1974) Development of the appreciation of verbal jokes. *Developmental Psychology, 10*, 13–20.

Simpson, G. B. (1981). Meaning dominance and semantic context in the processing of lexical ambiguity. *Journal of Verbal Learning and Verbal Behavior, 20*, 120–136.

Smith, E. E. (1978). Theories of semantic memory. In W. K. Estes (Ed.), *Handbook of learning and cognitive processes (Vol. 6)*. Hillsdale, NJ: Lawrence Erlbaum.

Smith, E. E., & Medin, D. L. (1981). *Categories and concepts*. Cambridge, MA: Harvard University Press.

Smith, E. E., Shoben, E. J., & Rips, L. J. (1974). Structure and process in semantic memory: A featural model for semantic decisions. *Psychological Review, 81*, 214–241.

Smith, P. T., & Sterling, C. M. (1982). Factors affecting the perceived morphemic structure of written words. *Journal of Verbal Learning and Verbal Behavior, 21*, 704–721.

Swinney, D. A. (1979). Lexical access during sentence comprehension: (Re)consideration of context effects. *Journal of Verbal Learning and Verbal Behavior, 18*, 645–659.

Taft, M. (1981). Prefix stripping revisited. *Journal of Verbal Learning and Verbal Behavior, 20*, 289–297.

Taft, M., & Forster, K. I. (1975). Lexical storage and retrieval of prefixed words. *Journal of Verbal Learning and Verbal Behavior, 14*, 638–647.

Taft, M., & Forster, K. I. (1976). Lexical storage and retrieval of polymorphemic and polysyllabic words. *Journal of Verbal Learning and Verbal Behavior, 15*, 607–620.

Talmy, L. (1975). Semantics and syntax of motion. In J. Kimball (Ed.), *Syntax and semantics (Vol. 4)*, (pp. 181–238). New York: Academic Press.

Talmy, L. (1985). Lexicalization patterns: Semantic structure in lexical forms. In T. Shopen (Ed.), *Language typology and syntactic description (Vol. 3)*, (pp. 57–149). Cambridge: Cambridge University Press.

Treiman, R., & Chafetz, J. (1987). Are there onset- and rime-like units in printed words? In M. Coltheart (Ed.), *Attention and performance XII: Proceedings of the twelfth international symposium on attention and performance*. Hillsdale, N.J.: Lawrence Erlbaum & Associates.

Treiman, R. (1988). The internal structure of the syllable. In G. Carlson and M. Tanenhaus (Eds.), *Linguistic structure in language processing*. Dordrecth, Holland: Kluwer.

Tweney, R., Tkacz, S., & Zaruba, S. (1975). Slips of the tongue and lexical storage. *Language and Speech, 18*, 388–396.

Tyler, L. K., Behrens, S., Cobb, H., & Marslen-Wilson, W. (1990). Processing distinctions between stems and affixes: Evidence from a non-fluent aphasic patient. *Cognition, 36*, 129–153.

Waxman, S. R., & Gelman, R. (1986). Preschoolers use of superordinate relations in classification. *Cognitive Development, 5*, 123–150.

Wells, R. (1951). Predicting slips of the tongue. *The Yale Scientific Magazine, 26*, 9–30. [Also in V. A. Fromkin (Ed.) (1973). *Speech errors as linguistic evidence*. The Hague: Mouton.]

Whorf, B. L. (1956). *Language, thought and reality: Selected writings of Benjamin Lee Whorf*. J. B. Carroll (Ed.). New York: Wiley.

Wittgenstein, L. (1953). *Philosophical investigations*. New York: MacMillan.

Zechmeister, E. B., & Nyberg, S. E. (1982). *Human memory: An introduction to research and theory*. Monterey, CA: Brooks/Cole Publishing Co.

Sentence Processing

ARTHUR WINGFIELD
Brandeis University

Introduction

In Chapter 4 we saw how individual words may be correctly recognized and their meanings activated. The power of language as a tool for communication, however, comes when these words are combined into sentences and collections of sentences. Collections of sentences that tell a story or convey sequences of events are referred to as **discourse**. This is the topic of Chapter 6.

The scope of *this* chapter lies between these two levels of language analysis. In this chapter we look at how people understand speech at the sentence level. We call this **sentence processing**; the question of how listeners rapidly decipher the structure of sentences and gain access to the meaning of the sentence as a whole.

One of the most striking features of connected speech is the very rapid rate at which it ordinarily arrives. Speech-rates in everyday conversation typically average between 140 to 180 words per minute (wpm), while a T.V. newsreader speaking from a prepared script can easily exceed 210 words per minute. Even these rates pale beside the rapid-fire delivery of many commercials or the fast talking T.V. weather persons with their charts and maps and little jokes. It is true that people generally find T.V. weather reports a perceptual and conceptual blur. But this is due more to the sensory overload caused by the charts and maps and little jokes than it is to the high speech rates *per se* (Wagenaar, Varey, & Hudson, 1984).

The rapidity of natural speech input is not the only problem the listener has to face. In fluent speech, individual words run in together and are often not as clearly articulated as they might seem to be. When speech scientists analyze the speech waveforms of ordinary speech, the waveforms often lack regular breaks between the words, phrases, and other linguistic elements of spoken sentences. The perceptual isolation of individual words that we hear as we listen to connected speech has to be imposed by the listener, often based on the meaning of the sentence as a whole.

To get a sense of this perceptual segmentation, try saying aloud the two sentences, "I *better* do my laundry," and "I *bet her* five dollars." If you say these sentences several times, and listen to yourself carefully, you may hear that the italicized segments are pronounced identically. It is the sentence context in which the sounds are imbedded that brings perceptual clarity to utterances such as these (Martin, 1990).

The surprising lack of clarity of articulation of many words in connected speech was demonstrated long ago by Pollack and Pickett (1964). They made tape recordings of people's conversations and then electronically spliced out single words and presented each of the words in isolation to different people. They wanted to see how recognizable the words might be when heard without their surrounding linguistic context. The results were dramatic. In many cases not only were the words unrecognizable, but they also barely sounded like words at all. When Pollack and Pickett played back the words again, but this time in their full sentence context, they now sounded crystal clear. The acoustic information was the same. What differed was the availability of surrounding semantic and syntactic context that the listener could use as part of the perceptual process. The other side of the coin is that speakers can adjust the clarity of their articulation depending on the predictability of the words in the sentence context (Hunnicutt, 1985).

In laboratory experiments we can use a computer to artificially accelerate speech without disturbing its pitch. We can use this technique to show that, depending on the speech materials, people can successfully comprehend speech at even twice normal speaking rates (Chodorow, 1979; Wingfield, 1975). Maximum speech-rates are limited more by the output capability of the speaker than they are by the perceptual needs of the listener.

In spite of these demands, listeners can, with apparent ease, segment the speech stream to isolate the "words," decode the grammatical structure of the sentences, and determine the semantic relations between the words—all at the very rapid rate at which speech normally arrives. As part of this task, the listener may also have to resolve semantic ambiguities, and draw logical inferences and implications that lie beyond the literal meanings of the sentences themselves.

Our goal in this chapter is to describe current theory and research on sentence processing, and to explain, among other things, how sentences can be processed at such rapid rates.

Structural properties of sentences

One reason why speech can be processed so rapidly is because of the way the processing system makes use of structure in natural language.

What do we mean by *structure* in language? We can define the structure of language in terms of sets of *rules* that tell us how words strung together can form a sentence and convey a meaning. When we speak of rules that give structure to language, we do not mean that these rules are consciously followed by a speaker when uttering the words of a sentence. As Levelt (1989) has said, "A speaker doesn't have to ponder the issue of whether to make the recipient of GIVE an indirect object (as in *John gave Mary the book*) or an oblique object (as in *John gave the book to Mary*)." Nor, he goes on to suggest, does the retrieval of common words require much time or conscious effort (Levelt, 1989, p. 22). These are "automatic" processes over which we exert little conscious control. Yet, for communication to occur, the speaker and the listener must share a common knowledge base, and each must have access to the same knowledge sets and rules.

Think for a moment of a simple "sentence" in the abstract, a sentence following the form, *noun-verb-noun*. Think now of the same "sentence" but in the form of an action, "The first noun verbed the second noun." Finally, let us instantiate this sentence with specific words, such as:

"The student read the book."
"The teacher graded the test."
"The teacher heard the student."

You will note that although all three sentences take the form of "The noun verbed the noun," the first two sentences are not reversible. That is, while you can say "The student read the book," or "The teacher graded the test," you cannot say "The book read the student," or "The test graded the teacher." Only the third sentence is reversible: You can just as easily say, "The student heard the teacher," as "The teacher heard the student." Some things in the world are possible, and some are not. Real world knowledge can supply constraints that operate as part of the structure of our language.

These properties of language give rise to regularities in the language that make possible a degree of statistical prediction whenever we listen to natural speech. To illustrate, let us begin with the fact that the average college-educated adult may have a speaking vocabulary of between 75,000 to 100,000 words (Oldfield, 1963). Suppose I was about to say a word to you, and you had to guess what the word might be. If all words in the language were equally probable, the odds of its being any particular word would be between .00001 and .000013. Now, clearly, each word is not equally probable. Some words tend to be used much more frequently than others. In writing, the most frequently used word is *the*, while in spoken telephone conversations, it is *I*. In fact, the 50 most commonly used words in English make up about 60 percent of all the words we speak, and about 45 percent of those we write. We can put this another way: On average, we can speak for only about 10 to 15 words before we repeat a word (Miller, 1951).

Thus, some words are more predictable than others, even out of context. When words are heard within a context, the effect is even further increased. Imagine I started to speak to you, but then stopped suddenly in midsentence. If I asked you what you thought the next word might be, you might have a good idea. You could at least tell me what part of speech the next word might be, whether it would probably be a noun, a verb, an adjective, and so forth. Indeed, there is a good chance that you would be able to tell me the word itself. If I said, "The train pulled into the. . . . ," you might say "station," or you might say "tunnel." From your knowledge of language, you would, in the very least, have a very high expectation for either a noun or an adjective.

Statistical approximations to English

We can capture this predictive quality of natural language by giving people a few words of a sentence and asking them to guess what they think the next word might be. We then show this set of words to another person and ask them to guess the next word, and so on. In this way one can see what people's linguistic intuitions look like with varying amounts of preceding context.

For example, Moray and Taylor (1960) showed a subject the five words, "I have a few little," and asked the subject to guess what he or she thought the next word of this sentence might be. The subject said *facts*. Moray and Taylor added the word *facts*, covered the first word, *I*, and then showed these five words to another subject:

". . . have a few little facts _____." This subject said, *here*. Subject number three now saw the last set of five words: ". . . a few little facts here _____," and was asked to guess the sixth word. This process was continued until an entire 150-word passage was constructed. This example is called a *sixth-order approxima- tion* to English, because each word was generated based on a context of five preced- ing words. Here is an extract from Moray and Taylor's sample. As you read it, it seems as if our artificial speaker is continually on the verge of saying something meaningful, but never quite does:

"I have a few little facts here to test lots of time for studying and praying for guidance in living according to common ideas as illustrated by the painting."

Somewhat less English-like would be a second-order approximation, where sub- jects had to guess the most likely word of a sentence based on seeing only one word of context: "The camera shop and boyhood friend from fish and screamed loudly men only when seen again and then it was jumping in the tree."

You might ask what would happen if one created approximations to English after giving subjects a specific context, such as telling them that the words are from a polit- ical campaign speech, a romantic novel, or a legal document. Following is a fourth- order approximation to English (each word is based on three words of prior context only) when respondents were told the words were taken from a mystery novel:

"When I killed her I stabbed Paul between his powerful jaws clamped tightly together. Screaming loudly despite fatal consequences in the struggle for life began ebbing as he coughed hollowly spitting blood from his ears" (Attneave, 1959, p. 19).

It has long been known that increasing the likelihood of words by increasing con- textual constraints, either with sentences or with statistical approximations to English, will make the words easier to remember (Miller & Selfridge, 1950), more audible under poor listening conditions (Rubenstein & Pollack, 1963), and more recognizable if they are presented visually for very brief durations (Tulving & Gold, 1963; Morton, 1964).

We can illustrate this with data taken from an early experiment by Miller and Selfridge (1950). Their goal was to test college students' ability to memorize "sentences" composed of word strings representing various orders of approximation to English. Figure 5.1 shows the percentage of words subjects could correctly recall from 20-word statistical approximations. To give you a feeling for the materials, some examples of the approximations they used are listed below the figure. (The first order strings were constructed by randomly sampling words from higher-order sets.)

Although we show only the data for 20-word strings, Miller and Selfridge also tested strings as short as 10 words, and materials as long as 50-word passages. In all cases, the shapes of the performance curves were the same. The more closely the word strings approximated true sentences, the better were subjects able to recall them. You will see that beyond third- or fourth-order approximations, the strings seem to be handled just about as easily as normal text. This is a typical finding in such experiments, regardless of whether one tests memory, as in the above case, or whether we test ease of learning or ease of perception. In all cases, people use quite effectively the structure of the materials, even when the materials convey no actual meaning.

Figure 5.1

Recall of 20-word "sentences" composed of word strings representing various orders of approximation to English. (Source: G. A. Miller & J. A. Selfridge, Verbal context and the recall of meaningful material. *American Journal of Psychology*, 1950, 63: Fig. 1, pg. 181.)

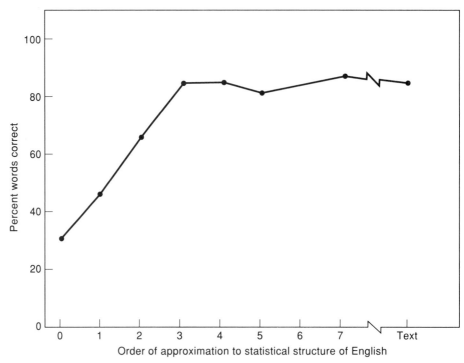

Examples of 20-word "Sentences" Used by Miller and Selfridge

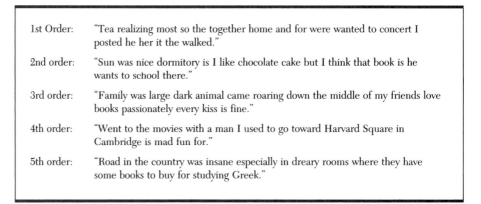

1st Order:	"Tea realizing most so the together home and for were wanted to concert I posted he her it the walked."
2nd order:	"Sun was nice dormitory is I like chocolate cake but I think that book is he wants to school there."
3rd order:	"Family was large dark animal came roaring down the middle of my friends love books passionately every kiss is fine."
4th order:	"Went to the movies with a man I used to go toward Harvard Square in Cambridge is mad fun for."
5th order:	"Road in the country was insane especially in dreary rooms where they have some books to buy for studying Greek."

Where do people pause when they speak?

Clearly, listeners know a great deal about the structure of their native language. The speech we hear also has an intonation pattern and rhythm to it that can give the listener hints about what is about to be heard. One of these hints can come from the periodic appearance of pauses in spontaneous speech, whether they are "filled" with *uhms* and *ahs*, or by silence. They occur as the speaker thinks of what it is he or she wants to say, and how to phrase it.

Some estimates suggest that as much as 40 to 50 percent of speaking time is occupied by pauses that occur as we select the words we wish to utter. What happens to these natural pauses when we reduce the planning demands on the speaker? Reading aloud from a script does reduce the proportion of pausing, but it may be impossible for a speaker to speak sensibly without pausing at least 20 percent of the time (Butterworth, 1989, p. 128).

Systematic studies verify that the pauses in connected speech tend to occur just before words of low probability in the context, the "thoughtful" words that do not represent a run of association. They suggest that, in fluent speech, we do not pause to take a breath. Rather, we take the opportunity to breathe during natural pauses that are determined by the linguistic content of what we are saying (Goldman-Eisler, 1968). In short, although speech that departs from an expected pattern will be harder to predict, the nature of the speech act itself can signal the listener that at least such an event is upcoming. Chapter 7 will discuss these and other issues in greater detail.

The lesson to be drawn from this discussion is that sentence perception is a surprisingly active process, even though it is ordinarily accomplished rapidly and without conscious effort. Sentence processing represents a continual analysis of the incoming speech stream to detect the structure and meaning of speakers' utterances as they are being heard. In order to discover how sentence processing takes place, we must understand how syntactic and semantic processing are accomplished by the listener. As we shall see, some theorists have claimed that syntactic structure and semantic analysis are conducted independently, while others have claimed that they are ordinarily processed at the same time, in an interactive fashion.

Syntactic processing

Syntactic resolution is needed for comprehension

Although the statistical properties of language say something about the consequences of the speaker's and listener's knowledge of language structure, they do not themselves explain this structure. The 1960s saw **transformational grammar** attempting to fulfill this goal. These attempts made two important points relevant to our discussion: the difference between surface structure and deep structure, and the difference between competence and performance.

Surface structure versus deep structure

The first point was a distinction between the *surface structure* and the *deep structure* of a sentence. The surface structure of a sentence is represented by the words you actually hear spoken or read; the specific words we have chosen to convey the meaning of what it is we wish to say. The task of the listener is to "decode" this surface structure to discover the meaning that underlies the utterance, what can be called the "deep structure" of the sentence.

Some sets of sentences have different surface structures, but the same deep structure. An example would be the pair of sentences, "The boy threw the ball," and "The ball was thrown by the boy." The specific words used, the surface structures of these sentences, are obviously different. The first sentence is a simple active declarative, and the second is a passive. In spite of this difference, both sentences focus on the fact that a boy threw a ball. The two sentences have different surface structures, but they convey the same meaning. They have the same deep structure.

By contrast, some sentences can have the same surface structure, but different deep structures. A well known example is the sentence, "Flying planes can be dangerous." This sentence could mean that it is dangerous to be a pilot, or it could mean that living near an airport can be dangerous.

The distinction between deep structure and surface structure makes an important point for our understanding of sentence processing. It tells us that sentence processing is conducted on two levels, in which the listener analyzes the surface structure, and uses this information to detect the deep structure. It is the latter that conveys the meaning of the sentence that is the primary goal of the communicator (Fodor, Bever, & Garrett, 1974).

Competence versus performance

The second point is that the way people produce language is not equivalent to what they know about language. Much of what we say consists of incomplete fragments that do not even approach a grammatical sentence (Goldman-Eisler, 1968). This does not mean that we do not have the knowledge to produce a complete sentence, or know the difference between an ungrammatical fragment and a grammatical sentence when we hear one. The specification of these rules is critical to an understanding of language *competence;* what the speaker knows about the structure of the language (Chomsky, 1957, 1965). For a theory of *performance,* we have to explain how we can understand speech, however incomplete and fragmentary it may be. A complete theory of sentence processing must thus take into account both competence and performance.

Syntactic structure and sentence parsing

In order to understand a sentence, it is necessary for the listener (or reader) to determine the syntactic structure of the sentence. The assignment of the words of a sentence to their relevant linguistic categories is referred to as *parsing* a sentence.

By way of example, take the simple declarative sentence, "The boy threw the ball." Figure 5.2 shows a tree diagram for this sentence that indicates the form-class (or, "part of speech") of each word, how the words can be grouped into phrases, and finally, how the phrase relationships form the structure of the sentence. That is, it tells us that this particular sentence is composed of two major phrases. The first is the *Noun Phrase* (NP), consisting of the article, or determiner (Det), "The," and the noun (N) "boy," followed by a *Verb Phrase* (VP), which is composed of the verb (V) "threw" and the noun phrase, "the ball."

This simple phrase-structure grammar shows that the noun phrase (the boy) and the verb phrase (threw the ball) form separate *units* of the sentence, in the sense that they derive from different higher-order nodes. The detection of such structures is an essential step for understanding the relationships between the objects and events within a sentence.

There are, of course, many sentences where the recognition of the correct constituent boundaries is less clear than in this example. Some of these are cases of phrase-structure ambiguities, where different hypotheses about the intended structure of a sentence could give rise to different meanings. An example of this would be the sentence, "They are eating apples." It is not immediately clear when you read this sentence whether *eating* is part of the verb, or whether *eating* is an adjective, modifying the noun *apples*; apples that are all right to eat on their own (*eating apples*), versus apples that are good only as ingredients in cakes and pies (*cooking apples*). We can express this parsing distinction with the two phrase structure diagrams for "They are eating apples" shown in Figure 5.3.

It is clearly the case that most sentences are more complex than even these simple examples. On the one hand, one could hear a sentence like that shown in

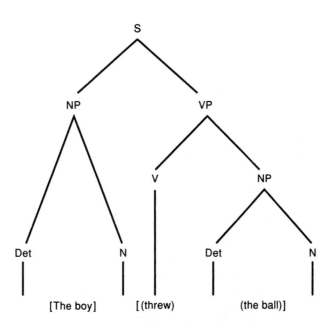

Figure 5.2

A phrase-structure grammar for the sentence, "The boy threw the ball."

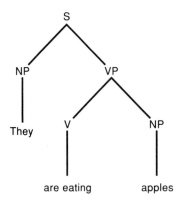

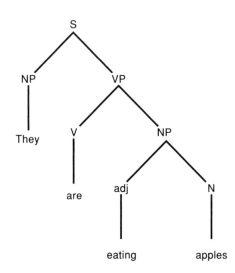

Figure 5.2 transformed into a passive version, (*The ball was thrown by the boy*), a passive negative version, (*The ball was not thrown by the boy*), a negative question, (*Did the boy not throw the ball?*), or a passive negative question, (*Was the ball not thrown by the boy?*) All of these versions derive from the basic active declarative, "The boy threw the ball." A part of the sentence processing task is to detect identities in underlying meanings of sentences in spite of differences in the surface structures represented by the different wordings of the sentences we might hear or read.

Complete understanding of a sentence must thus also take into account something referred to as "trace" theory. (The trace theory referred to here is a syntactic theory and is quite different from the TRACE model of speech perception in Chapter 3. See the glossary for definitions.)

Trace theory has three elements. The first is that linguistic constituents can move from one position to another as a speaker is organizing a sentence for production. The second is that this movement leaves a "trace" of the original constituent in the surface structure of the sentence. The third and final element is that detection of this trace by the listener is necessary for correct thematic role assignment. By this we mean that the sentence processor must reactivate the semantics of the correct lexical antecedent at the trace position (Chomsky, 1981; Nicol & Swinney, 1989). Although making some inferences about missing or moved elements of a sentence may require conscious effort, simple inferences, such as correctly activating the meaning of a pronoun referent, typically occurs rapidly and without awareness (Swinney & Osterhout, 1990).

An additional complicating factor is that many of the sentences with which we must deal have multiple clauses: "In order to achieve success, study and hard work are always necessary," or, "The mechanic who knows how to fix the car that my friend bought last year left on vacation." As we shall see later, sentences like these represent special processing problems.

Clausal processing

One way the perceptual system can reduce the processing load is to break up incoming sentences into their constituent clauses. To get a sense of this, take the sentence, "I was going to take a train to New York, but I decided it would be too heavy." The reason this old joke can still make people laugh is because of the way in which we processes complex utterances in terms of smaller, more manageable units. You will also see why comedians are referred to as having good "timing." This joke works best if the teller pauses for a few beats between delivering the two clauses.

Processing this sentence for meaning requires at least three operations. First, we take in and analyze the structure and meaning of the first clause, "I was going to take a train to New York," and temporarily store the product of this analysis in memory. Next, we analyze the second clause, "But I decided it would be too heavy," and temporarily store the product of this analysis. (A combined temporary memory and mental work space is sometimes called "working memory.") Finally, we retrieve the stored representation of the first phrase, and attempt to integrate it with the meaning of the second one. It is at this point that we begin to realize that it is funny. The delayed "double-take" people often exhibit after hearing this sort of joke—a look of confusion followed an instant later by amusement—is a measure of the time it takes for the incongruity to be appreciated.

This sense of processing speech by clauses is not just restricted to spoken language. When we look closely at people's reading strategies, we see that readers are also sensitive to boundaries between linguistic clauses. In a particularly interesting demonstration of this effect, Stine (1990) seated subjects in front of a computer which, when the space bar was pressed, would display on the screen the first word of a sentence the subject was told he or she would have to read, comprehend, and remember. With the next bar-press the first word of the sentence disappeared and the second word of the sentence appeared. This procedure continued, on a word-by-word basis, until the full sentence had been seen. Stine's interest was in the rate at which subjects felt ready for each subsequent word of the sentence. The computer automatically recorded subjects' word-by-word reading times as the time interval between successive bar-presses for each word.

Figure 5.4 shows an example of these data for a group of university students reading the sentence, "The Chinese, who used to produce kites, used them in order to carry ropes across the rivers." The jagged solid line running across the graph from left-to-right shows the average time (in milliseconds) that subjects dwelled on each word before pressing the bar for the next one. The dashed lines running above and below this average time show the range within which the majority of the reading times fell.

The pattern of word-by-word reading times across the sentence shows what we call a "scalloped" pattern: After reading the first NP (The Chinese), the subjects' time-per-word reading rates increased, until the completion of the first major clause boundary (ending with the word *kites*). At this point the reading rate slows presumably reflecting the readers' need for more time to process the clause content, and to integrate this content with the preceding NP. Once this point was passed, the

Figure 5.4

Average word-by-word
reading times (RTs) for
a sentence read by a
sample of college-age
readers. (The solid line
indicates median reading
time; dashed lines
indicate 25th and 75th
percentiles.)
(Source: E. A. L. Stine,
On-line processing of
written text by younger
and older adults.
Psychology and Aging,
1990, 5: Fig. 1, pg. 73.)

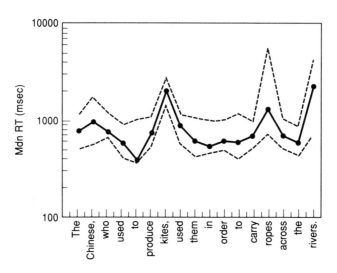

subjects' reading rate again increased, until the word *ropes* was reached. At this point subjects again dwelled on each word for a relatively long time, thus producing another scallop.

As Stine examined the patterns of reading times for many different sentences, she found an interesting generality. The more clauses (or chunks) a sentence contained, the higher was each successive peak, reflecting longer and longer processing times needed to integrate each new chunk into an increasingly rich coherence structure.

Although results like these have been shown before (Aaronson & Scarborough, 1977), Stine's experiment was particularly interesting because it took as its starting point the fact that elderly adults are often not as successful in remembering sentences as are young adults. For this reason, she also examined reading times for elderly adults matched with the young adults for years of education and general verbal ability. She found that subjects from both age groups were almost identical in the appearance of the scalloped pattern of their reading times: Both groups "chunked" the sentences into clauses in the same way. The difference was in the manner in which they allocated time at the peaks of the scallops, as the number of chunks increased. While the young adults showed an essentially linear increase in the time spent at each successive peak, the older adults did not.

To Stine, this analysis suggested that while the older adults allocated time to organize information between peaks (e.g., within clauses) just the way the young did, they did not allocate time to integrate the information across chunks as effectively as did the young. The fact that the two groups differed in subsequent memory for the sentence content might thus be attributable to the way the sentences were organized as they were originally being read (Stine, 1990).

In speech, especially when the syntactic structure or the semantic content is complex, we can often wish that speakers would pause for us at major clause boundaries, in order to give us time to digest what we have heard to that point. In reading, we can do this for ourselves by varying the dwell-time on the words as we read a sentence, with where we dwell, and for how long, depending on the structure of the sentence and the complexity of its content. We will return to the topic of clausal processing of spoken sentences later.

Meaning is the goal of sentence processing

The goal of sentence processing is to arrive at the meaning of the sentence. In formal terms, this means determining the semantic relationships between the rapidly arriving words. For this process to take place, the listener must analyze the acoustic information arriving at the ear in order to access the *lexicon*, the storehouse of our words and what we know about them, both on the semantic and syntactic level. Our ultimate goal is to develop the *propositional representation* of the utterance. This is the relationship among the objects, actions, and events described by the sentence.

Studies of sentence processing suggest that under ordinary circumstances we strive to comprehend the meaning of a sentence as quickly as possible, and then we discard the surface structure to retain only the meaning. In one study, Sachs (1967) had subjects listen to paragraph-length stories, which contained a critical test sentence. One story, for example, was about the invention of the telescope. It contained the target sentence, "He sent a letter about it to Galileo, the great Italian scientist."

As subjects listened to the passage, at a certain point a bell rang, and either the target sentence, or a sentence similar to it, was spoken. The subjects' task was to say whether or not this exact sentence had been heard in the passage.

The recognition sentences bore four possible relationships to the target sentence: (a) the *identical sentence*; (b) *Active/passive change*, in which the original sentence was changed from the active to passive form without changing the meaning (e.g., "A letter about it was sent to Galileo, the great Italian scientist."); (c) *Formal change*, in which the style of the wording was changed from the original sentence, but again without changing the meaning (e.g., "He sent Galileo, the great Italian scientist, a letter about it."); or (d) *Semantic change*, in which a sentence with similar wording to the original was presented, but with the meaning of the sentence changed (e.g., "Galileo, the great Italian scientist, sent him a letter about it.").

Figure 5.5 shows the subjects' accuracy of detecting changes of each kind, as a function of where in the original story the target sentence had occurred. When tested right after hearing the target sentence, any change from the original sentence was recognized by the subject. However, when the retention interval was increased, and filled with greater amounts of interpolated material, some changes were more difficult to detect than others. As time passed, subjects became less able to tell whether they were hearing the identical target sentence, or a sentence in which the wording had been changed without changing the meaning (*active/passive* or *formal* changes). By contrast, any semantic change from the original was easily detected, even after relatively long intervals. The semantic relations derived from the sentences are

212   *Sentence Processing*

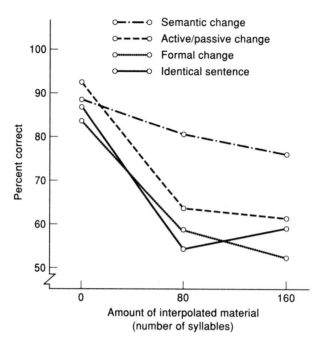

Figure 5.5

The ability to detect changes in a test sentence that involve either a change in wording without changing the meaning (an active/passive or a formal change), or a change in wording that does change the meaning (a semantic change). Accuracy is shown as a function of the amount of interpolated material received prior to testing. (Source: J. S. Sachs, Recognition memory for syntactic and semantic aspects of connected discourse. *Perception & Psychophysics*, 1967, 2: Fig. 2, pg. 441.)

important to people processing a sentence, and not the surface forms themselves. The former is durable in memory to a degree that the latter is not.

The importance of the meaning of a sentence over its surface form has been demonstrated many times in versions of Sachs' experiment (Bransford & Franks, 1971; Bransford, Barclay, & Franks, 1972).

Is there no memory at all for the specific words of a sentence after it has been heard? Under some circumstances this may be so. On the other hand, there may sometimes be retention of up to a sentence or two in a recoverable form, even if the trace is a rapidly fading one (Glanzer, Fischer, & Dorfman, 1984). As we shall see later, such a transient memory would be valuable in those cases where we initially misanalyze a sentence and must go back in memory to repair the mistake.

Numerous experiments have confirmed that immediate recall of sentences can be very accurate, but that we can usually recover from long-term memory only the meaning, or "gist," of what has been heard. Such experiments, however, do not necessarily mean that only the surface form of a sentence is initially stored in short-term memory. Indeed, Potter and Lombardi (1990) have argued that a conceptual representation of a sentence could be formed almost immediately, and that reproduction of the surface form could be accomplished by *regenerating* the original words from this representation. That is, the immediate recall of a sentence may not be due to accessing a short-term verbatim representation that can simply be "read off" word-for-word. It could be that short-term memory already holds a conceptual representation of the sentence and that apparent verbatim recall is the product of reconstructing the original sentence by piecing together in memory the sentence meaning and the fading traces of actual words and surface form.

If Potter and Lombardi are correct, this would imply that going back in memory to correct an initial parsing or interpretative error rests on our ability to correctly regenerate the original sentence, rather than simply reactivating a verbatim memory store. It is also possible that hearing a sentence is followed for a brief period by concurrent storage in memory of both semantic and surface representations, either of which can be tapped in a particular experiment.

Our point here is not that sentences may be represented conceptually in memory more quickly than some experiments might seem to imply. Our point is to reinforce the position that the goal of sentence processing is to extract meaning as quickly as possible, and that it is the conceptual representation of the utterance that is the primary focus of the memory system.

Is syntax processed separately from meaning?

At the time when modern psycholinguistics was first developing, psychology as a whole was largely dominated by "serial" models of mental operations. The possibility of massively parallel computers and neural network modeling was not yet on the horizon. Most theories of the time dwelled on the idea of simpler, more visualizable systems. In terms of language processing, it was common to see a four-stage model of sentence processing that followed the distinctions in general linguistics. These stages, which were assumed to operate in strict sequence, were processing at the level of phonology (the sound patterns of words), lexical processing (word identity or activation), syntactic processing (determination of grammatical structure), and semantic processing (processing the full utterance for meaning). Especially interesting was the proposal that syntactic processing must precede, and thus be conducted independently from, the semantic analysis of a sentence, where functional relationships are determined, and meaning of the utterance becomes available. This was sometimes referred to as the principle of *syntactic autonomy* (Garret, Bever, & Fodor, 1966).

In its earliest form, the idea of syntactic autonomy carried the implication that semantic analysis of a sentence could not begin until a major clause boundary or the end of the sentence had been reached. This view led to attempts to demonstrate the importance of syntactic clauses at the earliest stages of sentence processing.

A favorite technique was to insert a click into a recorded sentence and then ask listeners to say at which point in the sentence they thought the click had occurred (Fodor & Bever, 1965; Garret, Bever, & Fodor, 1966). For example, a subject might hear the sentence given below, which consists of a dependent clause, "In order to catch his train," followed by an independent clause "George drove furiously to the station." Subjects heard the sentence with a prerecorded click sound occurring either within the first clause (e.g., position [1]), at the boundary between the two clauses (e.g., position [2]), or somewhere in the second clause (e.g., position [3]).

"In order to catch [1] his train, [2] George drove [3] furiously to the station."

Over the course of hearing many such sentences, it was reliably demonstrated that subjects not only tended to be more accurate at saying where the click occurred when it had been presented between clauses than within a clause. When subjects made a mistake in saying where a click had occurred, they tended to report the click as having occurred either at the boundary, or closer to the boundary, than it actually did. Why did the subjective impression of where the click had occurred tend to "migrate" toward the major syntactic boundary of the sentence?

The so called "click studies" were originally interpreted as demonstrating that major linguistic clauses represent the *perceptual units* of sentence processing. When steps were taken to eliminate the pauses and changes in intonation pattern that usually accompany major clause boundaries, clicks located at clause boundaries were still more accurately localized than clicks presented within a clause (Garret, Fodor, & Bever, 1966). Thus it was argued that the perceptual isolation of the linguistic clause was the first step in sentence processing, and formal syntactic structure alone was sufficient to tell the listener where the clause boundary had occurred.

Few paradigms in psycholinguistics research drew as much fire as did the early click studies. The questions were not based on whether or not clauses are important elements in sentence structure. They clearly are. The questions were first, whether or not prosody is as unimportant to detecting syntactic boundaries of sentences as originally claimed, and second, whether these click effects reflected the way the sentences were actually perceived, or whether the click "migration" occurred in memory as the subject tried to recall where the click had occurred. For example, the migration effect is greatly reduced, although not completely eliminated, when subjects do not have to recall the entire sentence when saying where an extraneous sound had occurred, but instead are allowed to point at a script as they listen to the sentence (Wingfield & Klein, 1971).

The role of prosody in sentence processing

Prosody is a general term for the variety of acoustic features that ordinarily accompany a spoken sentence. One of these prosodic features is the *intonation pattern* of a sentence. Intonation refers to pitch changes over time, as when a speaker's voice rises in pitch at the end of a question, or drops at the end of a sentence. A second prosodic feature is *word stress* which is, in fact, a complex subjective variable based on loudness, pitch, and timing. Two final prosodic features are the pauses that sometimes occur at the ends of sentences or major clauses, and the lengthening of final vowels in words immediately prior to a clause boundary (Cooper & Sorensen, 1981; Lehiste, 1970; Streeter, 1978).

Prosody plays a number of important roles in language processing. Prosody can indicate the mood of a speaker (happy, angry, sad, sarcastic), it can mark the semantic focus of a sentence (Jackendoff, 1972), and it can be used to disambiguate the meaning of an otherwise ambiguous sentence, such as "I saw a man in the park with a telescope," (Beach, 1991; Wales & Toner, 1979).

A more subtle effect of prosody is the way it can be used to mark major clauses of a sentence. Consider the sentence, "In order to do well, he studied very hard." If you say this sentence aloud, you will notice how clearly the clause boundary (it is indicated here by the comma), is marked by intonation, stress, and timing. Note especially how speakers automatically lengthen the final vowel in the word just prior to the clause boundary (in this case, the word *well*).

Although a very ingenious splicing technique was used by Garrett and his colleagues to eliminate prosodic cues, this had the effect of underestimating their importance when such cues were present. When studies analogous to the "click" studies are conducted, but with the formal clause boundary and the prosodic marking for a clause boundary placed in direct conflict, "clicks" just as often migrate to the point marked by prosody as to the formal syntactic boundary (Wingfield & Klein, 1971).

Probably no experiment cast as dramatic doubt on whether or not the click studies were tapping on-line perceptual segmentation rather than reflecting a postperceptual response bias than a study conducted by Reber and Anderson (1970). They found results parallel to the original click studies even when subjects were falsely told that the sentences they would hear had "subliminal" clicks placed in them, and asked to say where they thought these clicks had occurred. Although no clicks were actually presented, subjects more often reported having heard them at clause boundaries than as occurring within clauses.

It is certainly the case that clauses are important to the way people remember speech. In one series of experiments, subjects heard a tape-recorded passage that was stopped without warning at various spots in the passage. The moment the tape was stopped, subjects were asked to recall as large a segment as possible of what had just been heard. Generally, subjects' recall was bounded by full clauses, just as one would expect if major linguistic clauses do have structural integrity (Jarvella, 1970, 1971). The importance of clause boundaries, and other syntactic constituents, can also be demonstrated by giving subjects tape-recorded passages and telling them to interrupt the tape whenever they want to immediately recall what they had just heard. In such cases, subjects reliably press the tape recorder pause button to give their recall at periodic intervals corresponding exactly with the end of major clauses and other important syntactic boundaries (Wingfield & Butterworth, 1984).

We should not dismiss all elements of an autonomy principle out of hand. Indeed, we will later review evidence for some degree of autonomous processing in the form of activation of word meaning independent of the sentence context in which the word is embedded. Few writers today, however, espouse the early version of syntactic autonomy that implied that analysis at the semantic level must await completion of a full clause or sentence boundary in the speech stream.

We do not want to suggest that clauses are unimportant units in sentence processing. Nor do we have to reject the idea of an active syntactic processor operating early in sentence perception, attempting to detect the completion of syntactic and functional relationships as early as possible (Flores d'Arcais & Schreuder, 1983).

Rather, our question is whether both syntactic and semantic analyses occur together, in a continuously interactive fashion, as a sentence is being heard. Let us examine the principles of an interactive view of sentence processing before returning to the arguments for processing autonomy still current in the literature.

On-line interactive models of sentence processing

We opened this chapter by stressing the speed with which spoken language must be comprehended when listening to everyday speech. In this regard we can see the attraction of an autonomy principle. The expression, "autonomy," means *independence*. Would the fastest system be one in which an autonomous syntactic processor was allowed to run independently at its own rate? This might be the case if we imagined a rapid parser that would only be slowed down if it had to continually cross-check its operation against possible semantic interpretations derived from prior context. Or would sentence processing be faster if information from all levels of analysis could interact freely with knowledge obtained at one level being allowed to facilitate on-line processing at other levels? This would be referred to as an **interactive model of language processing** (Tyler & Marslen-Wilson, 1977).

Both autonomous and interactive models would seem to have some virtue in a language processing system that features speed, interpretive accuracy, and the least possible demands in terms of processing resources. As we indicated, we will review evidence that initial lexical activation, even in a sentence context, may represent an autonomous, automatic process, that occurs free of interaction with other levels of sentence processing. On the other hand, there is equally persuasive evidence that, at least at the level of conscious awareness, listeners make excellent use of prior context in their analysis of what is being heard.

An interactive view of sentence processing begins with **bottom-up processing**. This refers to the way in which the listener's sensory apparatus detects and analyzes the acoustic speech signal, processing it upward from the level of the acoustic waveform, to the level of the recognition of phonemes, words, sentence structure, and finally, the recognition of semantic relations between the sentence elements that give rise to the sentence meaning. In our discussion of language structure, we also saw that listeners are quite adept at developing expectations of what they have yet to hear, based on the structure and meaning of what they have already heard to that point. The term **top-down processing** refers to the potential use of such knowledge in order to speed, clarify, or otherwise facilitate the processing of emerging information from bottom-up sources.

Imagine you were trying to understand an indistinct voice over a noisy telephone line. You have impoverished bottom-up information. To the extent that you could utilize linguistic context to supplement this degraded information, we would refer to your success as being the product of an effective *top-down/bottom-up interaction*. It is the contention of those who support an interactive model, that knowledge-driven, top-down information and sensory-driven, bottom-up information, continually interact not only when the signal source is degraded. It is also believed that all language processing is inherently interactive even when the signal clarity is good. Such models are called *on-line interactive models* because they assume that semantic processing co-occurs with syntactic processing as the speech is being heard. *Off-line* processes also occur, but these refer to later interpretive, or retrospective operations, that occur some time after the speech has been heard.

The comprehension system we are describing is one in which as much syntactic and semantic processing is carried out as possible, as each word of the sentence is heard. As the identity of each word is activated, its syntactic category is determined, and a hypothesis about the next syntactic element is generated. Encountering the determiner, *the*, you have an expectation that a noun is upcoming, either as the next word, or perhaps as the next word following an adjective modifying the upcoming noun. As each element arrives, full noun phrases and verb phrases are identified as soon as possible (Just & Carpenter, 1987; Thibadeau, Just, & Carpenter, 1982). An interactive model assumes not only that the meaning of the utterance is developed along with syntactic processing. It also assumes that prior semantic operations facilitate subsequent parsing decisions.

In such a system, all sources of information would be used. One source might be the phonological information that affects word recognition, such as the acoustic coloring of sounds that results from their syllabic environment. Other sources of information include the syntactic frame that leads you to expect a word of a certain form-class, as well as information based on the semantic constraints derived from the sentence meaning.

These interactions can account for the results of studies that show prior context has a significant effect on the speed and ease with which a word seen or heard in a linguistic context can be recognized (Morton, 1969, 1970; Marslen-Wilson & Tyler, 1987).

In some interactive models, expectations generated by the linguistic and real-world context are thought to operate by influencing the recognizability of likely words even before any of their sensory information has been received (Morton, 1969; Becker, 1980). In other interactive models, context is assumed to operate only *after* the sensory information supplied by the first part of the word (the "bottom-up" portion of the mix) has activated a mental list of potential candidates. It is proposed that no matter how powerful a particular context might be, it will not influence the number of candidates initially activated on the basis of bottom-up information. Context can only operate by quickly eliminating initially activated possibilities that do not fit the ongoing context (Marslen-Wilson & Tyler, 1987).

Interactive models are thus a major alternative to the early clausal hypothesis that assumed that syntactic and semantic analyses are conducted independently, and that analysis for meaning is not begun until a full sentence or clause boundary has been reached. In the interactive models, it is assumed that syntactic and semantic processing of sentences proceed together. The proponents of the interactive view believe that it is because we are able to mix the product of perceptual "bottom-up" analysis of the acoustic signal with "top-down" support from prior context that spoken sentences can be processed so rapidly.

"Shadowing" and "gating studies"

We can get a sense of top-down input whenever someone finishes a sentence for us. There is no claim in any of these interactive models, however, that this interactive process is conscious, or volitional, as it would be in this example. Rather, the interaction is assumed to be rapid, and inaccessible to conscious awareness. How can we get a window on this on-line interactive processing so as to test the contention that prior context automatically places constraints on the perception of lower level information?

One particularly ingenious study was conducted by Marslen-Wilson (1975) who had subjects listen to spoken passages, and to repeat what they were hearing as it was being heard. This is called "shadowing" or "echoing." It may sound difficult, but it is in fact quite easy, and subjects rarely lag much behind the speech they are shadowing. Marslen-Wilson found some subjects who were "close" shadowers; they were able to speak almost simultaneously with what they were hearing. (We have known some children to do this to adult speech just to annoy the adults.)

Marslen-Wilson found that even his close shadowing subjects would often spontaneously correct errors in pronunciation or grammar that had been intentionally placed into the recorded speech they were shadowing. To Marslen-Wilson, the important finding was that these unconscious corrections were made even before the incorrect word on the tape was fully completed. From the lags obtained, he estimated that recognition for words heard in context can occur within 200 milliseconds of their onset.

This time estimate was confirmed by Grosjean (1980) using a technique known as **gating**. Grosjean presented subjects with recorded sentences which included only the first 50 milliseconds of the last word in the sentence. The subject was asked to listen to the sentence and then to say what he or she thought the last word of the sentence was. If the subject was unable to do this the sentence was again presented, this time followed by the first 100 milliseconds of the last word, then the first 150 milliseconds, and so on, until the word could be correctly identified. This technique is called "gating" because in the early experiments an electronic "gate" was opened (and closed) to control the amount of the speech a subject would be allowed to hear.

Grosjean found that words in context could be recognized within 175 to 200 milliseconds of their onset, or when only half or less than half, of their full acoustic signal had been heard. The average time for words out of context was 333 milliseconds. Although this may seem surprising, the fact is that there are only a limited number of words in the lexicon that share the same initial sounds (the word-initial *cohort*). Further, this number decreases quite dramatically as more and more of a word onset is heard. For example, if one were to access a standard dictionary and count the total number of different picturable nouns, we would find an average of 115 different nouns that share the same sounds in the first 50 milliseconds of the spoken word. By the time the first 100 milliseconds of the word onset has been heard, the number drops to 43 words, then to 11 words after 200 milliseconds, and only 5 by 300 milliseconds (Wayland, Wingfield, & Goodglass, 1989). To put these figures in perspective, depending on speech-rate, typical one-, two-, and three-syllable words may average between 550 to 830 milliseconds in full duration.

The effect of context would presumably be to reduce the initial cohort of possible words based on word-onset sound, to those that could reasonably "fit" within the sentence frame heard (Tyler, 1984). Less clear is whether there is a reduction in cohort size based on context alone, without phonological information (Morton, 1969); if context begins to take effect only after the beginning sounds have activated the full cohort (Marslen-Wilson, 1987); or if context only operates after the word is fully specified and activated in the lexicon (Forster, 1979). The idea that context alone reduces cohort size is now thought unlikely: As Marslen-Wilson (1987) has suggested, real world survival demands a bottom-up priority to some degree in the processing system. It is important that we are able to detect sounds that signal danger, no matter how unlikely they might be in a particular context.

How on-line is gating?

The process we wish to understand, of course, is the real-time analysis of the speech input, and the automatized "core processes" involved in language understanding (Tyler & Wessels, 1985, p. 18). In gating, subjects typically have unlimited time to write down or to say aloud their answer after hearing a word-onset fragment. As we noted earlier, some theorists have argued that context only functions after the word has been accessed (Forster, 1979). If the subjects' responses in gating experiments are in fact produced only after a period of conscious (or unconscious) reflection, the effects of context seen in these studies could be occurring during a brief interval between the end of some automatic, context independent processes, and the subjects' overt responses.

Deciding whether gating taps on-line processes or later ones is not easy. Tyler and Wessels (1985) suggested that perhaps if subjects were forced to respond rapidly in a gating task, one might be on safer ground arguing that their responses did reflect the product of true on-line processing.

Their stimuli for this experiment consisted of gated words presented in the context of two prior sentences. The sentence pairs were selected such that one sentence of each pair would provide either a weak or a strong syntactic constraint, and the other sentence of the pair would have wording that would make the target word either semantically anomalous or else it would offer a minimal semantic context. (Because a very strong semantic context can make any word-onset information redundant, they used only a weak semantic context for this experiment.)

The sentence pairing possibilities are listed here in decreasing order of their value in reducing the amount of word-onset information necessary for correct identification of a gated word: (1) Minimal semantic constraint + Strong syntactic constraint (*Min Sem/Strong Syn*); (2) Minimal semantic constraint + Weak syntactic constraint (*Min Sem/Weak Syn*); (3) Anomalous semantic context + Strong syntactic constraint (*Anom/Strong Syn*); and (4) Anomalous semantic context + Weak syntactic constraint (*Anom/Weak Syn*). In a final condition, gated words were presented with no linguistic context whatsoever (*No-Context*).

Here are the three steps Tyler and Wessels took to get fast responses and more immediate reactions within the gating paradigm. First, instead of repeatedly presenting the context sentences with increasingly larger word-onset fragments of the target word, each subject heard a given word-fragment only once. The amount of word onset information needed for identification in the various context conditions was determined by using large numbers of subjects, with different subjects receiving word-onset fragments of different sizes. Second, Tyler and Wessels used two measures of word identification. The first was the *isolation point*, which was defined as the smallest average gate size which allowed subjects to give the correct answer, regardless of how uncertain they might be of their answer. The second was the *recognition point*. This is a later point at which subjects not only gave the correct word, but where they rated their confidence in their judgment fairly highly. Finally, Tyler and Wessels contrasted *nontimed responses*, where subjects were placed under no time pressure to give their responses, with *timed responses*, where they were asked to respond as quickly as possible. They argued that timed responses at the isolation point might come closer to tapping on-line processing than the usual procedures of nontimed responses at the higher-confidence recognition point. Their results are shown in Figure 5.6.

When subjects give an overt response in an experiment, we can never be sure what sorts of processes may have preceded that response at a level inaccessible to conscious awareness. As we shall see in the next section, this is a problem that has plagued psycholinguistics investigators since the earliest days. Although Tyler and Wessels did observe effects on gate sizes of timed versus nontimed responses, and of using isolation versus recognition points, they were even more impressed with the similarities in the gate sizes. Most important to them was that the pattern of the effects of linguistic context was the same, regardless of the length of the time-lag before the response was given. On the basis of this reasoning, they concluded that the gating technique can be used to tap on-line processes.

Why did syntactic form-class constraints have such a small effect on word identification times? When Tyler and Wessels first found this effect in an earlier study (Tyler & Wessels, 1983), they interpreted the finding in terms of cohort theory. They accepted the likelihood that form-class constraints might be expected to reduce the initial cohort to just those words that belong to one, or a few, possible syntactic categories. A syntactic constraint, however, would not ordinarily reduce the possible cohort size to the same degree as would a semantic constraint. To take a previous example, the semantic constraint offered by the sentence frame, "The train pulled into the. . . ." does more than constrain the next word to a noun, or to an adjective modifying a noun. It raises the likelihood of either one of two words occurring: *tunnel* or *station*.

There are cases where syntactic information can specifically isolate the correct meaning of an ambiguous word, such as *watch*. This would be the case simply by knowing from the sentence structure whether the word is a noun or a verb. Even in such cases, however, Tyler and Wessels suggest that syntactic constraints do not

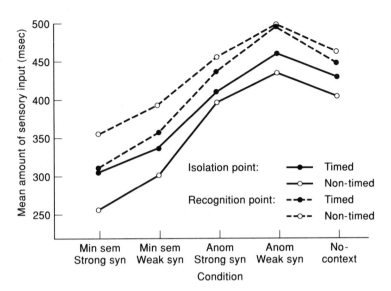

Figure 5.6

Mean isolation points and mean recognition points for gated words heard either with no context or with one of four combinations of types of linguistic context. Responses were either made at the subjects' own pace (nontimed) or when subjects were asked to respond as quickly as possible after hearing the target fragment (timed responses). (Source: L. K. Tyler & J. Wessels, Is gating an on-line task? Evidence from naming latency data. *Perception & Psychophysics*, 1985, *38*: Fig. 1, pg. 220.)

seem to operate immediately. Indeed, they cite data from Seidenberg, Tanenhaus, Leiman, & Bienkowski (1982), who claim that effects of syntactic form-class disambiguation of this kind can only be detected some 200 milliseconds after a word has been identified (Tyler & Wessels, 1983, p. 418).

Because syntactic constraints had a relatively small effect in the Tyler and Wessels experiment, we should not forget the importance of syntax in ordinary language processing. As we have seen, syntactic information plays a key role in the listener's ability to develop the meaning of a sentence. As Tyler and Wessels cautioned when they obtained a similar finding in an earlier experiment: "Perhaps one moral of the present study is that an information source that is important in one aspect of the system does not need to be important in every aspect" (Tyler & Wessels, 1983, p. 418).

Where does context operate?

Modularity theorists are those who believe that input processes, such as lexical activation, are cognitively impenetrable. That is, these operations are performed rapidly, automatically, and uninfluenced by prior or collateral information. In cognitive theory, such modular processes are thus said to be "informationally encapsulated" (Fodor, 1983).

Although this level of cognitive theory is beyond the scope of this chapter, let us see how a modular process would operate in sentence processing. One version can be derived from an early proposal by Forster (1979) who defined what he believed to be three separate processing systems devoted to language processing. (The model had other elements that need not concern us here.)

The first system he called the *lexical processor*. It activates particular lexical (word) entries based on input from peripheral systems that deal with phonological input in speech (or orthographic input in writing). The output of the lexical processor is passed to the next level, a *syntactic processor*. This processor extracts information from the lexical output level in order to conduct a syntactic analysis of the sentence leading to a surface structure representation. The final level of interest to us is that of a *message processor*. This was said to convert the linguistic representation into a conceptual, or meaning, structure that represents the semantic intention of the intended message.

In contrast with interactive models, in Forster's conceptualization, no processor would have any information from operations conducted by any of the higher level processors. In this scheme, for example, the lexical processor would work independently, or "autonomously," from both the syntactic and the message-level processors, and the syntactic processor would operate independently from the message processor. You can now see again the two contrasting views, both based on the speed of normal processing. The interactive model presumes that the only way people can handle speech so rapidly is because all levels of analysis are able to interact continuously with all other levels. The autonomous view suggests that lexical analysis is so rapid because it is not slowed by the need to integrate context as you are processing each word.

One way to view the autonomy question is to consider the possibility that while interactive processes might operate at a slower, conscious level of awareness of what we are hearing, the moment-to-moment analyses of the sentence's words are so fast and so automatic that the analysis at any one level is finished, and its output delivered to the next higher level before any information from the higher levels could possibly be brought to bear on them. Both positions presume multiple levels of processing. One assumes that all of these levels are constantly interacting with each other (e.g., that the lexical processor has at its disposal, and can be influenced by, semantic and message-level knowledge). The other position assumes that each processing level can be seen as an impenetrable, informationally encapsulated module, whose work is conducted autonomously from any other similarly modular process.

According to the autonomous theories, there is a clear limit on the way that contextual information could affect the bottom-up analysis at the word level. Specifically, linguistic or real world context could contribute to the evaluation of the output of the lexical processor, but it would not influence the operations of the lexical processor that led to this output.

How could we peek into automatic unconscious processing activity to see whether or not semantic context is operating on a word the instant it is being heard rather than later? For example, would an ambiguous word heard in a sentence context have only its contextually constrained meaning activated (as would be predicted by an interactive model), or are even unlikely meanings of a word initially activated the instant the word is heard (as would be predicted by an autonomous model)?

Cross-modal lexical priming

An experiment by Swinney (1979) suggested that, at an immediate automatic level, semantic activation takes place independent of the context that precedes it. Swinney's experiment made use of the phenomenon of *priming*, the somewhat unmodular fact that the processing of a word will be facilitated by having just seen or heard another word that is semantically related to it (Meyer, Schvaneveldt, & Ruddy, 1975; Neely, 1977). One way to show this priming effect is to measure the speed of naming (e.g., reading aloud) the second word. You will be faster reading aloud the word "nurse" flashed on a computer screen when it is preceded (either in writing or spoken through earphones) by the semantically related word "patient," than if it is preceded by the unrelated word "saucer." A second way to demonstrate semantic priming is to measure the speed with which you can decide whether or not a string of letters forms a real word. Using the above example, we could demonstrate the effect of semantic priming by showing that it takes you less time to decide that "nurse" is a real word (as opposed to the scrambled letters "surne") if it is preceded by "patient" than if it is preceded by "saucer." This word/nonword judgment is referred to as a **lexical decision** task.

Swinney used a version of this task referred to as **cross-modal lexical priming**. His goal was to see whether a local linguistic context would constrain access to just the appropriate meaning of an ambiguous word as implied by the context, or whether other meanings of the ambiguous word would also automatically be activated. For example, there are many words in English that have homophones. (*Homophones* are pairs of words that have different meanings but that share the same sound.) At a conscious level, if you were hearing the word "bark" in the context of someone telling you about their new puppy, you would probably not be distracted by, or even think of, the fact that "bark" also has another meaning as the outer covering of a tree trunk. Could it be, however, that—even though it is inaccessible to conscious awareness— at the instant you heard the word "bark," *both* meanings of the word were momentarily activated?

Swinney first made a tape-recording of a person reading the following passage in a natural tone at a normal rate of speech:

"Rumor had it that, for years, the government building had been plagued with problems. The man was not surprised when he found several spiders, roaches, and other bugs [1] in the [2] corner of the room."

The ambiguous word, of course, is the word *bugs*, which has at least two meanings known to most of us. One of these is the meaning of bugs in the sense of insects, and the other is the term for a hidden microphone, a term introduced into the lexicon by numerous espionage stories and movies.

At the moment the word *bugs* was heard, Swinney flashed on a screen for a lexical decision, a word that was either related to the contextually appropriate meaning of *bugs* (e.g., the word ANT), a word related to the contextually inappropriate meaning (e.g., SPY), or a control word that was unrelated to either meaning (e.g., SEW). These visual probes were presented either immediately after the ambiguous word, at the position marked as [1], or at a point several syllables later [2].

Swinney found that for subjects who saw the probe words presented at position [1], the lexical decisions for both ANT and for SPY were significantly faster than for lexical decisions to a semantically unrelated control word such as SEW. By the time several hundred milliseconds had passed (position [2]), however, only the word related to the contextually appropriate meaning of the word (e.g., the word ANT) was facilitated.

These results appear to support modularity at the lexical level. At the moment the spoken word was heard, there was a significant facilitation for lexical decisions to visually presented words that were related to both meanings of the ambiguous word, even when the word had been preceded by what should have been a highly constraining lexical-semantic context. Some time after the word had been heard (position [2]), activation was only present for the contextually appropriate meaning of the word, with the inappropriate meaning of the word having either rapidly decayed or rapidly been inhibited. Context did have an effect on meaning, but only after a first stage of automatic "modular" activation.

In a series of follow-up experiments, Onifer and Swinney (1981) confirmed this earlier finding by including ambiguous words where one meaning is ordinarily more common than the other, presenting them also in very strongly biasing contexts:

"The postal clerk put the package on the *scale* [1] to see if [2] there was sufficient postage."

or:

"The dinner guests enjoyed the specially prepared river bass, although one guest did get a *scale* [1] caught in his [2] throat."

The results showed that even for subjects who heard the first sentence, where the sentence context implied the more frequent meaning of the word "scale," both meanings of the word were activated at the instant in time indicated by position [1]. As before, for subjects who had the lexical decision tested at position [2], only the contextually appropriate meaning of the target word appeared to be activated.

These data are indicative of a sentence comprehension system composed of autonomous subsystems, called modules, that act automatically, and are uninfluenced by higher level processes. When an ambiguous word is heard, all of its meanings are activated. If a context is present, it operates only at a later point in time to select among possible meanings and to allow only the contextually appropriate one to come into conscious awareness. Although the technique of cross-modal lexical priming has received the most attention in the literature, a variety of experimental tasks have been used to support the general view that lexical access is automatic and uninfluenced, at least in its initial stages, by context. (See Simpson, 1984, for a review).

The cross-modal lexical priming technique has produced some interesting results, and has made the important point that many operations may be going on at an unconscious automatic level, about which we have no conscious access. Why would all meanings of an ambiguous word be activated regardless of context? Recall that these ambiguous words were homophones: words like *bug* or *scale*, that are really two different words in the sense that they represent two different concepts, but that, when spoken, share the same sound pattern.

As we noted earlier, even if top-down information is important to language processing at one level, at another level our real world survival would still demand a bottom-up priority in auditory processing. In times of danger we must be able to detect what is being heard, rather than what is expected to be heard (Marslen-Wilson, 1987). It would not be helpful to survival if the unlikelihood of encountering a lion in your back yard would prevent you from correctly identifying its roar when you heard it.

There is much to be said for a system that takes no chances, a system that activates every possible meaning of an acoustic input before using other information, such as context, to eliminate all but the appropriate interpretation. For nonhomophones that share only word-onsets, the picture seems fairly simple. For example, hearing a word that begins with the sound "cap" may activate both *captain* and *capital* (and hence, in a priming study, prime both *salute* and *money*). However, by the time you have heard the full word, only one of these possibilities remains. This process has been studied using techniques that combine features of both gating and cross-modal lexical priming (Marslen-Wilson & Zwitserlood, 1989).

Homophones, like *capital* and *capitol*, however, are an interesting case. The processing system cannot distinguish between them even when the full word has been completed. Can we extrapolate from the special case of homophones heard in a sentence context, to sentence processing in general? If we can, our conclusion would have to be that context does not come into play in lexical access as the speech is being heard, but that it influences our conscious perception of appropriate meaning.

The results from cross-modal lexical priming do not negate the importance of prior context in sentence processing. What they do is to suggest the displacement of the effects in time. Context acted not to prevent automatic activation of both word-meanings, but to allow the listener to select the correct one very quickly.

The view expressed here is an important one to modular theories of language processing, but the issue is not closed. There are those who suggest that selective (pre)activation of the dominant meaning might occur if the context is sufficiently constraining (Simpson & Krueger, 1991). Others argue a middle position: That sentence contexts do not preselect appropriate lexical entries, but that the process of eliminating the contextually inappropriate ones begins as the word is being heard (Zwitserlood, 1989).

As we conclude this section, the reader should know that both autonomous and interactive models have their adherents, and there is evidence in support of both. At issue is not whether top-down support is available to immediate speech processing, nor whether some processes are automatic and autonomous. What is at issue is the exact microstructure of events in the first few hundred milliseconds of on-line operations. We can only report that the search is underway for the right microscope.

Syntactic ambiguity: How do you parse an ambiguous sentence?

In the previous section we described experiments that focused on ambiguity about the meanings of words (e.g., *bug* in the sense of insects vs. *bug* as a term for a hidden microphone). As we have already seen, ambiguity occurs in syntactic and semantic domains, as well as in lexical domains. The occurrence of such ambiguities, and the fact that language comprehension runs along smoothly in spite of this, has long been of interest in psycholinguistics. As Connine, Blasko, and Hall (1991) point out, this is so because the way ambiguities are handled by listeners (and readers) can offer valuable insights into general processing principles in language comprehension.

Ambiguities about which of the two nouns you are hearing will certainly affect the implications of a sentence (whether to call the police or an exterminator if you find a bug in your room). However, such ambiguities will not affect the way you interpret the syntactic structure of the sentence. Mistaking a noun for a verb, or a verb for a noun, on the other hand, will. The "garden path" sentence, "The old man the boat," is confusing because people tend to assume that "The old man" is a noun phrase, which leads one to expect a following verb. Only if you correctly classify "The old" as the noun phrase and "man" as a verb (meaning "to operate") does the sentence now make sense.

The term *local ambiguity* is used to describe cases where the syntactic function of a word, or how to parse a sentence, eventually gets clarified as we hear the rest of a sentence (Frazier & Rayner, 1989). If we are forced to remain uncertain for too long, however, a sentence will be hard to understand. The sentence, "The rat the cat the dog chased bit ate the cheese," is difficult because we have to hold too many incomplete substructures before the sentence is finally complete and the full structure can be seen (Chomsky & Miller, 1963).

Abney and Johnson (1991) clearly summarize the complexities of memory requirements and parsing strategies in the resolution of local ambiguities. A parser could adopt a "wait and see" attitude, holding off making a decision until more information is available. This, however, would tax memory. On the other hand, a parsing strategy that keeps memory load to a minimum would run the risk of making many preliminary parsing errors at points of local syntactic ambiguity. Some theorists, like Frazier (1979), have emphasized the need to minimize memory requirements, while others, such as Marcus (1980), have emphasized the need to avoid local ambiguities, hence putting a greater burden on memory.

We would not, at this time, wish to delineate the possible parsing systems a sentence processor might employ. Good reviews of the highlights are given by Abney and Johnson (1991) and by Clifton, Speer, and Abney (1991).

The term *standing ambiguity* refers to cases of sentences that remain syntactically ambiguous even when all of the lexical information has been received. For example, the sentence, "The old books and magazines were on the bench," remains ambiguous even when the sentence is finished because it is not clear whether there should be a major syntactic boundary after "books" (the books were old, but the magazines may not have been), or whether the boundary should follow "magazines" (making it clear that both the books and the magazines were old). We can easily mark the intended boundary in speech by using such prosodic features as stress, intonation, and pauses (Beach, 1991).

The prosodic pattern in which the sentence is spoken could also be used to resolve local or temporary ambiguity: in principle, the idea of ambiguity might not even occur to a listener in the first place.

Beach (1991) illustrates this point by noting the way people spontaneously speak sentences that would certainly be syntactically ambiguous if you were reading them (Frazier & Rayner, 1982): "The city council argued the mayor's position forcefully," or "The city council argued the mayor's position was incorrect." The sentences are temporarily ambiguous because you do not know until after the word "position" whether or not there should be a clause boundary after "argued." When spoken aloud, natural stress can easily resolve such temporary ambiguity (Beach, 1991). Indeed, there is the view that prosodic cues can operate effectively at the earliest stages of parsing and interpretation in sentence comprehension (Marslen-Wilson, Tyler, Warren, Grenier, & Lee, 1992).

The role of memory in sentence processing

Although most sentence processing is conducted rapidly, as the speech is being heard, we have seen arguments for the necessity of a memory component in sentence processing to allow for necessary down-stream operations. Martin (1990) has divided these needs into three categories.

Speech perception and lexical identification

The first of these would be cases in connected speech where the acoustic input is ambiguous. We used one of Martin's examples earlier. This was the sentence pair, "I *better* do my laundry," and "I *bet her* five dollars," in which the italicized segments are pronounced identically. Martin points out that it is often the linguistic context that *follows* the ambiguous region that corrects the ambiguity. In a similar way, a poorly articulated word may not be recognized until more of the sentence following that word has been heard (Connine, Blasko, & Hall, 1991; Grosjean, 1985). For either forms of recovery to be possible, the phonological information would have to be retained, albeit for a short period, until the clarifying information has been reached.

Syntactic parsing and retention of phrases

In discussing the work of Sachs (1967) (Figure 5.5.), we saw that memory for phonological and syntactic information fades at a much faster rate than does the representation of meaning. The more quickly a listener can develop the propositional representation of a sentence, the less dependent the listener will have to be on the rapidly fading trace of the surface features.

As we have seen, however, the drive to determine functional relations as quickly as possible runs the risk of premature closure on an incorrect meaning that will have to be corrected as more information is received. Earlier we gave an example of a garden path sentence. These are sentences in which the wording (intentionally or not) invites people to take the wrong interpretive "path" at a point of local ambiguity. Such sentences are so hard to understand that people are convinced that they are ungrammatical. Consider the garden path sentence, "Since Jay always jogs a mile seems like a short distance to him." Either when reading the sentence, or hearing it spoken without clear prosodic marking, it would be easy to assign an incorrect structure in the ambiguous region around *a mile*: You might incorrectly assign *a mile* as the direct object of *jogs* (e.g., "Jay jogs a mile"), rather than as the subject of the main clause (e.g., "A mile seems a short distance to him.").

Frazier and Rayner (1982) measured eye-fixation times in reading sentences such as this one, and showed that the words following the ambiguous region were dwelled on much longer than for sentences where the wording better steered the reader toward the correct parsing (e.g., "Since Jay always jogs a mile this seems like a short distance to him.").

Although a reader can reread a part of a sentence where a parsing confusion may arise, listeners do not have this luxury. Martin (1990) suggests that a brief memory representation for the surface form of the sentence would be required for any hope of repairing the initial parsing error.

In addition to having the capability for correcting parsing errors, a transient memory representation is also needed to allow integration of phrases and clauses to develop full utterance meaning (van Dijk & Kintsch, 1983). When the speech input is especially rapid, or an unfamiliar word is encountered, words and phrases may continue to arrive even as we are still analyzing or attempting to integrate what has already been heard. Martin argues, quite reasonably, that some sort of memory buffer would be essential whenever on-line sentence processing lags behind the input.

Retention of semantic propositions

An erroneous initial parsing is not the only mistake an otherwise efficient sentence processor can make. No less costly to down-stream comprehension can be an initial misinterpretation of a lexically ambiguous word, such as *case* being interpreted as *case* as in *suitcase*, versus *case* as in *legal case*. This error would lead to the wrong semantic proposition being formed, and the propositions derived from that misinterpretation would in turn have to be corrected after the error was discovered. In this case a memory representation would be needed to allow the listener time to recover the original message for its reinterpretation at the propositional level. There may also be occasions where propositions derived from a passage are difficult to remember, such as when semantic coherence among the content words is not strong (Martin, 1990).

What kind of memory?

The necessity of some sort of short-term buffer memory for effective sentence processing seems persuasive. How then can we account for reports of brain-damaged patients with severe short-term memory deficits who nevertheless show good ability for at least some aspects of sentence processing (Linebarger, Schwartz, & Saffran, 1983; Martin, 1987)?

Martin (1987) examined sentence comprehension for a group of brain-injured patients whose memory span for materials such as word lists had been tested, and was known to be limited. The sentences she used varied in complexity from one-clause active sentences, "The boy pushed the girl," to one-clause passive sentences, "The boy was pushed by the girl," to sets of center-embedded relative clause constructions of the sort shown in Table 5.1.

Martin's task was to see whether a patient was able to assign a descriptive clause in a sentence to the correct person. For example, in sentence IV, who had black hair, the man or the woman? As you can see, this task is not easy. The correct answer requires that we overlook the long intervening clause, "that was pushed by the man," while focusing on the long distance dependency, "The woman . . . had black hair." Note also that one's grasp of the sentence structure must be strong enough to overcome the potentially distracting association of the adjacent words, ". . . the man had black hair." Role relations about the action verb were also tested: Did the man push the woman or did the woman push the man?

Relative clause sentences should put greater demands on memory than the one-clause sentences. Not only are they longer, they are also center-embedded constructions, in which the embedded clause occurs between the main clause (head noun) and the verb. Information about the incomplete main clause would have to be retained in memory while the embedded clause is being processed.

Not all of Martin's subjects showed good comprehension, but short-term memory span was not the defining predictor of adequate comprehension and thematic role assignment. For example, two subjects had a memory span of only 2.2 items, versus the 7 or so items most adults can recall. One patient scored only 57 percent

SENTENCE TYPE	EXAMPLE OF SENTENCE USED
I.	The woman that had black hair pushed the man.
II.	The woman that pushed the man had black hair.
III.	The woman that had black hair was pushed by the man.
IV.	The woman that was pushed by the man had black hair.
V.	The woman that the man pushed had black hair.

Table 5.1

Examples of relative clause sentence types used in a study of memory span and sentence comprehension by aphasic patients (from Martin, 1990, pg. 406)

correct on a comprehension test of role relations in the simple active and passive sentences, and 54 percent correct on the relative clause sentences. However, the other patient with exactly the same memory span scored 88 percent correct on the active and passive sentences and 93 percent correct on the relative clause sentences.

Other reports have also appeared in the neuropsychological literature describing patients with limited short-term memories, but with no apparent impairment in ordinary sentence comprehension (Butterworth, Campbell, & Howard, 1986). Indeed, Caplan and Waters (1990) claim that it may only be sentences that require a conscious "second pass," like garden path sentences, where patients with a short-term memory deficit may show impairment. It is clear that a great deal of sentence processing can be accomplished by individuals with very limited short-term memory spans. The same can be said for sentence processing and comprehension in normal aging where working memory capacity is often markedly limited (Stine & Wingfield, 1990).

Such results do not necessarily imply that memory is not important for sentence processing. What they do imply is that the memory structures used for temporary storage and recall of word lists or sentences are not the same memory structures used to support on-line syntactic parsing and propositional analysis in natural language processing (Martin, 1990; Caplan, Vanier, & Baker, 1986). You may recall Potter and Lombardi's (1990) point from earlier in the chapter that accurate short-term verbatim recall of a sentence does not mean that there is not yet a conceptual representation of the sentence in memory. At that time we raised the possibility that for a brief period there may exist concurrent storage of both semantic and surface representations of a sentence. It might thus be the case that there is one form of memory that is damaged in the sorts of patients described by Martin, and by Butterworth and his colleagues (a verbatim store that is measured by digit spans or word spans), and another form of memory (memory for semantic representations of sentences) that is not.

While memory is undoubtedly important in language processing, especially at the discourse level, it may be best to think not of a single memory system, but of a complex of structures with different representational characteristics and loss rates (Monsell, 1984).

A processing model of sentence comprehension

The beginnings of a very promising formulation of higher levels of analysis beyond syntax has been offered by Kintsch (1988; van Dijk & Kintsch, 1983). This model proposes that in active speech perception (or in reading), linguistic input is processed in cycles on a segment-by-segment basis. As the phonological (or orthographic) stream arrives, it is rapidly recoded into *propositions* (or "idea units") consisting of a relational term (the *predicate*) plus a set of concepts to be related (*arguments*). At the next stage, the connections among propositions are established, with this relationship among the propositions represented by a network referred to as a **coherence graph**. At this level, the most important propositions to the message structure are selected, and then other propositions connected to them are selected on the basis of shared arguments. Language is said to be coherent when its component propositions are rich in referential linkages.

Support for the belief that propositions serve as important units in sentence processing comes from the finding that the number of propositions contained in passages predicts the average reading time per word of written text (Kintsch & Keenan, 1973), and the speech rate at which rapidly spoken sentences can be understood and recalled (Stine, Wingfield, & Poon, 1986). It has also been shown that propositions at higher levels on a coherence graph are more likely to be recalled than propositions lower on the coherence graph. This would be a consequence of higher-level items receiving more processing cycles in working memory (van Dijk & Kintsch, 1973).

The importance of this model to our present discussion is the notion that in language processing, propositions are distributed across sentences, as well as within sentences. Language comprehension across sentences is referred to as **discourse**. It is to this topic that we now turn in Chapter 6.

Summary

The focus of this chapter was on sentence processing; the question of how listeners rapidly decipher the structure of sentences and gain access to their meaning. We saw that one striking feature of this process is the speed with which it is ordinarily conducted. Listeners have the ability to comprehend and integrate sentences and sentence elements as they are being heard, even though the sentences in ordinary conversation arrive at speech rates in excess of 100 words per minute.

Early studies of the statistical properties of language illustrated the way in which knowledge of linguistic structure can be used to develop expectations about the structure and meaning of what is being heard. Such contextual constraints can facilitate rapid recognition of the speech input, as well as serving to guide its later recall.

Determination of the syntactic structure of sentences is an essential step for understanding the meaning of a sentence. Experimental studies show that listeners ordinarily strive to determine the meaning of an utterance as quickly as possible, and then to quickly discard from memory its surface form.

Many theorists believe that sentence comprehension is an active process in which the perceptual system attempts continually to determine the structure and meaning of the sentence as it is being heard. Others argue that early levels of sentence processing, such as activation of word meaning, may be conducted independently of knowledge potentially available from prior linguistic context. These questions, as well as the role of memory processes in sentence comprehension, remain important questions for future research.

References

Aaronson, D., & Scarborough, H. S. (1977). Performance theories for sentence coding: Some quantitative models. *Journal of Verbal Learning and Verbal Behavior, 16,* 277–304.

Abney, S. P., & Johnson, M. (1991). Memory requirements and local ambiguities of parsing strategies. *Journal of Psycholinguistic Research, 20,* 233–250.

Attneave, F. (1959). *Applications of information theory to psychology.* New York: Holt, Rinehart and Winston.

Beach, C. M. (1991). The interpretation of prosodic patterns at points of syntactic structural ambiguity: Evidence for cue trading relations. *Journal of Memory and Language, 30,* 644–663.

Becker, C. A. (1980). Semantic context effects in visual word recognition: An analysis of semantic strategies. *Memory and Cognition, 8,* 493–512.

Bransford, J. D., Barclay, J. R., & Franks, J. J. (1972). Sentence memory: A constructive versus interpretive approach. *Cognitive Psychology, 3,* 193–209.

Bransford, J. D., & Franks, J. J. (1971). The abstraction of linguistic ideas. *Cognitive Psychology, 2,* 331–350.

Butterworth, B. (1989). Lexical access in speech production. In W. Marslen-Wilson (Ed.), *Lexical representation and process* (pp. 108–135). Cambridge, MA: MIT Press.

Butterworth, B., Campbell, R., & Howard, D. (1986). The uses of short-term memory; A case study. *Quarterly Journal of Experimental Psychology, 38A,* 705–737.

Caplan, D., Vanier, M., & Baker, C. (1986). A case study of reproduction aphasia: II. Sentence comprehension. *Cognitive Neuropsychology, 3,* 129–146.

Caplan, D., & Waters, G. (1990). Short-term memory and language comprehension: A critical review of the neuropsychological literature. In G. Vallar & T. Shallice (Eds.), *Neuropsychological impairments of short-term memory.* Cambridge: Cambridge University Press.

Chodorow, M. S. (1979). Time-compressed speech and the study of lexical and syntactic parsing. In W. E. Cooper & E. C. T. Walker (Eds.), *Sentence processing: Linguistic studies presented to Merrill Garrett* (pp. 87–111). Hillsdale, NJ: Erlbaum.

Chomsky, N. (1957). *Syntactic structures.* The Hague: Mouton.

Chomsky, N. (1965). *Aspects of a theory of syntax.* Cambridge, MA: MIT Press.

Chomsky, N. (1981). *Lectures on government and binding.* Dordrech, The Netherlands: Foris.

Chomsky, N., & Miller, G. (1963). Finitary models of language users. In R. D. Luce (Ed.), *Handbook of mathematical psychology, Vol II.* New York: Wiley & Sons.

Clifton, C., Speer, S., & Abney, S. P. (1991). Parsing arguments: Phrase structure and argument structure as determinants of initial parsing decisions. *Journal of Memory and Language, 30,* 251–271.

Connine, C. M., Blasko, D. G., & Hall, M. (1991). Effects of subsequent sentence context in auditory word recognition: Temporal and linguistic constraints. *Journal of Memory and Language, 30,* 234–250.

Cooper, W. E., & Sorensen, J. (1981). *Fundamental frequency in sentence production.* Berlin: Springer-Verlag.

Flores d'Arcais, G. B., & Schreuder, R. (1983). The process of language understanding: A few issues in contemporary psycholinguistics. In G. B. Flores d'Aracais & R. J. Jarvella (Eds.), *The process of language understanding* (pp. 1–41). New York: John Wiley & Sons.

Fodor, J. A. (1983). *Modularity of mind.* Cambridge, MA: MIT Press.

Fodor, J. A., Bever, T. G., & Garrett, M. F. (1974). *The psychology of language.* New York: McGraw-Hill.

Forster, K. I. (1979). Levels of processing and the structure of the language processor. In W. E. Cooper & E. C. T. Walker (Eds.), *Sentence processing: Psycholinguistic studies presented to Merrill Garrett* (pp. 27–85). Hillsdale, NJ: Erlbaum.

Frazier, L. (1979). *On comprehending sentences: Syntactic parsing strategies.* Bloomington, IN: Indiana University Linguistics Club.

Frazier, L., & Rayner, K. (1982). Making and correcting errors during sentence comprehension: Eye movements in the analysis of structurally ambiguous sentences. *Cognitive Psychology, 14,* 178–210.

Frazier, L., & Rayner, K. (1989). Selection mechanisms in reading lexically ambiguous words. *Journal of Experimental Psychology: Learning, Memory and Cognition, 15,* 779–790.

Garrett, M. F., Bever, T. G., & Fodor, J. (1966). The active use of grammar in speech perception. *Perception and Psychophysics, 1,* 30–32.

Glanzer, M., Fischer, B., & Dorfman, D. (1984). Short-term storage in reading. *Journal of Verbal Learning and Verbal Behavior, 23,* 467–486.

Goldman-Eisler, F. (1968). *Psycholinguistics: Experiments in spontaneous speech.* New York: Academic Press.

Grosjean, F. (1980). Spoken word recognition processes and the gating paradigm. *Perception and Psychophysics, 28,* 267–283.

Grosjean, F. (1985). The recognition of words after their acoustic offset: Evidence and implications. *Perception and Psychophysics, 38,* 299–310.

Hunnicutt, S. (1985). Intelligibility versus redundancy—Conditions of dependency. *Language and Speech, 28,* 47–56.

Jackendoff, R. (1972). *Semantic interpretation in generative grammar.* Cambridge, MA: MIT Press.

Jarvella, R. J. (1970). Effects of syntax on running memory span for connected discourse. *Psychonomic Science, 19,* 235–236.

Jarvella, R. J. (1971). Syntactic processing of connected speech. *Journal of Verbal Learning and Verbal Behavior, 10,* 409–416.

Just, M. A., & Carpenter, P. A. (1987). *The psychology of reading and language comprehension.* Newton, MA: Allyn & Bacon.

Kintsch, W. (1988). The role of knowledge in discourse comprehension: A construction-integration model. *Psychological Review, 95,* 163–182.

Kintsch, W., & Keenan, J. (1973). Reading rate and retention as a function of the number of propositions in the base structure of sentences. *Cognitive Psychology, 5,* 257–274.

Lehiste, I. (1970). *Suprasegmentals.* Cambridge, MA: MIT Press.

Levelt, W. J. M. (1989). *Speaking. From intention to articulation.* Cambridge, MA: MIT Press.

Linebarger, M., Schwartz, M., & Saffran, E. (1983). Sensitivity to grammatical structure in so-called agrammatic aphasics. *Cognition, 13,* 361–392.

Marcus, M. (1980). *A theory of syntactic recognition for natural language.* Cambridge, MA: MIT Press.

Marslen-Wilson, W. D. (1975). Sentence perception as an interactive parallel process. *Science, 189,* 226–228.

Marslen-Wilson, W. D., & Tyler, L. K. (1987). Against modularity. In J. Garfield (Ed.), *Modularity in knowledge representation and natural language understanding.* Cambridge, MA: MIT Press.

Marslen-Wilson, W. D., Tyler, L. K., Warren, P., Grenier, P., & Lee, C. S. (1992). Prosodic effects in minimal attachment. *Quarterly Journal of Experimental Psychology. 45A,* 73–87.

Marslen-Wilson, W. D., & Welsh, A. (1978). Processing interactions and lexical access during word recognition in continuous speech. *Cognitive Psychology, 10,* 29–63.

Marslen-Wilson, W. D., & Zwitserlood, P. (1989). Accessing spoken words: The importance of word onsets. *Journal of experimental psychology: Human perception and performance, 15*, 576–585.

Martin, R. C. (1987). Articulatory and phonological deficits in short-term memory and their relation to syntactic processing. *Brain and Language, 32*, 159–192.

Martin, R. C. (1990). Neuropsychological evidence on the role of short-term memory in sentence processing. In G. Vallar & T. Shallice (Eds.), *Neuropsychological impairments of short-term memory* (pp. 390–427). Cambridge: Cambridge University Press.

Meyer, D. E., Shvaneveldt, R. W., & Rudy, M. G. (1975). Loci of contextual effects on visual word recognition. In P. M. A. Rabbit & S. Dornic (Eds.), *Attention and performance V.* London: Academic Press.

Miller, G. A. (1951). *Language and communication.* New York: McGraw-Hill.

Miller, G. A., & Selfridge, J. A. (1950). Verbal context and the recall of meaningful material. *American Journal of Psychology, 63*, 176–185.

Monsell, S. (1984). Components of working memory underlying verbal skills: A "distributed capacities" view. In H. Bouma & D. G. Bouwhuis (Eds.), *Attention and performance X: Control of language processes* (pp. 327–350). Hillsdale, NJ: Erlbaum.

Moray, N., & Taylor, A. (1960). Statistical approximations to English. *Language and Speech, 3*, 7–10.

Morton, J. (1964). The effects of context on the visual duration threshold for words. *British Journal of Psychology, 55*, 165–180.

Morton, J. (1969). Interaction of information in word recognition. *Psychological Review, 76*, 165–178.

Morton, J. (1970). A functional model of human memory. In D. Norman (Ed.), *Models of human memory.* New York: Academic Press.

Neeley, J. (1977). Semantic priming and retrieval from lexical memory: Evidence for facilitatory and inhibitory processes. *Memory and Cognition, 4*, 648–654.

Nicol, J., & Swinney, D. (1989). The role of structure in coreference assignment during sentence comprehension. *Journal of Psycholinguistic Research, 18*, 5–19.

Oldfield, R. C. (1963). Individual vocabulary and semantic currency: A preliminary study. *British Journal of Social and Clinical Psychology, 2*, 122–130.

Onifer, W., & Swinney, D. (1981). Accessing lexical ambiguities during sentence comprehension: Effects of frequency-of-meaning and contextual bias. *Memory and Cognition, 9*, 225–236.

Pollack, I., & Pickett, J. M. (1964). Intelligibility of excerpts from fluent speech: Auditory versus structural context. *Journal of Verbal Learning and Verbal Behavior, 3*, 79–84.

Potter, M. C., & Lombardi, L. (1990). Regeneration in the short-term recall of sentences. *Journal of Memory and Language, 29*, 633–654.

Reber, A. S., & Anderson, J. R. (1970). The perception of clicks in linguistic and nonlinguistic messages. *Perception and Psychophysics, 8*, 81–89.

Rubenstein, H., & Pollack, I. (1963). Word predictability and intelligibility. *Journal of Verbal Learning and Verbal Behavior, 2*, 147–158.

Sachs, J. S. (1967). Recognition memory for syntactic and semantic aspects of connected discourse. *Perception and Psychophysics, 2*, 437–442.

Seidenberg, M., Tanenhaus, M., Leiman, J., & Bienkowski, M. (1982). Automatic access to the meanings of ambiguous words in context: Some limitations of knowledge-based processing. *Cognitive Psychology, 14*, 489–537.

Simpson, G. B. (1984). Lexical ambiguity and its role in models of word recognition. *Psychological Bulletin, 96*, 316–340.

Simpson, G. B., & Krueger, M. A. (1991). Selective access of homograph meanings in sentence context. *Journal of Memory and Language, 30*, 627–643.

Stine, E. A. L. (1990). On-line processing of written text by younger and older adults. *Psychology and Aging, 5,* 68–78.

Stine, E. A. L., & Wingfield, A. (1990). How much do working memory deficits contribute to age differences in discourse memory? *European Journal of Cognitive Psychology, 2,* 289–304.

Stine, E. A. L., Wingfield, A., & Poon, L. W. (1986). How much and how fast: Rapid processing of spoken language by older adults. *Psychology and Aging, 86,* 303–311.

Streeter, L. A. (1978). Acoustic determinants of phrase boundary perception. *Journal of the Acoustical Society of America, 64,* 1582–1592.

Swinney, D. (1979). Lexical access during sentence comprehension: (Re)consideration of context effects. *Journal of Verbal Learning and Verbal Behavior, 18,* 645–659.

Swinney, D., & Osterhout, L. (1990). Inference generation during auditory language comprehension. In A. C. Graesser & G. H. Bower (Eds.), *Inference and text comprehension: The psychology of learning and motivation.* Vol. 25 (pp. 17–33) San Diego: Academic Press.

Thibadeau, R., Just, M. A., & Carpenter, P. A. (1982). A model of the time course and content of reading. *Cognitive Science, 6,* 157–203.

Tulving, E., & Gold, C. (1963). Stimulus information and contextual information as determinants of tachistoscopic recognition for words. *Journal of Experimental Psychology, 66,* 319–327.

Tyler, L. K. (1984). The structure of the initial cohort: Evidence from gating. *Perception and Psychophysics, 36,* 417–427.

Tyler, L. K., & Marslen-Wilson, W. D. (1977). The on-line effects of semantic context on syntactic processing. *Journal of Verbal Learning and Verbal Behavior, 16,* 683–692.

Tyler, L. K., & Wessels, J. (1983). Quantifying contextual contributions to word-recognition processes. *Perception and Psychophysics, 34,* 409–420.

Tyler, L. K., & Wessels, J. (1985). Is gating an on-line task? Evidence from naming latency data. *Perception and Psychophysics, 38,* 217–222.

van Dijk, T. A., & Kintsch, W. (1983). *Strategies of discourse comprehension.* New York: Academic Press.

Wagenaar, W. A., Varey, C. A., & Hudson, P. T. W. (1984). Do audiovisuals aid? A study of bisensory presentation on the recall of information. In H. Bouma & D. G. Bouwhuis (Eds.), *Attention and performance X: Control of language processes.* Hillsdale, NJ: Erlbaum.

Wales, R., & Toner, H. (1979). Intonation and ambiguity. In W. E. Cooper & E. C. T. Walker (Eds.), *Sentence processing: Psycholinguistic studies presented to Merrill Garrett.* Hillsdale, NJ: Erlbaum.

Wayland, S. C., Wingfield, A., & Goodglass, H. (1989). Recognition of isolated words: The dynamics of cohort reduction. *Applied Psycholinguistics, 10,* 475–487.

Wingfield, A. (1975). Acoustic redundancy and the perception of time-compressed speech. *Journal of Speech and Hearing Research, 18,* 139–147.

Wingfield, A., & Butterworth, B. (1984). Running memory for sentences and parts of sentences: Syntactic parsing as a control function in working memory. In H. Bouma & D. G. Bouwhuis (Eds.), *Attention and performance X: Control of language processes.* Hillsdale, NJ: Erlbaum.

Wingfield, A., & Klein, J. F. (1971). Syntactic structure and acoustic pattern in speech perception. *Perception and Psychophysics, 9,* 23–25.

Zwitserlood, P. (1989). The focus of the effects of sentential-semantic context in spoken-word processing. *Cognition, 32,* 25–64.

Conversational Discourse

SUSAN ERVIN-TRIPP
University of California, Berkeley

Introduction

A woman collides on a sidewalk with a stranger:

Introduction

(1)   a   Woman to man: Oh, I'm sorry.

        b   Man to woman: I still say he's wrong about that, Jim.
                      Anyway, honey, it's Tuesday.

What can you make of this imaginary encounter? The grammar of each sentence is acceptable. The woman's speech is an apology for the collision. Her "Oh," marks surprise, appropriate to an accident. But the man's speech is bizarre. He doesn't respond to the apology or make one himself. "Jim," and "honey," are address terms respectively to a man, and to a woman or child, so they are incoherent together to an adult woman. The address terms imply familiarity, but these are strangers. His topics do not follow either from the context or from any introduction of theme, so the topical sequence is incoherent. "Anyway," indicates recovery from a distraction, but there was no prior topic. "Still," is a third-turn form, which refers back to something the speaker said on an earlier turn or earlier encounter, yet there was none. "He" and "that" have no antecedents, so the reference is lost. Thus the conversation doesn't seem coherent, cooperative, or even interactive.

Linguists often ask listeners or readers to make sense, or to make judgments, about isolated invented sentences. As listeners in such tasks, we must invent contexts to try to make sense. This is to say that in our understanding of speech, as well as in our creation of speech, we bring our knowledge of the participants and of what is going on.

The analysis of utterance production begins with observing a talk in context rather than an isolated sentence, for sentences are an outcome of the talk situation, and both their structure and their meaning are changed by the purposes of talk. In this chapter we will examine what we mean by context, what the dimensions are by which discourse is structured, and how these affect the text.

In example (1) we have identified the events in the context, the relation of the participants to address terms, the turn structure, topic sequence, action (apology), and cohesion of pronouns with antecedents and appropriateness of markers with context as all affecting the listener's judgment. These domains are discussed below.

When people are engaged in talk, commonly they have a sense of a joint "activity" they are in, whether it is a baseball game or a conversation at a party. They alternate or collaborate in talking, or remain as audience, establishing a **participation structure**. Within the activity which sets up the talk, they have goals with respect to ideas and action, which we refer to below as the **ideational** and **action** levels. These may be shared or not; participants also contribute separately to defining the larger activity context, allowing situational shifts. The outcome is a **text**. The structure of the joint text is closely knit by structural knowledge, style, and also by aesthetic skill. The syntactic and lexical features of these texts are what psycholinguists who examine production often study.

When a person comes to say something, even to a stranger, what we hear is not a random set of grammatical utterances. What is likely to occur can in part be known by shared context. Context, which is known before speech occurs, affects strongly what is likely to be said, how it is said, and how it is understood. At a baseball game you do not expect the umpire to shout recipes. Even in a noisy environment, what he says is sufficiently predictable as to be understandable most of the time.

The contextual features that make the biggest difference to speech are those of situation, participant status, participant social relations, and shared environment and knowledge. In turn, the interaction redefines or confirms these features. The reason we have any stable expectations in the social world is precisely because interaction occurs as it does. What is psycholinguistic about discourse then takes place within a powerful social nexus.

Context of situation

Erving Goffman (1963) made important distinctions between types of encounters between speakers and listeners which are basic to the construction of talk. He distinguished *civil inattention*, in which the other is normally ignored, from *unfocussed interaction*, where people follow norms of public demeanor, and glance at one another as they pass into and out of view, and *focussed interaction*, where people cooperate with a common focus of attention. Goffman made acute observations about the problems of entering into and terminating focussed engagement, and about the issues of attention which constitute breaches, such as distractions during focussed engagement (e.g., looking in a mirror) or incursions of undesired involvement, such as street remarks from strangers. A street remark presents an unresolved dilemma to women, who must breach the etiquette of responding to summons or collude in an unwelcome exchange which breaches civil inattention (Gardner, 1984).

A situation can be recognized by the setting, personnel, and activities. Settings may have spatial organization, objects, and **standing behavior patterns** (Barker & Wright, 1954). These patterns can be instantiated in activities. For instance, a classroom normally is a setting for a class, but it could be the setting for a party, for a political speech, or for intimate conversation, which are different activities. We recognize these situational switches by the properties of the talk we hear. The personnel also have implications for activities. A two-year-old is less likely to be giving instruction than an adult.

Situations with names like classes, church services, trials, job interviews, and football games often are *conventional situations*. These involve norms, so violations of constraints on actions and speech are recognized and talked about in a community. During wartime or other civic crises, there has been debate in American colleges about whether a college professor or the students are on strike when the class moves to a different site or changes the topic to current affairs or history. Such debates are only possible because norms exist for these conventional situations. They can be considered formal, in the sense they have a predefined structure and may entail *planned discourse*, such as graduation speeches.

Many of these conventional situations are complex in structure, containing subparts or episodes, which have names, roles, and special activities. A church service is a complex speech event; the congregation has different activities and even postures during prayers, sermons, hymns, and responsive readings so that a newcomer has to watch carefully to know when and how to participate as a speaker. The structure of participation, and the content and the language or register are shifted in each episode. The same can be said of a trial. The speech on these occasions is sometimes called a **genre** since it has recognizable features. It is by hearing the genre change that the congregation knows when the church service has passed from prayer to sermon, and that they can sit down.

Familiar situations, on the other hand, are those in which participants come to recognize shared goals, but the event may have no name, and there is no accountability for norms. Changes don't usually invite criticism. An example might be bringing groceries into the kitchen, or washing up. Because these activities are familiar, participants may come to share some assumptions about action trajectories and roles, as they do in conventional situations. If everyone shares in putting groceries away, then "This goes next to the cereal" can be heard as a directive or request. With extreme routinization some familiar situations can become conventional, so that deviation is noticed and generates interpretations.

Phone conversations are good examples. In a multiperson household, anyone might answer the phone. Since typically phone calls are two- rather than multiparty, the primary target for the call remains to be known. "Is Sybil there?" will be heard by an experienced listener as a request for action to go and bring Sybil to the phone. This is such a familiar pattern that it can be used strategically for other goals:

(2)   (Phone rings in household. Teenage girl picks it up, listens, covers the mouthpiece.)

Hey [**stooopid! (loud)]   [SUMMONS]

(Older brother comes to the phone.)   [RESPONSE]

                                                         TR78

The sister has played with the familiar structure to accomplish two acts at once. By using an insult as a summons, she traps her brother into complicity with the insult through compliance with the summons.

Activities

Activities are fundamental to talk because they make evident whether talk is possible or necessary, establish roles that create speech options for participants, and in task-oriented situations, set up goals that constrain relevance. The activity of teaching, in a conventional classroom, constrains topics by roughly showing what is relevant and what is a sidetrack. Talk differs considerably when it is goal-oriented or transactional, or when it is personal.

Activity may be verbal or nonverbal—chatting is an activity. Jumping rope, disputing, cooking, and telling a story are activities. Activities may be parallel or joint between participants, and joint activities may involve complementary or similar roles. Knitting is a parallel activity, requiring no coordination between participants, so it allows unrelated talk at the same time. Bringing in groceries from the car is a joint activity, in which there can be similar or complementary roles—carrier and putter-away. Joint activities typically require some shared goals and shared notions about roles. The trajectories in joint activities allow speech to be used to direct during talk-in-action. In complementary roles, the speech of participants reflects role. Control over participation structure—talk time and type of talk—is not the same for teacher and student, priest and congregation, lawyer and client, or doctor and patient. In language during a soccer game, for instance, there are recognizably different speech types occurring in the players, the coach, the umpire, and the onlookers because the function of talk is different for each role, though there may be overlap, such as coach-talk from teammates and onlookers.

Overlapping situations occur whenever there are two types of co-occurring activities with the same participants, such as knitting and talking. If one task requires no talk and little concentration, the situation is ideal for sociability, or overlapping personal talk, as in quilting or sewing or sorting in a cannery. It is possible for a passenger in a car to intersperse sociable talk with route directions and for a driver to concurrently engage in sociable talk and drive. But there are limits; engrossing talk can disrupt driving or cooking. In overlapping situations, participants can choose which to foreground in talk. Mealtimes are familiar situations of overlapping activities. Managerial talk about allocation of places, offering of food, or offering help may overlap with task- or sociable-talk.

In the following example of Thanksgiving dinner conversation with friends rather than family, consider how participants can identify which of the two overlapping contexts is at issue. (In these texts, = = brackets overlaps, == is for latching or fast replies, (xx) was unintelligible, * indicates emphasis):

(3) a   Peter: = (xxxxx) cranberry sauce =
     b   Deborah: I wonder how *our = *grandparents and *parents =
     c   Deborah: felt about Thanksgiving.
. . . .
     k   Steve: Could we get this off the table?
     l   Deborah: Y'know if they used to do it for the
     m   Deborah: = kids, or whether they really = *felt it.
     n   Peter: = I'd like it off the table   =
     o   Steve: It *keeps coming back on the *table.
          Steve: It *must have a will of its own.
                                        Tannen, 1986, p. 91

There are three topics mentioned: the food, the tape recorder, and the history of Thanksgiving. Pronouns refer back to these items separately, so Deborah's "it" is not the same as Peter's and Steve's "it."

Contextualization.   In order to know how participants identify their situation, or if there is overlap, what is foregrounded at the moment, we look for cues, such as posture, vocal indicators, register, code, and topics. Of course some situations can't be changed; it would be hard to turn a baseball game into a mass because of setting and personnel constraints. But it is not hard to turn a tutoring session or work conference into seduction. Learning how to alter situations verbally may be a practical defense.

Personnel

The number of participants in focussed engagement affects the dynamics. Two have an incentive to resolve conflicts, but in a group of four, there can be alliances, and in a triad, one can be excluded, so interactional structure differs in these group forms (Simmel, 1902). A crucial factor in the dynamics of interaction is status equality or inequality.

Participant status.   Just as there may be a situation suggested by a setting, but another developed by the participants (the classroom that is a site for a party), there can be participant status brought to the setting, in contrast to statuses constituted by the talk itself. Noticeable at the outset are clothing, gender, and physical attributes. You know whether the stranger before you is child or adult; baby talk is unlikely to an unfamiliar able-bodied adult (though nurses use it to adult patients). The importance of these first features in steering interaction may be why we can be surprisingly confused when we cannot tell if a longhaired stranger is man or woman.

Ethnicity, national or regional background, social class, and education may become apparent through talk itself, since grammar, vocabulary, and pronunciation all are sensitive indicators of social identity (Fasold, 1990). In an American high school, for instance, the pronunciation of vowels in peer talk can reveal not only clique membership, but also centrality in a clique (Eckert, 1989).

The division of labor demanded by a new situation may alter the relevance of prior status features. In an emergency, knowledge of CPR or of first aid may be more relevant than whether or not the participant is a teenager or an aged artist. The new context can demand a division between organizers, supervisors who control activities of others, and enablers who permit access to materials and information. On the other hand, status contrasts brought into a situation may be reinforced within. Juries tend to select as foreman those with high external social status. In the case of a jury there is an explicit vote, but other roles are self-nominated. The person with confidence who chooses to sit at the head of a table gains an advantage in dominating the talk. The speech may reveal to participants who has taken up what role—the role of organizer or supervisor may only be visible when one person begins to order others about.

Social relationships.   Participants bring to the encounter relations with each other—strangers, friends, bosses, or parents, which differ along dimensions of power and of solidarity or distance. They can choose to foreground these relations or not, according to the situational context. Friendship deeply alters many features of talk; many generalizations in psycholinguistic research apply only to strangers.

Shared knowledge. The physical context of talk when people are copresent provides a common basis of reference with definite articles, pronouns, and gesture as in Text 4. We can talk about "the" sun because we all believe there is only one; it is hazardous to agree to meet at "the" airport if there is more than one, and experience shows disagreement about which is presupposed. Friends assume they share ideas; they rely on allusions and metaphors which presuppose common experience. When information is to be conveyed, strangers more often use subordination, conjunctions, adverbial connectives in becoming more explicit. In contrast, stories to friends leave semantic relations implicit, but mark pragmatic relations and emotions more than stories to strangers. Thus stranger talk is more formal, ideationally focused, and complex in its language; to friends we use more emotive and vivid speech such as dramatizing dialogue in stories (Redeker, 1990; Tannen, 1989). Some of the theoretical reasons for these differences have been explored in a broad survey of language use by Clark (1985). Some similar contrasts have been found to differentiate middle- and working-class speech to strangers, with working-class speech to strangers more like familiar speech (Hemphill, 1989).

Participation structure

Turntaking by participants changes in various speech events, and roles in speech from audience to addressee to speaker. While turntaking is highly ritualized in some settings, such as church services, how do we manage to have organized timing in casual conversations? Conversational competence seems to require both paying attention to what partners say and making appropriate replies. Since all participants share the same speech stream, listening to another speaker might mean you have to be quiet until each speaker finishes. In a group, this requires everyone to pay close attention to others.

Mutual gaze, minimal speech overlap, and speech that is contingent on the other's in form, function, and topic—these are the clues used to show competent conversational engagement in an idealized view. An incompetent listener, in this view, would not gaze at the speaker, would display random gaps and overlaps in conversation, and would talk without regard to what was just said. What actually happens?

Detailed work on verbal turntaking has been provided by temporal studies of talk between American strangers in phone conversations (Brady, 1969) and in interviews (Jaffe & Feldstein, 1970), and by analysis of American natural conversations (Jefferson, 1973; Sacks, Schegloff, & Jefferson, 1974). In these studies, it was observed that adult Americans:

1. Overlap only briefly. Average overlap lengths in phone conversations of 0.25 seconds (Brady, 1968) and in interviews of 0.40 seconds (Jaffe & Feldstein, 1970) occupied only 4.49% or 3.29% of the speech time, respectively. Thus in these studies, over 95% of the time one speaker is talking at a time.

2. Allow very short gaps. Averages reported for stranger dyads were gaps of 0.40 seconds in adult phone conversations and 0.77 seconds in interviews. But a quarter of the time in stranger talk, there was silence. Sacks, Schegloff, and Jefferson called this feature "precision-timing" and pointed out that it is possible only if speakers can anticipate the end of a turn or are responsive to cues of termination, and if effective locally managed devices for next speaker selection exist in multiparty conversation.

3. Overlap as competing first starts or at a "transition-relevant place." Sacks, Schegloff, and Jefferson (1974) and Jefferson (1973) noted that overwhelmingly listeners break in at points which would be plausible stopping places. They either interrupt just briefly with feedback, or they overlap at predictable tags (like O.K.), routines, or address terms. These may be cued by prosody or other surface indicators, or by content suggesting the speaker is ending the informational segment. Listeners have to be able to project such places and be ready to enter. Even requests for repairing poorly heard speech await the transition relevant place.

4. Remedy overlaps. When important material is overlapped, Sacks, Schegloff, and Jefferson noticed that speakers remedy by increasing volume, lengthening syllables, repeating, slowing down, or stopping. These remedies imply that speakers are concerned that speech be audible.

5. Select the next speaker in the group by name, gaze, body orientation, topic selection, or a "first" in a pair such as a question requiring an answer. Gaps at such points are the silences belonging to the next speaker. But selection isn't absolutely necessary, as we learn from the relative success of large group telephone conference calls, in which the only conscious adjustment is self-identification.

There has been a debate between those arguing that cues control turns (Duncan, 1972; Duncan & Fiske, 1977; Kendon, 1967) and those who suggest neither gaze nor prosodic cues are enough to explain success (Ellis & Beattie, 1986; C. Goodwin, 1981), who insist that there is a social system at work.

The fast response feature of turntaking clearly makes strong demands on the processing of language by participants. Perhaps you have noticed how hard it is to interrupt with relevance in seminars. We see this problem in young children who have the greatest difficulty locating appropriate breaks in two-party talk so they can intervene (Ervin-Tripp, 1977). What seems to be required is not only an awareness of clause structure, but also following the topic sequence enough to notice when macro-units of talk are ending and there is no outstanding unfinished business like unanswered questions. That requires more than just attention; it requires figuring out the conversational structure.

Why does orderly turntaking exist? One explanation is utilitarian; speakers are really interested in what other people say. If this is the reason, we would predict more overlaps when speech is predictable or redundant. Jefferson (1973) noticed that in police phone conversations overlaps occurred during optional segments after crucial information, during recognition and acknowledgement of the information, or conversation-closing sequences. We would expect differences in overlap between different types of speech events or situations, expecting more overlap during redundant or predictable events such as praying or sports events. We would also expect more overlaps in sociable talk between intimates who share most information. We would expect overlapping of inferiors and children whose information is less valuable; West and Zimmerman (1983) found that men interrupt women more, though this may reflect another factor: dominance. West has found that some male patients interrupt even women doctors more, gender outweighing professional status (West, 1984). Ervin-Tripp (1977) noted that small children were interrupted more by older children and adults even when relevance of their talk was controlled. In such studies, age, acquaintance, and other factors affecting both status and overlapping must be controlled.

Another argument for turntaking has to do with politeness rather than utility or interest. But this leads to ambiguous predictions, since there are, according to R. Lakoff (1973) and Brown and Levinson (1987), two kinds of politeness. Lakoff calls these rapport and deference; Brown and Levinson call them positive and negative politeness. If we want to be polite-positive we compliment by showing common interests and shared perspective. This effort can lead to fast replies with a minimum of gaps, revealing familiarity and what Tannen (1984) calls the "high-involvement style." But if we want to be deferent, we risk long gaps to avoid interruptions and allow speakers to continue. This leads to the prediction that intimacy and rapport lead to gap-minimizing and some overlaps, and deference to gap-maximizing with a minimum of overlaps.

Studies of different cultural groups have shown quite a lot of contrast in this dimension. Warm Springs Indian style (Philips, 1972) maximizes gaps and calls for distance cues like gaze aversion, while East Indian English (Agrawal, 1976) and New York Jewish speech maximize overlaps (Tannen, 1984) and call for signs of involvement such as acknowledgements, simultaneous completions, accelerating pace, latching (immediate responses), agreements, and repetitions. In the positive politeness cultures, overlaps are favored as a sign of cooperative, attentive listening. And of course we all recognize personal style differences here.

Speakers from low involvement communities find the high degree of overlap and the intensely paced talk of high involvement speakers to be rude. On the other hand, high involvement speakers regard not attending to topic, not following themes, monologuing, and allowing long gaps to be rude and inattentive.

The following text illustrates the high involvement style between two Californian college-age sisters, Mimi and Rae. In this case, the overlaps (bracketed by = =) appear to result from intimacy. Asterisks in the text indicate extra emphasis and periods indicate pauses. To get the flavor of this conversation read it aloud with another person:

(4) a   M: hey there's what's her face she has a boyfriend . . um . .*Joey.

    b   R: [laughs] [soft] oh yeah it *might be her boyfriend from Fresno

    c   M: = yeah = . . . she's cute.

    d   R: = (xxx) =   so you decided to call Cindy?

    e   M: yeah. . . . it's weird cause she's kinda-   I don't know

    f   M: don't you think that she's kinda *standoff-   she's she's kinda g   R: = she left this message =

h   M: = her'n   = *her'n *Jack are both kinda weird
        I think

i   R: = she always goes she goes = ([slow whiney] I'm calling for
        **Mii*mii)

j   M: = they're like   =
     M: she's she = calls me *Mii*mii   =

k   R: = did you hear her message? =

l   M: yeah.

m   R: she goes ([slow whiney] I'm calling for *Mii*mii um if you
        want you can work at the music store. um tell her to call me. bye
        *Mii*mi). [laughs]

n   M: ==mhm mhm the thing is like . . here I know they're gonna
        hire me. and the thing is . . like I don't- I mean they have
        other people but she said = oh I'll call tomorrow   =

o   R: = I'm totally like that though = I'll say.
                                         UCBDisclab.SISTR

In this text there is one latch or fast reply, in line (n), and five overlaps, in (cd), (gh), (ij), (jk), and (no). The first overlap fits the pattern of uninformative agreement, a feedback. In the two next overlaps, (g) and (j), the speaker with the floor was repeating, not producing new information. The last overlap by Rae fits neither pattern but occurs when Mimi is thinking outloud about information Rae already knows. Turn (k) called for a reply, which we find in turn (l), suggesting no interference with comprehension. These latches and overlaps and the fast pace of the conversation are typical of intimate talk of close friends or sisters, who share most of the same information. It has been argued that timing coordination or synchrony is a reflection of participants' intimacy or at least of sympathy (Ellis & Beattie, 1986, p. 132).

Dimensions of choice in discourse

Speakers do more than divide the talk time. We will distinguish six levels at which choices are made by speakers, all of them consequential in talk: the level of **topics, propositions, action, social features, key**, and sometimes **genre**. All of these create the resulting text. The evidence suggests that we remember these features of speech better than the actual words used (Sachs, 1974; Hickman & Warden, 1991). Even when some of these levels are more salient, choices may occur on others. In a hilarious conversation with lots of wisecracks the genre and key may be paramount; in children's role-play, action may predominate; in a history classroom, the ideational or propositional level may be salient to major organization; in encounters at a party, social relations may be at issue. But each conversation can have values on all of these dimensions.

Thematic structure

Conversational interaction involves a structure of topics. The choice of topic or ideational content is made at every point in the conversation except during fixed routines. We can ask who can initiate topics, how stable topics are in coherent speech, and how topics are supported or changed through propositional material.

Topic control is a factor in conversational power and inheres in some asymmetrical roles like teacher or presider. Topic uptake is a form of compliance, so it is not surprising that power is reflected in getting others to support one's topics. In some American studies (Fishman, 1983), women who initiate new topics are often less successful in getting topic uptake than are men. Role-derived privileges in topic choice include the right to initiate the first topic when you have summoned the hearer, as in a phone call. While topic control in transactional encounters is likely to be ascribed by status, in personal encounters between peers it is negotiated, and asymmetrical dominance can create tension.

Topics are initiated, supported, or changed. Clark and Schaefer (1989) have noted that participants must collaborate in starting and grounding a topic to establish shared belief that there has been mutual comprehension. Without this grounding, continuation on the topic cannot occur. Next turns, if there are no repairs, then display this shared understanding.

Side sequences for clarifying or repairing occur when there is some obstacle to this goal of comprehension. These practical repairs are of five types: (a) There is a preference for self repair, such as we saw in conversation (4); (b) An addressee may make hearing or channel queries (hunh?); (c) An addressee may make confirmation checks by repeating the prior turn or part of it; (d) The addressee can solicit or add extra information, supporting the first speaker's continuation; or, finally (e) The partner may expand a theme from a prior speaker, taking it over. A side sequence can carry out each practical repair (Cheepen, 1988; Levinson, 1983; Jefferson, 1972). These side sequences are typically marked in a way that sets them off as units deviant from the thematic focus. "Oh," "anyway," and so on, are called by Redeker (1991) sequential transition markers. They help the listener to know whether to assume a topic and related thematic materials should be put on hold, or recovered and reestablished.

If we look back at the sisters' conversation (4), we see two distinct topic sections. The first three turns are stimulated by a contextual event, seeing a friend.

(5) a   M: Hey there's what's her face she has a boyfriend . . um . . *Joey.
     b   R: [laughs] [soft] Oh yeah it *might be her boyfriend from Fresno
     c   M: = yeah = . . . She's cute.

Though Mimi introduced this topic, Rae collaborated, confirming the topic with a feedback "yeah," and adding information. The confirmation response "yeah" was followed by an assessment in line (c) as a topic terminating move. In turn (d), Rae changed to a new topic by an elicitation oriented to Mimi's interests: Mimi's phone call to a friend about a job. This shift has a marker, "so."

(6)   R : So you decided to call Cindy?

In the next lines there appears to be a common topic—the woman who was called—but the focus of the two speakers looks different. Mimi replied to the elicitation question by discussing the personality of Cindy.

(7) e   M: Yeah. . . . it's weird cause she's kinda- I don't know/
            don't you think that she's kinda she's kinda *standoff-
            she's kinda- her'n Jack are both kinda weird I think/

Rae responded to the first statement by interrupting and moving directly to an example, making fun of Cindy by mimicking her phone message. Her focus through the next lines is in getting this story produced. This vivid quote is an example of the informal narrative style used with friends.

(8) g   R : She left this message.
     i   She always goes she goes ([slow whiney] I'm calling for
            **Mii*mii)
     k   Did you hear her message?
     m   She goes ([slow whiney] I'm calling for *Mii*mii um if you
            want you can work at the music store. um tell her to call me.
            bye *Mii*mi). [laughs]

The two speakers overlapped a good deal, so line (k) was Rae's move to get the floor to display the story about Cindy's weird message, which was at the same time a dramatic rendition, a confirmation of Mimi's assessment, and laughable.

In line (n) Mimi changed key and moved to a serious topic, the job mentioned in the phone message story. The next turn of Rae was a statement of solidarity which confirmed Mimi's topic. The topic of the job then preoccupied Mimi during a long turn after this segment.

(9) n M: ==mhm mhm the thing is like . . here I know they're gonna
              hire me. and the thing is . . like I don't-   I mean they have
              other people but she said = oh we'll call tomorrow   =

     o R: = I'm totally like that though = I'll say.

The close knitting of topic offering, confirmation, and elaboration shows how good joint understanding was despite the large amount of overlapping. There were no examples of repairs of the sort illustrated by Clark and Schaefer except some false starts.

Continuity of topic ranges from strong maintenance in formal, task-oriented encounters to the very loose constraints of personal talk among intimates during non-verbal activity, such as sewing, knitting, or fishing. In some texts of this sort, speakers follow their own topics and seem not to be constrained by the partner's topic, as if using the other merely as audience in talking to oneself. Studies of differences in topical focus show it to be a cultural feature; for example, American girls have been found to have more topical continuity and topic focus than boys in conversations with best friends (Tannen, 1990).

In personal conversations topics can be individually created and relatively coherent, as in narrative rounds, or they may show gradual drift. In types of talk having topical constraints, global topic shifts may be revealed by sequential markers like "okay," and "so" before shifts or summaries, even in monologues.

Within topics, the structure of support, continuation, and disagreement is maintained by propositional relations marked by discourse operators, "a word or phrase—for instance, a conjunction, adverbial, comment clause, interjection," (Redeker, 1991) such as "but," "however," "if," and "then," or, sometimes, "still."

Action

Adjacency pairs

Conversational engagement is expressed through **adjacency pairs**. These are sequences of moves; when a first occurs, the second is awaited. This second is usually matched at several levels, or it will be heard as incoherent. If there is a mismatch, the hearer still seeks a match by inferring a link, or by soliciting the second turn or some account for its absence (Schegloff & Sacks, 1973, pp. 295–296; Heritage, 1984, pp. 245–253).

The basic structure is well illustrated by phone conversations:

(10) a C [ring]   [SUMMONS]
      b R Hello.   [RESPONSE]

c   C Hi.   [GREETING]
d   R Oh hi::   [GREETING]

Levinson, 1983, p. 311

In this example, the initial summons-response is in turns (a-b). In turn (c), which is typical of American phone calls, (C) greets with a familiar form. A return greeting is obligatory for (R), who is supposed to recognize (C)'s voice. There are thus two adjacency pairs, (a-b) and (c-d).

Is this phone call pattern universal? In England a common (b) response is to give the respondent's name "Smith here." Some French consider Americans' use of turn (c) to be rude; they would supply a self-identification with the caller's greeting, even when the person who picks up the phone isn't the ultimate target of the call (Godard, 1977). Everywhere summons obligate replies, but the requirement to presuppose or supply particular information seems to be culture specific. Cross-cultural, cross-ethnic, and cross-regional studies are an important facet of the study of conversational features.

When we examine the turns in a dialogue like (11), we notice that they do seem to be paired as initiations and responses. New initiations can occur in the same turn with a response, making a closely knit dialogue. In the following conversation, each turn by Ann reinstantiates the request, and each turn by the mother makes a refusal.

(11)   [family valentine construction. Ann is 7.5]
    a   Ann: Mommy I don't want to make 18 so why don't you help
              me. I mean twenty eight I have to make.   [REQUEST]
    b   Mot: Hm? You can do that.   [REFUSE]
    c   Ann: Mother!   [REQUEST]
    d   Mot: You have a whole week.   [JUSTIFY REFUSAL]
    e   Ann: I know but we're supposed to all make em
              today.   [DENY/ASSERT]
    f   Mot: No you don't have to make them all today.   [DENY]
                                              UCBDisclab:Cannon11

This conversation began a series of 12 requests and hints from Ann to try to capture her mother's help. As the first in an adjacency pair, (a) sets up an expectation that the mother must soon respond to the request. Turn (b) can be heard as a refusal by inference, because it follows (a), is spoken by the person addressed in (a), and will therefore first be interpreted as relevant to (a). Though mother does not explicitly say, "I won't help you," the turn is interpreted as a refusal since "you can do that" removes a reason for helping, and therefore recognizably justifies a refusal in this cultural milieu where direct refusals are avoided.

Each move Ann makes can be heard as reinstantiating her request, and each reply by the mother as strengthening her refusal, but these relations are in each case not explicit. They are accomplished by inference.

Exchanges

The action structure of a speech event concerns the function of talk in getting things done. Our language has many names for these speech acts: requests, commands, assertions, compliments, lies, promises, threats and so forth. While many of these acts take on conventional forms—"hi" is unambiguously a greeting—others are less obvious. We shall see that their formal diversity arises from the fact that they can serve several action functions at once, and also convey social relations and affect.

In a commercial shop, "It's six" could imply "lock up." The speech events in which we talk set up expectations for many action implications. Even many children of age five tell us that, "Is the door open" will get someone to open a door for a mom with a big bag of groceries. They can understand enough about a familiar situation to look for what needs to be done.

Many of these moves seem to call for typical replies, building up a series of exchanges. Summons call for responses, greetings call for greetings, invitations for acceptance or rejection, questions for answers, requests for compliance or refusal. This is a system of norms recognizable by reactions to an unexpected reply.

The exchange system is a local system, which is managed turn by turn. The evidence that participants orient to these expectations is strong. Unless there is an excuse, the next turn by whoever speaks next, if the addressee is not specified, is taken as conditionally relevant. That is, the next turn might be viewed as a possible reply. Not speaking is heard as a selected addressee's silence; such a pause is likely to be interpreted as a problem. If no candidate reply occurs, the expectation is maintained, so that there can be insertion sequences, typically for repair, and still there is a return to the suspended action.

(12)   Ordering beer.
    a A: May I have a bottle of Mich?   [REQUEST]
    b B: Are you 21?   [SIDE QUERY]
    c A: No   [SIDE RESPONSE]
    d B: No   [REFUSE]

Merritt, 1976, p. 333

In this sequence, the second turn is clearly not a reply to the first. The reply to the query in (a) is suspended until there is a reply to a contingent query in (b); we see the contingent query and response as an insertion sequence (b-c) inside the adjacency pair (a-d). In some cases these insertions are quite complex, but participants succeed in keeping track.

The principle of adjacency pairs has reflexes in the participant structure of the talk; the first part implies a turn soon to come so it creates dialogue. The other reflex is in the action structure. When the first part is conventional or "on record," the addressed or implicated participant is constrained in terms of verbal response types. When the action is merely implied, the addressee has the choice of completely ignoring it (unless it is a question), or of responding to the manifest text level only, or to the action proposal, or to both. If I say, "Do you know where the Post Office is?" and your reply is "Yes," you are responding to the manifest text level only and ignoring the implied request, which is for location information.

In a telephone study in California, Clark (1979) separated these two levels. He had people call merchants with various formats of questions (See Table 6.1) At the text or literal level, question (A) calls for a specific time reply and question (C) calls for a yes/no reply. However, in an indirect culture, where the listener is supposed to make cooperative inferences about goals, the respondent to a yes/no question might also guess the desire to know the time, and give a dual answer. "No, at ten" gives a first answer cohesive with the surface form, and a second answer compliant with an implied information request.

In the following results, P is surface cohesion by a polarity yes/no reply and T is a response to an inferred time request:

Table 6.1

Literal and Inferential Responses

	P	T	BOTH
A Could you tell me the time you close?	0	100%	0
B Would you mind telling me the time you close?	0	96%	24%
C Do you close before seven?	19%	23%	58%

In (A), "Could you?" is just heard as a polite marker by all the respondents, who ignore the surface form of the polarity question (e.g., "At 8"). The more elaborate and less frequent form of (B) calls attention to the question format and leads to an additional surface answer cohesion by a quarter of the respondents, "No, we close at 8." Question (C) does not make explicit the request for exact closing time, yet even with a very explicit polarity question, most not only answered the surface question, but went beyond to add surplus information "No, we close at 8."

There are two contrasting theories about how this kind of understanding of what speakers want can occur. One theory is based on a set of principles of conversation, which allowed listeners to go beyond what is said by making inferences (Levinson, 1983, pp. 97–106). This theory was developed by Grice, who stated "maxims" about what people assume conversation is like. He believed that deviation from what is culturally expected pushes people to make inferences. The themes of these expectations include cooperation, brevity, truth, and relevance. In this view listeners try to account for unexpected features on these dimensions and thus discover nonliteral, indirectly expressed meanings. It seems to be the cooperativeness of addressees that leads them to seek for goals in conversation beyond those stated explicitly, and to provide the additional information noted by Clark and Schaefer. Another theory is that understanding is "locally negotiated," based on the informational detail in adjacency pairs. The preference system illuminates this approach.

Preference system

Close study of American adult talk has shown that there is an asymmetry in adjacency pair second parts. One type of reply is different in that it is quicker, so it looks more spontaneous. This has been termed the *preferred* response. Preferred responses include accepting an invitation, answering a question, complying with a request, accepting an offer, agreeing with an assessment, disagreeing with other's self-deprecation, thanking for a compliment, and denying blame, (just as denial of guilt is preferred in the legal system). On the other hand, turning down an invitation, side-stepping a question, refusing an offer, disagreeing, agreeing with another's self-criticism, accepting blame seem to be marked, or dispreferred (Atkinson & Drew, 1979, p. 112; Heritage, 1984, pp. 265–280). How can we tell?

The dispreferred second turns found in American and English texts were delayed or displaced, and were marked or elaborated by preface markers like "well . . . ," token agreements, apologies, mitigations, hedges, indirection, explanations, or excuses. Speakers seeking agreement or compliance from partners can use this knowledge of preference marking. If they expect immediate and overlapped agreement, they note the presence of a delay or of dispreference markers and make remedies even while in the first turn in the exchange (Pomerantz, 1984). Quick dispreferred responses without these added markers of norm awareness can be heard as rude—though of course they can be done as wit. This system maximizes the likelihood of socially solidary moves, by delaying disaffiliative moves, according to sociologists (Heritage, 1984, p. 276).

If we examine answers to WH-questions and compare expected and unexpected replies, we can find support for this analysis of dispreference. The marker "well" occurs in 56% of answers to Wh-questions that don't give an expected reply, but occurs in 14% of expected answers. Simple yes/no replies to polarity yes/no questions almost never are prefaced by "well" but we find this dispreference marker in 48% of the other types of replies (Schiffrin, 1987, p. 107). The less in agreement the answer with the questioner's framework, the more likely one will find "well." This is an example of a pragmatic discourse marker which marks both a turn unit and a feature of action.

What is especially valuable in this reliance on local cues of preference analysis is that it allows us to check for preferences in any cultural environment by observing rather than just interviewing. We have to start with some obvious case and see what the features that identify the *dispreferred* reply are for this group of speakers, then look at all the other examples to identify what is the cultural or group *preference*.

A nice example of cultural factors is the problem of compliments. What is the quick or "preferred" response to a compliment? East Asian immigrants to the United States are surprised to see the preference for agreement dominant in giving thanks for compliments; for many of them, immediate disagreement and self-depreciation is required by the valuing of humble self-presentation.

Closing

A common example of the structure of action is the closing of conversations. In phone conversations, the caller gets to bring up the first topic, but some topics are delicate and may be hard to introduce in an appropriate and coherent way, so they may still be pending at parting. In phone closings, people don't just suddenly say "goodbye" unless interrupted. Instead, there are several turns in the closure, as in this example:

(13)   [B has called to invite C, but C is going out to dinner]
   a B: Yeah. Well get on your clothes and get out and collect some
   b   of that free food and we'll make it some other time Judy then.
   c C: Okay then Jack.
   d B: Bye bye.
   e C: Bye bye.

Schegloff and Sacks, 1973, p. 87

In this text, turn (a) anticipates closure of the conversation with "well," and by projecting a vague future encounter, and leaves an opening if (C) has more to say. A new topic could be introduced at this point, but it would be marked as dispreferred. Only when the "O.K." in turn (c) ratifies agreement on closure and reveals that there is no topic on the table, can they proceed to say goodbye. This closing exchange involved only two adjacency pairs.

Four steps have been found in such closures in American phone conversations (Schegloff & Sacks, 1973): finishing a topic; topicless passing turns to ensure there is nothing left to say; optional appropriate ends like an apology, summary, or "thank you" and various warrants for closing; the final farewells. In the above example we see only the summary, passing turn, and farewells.

Pre-sequences

The first line of conversation 13 is called a preclosing since it indicates a closure is coming. There are also preinvitations, such as "Are you busy Tuesday?" and prerequests like "Is there any coffee left?" (Schegloff, 1980). These presequences are an indirect means of avoiding embarrassment to the speaker. They give an opening to the addressee to make an offer, or avoid having one's invitation turned down or having a request refused (Levinson, 1983, pp. 356–364). In this ingenious analysis, the form of **indirect requests** such as "Can you help me?" suggests they began as prerequests and became conventionalized. By raising questions about ability and availability, a speaker can suggest a trajectory of action without specifying it on record, and thus save face by avoiding refusal.

"Is there any coffee left?" or "Is Sybil there?" "Have you got the time?" have become familiar in place of on-record requests (Ervin-Tripp, 1976; Brown & Levinson, 1987). They may lead directly to compliance, but as adjacency pairs they do not call conversationally for the "O.K." of compliance, so they are distinguishable from conventional requests like "Can you help me?" or "Could you tell me the time you close?" This difference tells us that though they are unambiguous as requests in context, they are nonetheless off-record as the first of an adjacency pair. On the other hand, in recalls, they are reported as requests, for example, "He asked for Sybil" (Hickmann & Warden, 1991). As we shall see, these contrasts play a role in social relations.

Social features

The social dimensions which are at issue in linguistic marking of social relations have been identified in two different theories. Brown and Gilman (1960) called them *power* and *solidarity*, when they analyzed the European pronominal contrasts which use a high form like "usted" or "vous" in Spanish and French both to superiors in age or rank, and to strangers (Brown & Gilman, 1960). P. Brown and S. Levinson (1987) elaborated the notion of "face," originally an Asian idea about one's reputation, which had been taken up as a theme of social self-presentation by Goffman. They altered the idea in two ways. First, it had been a notion of the speaker's own face, which combined dignity of demeanor with appropriateness in behavior to others. They changed the notion of face to an attempt to help satisfy an addressee's needs. Taking up a proposal of R. Lakoff, they suggested two dimensions: avoiding imposition/ intrusion and maintaining the addressee's autonomy, which they called "negative face." Expressing positive affect and esteem was the other, which they called "positive face." These dimensions are important when speakers "threaten face" by requests, offers, and so on, and thus must remedy the threat by a variety of tactics which they have found in many languages (Brown & Levinson, 1987). The poles they discuss seem to express the solidarity-distance dimension of R. Brown, but not the power dimension, which is more indirectly involved in verbal choices in their analysis than in Brown and Gilman's.

Address terms

Recall the conversation in which the sister, answering the phone, summons her brother with "Hey stoopid!" The action involved, a summons, is obvious because it followed the phone ring, it was prefaced by an attention getting "hey," and it was shouted. The summons is accomplished by an address term which has social content, an insult. Address terms may be used to get someone's attention, but they also occur for other functions. In persuasion and in arguments, address terms can increase in frequency. Names always do two things at once; they serve a function such as calling attention; they also convey information about social relations or about emotion or both.

In every society, naming is the outcome of a semantic choice system, typically involving setting (Your Honor), age of addressee (Bobby), kinship, relative status, gender, occupation, and possibly marital status (Ervin-Tripp, 1973). In any extended family, a list of the address terms will contain indicators of familiarity, distance, and generation. Overlaid on these regular names are variants which reflect situational and affective factors, for example the contrast between choice of nicknames and endearments in families.

Reference to people (Judge Barrows, Joe, Dad, Gramps, Honey, Uncle Joe) displays similar variation (Ervin-Tripp, 1973), and the use of "we" and "you" is sensitive to issues of classification, inclusion, and exclusion. "Why do you vote that way?" may imply the general "you," the specific single "you" of the addressee, or the "you" of a

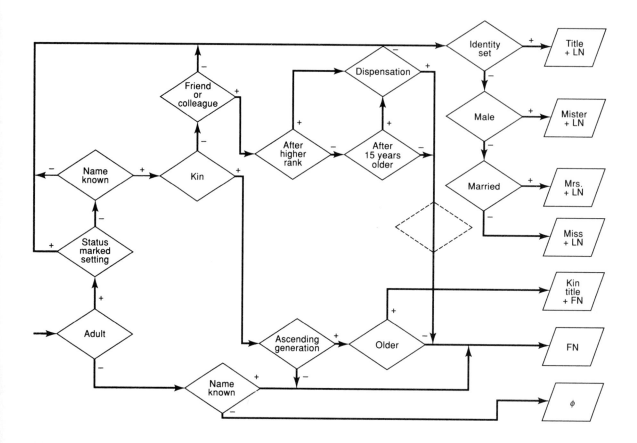

Figure 6.1

An American address system

group the speaker doesn't belong to. Speakers of European languages which have two or more pronouns of address (sie, vous, usted, vs. tu, du) will note that many of the same social features select these choices—relative age, respect, distance, intimacy and so forth. Brown and Gilman wrote about the pronouns of power and solidarity, which also delicately nuance literature, even in the English of Shakespeare, as a choice between "thou" and "you."

In these systems, markers of distance and of respect are collapsed, so a 60-year-old woman cannot tell when she is first-named by a car salesman or a dentist if it is through friendliness, lack of respect, or condescension. The baby talk she receives in a nursing home or hospital is easier to interpret.

But European systems are relatively simple. In Asia, two Korean women who meet for the first time must spend time establishing age of graduation, marital status, and if relevant, job status and number of sons. This stage is necessary to know how to talk. In Southeast Asia (e.g., Japan, Korea, Java), style level in terms of syntax and vocabulary throughout all speech is tuned to context and to the social features of the relationship of the speaker to the addressee as well as to persons named in the talk. A Vietnamese or Korean child who does not speak with respect features to an older person would be punished. The contrasts, which in Korean mark every verb and many nouns, are very obvious.

Requests

(14) Constructed examples
   a. Hey lady move your car.
   b. Ma'am, if you could move that car.
   c. Pardon me, that car is in the way.

The function of address terms is usually clear enough so the address term can be used just to convey social meaning. Requests are far more complex because the hearer must figure out both the social message and the action message. If I say "it's cold here," do I want you to do something about it or not? (Ervin-Tripp, 1976).

When speakers are in a cooperative relationship, or when the trajectory of action is obvious or conventional, speakers can use minimal cues and the action will be understood, leaving the form free to carry social and affective information.

Typically, a request is fitted into a sequence which includes attention-getters, framing moves, the request itself, supporting information which precedes or follows, and a reply along with its justifications. And there may be remedies if the reply doesn't fit the initiator's needs.

(15) [Two friends are indoors at a birthday party, Eliza (6) is outdoors with an adult]

   a Ann (7):   Oh, they're going in the back yard!
   . . . .
   i   [Hester (8) knocks on the window.]   [SUMMONS]
   j   Hester: No! Eliza No!   [PROHIBITION]
   k   Ann: Hester, don't open the . . . [grabs arm. H stops]
   l   Hester: No, don't show her. Don't show her!
                   Don't show her.   [EXPLICIT PROHIBITION]
   m   Hester: ([pleading voice] It's secret.)   [JUSTIFICATION]
                                             UCBDisclab:Cannon21

In this scene, Hester's awareness of a problem was evoked in turn (a), but it was not until turn (i) that she made an inference and moved into immediate action with an attention-getter, a loud and simple prohibition, and a justification.

Tactics such as the use of prerequests or hints can forestall making a conventional request. Often these seem emergent, not planned. They include giving reasons, forestalling intervention, neutralizing obstacles, changing the context, and getting the hearer to be aware of the speaker's goals. These hints were found most often either in cases where the speaker didn't feel authorized to make a request, or when there was such cooperative interaction there was no need to be explicit.

A request can be formulated as an order, as an offer, or as a permission request, with different social implications. Requests which are expressed as an offer or permission request give the hearer the right to refuse, in form if not in reality.

Conventional requests include imperatives, needs and wants, and requests which are qualified with deference markers like conditionals and modals.

(16)   Cleaner to older boss: I could use some furniture polish.

Ervin-Tripp, 1976, p. 30

The elaboration of these mitigating features leads to the possibility of marking social relations overtly while keeping the request explicit:

(17)   Teenager to friend's mother:
        Do you have any water that I could drink?

This question contains both an availability prerequest, and a permission request containing a conditional. These three features together make a strong social statement.

Social variation.   The form of requests is delicately related to social features, as the following example supplied by H. Sacks reveals:

(18)   A couple is tasting herring with a stepfather:
        a   W: Bring some out, so that Max could have some too.
        b   W: Geschmacht. Hmm. Oh it's delicious!
             Ben could you hand me a napkin please?

The imperative in (a) is permitted by the shared host role with a common goal of benefitting a guest. In (b) when the beneficiary is herself, and the task is not part of the expected role of the hearer, the conventional polite request, conditional, and "please" are all used. Possibly the address term, too, is a mitigator.

In American English, usage varies with region and class. In middle-class adult speakers, subordinates are most likely to be given statements of need and imperatives; equals are likely to be given hints allowing for humor and sharing of assumptions, unless explicitness is needed so they use imperatives. To superiors, questions and hints appear when compliance is not certain; otherwise we choose permission requests and conventionally polite requests "Could you, would you mind . . ." which contain overt markers of politeness (Ervin-Tripp, 1976). Such mitigations are characteristic of demands made outside the normal role of the addressee—that is, for special favors. Mitigating features in cases where compliance is doubtful begin to appear in preschool children even in usage with other children, and in role play where they symbolize status (Ervin-Tripp, Guo, & Lampert, 1990). Of course, aggravation is a direction of social modification which can be richly elaborated, too, especially when rights are violated or the addressee is of lower power. We found good examples from U.S. Marine sergeants.

Since the form of requests corresponds to social relationships, requests can be a good territory for status haggles; Goodwin found that in boys' groups, directness, aggravation, and hierarchy were apparent in directives. In girls' groups, there were more suggestions for future action, and less hierarchical differentiation by directives—except when girls talked to boys or younger children, or took on roles in play (M. Goodwin, 1990).

Mitigation upward is so automatic in adults that it can actually be life threatening. In a study of flight crew communications in airplane accidents, Linde (1988) found that lower status members of flight crews tended to use indirect, mitigated suggestions to the pilot, and that these warnings were the least likely to be understood.

Key

The key of an interactional situation is the general tone of seriousness, task orientation, levity, playfulness, which can affect the interpretation of particular moves, and alter distance or solidarity. Rae's whining tone in *marking* Cindy in example (4) affects our interpretation of the quotations. Key constitutes a major contextualization cue for deciding how to interpret meaning. "When you say that, smile" refers to the many terms which can be intimate in one key and insulting in another, such as *bitch* and *bastard*. One way to check on the cues of key is to examine how you know when someone is joking. Requests, for example, can be serious or mock. The key of a conversation can shift, affecting a whole situation or text.

Telling jokes can be an activity, but much more often wit occurs in personal conversations, to serve other purposes by the construction of something laughable, as in the example below of spontaneous humor. This exchange followed a long description by Helen of how she made cappuccinos at her job in a cafe, and how Bill had been served a bad one. It was topically relevant but changed the key:

(19) a   Edie: == I can't wait until mcdonald's gets *espressos and *cappuccinos they *will

b   Helen: == Yeah

c   Lynn: That'll really be *good

d   Edie: mac mc = mcspresso =   = mc mcspresso =

e   Helen: = mc   =

f   Lynn: = mc mcpuccino =

g   Edie: (laughs) mcpuccino   = mcspresso   =

h   Bill: = mcpuccino o my god =

i   Lynn: It sounds like = uh   al = pacino (laughs).

j   Edie: = al pacino =

k   Edie: Yeah [laughs] yeah they'll have al *pacino do the *publicity for it **yeah [laughs]

(UCBDisclab: CCON2)

The joint construction of humor in this passage is typical of friendly groups (all were females except Bill, who provided the evaluation). *Duetting* (Falk, 1980) occurs in (i-j), where Edie completed the sentence Lynn had begun before Lynn finished.

The success of humor depends strongly on shared attitudes and knowledge. In this case, awareness of the naming creativity of the McDonald's chain and of movie stars like Al Pacino were necessary. Humor depends so delicately on the timing of awareness that shared knowledge cannot be created by explicitness as it can in disputes, narratives, or other genres. *Explaining* a joke often destroys its humor.

Text

What we finally hear is the text of the conversation, the actual words that we study as a transcript, including intonation, vocal qualities and gestures, which all contribute to the meaning the hearer interprets.

Sometimes the surface features cluster in recognizable types we call **registers**, such as sportscaster talk, sermons, and stewardess style, which are identified with a speech event, genre, or role. The characteristics of these genres are so recognizable they can be parodied.

(20) a About ready to replace the wiring, Eric?

      b That's right, Bob. I've run the wiring around the joists and I'm about ready to shimmy the grout into the holes I've made with my inch-and-a-half obverse punch.

J. Carroll, S. F. Chronicle 3/22/91

This text is from a column making fun of home repair television shows. We recognize that this is too wordy for normal talk while doing everyday repairs; it is hyperexplicit instructional talk. The oddness is enhanced by specialized vocabulary possibly invented and known only to experts.

In a sketch recorded by improvisational artists Elaine May and Mike Nichols, May played a flight attendant whose husband expressed despair at her emotional distance. Her voice has the calm, cheery sing-song of flight attendants, the comedy lying in the inappropriateness of tone to the marital crisis.

(21) a W: I *am preparing *breakfast, but if you'd *rather go *without it I'll certainly hold it *back for you.

      f H: = No, look = I can't *stand it any more, do you *understand me I can't *bear it, I'm getting *out, I *quit, I want a *divorce.

      g W: We-ell, if you *do feel that *way about it, I'd *suggest that you *wait until perhaps *3 pm when I *will be back from shopping at the beautiful *Saks Fifth Avenue.

Nichols & May, 1959

These different types of talk, varying in vocabulary, sentence types, sometimes also in pitch and pronunciation, are called registers. Baby-talk, the speech you use to two-year-olds, is a good example, familiar to everyone. But special registers appear in many job contexts. The test is whether they are recognizable out of context. The choice of register is based on contextual factors, which is why misplacement is funny (courtroom speech to a baby, baby-talk to a judge, flight attendant style to a husband). Register is a coherent choice, so that speakers do not shift register within a setting without conveying social meaning.

Within communities of multilingual speakers **code-switching** between languages refers to language choice. *Situational code-switching* involves switching at the boundaries of change in major situational factors like setting, addressee, or situation. In Puerto Rico, English is required by law in the federal court, but Spanish might be used between speakers off the record. A public lecturer using classical Arabic switches to colloquial Arabic to talk informally face-to-face about the same topic (Ferguson, 1959). *Conversational code-switching* refers to juxtaposition within the same speech exchange of passages with features from different language systems. Switching occurs unconsciously and automatically in informal conversations on the basis of personal meaning, for example, it might occur between greeting and first topic, between a command and persuasive justification or a repeated insistence.

(22)
      Come here, come here. Ben aca!

Gumperz, 1982

Switches occur for quotations, to specify addressee, as interjections, to get attention, to intensify by repetition, to elaborate, qualify, personalize or objectify, to change function or action or topic. The most general effect of code-switching is to provide a contextualization cue of the cultural or personal framework for the interpretation of the content (Scotton & Ury, 1977; Gumperz, 1982, pp. 59–99).

Bilingual code-switching is not structurally random; it provides a nice marker of the seams of speech for psycholinguists. Switching most often occurs before nouns (as borrowings), between large units like clauses, noun phrase subjects and predicates (but not between pronominal subjects and predicates or in ellipsis), between nouns and prepositional phrases, between conjunctions and clauses, but not within integrated units like idiomatic phrases, nor can switching oscillate within a list or a phrase. Generally each segment must have some semantic independence and permit emphasis (Gumperz, 1982; Poplack, 1980).

(23)   [making valentines]

(7.5) a A: Mommy I don't want to make 18 so why don't you help me.

      b A: I mean 28 I have to make.

      c M: Hm?You can do that.

      d A: Mother!

      e M: You have a whole week.

      f A: I know but we're supposed to all make 'em today.

      g M: No you don't have to make them all today.

UCBDisclab:Cannon11

Texts often are **coherent**, in the sense that their structure of actions lead to the same goals, or the ideational structure contains topics and propositions that fit together. Of course, in casual conversation, especially secondary to other activities, frequent topic jumps are common and conversations may not appear to be coherent. Texts are also often structurally **cohesive**, in that there are linguistic features which co-refer, substitutions, ellipsis, and connectives (Halliday & Hasan, 1976). "That," in turn (c) co-refers with the verb identified in line (b). "Them" in lines (f) and (g) corefers with 18 and 28 valentines, which have been talked about earlier in (a) and (b). Valentines are also referred to by ellipsis in (a) and (b) where numbers are used but "Valentines" are understood. A more complex ellipsis that relies on the text for interpretation is "You have a whole week 'to make the valentines.'" The "I know" of (f) implies the preceding turn = 'I have a whole week,' and the turn in (g) is a negative repetition of (f).

Another structural way to make a cohesive text is through the use of reply markers and connectives. In this short text there are three reply markers: "hm," "I know," and "no," and three connectives: "so" which conveys that the first clause supplies a justification for the second, "but" which implies a contradiction, and "I mean" which marks a repair. These connectives thus supply not only cohesion but information about the ideas in dispute, that is, the propositional structure (Schiffrin, 1987).

These markers and connectives sometimes mark turn starts, that is the participation structure, sometimes mark pragmatic relationships such as compliance with a request, sometimes mark propositional relationships such as temporal sequence, and sometimes mark the global structure of the discourse, by indicating new topics, repairs, side sequences, interruptions, or restarts.

Genre

Conversation 23 can also be analyzed as a **dispute** in which there is a set of moves and responses thematically related. In a dispute there is a disagreement through three turns. In move (a), Ann supplies a justification for the help she explicitly requests. Her mother's response move takes two turns, (c) and (e) which are linked in the propositional system by an implicit causal relation. In (f), Ann rejects her mother's argument, trying to remove her mother's reasons for refusal. In (g), the mother in turn rejects the argument in (f).

This is a typical dispute, which moves through a series of linked arguments. These arguments, which are at the ideational level of the structure of interaction, have reflections in the text forms. The forms particularly relevant to disputes are the "so" identifying a relation of justification to request, the "I know but" which marks agreement plus the elaboration of a new argument which implies a disagreement, and the "No you don't . . . " + repetition, which directly contradicts the previous turn. These forms help us identify that the genre involved is a dispute.

Sometimes the first thing we recognize about a text is what is called its genre—whether it is a dispute, a joke, a riddle, a story, a poem, or a news report. Certain genres are systematically situated in speech events. The sermon and the prayer are parts of church services, the cross-examination is part of a trial, a joke can begin an after-dinner speech, the story can occur at bedtime. Others arise in the course of other talk, as strategies. The dispute in (24) was incidental to an unsatisfied request.

Stories can be used to support or contradict claims, to persuade, to joke, to support requests or settle disputes (M. Goodwin, 1990). All of these types of talk may serve more complex purposes in discourse.

How do we recognize a genre? Consider the following text:

(24) a   L: . . . you have had sexual intercourse on a previous occasion haven't you?

b   W: Yes.

c   L: On many previous occasions?

d   W: Not many.

e   L: Several?

f   W: Yes

g   L: With several men?

h   W: No.

i   L: Just one?

j   W: Two.

k   L: Two. And you are seventeen and a half?

l   W: Yes.

Levinson, 1979, p. 380

What makes this obviously a *cross-examination* is three properties. The language in (a) is formal and explicit, with none of the slang, humor, indirectness, hesitation, and markers of surprise or of affect that might mark personal or friendly talk on such a topic. The participation structure is question and answer, with minimal replies. The questions are not open-ended and neutral, but are built with presupposed replies to suggest a particular inference—in this case, the experience of the woman in relation to her age. Contrast this recognizable genre with the next, also in a transactional or nonpersonal conversation:

(25) a   I: What was it leading to?

b   A: It was leading to the technician apprenticeship I mentioned.

c   I: Oh I see, yeah.

d   A: Yeah.

e   I: Yeah. Right. And . . did you complete, you completed that?

UCBDisclab:JOB07

In this very different type of stranger text, an interview, a job training center interviewer used a relatively relaxed, informal style, displaying surprise in (c), and hesitation, topic boundary marking, and rewording in (e). She proceeded slowly, rather than trying to get the candidate off-guard by rapid questioning. The interviewer's first question is unslanted and solicits formulation by the candidate. The agreement feedback in (c) and the echoing in (d) and (e) suggest affective coopera-tion. Solidarity features can also be found in commercial contexts when commit-ments are sought. The recognizability of the genre of cross-examination arises both from the adversarial relationship and the institutional features of the court.

Stories

In contrasting decontextualized sentences and those in authentic texts among friends, the most striking shift is in the degree of ellipsis, or omission of surface elements, and of cohesion that occurs. The following text belonged to a set of rounds of **narratives** about a recent earthquake. Art and Neal are English brothers who are students in California, Olga is Neal's female friend, Cass is her roommate.

(26) a　Art: You know . . you know that that nice glass china display
　　　　　　　case in our dining room?

　　　b　Neal: == in the dining room.

　　　c　Cass: oooooh.

　　　d　Neal: trashed

　　　e　Cass: forget it

　　　f　Neal: absolutely trashed

　　　g　Art: == whole thing a=bsolutely . . yeah　　　　　　　　　=

　　　h　Neal:　　　　　　= every single bit of glass and pottery in th- =

　　　i　Olga: == and crystal?

　　　j　Neal: == all the crystal trashed

　　　l　Art: == crystal

　　　m　Neal: == everything trashed

　　　n　Cass: oooh my *gaaawd

　　　　　　　　　　　　　　　　　　　　UCBDisclab: QUAKE

This text is an example of *duetting* (Falk, 1980), a participation structure in which several people collaborate to produce utterances. There are two duetting story tellers; an evaluation from Cass (c, n) and a prompt from Olga (i). The repetition with elaboration by the story tellers gives dramatic emphasis by a kind of acceleration. The first line sets the scene by identifying the *characters* in a typical story introduction. The event telling begins with a single predicate, "trashed" in (d), then expansion of the predicate comes with an adverb, "absolutely trashed" (f), next, expansion of the subject "whole thing absolutely" in (g), then a clause spelling out "whole thing" in detail (g, h), to which the prompt "and crystal?" allows an addition in (j). Line (m) provides a summary and the fourth repetition of the refrain: "trashed."

The strong sense of cohesion arises from the rhythmical pairing of topics with elliptical predicates: "crystal" + "everything trashed." The heavy use of repetition is a common feature of narratives by close friends (Tannen, 1989). This story illustrates well that narrators do not act alone. "It is hearers of the story who ultimately provide the turn, realize the point, and endorse the action," (Schiffrin, 1987, p. 17).

This brief text illustrates the basic structure of a story. It was in a round of stories about earthquake damage, so it was not elicited by a participant's question or started with an introduction or framing as a story, such as "You know what happened the other day?" or by an introductory abstract. In rounds, "When an event of one type occurs, it becomes grounds for a second contribution of the same type," (Ryave, 1978; Tannen, 1984). But stories occur in many contexts—for instance, to support requests, to shift frames in a dispute (M. Goodwin, 1990). Since many studies of narratives elicit them in a laboratory or extract them from their context, we don't know much about how these different contexts affect the structure of stories.

Stories contain information about the temporal location and characters, as in line (a), narrative clauses which recount a past, future, or fantasied happening or event, and evaluations, such as the last line. Some also have a **coda** which closes the story (Labov & Waletsky, 1967). Perhaps the summary in (m) provides the coda for this simple narrative. Stories are cultural products; participation expectations such as joint construction with the *audience*, and structural expectations vary (Polanyi, 1989; C. Goodwin, 1981).

Goodwin gives us a narrative example used as a strategy in a dispute between Chopper and Tony:

(27)

a	Chopper:	*Guess what. ([rapid] *Lemme tell ya) Guess what.
b		(0.8) We was comin home from *practice.
c		(0.4) and, three boys came up there. and
d		([rapid] asked us for money and Tony did like this.)
e		(016) [raises hands up]
f		([loud] I ain't got) ([laughing] = no money) =
g	Others:	= [laugh] =

Goodwin, 1990, p. 243

Reference.   In many stories, the first time a character appears, there is identifying information or an orientation. The later references to characters are by pronoun or ellipsis (also called zero anaphora). In (d) the boys are left out of the second clause, but Tony is named. In adult speech, the coordinate clauses of the narrative may use such coordinate predicates, which involve a kind of subject ellipsis. In languages like Japanese and Korean, reference to what has been mentioned before is usually absent, since in these languages ellipsis is rife. Subjects and objects can be understood and omitted. In stories, pronouns or ellipsis are most common when referents (a) are present at the time of speech, (b) have been mentioned before, and (c) were mentioned in the same chunk or episode in the story. Studies in English and French (Karmiloff-Smith, 1979) suggest that speakers like to keep the same subject through an episode, even using passives if they refer to undergoing action, just to keep the same subject throughout the episode. In side sequences or orienting clauses pronouns are used also.

But when a new episode occurs, a change in characters' role, or reappearance of a character, a noun occurs. There is, however, social variation depending on the familiarity, class, and other cultural features. This is when gestural pointing occurs too, not during the episodes where the subject is already set up (McNeill, 1987, p. 53). Even children make this global adjustment, changing verb tenses to mark episode boundaries (Bamberg, 1987).

Backgrounding.   Stories typically alternate states and events. The events in a story may be temporally located. In (27b) the temporal and spatial location of the story is suggested. Sometimes the narrative clauses are separate, or just loosely

linked by "and" or "and then" as in (27). In such stories there is just a chain of parallel or coordinate serial clauses like route directions or recipes. Verbs are similar in marking and noun ellipsis increases. Another, more complex strategy is to highlight or foreground these narrative happenings, by putting them into main clauses, and putting the orienting information contained in descriptions of states or activities, goals or causes into subordinate clauses. Even very young children begin to make this contrast:

(28) (2:9 years)
       When I was sick, I couldn't have any birthday cake.

UCB:Disclab SM

(29) (5 years)
       When I was walking down the street, I saw this piece of glass and picked it up.

UCBDisclab: BO5

This structure has the result that "unbounded states, habituals, generics and also negated propositions are generally excluded from the main structure of the narrative" (von Stutterheim & Klein, 1989, p. 50). These become the backgrounded information about places, times, and people's states of mind, wishes, and habits which help situate or motivate the narrative events. Between the subordinate or backgrounded clauses and the main or foregrounded clauses we see many contrasts. More kinetic gestures are used with the main clauses (McNeill & Levy, 1982). Verbs in main and subordinate clauses are contrasted, not parallel and similar, and pronouns rather than ellipsis are used for the nominal information in backgrounded clauses.

Are these structural contrasts in the texts peculiar to stories? In other types of texts, contrasts between clause types, verb types, nouns, pronouns and ellipsis, word order and connective forms seem to reflect topic organization. A story involves a sequence of events with a focus on an actor. A description of your apartment involves a sequence of locations with information about relative spatial position. A route direction such as directions on how to find your house involves a sequence of commands about space with a focus on the moving person. A recipe contains commands about quantities and actions. Even though this general contrast remains the same, the sentence structure of such texts is different because of the focus on place in descriptions, on moving persons in route directions, and on actors in stories (von Stutterheim & Klein, 1989). In these ways, the linguistic structure of texts reflects the goals in the activity that called for speech. The result is a type of coherence which derives from the ideational, or propositional structure of a text, whether it be within a genre or just within a topic in a more loosely structured interaction (Levelt, 1989).

Summary

The development of talk in dialogue occurs in sociable or in task contexts where people bring notions of what the activity is, their goals, and their social relations to each other. The speech may confirm or change these. Dialogue cannot be seen as a sequence of turns at monologue, but as a joint product. The turntaking creates chances to make change through choices of topics, propositions, actions, and social meaning. Each is altered by what went before, because there are strong structural expectations, and discourse markers of the global topical, propositional, action, and sequential structure which members can recognize. All of these create the resulting text.

References

Agrawal, A. 1976. Who will speak next. *Papers in Linguistic Analysis*. (Department of Linguistics, University of Delhi) *1*, 58–71.

Atkinson, J. M., & Drew, P. (1979). *Order in court: The organization of verbal interaction in judicial settings*. London: Macmillan.

Bamberg, M. G. W. (1987). *The acquisition of narratives; learning to use language*. Berlin: Mouton de Gruyter.

Barker, R. G., & Wright, H. F. (1954). *Midwest and its children: The psychological ecology of an American town*. New York: Appleton-Century-Crofts.

Brady, P. T. (1969). A statistical analysis of on-off patterns in 16 conversations. *Bell System Technical Journal, 47*, 73–91.

Brown, P., & Levinson, S. C. (1987). *Politeness*. Cambridge: Cambridge University Press.

Brown, R., & Gilman, A. (1960). The pronouns of power and solidarity. In T. Sebeok (Ed.), *Style in language* (pp. 253–276). Cambridge, MA: MIT Press.

Cheepen, C. (1988). *The predictability of informal conversation*. London: Pinter.

Clark, H. H. (1979). Responding to indirect speech acts. *Cognitive Psychology, 11*, 430–477.

Clark, H. H. (1985). Language use and language users. In G. Lindzey & E. Aronson (Eds.), *Handbook of social psychology* (3rd ed.). Hillsdale, NJ: Random House.

Clark, H. H., & Schaefer, E. G. (1989). Contributing to discourse. *Cognitive Science, 13*, 159–294.

Clark, H. H., & Wilkes-Gibbs, D. (1986). Referring as a collaborative process. *Cognition, 22*, 1–39.

Clark, H., & Carlson, T. (1982). Hearers and speech acts. *Language, 58*, 332–373.

Duncan, S. (1972). Some signals and rules for taking speaking turns in conversation. *Journal of Personality and Social Psychology, 23*, 283–292.

Duncan, S., & Fiske, D. W. (1977). *Face to face interaction: Research, methods and theory*. Hillsdale, NJ: Lawrence Erlbaum.

Eckert, P. (1989). *Jocks and burnouts: Social categories and identity in the high school*. New York: Teachers College Press.

Ellis, A., & Beattie, G. (1986). *The psychology of language and communication*. London: Weidenfeld and Nicolson.

Ervin-Tripp, S. (1973). *The acquisition of communicative choice*. Stanford: University Press.

Ervin-Tripp, S. (1977). Children's verbal turn-taking. In E. Ochs & B. B. Schieffelin (Eds.), *Developmental Pragmatics* (pp. 391–414). New York: Academic Press.

Ervin-Tripp, S. (1976). Is Sybil there? The structure of some American English directives. *Language in Society, 5*, 25–66.

Ervin-Tripp, S., Guo, J. & Lampert, M. (1990). Politeness and persuasion in children's control acts. *Journal of Pragmatics, 14*, 307–332.

Falk, Jane. (1980). The conversational duet. *Proceedings of the Sixth Annual Meeting of the Berkeley Linguistics Society, 6*, 507–514.

Fasold, R. W. (1990). *The sociolinguistics of language*. Oxford: Blackwell.

Ferguson, C. A. (1959). Diglossia. *Word, 15*, 325–340.

Fishman, P. M. (1983). Interaction: The work women do. In B. Thorne, C. Kramarae, & N. Henley, (Eds.), *Language, gender and society*. Rowley, MA: Newbury House.

Gardner, C. B. (1984). Passing by: Street remarks, address rights, and the urban female. In J. Baugh & J. Sherzer (Eds.), *Language in Use* (pp. 148–164). Englewood Cliffs, NJ: Prentice-Hall.

Godard, D. (1977). Same setting, different norms: Phone call beginnings in France and the United States. *Language in Society, 6*, 209–220.

Goffman, E. (1963). *Behavior in public places*. New York: Macmillan Free Press.

Goodwin, C. (1981). *Conversational organization: Interaction between speakers and hearers*. New York: Academic Press.

Goodwin, M. H. (1990). *He-said-she-said: Talk as social organization among black children*. Bloomington: Indiana University Press.

Gumperz, J. J. (1982). *Discourse strategies*. Cambridge: Cambridge University Press.

Halliday, M. A. K., & Hasan, R. (1976). *Cohesion in English*. London: Longman.

Hemphill, L. (1989). Topic development, syntax, and social class. *Discourse Processes, 12,* 267–286.

Heritage, J. (1984). *Garfinkel and Ethnomethodology*. Cambridge: Polity Press.

Hickmann, M., & Warden, D. (1991). Children's strategies when reporting appropriate and inappropriate speech forms. *Pragmatics, 1,* 27–70.

Jaffe, J., & Feldstein, S. (1970). *Rhythms of Dialogue*. New York: Academic Press.

Jefferson, G. (1972). Side sequences. In D. Sudnow (Ed.), *Studies in social interaction*. New York: The Free Press.

Jefferson, G. (1973). A case of precision timing in ordinary conversation: Overlapped tag-positioned address terms in closing sequences. *Semiotica, 9,* 47–96.

Karmiloff-Smith, A. (1979). *A functional approach to child language*. Cambridge, England: Cambridge University Press.

Kendon, A. (1967). Some functions of gaze direction in social interaction. *Acta Psychologica, 26,* 22–63.

Labov, W. & Waletsky, J. (1967). Narrative analysis: Oral versions of personal experience. In J. Helm (Ed.), *Essays on the verbal and visual arts*. Seattle: University of Washington Press.

Lacoste, M. (1981). The old woman and the doctor: A contribution to the analysis of unequal linguistic exchanges. *Journal of Pragmatics, 5,* 169–180.

Lakoff, R. (1973). The logic of politeness; or minding your p's and q's. *Papers from the Ninth Regional Meeting of the Chicago Linguistic Society, 9,* 292–305.

Laver, J., & Hutcheson, S. (Eds.) (1972). *Communication in face–to–face interaction*. Harmondsworth, Middlesex: Penguin.

Levelt, W. J. M. (1989). *Speaking: From intention to articulation*. Cambridge, MA: MIT Press.

Levinson, S. (1979). Activity types and language. *Linguistics, 17,* 356–399.

Levinson, S. (1983). *Pragmatics*. Cambridge: Cambridge University Press.

Linde, C. (1988). The quantitative study of communicative success: Politeness and accidents in aviation discourse. *Language in Society, 17,* 375–401.

McNeill, D. (1987). *Psycholinguistics: A new approach*. New York: Harper and Row.

McNeill, D., & Levy, E. (1982) Conceptual representations in language activity and gesture. In R. Jarvella and W. Klein (Eds.), *Speech, space and action: Studies in deixis and related topics*. Chichester: Wiley, pp. 271–295.

McTear, M. F. (1979). Is conversation structured? Towards an analysis of informal spoken discourse. In W. Wolck & P. L. Garvin (Eds.), *The Fifth Lacus Forum*, Columbia, SC: Hornbeam.

Merritt, M. (1976). On questions following questions (in service encounters). *Language in Society, 5,* 315–357.

Nichols, M., & May, E. (1959). Improvisations: Conversation at breakfast. *Echo Magazine*.

Philips, S. (1972). Participant structures and communicative competence. In C. Cazden, V. John & D. Hymes (Eds.), *The functions of language in the classroom* (pp. 370–394). NY: Teachers College Press.

Polanyi, L. (1989). *Telling the American story: A structural and cultural analysis of conversational storytelling*. Cambridge, MA: MIT Press.

Pomerantz, A. (1984). Agreeing and disagreeing with assessments: Some features of preferred/dispreferred turn shapes. In J. M. Atkinson & J. Heritage (Eds.), *Structures of social action* (pp. 57–101). Cambridge: Cambridge University Press.

Poplack, S. (1980). Sometimes I'll start a sentence in Spanish y termino en espanol: Toward a typology of code-switching. *Linguistics, 18,* 561–618.

Redeker, G. (1990). Ideational and pragmatic markers of discourse structure. *Journal of Pragmatics, 14,* 367–381.

Redeker, G. (1991). Linguistic markers of discourse structure. *Linguistics*, 29, 1139–1172.

Ryave, A. L. (1978). On the achievement of a series of stories. In J. Schenkein (Ed.), *Studies in the organization of conversational interaction* (pp. 113–132). New York: Academic Press.

Sachs, J. S. (1974). Memory in reading and listening to discourse. *Memory and Cognition. 2*, 95–100.

Sacks, H., Schegloff, E., & Jefferson, G. (1974). A simplest systematics for the organization of turn-taking in conversation. *Language, 50*, 696–735.

Schegloff, E. A. (1980). Preliminaries to preliminaries: "Can I ask you a question?" Language and social interaction. In D. H. Zimmerman & C. West (Eds.), *Sociological Inquiry, 50*, 104–152.

Schegloff, E. A., & Sacks, H. (1973). Opening up closings. *Semiotica, 8*, 289–327.

Schiffrin, D. (1987). *Discourse markers*. Cambridge: Cambridge University Press.

Scotton, C. M., & Ury, W. (1977). Bilingual strategies: The social functions of code-switching. *International Journal of the Sociology of Language, 13*, 5–20.

Simmel, G. (1902). The number of members as determining the sociological form of the group. *American Journal of Sociology, 8*, 1–46, 158–196.

Stutterheim, C. van, & Klein, W. (1989). Referential movement in descriptive and narrative discourse. In R. Dietrich & C. F. Graumann (Eds.), *Language Processing in Social Context* (pp. 39–76). Amsterdam: North-Holland.

Tannen, D. (1984). *Conversational style: Analyzing talk among friends*. Norwood, NJ: Ablex.

Tannen, D. (1990). Gender differences in conversational coherence: Physical alignment and topical cohesion. In B. Dorval (Ed.), *Conversational organization and its development* (pp. 167–206). Norwood, NJ: Ablex

Tannen, D. (1989). *Talking voices: Repetition, dialogue, and imagery in conversational discourse*. Cambridge: Cambridge University Press.

West, C. (1984). *Routine complications: Troubles with talk between doctors and patients*. Bloomington: Indiana University Press.

West, C., & Zimmerman, D. H. (1983). Small insults: A study of interruptions in cross-sex conversations between unacquainted persons. In B. Thorne, C. Kramarae, & N. Henley (Eds.), *Language, gender, and society* (pp. 86–111). Rowley, MA: Newbury House.

Speech Production

VICTORIA A. FROMKIN
UCLA

Introduction

In this chapter, the process by which a speaker turns a mental concept into a spoken utterance is discussed. It is more difficult to study speech production than to investigate speech perception or comprehension because experimental tasks which can reveal the complex steps in the process are not easily constructed. Thus, psycholinguists interested in the speech production process must use more indirect methods to gain insight into how this is accomplished. Researchers have historically relied on two kinds of data in the construction of speech production models—speech errors and speech disfluencies. These data have provided evidence for the units used in generating speech and for the stages which lie between the message the speaker wishes to convey and its spoken expression. The data and their contribution to understanding production will be discussed.

As Chapter 1 notes, knowing a language means knowing how to produce and comprehend an unlimited set of utterances. A competent speaker/listener does this effortlessly, without conscious knowledge of the complexities involved in the process. The internalized knowledge which permits one to simultaneously be both a speaker and a listener is referred to in linguistics as the mental grammar which makes linguistic performance possible. Analysis of speech errors allows insight into the nature of this mental grammar.

From concept to expression

Speech[1] communication may be viewed as a "chain of events linking the speaker's brain with the listener's brain," as illustrated in Figure 7.1 (Denes & Pinson, 1963).

Most of what is shown in Figure 7.1 symbolizes the nonlinguistic aspects of the speech chain, starting "in the speaker's brain (where) . . . appropriate instructions, in the form of impulses along the motor nerves, are sent to the muscles of the vocal organs, the tongue, the lips and the vocal cords," which in turn produce speech sounds waves. In the case of signed communication, the neuro-motor commands to the hands will produce signed gestures. We know a great deal about the physiological, articulatory, and acoustic aspects of these stages of speech production as a result of experimental phonetic research. But we are still far from understanding the processes by which speakers put the message they wish to convey into linguistic form, or how their words and phrases are selected, constructed, and ordered. Nor do we fully understand what intermediate representations of the message look like at the different stages prior to neural excitation of the muscles.

---

[1]Linguistic communication may occur either via spoken or signed utterances. "Speech" or "speech production" as used here, therefore, refers to either the production of sounds or gestures, unless otherwise indicated.

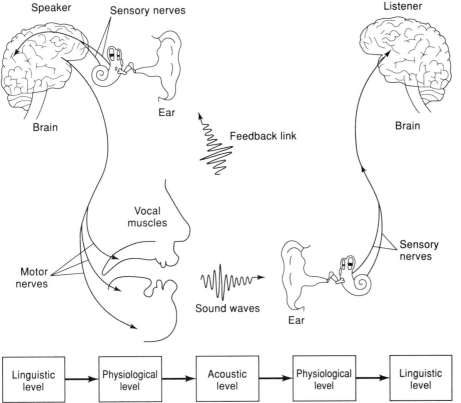

Figure 7.1

The Speech Chain

The different forms in which a spoken message exists in its progress from the mind of the speaker to the mind of the listener.

| Linguistic level | Physiological level | Acoustic level | Physiological level | Linguistic level |

The final stages of this "speech chain" (how the listener responds to the spoken message) were discussed in Chapters 3 through 5 on speech perception, lexical processing, and sentence processing, respectively. This chapter considers the process from the point of view of the speaker, who "Has to . . . arrange his [sic] thoughts, decide what he wants to say and put what he wants to say into *linguistic form* . . . by selecting the right words and phrases to express its meaning, and by placing these words in the correct order required by the grammatical rules of the language . . ." (Denes & Pinson, 1963, p. 3).

The diagram of the speech chain in Figure 7.1 omits the initial and final stages of the process—the thoughts or nonlinguistic message which the speaker wishes to convey to the listener who, if all goes well, will receive that same message. As Pillsbury and Meader observed, " . . . man thinks first and then expresses his thought in words by some sort of translation . . . Speech has its origin in the mind of the speaker . . . and the process . . . is completed only when the word uttered or spoken arouses an idea in the listener . . . " (1928, pp. 92–93). Although philosophers through the ages have speculated about the "language of thought" (Fodor, 1975), knowing how concepts are represented in the mind remains a problem. A number of alternative views have been posited, with little empirical evidence to support one as opposed to another. This chapter will therefore simply assume that speakers have some notion, concept, or message that they wish to convey, but will not attempt to specify how it is represented before being encoded into linguistic form.

Sources of data for models of speech production

Speech errors

It is of course no simple matter to try to understand any aspect of the mental processes involved in speaking. Lashley (1958) noted that "When we think in words, the thoughts come in grammatical form with subject, verb, object and modifying clauses falling into place without our having the slightest perception of how the sentence structure is produced." Although Lashley was basically correct, it is not always the case that the thoughts come in correct grammatical form or that we always select "the right words . . . to express (the) meaning" we wish to convey. All of us have experienced, either as speakers or hearers, utterances which seem to have gotten "mixed-up" on their way out. Consider the following examples, in which we can compare what was actually said to what the speaker intended:

> *You have missed all my history lectures* (intended utterance) → *You have hissed all my mystery lectures.* (utterance actually produced)
> *Noble sons of toil* → *noble tons of soil.*
> *You have wasted the whole term* → *You have tasted the whole worm.*
> *The dear old Queen* → *The queer old dean.*

Such errors in production, called **speech errors** or **slips of the tongue**, occur regularly in normal conversation. All the examples above are attributed to the Reverend William A. Spooner, the Warden (head) of New College in Oxford from 1903 to 1924. Because he became "famous" for producing such errors, they are often called "spoonerisms."

While such errors may be funny (to the listener) or embarrassing or frustrating (to the speaker), they provide indirect evidence for the units, stages, and cognitive computations that are involved in speech production. It is of interest to note that in a study of the speech produced in seminars, classes, business meetings and similar contexts, in both planned talks and spontaneous conversation, Deese (1978, 1980) found that speakers used complete sentences, 98 percent of which were grammatically correct. Yet an examination of the relatively small number of errors that people produce when speaking has led to greater insights into the production process than the study of error-free utterances. A number of collections of errors are now used for analysis. Two of the largest collections are the UCLA corpus (Fromkin, 1988) and the MIT corpus (Garrett, 1988; Shattuck-Huffnagel, 1986).

Rev. William Spooner was well known for his slips-of-the-tongue.

Disfluencies

In addition to speech errors, many utterances are characterized by hesitations, repetitions, false starts, and "filler" words such as *um, well,* or *you know*. Such disfluencies or nonfluencies are actually more common than we generally perceive them to be—we tend not to notice them. Work done by Goldman-Eisler (1968) suggests that hesitations, sometimes called unfilled pauses, occur roughly every five words when people describe pictures. If speakers are conversing naturally, hesitations may appear every seven to eight words. However, their presence is rarely noted. As we shall see, such lapses in fluent speech production actually provide valuable insights into the units of speech production and permit us to evaluate how much of speech is mentally planned in advance of its production.

Issues in speech production

In trying to explicate what is known about the complex speech production process, a number of questions arise: What are the basic elements, units, or hierarchy of units into which the conceptual message is translated? How are these units combined? What are the stages in real time by which a thought is translated or encoded into an

utterance? By what processes are both well-formed and ill-formed structures (errors) produced? Do speech errors provide evidence to suggest that the units, components, and rules posited by linguistic theory to be part of the mental grammar are used during the process of speech production? These questions, which various models of speech production attempt to answer, are the focus of this chapter.

What are the units of speech production?

When we produce an utterance corresponding to some thought we wish to convey, we cannot go to a mental storage unit and pull out the appropriate stored message. The brain's finite storage capacity cannot warehouse an infinite set of utterances, and most of what we say has never been said in just that way before. Thus, speech is produced by stringing together, arranging and rearranging a limited number of stored items. A major question in trying to understand the production process is to determine the size and nature of these units. Even a long memorized passage, such as the *Gettysburg Address* or *Mary Had a Little Lamb*, must be mentally represented by its constituent parts including sentences, clauses, phrases, words, morphemes, syllables, phonemes, and even phonological features, since, as we will see below, all of these units represent items which may be disordered or forgotten or remembered as fragments. As this chapter will explore, these units of language, which linguists use in describing the structure of language, have been shown to be just those discrete units out of which the semicontinuous physical speech signal is composed during the process of speech production.

The first known linguistic work to deal with speech errors was published in the eighth century by the Arab linguist Al-Ki-sa'i. More recently, speech errors have been analyzed by linguists and psycholinguists working under the assumption that these errors ". . . can give some clues to the particular mechanisms of language production, which in the abnormal case—in accordance with a general methodological principle—can lead to conclusions about the factors involved in normal functioning" (Bierwisch, 1982, p. 310).

Analysis of such errors shows, first of all, the discreteness of the units which cannot normally be observed in error-free utterances. As Chapter 3 observed, the speech signal is quite continuous, and locating the boundaries of any speech unit is difficult. However, when segments such as sounds or words are produced incorrectly or shift position within the utterance, they are more readily identifiable as separable units. Errors also reveal that utterances are composed of units of differing sizes and classes, since segments of varying sizes appear to be vulnerable to slips of the tongue.

Phonemic segments

The literature on speech errors, going back to the first major collection of over 8,000 German errors published by Meringer and Mayer (1895), provides countless examples of phonological errors in which single phonemic-sized segments are **anticipated** or **persevere**. In anticipation errors, sounds which will come later in the utterance inappropriately appear earlier than intended. In perseveration errors, a sound produced early in the utterance reappears in an incorrect location later in the utterance. In other types of errors, phonemes are deleted or added or exchanged (reversed), as illustrated in the examples given in (1).

(Note: The intended utterance occurs to the left of the arrow; the actual utterance with the error appears on the right. C = consonant, and V = vowel in these examples.)

(1)   a.   *A reading list → a leading list* (C anticipation)
  b.   *a phonological rule → a phonological fool* (C perseveration)
  c.   *brake fluid → blake fruid* (C cluster division and C exchange)
  d.   *speech error → peach error* (C deletion)
  e.   *box of flowers → blocks of flowers* (C anticipation and insertion; C cluster division)
  f.   *fill the pool → fool the pill* (vowel exchange)
  g.   *Sue weeded the garden → sea weeded the garden* (V anticipation)
  h.   *annotated bibliography → annotated babliography* (vowel perseveration)
  i.   *drop a bomb → bop a dromb* (consonant cluster—C exchange)
  j.   *when you get old your spine shrinks → your shrine spinks* (consonant cluster exchange)

It's impossible to account for such errors without positing that, for example, consonant clusters like the /br/ and /fl/ in example (c) are composed of individual segments which in the process of speaking are "split" and reversed. Note, however, that in examples (i) and (j), consonant clusters can also be disordered as a unit. The speech errors above illustrate an important point about the basic units of speech production: at some level, they correspond to our notions of phonetic segments, such as consonants, vowels, and consonant clusters. One can divide the physical acoustic signal in the middle of a vowel, but such division does not occur when we speak, even when we "catch ourselves" in a false start or an error.

Phonetic features

The examples below in (2) illustrate that the *quark*, or most elementary unit of speech production, is even smaller than the segment, since *phonetic features* can independently be disordered. Phonetic features, sometimes called distinctive features, are the attributes which combine to define the phonemes of a language. For example, [b] can be described as having the features + consonantal, = continuant, + oral, + voice, and so forth. Taken together, these features define the segment [b]. Now consider the following speech errors:

(2) a. *big and fat* → *pig and vat* (voicing reversal; + voicing → −voicing)
     b. *Cedars of Lebanon* → *Cedars of Lemadon* (nasality reversal; − nasal → + nasal)
     c. *is Pat a girl* → *Is bat a curl* (voicing reversal)
     d. *he's a vile person* → *he's a file person* (voicelessness anticipation, + voice → − voice)

In (a), the /b/ in the intended word *big* is a voiced bilabial stop and the /f/ in *fat* is a voiceless labio-dental fricative. The /b/ and /f/ were not reversed; only the voicing feature was exchanged, which resulted in the production of the voiceless bilabial stop /p/ and the voiced labio-dental fricative /v/. If we represent each feature as having a binary value, for example [+/−voicing], then in (a), we see that the [+ voicing] value of /b/ and the [− voicing] value of /f/ are reversed; all other feature values remain as the speaker intended. Thus, features must also be units in speech production.

One interesting finding about phonological feature errors is that one never finds features of consonants exchanging with or influencing the features in vowels and vice versa. This fact supports the more recent views in phonological theory which suggest that segments have hierarchical structure, as opposed to earlier views that segments are bundles of unordered features (Clements, 1983; Archangeli, 1988; McCarthy, 1982).

Errors occurring in the production of American Sign Language are similar to the kinds of errors discussed above. Thus, in Figure 7.2, we see that the signer exchanged the hand configurations of two signs, keeping other aspects of the sign as originally intended.

The syllable

It has been suggested that in addition to segments and features, syllables constitute "unit(s) in the phonemic programming system" (Nooteboom, 1969; MacKay, 1969; MacKay, 1970a; Fromkin, 1968, 1971). Errors do occur in which syllables that have no morphemic status (have no meaning by themselves) are disordered as in (3).

(3) a. *unanimity of opinion* → *unamity of opinion* (syllable deletion)
     b. *Morton and Broadbent point out* → *Morton and Broadpoint*
     c. *Stockwell and Schacter* → *Schachwell and Stockter*

Figure 7.2

Signed Errors

Sick

Bored

Error

Error

Errors such as those in (3), in which nonmorphemic syllabic strings are disordered, are very rare compared to other types of segmental errors. The major argument in support of the syllable as a processing unit is based on the fact that exchanged syllables seem to "obey a structural law with regard to syllable place"; that is, initial segments replace initial segments, and final syllables exchange with final syllables (Boomer & Laver, 1968). MacKay (1969) also found that the "syllabic position of reversed consonants was almost invariably identical."

The fact that in errors, syllable initial segments interact with initial segments, medial with medial, and final with final supports the "contemporary metrical theory (of phonology) in a straightforward way" (Garrett, 1988), further showing that linguistic theory and psycholinguistic processing interface in critical ways.

Stress

There is continuing controversy as to whether word and phrasal stress are manipulatable processing units. Fromkin (1977) argues, again from speech error data, that since stress can be disordered like other phonemic features, it should be viewed as an independent production unit. Such errors are exemplified in (4).

(The stressed syllable is given in upper case letters.)

(4) a. *apples of the Origin* → *apples of the oRIgin*
     b. *moBILity* → *mobiLIty*
     c. *eCONomists* → *ecoNOMists, I mean, eCONomists*
     d. *phoNEtic* → *PHOnetic*

Gandour (1977), in his study of speech errors in Thai, a tone language in which the pitch of a syllable may contrast meaning, shows that tone can also be disordered in slips of the tongue.

Cutler (1980), however, argues that what appears to be disordering of stress might really be a lexical error in which the wrong derived word is selected. For example, she would explain the stress error in (c) as one in which the speaker incorrectly selected the word "ecoNOmics" instead of "eCONomists," and then corrected the selection error. However, one does find stress errors in which it is difficult to find related words with a different stress pattern.

Word, morpheme, and phrase units in speech production

Both speech error and disfluency patterns provide information about possible basic units used in generating sentences. We will review each of these types of data, explaining how each contributes to an understanding of how a thought is eventually encoded into spoken utterances.

Word selection and placement errors

No one would question that words are discrete units in the production process, even if errors such as those in (5) were rare (which they are not).

(5) a. *tend to turn out* → *turn to tend out* (word exchange)
     b. *I love to dance* → *I dance to love* (exchange)
     c. *I really must go* → *I must really go* (word movement)

In other kinds of speech errors, words are also misselected, which provides interesting evidence for the nature of lexical retrieval and the representation and organization of our mental dictionaries, issues which are discussed in Chapter 4.

Lexical search and pausal phenomena

Lexical search, or the process by which the individual words are retrieved from the mental dictionary, is also reflected in patterns of speech disfluency. For example, hesitations (unfilled pauses) are more likely to occur before content words, such as nouns, verbs, and modifiers, than before function words, such as articles, helping verbs, and so forth (Maclay & Osgood, 1959). Pauses are also longer before content words than function words (Boomer, 1965). Such patterns suggest that the speaker does not yet have his lexical target available for the next stage in the production process. Further, hesitations are more likely to occur before less commonly used words in the language, suggesting a more difficult process of lexical access than for more frequently used words.

Morpheme and speech errors

Since the basic unit of meaning in language is not the word, but the morpheme, it is not surprising that all categories of morphological units serve as production building blocks. Stem morphemes, such as *easy* in the word *easily*, derivational morphemes such as the *-ly* in *easily* or *un-* in *unhappy*, and inflectional morphemes such as the plural endings in *ministers*, *churches*, or *priests* undergo rearrangement in different kinds of errors.

The separation of stem morphemes from affixes (inflectional or derivational prefixes or suffixes) shows that such affixes function as independent processing units, as the examples below in (6) reveal. Furthermore, the production of "possible" but nonoccurring derived forms show that, at least in some cases, complex words may be formed during speech in addition to being selected from the mental dictionary.

(6) Inflectional morpheme errors
  a. *rules of word formation* → *words of rule formation*
  b. *we have a lot of ministers in our church* → *we have a lot of churches in our minister*
  c. *I'd forgotten about that* → *I'd forgot abouten that*
  d. *cow tracks* → *track cows*
  e. *it's not only us who have screws loose* → . . . *have screw looses*
(7) Derivational morpheme errors
  a. *easily enough* → *easy enoughly*
  b. *the introduction of the subject* → *the introducting of the subject*
  c. *there's a good likelihood* → *there's a good likeliness*
  d. *they can't quite make it* → *they can't quitely make it*

Grammatical rules

Rules of inflectional and derivational morphology *surface* in speech errors through production of nonoccurring morphologically complex forms, and errors in morphological rule application (nonapplication when a rule applies; application when it should not). Some instances in which one can observe misapplied grammatical rules are shown in the following examples:

(8) a. the last I *knew* about it → . . . I *knowed* about it
  b. I don't know that I'd *know* one if I *heard* it → . . . that I'd *hear* one if I *knew* it
  c. bunnies [s = /z/] don't eat steak → steaks [s = /s/] don't eat bunny
  d. an aunt's (/s/) money → a money's (/z/) aunt
  e. he always keepS a pack → he always packS a keep
  f. a watchED (/t/) pot never boils → a potted (/ad/) watch never boils

The phrase as a planning unit

The phrase as a unit in slips of the tongue.   There are various kinds of evidence to support the view that even larger linguistic structures function as units in the speech production process. We discuss below how these units are formed and the role they play in what has been called the planning aspects of speech; here we simply wish to point out that sentence constituents such as noun phrases, verb phrases, prepositional phrases are in some fashion *marked off* as units when we speak. Consider, for example, the speech errors in (9), in which more than one word is involved.

(9)   a.   *a hummingbird* was attracted by *the red color* of the feeder → *the red color* was attracted by *a hummingbird* of the feeder

   b.   *my sister* went to *the Grand Canyon* → *the Grand Canyon* went to *my sister*.

The two examples in (9) show the exchange or reversal of two noun phrases. Interestingly, the noun phrases retain their internal organization, and two identical types of grammatical constituents are exchanged; one never finds errors in which the final word of one constituent phrase and the first word of a following phrase are disordered, as in (9). That is, (9) represents a theoretically possible, but never seen type of speech error.

(9)   b.   → my *Canyon* to the grand *sister went*.

The absence of such speech errors suggests that notions such as noun phrase, verb phrase, prepositional phrase, and so forth, represent types of units which play some role in the speech production process, and which may be inadvertently exchanged.

Self-corrections and retracings.   It has also been observed that when a speaker notices an error and proceeds to correct it, the correction is more apt to occur at the beginning of the syntactic constituent in which it occurs than at the actual error site. The speaker "backtracks" to the beginning of the constituent containing the speech error. Clark and Clark (1977) suggest that a speaker will correct himself by saying, "The doctor looked up Joe's nose—that is, up Joe's left nostril," rather than saying, "The doctor looked up Joe's nose, that is, left nostril." While this is not always the case, the fact that most corrections do take place at the beginnings of syntactic phrases supports such units as one type of building block in the speech production process.

Similar findings were obtained in an earlier study conducted by Maclay and Osgood (1959) of repetitions in the recorded speech of speakers at a conference. They also found that when a speaker repeats himself, he most often goes back to a constituent break to begin the repetition. Thus, if a speaker intends to say, "Speech errors provide evidence for constituent boundaries" and stops after "evidence," he will then say, "Speech errors provide evidence—(pause) provide evidence for . . . ," rather than, "Speech errors provide evidence (pause) evidence for . . . "

Pausal phenomena. Pauses serve many functions in connected discourse. It is obvious that speakers need to take breaths every so often between utterances, and that this is reflected in pause time. However, pausing is also a reflection of the language encoding process. Pauses are likely to occur at clause boundaries or other major structural breaks, as well as before certain lexical decision points, as discussed above (Goldman-Eisler, 1968; Boomer, 1965). This distribution is evident even when speakers are asked not to breathe during the production of short messages, thus removing the need to breathe as a factor in pausal phenomena (Grosjean, Grosjean, & Lane, 1979). Such positioning implies that speakers may be using the pause time to encode the following clause. Research by Lindsley (1975) suggests that speakers attempt to preplan their utterances before uttering them, and that such a strategy may demand a leadtime. Specifically, subjects in Lindsley's experiments took longer to initiate subject-verb captions for pictures than simpler subject captions. Such latency behaviors presumably reflect speakers' tendencies to pre-encode the verb that follows before producing sentential subjects.

Syntactically more complex speech tends to be characterized by more hesitations and filled pauses (Rochester & Gill, 1973; Cook, Smith, & Lalljee, 1974), suggesting that more difficult constructions require more planning time for their execution. Indeed, there is experimental evidence to suggest that some degree of pausing is *necessary* for successful speech production. Beattie and Bradbury (1979) designed an experiment in which speakers received feedback (in the form of a light) whenever they produced a pause of more than 600 milliseconds duration while narrating stories. The speakers, however, were not aware that this was the basis for the feedback; rather, they were told that the appearance of the light indicated poor story-telling. Even though speakers were instructed to view the light as indicative of story-telling ability, long pauses were decreased by approximately 35 percent during the course of the experiment. However, the accuracy and quality of the speakers' output was diminished in other respects, showing increased repetition and backtracking. By encouraging the speakers to avoid pauses, the experiment led to a greater number of production errors. Such a finding strongly suggests that pauses reflect active sentencing planning effort on the part of speakers.

How far ahead do we plan?

Syntactic phrases have hierarchical structure, that is, larger phrases include smaller phrases. A sentence or clause may be composed of constituent clauses, which in turn are composed of various syntactic phrases. An examination of speech errors in which words are exchanged, such as those in section (5) earlier, reveal that the largest percentage of such errors involve words in the same clause. Garrett (1975, 1976) found that 85 percent of word exchange errors involved elements within a single clause; in Fromkin's corpus, 79 percent of such errors involved words in the same clause. This implies that speech is planned in clausal units. It must be noted, however, that 15 percent of the word exchange errors in Garrett's corpus and 21 percent of those in the Fromkin corpus involved elements from more than one clause, showing that prior to producing speech, the speaker plans quite far ahead and builds syntactic structures in advance.

Thus, both by observing spontaneous speech and through controlled experiments, the units involved in speech production are revealed: phonological segments and features, morphemes and words, and syntactic phrases and clauses.

What speech error data suggest about the process of speech production

Even if we just try to determine the units used in production, we see that speech production is highly complex. The complexity is increased by the ways in which these units are accessed, selected, manipulated, and organized into hierarchical structures; they are not simply strung together as beads on a string, and even in the errors we produce there are constraints on what can occur. The question that any theory or model of speech production must address is how a speaker's intended message is constructed out of these units. What are the stages of this process?

In trying to answer these questions, linguists and psycholinguists have constructed speech production models. A scientific model is only viable to the extent that it can account for the observable phenomena of interest, and can predict further phenomena. Models can be simply descriptive or theoretical; the long-range goal in any empirical science is the construction of theoretical, explanatory models.

Speech is planned in advance

Before examining some of the speech production models that have been developed, it may be helpful to summarize the data that such models must account for. First, anticipation and exchange errors (whether phonological, lexical, or syntactic) show that speech is not produced one unit at a time. As Lashley (1951) pointed out, prior to articulation, the speaker must have access to a representation that includes more than one word, and in fact may include more than one clause. Furthermore, he showed by using "speech (as) . . . the only window through which the physiologist can view the cerebral life," that an associative stimulus/response chain theory cannot account for the "multiplicity of integrative processes" underlying speech production and proposed "a series of hierarchies or organization: The order of vocal movements in pronouncing the word, the order of words in the sentence, the order of sentences in the paragraph," (Fournie 1887, quoted by Lashley). The levels in this hierarchy can be viewed as stages in the production process, with the possibility of disordering occurring at any stage. A viable model of production must, therefore, posit all and only the necessary stages, showing which errors (and other dysfluencies) could occur at which level or stage, and predict the form of the utterance representation at that level.

The lexicon is organized both semantically and phonologically

Second, in word substitution errors and word blends, the words involved are semantically and/or phonologically similar. Fay and Cutler (1977), Cutler and Fay (1982), and Hurford (1981) show that, in such speech errors, the target word and substituted word share significantly similar initial segments, stress placement, morphological structure, and phonological form. Other studies (Fromkin, 1973, 1988; Garrett, 1988) also note the semantic similarities of affected words in slips of the tongue. Examples are illustrated in (10):

(10) a. *that's a horse of another color* → . . . *a horse of another race* (semantic substitution)

   b. *too many irons in the fire* → . . . *too many irons in the smoke* (semantic substitution)

   c. *white Anglo-Saxon Protestant* → . . . *prostitute* (phonological substitution)

   d. *grab/reach* → *greech* (semantic blend)

   e. *gin and tonic* → *gin and topic* (phonological)

   f. *arrested and prosecuted* → *arrested and persecuted* (phonological/semantic)

   g. *at 4:30 we're adjourning the meeting* → *we're adjoining the meeting* (phonological)

   h. *stiffer/tougher* → *stougher or stuffer* (semantic/phonological blend)

   i. *edited/annotated* → *editated* (semantic blend)

Chapter 4 discusses the representation and organization of morphemes and words in the mental lexicon and how these are accessed and retrieved during speech production and comprehension. The models of speech production that we will now discuss assume that errors in lexical selection (retrieving the wrong word for a concept) are accounted for by the nature of lexical organization. That is, the choice of inappropriate lexical items may occur because synonyms, antonyms, and similar sounding words are stored in close proximity to a given target word, and thus may be retrieved in error. Such erroneous selection, however, must occur at a stage after the syntactic form class of the target words have been determined, since word substitutions and blends do not create ungrammatical strings, as the examples in (10) reveal. These examples illustrate that nouns substitute for nouns, verbs for verbs, and so forth. Such behavior indicates that the speaker has already determined the grammatical form class of a target word.

Some lexical selection errors seem to fall into the category of "Freudian slips," the result of unconscious "competing plans" (Baars, 1980), or nonlinguistic interference, either internally or externally induced. Such external influences may combine with linguistic factors, which could help to trigger their occurrence. A speaker's comment, "He made hairlines," produced in place of the intended "He made headlines," when referring to a barber may be such an error. We know very little about the ways in which linguistic and nonlinguistic factors intersect during speech and will thus leave this interesting issue until further research provides us with some answers.

Morphologically complex words are assembled

Other errors in which possible, but nonoccurring morphologically complex words are produced also occur, as in (11).

(11) a.   *a New Yorker* → *a New Yorkan* (cf. America/American)
      b.   *the derivation of the surface form* → *the derival of the surface form*
           (cf. recital or quittal)

As in the case of word substitution errors, one can assume that these derivational errors occur in the lexicon prior to *lexical insertion* (the stage at which words are placed into the intended utterance). What they show is that the morphological rules for word formation posited by linguists are actively engaged during speech production, and that morphologically complex items are compiled, even if they are stored as wholes (with morphological boundaries included).

Some word substitutions occur which appear to be influenced by previous words in the string, that is, they appear to be horizontally or *syntagmatically* conditioned, as shown in (12).

(12) a.   *it spread like wild fire* → *it spread like wild flower*
      b.   *sesame seed crackers* → *sesame street crackers*
      c.   *chamber music* → *chamber maid*
      d.   *gave birth at midnight* → *gave birth at midwife*

Examples (a), (b), and (c) appear to be lexical selection errors similar to those in 11, if one assumes that *wild flower, Sesame Street*, and *chamber maid* are listed as noun compounds in the mental dictionary. One may then posit that the speaker selected a lexical entry that was listed in close proximity to the intended item. In (d), however, the semantic relatedness between *birth* and *midwife* suggests that after *birth* was selected, as well as the intended *midnight, midwife* was incorrectly selected because of its phonological similarity and its active priming.

Errors involving word stem and affix morphemes were discussed in an earlier section. In particular, speech errors involving affix placement suggest that inflectional and derivational morphemes are stored and processed differently from words and word stems in the speech production process.

First, although words and stems are often involved in exchanges or reversals, neither inflectional (e.g., past tense, plural) or derivational (e.g., the *-er* of *singer*) morphemes are. For example, a past tense marker does not appear to exchange position with a comparative form.

Examples of such exchanges are given in (13). (Note that prepositions sometimes are exchanged, and pronouns, while primarily exchanging with pronouns, also may exchange with nouns or noun phrases.)

(13) a. *rules of word formation → words of rule formation*
      b. *I left the cigar in my briefcase → I left the briefcase in my cigar*
      c. *I don't know that I'd know one if I heard it → I don't know that I'd
          hear one if I knew it*
      d. *rubber hose and lead pipe → rubber pipe and lead hose*
      e. *when the story hits the paper → when the paper hits the story*

but **not**: f. *a big bird in the alder tree → the big bird in an alder tree.*

Note that in (c), that the verbs *know* and *hear* are shifted, but not in their inflected form, since *heard* becomes *hear* and *know* becomes *knew*. That is, the verbs were exchanged (but the past tense marker meant to be applied to *hear* remained behind) before the past tense marker was applied to yield the final appropriate form of the new word, *knew*. Sentence (c) could only result from a discrete stage at which affixes are combined with their roots. This will be discussed again below.

In examples (a) and (c) above, and in those in (14), it can be seen that in exchange errors, inflectional morphemes may be "stranded" (left behind); they are, however, seldom involved in exchanges.

(14) a. *cow trackS → track cowS*
      b. *ministerS in our church → churchES in our minister*
      c. *I hopeD he would like Chris → I likeD he would hope Chris*

but **not** d. *the boyS are goING → the boyING are goeS*

Stranding errors reveal another phenomenon that must be accounted for in a viable production model. When grammatical morphemes are stranded, they are "fixed up" according to the phonological and morphological rules of the language (Fromkin, 1971; Bierwisch, 1982). Such "accommodations" also occur with some grammatical morpheme substitutions, anticipations, or perseverations, as illustrated in (15).

(15) *An eating marathon → A meeting arathon*

Note that in (15), when the initial segment of *marathon* is anticipated and inserted at the beginning of *eating*, the indefinite article does not surface as *a* (as it would have in the intended utterance) but as *an*, in keeping with the morphological rules of English. Similarly, when the stems in (14a) are exchanged, the stranded plural morpheme attached to *cow* is phonetically /z/, although had the exchange not occurred, the plural suffix for *track* would have been /s/. Thus, at the stage where the accommodation process occurs, these units must be marked as grammatical morphemes or the rule for appropriate phonological realization would not apply.

Affixes and functors behave differently than content words in slips of the tongue

Garrett (1976, 1984, 1988) points out that affix morphemes and minor sentence elements (adverbs, intensifiers, determiners) may be "moved" or "shifted," whereas the major category stems and words (nouns, verbs, and adjectives) tend to be involved in exchange errors but seldom participate in shift errors. The examples in (16) illustrate this tendency. Another difference between the two types of speech errors is pointed out by Cutler (1980), who notes that, whereas "exchanges preserve (phrasal) stress, shifts often distort it."

(16) a. *I frankly admit to being subjective → I Ø admit to frankly being subjective*
      b. *Did you stay up very late last night? → did you stay up late very last night?*
      c. *I'd forgotten about that → I'd forgotØ abouten that*
      d. *That would be the same as adding ten → as addØ tenning.*
      e. *if she wantS (-/s/) to come here → if she wantØ to comeS (/-z/) here*
      f. *Jerry'S (/-z/) Pancake House → JerryØ Pancake'S (/-z/) House*

Speech errors reflect rule knowledge

The remaining phenomena which have to be accounted for in a viable production model concern different categories of grammatical rules. It has already been shown that rules of inflectional and derivational morphology "surface" in speech errors through accommodation mechanism and the creation of nonlexicalized morphologically complex words. The productive use of such rules (or constraints on well formedness) are also shown in utterances where a regular rule has applied to an irregular or exceptional form, when a rule which should apply does not, or when a rule is mistakenly applied, all of which are illustrated in (17).

(17) a. the last I KNEW about it → . . . I KNOWED about it
      b. he SWAM in the pool → he SWIMMED in the pool
      c. the CHILDREN are in the park → the CHILDS are — I mean the children are in the park
      d. she was so DRANK when she called him
      e. I don't know whether anyone has SAW the review
      f. it took you longer to read it than it took me to WROTE it
      g. how angry he is → how angry he AM

Such phonological specification of inflectional morphemes must occur at the same level as that at which the accommodation of stranded morphemes occurs—at the stage of representation before the **phonemicization** of these morphemes, the point at which the phonological composition of the target morphemes is specified.

The mental grammar accessed during production also includes syntactic rules and constraints that determine which sentences in a language are well formed or grammatical and which are not. These include movement rules, subcategorization constraints (e.g., that a transitive verb must be followed by a noun phrase object), selectional restrictions (e.g., that some verbs, such as *love* or *cry* must co-occur with an animate subject), among others. When these constraints are violated by speakers who "know better," they result in ungrammatical sentences or syntactic speech errors, examples of which are given in (18).

(18)   a.   *does it sound different → does it hear different*
          b.   *she swore me to secrecy → she promised me to secrecy*
          c.   *they seem to know where the problem is → they seem they know . . .*
          d.   *Turkish and German don't have the third dimension, so does Swedish*
          e.   *it would be of interesting to see*
          f.   *she made him to do the assignment over*
          g.   *John is going, isn't it?*
          h.   *This is something that we should discuss about*
          i.   *he not seem happy now*
          j.   *it's almost all finished → it's all almost finished*
          k.   *she was waiting her husband for*
          l.   *but when you will leave?*

Some of these syntactically deviant sentences may be the result of sentence blends, a combination of two sentence options into one. Example (c) may be a blend of *they seem to know/they know* and (e) might be a blend of *it would be interesting/it would be of interest.* Such ill-formed syntax must arise at the level or stage in speech production when the syntactic structure of the utterance is being planned and constructed.

Speech production processing models

Until investigators began to seriously examine speech error and other disfluency data, psycholinguistic processing was, for the most part, limited to the comprehension side of the speech chain. In 1976, MacNeilage and Ladefoged wrote: "Very little is known about the production of language" as opposed to the production of speech sounds. Only two pages in a basic introductory textbook on psycholinguistics by Glucksberg and Danks (1975) were devoted to production. The first speculative model which attempted to specify stages and representations in production (Fromkin, 1968) was limited to the mapping of phonemic representations onto motor commands to the muscles.

In 1971, the first model which attempted to account for the major stages and levels of representation was published (Fromkin 1971, 1973), followed by a similar and more detailed model by Garrett (1976). Both were heavily based on speech error data, and can be considered to take a linguistic, as opposed to psychological perspective on the process of speech production (Garrett, 1982; Garman, 1990). Other models more narrowly concerned with subsections or subprocessors of the overall model have been proposed. Shattuck-Hufnagel (1986) was concerned with accounting for phonological segmental errors; Fay and Cutler (1977) provide a detailed account of word substitution errors. In the next sections, we will review three alternative accounts of the speech production process.

The Utterance Generator model of speech production

The *Utterance Generator model* proposed by Fromkin (1971) is presented in Figure 7.3. It attempted to account for most of the speech error patterns we have previously discussed (Fromkin, 1971).

The Fromkin model distinguishes six stages at which different representations of the utterance occur. The rectangular boxes in the diagram stand for the representations at each level; the diamonds symbolize the processes which translate each level of representation into the one below. It is a top-down generator without any feedback loops. The large rectangular box labeled "Lexicon" will become better specified through aphasia research, further analysis of speech errors, and psycholinguistic experiments. As Chapter 4 and this chapter demonstrate, speech errors give us a much better idea about the organization and representation of lexical items (Fromkin, 1986, 1987, 1990; Emmorey and Fromkin, 1988).

The stages, representations, and processes which are specified in the 1971 model are summarized below.

Stage I. A 'meaning' to be conveyed is generated.   As mentioned earlier, we know little about the form of the conceptual message and we therefore cannot specify what it looks like or how it is compiled. Butterworth (1980) feels that an adequate model of speech production should account for "competing plans" at the conceptual level or at other levels, the kinds of competing plans which might produce Freudian slips. The model could also allow the generation of more than one message at Stage I which could be mapped onto one or more syntactic structures at Stage II. This could lead to speech errors such as the syntactic blends in examples (19a-1), or allow multirepresentations at any of the other levels.

Stage II. The message is mapped onto a syntactic structure.   A syntactic outline of the message is created. Semantic features or constellations of such features will later be mapped onto these structures. One reason for generating the syntax before selecting words or stems from the lexicon is because the syntactic structure determines the form and grammatical category of the words which may be chosen. The representation of the utterance at this level is thus a semantic-syntactic structure, with semantic and syntactic features marked at lexical nodes in the phrase marker.

Stage III. Intonation contours (sentence and phrasal stress) are generated on the basis of the syntactic representations.   Intonation must be assigned before lexical selection occurs, because the syntactically determined primary stress and intonation contours and lexical stress are independent of one another, and exist on different prosodic tiers.

Stage IV. Words are selected from the lexicon.   The message is now represented as a syntactic structure, with semantic and syntactic features specified, and sentence and phrasal stress marked. Lexical items are now chosen on the basis of

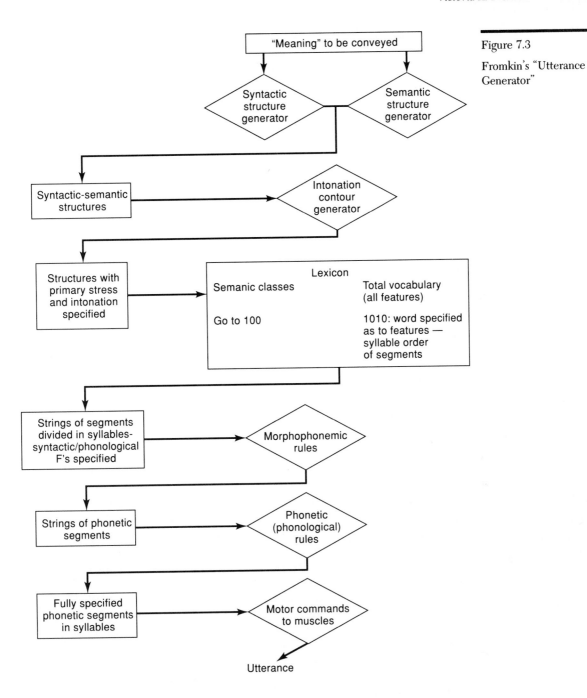

Figure 7.3

Fromkin's "Utterance Generator"

these semantic features and syntactic categories. The lexical items that are entered into this representation of the utterance are not fully specified, in the sense that their morphological affixes are not "spelled out" phonologically; the stems, however, are represented by phonemic segments, with features specified, and syllable positions serially ordered. Speech error data discussed earlier show that the eventual phonological forms of the grammatical morphemes are not yet determined; in slips of the tongue, accommodations are made to match morphological affixes to their stems using morphophonemic rules. Thus, the model proposes that grammatical morphemes are entered in their phonological shape at a later stage.

At this stage, errors may occur in which semantically or phonologically similar words may be selected instead of the intended words. It is also possible that in mapping these words onto the syntactic structures, phonological segments or features may be dislodged out of their specified sequential place.

Stage V. Phonological specification.   At this level of representation, phonological pronunciation rules apply, producing fully specified phonetic segments in syllables as the output.

Stage VI. Generation of the motor commands for speech.   The phonetic feature bundles (of segments or full syllables) are mapped onto motor commands to the muscles of the vocal tract to produce the intended (or deviant) utterance.

Such a model accounts for a large part of the data that were shown above to be critical for a viable speech production model. It specifies discrete planning units, and explains why word substitutions tend to share phonological or semantic similarity. It accounts for the fact that phrasal stress is not disrupted when words shift or exchange position. The model predicts that grammatical morphemes could be stranded, as well as the phonological accommodation which occurs when this happens. It implicitly predicts the inclusion of words and stems and the exclusion of inflectional affixes in exchange errors, by positing that at the stage where words and stems exchange, the grammatical morphemes are not yet phonologized. However, the model above does not account for the fact that major categories (nouns, verbs, adjectives) are not moved or shifted, whereas minor categories and inflectional morphemes are.

Sentences that result from possible sentence blends, such as, "Where is the Grand Ball Room by any chance?"—a possible blend of "Where is the Grand Ball Room?" and "Do you know where the Grand Ball Room is by any chance?"— can be accommodated within the model, by assuming the early attempt to generate more than one sentence, which become blended at a later stage. But as Butterworth (1982) points out, if the model allows initial generation of more than one sentence, one presumes that "there will be an enormous proliferation of representations at lower levels which requires the postulation of new mechanisms to sort them out in an appropriate way." Thus, the model still requires correction and enhancement.

The Garrett model

In 1975, Garrett proposed a speech production model, also based on speech error data, that made explicit some of the implicit aspects of the Fromkin model and filled in some gaps in the model. Although it too requires refinement, this model has provided a major framework for further research in the field. Figure 7.4 presents the first version of the Garrett model, and Figure 7.5 the latest construction of the model (1984). The earlier model is presented because it includes statements of what the levels attempt to account for (Garrett, 1975, 1984).

It will be evident that there is much overlap between the Fromkin and Garrett models. Both distinguish between three levels—"a conceptual level, a language-specific sentence level, and a motor level of articulatory control" (Garrett, 1980). At the conceptual level, Garrett's Message Source (Figure 7.4) and Inferential Processes and Messages (Figure 7.5) correspond to Fromkin's "'meaning' to be conveyed."

At the sentence level, Garrett distinguishes between a *functional level*—"a multiphrasal level of planning in which the assignment of major lexical-class items to

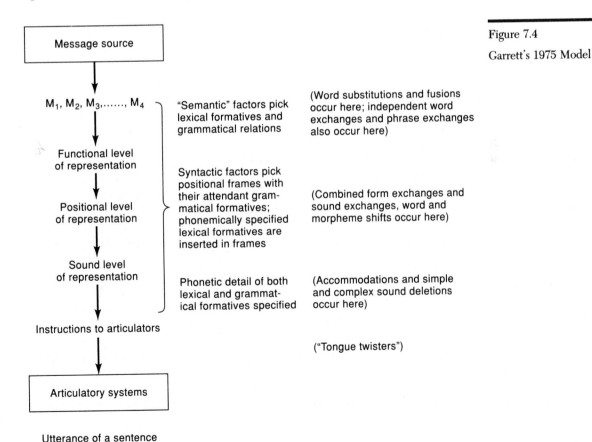

Figure 7.4

Garrett's 1975 Model

Figure 7.5
Garrett's 1984 Model

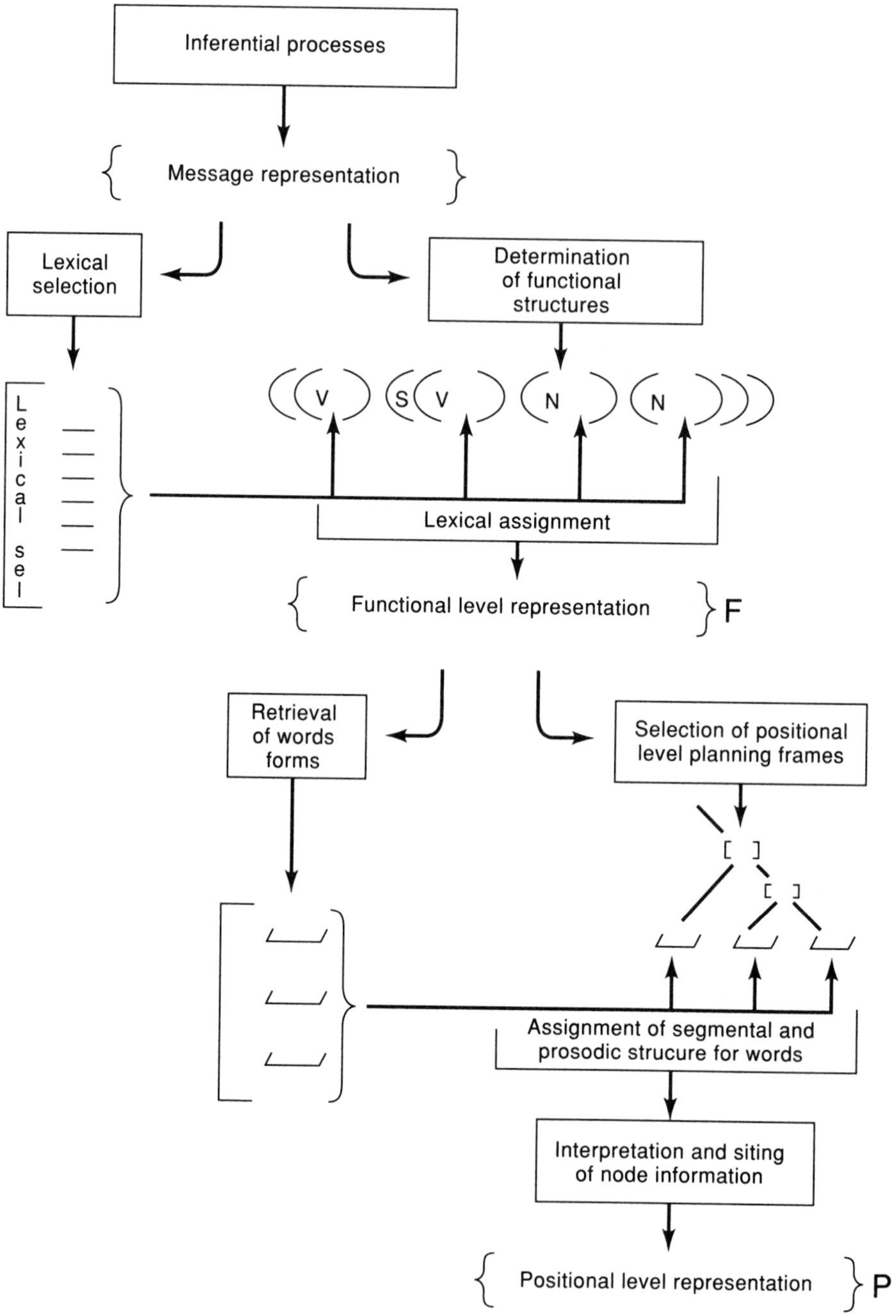

phrasal roles is accomplished" (1984). It is at this level that word exchanges involving words that have the same grammatical role occur.

A pronunciation-oriented representation occurs at the *positional level*, whereas in the Fromkin model, lexical items are retrieved with phonological form specified. In this model, it is at this level that sounds in words and sentence elements are assigned locations in the eventual surface sequence (Garrett, 1984, p. 177). At this level, form-based word substitutions (which are similar in form but not meaning) occur, as well as sound exchanges, stranding exchanges, and word and morpheme shifts.

In the Garrett model, the phonologization of grammatical morphemes takes place at the level of phonetic representation; this level is required to account for errors which show apparent alteration so that the eventual output conforms to the regular phonological constraints of the language.

Garrett's articulatory level corresponds to Fromkin's final Stage VI, in which the motor commands to vocal tract produce the acoustic representation of the message.

Levelt's model

The final model we will discuss has been advanced by Levelt (1989). In this model, message generation is initiated by the conceptualization of the utterance. During this early phase, an intention is conceived. The output of this stage is called the *preverbal message*, which is fed to the *formulator*. The formulator is divided into two sub-components. The first is a grammatical encoder, which retrieves lexical items. Levelt distinguishes between the semantic and syntactic properties of items in the lexicon, bundled together to form **lemmas**, and the phonological information about the lemmas, which he believes are stored and accessed separately. Thus, a lemma contains an item meaning, as well as its syntactic properties, which are used to generate appropriate phrase structures. The grammatical encoder produces an appropriately ordered string of lemmas. The phonological encoder then takes the syntactic outline and generates a phonological plan for the utterance, which includes its eventual intonation and stress patterns. The *articulator* then executes the phonetic plan by conveying instructions to the neuromuscular system.

Levelt further distinguishes a *speech-comprehension system* within his model of speech production. Its primary role is to monitor the output for errors. Levelt (1983, 1989) notes that attempts at *self-correction* while speaking suggest that speakers actively attend to (*self-monitor*) both intermediate forms of their intended utterances during processing, as well as their output. Nooteboom (1980) estimated that speakers detect up to about 75 percent of their phonological errors, but only about half of their lexical errors. Levelt offers the following utterances for example:

(19) a. To the left side of the purple disk is a v-, a horizontal line.
  b. How long does that has to—have to simmer?

The first suggests an error discovered before full articulatory realization, while the second demonstrates recovery from an error in a fully realized utterance.

Evidence for a monitoring function of speech can be found from many sources. One type of evidence arises from experimental attempts to induce speakers to make

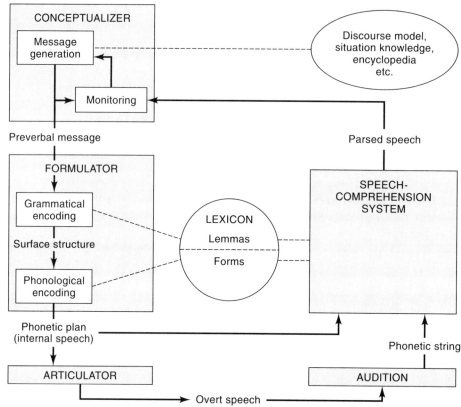

Figure 7.6
Levelt's Model

speech errors. Baars, Motley, and MacKay (1975) *phonetically biased* speakers by having them silently read lists of two-word strings, such as *ball-dome*, *bath-dog*, and so forth. When subjects were then asked to read aloud pairs which followed an inverted pattern, such as *darn-bore*, they occasionally responded *barn-door*. However, it is much less likely that a string such as *dart-board* will be produced as *bart-doard*, presumably because the self-monitoring function checks to see if the output is lexically permissible. However, if stimuli presented to the subjects in the experiment consist of nonsense words such as *bick-rint*, an error resulting in *rick-bint* (nonsense forms) is as likely to occur as actual words produced, showing that the monitor "recognizes" that nonoccurring words are acceptable under these conditions.

Summary

This chapter has been concerned with elucidating the planning units and stages that are the bridge between a speaker's concept and its grammatical expression. The processes involved on the speaker's end of the speech chain elude easy description and explanation. One cannot go into speakers' brains and examine the mental processes and computations that are taking place when they are producing an utterance. Even with the latest advances in CAT and PET scans, blood flow analysis, and Magnetic Resonant Imaging, which all provide some idea of the neural activity in the brain when we are thinking, speaking, or listening, cannot tell us whether the speaker is constructing a noun phrase or a verb phrase, at what moment phrase construction occurs, or how it is accomplished.

In the attempt to understand this process, more and more linguists and psycholinguists have turned to speech error and other speech disfluency data. Deviant utterances serve as windows into the mind, showing that the semicontinuous speech signal is composed of discrete units of different sizes and kinds, that speech is not produced simply by uttering one sound, or syllable, or word at a time. Rather, these serially ordered elements are put together by means of a number of fixed stages. By examining the constraints on the kinds of errors which occur, we have been able to construct models and posit what levels of representation and what computations can occur at each stage.

The models presented in this chapter still do not reveal all the complexities and constraints and kinds of representations that are computed in the course of producing even a single short utterance. However, by attempting to explain not only errorless production, but also those utterances which contain slips of the tongue or fluency failures, they point to the questions about the speech production process that are still unanswered, which is always the first step in the quest for understanding.

References

Archangeli, D. (1988). Aspects of underspecification theory. *Phonology 5*, 183–207.

Baars, B. J. (1980). The competing plans hypothesis: An heuristic viewpoint on the causes of errors in speech. In H. W. Dechert and M. Raupach (Eds.), *Temporal variables in speech*. The Hague: Mouton

Baars, B., Motley, M., & MacKay, D. (1975). Output editing for lexical status from artificially elicited slips of the tongue. *Journal of Verbal Learning and Verbal Behavior, 14*, 382–391.

Beattie, G., & Bradbury, R. (1979). An experimental investigation of the modifiability of the temporal structure of spontaneous speech. *Journal of Psycholinguistic Research, 8*, 225–248.

Bierwisch, M. (1982). Linguistics and language error. In A. Cutler (Ed.) *Slips of the tongue and language production* (pp. 29–72). Amsterdam: Mouton.

Bond, Z. S. (1969). Constraints on production errors. *Proceedings of the Chicago Linguistics Society, 5*, 302–305.

Boomer, D. S. (1965). Hesitation and grammatical encoding. *Language and Speech, 8*, 148–158.

Boomer, D. (1965). Hesitation and grammatical encoding. *Language and Speech, 8*, 148–158.

Boomer, D. S., & Laver, J. D. M. (1968). Slips of the tongue. *British Journal of Disorders of Communication, 3*, 1–12.

Boomer, D. & Laver, J. (1968). Slips of the tongue. In Fromkin (1973) 120–131.

Butterworth, B. (1980). Some constraints on models of language production. In B. Butterworth (Ed.), *Language production (Vol. 12): Speech and talk* (pp. 423–459). London: Academic Press.

Butterworth, B. (1981). Speech errors: Old data in search of new theories. *Linguistics, 19,* 627–662.

Butterworth, B. (1982). Old data in new theories. In A. Cutler (Ed.), *Slips of the tongue and language production* (pp. 73–108). Amsterdam: Mouton.

Clark, H. H., & Clark, E. V. (1977). *Psychology and language.* New York: Harcourt Brace Jovanovich.

Clements, G. N. (1988). Towards a substantive theory of features specification. In *Proceedings of the 18th Annual Meeting of the North East Linguistics Society.* Amherst, MA.

Clements, G. N., & Keyser, S. J. (1983). *CV phonology: A generative theory of the syllable.* Cambridge, MA: MIT Press.

Cook, M., Smith, J., & Lalljee, M. (1974). Filled pauses and syntactic complexity. *Language and Speech, 17,* 11–16.

Cooper, W. E., Paccia, J. M., & Lapointe, S. G. (1978). Hierarchical coding in speech timing. *Cognitive Psychology, 10,* 154–177.

Cowan, N., Braime, J. D. S., & Levitt, I. (1985). The phonological and metaphonological representation of speech: Evidence from fluent backward talkers. *Journal of Memory and Language, 24,* 689–698.

Cutler, A. (1979). The psychological reality of word formation and lexical stress rules. *Proceedings of the Ninth International Congress of Phonetic Sciences (Vol. 2)* 79–85. Copenhagen: Institute of Phonetics.

Cutler, A. (1980a). Syllable omission errors and isochrony. In H. W. Dechert and M. Raupach (Eds.), *Temporal variables in speech,* (pp. 183–290). The Hague: Mouton.

Cutler, A. (1980b). *Errors of stress and intonation.* In Fromkin (1980) 67–80.

Cutler, A. (1982). (Ed.). *Slips of the Tongue and Language Production.* Amsterdam: Mouton.

Cutler, A., & Fay, D. (1982). One mental lexicon, phonologically arranged: Comments on Hurford's comments. *Linguistic Inquiry, 13,* 107–113.

Deese, J. (1978). Thought into speech. *American Scientist, 66,* 314–321.

Deese, J. (1980). Pauses, prosody and the demands of production in language. In H. W. Dechert and M. Raupach (Eds.), *Temporal variables in speech.* The Hague: Mouton

Denes, P. B., & Pinson, E. N. (1963). *The Speech Chain.* Baltimore: Waverly Press.

Emmorey, K., & Fromkin, V. A. (1988). The Mental Lexicon. In F. Newmeyer, (Ed.), *Linguistics: The Cambridge Survey III* (pp. 124–149). Cambridge: Cambridge University Press.

Fay, D., & Cutler, A. (1977). Malapropisms and the structure of the mental lexicon. *Linguistic Inquiry, 8,* 505–520.

Fodor, J. (1975). *The Language of Thought.* New York: Thomas Crowell.

Fodor, J., Bever, T., & Garrett, M. G. (1974). *The Psychology of Language: An Introduction to Psycholinguistics and Generative Grammar.* New York: McGraw-Hill.

Fromkin, V. A. (1968). Speculations on performance models. *Journal of Linguistics, 4,* 47–68.

Fromkin, V. (1971). The nonanomalous nature of anomalous utterances. *Language, 47,* 27–52.

Fromkin, V. (1973). *Speech errors as linguistic evidence.* The Hague: Mouton.

Fromkin, V. A. (1977). Putting the emPHasis on the wrong sylLAble. In L. M. Hyman (Ed.), *Studies in stress and accent,* 15–26. Southern California Occasional Papers in Linguistics #4.

Fromkin, V. A. (1980). (Ed.). *Errors in linguistic performance: slips of the tongue, ear, pen, and hand.* New York: Academic Press.

Fromkin, V. A. (1985). Evidence in Linguistics. In R. H. Robins and V. A. Fromkin (Eds.), *Linguistics and Linguistic Evidence* (pp. 18–38). Newcastle upon Tyne: Grevatt & Grevatt.

Fromkin, V. A. (1987). The lexicon: Evidence from acquired dyslexia. *Language, 63,* 1–22.

Fromkin, V. A. (1988). The grammatical aspects of speech errors. In F. J. Newmeyer (Ed.), *Linguistics: The Cambridge Survey, (Vol. II)* (pp. 117–138). Cambridge University Press.

Gandour, J. (1977). Counterfeit tones in the speech of Southern Thai bidialectals. *Lingua, 41,* 125–143.

Garman, M. (1990). *Psycholinguistics.* Cambridge: Cambridge University Press.

Garrett, M. (1975). The analysis of sentence production. In G. Bower (Ed.), *Psychology of learning and motivation: Volume 9.* New York: Academic Press.

Garrett, M. (1982). Production of speech: observations from normal and pathological language use. In A. Ellis (Ed.) *Normality and pathology in cognitive functions.* London: Academic Press.

Garrett, M. (1976). Syntactic processes in sentence production. In R. Wales and E. Walker (Eds.), *New approaches to language mechanisms* (pp. 231–256). Amsterdam: North Holland

Garrett, M. (1980a). The limits of accommodation. In Fromkin (Ed.) *Errors in linguistic performance: Slips of the tongue, ear, pen and hand.* NY: Academic Press, pp. 263–271.

Garrett, M. (1980). Levels of processing in sentence production. In B. Butterworth (Ed.), *Language Production I.* (pp. 177–220). London: Academic Press.

Garrett, M. F. (1984). The organization of processing structure for language production. In D. Caplan, A. R. Lecours, and A. Smith (Eds.), *Biological Perspectives on Language* (pp. 172–193). Cambridge: MIT Press.

Garrett, M. F. (1988). Processes in language production. In F. J. Newmeyer (Ed.), *Linguistics: The Cambridge Survey III. Language: Psychological and Biological Aspects* (pp. 69–96). Cambridge: Cambridge University Press.

Glucksberg, S., & Danks, J. (1975). *Experimental psycholinguistics.* Hillsdale, NJ: Erlbaum.

Goldman-Eisler, F. (1968). Psycholinguistics: Experiments in spontaneous speech. New York: Academic Press.

Grosjean, F., Grosjean, L., & Lane, H. (1979). The patterns of silence: Performance structures in sentence production. *Cognitive Psychology, 11,* 58–81.

Hurford, J. R. (1981). Malapropisms, left-to-right listing, and lexicalism. *Linguistic Inquiry, 12,* 419–23.

Lapointe, S. G., and G. S. Dell. (1989). A synthesis of some recent work in sentence production. In G. N. Carlson and M. K. Tanenhaus (Eds.), *Linguistic Structure in Language Processing* (pp. 107–156). Dordrecht, Boston, London: Kluwer.

Lashley, K. S. (1958). Cerebral organization and behaviour in the brain and human behaviour. *Proceedings of the Association for Research in Nervous and Mental Diseases, 36,* 1–18.

Lashley, K. S. (1951). The problem of serial order in behaviour. In L. A. Jeffress (Ed.), *Cerebral mechanisms in behaviour.* New York: Wiley, pp. 112–136.

Levelt, W. (1983). Monitoring and self-repair in speech. *Cognition, 14,* 41–104.

Levelt, W. (1989). *Speaking: From intention to articulation.* Cambridge, Massachusetts: MIT Press.

Lindsley, J. (1975). Producing simple utterances: How far ahead do we plan? *Cognitive Psychology, 7,* 1–19.

MacKay, D. (1969). Effects of ambiguity on stuttering: Towards a model of speech production at the semantic level. *Kybernetick, 5,* 195–208.

MacKay, D. (1970). Spoonerisms: the structure of errors in the serial order of speech. *Neuropsychologia, 8*, 323–350. Reprinted in V. Fromkin (Ed.) (1973). *Speech errors as linguistic evidence*. The Hague: Mouton.

MacKay, D. (1972). Lexical insertion, inflection, and derivation: creative processes in word production. *Journal of Psycholinguistic Research, 8*, 477–498.

Maclay, H., & Osgood, C. E. (1959). Hesitation phenomena in spontaneous English speech. *Word, 15*, 19–44.

MacNeilage, P. & Ladefoged, P. (1976). The production of speech and language. In E. C. Carterette and M. P. Friedman (Eds.), *Handbook of Perception, 7*, 75–120. New York: Academic Press.

McCarthy, J. (1982). Prosodic templates, morphemic templates, and morphemic tiers. Part I. H. van der Hulst and N. Smith (Eds.), *The Structure of Phonological Representations, I and II*. Dordrecht: Foris.

Meringer, R. (1908). *Aus dem Leben der Sprache*. Berlin: Behrs Verlag.

Meringer, R., & Mayer, K. (1895). Versprechen und Verlsen. In A. Cutler and D. Fay. (Eds.), *Stuttgart. Goschensche Verlagsbuchhandlung*. New edn 1978. Amsterdam: Benjamins.

Nooteboom, S. G. (1969). The tongue slips into patterns. In A. G. Sciarone, A. J. van Essen, & A. A. van Raad (Eds.), Nomen Society, *Leyden studies in linguistics and phonetics* (pp. 114–132). The Hague: Mouton.

Nooteboom, S. (1980). Speaking and unspeaking: detection and correction of phonological and lexical errors in spontaneous speech. In V. Fromkin (Ed.) *Errors in linguistic performance*. New York: Academic Press.

Pillsbury, W. B., & Meader, C. L. (1928). *The psychology of language*. New York: D. Appleton

Rochester, S., & Gill, J. (1973). Production of complex sentences in monologues and dialogues. *Journal of Verbal Learning and Verbal Behavior, 12*, 203–210.

Shattuck-Huffnagel, S. (1986). The role of word-onset consonants: speech production priming. In E. Keller and M. Moprik (Eds.), *Motorsensory processes*. Hillsdale, NJ: Erlbaum.

Stemberger, J. P. (1982). The nature of segments in the lexicon: evidence from speech errors. *Lingua, 56*, 235–259.

Stemberger, J. P., & Treiman, R. (1986). The internal structure of word-initial consonant clusters. *Journal of Memory and Language, 25*, 163–180.

Treiman, R. (1983). On the status of final consonant clusters in English syllables. *Journal of Verbal Learning and Verbal Behavior, 23*, 343–356.

Treiman, R. (1983). The structure of spoken syllables: evidence from novel word games. *Cognition, 15*, 49–74.

Language Development
in Children

JEAN BERKO GLEASON
Boston University

NAN BERNSTEIN RATNER
University of Maryland at College Park

> *H*e wanted to learn thereby, when the indistinct babblings of infancy were past, what word they would first speak
>
> (Herodotus, *Euterpe*, Book II)

Introduction

Adults have always been fascinated by the almost miraculous unfolding of language in children. Although babies are born completely without language, by the time they are three or four years old, children have typically acquired thousands of vocabulary words, complex grammatical and phonological systems, and equally complex rules for how to use their language appropriately in many social settings. These accomplishments occur in every known society, whether literate or not, in every language from Afghan to Zulu, and in almost all children, regardless of the way in which they are raised. The tools of modern linguistics and psychology have enabled us to say a good deal about *what* children learn, and the stages they may go through on the way to adult communicative competence. But we still have many unanswered questions about *how* children actually acquire language. Nor is there really agreement among researchers as to *why* children learn language: Do children learn language because adults teach it to them? Or because they are genetically programmed to acquire language? Do they learn complex grammar simply because it is there, or do they learn in the service of some need to communicate with others? *Developmental psycholinguistics* is the discipline devoted to the study of language acquisition by children, and it is the topic of this chapter. Developmental psycholinguists have described the way that children acquire language, which turns out to be quite an orderly process, and they have attempted to discover the *biological* and *social processes* that make language development possible, or, perhaps, inevitable.

This chapter is divided into four major sections. The first section describes the *methods* that are used in studying children's language, followed by a description of what is currently known about *the course of language acquisition* in English and other languages. In the third section we present some of the principal *theories* that have attempted to account for language development. Finally, on the basis of the data we have about children's language, we return to some of the theoretical claims in a section on *perspectives*.

Methods: How do we know what we know?

"Pre-Chomskyan" methods

Interest in language development has been with us since ancient times, but the systematic study of children's language is recent (see Gleason, 1993, for a review). Until relatively recently, the *structural* nature of language was not well understood, and most studies concentrated on the kinds of things that children *said* rather than on their acquisition of language as a system.

Diaries

The first studies—some as early as the eighteenth century—were almost invariably based on observations of the author's own children and were kept in the form of diaries. During the nineteenth century and the first half of the twentieth century, many psychologists kept diary records of their children. (A number of fascinating early studies, such as Charles Darwin's careful notes on his son's language development, are summarized in Bar-Adon and Leopold, 1971.) Diaries remain a valuable way to trace the development of language in individual children. One of the most famous diary studies was conducted by Werner Leopold (1948), whose work traced his daughter Hildegarde's acquisition of both English and German. He then made more general observations about the nature of language development based on the diary entries, such as the following:

> *Hildegarde was from birth exposed to two languages, English and German, simultaneously, and built her own early speech from selected vocabulary items from both languages. . . . In examining Hildegarde's vocabulary it is necessary to keep in mind that meanings are necessarily hazy and vague at first . . .*
>
> (Leopold, 1948, p. 174)

Diaries can be a valuable adjunct to other research on children's language. By themselves, they can be misleading, since the temptation to write what is unusual or interesting, rather than what is daily and ordinary, is hard to resist. More recently, a number of researchers have found ways to augment and improve diary studies, by giving parents who are participating in language studies checklists of the words that their children are likely to acquire during their first years (Dale, 1991). The checklists help parents organize their observations and remind them of the more ordinary, but important, things their children say that they might otherwise overlook.

Wild children

Most older child language studies consisted of diary records of the author's own children. One exception to this general rule was research conducted on **feral children** (children raised in the wild, supposedly by animals) or on children kept in *isolation* without exposure to language. There is continuing philosophical interest in the effects of isolation on language development. Perhaps the most famous feral child was Victor, the "wild boy of Aveyron," studied in the eighteenth century by a French doctor, Itard (Lane, 1976). Victor was found near the city of Aveyron, running through the woods on all fours; Dr. Itard took him in and was able to teach him a great deal, but Victor never learned to say more than a few words, including "Dieu!" *God!* and "lait," *milk.*

An example of an *isolated child* came to the attention of authorities in Los Angeles a few years ago when they found Genie, a girl whose parents had kept her locked in a room for years and never spoke to her (Curtiss, 1977; see also Chapter 2.). Genie also acquired some language, but had difficulty speaking and there was some evidence that she was relying on her right cerebral hemisphere, rather than the left, even though she was right handed. Studies of feral and isolated children were at one time thought to be the way to answer our questions about possible **critical periods** for first language acquisition, but children who have suffered such terrible deprivations inevitably have so many compounding problems that it is difficult to attribute a failure to develop language to animal companions or isolation alone.

Assessment

In contrast to diary studies, assessment is based on data drawn from many subjects. Children's language has been studied to arrive at clinically and educationally useful *norms* for the achievement of given milestones (e.g., average length of sentence produced by four-year-old children), to describe *gender* and *social class differences* and to seek answers to the puzzles posed by *developmental difficulties*. Group tests using large numbers of children provide the basis for the norms. Assessment is a tool that is still used in research: For instance, a standard instrument such as the *Peabody Picture Vocabulary Test* (Dunn & Dunn, 1981) might be given to different groups of children to compare their vocabularies, or it might be used as an outcome measure to gauge the effectiveness of an intervention program designed to improve vocabulary.

Contemporary methods

The traditional methods of studying language changed dramatically beginning in the late 1950s. Newer theories of grammar (previously discussed in Chapter 1) provided a novel framework within which to view the process of language development. Linguists such as Chomsky (1957, 1965) increasingly demanded that linguistics account not only for the structural properties of language, but also for its relatively effortless, rapid, and accurate acquisition by children. Furthermore, the new **transformational generative grammar** proposed by Chomsky and elaborated on in succeeding years by Chomsky and other linguists suggested new opportunities for viewing the language acquisition process. Increasingly, the acquisition of language was viewed as a **generative process**. Children were seen as creators of interesting and systematic language, rather than as imperfect imitators of adult speech.

Developmental psycholinguists began to collect tape-recorded *observational data* on children's language and to conduct experimental research based on children's abilities to produce and comprehend specific structures of English. The goal of much of this research was to reconcile the findings of such observational and experimental research with the predictions made by the new transformational grammars.

Some of the landmark work in developmental psycholinguistics is based on a very small number of children who were intensively observed over a number of months or years. In the 1960s at Harvard University, Roger Brown headed a project that studied the language of three children who were called Adam, Eve, and Sarah (Brown, 1973). Researchers recorded the children once a month in their homes and brought the tape recordings back to the laboratory to be transcribed. The transcriptions were studied in a weekly seminar that led to a large number of early studies of children's developing grammatical systems. Adam, Eve, and Sarah's earliest attempts at language fostered our earliest understanding of how children acquire basic sentence structures in English, such as questions and negatives, how they acquire the grammatical morphology of English, and the possible role of adult models and feedback in the process of language development. Their efforts were reported by Brown and various colleagues and students in a broad array of publications (for a complete account, see Brown, 1973; Kessel, 1988).

Similar intensive observational studies of small numbers of English-speaking children constituted the bulk of much child language acquisition research during the 1960s (Braine, 1963; Bloom, 1970; Miller & Ervin, 1964). While other research methods using larger numbers of subjects have characterized the study of child language both during and since that time, intensive scrutiny of small numbers of children has continued to be a major research paradigm in child language development. This is due to a number of factors. First, it is often necessary to study a child's linguistic attempts intensively over time to obtain a representative sample of his or her abilities. We cannot ask children to produce their current version of an imperative or question by simply requesting, "Ask me a question," for example! Thus, it is difficult to construct a study which will examine the typical question asked by 100 two-year-old children. Second, because children's earliest attempts at language are nonadult-like in both structure and pronunciation, great care must be taken to annotate in a transcript what the researcher believes the child *meant to say*, as well as how he said it. The current context, previous context, responses of adults in the environment and factors such as pronunciation and gestural support may all be extremely relevant to understanding the child's behavior. Such a broad array of concerns are not easily coded when large numbers of children are being observed. Thus, the study of child

Eve

Adam

Sarah

language development can be seen as relatively detail-intensive, which has led many researchers to confine their observations to small numbers of children. Thankfully, the results of such "small N" studies are not usually in great disagreement. We will note here, and discuss in further detail later in the chapter, the rather remarkable finding that many of the behaviors observed in Adam, Eve, and Sarah's speech were in fact consistent with the results of studies of many other children observed in later years. We will describe the research findings in greater detail in the next section of the chapter.

By the mid-1980s, a large number of finely detailed transcripts of early child language attempts had been compiled, many of which could be used to investigate questions the original researcher had not necessarily envisioned. The Child Language Data Exchange System (CHILDES) was developed to enable child language researchers to examine and pool language transcripts already in existence (MacWhinney & Snow, 1985). Thus, Brown's transcripts are now available to the entire child language research community, and continue to provide data for current research questions (Pinker, 1991).

CHILDES collects data in many languages and on normally and atypically developing children. The computerized databank makes it possible for researchers to test their hypotheses on many subjects and it provides increased precision, standardization, and automation of the many data analyses which have been concurrently developed to describe the samples. A more detailed guide to the CHILDES database and the computer programs designed to analyze the computerized transcripts can be found in MacWhinney (1991). A sample transcript is shown in Figure 8-1.

Thus, over the years, many small sample studies of child language have contributed to a novel large scale data base, in which the language development of hundreds of children is profiled.

Research design

The design of studies can be either *cross-sectional* or *longitudinal*. Longitudinal studies—like Brown's study of Adam, Eve, and Sarah—track development in the *same* subjects as they grow older. Longitudinal designs must be used to answer certain kinds of questions, such as those that deal with the effects of children's early linguistic environment on their later acquisition of language. For instance, a longitudinal design was used to show that infants whose mothers spoke to them frequently and in short sentences at 9 months (time 1) performed better on tests of language comprehension at 18 months (time 2) than did infants of less talkative mothers (Murray, Johnson, & Peters, 1990). Longitudinal studies are usually limited in the number of individuals they can study.

Cross-sectional studies are concerned with asking questions such as "How do 2-, 3-, and 4-year-old children interpret passive sentences?" and do not follow an individual two-year-old over time to determine the answer; rather they gather groups of two-, three-, and four-year-old children and assess their abilities on the task in question. They are able to obtain a great deal of data in a short time, rather than over

```
@Begin
@Participants:   CHI Adami Child, MOT Nan Mother, SIS Jamie Sister, FAT Bob Father
@Age of child:   4;3.
@Date:   10-APR-1991
@Coder:   Rachel Brown
@Coding:   CHAT 1.0
*CHI:   toy-s.
%pho:   toiz.
%mod:   toiz.
*CHI:   after [*] my book.
%pho:   afU mai bUk.
%mod:   &ft3 mai bUk.
%gls:   we will play after my book.
*CHI:   this [*] is not [*] my book.
%pho:   dIs Iz nad mai bUk.
%mod:   DIs Iz nat mai bUk.
%gls:   this is not my book.
*MOT: this is not your book?
*CHI:   you-'re [*] just say-ing it.
%pho:   n3r dZAS SejIN It.
%mod:   j3r dZAs sejIN It.
%gls:   you're just saying it.
*MOT: Well these are the pictures of our trip to Disney World.
*CHI:   i want [*] two april-s in my xxx.
%pho:   ai wAnt tu eprOlz In mai xxx.
%mod:   ai want tu eprAlz In mai xxx.
%gls:   i want two aprils xxx.
*CHI:   xxx.
%pho:   In dIs bO.
%mod:   xxx.
%gls:   xxx.
*MOT: you want two aprils?
*MOT: maybe we can give Jamie a different april.
*MOT: i might have a different april.
*MOT: what did you say about april?
*MOT: what's funny about april's name?
*CHI:   me tell april.
%pho:   ni [*] ter [*] eprO [*].
%mod:   ai tEl eprAl.
%gls:   I tell april.
*MOT: you did what April?
*CHI:   me [*] tell [*] april [*] ‹is› [/] is on a calendar [*] day.
%pho:   ni ter eprO iz iz an e kaundO de.
%mod:   mi tel eprAl iz iz an e k&lInd3 de.
%gls:   i tell april she is a calendar day.
*MOT: you're going to tell april that her name is on a calendar?
*CHI:   yes.
%pho:   jEs.
%mod:   jEs.
%gls:   yes.
%com:   mother laughs.
```

Figure 8.1

A sample CHILDES transcript.

months or years. Studying many subjects also makes it more likely that study results can be generalized, rather than perhaps particular to a small group of children. Cross-sectional studies include at least two groups of subjects: in order to study the development of tag questions cross-sectionally, for instance, the speech of a group of 3-year-olds and a group of 4-year-olds could be compared for their use of the tags.

Cross-sectional and longitudinal studies can be either *observational* or *experimental*. In observational studies, the researcher tries not to interfere with a child's natural use of language, and in *naturalistic observational studies*, the focus is on real life situations. One example is the use of routines such as "What's the magic word?" in the speech of 24 families at home having dinner (Gleason, Perlmann, & Greif, 1984). Such studies provide insight into the experiences which shape the child's linguistic socialization.

Controlled observational studies are often administered in a laboratory playroom where the setting and props are the same for all subjects. In an illustrative study, differences were observed between fathers' and mothers' speech to young language learning children. Men and women were asked to play with their children in a laboratory playroom using particular toys provided by the research project (Ratner, 1988). Fathers used less common vocabulary than did mothers, and repeated the names of items less often. The impact of parental input style on children's language development continues to be of great interest to many researchers, as we will discuss later in the chapter. A different type of controlled observational study might ask children to repeat adult sentences to see how well they can approximate the model (e.g., Slobin & Welsh, 1971; Tager-Flusberg & Calkins, 1990). Research of this type tends to suggest that children's imitations reflect the grammatical tendencies of their spontaneously generated speech.

Experimental studies, by contrast, involve interference on the part of the researcher to discover if a particular condition does cause a predicted outcome. The *experimental group* of subjects receives a treatment chosen by the experimenter, and for comparison purposes, there is a *control group* of subjects that receives no special treatment. If a researcher wanted to know if training can make a difference in children's acquisition of tag questions, for instance, she could divide a group of three-year-olds in half into a control group and an experimental group. The experimental group would receive some sort of training: They might be read stories in which many kinds of tag questions are modeled. The control group would get no special treatment. Finally, both groups could be engaged in puppet play in which the child is asked to make the tag questions to statements made by the examiner: "John can ride a bike, *can't he*?" "The dog isn't very big, *is it*?" and so forth. (See Dennis, Sugar, & Whitaker, 1982, for an actual study of tag question acquisition.) If the trained group performs significantly better than the control group there is evidence that training can cause earlier development of tag questions. Many such positive studies would have implications for theories that claim that grammatical development is innately determined and unaffected by environmental factors. In the example provided in the section above, we would have to overtly train parents to use different kinds of vocabulary with children and compare the children's pre- and postexperimental vocabulary patterns to ascertain what effect different naming strategies have on language development.

Some studies attempt to replicate the natural settings for language acquisition.

Interviews

In general, we explore children's language systems indirectly, at least in part because it would be difficult to ask them what their rules are or what they find acceptable; their metalinguistic capacities are limited. A classic example is provided by a researcher's query of Adam:

> *Interviewer: Now Adam, listen to what I say. Tell me which is better . . . some water or a water.*
> *Adam: Pop go weasel.*

(Brown & Bellugi, 1964)

However, when we want to study children's **metalinguistic** development, it is appropriate to ask direct questions—the nature of the child's response enables us to ascertain the stage of metalinguistic development. In one famous metalinguistic study, Papandropoulou and Sinclair (1974) asked children metalinguistic questions (questions *about language*) such as "What is a word?" "What is a long word?" and "What is a short word?" They found that young children gave responses like *river* for the long word, and only later came to understand that there is a difference between the word and its referent. If you ask a three-year-old "What is your favorite word?" she is liable to say *candy*. A child of six or seven is more likely to produce a word whose phonetic form appeals to her, even if its referent does not. One of our favorite words (not things) is *pumpernickel*. Our least favorite, most unappetizing, word is *luscious*.

The course of language development: What do we know?

In this section, we will provide a necessarily brief introduction to the course of language development in English. To date, much more is known about what children are able and incapable of doing at particular stages of development than how these patterns evolve, which is a major concern of the psycholinguist.

In all parts of the world children say their first words around their first birthdays. But long before they speak, infants are engaged in communication with those around them. Human infants have special capacities that make later language development possible, and in all the societies that have been studied adults make special accommodations to infants when speaking to them.

Before speech: Early communicative development

The course of early communicative development has been summarized by Sachs (1993), who notes many of the following hallmarks:

Between her first and sixth birthdays, this child will master a large proportion of her adult language capacity.

Babies hear a special kind of language

Before discussing what children acquire and when, it is important to realize that the speech they hear is different in many ways from the language shared between adult speakers. What are these differences, and what are their implications? The work of Fernald (1985) has shown that mothers use very typical intonation patterns in speaking to infants and that it is the prosodic envelope that carries information about such things as approval or disapproval in the early weeks. Fernald's work in several language communities has shown that mothers use quite similar patterns to tell their children "no," or to encourage them. Additionally, research examining the prosody of speech addressed to infants suggests that it may facilitate the segmentation of major syntactic units by the young language learner (Kemler-Nelson, Hirsh-Pasek, Jusczyk, & Cassidy, 1989; Ratner, 1986).

Speech to infants in our society is marked by *slow rate, exaggerated intonation, high fundamental frequency*, many *repetitions, simple syntax*, and a *simple* and *concrete vocabulary* (Snow & Ferguson, 1977). Parents say things like, "See the birdie? Look at the birdie! What a pretty birdie!" These features probably make it easier for the infant to decode the language than if they heard, "Has it come to your attention that one of our better looking feathered friends is perched upon the windowsill?"

Child directed speech (CDS) or *babytalk (BT)* exists in one form or another in all societies that have been studied. But it is not uniform from society to society; rather, it is culturally determined. CDS is one of a number of speech registers available to speakers of a language. Although it has some features that are determined by the needs of the hearer infant, it varies from society to society. For instance, high fundamental frequency appears to be a feature that appeals to infants (perhaps high voices are less threatening than low voices) and it is frequently a feature of CDS, but there are some languages in which high fundamental frequency is reserved for other purposes (Bernstein Ratner & Pye, 1984). In Quiche Mayan the babytalk register is characterized by *low* fundamental frequency, and high fundamental frequency is used in speech to social superiors. However, Quiche Mayan utilizes its own particular BT register, designed to call the child's attention to ways of producing well formed Quiche utterances. Thus, babytalk registers are pervasive, though their individual forms vary. Gleitman, Gleitman, Landau, and Wanner (1988) propose that, "There is a natural coadaptation at work here, in which the mothers are inclined to provide a particular data base, and the babies are inclined to attend particularly to this." Whether BT is necessary, helpful or irrelevant to the process of language development is still a matter of spirited debate. The relative contribution made by the BT register to the process of language acquisition continues to be one of the critical questions in developmental psycholinguistics.

Infants learn about conversations long before they can talk

Adults assign meaning to infants' early burbles, and engage them in "conversations" long before babies have language. For instance, the adult may treat the baby's burp as a *conversational turn*, and respond to it:

Mother: There's a nice little smile.
Infant: (burps)
Mother: What a nice wind as well!
    Yes, that's better, isn't it?

(Snow, 1977)

As infants begin to acquire language, adults become *more demanding* in what they will accept as a conversational turn. Screaming "Wawwee!" won't do when you are 2. These increasing parental expectations increase the amount of vocalizations produced by infants, and teach them conversational turn-taking. Parents respond to inadequate or poorly formed early utterances in many ways, seeking clarification from their child, "What do want? Do you want the ball?" or imitation "Can you say, *block*?" among other responses. Even the loving provision of the wrong item provides the child with important feedback about the adequacy of her message.

Before they are able to speak, infants can communicate their intentions

Parents in our society tend to anticipate their children's competencies. Not only do they assume that burps are conversational turns, they also *impute intentions* to their children well before the intentions are actually there. For example, they may say of a howling 2-month-old, "She wants her daddy." Late in the first year infants begin to demonstrate true intentions and to express them in a variety of prelinguistic ways: They *gesture* or point at what they want, they may make *consistent word-like sounds*, use their *eyes* expressively, and become *persistent* when misunderstood. We cannot always tell what an infant may be trying to express, but researchers believe that these early attempts at communication include both *proto-declaratives* (language about something) and *proto-imperatives* (requests that something be done for or given to the infant) (Bates, 1979).

Infants have special abilities to perceive speech sounds

As early as the first weeks of life infants are able to make fine distinctions among speech sounds, to distinguish, for example, between voiced and unvoiced phonemes such as /p/ and /b/ in English. In fact, infants are able to make distinctions that adults cannot: Janet Werker (1984) and her colleagues have shown that Canadian babies can distinguish Czech /ř/ from /ʒ/, even though Canadian adults cannot hear the difference between these sounds (the first is a combination of [r] and [ʒ], as in the composer *Dvořak's* name, and the second is the sound [ʒ], as in the word *azure*). Thus, Werker and her colleagues have shown that infants from 8 to 10 months of age have the ability to discriminate phonemes that are not in the local language, whereas the adults in the community cannot. This ability begins to disappear by the end of the first year, when the infant has begun to learn the sounds of the language around her. Apparently infants come prepared to hear all possible distinctions, since they cannot know what language community they will be born into; once they learn their native language this special phonetic sensitivity vanishes. Work recently completed by

Kuhl, Williams, Lacerda, Stevens, and Lindblom (1992) suggests that infants are beginning to narrow their perception of sounds to those in their target native language before they even begin talking, much earlier than had been previously presumed.

Changes in infant eye gaze can signal discrimination of sound differences.

Speech sounds show a typical maturational pattern in infancy

Babbling, sometimes called *vocal play*, appears on a fairly predictable timetable when babies are a few months old. Stark (1980) has described typical developmental stages of vocal behavior:

In a typical infant, until about the age of 2 months, sounds produced are mostly either *reflexive* (e.g., basically uncontrolled) like crying or *vegetative sounds* (resulting from some physical activity) like burps and yawns.

Beginning when they are about 2 months old, babies begin to *coo* and *laugh*.

At five or six months they begin to engage in the sort of *vocal play* with sounds and syllables that is usually recognized as babbling.

Around the first birthday the babbling contains many *reduplicated syllables* such as "mama," and "dada." Many infants begin to say their first words around this time (either because they have intentionally used one of these forms referentially, or, perhaps because the adults around them have imputed meaning to the reduplicated babble: e.g., the baby babbles "dada" and the adults excitedly decide that she has called for her father).

For many babies there is a later stage of babbling called *jargon babbling*. Jargon has the intonation patterns of sentences and may be produced so convincingly that adults feel that the child is surely speaking, if they could only understand. Jargon babbling may last well into the second year and overlap with actual speech. Some infants never engage in jargon babbling, and seem to prefer to produce one careful word at a time.

Early language

First words

The first words spoken by children in very diverse communities of the world are very similar, both in their *phonetic form* and in the *kinds of meanings that underlie them*. First words, for instance, rarely contain consonant clusters, and are more likely to consist of *open syllables* (a consonant followed by a vowel) rather than closed syllables, or syllables ending in consonants. Nelson (1973) noted that early words tend to refer to things within the child's environment which the child could actively interact with. Thus, for both phonological and semantic reasons, a word such as *"carpet"* is an unlikely candidate for first word. A single word, such as *"more,"* may be produced with an adult like questioning intonation contour, and function as a reduced version of the adult request, *"May I have more please?"* The one-word stage of language development is sometimes called the **holophrastic** stage, to describe this use of single word "sentences."

Once language development is under way, researchers have noted very regular patterns in the ways young children progress toward full adult competence. The work of Brown and his colleagues has revealed that children's early utterances in a great variety of languages around the world are very similar (Brown, 1973; DeVilliers & DeVilliers, 1973; Slobin, 1985). At the earliest stage, children produce one meaningful word at a time, and that word is inevitably a concrete *content word* (such as "*kitty*" or "*mommy*," but certainly not a *function word* like "*of*" or "*the*," or an abstract word like "*truth*"). Early words are embedded in the child's environment, or the "here and now."

Even at the single word stage, children appear to be using their language to signal a variety of intentions, such as *negation, recurrence, nonexistence,* and *notice*. In other words, they can refuse something ("No!"), ask for more of something ("More!"), comment on the disappearance of something ("Gone!") or call attention to something or someone ("Hi!").

Comprehension precedes production of longer utterances

Children whose communicative output is limited to single word utterances appear to understand more complex language than they are able to produce. Golinkoff, Hirsh-Pasek, Cauley, and Gordon (1987) used an innovative technique to measure comprehension of basic Subject-Verb-Object (SVO) order in English by 17-month-old children. Children watched simultaneous, competing videotape loops while listening to utterances such as "Cookie Monster tickles Big Bird," or "Big Bird tickles Cookie Monster." Selective looking responses indicated that infants focused on those video segments which matched the word order pattern of the audio message.

The meanings of early words

What do words such as "horse," "daddy," and "chair" mean? Most adults will agree on their general definition or meaning. Yet a very young child may call a cow or zebra "horsie," any man "daddy," and anything which can be sat upon a "chair." The use of words to refer to a larger than appropriate set of referents is called **overextension**. Some researchers hypothesize that young children have not yet specified all of the necessary features which define the meaning of a word. Thus, the child who will call zebras "*cows*" or large dogs "*horsie*" has failed to incorporate the relevant features which distinguish horses from these other animals (Clark, 1973). While it has been argued that overextension is seen only in children's expressive languages some experimental evidence suggests that children's understanding of words may be overly broad as well (Fremgen & Fay, 1980). M. Bernstein (1983) showed that some very young children were apt to sort any items which could be sat on (such as sofas, benches, and swings) as "*chairs*." Rescorla (1980) has estimated that as many as one-third of the child's earliest lexical items may be overextended.

Early sentences

Some time during their second year, after children have about 50 of these early words in their vocabularies, they begin to put them together into rudimentary two-word sentences (Brown, 1973). Words that they said in the one-word stage are now

Figure 8.2

Even before they can construct sentences, infants recognize S-V-O constructions in English by gazing at the T.V. image which matches an audio message.

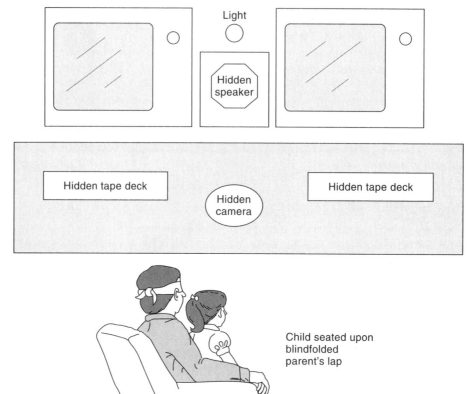

combined into short utterances. In English, such utterances lack articles, prepositions, inflections, or any of the other grammatical modifications that well formed adult language requires.

An examination of children's two-word utterances in many different language communities has suggested that everywhere in the world children at this age are expressing the same kinds of thoughts and intentions in the same kinds of utterances (Brown, 1973). The first two word utterances tend to have the same kinds of meanings that the child expressed in the one word stage:

> *Negation*: They say "no" to something: "No bed."
> *Recurrence*: They ask for more of something: "More milk."
> *Nonexistence*: They notice that something has disappeared: "Allgone cookie."
> *Notice*: They call attention to something: "Hi, Daddy."

A little later in the two-word stage, another dozen or so kinds of meanings appear:

> They name an *actor and a action*: "Daddy eat."
> They *modify a noun*: "Bad doggie."
> They indicate *possession*: "David shoe."

They *specify a location*: "Kitty table."
They describe an *action* and a *location*: "Go store."
They name an *action* and an *object*, leaving out the subject: "Eat lunch."

They also produce some sentences consisting of an *actor* and *object*, leaving out the verb or action: "Mommy . . . lunch," (meaning mommy is eating lunch).

At this stage, children acquiring English express these basic meanings, but they cannot use the grammatical forms of the language that indicate number, gender, and tense. Words that were previously uttered singly are produced in **telegraphic** combinations like, *"Nice kitty"* and *"More cookie"* (they sound like a telegram: "Send money car broke.") The sentences are limited in meaning (e.g., they are not generally about events in the past or future) and are produced without function words or inflections.

As we discuss regular patterns of development here and elsewhere within this chapter, it is important to note that language acquisition is marked by individual variation, as well as generalized developmental trends. Thus, some children seem to appreciate the "gestalt" of adult language patterns before being able to reproduce aspects of the grammar; such children may use adult-like prosody and "dummy syllables" to fill in between those vocabulary items they are capable of producing, saying, [wan ə kʊki] for *"I want the cookie."* Children with a more analytic style appear comfortable producing *"Want cookie,"* until they can incorporate the additional grammatical elements into their output. Similarly, even when children use only single words to communicate, stylistic variation in the kinds of words most frequently used by children can be seen. Some children appear to build their initial lexicons by incorporating many names for things; other children may include proportionately more "social" items, such as *hi, bye, please*, and so forth.

While English speaking children's early utterances are markedly devoid of grammatical inflections, children learning certain other kinds of languages use such inflections earlier in the course of their language development. In languages which have a much richer system of bound morphology, such as Turkish (Aksu-Koc & Slobin, 1985), Hungarian (MacWhinney, 1978), or Spanish (Johnson, 1991), much of the morphological system is used relatively without error by age 2. Why should this be? Let us consider the case of English verbs. We (and the child) can say *talk* (which we will call the *bare stem* version of the verb), as well as *talked, talking, talks*, and so forth. Additionally, the word *talks*, as in "She talks," represents a deviation from our otherwise regular pattern which permits the bare stem form of the verb in the present tense (e.g., *I talk, you talk, we talk*, etc.). In a language such as Spanish, bare stems are not permissable. That is, one must say *hablo, hablas, hablamos, habla*, and so forth, when using the verb in any tense, be it present, past, or future. The underlying root, *habl-*, cannot exist in its uninflected form. Thus, children learning English and Spanish receive different cues regarding the importance of grammatical suffixes. A child learning Spanish quickly comes to appreciate the need for them because they are so pervasive; a child learning English, because he hears both inflected and uninflected forms of the root, may take longer to learn when they are necessary and when they are not.

Early grammar

Slobin (1985) proposes as one of his *operating principles* which govern child language acquisition that, "the more pervasive a morphological category is in a language, the more readily it will be learned," (p. 1194). He cites the example of Hebrew, in which gender must be marked in every utterance, and which affects proper formation of subjects, verbs, modifiers, and plurals (Berman, 1985). In a language such as French where gender is marked less obviously, and multiple forms share the same pronunciation, children acquire gender marking later than those learning Hebrew (Clark, 1985).

In general, research such as that compiled by Slobin (1985, and in press) suggests that the emergence of grammar will be determined by a number of factors, including the *pervasiveness* and *regularity* of a language's grammatical constructions, the degree to which they "make semantic sense" (Slobin, 1973), and the relative *salience* of the grammatical concept. Those grammatical forms which are *stressed* are almost universally acquired before those which are not. Below, we will explore how such proposals accommodate general patterns of grammatical development in English and other languages.

Although the two-word stage has some universal semantic characteristics across all languages, what is acquired once children begin to acquire inflections and **function words** depends on the features of the language being learned. English-speaking children learn the articles *a* and *the*. But in a language such as Russian there are no articles. Russian grammar, conversely, has features that English does not, such as different past tense endings depending on whether the verb's subject is a male or a female.

Some theorists (Hyams, 1986) believe that Universal Grammar (introduced in Chapter 1) not only specifies **parameters** or switches for some variable features of language, but that the parameters also have *default settings*. For instance, languages vary in respect to whether they require that the subject be expressed in any given declarative sentence. All English sentences require a subject, even when there is no real referent for the subject (such as the *it* in "It is raining.") Spanish, by contrast, is a *null subject* (so-called *pro-drop*) language and does not require a subject: One may and usually does say things such as *"Esta lluviendo,"* (literally "Is raining."). Hyams (1986, 1990), after surveying the early, often subjectless, utterances of English-speaking children, hypothesizes that all children initially assume that their language is a pro-drop language; later evidence will cause English language learners to reset their parameter to accommodate the mandatory expression of subjects in English declaratives.

Once children learning a particular language begin to acquire grammatical markers, most of them do so in basically the same order within that language. In English, for instance, children tend to learn *in* and *on* before other prepositions such as *under*, and they learn the progressive tense (*-ing*) before other verb endings, such as the past tense marker (*-ed*). Brown (1973), using data from Adam, Eve, and Sarah, proposed a uniform sequence of development in which phonologically regular and semantically simple concepts such as the present progressive (*-ing*) emerge before the past tense (which has multiple phonological representations—*walked:* -ed = /t/; *played:* -ed = /d/; and *patted:* -ed = /əd/). In turn, the past will be acquired before the rather arbitrary *third person singular* marker (e.g., "*John walks*"), which has both regular and irregular realizations (e.g., *do/does*). The plural, which is conceptually simple, emerges before the possessive, which is somewhat more abstract. Rather arbitrary, unstressed and semantically empty elements such as auxiliary verbs ("*He is walking*") are relatively late acquisitions.

Because English contains relatively few grammatical morphemes, but uses them in the vast majority of well formed sentences, Brown and other researchers have found it useful to track language development by reference to a measure known as **mean length of utterance (MLU)**. This measure calculates the average length of a child's utterance in *morphemes*, rather than words, and tends to define stages of very early language development.

After children begin to learn the regular plurals and pasts like *horses* and *skated*, they create some regularized forms of their own, like *mouses* and *eated*. This is generally referred to as *overregularization*, and it is excellent evidence that children are learning the *systems* of their language, since they are producing words according to the basic *rules* of the language, rather than by simple imitation of the language they hear. Contributors to Slobin's (1985) volumes surveying language development cross-linguistically find overregularization of grammatical rules in all of the languages studied, including Hebrew, German, French, Hungarian, Japanese, Samoan, Polish, Turkish, Kaluli, and American Sign Language.

Learning to make sentences in English

Certainly, acquisition of morphological markers such as verbal inflections, articles, plurals, and so forth is necessary for the creation of well formed sentences in English (and other languages). However, as Chapter 1 noted, there are many types of sentences in English: those which negate, question, or take the form of the imperative. Additional major simple sentence types are passives ("*The baby was frightened by the loud noise.*"), in which subject and object are inverted, or datives ("*The man showed the student the room.*"), in which direct and indirect objects are inverted. Finally, English is characterized by varieties of *compound sentences*, in which conjunctions link multiple phrases ("John and Sue hike."; "Mary saw Tom and Joe."; "I will be late *because* I overslept."), and by *complex sentences*, in which clauses are embedded within phrases ("The man *who lives down the street* is a doctor."; "I know the woman *whom you saw*."; "*That John passed any courses* surprised me."). In the next few sections, we will briefly review acquisition of these many constructions. Research regarding the stages leading to mastery in the production and comprehension of these structures often suggests complex interactions between the syntactic and semantic complexity of such structures, their relative frequency (or lack of frequency) in conversational English, and children's use of non-linguistic strategies in interpreting difficult constructions. More extensive reviews are provided by Tager-Flusberg (1993) and DeVilliers and DeVilliers (1985).

Learning to say no.   The development of negative sentence forms in English was originally traced by Bellugi (1967), using data from Adam, Eve, and Sarah. Most subsequent studies have generally agreed with her findings, which suggested three major stages in negative formation. These stages are not discrete and discontinuous,

Figure 8.3

Rules for Calculating Mean Length of Utterance. (From *A First Language* [p. 54] by R. Brown: 1973. Cambridge, MA: Harvard University Press. Reprinted by permission.)

1. Start with the second page of the transcription unless that page involves a recitation of some kind. In this latter case start with the first recitation-free stretch. Count the first 100 utterances satisfying the following rules.

2. Only fully transcribed utterances are used; none with blanks. Portions of utterances, entered in parentheses to indicate doubtful transcription, are used.

3. Include all exact utterance repetitions (marked with a plus sign in records). Stuttering is marked as repeated efforts at a single word; count the word once in the most complete form produced. In the few cases where a word is produced for emphasis or the like (*no, no, no*) count each occurrence.

4. Do not count such fillers as *mm* or *oh*, but do count *no, yeah,* and *hi*.

5. All compound words (two or more free morphemes), proper names, and ritualized reduplications count as single words. Examples: *birthday, rackety-boom, choo-choo, quack-quack, night-night, pocketbook, see saw*. Justification is that there is no evidence that the constituent morphemes function as such for these children.

6. Count as one morpheme all irregular pasts of the verb (*got, did, went, saw*). Justification is that there is no evidence that the child relates these to present forms.

7. Count as one morpheme all diminutives (*doggie, mommie*) because these children at least do not seem to use the suffix productively. Diminutives are the standard forms used by the child.

8. Count as separate morphemes all auxiliaries (*is, have, will, can, must, would*). Also all catenatives: *gonna, wanna, hafta*. These latter counted as single morphemes rather than as *going to* or *want to* because evidence is that they function so for the children. Count as separate morphemes all inflections, for example, possessive [s], plural [s], third person singular [s], regular past [d], progressive [In].

9. The range count follows the above rules but is always calculated for the total transcription rather than for 100 utterances.

and children do not suddenly catapult from one to the next; rather, there is a steady progression, characterized by frequent use of a particular strategy as the child attempts to master the eventual adult form. In the first stage of negative formation, negative markers such as *no* and *not* simply precede the utterance, as in "No cars there," and "Not Fraser read it." In the next stage, as MLU approaches 3.0, negatives follow the main verb, and *can't* and *don't* appear within sentences, although they appear to be used as unanalyzed elements (since *can* and *do* are not present in any utterances). Thus, the child may produce, "That not mine," "I no eat it," "I can't see." As children enter later stages of language development (roughly MLU 3.5-4.0 and beyond), they acquire the ability to place negative markers on the verbal auxiliary, creating forms such as *isn't*.

Learning to ask questions. Although it is possible to simply use a declarative sentence and modify its intonational structure when asking a question (e.g., "He's

**Mean Length of Utterance and
Chronological Age for Three Children
(From A First Language by R. Brown,
1973, Cambridge, MA: Harvard University
Press. Reprinted by permission.)**

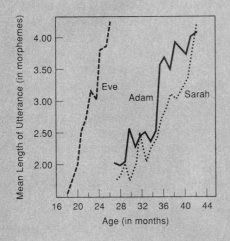

**Average Order of Acquisition of 14
Grammatical Morphemes by Three
Children Studied by Brown.**

1. present progressive
2/3. prepositions *(in/on)*
4. plural
5. irregular past tense
6. possessive
7. copula, uncontractible
8. articles
9. regular past tense
10. third person present tense, regular
11. third person present tense, irregular
12. auxiliary, uncontractible
13. copula, contractible
14. auxiliary, contractible

coming?"), the usual question formation in English requires reordering of the subject and auxiliary of the corresponding declarative form. In general, well formed *Yes/No* questions (e.g., "Is Daddy going?") precede *Wh-* questions (such as "Where is Daddy going?"), which require knowledge of the relevant *wh-* word as well as inversion of the subject and auxiliary. A number of studies suggest that the relative semantic difficulty of words such as *why, how,* and *when,* which require understanding of causal and temporal concepts, causes them to emerge at a later stage in both production and appropriate comprehension than words such as *what, where,* and *who* (see DeVilliers and DeVilliers, 1985 for summary discussion).

The role of word order strategies in sentence formation and comprehension. We have said that English primarily utilizes Subject-Verb-Object word order in its sentences. Children exposed to English quickly appreciate this pattern, as Golinkoff, et al.'s study of infants dramatically illustrates. The assumption that well formed sentences will use S-V-O ordering has consequences for the acquisition of some sentence types which do not utilize S-V-O order, such as the *passive, dative,* and certain types of *complex sentences.*

Many studies suggest that children younger than the age of 5 will use either an *S-V-O word order strategy* or *event probability* to comprehend passives and datives, which not only violate S-V-O ordering, but are rarely used in parental speech models to children. Thus, if the child can use knowledge of real-world events to properly interpret "The mouse was chased by the cat," or "Mary baked John a cake," (since Mary cannot bake John), she will do so, perhaps even at a very young age (Bridges, 1980). However, when the meaning cannot be derived without properly analyzing the syntax (such as in "The boy was hit by the girl," or "The mother showed the girl the baby."), children are likely to interpret the sentences as S-V-O constructions (Bever, 1970; Osgood & Zehler, 1981). Thus, they will act out or point to a picture of a boy hitting a girl, and a woman showing a girl *to* a baby. Similar problems may arise when a sentence's S-V-O structure is disturbed by an embedded clause, as in "The man who lives next to my sister is a doctor." Children may assume that the object of the main clause (*sister*) operates as the subject of the phrase *is a doctor.*

Combining sentences.   Children's first efforts to create compound sentences are likely to utilize the conjunction *and*, and link objects, as in "I like cookies and cake," (which is presumably based on the underlying notions *I like cookies and I like cake*). Those which link subjects, as in, "Adam and Eric want to come" emerge later; earlier attempts are likely to resemble, "Adam wants to come, and Eric wants to come too." More languages of the world permit the first type of conjoined structure, which is thought to involve *forward deletion* of the redundant subject-verb sequence *I like*, than the second, which requires *backward deletion* of the first verb phrase, and adjustment of the verb.

The use of other conjunctions, such as *because, but, if, before/after*, and so forth will require children to understand their particular meanings. Children may use them in appropriate syntactic frames, yet fail to appreciate their semantic roles, as in *"I fell down because I hurt my knee,"* (Bloom, Lahey, Hood, Lifter, & Fiess, 1980; Menyuk, 1969). In many cases, an *order of mention strategy* appears to apply both to production and comprehension of such strings, in which the event in the first clause is simply presumed to occur before the second.

Young children rarely produce embedded clauses in their conversational speech. Most of the research on acquisition of such structures has addressed the degree to which children are able to comprehend them.

As Hamburger and Crain (1982) have noted, these sentences pose great difficulty for children, probably for a number of reasons. Studies disagree both on the relative difficulty of the constructions, as well as the ages at which they tend to be accurately interpreted by the majority of child subjects. It is safe to say that children below the age of 6 do not find it easy to accurately interpret such structures.

This whirlwind tour through the basic accomplishments of young children acquiring a first language cannot begin to touch upon the complexity of their task, and the great wealth of information which has become available on the topic during the past two decades. Readers interested in a more complete picture of children's

ROLE OF COMPLEX NP IN MATRIX SENTENCE (EMBEDDEDNESS)	ROLE OF HEAD NOUN IN RELATIVE CLAUSE (FOCUS)	ABBREVIATION	EXAMPLE
subject	subject	SS	The cat that bit the dog chased the rat.
subject	object	SO	The cat that the dog bit chased the rat.
object	subject	OS	The cat bit the dog that chased the rat.
object	object	OO	The cat bit the dog that the cat chased.

Table 8.1

Types of Relative Clauses

progress toward language competence may wish to refer to Gleason (1993), DeVilliers and DeVilliers (1985), or Owens (1992), among other sources.

Form and function as bases of language development

Researchers have varying ways of accounting for children's early utterances. The work of the 1960s, inspired by the grammatical theory of Chomsky (1957, 1965) interpreted early word combinations as evidence that the child was learning syntax and developing a grammatical system. More recently, the child's intentions and attempts to attain certain pragmatic goals in the world have dominated the research, at least in some quarters. The list of typical early sentences we have included in the previous section is based on a functional view—for example we interpret the utterances as having some functional goal (such as getting the child to do something) rather than as abstract expressions of grammatical capacity.

Early social uses of language

When we speak of *psycholinguistics* we tend to think of memory, attention, intelligence, and cognitive processing as the psychological components that underlie language. While children are developing cognitively and linguistically they are also developing affectively and socially, and these are also facets of psychological development that play a role in language development.

Once they have acquired linguistic principles such as conversational turn-taking and many semantic relations, much of children's early speech is directed toward maintaining contact with caregivers and getting others to do things for them. These early *social intentions* have been described by researchers studying the pragmatic aspects of language (Bates, 1976; Halliday, 1975) and include: *drawing attention* to the self (a good example at the one-word stage is *hi*); *showing objects* (*see, ball*);

offering (e.g. "There!" said as the child offers the adult a toy); and, *requesting* objects or activities (e.g., "More!"). The purely social expression "Bye-bye," is, in fact usually the first conventionalized communicative act that an infant engages in, in our society.

Many researchers have suggested that some children are more social than others in their use of language, yet these reported stylistic differences are difficult to interpret. For instance, Nelson (1973) found that some children are *referential* whereas others are *expressive*. The expressive children were thought to be more social in orientation, and the referential children more interested in labeling the world. Perhaps the child who spends her time labeling her environment is actually motivated by primarily social (and not taxonomic) reasons—perhaps it is just this behavior that attracts and holds the attention of her achievement-oriented, middle-class family.

Research on the potential contributions of the early social characteristics of children suggests that the acquisition of grammatical forms may not be determined exclusively by the syntactic, semantic or cognitive complexity of the form (Brown, 1973; Slobin, 1985). The social motivational propensities of children and the adults with whom they interact may also influence what and when particular linguistic forms are acquired. Cross-linguistic research provides many examples to support this position. Acquisition of Samoan provides one illustration. Samoan is an *ergative* language in which special marking of transitive subjects distinguishes them from intransitive subjects. Ochs (1982) notes that ergative case marking is acquired late by Samoan children for what appear to be social rather than linguistic reasons. In Samoan, the ergative case is more characteristic of men's than of women's speech. "Samoan children do not acquire this marking early largely because they are not exposed to it in their social environment, the household setting, where women and other family members are primary socializing agents," (p. 77). Ochs points out that this contrasts with the acquisition of ergatives by Kaluli-speaking children in New Guinea, who acquire ergatives early. Clancy (1985) also describes the importance of sociolinguistic factors in the acquisition of Japanese and how pragmatic factors pervade the grammar of the language. "The child who masters the syntax and morphology of Japanese has also mastered a subtle pragmatic system for regulating the flow of information to listeners in accordance with their needs in the speech context through word order, ellipsis, and sentence-final particles, as well as an elaborate system of socially defined statuses and roles which are expressed in verb morphology, pronouns, and sentence-final particles," (p. 377). Grammatical forms which express deference, politeness and other social proprieties may be acquired early not because they are syntactically or cognitively less complex, but because they are a social necessity.

Children's acquisition of varied *polite forms* occurs in conjunction with explicit teaching on the part of adults (Snow, Gleason, & Perlmann, 1990). It seems obvious that children acquire polite forms partly as a result of their increasing cognitive capacities and partly because they are motivated (at some level) to be socially acceptable, and hence polite, people. Additionally, active and explicit teaching on the part of adults to assure that pragmatic socialization takes place appears to be pervasive. In a study of eight families at dinner (Gleason, Greif, & Perlmann, 1984), even when the dinner was only 13 or 14 minutes long, the adults in every family structured explicit teaching episodes regarding how children should comport themselves. Every family used at least some politeness routines, such as *"Thank you,"* and *"May I please be excused?"* Six of th⸻ l prompting techniques with their children, ⸻ord?" or "What do you say?" When ques-⸻uired form, parents often modeled it for ⸻ from a family with a 4-year-old daughter,

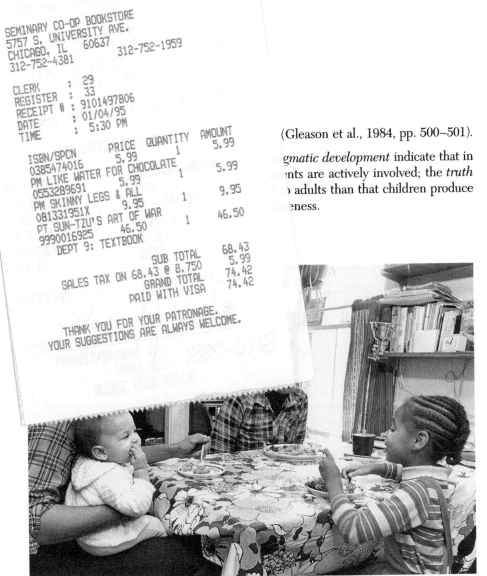

(Gleason et al., 1984, pp. 500–501).

⸻*gmatic development* indicate that in ⸻nts are actively involved; the *truth* ⸻ adults than that children produce ⸻eness.

Appropriate use of language requires social interaction and feedback

In concentrating our attention on the generative and productive aspects of language it is important not to neglect the social forms that children must acquire in order to be accepted in society and the influence of social and affective factors on the acquisition of linguistic rule systems.

Theories of language acquisition: What are the questions?

General features of theories

Developmental psycholinguistics is filled with lively theoretical controversy about how best to account for language development. At one extreme, scholars claim that language is a *learned behavior* that parents teach to children, and at the other end of the theoretical spectrum equally dedicated researchers claim that the principles that underlie language are *innate*, or present at birth as part of the child's biological heritage.

Most people today who have not studied psycholinguistics also have a folk theory of language development: They theorize that children acquire language by *imitating* the adults around them. Children do imitate many adult behaviors, both naturally and experimentally. In a famous study, Bandura, Ross, and Ross (1963) showed preschoolers an attractive person who punched and beat a doll. When left alone with the doll later, the children also punched the doll, occasionally using the adult model's words when they did so. Although imitation or, more broadly, social learning theory seems quite plausible, and surely accounts for part of language development, some of the problems with assuming that imitation is a *sufficient* explanation can be seen if one simply tries to imitate an unknown language, for instance a Greek radio program on any Sunday morning, or a simple conversation between two waiters in a Chinese restaurant. Under those circumstances, imitation does not seem to be a very easy or obvious way to learn a language, and we must turn to more powerful theories to account for children's remarkable linguistic accomplishments.

Major dimensions of theories of language development

Theories of language development differ in the weight that they ascribe to various dimensions that characterize language. Each of the following questions asks which end of the continuum is more important:

Nature or nurture?

Perhaps this is the major question that divides psycholinguists: To what extent is language *hard wired* into the human brain (nature), and to what extent is it learned through interaction with the environment (nurture)? Do parents teach children language, or does language simply unfold according to a genetic program?

Continuity or discontinuity?

Does language develop in a seamless flow, smoothly and with barely perceptible transitions, or does it proceed in stages that are clearly distinct from one another? For instance does the infant's babbling slowly turn into words, or is there a stage where the babbling ceases, followed by a stage in which talking begins?

Universal competence or individual variation?

Is linguistic competence basically *invariant*? That is, can we assume that all speakers of the language who are not in some way impaired share the same linguistic knowledge? Or is there a great deal of variation in what individuals know? Do all children acquire language in the same way? For instance, if we collect the first words and then the first sentences of 50 or 100 children learning English, will they all be basically the same?

Structure or function?

In studying language development should we concentrate on *structure*, the grammar of the language that children acquire, or should we pay more attention to function, the way that language is used in various situations? For instance, if a 4-year-old says, "It's hot in here, isn't it?" is it of greater interest that she is able to make the complex syntactic *tag question*, or should researchers study the interpersonal situations in which children learn to mitigate or hedge their statements with tag questions? (See Chapter 1 for a description of the grammatical rules that underly formation of tag questions in English. Note that English makes it particularly difficult for children to learn tags, whereas in languages such as French or German tags require no grammatical modulation at all: one simply appends "N'est-ce pas?" or "Nicht Wahr?" to any appropriate sentence.)

Autonomy or dependency?

Is language a separate faculty of the human mind? Or is language development dependent on or a part of other kinds of development? For instance, are there cognitive prerequisites for language, or can language be learned by an individual who will never pass the usual cognitive milestones of childhood?

Rules or associations?

Is the child who is acquiring language internalizing a set of abstract cognitive principles, or can language be learned without recourse to *rules*, but merely as a set of *connections* or associations built on past experience? For instance, when a child learns that the past tense of "melt" is "melted," has she learned a *rule* for adding the ending, or has she simply processed the statistical observation that words ending in /t/ tend to be followed by /əd/ if they are conveying past tense information?

These are just some of the kinds of questions that have led to research, theory, and heated controversy in the field of developmental psycholinguistics.

Theoretical approaches to the study of language acquisition

There are specialized theories that deal with each subcomponent of language, for example, *syntactic theory, phonological theory,* or *semantic theory.* There are also more general theories which attempt to account for broad aspects of linguistic development, and they are based on at least five major theoretical perspectives: *innatist theory, learning theory, cognitive theory, social interactionist theory,* and *connectionist theory.*

Linguistic/innatist theory

The quotation at the beginning of this chapter refers to events that took place in Egypt in the fifth century B.C. According to the Greek historian Herodotus, who was a contemporary of the playwright Sophocles, a king named Psammetichus, performed an experiment in order to find out which human language was the first. Psammetichus gave two infants to a shepherd, who was instructed to treat them well, but to keep them in isolation and never to speak to them. The king wanted to know what the children's first words would be if they were left to their own devices in this way. (This is an unethical experiment! The ancient Egyptians did many things that the National Institutes of Health would never allow.) This king's linguistic theory was perhaps the first and most extreme example of *innatism*: He believed that at a given moment the children would simply begin to speak the language that was innate to them (*innate* really means *present at birth*), and he hoped that the language would be Egyptian, because that would back up his proud claim that the Egyptians were the original race of humans.

According to Herodotus, the shepherd arrived to take care of the children one day, "after the indistinct babblings of infancy were past," and they held out their hands and said "bekos," which was a word he had never heard. The shepherd went to the king, who made inquiries all over the country, and eventually was told that "bekos" was the Phrygian word for bread. The king then claimed that the Egyptians were surely the *second oldest* race, since obviously the Phrygians must have come first.

No researcher today believes that a particular language is inscribed on our neurons, but linguistic/innatist theorists do believe that the principles of language are inborn, and not learned. Why is such an assumption made? Most simply put, it is because "one . . . still want(s) to know why young children arrive at successful grammars so much more readily than professional linguists" (Lightfoot, 1982). Children universally acquire the major proportion of their mature language capacity within a very short time frame, between approximately 1 and 6 years of age. They do so,

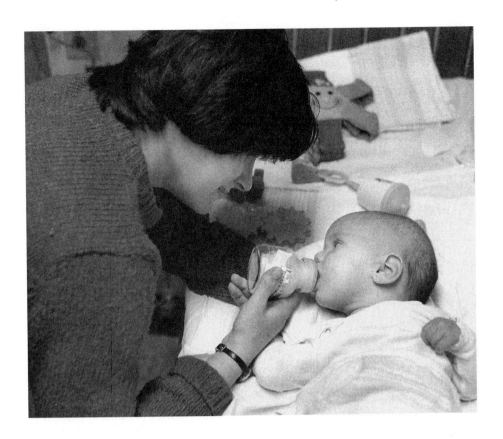

according to some observers, without access to either the kind of models or responses to poorly formed attempts at language which should permit rapid achievement of such a complex system of behavior. In a modern day parallel to Psammetichus' experiment, they point to research on deaf children who have not been exposed to any language; a group of children like this was studied by Goldin-Meadow and her colleagues (Butcher, Mylander, & Goldin-Meadow, in press; Goldin-Meadow & Mylander, 1990). The children's parents did not want them to learn sign language, and the children had not yet entered a program that would teach them lip reading and oral skills. Goldin-Meadow found that the deaf children, even with no exposure to any kind of language, developed their own systems of manual *sign communication* that incorporated many of the formal features of language.

Other evidence of children actually creating language is offered by Bickerton (1984), who studied the properties of Hawaiian pidgin. A *pidgin* language is typically one that develops in a situation where speakers of many different languages need to find a common means of communication; as such, the pidgin may be quite simplified and lack features found in complete languages (Mülhaüsler, 1986; Romaine, 1988). Bickerton found that Hawaiian children who heard only pidgin gradually transformed that pidgin into a *creole*, which is a true language, and actually produced grammatical forms that were more complex than those in their parents' speech. The work of Goldin-Meadow and Bickerton is controversial, since, for instance, Goldin-Meadow studied only a small number of children, and Bickerton inferred the course of creole evolution from historical data, but both provide provocative support for the notion that some linguistic categories may be part of the way humans will inevitably want to organize their experience.

Of course, most children do not acquire language under the conditions studied by either Goldin-Meadow or Bickerton. Even so, many researchers are concerned that children could not extrapolate all of the rules of their language and only the rules of their particular language merely by reliance upon adult models or adult feedback to linguistic efforts. Lightfoot (1982) lists three major concerns which underlie the assumption that language learning is critically dependent upon specific biologically determined abilities and processes. All of them contribute to the deficiency or *poverty of the stimulus* problem.

First, some observers note that not all language addressed to or overheard by young children consists of complete, well formed utterances. Given the fact that children cannot, at the beginning, distinguish between good and poor examples of language use, how do they proceed? Lightfoot provides the analogy of attempting to learn chess by watching large numbers of games into which a small number of illegal moves are introduced, without being labeled or penalized. Second, children come to use and understand sentences which presumably never occur in their language-learning environment, such as multiple clauses strung together endlessly, as in, "The horse the cow kicked was chased by the bull the farmer bought," and so forth. Perhaps most importantly, since children do eventually master language structures they have probably not heard before, why is it that they do not, at least in syntax, attempt to form certain ungrammatical constructions? Some people have called this last problem one of *negative evidence*: No one supposedly ever tells you, "And by the way, don't try doing the following things in English, they're not grammatical." Pinker (1991) discusses these limitations on the cues provided by the child's environment in detail.

Even when adults in the child's environment do attempt to actively teach language, linguists note that children do not seem predisposed to make use of such information at particular stages of linguistic development, when the child presumably cannot profit from the feedback. McNeill's (1966) example has become perhaps the most often cited example of the phenomenon:

Child: Nobody doesn't like me.
Mother: No, say, "nobody likes me."
Child: Nobody doesn't like me.
(eight repetitions of this dialogue)
Mother: No, now listen carefully: say "Nobody likes me."
Child: Oh, nobody don't likes me.

(McNeill, 1966, p. 69)

Linguistic theorists rely heavily on theories of mind, and on special abstract mental mechanisms, such as a postulated **LAD** or **Language Acquisition Device** (Chomsky 1965, 1972, 1982) to reconcile rapid, successful language acquisition with these deficiencies in the data to which the child is exposed. The Language

Acquisition Device, according to Chomsky, makes it possible for children to *attend* to the language that the adults around them speak, *make hypotheses* about how it works, and *derive an appropriate grammar*. Chomsky himself eschews the term "innateness" when discussing the theory of language acquisition. As he points out, all theories of learning presume some innate capacities which are probably unique to the human experience. A horse cannot be trained either to use language or to calculate the odds on horse races. Thus, a linguist finds it noncontroversial to assume that the human mind possesses certain inherent properties, tendencies and initial assumptions. The task is to specify them. Innatist theory claims that many aspects of language development are *preprogrammed* in the individual, and that explicit teaching or experience is not required in order for a child to acquire language. The language that infants hear provides data for their grammatical hypotheses, but the LAD does not require *specialized input* to do its job—any reasonable sample of language will do, according to the theory. Thus, nativists view language as a hard-wired *bioprogram* that will develop once the infant is *exposed* to language.

The principles which underly all possible human languages are considered to be innate, and constitute the concept known as Universal Grammar. Chomsky (1975) defines **Universal Grammar (UG)** which we first discussed in Chapter 1, as "the system of principles, conditions and rules that are elements or properties of all human languages not merely by accident but by (biological) necessity . . . ," (p. 29). Because UG specifies the basic linguistic possibilities from which individual languages derive, and because language reflects properties of the human mind, one can hypothesize certain initial states and paths toward language competence.

Linguists point out that children everywhere learn to talk—in fact it is just about *impossible to suppress* the development of language (Lenneberg, 1967). Since children around the world are raised in societies where thousands of different languages are spoken and different child care practices prevail, and since they come with obvious individual differences in intelligence, temperament, motivation, personality, and so forth, universal patterns of language development provide strong evidence that the *mechanisms* underlying language development are inborn or innate. Thus, acquiring language is rather like learning to walk—something that happens in just about every intact individual, with or without explicit training.

Of course, every child learns a particular language, and it is necessary to explain *how* the child proceeds from the initial state (which specifies more structural possibilities than any individual language will permit) to competence in the language spoken in his community. According to the linguistic view, infants may be innately endowed with linguistic switches or *parameters* that they set once they hear the adult language around them; for instance, they may note that English is a subject-verb-object or S-V-O language, or that it has articles before its nouns (Hyams, 1986), and set their parameters accordingly.

In the linguistic view, language is an *autonomous* faculty, separate from intelligence; and infants are innately driven to acquire it. The various subsystems of language are internalized as sets of algorithms or rules that allow the child to produce new utterances that she has never heard before. For instance, a child of 3 or 4 can produce the plural of a nonsense word "*gutch*" that she has never heard before:

If a child knows that the plural of *witch* is *witches* he may simply have
memorized the plural form. If, however, he tells us that the plural of *gutch* is
gutches, we have evidence that he actually knows, albeit unconsciously, one of
those rules which the descriptive linguist, too, would set forth in his grammar.

(Berko, 1958; p. 47)

Language acquisition involves the internalization of the rules that underlie the
various subsystems of the language. Knowing one set of rules (the phonology, for
instance) can occur even in the absence of another set of rules (the inflectional system, for instance). In this sense linguistic knowledge is *modular*—the units are to a
large degree independent of one another.

According to linguistic/innatist theory there may be a *critical* or *sensitive period*
during which the language acquisition device and parameter setting can optimally
function. Once the critical period has passed (usually when the individual reaches
puberty) acquiring a first language may become difficult or even impossible.

Learning theory

Behaviorists, or *learning theorists* (e.g., Skinner 1957, 1969; Whitehurst, 1982), claim
that language is acquired according to the *general laws of learning* and is similar
to any other learned behavior. Behaviorists see spoken language development as
a result of adults' *reinforcement* and gradual *shaping* of infants' babbling, and
they apply the general principles of learning to later developments—for example,

This is a Gutch.

Now there is another one.
There are two of them.
There are two _____ .

Figure 8.4

When a child pluralizes a nonsense word, she demonstrates knowledge of a rule of English.

learning how to make a past tense of a new verb is a result of *generalization* based on past experience with similar words.

No special internal capacities are postulated, since *external behavior* rather than mental activity is the object of study. Learning theorists do not deny that there may be neuropsychological mechanisms that underlie language, but they deny the usefulness of *mentalistic* approaches. These theorists assert that speakers can only be said to have linguistic *"rules"* if they can actually describe them (Skinner, 1969). If you were unable to provide the rule for the formation of *tag questions* in Chapter 1, then you do not have a rule, even if you are an impeccable tag-question maker.

Learning theory includes at least three kinds of learning: *classical conditioning*, *operant conditioning*, and *social learning*. Each of these kinds of learning can be called upon to explain some part of language development.

Classical conditioning   An infant may learn the meaning of a word through classical conditioning. In the famous conditioning experiments conducted by Pavlov (1927) dogs learned (were *conditioned*) to react to a bell as if it were meat powder. Initially, the dogs were presented with meat powder (the *UCS* or *unconditioned stimulus*) and their *unconditioned response* or *UCR* was to salivate. The experimenter then rang a bell (the *conditioned stimulus*) just before giving the dogs meat powder. Eventually, ringing the bell alone caused the dogs to salivate (the *conditioned response*). In a sense, the dogs reacted to the bell as if it were the meat (even though their response was not complete—they did not attempt to eat the bell). In the beginning, the meat powder was the *stimulus*, and salivation was the *response*. Soon, through *association* with the meat powder, the bell alone became sufficient to evoke the salivation response.

Learning the meaning of a word is thought to be a similar process. An infant fed with a bottle, for instance, has many reactions to the bottle, such as anticipation of drinking (or perhaps even salivation). If every time she is fed, her mother holds up the bottle and says "Bottle," the child begins to *associate* the word *bottle* with the object. Ultimately, when someone says "bottle," the child responds to the word in some sense as if it were the thing—by expecting to see a bottle, becoming physiologically prepared to drink, (perhaps salivating) and so on. The word now evokes the same response as the bottle, and in this sense she knows the meaning of the word.

Operant conditioning.   The basic principle of operant conditioning (also called *instrumental learning*) is that behavior that is rewarded, or *reinforced*, will be *strengthened*. This kind of learning is called "operant" because the subject "operates" on the environment in order to get a reward, or *reinforcement*. Behavior that is not reinforced will become *extinguished*. In the behavioral view, parents and others teach children language through operant conditioning by *rewarding* their early attempts at language. At first, parents are happy and react with reinforcing smiles and attention if their child makes any language-like noises at all, but in time the parents become more demanding and only reward closer approximations of the target language. This *selective reinforcement* gradually *shapes* the child's linguistic behavior.

For instance, an infant who wants some water may say something that sounds like "Wawweee!" and get results from happy parents. At the age of 3, if the child says "wawwee," the parent is liable to say, "What did you say? What do you want?" and not react favorably until the child says "Water!"

By the time the child is 4 or 5, "Water!" won't do any more; now the parent says something like "What's the magic word?" and holds out until the child says "Please, may I have some water?" The child's early utterances have gradually been *shaped* until they reach adult form.

Social learning.   Social learning is a kind of learning that takes place when the child *observes* and *imitates* others. The basic principle involved is that children need not be rewarded themselves in order to acquire a behavior—they also learn to behave like appropriate *models*. Older people who are seen as *powerful, nurturant*, and *similar* to the child (e.g., the same gender) are most likely to be imitated. Little boys learn to talk like their fathers, and little girls imitate the speech (and other behaviors, of course) of their mothers. Thus, through a combination of *classical* and *operant conditioning*, as well as imitation and *social learning*, the child moves from babbling infant to speaking adult, according to learning theory. Since *observable* and *measurable behavior* provide the data for learning theorists, they are not concerned with abstractions such as whether children or adults at any stage have *concepts* underlying their language.

As we noted in Chapter 1, many aspects of children's language acquisition cannot easily be explained by learning theory models, since children: 1) say things they have never heard before, like, "I holded the baby rabbits"; and 2) do not say some of the things they hear most commonly—for instance infants' first utterances do not contain articles, even though *a* and *the* are the most common words in the English language. As a human activity, language development cannot be impervious to the laws of learning, however. What seems likely is that some parts of language (e.g., the politeness system or other social routines) may be explicitly taught, whereas others (e.g., the phonology and syntax) may be acquired in a less obvious way.

Moerk (1990), in a reanalysis of Brown's original transcripts of Eve and her mother, has urged a reconsideration of stimulus-response-reinforcement mechanisms in language acquisition. In his alternative view, which contains elements of both operant conditioning and social learning paradigms, maternal utterances serve as model and stimulus, the child's utterances, which tend to be highly imitative in part or whole are considered responses, and the following maternal response is considered reinforcement. If reinforcement is operationally defined as an acknowledgement (*yeah, right*, etc.), evidence from Eve's interactions suggest a high proportion of self-repetition of rewarded utterances, an increase in the rewarded behavior. Similarly, maternal expansions of the child's utterances, which are extremely frequent, are hypothesized to provide reinforcement to the child's attempts, as well as corrective feedback.

Cognitive theory

Cognitive theorists (Bates, 1979; Bates & Snyder, 1985; Macnamara, 1972; Piaget, 1926, 1954; Sinclair-deZwart, 1973) believe that language is a subordinate part of cognitive development, dependent on the attainment of various concepts. According to this view, children learn about the world first, and then map language onto that prior experience. For example, an infant attains the concept of *object permanence* first, and then begins to note the disappearance of objects (such as milk) by saying, "All gone," (Gopnik & Meltzoff, 1987). Or an infant has experience with the family cat, knows that it meows, is warm and furry, eats in the kitchen; she develops a cat *concept* first, and then learns to map the word *kitty* onto that concept.

In developing theories of language acquisition, we are faced with special problems because children are developing in many ways at the same time. It is difficult to know to what extent language development is dependent on, or part of, other development, and to what extent it is separate, or *autonomous*. Adults learning a second language, for instance, already have their basic concepts in place: For an English speaker to learn that a horse is called *cheval, caballo, pferd*, or *ló* in French, Spanish, German, or Hungarian requires learning some new sounds, but we already have the concept *horse*, on which to map these new words. Children who are acquiring their first language are acquiring their first concepts at the same time.

There are obvious grounds for controversy among researchers about to what extent the developments that take place in cognition as well as in other spheres are necessary before language can blossom. The temptation to mistake *correlation* for *causation* is particularly strong when we study children—because different kinds of developmental milestones may occur at about the same time. For example, children's first words and first steps occur at around their first birthdays, and children's first word combinations, late in the second year, often occur around the time they gain sphincter control. Though these events are closely correlated in time, few would argue that toilet-training "causes" language development. It is certainly easy to assume, however, that before a child can converse about something she needs to *know* what it is. Or that there are general *cognitive prerequisites* for language: For instance that the ability to use the future and past tenses depends upon a prior understanding that there *is* a future or past. Cognitive theorists believe that language is just one aspect of human cognition (Piaget, 1926; Sinclair-deZwart, 1973). According to Piaget and his followers, infants must learn about the world around them, which they do through active experimentation and *construction*. For example, the infant crawls around the floor, observes objects from all angles, and slowly develops a *sensorimotor* (literally, through the senses and motor activity) understanding of the space in which she lives. Primitive notions of *time* and *causality* develop, as well as an understanding that people and objects continue to exist, even when they are out of sight (*person permanence* and *object permanence*). According to a Piagetian perspective, language is mapped onto an individual's set of prior cognitive structures, and the principles of language are no different from other cognitive principles.

A number of studies have observed parallels between linguistic and cognitive development. For the most part, researchers have attempted to link Piagetian stage acquisition with the emergence of language skills in children. For example, Kelly and Dale (1989) suggest that late stage 4 or early stage 5 sensorimotor skills appear to signal the onset of single word utterances by children. Stage 6 sensorimotor capacity closely precedes the emergence of combinatorial language. Bates, Bretherton, Snyder, Shore, and Volterra (1980) linked symbolic play behavior to greater progress in language development in children.

More recently, some have suggested that attempting to evaluate the role of cognition in language development by defining children's cognitive progress solely in Piagetian terms may obscure real relationships between the two domains (Cromer, 1991). Further, some researchers maintain that it is *skill*, rather than *stage* mastery which sets the stage for the acquisition of particular linguistic behaviors. For example, *object permanence* may be required before words such as *all gone* are used (Gopnik & Meltzoff, 1987).

Cognitive theory is challenged when cases arise that suggest that there can be a *dissociation* between cognitive and linguistic development—for example some children who were born during the 1950s to mothers who had taken a supposedly mild tranquilizer, *thalidomide*, during their pregnancies had limbs missing and were unable to have the sensorimotor experiences thought to be prerequisite to language development. Yet they developed full, sophisticated language capacity. More recently there have been reports of children with very substantial intellectual impairments (such as an IQ of only 50) who have complete and sophisticated language capacity (Curtiss, 1982; Yamada, 1990).

> Mother: *Adami, you are talking ever so much better in kindergarten than you
>   did in nursery!*
> Adami: *(shrugs his shoulders and smiles) Yeah, well, you teached me!*

Social interactionist theory

Social interactionists (e.g., Bruner, 1985; Gleason, Hay, & Cain, 1989; Farrar, 1990;
Snow, 1981) do not deny the existence of special *neuropsychological endowments*,
but they also hold that biological factors, while *necessary*, are *not sufficient* to ensure
that language will develop. They place less reliance on postulated hard-wired and
time-limited neural structures (such as the Language Acquisition Device) for which
there is no anatomical evidence.

According to some social interactionists, a biological "critical period" for language acquisition does not exist (Snow, in press). They point out that *some* parts of
language, such as a *native-like accent*, may be more difficult to learn as one gets
older, but that there is little evidence that adults are worse language learners than
children. Nor is language development seen as simply one aspect of cognitive development. Instead, social interactionists view language as a facet of *communicative
behavior* which develops through *interaction* with other human beings. Bruner
(1983) offers the term LASS (Language Acquisition Socialization System) as an alternative to Chomsky's LAD.

According to this interactionist view, children acquire language in part through
the *mediation* and help of others, rather than purely through their own mental activity in processing adult language. Thus, *interaction*, rather than *exposure*, is seen as
necessary. Children cannot acquire language simply by observing adults in conversation with one another, or by watching television or listening to the radio. Social interactionists point to the fact that there are *special ways of talking to young children* all
over the world and that the special language used by adults appears *tailored* or *fine
tuned* to the cognitive and communicative needs of the children. This Child Directed
Speech is believed to make the job of *segmenting* the speech stream and *decoding*
the language easier for children acquiring language (Kemler Nelson, Hirsh-Pasek,
Jusczyk, & Wright Cassidy, 1989; Ratner, 1986).

According to this view, children are not little grammarians, motivated to decode
the syntax of the language around them through the operation of their LAD, but
social beings who acquire language in the service of their needs to communicate with
others. In stressing the *functional basis* of language, interactionists study the *interpersonal reasons* that children have for speaking in the first place, the ways that older
speakers tailor their linguistic interactions with infants in order to facilitate language
acquisition, and the effect of different kinds of input on children's developing
language.

Social interactionists disagree with the view that children receive no *negative
evidence* about their ungrammatical utterances, because research has shown that
parents tend to respond in a variety of ways to unsuccessful language attempts. They
are apt to react with puzzlement to ill–formed utterances, to *recast* them (or repeat
them in corrected form), and to provide other cues to grammar (Bohannon,
MacWhinney, & Snow, 1990; Farrar, in press). Additionally, social interactionists

focus additional attention on those aspects of language competence less often studied by proponents of linguistic theories of language development, who generally study the acquisition of syntactic ability. They focus on additional areas such as phonology (Ratner, in press), the lexicon (Masur & Gleason, 1980; Kavanaugh & Jirkovsky, 1982), and pragmatics (Gleason, Hay, & Cain, 1989). Data suggest that parents make efforts to tailor articulation to young children to maximize phonemic contrasts (Ratner, 1985) and respond to immature pronunciation (Ratner, 1992). Further, the acquisition of a lexicon (vocabulary) seems inherently tied to interactional experience; one cannot extrapolate the name for an item using rules, unlike syntax or morphology. Finally, the very nature of pragmatic competence suggests the inherent role of social interaction within one's language community in its development.

Connectionist models

Connectionist or **parallel distributed processing (PDP) models** explore how *information* may be built into a system (in this case the child's brain) through *neural connections*. In particular, the human ability to make connections or associations between elements distinguishes the human mind from computer memory, which holds discrete bits of information at a specified address, available for retrieval and input to computations. To illustrate a nonconnectionist system, Potter (1990) uses the analogy of a television screen, in which a meaningful display can be generated by turning pixels off and on at discrete locations. The pixels' activity, however, is controlled by commands to each, and the pixels do not communicate with each other. People are different from computers and T.V.s; it is clear that activation of one concept in our minds has the capacity to bring up another.

Human memory for experiences appears to be distributed widely across what may be termed *processing units*. These units "are a little like idealized brain cells. They can perform only the same simple computation. The power of the system comes from how the units are connected," (Johnson-Laird, 1988; p. 174). In people, such connections are developed over time as the child is exposed to the forms of the language associated with external events. For example, a child may hear the word *bottle* under varying circumstances and thereby establish neural associations to the word, to the initial sound /b/, to the word *milk*, and so forth. Ultimately those interconnected associations become the "meaning" of the word. Information in such a *neural network* is conveyed through many interconnected units or nodes. The nodes have activation levels or thresholds that can turn them on or off, and learning consists essentially of adjusting the strengths of the connections in a direction that produces the desired outputs. In the case of word recognition, for example, the word's stimulus properties activates a number of nodes and their corresponding connections to produce a pattern or state of activation. When this pattern reoccurs, the system can be said to "recognize" the stimulus. Eventually, even an incomplete or degraded stimulus may be sufficient to activate the full pattern.

In such a model, many operations can take place simultaneously, or *in parallel*. No manipulation of symbols or higher "cognitive" activity is required. *Connectionist* theories thus model language acquisition at the *neuronal level*. In particular, they have been used to describe how particular grammatical structures such as the *inflectional system* may be acquired (McClelland, Rumelhart, & PDP Group, 1986).

Connectionist theory assumes that sufficient exposure will lead to the establishment of neural networks, and McClelland and his colleagues have somewhat successfully modelled in a computer how a child might acquire simple past tenses in English. In doing so, the "processor" (child or machine) simply tallies the input frequencies of the phonological characteristics of word stems and the corresponding phonological patterns in the suffix. If a particular sequence is statistically likely, the model will extend previously noted regularities to the new data. Thus, *showed, mowed, towed, glowed* may imply the statistical likelihood that *growed* is the correct past tense of *grow*. In particular, forms such as *growed, maked,* and *goed* seem to appear (in either computer simulations or actual children) after the initial lexicon (consisting of very frequent, but typically irregular verb forms) undergoes dramatic expansion, resulting in the input of a wider array of forms which follow more predictable patterns of root affixation. PDP models assert that connections, not "rules," underlie language development:

> *We have, we believe, provided a distinct alternative to the view that children learn the rules of English past tense formation in any explicit sense. We have shown that a reasonable account of the acquisition of past tense can be provided without recourse to the notions of a "rule" as anything more than a description of the language. . . . the child need not figure out what the rules are, nor even that there are rules.*
>
> (Rumelhart & McClelland, 1986, p. 267)

A rare introductory level discussion of parallel distributed processing models is provided by Johnson-Laird (1988). Pinker (1984, 1989, 1991) and his associates, however, argue that connectionists have not modelled everything that even a 4-year-old can do, and that the most parsimonious explanation for the acquisition of grammar is still that the child internalizes a set of *rules* or principles. In his most recent formulation, Pinker (1991) has proposed that connectionist models can explain children's acquisition of *irregular past tenses*, and why children and adults in "wug"–like experiments will create nonsense irregular forms, rather than regulars when confronted with a hypothetical phrase such as, "This man is fringing; Yesterday, he _____ ." He suggests, however, that rule induction underlies the *regular inflectional system*, and that children do possess important underlying knowledge about verbs which goes beyond mere tallies of their phonological properties. For example, [rɪŋ] is the present tense pronunciation of *ring* (as in a bell, or to border something), as well as *wring*. These three verbs take three separate past tenses, implying the necessity for more sophisticated analysis of past tense formation, which may, as Pinker suggests, require knowing whether a verb is irregular or has been historically derived from a noun root.

This controversy about the nature of mental representation may appear to be very abstract, but it underlies much current thought in psycholinguistics. If children are acquiring rules and principles, then language can be seen, as Pinker has said, as the "jewel in the crown" of cognitive development; if they are simply establishing neural connections which are automatic and unrelated to their higher abstract abilities, then language loses some of its special status. Pinker is impressed with children's sensitivities to principles of language which are not easily captured in statistical terms.

It has become increasingly plausible, to many researchers, that multiple mechanisms may be involved in the full range of language skill acquisitions (MacWhinney, 1978, 1982; Moerk, 1989). Thus, rote learning, pattern abstraction and rule learning may all contribute to the eventual development of language by children.

It should be clear at this point that there is another feature of theories that we should add to the list presented in the first section of this chapter: theories are *selective*. Each of them concentrates on only some of the phenomena under consideration, and has very little to say about the others.

Theories, of course, ultimately require data. Since young children do not possess the *metalinguistic* ability that would allow them to tell us what their linguistic systems are like, we rely upon various forms of observation, experimentation, and assessment in the study of children's acquisition of language. Thus, the search for new sources of data, and new ways to evaluate old sources of data continues.

Perspectives: What do the data tell us about the theories?

We come to this point in the chapter having discussed a variety of theories. We have also listed some of the major questions that divide otherwise friendly groups of psycholinguistic researchers. For some questions there are no answers, but our rapidly growing understanding of psychology and linguistics points us toward ways to synthesize certain types of information.

Nature or nurture?   Clearly the answer to this question is a resounding, "Both." Clearly, some properties of the human mind must guide the child through her rapid acquisition of this immensely complex system of behavior. However, certain types of knowledge, such as vocabulary and the social use of language, are clearly "taught," either explicitly, or through directed exposure. Additionally, even in the area of syntax, particular parental language models do appear to affect some aspects of children's language development. For example, frequent parental use of yes-no questions does appear to facilitate the child's acquisition of the verbal auxiliary system in English (Newport, Gleitman, & Gleitman, 1977).

Biological bases.   Research over the last 30 years has provided us with a large data base as well as evidence of *universal processes* in language development. Linguistic capacity relies upon, among other things, *neuroanatomical structures* that are unique to our species. (See Chapter 2.)

Left hemisphere specialization for language appears to be innate; *cerebral asymmetries* have been noted as early as the eighteenth week of gestation (Witelson,

1977). In particular, the *planum temporale* (temporal plane) of the left hemisphere is larger than its homologue on the right; ultimately, the left temporal plane develops into **Wernicke's area** (in the medial and superior left temporal lobe; see Chapter 2). Wernicke's area is known to be involved in the processing of *incoming speech*, and damage to Wernicke's area in an adult speaker results in a typical language deficit, Wernicke's aphasia. Other areas of the brain are also known to be intimately involved with language: These include **Broca's area** in the posterior inferior left frontal lobe, and the **arcuate fasciculus**, which is a band of subcortical fibers that connects Wernicke's area to Broca's area.

Thus, human infants are born with neuropsychological endowments in place that make ultimate perception, comprehension, and production of language in all its forms possible. There is no evidence that any other creatures have this kind of linguistic capacity, not even our close relatives the chimpanzees.

Biological, cognitive, and social interaction.   Assuming an intact neurological system, infants' *cognitive* and *affective* propensities lead them to acquire language relatively rapidly during the first few years of life, and with remarkable similarity across languages. As we have noted, during the first year of life children progress through some typical early communicative stages and much of this development is maturational or determined by neuropsychological development.

It is possible for someone who is unfamiliar with the immense research literature in developmental psychology to think that during a baby's first year she is best described as merely "prelinguistic," as if the main task of that period were to lie about engaged in phoneme discrimination, learning to babble, and so forth. But it is important to emphasize that during the period of infancy children are also developing socially and emotionally. These social and affective characteristics may actually *cause* changes in the psychological mechanisms that undergird language and make language development possible.

Babies' innate social and affective dispositions lead them to be intensely interested in other human beings and to seek and maintain social contact with them. For example, there is much research which indicates that babies are more interested in people than in objects. They are especially interested in the normal human face, which they prefer to look at when given a choice of various stimuli. They prefer an undistorted human face to a rather Picasso-like "face" with scrambled features, and they prefer the scrambled-feature face to a similarly complex but inanimate picture (Fantz, 1961; Lamb & Sherrod, 1981).

Infants' ability to hear fine auditory distinctions was noted earlier. Their preference for the human voice also appears very early on; in fact, it seems quite likely that infants are innately predisposed to attend preferentially to human speech versus other sounds (Gibson & Spelke, 1983). Even more remarkable is the finding of DeCasper and Fifer (1980) that newborn infants prefer to hear their own mothers' voices! Infants were given the opportunity to suck a pacifier in order to evoke either the voice of the mother or that of a stranger; eight out of ten newborns adjusted the pauses in their sucking in such a way as to hear their own mother's voice. It is thus possible that children become attached to their own mother and their own mother's voice while still *in utero*, and thus begin their language development *prenatally*.

Language development is dependent on much more than cognitive attainment—it is predicated on a complex base of social and emotional development as well, and it arises in an intensely interactive arena.

Interpretation of the same child language data varies with the theoretical stance of the researcher. How, for instance do we interpret the actions of a child just learning to talk who points at her favorite toy, high on a shelf, and says, "Want dolly"? According to learning theory, the child has been rewarded in the past for speaking, and has been reinforced for producing successive approximations of the phrase *want dolly* in the presence of the toy and a listener.

This behavior is explained by cognitive theorists and innatists as an example of the child's exercise of cognitive and linguistic proclivities: The child is seen as driven to categorize and name concepts, and to understand the permissable organization of nouns and verbs in sentences in her language.

A social interactionist theorist sees this behavior as socially and emotionally motivated as well: The child uses language to get and hold the attention and affection of another person, and to achieve a goal. This is not to deny cognitive activity, or the fact that the child is learning to categorize the world and acquire the lexical system of English, but the act of requesting the toy is also an interactional phenomenon, and is a behavior that is extraordinarily successful in capturing the notice of parents and others. Like other attachment behaviors (smiling, following the parent, crying when the parent leaves) early language serves the social and affective needs of both infants and their parents. Like language itself, attachment is a universal phenomenon and is biologically based (Bowlby, 1969).

Continuity or discontinuity?　This is one question to which there appears to be an answer, and the evidence is on the side of continuity in the domains that have been investigated, most particularly in children's progression from babbling to speech. Earlier theorists had postulated that there was a stage of babbling, followed by a silent period, and that only then did true speech evolve (Jakobson, 1968). Current studies of babbling reveal a considerable overlap between babbling and speech (DeBoysson-Bardies & Vihman, 1991). Likewise, children's acquisition of syntax, while characterized by stages, does not appear to be markedly discontinuous, changing radically in underlying organization. Language is unlikely to be a "today you're a tadpole, tomorrow you're a frog" phenomenon.

Universal competence or individual variation?　We all learn to talk, just as we all learn to walk. But beyond the fundamentals we share, there is variation in language, as there is in gait. Much of psycholinguistic theory and research is based upon a belief that all speakers are alike and share identical representations of language. Early child language studies also sought to find these universally shared aspects of language, and it is clear that there are universal, possible innate, constraints on what an infant can acquire. However, even if language were entirely innately determined, we would expect it to vary from individual to individual. No two individuals have the same brain (Lieberman, 1991). Nor do they share exactly the same experiences. Studies of children's language reveal increasingly that there are differences in their style, rate, focus, and ultimate communicative competence (Goldfield & Snow, in press).

Structure or function?   How shall we understand the bases of language development? Are children acquiring syntactic structures, or are they learning to communicate? Clearly, they are doing both. There may be grammatical mechanisms set in motion when they hear language over which they have no control. At the same time, they are driven by social and affective forces that lead them to want to use language to establish and maintain contact with other humans. The adults in a child's environment also have certain beliefs about their own role in their child's language development, as well as what the child should be able to do to perform adequately within society at various stages of maturation. We cannot say what researchers *should* study: information about *syntax, phonology, the lexicon, morphology,* and *the social uses of language* are all needed to complete our understanding of language acquisition.

Autonomy or interaction?   Is human language a separate faculty, or is it just one of the mightier weapons in our general cognitive armamentarium? Are complex vocabulary and syntax our crowning intellectual achievement, evidence of abstract abilities, and advanced cognitive development? This is one of the most intriguing puzzles that faces the developmental psycholinguist. Innatist/linguistic theorists believe that linguistic capacity is *autonomous,* whereas others see it as dependent on social or cognitive factors. To answer this question, much more information on atypical populations is needed.

A number of recent studies (Yamada, 1991) have described *dissociations* between linguistic and other development: For example, a young woman named Laura was studied by Yamada. When asked at the age of 16 years to name some fruits, Laura responded with *pears, apples*, and *pomegranates*. In referring to a recent distressing event at around the same time, she said: "He was saying that I lost my battery powered watch that I loved; I just loved that watch."

These responses are unremarkable—except that Laura is a retarded person, with a full scale IQ of just 41. Laura was given extensive batteries of tests of linguistic, cognitive, and neuropsychological functioning, and her language was analyzed. Her language has always been far in advance of her other abilities. Data of this nature support at least in part the conclusion that language is an independent, or *modular,* ability. At the time of testing, even though Laura could talk about pomegranates and produce complex sentences with multiple embeddings such as the one cited above, she performed essentially at the preschool level in most standardized tests of intellectual functioning. She could not read or write or tell time. She did not know who the president of the United States was or what country she lived in. Her drawings of humans resembled potatoes with stick arms and legs, and, unlike many 2-year-olds, she did not know her own age.

Ultimately, our theories will have to account for the remarkable dissociations that can exist between an individual's understanding of the world and his or her ability to produce complex language.

Rules or associations?   How do human beings represent language mentally? As we noted earlier, this is one of the most contentious areas of modern linguistics. Some of our own early work was predicated on the notion that children acquire rules (indeed, in another incarntion one of us wrote the statement quoted earlier that if a child can tell us that the plural of *gutch* is *gutches* we have evidence that he has a rule for the formation of the plural).

Now there are models of plural formation that call upon neural nets rather than abstract principles, and they are also persuasive. Perhaps, for the time, our best answer is to say, as we did at the beginning of this chapter, "We can describe *what* children learn, but we don't really know *how* they do it."

The answer to how they do it will involve understanding not just the complexity of linguistic systems, but children's unique biological endowments, as well as an understanding of the cognitive and social characteristics that they bring to the task.

Summary

Young children acquire language rapidly and apparently effortlessly during their first three or four years. Researchers do not agree on how to account for language development, and there are a variety of theories that have been called upon. These include linguistic/innatist theory; behavioral/learning theory; cognitive theory; information processing theory; and social interactionist theory. Each of them has something to offer, but none of them is complete. Psycholinguistic research can be conducted experimentally or observationally; early studies consisted mainly of diary reports, but contemporary researchers are able to study data on many children by using the Child Language Data Exchange System (CHILDES). Research on children reveals universal characteristics in early words and early sentences. Once children begin to acquire the grammar of their own language, they all tend to follow roughly the same course. Language development relies upon both innate mechanisms that are specific to language, such as specialized parts of the brain, and more general propensities of children, such as the need to form bonds of attachment with their caregivers. In this sense, language is a biologically based attainment that relies upon social, cognitive, and affective processes.

References

Aksu-Koc, A., & Slobin, D. I. (1985). The acquisition of Turkish. In D. I. Slobin (Ed.), *The crosslinguistic study of language acquisition: Vol. 1: The data*. Hillsdale, NJ: Erlbaum.

Bandura, A., Ross, D., & Ross, S. (1963). Transmission of aggression through imitation of agressive models. *Journal of Abnormal and Social Psychology, 63*, 3–11.

Bar-Adon, A., & Leopold, W. F. (1971). *Child language: A book of readings*. Englewood Cliffs, NJ: Prentice Hall.

Bates, E. (1976). *Language and context: the acquisition of pragmatics.* New York: Academic Press.

Bates. E. (1979). *The emergence of symbols: Cognition and communication in infancy.* New York: Academic Press.

Bates, E., Bretherton, I., Snyder, L., Shore, C., & Volterra, V. (1980). Vocal and gestural symbols at 13 months. *Merrill-Palmer Quarterly, 26,* 407–423.

Bates, E., & Snyder, L. (1985). The cognitive hypothesis in language development. In I. Uzgiris & J. M. Hunt (Eds.), *Research with Scales of Psychological Development in Infancy.* Champaign-Urbana: University of Illinois Press.

Bellugi, U. (1967). *The acquisition of negation.* Unpublished doctoral dissertation. Harvard University.

Berko, J. (1958). The child's learning of English morphology. *Word, 14,* 47–56.

Berman, R. (1985). The acquisition of Hebrew. In D. I. Slobin (Ed.), *The crosslinguistic study of language acquisition: Vol. 1: The data.* Hillsdale, NJ: Erlbaum.

Bernstein, M. (1983). Formation of internal structure in a lexical category. *Journal of Child Language, 10,* 381–399.

Bernstein Ratner, N., & Pye, C. (1984). Higher pitch in babytalk is *not* universal: Acoustic evidence from Quiche Mayan. *Journal of Child Language, 11,* 515–522.

Bever, T. (1970). The cognitive basis for linguistic structures. In J. Hayes (Ed.), *Cognition and the development of language.* New York: Wiley.

Bickerton, D. (1984). The language bioprogram hypothesis. *Behavioral and Brain Sciences, 7,* 173–221.

Bloom, L. (1970). *Language development: Form and function in emerging grammars.* Cambridge: MIT Press.

Bloom, L., Lahey, P., Hood, L., Lifter, K., & Fiess, K. (1980). Complex sentences: Acquisition of syntactic connectors and the semantic relations they encode. *Journal of Child Language, 7,* 235–262.

Bohannon, J. N. III, MacWhinney, B., & Snow, C. E. (1990). No negative evidence revisited: Beyond learnability, or who has to prove what to whom. *Developmental Psychology, 26,* 221–226.

Bohannon, J. N. III, & Warren-Leubecker, A. (1989). Theoretical approaches to language acquisition. In J. Berko Gleason (Ed.), *The development of language.* Columbus, OH: Charles E. Merrill.

Bowlby, J. (1969). *Attachment and loss: Vol. I: Attachment.* New York: Basic Books.

Braine, M. (1963). The ontogeny of English phrase structure: The first phase. *Language, 39,* 1–13.

Bridges, A. (1980). SVO comprehension strategies reconsidered: The evidence of individual patterns of response. *Journal of Child Language, 7,* 89–104.

Brown, R. (1973). *A first language: The early stages.* Cambridge, MA: Harvard University Press.

Brown, R., & Bellugi, U. (1964). Three processes in the child's acquisition of syntax. *Harvard Educational Review, 34,* 133–151.

Bruner, J. (1983). *Child's talk: Learning to use language.* New York: Norton.

Butcher, C., Mylander, C., and Goldin-Meadow, S. (In press). Displaced communication in a self-styled gesture system: Pointing at the non-present. *Cognitive Development.*

Chomsky, N. (1957). *Syntactic structures.* The Hague: Mouton.

Chomsky, N. (1965). *Aspects of a theory of syntax.* Cambridge, MA: MIT Press.

Chomsky, N. (1972). *Language and mind.* New York: Harcourt Brace Jovanovich.

Clancy, P. (1985). The acquisition of Japanese. In D. I. Slobin (Ed.), *The crosslinguistic study of language acquisition: Vol. 1: The data.* Hillsdale, NJ: Erlbaum.

Clark, E. (1973). What's in a word? On the child's acquisition of semantics in his first language. In T. Moore (Ed.), *Cognitive development and the acquisition of language*. New York: Academic Press.

Clark, E. (1985). The acquisition of Romance, with special reference to French. In D. I. Slobin (Ed.), *The crosslinguistic study of language acquisition: Vol. 1: The data*. Hillsdale, NJ: Erlbaum.

Cromer, R. (1991). *Language and thought in normal and handicapped children*. Cambridge, MA: Blackwell.

Curtiss, S. (1977). *Genie: A psycholinguistic study of a modern day "wild child."* New York: Academic Press.

Curtiss, S. (1982). Developmental dissociations of language and cognition. In L. Obler & L. Menn (Eds.), *Exceptional language and linguistics*. New York: Academic Press.

Dale, P. (1991). The validity of a parent report measure of vocabulary and syntax at 24 months. *Journal of Speech and Hearing Research, 34,* 565–571.

Dale, P. (In press). The validity of a parent report measure of vocabulary and syntax at 24 months. *Journal of Speech and Hearing Sciences.*

DeBoysson-Bardies, B., & Vihman, M. M. (1991). Adaptation to language: Evidence from babbling and first words in four languages. *Language, 67*(2), 297–319.

DeCasper, A. J., & Fifer, W. P. (1980). Of human bonding: Newborns prefer their mother's voice. *Science, 208,* 1174–1176.

Dennis, M., Sugar, J., & Whitaker, H. (1982). The acquisition of tag questions. *Child Development, 53,* 1254–1257.

DeVilliers, J. G., & DeVilliers, P. A. (1973). A cross sectional study of the acquisition of grammatical morphemes in child speech. *Journal of Psycholinguistic Research, 2,* 267–278.

DeVilliers, J. G., & DeVilliers, P. A. (1985). The acquisition of English. In D. I. Slobin (Ed.), *The crosslinguistic study of language acquisition: Vol 1: The data*. Hillsdale, NJ: Erlbaum.

Dunn, L., & Dunn, L. (1981). *The Peabody Picture Vocabulary Test-Revised*. Circle Pines, MN: American Guidance Service.

Fantz, R. L. (1961). The origin of form perception. *Scientific American, 204,* 66–72.

Farrar, M. J. (1990). Discourse and the acquisition of grammatical morphemes. *Journal of Child Language, 17,* 607–624.

Farrar, M. J. (In press). Negative evidence and grammatical morpheme acquisition. *Developmental Psychology.*

Fernald, A. (1985). Four-month-old infants prefer to listen to motherese. *Infant Behavior and Development, 8,* 181–195.

Fremgen, A., & Fay, D. (1980). Overextensions in production and comprehension: A methodological clarification. *Journal of Child Language, 7,* 205–211.

Gibson, E. J., & Spelke, E. S. (1983). The development of perception. In J. H. Flavell & E. M. Markman (Eds.), *Handbook of child psychology: Cognitive Development: Vol. 3*. New York: John Wiley & Sons.

Gleason, J. Berko (Ed.). (1989). *The development of language* (2nd ed.). Columbus, OH: Charles E. Merrill.

Gleason, J. Berko (Ed.). (1993). *The development of language* (3rd ed.). New York: Macmillan.

Gleason, J. Berko, Hay, D., & Cain, L. (1989). The social and affective determinants of language development. In M. Rice & R. Schiefelbusch (Eds.). *The Teachability of Language* (pp. 171–186). Baltimore: Paul Brookes.

Gleason, J. Berko, Perlmann, R. Y., & Greif, E. B. (1984). What's the magic word? *Discourse Processes, 7,* 493–502.

Gleitman, L., Gleitman, H., Landau, B., & Wanner, E. (1988). Where learning begins: Initial representations for language learning. In F. Newmeyer (Ed.), *Linguistics: The Cambridge Survey. Volume III. Language: Psychological and biological aspects.* Cambridge: Cambridge University Press.

Goldfield, B. & Snow, C. E. (1993). Individual differences in language acquisition. In J. Berko Gleason (Ed.) *The Development of Language* (3rd ed.) New York: Macmillan.

Goldin-Meadow, S., & Mylander, C. (1990). Beyond the input given: The child's role in the acquisition of language. *Language, 66,* 323–355.

Golinkoff, R., Hirsh-Pasek, K., Cauley, K., & Gordon, P. (1987). The eyes have it: Lexical and syntactic comprehension in a new paradigm. *Journal of Child Language, 14,* 23–46.

Gopnik, A., & Meltzoff, A. N. (1987). Early semantic developments and their relationship to object permanence, means-end understanding, and categorization. In K. E. Nelson & A. van Kleeck (Eds.), *Children's language: Vol. 6.* Hillsdale, NJ: Lawrence Erlbaum Associates.

Halliday, M. (1975). *Learning how to mean: Explorations in the development of language.* New York: Arnold.

Hamburger, H., & Crain, S. (1982). Relative acquisition. In S. Kuczaj (Ed.), *Language development: Syntax and semantics.* Hillsdale, NJ: Erlbaum.

Hirsh-Pasek, K., Kemler Nelson, D., Jusczyk, P., Cassidy, K., Druss, B., & Kenedy, L. (1987). Clauses are perceptual units for young infants. *Cognition, 26,* 269–286.

Hyams, N. M. (1986). *Language acquisition and the theory of parameters.* Dordrecht: D. Reidel.

Hyams, N. M. (1989). The null subject parameter in language acquisition. In O. Jaeggli & K. Safir (Eds.), *The null subject parameter.* Dordrecht: Kluwer.

Jakobson, R. (1968). *Child language, aphasia, and phonological universals.* (A. R. Keiler, Trans.) The Hague: Mouton.

Johnson, C. (1991). *Emergence of "subject" in monolingual acquisition of Mexican Spanish.* Unpublished doctoral dissertation, University of Maryland at College Park.

Johnson-Laird, P. (1988). *The computer and the mind: An introduction to cognitive science.* Cambridge, MA: Harvard

Kavanaugh, R., & Jirkovsky, A. (1982). Parental speech to young children: A longitudinal analysis. *Merrill-Palmer Quarterly, 28,* 297–311.

Kelly, C., & Dale, P. (1989). Cognitive skills associated with the onset of multiword utterances. *Journal of Speech and Hearing Research, 32,* 645–656.

Kemler-Nelson, D., Hirsh-Pasek, K., Jusczyk, P. & Wright-Cassidy, K. (1989). How the prosodic cues in motherese might assist language learning. *Journal of Child Language, 16,* 55–68.

Kessel, F. (1988). *The development of language and language researchers.* Hillsdale, NJ: Erlbaum.

Kuhl, P., Williams, K., Lacerda, F., Stevens, K., & Lindblom, B. (1992). Linguistic experience alters phonetic perception in infants by six months of age. *Science, 255,* 606–608.

Lamb, M., & Sherrod, L. (1981). *Infant social cognition.* Hillsdale, NJ: Erlbaum.

Lane, H. (1976). *The wild boy of Aveyron.* Cambridge, MA: Harvard University Press.

Lenneberg, E. (1967). *The biological foundations of language.* New York: Wiley.

Leopold, W. (1948). Semantic learning in infant language. *Word, 4,* 173–80.

Lieberman, P. (1991). *Uniquely human: The evolution of speech, thought, and selfless behavior.* Cambridge, MA: Harvard University Press.

Lightfoot, D. (1982). *The language lottery: Toward a biology of grammars.* Cambridge: MIT Press.

Macnamara, J. (1972). Cognitive basis of language learning in infants. *Psychological Review, 79*, 1–13.

MacWhinney, B. (1975). Rules, rote and analogy in morphological formations by Hungarian children. *Journal of Child Language, 2*, 65–77.

MacWhinney, B. (1978). The acquisition of morphology. *Monographs of the Society for Research in Child Development, 43.*

MacWhinney, B. (1982). Basic syntactic processes. In S. Kuczaj II (Ed.), *Language development: Vol. 1: Syntax and semantics*. Hillsdale, NJ: Erlbaum.

MacWhinney, B., & Snow, C. (1985). The child language data exchange system. *Journal of Child Language, 12*, 271–296.

Masur, E. & Gleason, J. B. (1980). Parent-child interaction and the acquisition of lexical information during play. *Developmental Psychology, 16*, 404–409.

McClelland, J., Rumelhart, D., & PDP Research Group (1986). *Parallel distributed processing: Explorations in the microstructure of cognition: Vol. 2*. Cambridge, MA: Bradford.

McNeill, D. (1966). Developmental psycholinguistics. In F. Smith & G. Miller (Eds.), *The genesis of language*. Cambridge: MIT Press.

Menyuk, P. (1969). *Sentences children use*. Cambridge: MIT Press.

Miller, W., & Ervin, S. (1964). The development of grammar in child language. In U. Bellugi & R. Brown (Eds.), *The Acquisition of Language: Monographs of the Society for Research in Child Development, 29*, 9–34.

Moerk, E. (1990). Three-term contingency patterns in mother-child verbal interactions during first-language acquisition. *Journal of the Experimental Analysis of Behavior, 54*, 293–305.

Moerk, E. (1989). The LAD was a lady and the tasks were ill-defined. *Developmental Review, 9*, 21–57.

Mülhäusler, P. (1986). *Pidgin and creole linguistics*. Oxford: Basil Blackwell.

Murray, A. D., Johnson, J., & Peters, J. (1990). Fine-tuning of utterance length to preverbal infants: Effects on later language development. *Journal of Child Language, 17*, 511–526.

Nelson, K. (1973). Structure and strategy in learning to talk. *Monographs of the Society for Research in Child Development, 38.*

Newport, E., Gleitman, L., & Gleitman, H. (1977). Mother, I'd rather do it myself: Some effects and non-effects of maternal speech style. In C. Snow & C. Ferguson (Eds.), *Talking to children: Language input and acquisition*. Cambridge: Cambridge University Press.

Ochs, E. (1982). Talking to children in Western Samoa. *Language and Society, 11*, 77–104.

Osgood, C. E., & Zehler, A. (1981). Acquisition of bitransitive sentences: Prelinguistic determinants of language acquisition. *Journal of Child Language, 8*, 367–383.

Owens, R. (1988). *Language development: An introduction* (2nd ed.). Columbus, OH: Charles Merrill.

Papandropoulou, I., & Sinclair, H. (1974). What is a word? Experimental study of children's ideas on grammar. *Human Development, 17*, 240–258.

Pavlov, I. (1927). *Conditioned Reflexes*. (G. Anrep, Trans.) New York: Dover.

Piaget, J. (1926). *The language and thought of the child*. New York: Harcourt Brace Jovanovich.

Piaget, J. (1954). *Origins of intelligence*. New York: Basic Books.

Pinker, S. (1984). *Language learnability and language development*. Cambridge, MA: MIT Press.

Pinker, S. (1989). *Learnability and cognition*. Cambridge, MA: MIT Press.

Pinker, S. (1991). Rules of language. *Science, 253*, 530–535.

Potter, M. (1990). Remembering. In D. Osherson & E. Smith (Eds.), *An invitation to cognitive science: Vol. 3: Thinking.* Cambridge, MA: MIT Press.

Ratner, N. (1986). Durational cues which mark clause boundaries in mother-child speech. *Journal of Phonetics, 14,* 303–309.

Ratner, N. (1988). Patterns of parental vocabulary selection in speech to young children. *Journal of Child Language, 15,* 481–492.

Ratner, N. (in press). Maternal input and unusual phonological behavior: A case study and its implications. *Journal of Child Language.*

Rescorla, L. (1980). Overextension in early language development. *Journal of Child Language, 7,* 321–335.

Romaine, S. (1988). *Pidgin and creole languages.* London: Longman.

Rumelhart, D. E., & McClelland, J. L. (1986). On learning the past tenses of English verbs. In J. L. McClelland, D. E. Rumelhart, & the PDP Research Group (Eds.), *Parallel distributed processing: Explorations in the microstructure of cognition: Vol. 2: Psychological and biological models.* Cambridge, MA: Bradford Books/MIT Press.

Sachs, J. (1993). The emergence of intentional communication. In J. Berko Gleason (Ed.), *The development of language* (3rd ed.). New York: Macmillan.

Sinclair-deZwart, H. (1973). Language acquisition and cognitive development. In T. Moore (Ed.), *Cognitive development and the acquisition of language.* New York: Academic Press.

Skinner, B. F. (1957). *Verbal Behavior.* Englewood Cliffs, NJ: Prentice-Hall.

Skinner, B. F. (1969). *Contingencies of reinforcement.* New York: Appleton, Century, Crofts.

Slobin, D. I. (1973). Cognitive prerequisites for the development of grammar. In C. Ferguson & D. I. Slobin (Eds.), *Studies of child language development.* New York: Holt, Rinehart & Winston.

Slobin, D. I. (Ed.) (1985). *A cross linguistic study of language acquisition.* Hillsdale, NJ: Erlbaum.

Slobin, D. I., & Welsh, C. (1971). Elicited imitation as a research tool in developmental psycholinguistics. In C. Lavatelli (Ed.), *Language training in early childhood education.* Urbana: University of Illinois Press.

Snow, C. E. (1977). The development of conversation between mothers and babies. *Journal of Child Language, 4,* 1–22.

Snow, C. E. (1981). Social interaction and language acquisition. In P. Dale & D. Ingram (Eds.), *Child language: An international perspective.* Baltimore: University Park Press.

Snow, C. E. (In press). Relevance of the notion of a critical period to language acquisition. In M. Bornstein, (Ed.), *Sensitive periods in development.* Hillsdale, NJ: Erlbaum.

Snow, C. E., & Ferguson, C. A. (1977). *Talking to children: Language input and acquisition.* Cambridge: Cambridge University Press.

Snow, C. E., Perlmann, R. Y., & Gleason, J. Berko. (1990). Developmental perspectives on politeness: Sources of children's knowledge. *Journal of Pragmatics, 14,* 289–305.

Stark, R. (1980). Stages of speech development in the first year of life. In G. Yeni-Komshian, J. Kavanaugh, & C. Ferguson (Eds.), *Child phonology: Vol. 1: Production.* New York: Academic Press.

Tager-Flusberg, H. (1993). Putting words together: Morphology and syntax in the preschool years. In J. Berko Gleason, (Ed.), *The Development of Language* (3rd ed.). New York: Macmillan.

Tager-Flusberg, H. & Calkins, S. (1990). Does imitation facilitate the acquisition of grammar? Evidence from a study of autistic Down's syndrome and normal children. *Journal of Child Language, 17,* 591–606.

Valian, V. (1990). Null subjects: A problem for parameter-setting models of language acquisition. *Cognition, 35,* 105–122.

Werker, J., & Tees, R. C. (1984). Cross-language speech perception: Evidence for perceptual reorganization during the first year of life. *Infant Behavior and Development, 7,* 49–64.

Whitehurst, G. (1982). Language Development. In B. Wolman (Ed.), *Handbook of Developmental Psychology.* Englewood Cliffs, NJ: Prentice-Hall.

Witelson, S. F. (1977). Early hemispheric specialization and interhemispheric plasticity: An empirical and theoretical review. In S. J. Segalowitz & F. A. Gruber (Eds.), *Language development and neurological theory.* London: Academic Press.

Yamada, J. (1990). *Laura: A case for the modularity of language.* Cambridge, MA: MIT Press.

A Psycholinguistic Account
of Reading

MARYANNE WOLF
Tufts University

FRANK VELLUTINO
State University of New York, Albany

The relation between thought and word is a living process.

Lev Semenovich Vygotsky, 1962

The simple single principle of a truly adequate literacy . . . is that the way we use language constitutes what and how we think . . . language is not the arbitrary external form of thinking . . . but rather the substance.

Leon Botstein, 1990, p. 57

Introduction

Just as the development of oral language made us a unique species, the acquisition of written language changed our species in a number of ways: cognitively (Olson, 1980, 1986); epistemologically (Havelock, 1974); and possibly even neuroanatomically (Geschwind, 1974). Perhaps no other human activity has so altered the course of individual and cultural development. The structure and development of written language, and our remarkable ability to process it—to read—are the content of this chapter. We will begin with a brief *historical overview of writing systems*. A *psycholinguistic account of the many subprocesses that underlie reading* follows. In a third section, we present a *natural developmental history of reading acquisition*. The chapter concludes with a discussion of *current models of skilled reading*. In several places we provide examples of what occurs when written language is largely inaccessible, for instance in individuals with dyslexia. In examining examples of written-language loss, our goals are to underscore by illustration the extraordinary complexity of the reading process, and to bring to life its invaluable place in human activity.

Throughout this chapter our efforts to chart connections between oral and written language development will be transparent. It is our position that only when these systems are studied in tandem will the development of written language be understood properly.

A history of writing systems

We begin with an historical view of the move from oral to written language. Indeed, this history is relatively recent and varies somewhat in chronology; early writing appears to have evolved independently in different parts of the world. The earliest system we know of was devised by the ancient Sumerians, who used **pictographs**, or pictures, to represent an object or concept; this first "formal" precursor to writing originated in the latter part of the fourth millennium B.C. Chinese **ideograms** (pictures that symbolize ideas or things, but not particular words for them) found on bone and turtle shells trace to the second millennium B.C. and were used to ask questions of the divinities—questions perhaps best unuttered in oral language. An early Mayan picture writing system emerged as a means to chronicle major events. Each of these precursor writing systems became a way to preserve, accumulate, and transmit cultural knowledge across distance and time (S-Y Wang, 1991), a feat which the constraints of oral history could not allow.

With time these early systems became less picture-like and began to represent actual words of the language rather than objects or ideas. This step to "one-word–one-symbol" marks the beginning of true writing systems (Ellis, 1984, p. 3). Various scholars have proposed a relatively orderly progression in the development of writing systems from concrete pictographs, to somewhat abstract **logographs** (e.g., Egyptian hieroglyphs which correspond to words and sounds), culminating in **syllabaries** (e.g., the Japanese Kana writing system, where a visual symbol conveys each syllable in the language); and **alphabets** like our own (e.g., a set of symbols in which **graphemes** or written letters represent each **phoneme** in the language, as well as underlying lexical relationships among words).

A major assumption of these historical approaches to the development of writing was that with each transformation in writing systems came more abstraction, more efficiency, and more cognitive requirements for the learner. The reality is more complex. As Schmandt-Besserat (1991) contended, the early Sumerian systems were token systems used for various transactions and were arguably more abstract, since they may not have represented particular words. Furthermore, logographic systems, as exemplified by present-day Chinese, make greater phonological demands than previously realized (Mann, 1986) and make immense memory demands upon the learner. For example, at least 3,000 symbols are needed in Chinese for basic literacy (Stevenson, Stigler, Tucker, Lee, S.Y. Hsu, & Ketanusa, 1982). The syllabaries, by comparison, make relatively few demands upon memory, and the alphabet still fewer; thus, both of these systems increase cognitive efficiency. On the other hand, the alphabet, as we detailed, makes increased demands on the learner's *representation abilities*, particularly during the acquisition stages. There are two critical points in this very brief history of writing: First, writing systems used around the world today reflect culture and oral language in uniquely different ways and make very different requirements of the learner. Second, as Adams (1990, p. 43) wrote, the discovery that "symbols can represent the sounds of language, rather than its referents," transformed the history of writing.

The alphabet

Nowhere is this transformation more obvious than in the introduction of the Greek alphabet, upon which all modern alphabets are based. The emergence of the Greek alphabet represented "a psychological and epistemological revolution" (Havelock, 1974, p. 49) in Western culture and thought. In brief, the Greeks took a syllable-based Phoenician system, adapted it to provide a separate character for each phoneme, and invented the alphabetic principle (Ellis, 1984). Havelock proposed three conditions for a true alphabet: 1) each phoneme in the language must be "covered," or represented, by the writing system; 2) ideally, there should be an

unambiguous one-to-one correspondence between phoneme and grapheme; and 3) the total number of graphemes must be limited so as not to tax memory processes, with an ideal number between 20 and 30 if literacy is to be "democratic" (that is, accessible to most human beings). Havelock added that if the last condition is met, then the act of reading can attain the status of "unconscious reflex" (1974, p. 24) or what cognitive and psycholinguistic theory refer to as **automaticity** or **fluency** (see discussions in LaBerge & Samuels, 1974; Logan, 1988; Stanovich, 1990; Wolf, 1991a). Pre-Semitic and Semitic syllabaries met the first condition, but only the Greek alphabet was able to achieve all three, and in the process "invented literacy and the literate basis of modern (Western) thought" (Havelock, 1974, p. 44):

> *The alphabet, making available a visualized record . . . abolished the need for memorization and hence for rhythm [with rhythm's] severe limitations upon what might be said, or thought. . . . The mental energies thus released, by this economy of memory, have probably been extensive, contributing to an immense expansion of knowledge available to the human mind. . . . The alphabet therewith made possible the production of novel or unexpected statements, previously unfamiliar and even "unthought."*

(Havelock 1974, pp. 49–50)

GREEK ALPHABET.	HIERATIC SIGNS.	PHŒNICIAN ALPHABET.	GREEK ALPHABET.	HIERATIC SIGNS.	PHŒNICIAN ALPHABET.
A			Λ		
B			M		
Γ			N		
Δ			Ξ		
E			O		
F			Π		
Z					
H			Ο		
Θ			P		
I			Σ		
K			T		

With the dissemination of the alphabetic principle, Olson (1980) contended, writing began to make explicit some of the *tacit* aspects of knowledge carried by oral language. In the process, he argued, two critical consequences resulted across cultures: First, there was an ordering, and thus a rethinking, of previous knowledge. Second, a new distinction between a) factual information and b) its interpretation was made visible by text (Olson, 1986). Olson described how writing "split the comprehension process into two parts; that part preserved by text, the given, and . . . interpretation" (1986, p. 120). The consequences of such a split are the basis, he continued, for modern science and an awareness of subjectivity, two of the most fundamental aspects of Western education and thought. Becoming literate makes it more likely that an individual can distinguish between what he actually knows to be a fact and what he only believes or supposes. Scientific thought is not possible in the absence of this distinction.

Alongside the overwhelming contributions of the alphabetic principle to intellectual growth, the cognitive costs must also be considered. The alphabetic principle may be difficult to acquire, depending on the language. For example, on the one hand, Serbo-Croatian is easier to acquire because there is a "transparent" relationship between a word's spelling and its pronunciation. That is, there is a more invariant correspondence between the graphemes (written letters) and phonemes

(abstract representation of individual speech sounds) in the language. On the other hand, English orthography with its many irregular spellings barely approximates Havelock's (1976) second condition for an alphabet that there be an unambiguous one-to-one correspondence between grapheme and phoneme. A major reason for this apparent lack of orderliness is historical: The English language system attempts both to map all phonemes in the sound system and to preserve lexical or etymological relationships among its morphemes (basic units of meaning) (Chomsky & Halle, 1968; C. Chomsky, 1972). Thus, words like *signature* and *sign*, *bomb* and *bombardier* are orthographically connected to their etymological root, which would not be the case if all words were spelled strictly phonetically—for example we might not recognize the relationship between *sign* and *signature* if the word were spelled *sine*. Ellis wrote that "in the case of English spelling it is as if a tension has existed between the demand of an alphabet for transparency and a wish to retain something of the old logographic principle" (1984, p. 7).

The underlying requirements of reading

And so to completely analyze what we do when we read would almost be the acme of a psychologist's achievements, for it would be to describe very many of the most intricate workings of the human mind, as well as to unravel the tangled story of the most remarkable specific performance that civilization has learned in all its history.

(E. B. Huey, 1908/1979, p. 6)

As we shall see in this section, the number of processes involved in reading, the complex nature of each, and the daunting demands posed by their rapid interaction, provide ontogenetic evidence for Olson's historical claims, and help us understand the difficulty of acquiring the alphabetic principle. This discussion will be divided into a description first of the *representational systems* that support *word recognition* within an alphabetic orthography, and second of the *cognitive systems* involved in reading and learning.

Representational systems in word identification

Learning systems

As a child learns to read, printed words gradually become invested with different types of linguistic properties, which may be more or less salient, depending on the child's stage of reading development. These properties are derived from corresponding linguistic *codes*, which are abstract mental representations of the different attributes of the units of language: *semantic codes, phonological codes*, and *syntactic/ grammatical codes*.

Semantic coding.   Semantic codes are the interconnected mental representations of the meanings assigned to units of language. They have reference either to the meanings of individual words or to the broader meanings conveyed by groups of words. In order to learn to associate a spoken word with its counterpart in print, children must have an adequate grasp of the meaning of that word, both in and out of sentence contexts. They must also be able to make clearcut distinctions between the word's meaning and the meanings of other words, for example, words that are similar either in referential meaning (e.g., *cat* and *kitten*) or functional meaning (e.g., *add* and *plus; him* and *he*). Adequate knowledge of the meanings of spoken words is important at the beginning stage of reading, because the child relies heavily on word meanings in learning to identify words initially encountered (Biemiller, 1970; Ehri, 1992; Vellutino, Scanlon & Tanzman, 1990; Vellutino, Scanlon, DeSetto, & Pruzek, 1981; Weber, 1970). Semantic coding becomes increasingly important as the number of new words encountered in print expands, especially in learning to identify those that cannot be readily decoded using regular spelling-sound correspondence rules (e.g., *was, saw, their*, etc.).

Phonological coding.   Phonological codes are abstract mental representations of the sound attributes of spoken and written words, in the form of individual units of speech—that is, the previously referred to phonemes—along with implicit rules for ordering and combining them (Chomsky & Halle, 1968). As Chapter 8 on the development of language made clear, in order to acquire words in a language, children must be able to discriminate and represent the phonemes of the language. In other words, they must be able to code information phonologically.

Phonological coding ability is also important in learning to identify printed words and it supports this activity in several different ways. One way is that it aids the process of associating a known (oral) name with a printed word as a whole unit. Phonological coding also aids **segmentation** of spoken and printed words and thus facilitates detection and use of grapheme-phoneme and other spelling-sound invariants that can be used for word decoding (e.g., to distinguish between *cat* and *fat*; *train* and *pain*). In addition, it facilitates use of letter sounds to aid in discriminating and sequencing letters in words (e.g., *pot* vs. *top*). Still another is to promote development of **morphophonemic production rules**. These rules help a child arrive at correct pronunciations of *derived words*—these are words that have common root morphemes, but vary in form class (e.g., *decide, decision*). A final function of this phonological knowledge is that it aids the process of attaching the appropriate sounds to common segments such as bound morphemes (*-ed, -ing*) and syllables (*-ove* in *love* and *dove*). Thus, facility in phonological coding is critically important in learning to identify words in an orthography based on an alphabet.

Syntactic/grammatical coding.   *Syntactic codes* are abstract representations containing rules for ordering words in the language, the rules for making sentences. *Grammatical codes* are representations of a word's form class (e.g., noun, verb, etc.) and they define its function in sentences. Related to both of these codes are representations of **bound morphemes** (usually inflectional morphemes) which modify words for case, gender, tense, mood, and so forth. In order to comprehend and generate sentences, the child must learn to apply syntactic rules in order to segment the sentences into their grammatical constituents, and then determine how those constituents are related to one another. The grammatical constituents contain the substantive components of a sentence, and the syntactic rules order them in ways that facilitate comprehension.

Competence with the grammar and syntax of language facilitates word identification in at least three different ways. First, competence facilitates sentence comprehension and aids the child in using the sentence context to anticipate which words might appear in given sentence frames, as well as to monitor accuracy in word identification. Second, competence aids the process of assigning to printed words what might be called *function codes*. Function codes are representations that define or "mark" a word's unique role in sentences. Function codes are especially important in distinguishing among noncontent, function words, such as *if, and, for, from*, and *of*. They, along with phonological codes, are also important in acquiring morphophonemic production rules that facilitate correct pronunciations of derived words such as *bomber* and *bombardier* and inflections such as *-ed* and *-ing*. The acquisition of morphophonemic production rules is a third way in which grammatical and syntactic competence aids printed word identification.

The visual system

In order to learn to read, children must come to discriminate among (literally) thousands of printed words, some differing in only a small feature of one letter (e.g., *snow/show*), or in the way their letters are ordered (e.g., *was/saw*). Children must also learn to recognize words written in different cases, fonts, and writing styles. How can developing readers accomplish this feat relying on visual memory alone? The answer is that they do not rely on visual memory alone, simply because they cannot do so, at least not in an alphabetically derived orthography where there is so much visual similarity. The load on visual memory is much too formidable. And, a case could be made that some children who attempt to rely exclusively on visual memory for words as wholes will encounter significant difficulties in learning to read.

Successful developing readers negotiate the complexities of the orthography by acquiring a number of synthesizing strategies that reduce the load on visual memory; and they do so with the aid of the language systems, especially the phonological system. Provided children are exposed to instruction that facilitates discovery and use of the alphabetic principle (e.g., that a letter on the page stands for a sound in their spoken language), and assuming adequate ability in phonological coding, they soon learn to take advantage of frequently encountered spelling-sound correspondences and begin: (1) storing rules for the order in which letters may occur in the orthography; (2) storing rules for ordering the letters in words (e.g., grapho-phonemic rules); (3) storing representations of redundant combinations of letters with invariant spellings and pronunciations (e.g., *at* in *cat* and *fat*); (4) making increasingly fine-grained discriminations among visually similar words; (5) storing unitized representations of sub-word morphophonemic units that have invariant spellings and pronunciations (e.g., *ing, tion*); (6) storing unitized representations of redundant combinations of letters (e.g., *th, sh, ch*); and (7) identifying new words generatively and through recombination of elements they already know.

Each of these helps to reduce the load on visual memory in a slightly different way. Collectively, they constitute a powerful set of mechanisms that not only aid the child in negotiating the written system, but also assist in the process of internalizing representations for identifying words that are familiar and those that are unfamiliar.

Research indicates that in word identification the visual system takes its lead from the language systems, this relationship being dictated by the nature of the reading process. It is the language systems that confer meaning on the visual symbols representing printed words and determine how they will be analyzed and thereafter represented. It is also the language systems and the heuristics and algorithms generated by the language systems that facilitate synthesis of the vast amounts of visual information that must be stored in order for the child to acquire fluency in word identification. This suggests that reading may be acquired by children with a wide range of individual differences in visual ability, provided that they have the linguistic coding abilities that enable them to capitalize on the spelling-sound redundancies inherent in the orthography, and to utilize code-oriented as well as meaning-based strategies for word identification.

Motor systems

Children typically learn to read using an oral reading method, and they learn to relate visual symbols to internalized representations of the *speech-motor executions* used in vocalizing the names associated with those symbols. It is our opinion that the role of the motor systems in learning to read is actually quite minimal. While we have no doubt that speech-motor and *visual-motor* representations normally become part of the information stored in memory about a printed word, we are inclined to believe that success in word identification does not depend significantly on the availability of high quality representations of speech-motor and visual-motor executions. We think it is more important for the child to grasp the concept that letters have sounds, as a prerequisite to success in alphabetic mapping, than to articulate these sounds physically.

Cognitive processes involved in reading and all learning

In addition to the representational systems and processes that are specifically involved in reading, there are several cognitive processes that are involved in learning to read, as well as in all learning. These might be profitably discussed, both to enhance our understanding of the word identification process, and because dysfunction in each of these processes has been hypothesized to be a cause of reading disability.

Attention

Success in learning any new relationship depends initially on our ability to *attend selectively* to the distinguishing attributes of the things we are attempting to relate. It is also important that we come to distinguish between *variant* and *invariant dimensions* in these things so as to become increasingly efficient in how we search for their distinguishing attributes. Gibson (1969) calls this type of processing **perceptual learning** to underscore this tendency to become increasingly efficient in attending selectively. However, as she points out, efficiency is not insured simply by looking at or listening to the things one attempts to discriminate. Efficiency requires an extensive period of analysis that is influenced by three related contingencies: (1) by the ability to attend as determined by one's affective or emotional state; (2) by conscious motivation or interest in attending; and (3) by the extent to which one has acquired knowledge that would facilitate selective attention of the sort that leads to critical discriminations.

The first contingency relates to the intactness of those components of the central nervous system that are responsible for degree of emotional arousal.

The second contingency relates to the child's volition and deliberate intent. Without sufficient interest in acquiring knowledge in a given domain, it becomes difficult to attend in a way that optimizes the likelihood of learning. There are, no doubt, many children who have difficulty learning to read because of a lack of inherent motivation.

The third contingency is more subtle. It involves the role of prior knowledge in determining one's processing attitudes in new learning situations. For instance, young children who are familiar with the printed word *lion*, when first presented with the new word *loin*, are apt to misname this word because of their prior experience with its visually similar counterpart. After they add *loin* to their vocabulary, they begin to attend to the way its medial letters and those in *lion* are ordered. Subsequently, their means of processing these two words changes in a way that insures selective attention to the order of their medial letters.

During the initial stages of discrimination, processing requires a good deal of cognitive effort, but over time it becomes *automated*. LaBerge and Samuels (1974) have shown that accurate discrimination of distinguishing attributes and selective and effortless attention to those attributes are related benchmarks of automatic processing of letters and words (see also Perfetti, 1985; Stanovich, 1991; Wolf, 1991b). Conversely, less accurate discrimination of distinguishing attributes and non-selective and effortful attention in searching for those attributes are benchmarks of non-automatic processing. It follows that the child who does not steadily and systematically acquire the types of knowledge that lead to more precise analysis of the orthography (knowledge such as word meanings, spelling-sound rules, etc.) will have difficulty attending selectively to critical differences in letters and words. The child who acquires this knowledge becomes increasingly more efficient in attending selectively to distinctions among letters and words.

Associative learning

The ability to associate one entity with another is a basic cognitive mechanism that is critically important for learning in general, and for word identification in particular. It underlies one's ability to establish connective bonds between written language and its counterparts in spoken language. In a very real sense **association** underlies one of the most rudimentary and ubiquitous of all of our cognitive abilities, specifically, the ability to *symbolize*. When we symbolize, we have one thing represent another; and each may prompt a reaction common to both. For example, we attach the same meaning to a word, regardless of whether it is spoken or printed. How one learns associative relationships, whether through *insightful discovery* of the distinguishing and mediating attributes, or through gradual accretion of *connective bonds* through practice and reinforcement, is a controversial issue with a long history that we need not address here (Gibson, 1969). Contemporary theories of learning and memory suggest that each of these conceptualizations may have some validity.

Associative learning seems to involve something akin to a search for and "discovery" of **implicit mediators** (often called *retrieval cues*) that may link two associates in a component of memory called the **semantic network** (Tulving & Pearlstone, 1966). Moreover, associative learning often appears to be gradual, perhaps because of the need to eliminate competition from associates with similar attributes. This entails explication and encoding of distinguishing attributes, and may require several "passes" through the semantic network. What is not controversial, however, is the fact that we come by this associative capability quite naturally, assuming that we are developing normally.

Cross-modal transfer

When connective bonds are established between encoded information stored in different representational systems, and when accessing one type of information from memory becomes the occasion for accessing the other, we have an instance of what has been alternately called **cross-modal transfer** and **intersensory integration** (Bryant, 1974; Gibson, 1969). Learning to identify printed words is one type of cross-modal transfer: It entails associating visual symbols with linguistic symbols.

The ability to associate symbols that are stored in different representational systems is a basic mechanism for learning that is available very early in life (Bryant, 1974; Gibson, 1969). Reading typically involves the use of rather arbitrary sets of visual symbols, but it could as readily involve the use of other types of symbols, as in learning to read tactile symbols such as braille. Moreover, the types of cross-modal equivalences that are established vary with the writing system. For example, the types of equivalences established in a logographic writing system such as Chinese differ from those established in an alphabetic writing system such as English, and the way in which those equivalences are established is different in each system. Whereas logographic systems rely primarily on word names and meanings to form connective bonds between visual and linguistic symbols, alphabetic systems rely more heavily on connections between visual symbols and letter sounds.

Pattern analysis and rule learning

One of the most important of all of our cognitive abilities is the ability to detect *patterned invariance*. Gibson (1969) suggests that humans are naturally inclined to "search for invariance" in new learning situations to aid them both in reducing the amount of information they would otherwise be required to store, and to facilitate detection of distinguishing attributes in things having overlapping features. She also suggests that we are naturally endowed with mechanisms that allow us to store representations of invariant relationships in the form of rules and *algorithms* that can be used generatively. In regard to reading, she argues that the ability to detect and use patterned invariance makes word identification, as a developmental phenomenon, something more than simple paired associate learning. Thus, she suggests that developing readers will eventually detect and utilize spelling-sound correspondences and other forms of orthographic redundancy, even if they are not explicitly attuned to such redundancy, because they are naturally *programmed* to search for invariance.

We are inclined to agree with this analysis. Indeed, we intuit that the ability to detect and represent invariance may well be the foundation of our cognitive abilities and intelligent behavior in general.

Serial memory

A question of some importance to students of cognition—psycholinguists and practitioners alike—is just how one remembers the order in which things occur. A related question is whether or not memory for the individual elements in a given array or system is psychologically distinct from memory for the order in which those elements occur. Some suggest that **serial memory** is a generalized ability that determines the order in which all information is processed. For example, largely on the basis of clinical studies of neurologically impaired adults, some investigators (e.g., Luria, 1966) have assumed that serial memory in general is a neurologically distinct capability that depends upon the integrity of the left hemisphere (Das, Kirby, & Jarman, 1975). According to this point of view, the left hemisphere has the responsibility of representing and processing ordered information of all types (see Tzeng & Wang, 1984). This entails representing such diverse types of information as the order in which elements of a stimulus array are presented on memory tasks, the ordering rules for complex systems such as the language systems, mathematical systems, and so forth. By the same account, the right hemisphere is responsible for representing and processing simultaneously arrayed information, for example, spatial concepts. This division of labor has been called *successive* and *simultaneous processing*, respectively, following Luria (1973). An alternative view of serial memory is that there are different neurological structures supporting *modality-specific* sequencing abilities (Johnson & Myklebust, 1964). Thus, the ability to sequence visual information is seen as distinct from the ability to sequence auditory information.

Although clinical descriptions of *ordered recall* have fostered the idea that serial memory may be either a general ability or a collection of modality specific abilities, research conducted by cognitive psychologists would lead to a different conclusion. In fact, certain generalizations have emerged from this research which suggest that serial processing is a rather generic cognitive function that varies with the type of information serialized. First, the evidence suggests that the ways one represents the actual items in an ordered set and the serial order in which those items occur are distinctly different (see Bower & Minaire, 1974; Healy, 1974; Houston, 1976; for experimental documentation). This facet of cognition is illustrated by the distinction between the semantic and syntactic components of natural languages: semantics embodies the meanings of words in the language in terms of their conceptual attributes, and syntax embodies abstract rules and algorithms which set constraints on the ways those words may be ordered. A more relevant illustration for our discussion is the distinction between the letters that make up a printed word and the invariant order in which these letters appear. It is clear that the rules of serializing the letters in words are not inherent in the encoded representations of the letters themselves, but, rather, in the writing system. The system contains orthographic conventions that are largely determined by the various ways that the alphabetic characters map onto their sound counterparts.

Another important generalization that has emerged from the study of item and order processing is that there is no invariant means by which one serializes information. Patterned information is typically serialized by implicit ordering devices in the form of rules or principles that are inherent in a particular representational system. For example, the syntactic rules for the order of words in a language are quite different from the mathematical rules that order the quantities in a number system. Thus, learning to serialize a given type of information necessitates acquisition of the ordering rules inherent in the system representing that information. However, when one is confronted with information for which there are no inherent ordering rules, then serialization strategies must be devised, and those employed will vary both with the unique properties of the ordered set and with one's particular organizational and coding abilities. Such strategies will, therefore, be highly individualized.

The strategies one uses in serializing randomly ordered arrays have, in fact, been the object of extensive inquiry by memory researchers (see Bower & Hildgard, 1981, for a review), but space does not permit detailed discussion of this research. It will suffice to note that the two strategies most often used to serialize random arrays are *chunking* and *recoding*, which are typically used in concert with one another. Chunking involves reducing the size of an array into units that more readily lend themselves to position coding. Recoding involves assigning these units superordinate codes that facilitate recovery of position as well as item information. This is essentially what we do when we learn the order of digits in new phone numbers or the letters and numerals imprinted on new license plates.

These latter points bring into focus a final generalization that has emerged from the study of serial memory in cognitively based research, specifically, that serial recall is almost always rule-based. If the material to be ordered does not exceed the limit of short-term memory and is reasonably familiar (memory span for nonsense words is less than memory span for digits and meaningful words), then verbatim serial recall is readily accomplished without the aid of organizational and coding devices. But when the material to be ordered exceeds short term-memory limits, it is ordered by rules and algorithms that are implicit, induced, or invented anew. It should be apparent that, in learning to read, the child serializes the letters in printed words largely by encoding representations of spelling-sound relations and orthographic redundancy and not by some inherent ability to serialize in the general sense.

Two questions inevitably emerge as a result of this discussion of constituent processes in word recognition. First, how does the child come to use each of these underlying systems in the various stages of reading acquisition? Second, how do these processes interact with the rapidity necessary to produce skilled reading? These two questions will frame the next two sections on reading development and models of the reading process.

The development of reading

The relation between oral and written language is a living process.
Maryanne Wolf and Frank Vellutino

The protoliteracy period

The attainment of reading by the child, as in the species, emerges over a long period and is rooted in spoken words. Several decades of crosscultural research indicate that the most powerful predictors of later reading achievement are a child's phonological skills and ability to recognize letters (Adams, 1990; Bradley & Bryant, 1983, 1985; Chall, 1967, 1983; Liberman, Shankweiler, Fischer, & Carter, 1974; Roswell & Natchez, 1971; Snow, 1973; Vellutino & Scanlon, 1987).

Perhaps the greatest influence on the development of these abilities is simply the experience of being read to as a child. Within the seemingly simple experiences of watching a person turn pages of print and listening to stories and Mother Goose rhymes, a wealth of perceptual, cognitive, and linguistic precursors are found. First, the earliest correspondence between print and sound is made; this prepares the child to extract meaning from print (Marsh & Desberg, 1983). Second, in the phonological domain, a sense of rhyme, alliteration, and sound segmentation are introduced: the child gains the tacit knowledge that words are made of phonological parts. Bradley and Bryant (1983) have shown this knowledge to be a powerful predictor of early reading (see also Bowey & Patel, 1988; Bryant, Maclean & Bradley, 1990). Third, vocabulary knowledge, a foundation for all later reading, is exponentially increased.

Marsh and Desberg (1983) suggest that some of the earliest reading experiences occur when children turn from listening to others to making attempts of their own to read the pictured texts; this *linguistic guesswork* is the basis for children's first understanding of meaning-print connections. Another important kind of linguistic guessing that can prepare children to read is found in some children's *invented spelling* (Read, 1981). Read (1981) and Snowling (1987) demonstrated that children's earliest spelling often reflects what they hear or do *not* hear in the speech stream. For example, nasal consonants are difficult to detect in speech and are often omitted in children's invented words: *numbers* is written *nubrs*. Frequently children use the letter name as the basis of their efforts: *lady* is written *lade*, and *genius* becomes *gnus* (Bissex, 1980).

Phonological skills

Barron (1992) described this early period when the precursors of written language are being laid down as the *protoliteracy period*. He emphasized that during this time phonological awareness does not emerge as a whole, but rather as a heterogenous set of skills. For example, as Snowling (1987) and Treiman (1985) have suggested, segmentation skills are not an "all or none phenomenon." Rather, Treiman's work demonstrated that the ability to segment *syllables* is acquired first, followed by an intermediate level where the *onset* (e.g., initial consonant of the syllable) and *rime* (e.g., vowel and final consonants) are learned, followed by a final ability to segment individual phonemes.

Barron suggested that each level of segmentation skills has a particular relationship to different aspects of reading development. He and others have emphasized the *bidirectional character* (Barron, 1992) of the segmentation/reading relationship, whereby some levels of segmentation proficiency influence the acquisition of reading and some are then themselves influenced by reading practice (Bertelson & De Gelder, 1989; Wolf & Dickinson, 1985; Perfetti, Beck, Bell & Hughes, 1987). A fascinating example of this bidirectional character is seen in cross-cultural comparisons of segmentation skills. Chinese speaking adults who are literate in their logographic system (Read, Yun–Fei, Hong-Yin, & Bao-Qing, 1986) and Japanese children fluent in syllabaries (Mann, 1986) cannot initially segment words at the *phonemic* level which English speaking children can do by grade two after exposure to the alphabet. Another example is found in a study by Vellutino and Scanlon (1987) who showed that segmentation training can improve the reading acquisition process in young disabled readers. Thus, we see the developmentally interactive, level-specific nature of the relationships between specific phonological skills and later reading.

Vocabulary knowledge

Similar developmental, bidirectional relationships with reading are found in the formation of both vocabulary and letter-recognition/letter-naming skills. Beck, Perfetti, and McKeown (1982) suggested that development of vocabulary knowledge represents a continuum whereby individual words move from unfamiliar, to acquainted, to established categories (see also, Kameenui, Dixon, & Carmine, 1987). This vocabulary development both pushes and is pushed forward by reading acquisition.

Curtis (1987) also described the interconnectedness of reading and vocabulary development, where advances in each influence the other. Conversely, Stanovich (1986) described a *reciprocal causation* relationship that exists in older impaired readers, where these readers developed problems in vocabulary knowledge as the result of delays in reading, which then became further impeded because of increasing vocabulary deficits.

Letter recognition and naming speed abilities

Numerous letter-recognition studies have shown the predictive nature, apart from phonological skills, of the simple ability to recognize letters (Vellutino & Scanlon,

1987). Stanovich and West (1989) have shown that even in adulthood, orthographic skills accounted for the observed variance in word recognition—quite independent of phonological abilities. Recently, Barron (1992) discussed the particular predictive importance of one form of protoliteracy skill: That is, knowing the difference between letters and their names (B—pronounced *bee*) and letters and their sounds (B—pronounced *buh*) (Barron, 1992, p. 16).

The predictive value of *letter-naming*—which requires rapid integration of letter-recognition, letter-sound associations and phonological skills—has been the subject of considerable discussion (Walsh, Price & Cunningham, 1988). Most recently in a seven year longitudinal research study, Wolf (1991a) demonstrated that the *speed* of naming either letters *or* numbers was a singularly powerful predictor in kindergarten children of later reading, specifically, of word-recognition. Further, Wolf and her colleagues (Wolf, Bally & Morris, 1986) have demonstrated that after reading is acquired for average readers, the speed of letter-naming quickly reaches almost adult levels of fluency or automaticity, a finding suggestive of the bidirectional influence of reading on naming.

By contrast, numerous studies now document that a deficit in naming speed is a *specific* core deficit (independent of phonological problems) found in dyslexic readers from kindergarten to adulthood. Most recently, Bowers and Wolf (in press) have argued that this early separate deficit in naming speed may be linked to later failure in orthographic skills.

What emerges from the research in the protoliteracy period is that the child brings to the reading acquisition process a vast number of phonological, semantic, and orthographic skills which both influence development and, in turn, are influenced by it as these skills become practiced, integrated, and established over time.

Stages of literacy

The actual stages of the acquisition of literacy are a matter of continuing discussion. It should be clear from previous sections that considerable variation in learning to read exists, based on such factors as early exposure to print, individual learning strategies, patterns of strength and deficit, and method of teaching. Within this context, three theoretical accounts of stages of reading development will be considered. These three accounts were chosen both for their areas of overlap, which reinforce one another and for their differences, which complement one another and provide a fuller picture.

In the earliest stage in both Ehri's (1985) and Chall's (1983) accounts, letter discrimination and knowledge are emphasized, with the child recognizing a few rudimentary words (like the child's own name). Ehri and her colleagues (Ehri, 1985; Ehri & Wilce, 1985) have suggested that for young children, letters act as symbols for their particular sounds and that children build up a repertoire of letter-sound associations which provides the basis for their move from pre-reader to reader. Chall (1967, 1983) emphasized the importance at this stage of letter-naming and the skills discussed earlier (Wolf, 1991a).

In the next stage, characterized as the **logographic phase** by Frith (1985), highly familiar words are recognized visually, but novel or unknown words are inaccessible. Bradley and Bryant (1978) demonstrated that during this general period there can be a dissociation between reading and spelling strategies. Some readers use *visual* strategies for reading, but phonological strategies for spelling. For these children their invented spelling progresses, but they cannot read the very words they spell. For other children there is little spelling during this stage. Ehri's *semi-phonetic strategies* begin to emerge during this time as the child begins to apply some phonemic knowledge in both reading and spelling.

Chall's (1983) first formal reading stage begins at the point when the child begins a more systematic learning and application of these grapheme-phoneme rules. Frith (1985) refers to this period as the *alphabetic phase*. Decoding is the central emphasis (across all three theories), as the lower-level skills in reading (e.g., feature extraction, letter/pattern recognition, grapheme-phoneme correspondence, word recognition, lexical retrieval) are practiced and made automatic.

This alphabetic stage is characterized by changes in both reading and spelling. The child has begun to learn the specific connections between particular letters and sounds (e.g., grapheme-phoneme correspondence rules).

Mechanisms underlying the move from the logographic to the alphabetic phase, when children learn correspondence rules and "crack the code," are insufficiently understood (Snowling, 1987, p. 40). This move is more or less difficult depending on the invariant nature of correspondence in the various language systems. Indeed in English there are, according to Gough and Hillinger (1980), approximately 577 letter-sound correspondence rules. (Recall George Barnard Shaw's famous lament that in the English language *ghoti* can spell *fish*: e.g., *gh* as in *laugh*; *o* in *women*; and *ti* in *tion*!) Although, as discussed, English orthography embodies a living etymological history, the resulting lack of invariant correspondence rules is a major impediment in learning to read for English-speaking children. Gough and Hillinger (1980) suggested that we look at reading in these early acquisition stages as an "unnatural act," which inevitably needs intervention (teaching) by an outsider, who pushes the child from an early paired associate form of learning towards analytic processing. This characterization underscores an important, historical dispute in reading theory: whether the achievement of word recognition skills proceeds from "bottom up processes of spelling-to-sound decoding and direct visual recognition, or (from) top down processes of expectancy generation and contextual prediction" (Stanovich, 1992, p. 2).

While the substance of this debate will be elaborated in discussion of models of skilled reading in the next section, the question of how developing readers access their mental lexicon is important to consider within a developmental framework. Many models of fluent reading (Coltheart, 1982; Humphrey & Evetts, 1985) suggest a central concept—the notion of dual routes to lexical access. Within the dual route view there are two possible access procedures in reading: an indirect (nonlexical) route via phonology, "where a phonological representation of the word is assembled by application of letter-sound correspondence rules"; and a direct (orthographic or lexical) route "which involves no phonological recoding and uses an orthographic input register" to access information (Bertelson, 1986, p. 14) (see fuller treatment in Humphrey & Evetts, 1985, and the subsequent Open-Peer commentary). More simply, in direct access models, the reader is able to go directly from the printed word to meaning, without having to access the word's phonological representation. In the phonological, indirect access route, it is necessary to access the word's phonological representation to get to meaning.

Barron (1986) reviewed evidence supporting various hypotheses concerning whether children employ a direct or indirect route or, in fact, use both in the reading acquisition process. He found that "rudimentary letter-sound/name knowledge and knowledge obtained from applying analogies" (e.g., learning new words by using the sound and spelling similarity between the new word and a known word) are most central to the reading process (Barron, 1985, p. 110); (see work on analogies by Goswami, 1985; Marsh & Desberg, 1983). These types of knowledge, in turn, correspond to two basic types of orthographic units used by children: 1) letter-sound units (e.g., consonants); and 2) letter-cluster sound units that represent the medial and final portions of a syllable. Barron (1985) contended that neither direct nor indirect routes appeared to be a "satisfactory characterization of these units in the orthographic lexicon of beginning readers" (p. 111). He went on to suggest a single route model of lexical access that allowed for 1) the retrieval of different levels of orthographic units; 2) the application of grapheme-phoneme correspondence rules, in various stages of development; and 3) the interaction between phonological and orthographic information.

Debate over whether children learn to read using an indirect, bottom up route, or a direct, top-down route, or both at different times, has become polarized because of the implications for methods of reading instruction (Adams, 1990; Chall, 1967, 1983). If an indirect bottom-up route is assumed, then phonics instruction with its explicit teaching is emphasized (see work by Liberman, Liberman, Mattingly & Shankweiler, 1980). If top-down, direct-access, is assumed, then look-say (whole word or whole language) approaches are used (see work by Goodman & Goodman, 1980; Smith, 1980). The best evidence to date, the complexity of the reading process, and the developmental individual differences among readers support the narrow, exclusive use of neither approach, but rather the thoughtful combination of *both* (see Adams, 1990; Nicholson, 1991; Vellutino, 1991b).

Many investigators believe that there are developmentally influenced transitions —characterized by reliance on one or the other access procedure—that depend on the child's individual learning strategy, background, and instructional experience (see also reviews in Bertelson, 1986; Jorm & Share, 1983). To bring to life some of the complexities involved, one need only imagine an average child with significant exposure to print beginning with a rudimentary direct-access, paired-associate strategy for word identification; then as phonics instruction progresses, moving to a more analytic, indirect strategy for most but not all words. Finally, as she acquires fluency in word identification, direct-access procedures may be utilized predominantly and supplemented with indirect procedures when difficult or low-frequency words are encountered. The literature reviewed in the next section will elaborate upon the actual complexity of this last transition.

The final stage of literacy acquisition is characterized by increasingly greater fluency in word identification along with greater emphasis on comprehension processes. In Frith's schema this move into a final **orthographic phase** is character-ized by the use of analogies, pronunciation rules dictated by context, morphophone-mic knowledge, and what she calls *fluent, orthographic reading*. Ehri (1985) emphasized both the use of *morphemic strategies* and the consequent shift from sight vocabulary to *orthographic neighborhoods* of related words in this transition. Chall (1983) breaks this period into several stages: Stage 2 (grades 2½ to 4) where attention is increasingly directed to meaning and the use of inferential skills; Stage 3 (grades 4 to 8) where lower-level processes are now consolidated and comprehension of various kinds of material is the focus; Stage 4 (secondary school) where inference, and recognition of perspective dominate in comprehension processes; and Stage 5 (college and beyond) where comprehension involves the active synthesis, integration, and critical analysis of different bodies of knowledge and the formation of novel thought.

Chall's final stage of reading in adulthood invokes Havelock's (1974) and Olson's (1986) powerful discussions of the ultimate contribution of literacy—that is, the pro-duction of the "novel or unexpected statement, previously unfamiliar and even 'untaught' " (Havelock, 1974, p. 50). In our final section on models of skilled reading, we examine the complexity of fluent adult reading, the true basis for the production of most new or novel thought.

Models of skilled reading

Research with skilled readers has been primarily concerned with the question of how one recognizes and identifies printed words.[1] This focus is well motivated, since reading is critically dependent on facility in word recognition (Just & Carpenter, 1987; Perfetti, 1985; Rayner & Pollatsek, 1989). Accordingly, we describe briefly the major word recognition models that have been influential in establishing facts about reading. Each of the models is defined in terms of the assumptions it incorporates in addressing one or more of the following related questions: (1) whether words are recognized by accessing whole word representations in the mental lexicon, or sub-word representations such as features, letters or syllables; (2) whether words are ulti-mately identified through direct access or through phonologically mediated access to word meanings; (3) whether word recognition entails serial or parallel (simultaneous) processing of letters; (4) whether recognition is primarily a context-driven "top-down," stimulus-driven "bottom-up" or interactive process; (5) whether recognition entails the use of a single mechanism for accessing the lexicon, or multiple mecha-nisms for doing so; and (6) whether word recognition takes place through activation or through "search" processes.

---

[1]Strictly speaking, the term "word recognition" refers to the process whereby a word is perceived as a familiar stimulus, whereas the term "word identification" refers to the process whereby a familiar word is assigned its proper name and meaning. However, since in skilled readers, recognition typically implies identification, the terms are used interchangeably.

Because of space limitations, our discussion of the various models must necessarily be brief. Moreover, we will not consider here models of reading comprehension, but refer the reader to discussions of language comprehension in the chapter on sentence processing (see also an excellent treatment in Just & Carpenter, 1987).

Context-driven "top-down" models

Context-driven models of word recognition assume that higher level contextual information can directly affect the way lower level stimulus information is perceived and interpreted. By contextual information we mean domain-specific knowledge, knowledge of the semantic and syntactic constraints inherent in language, and implicit knowledge of orthographic redundancies and constraints (e.g., *u* always follows *g*; *th* occurs frequently; *xz* never occurs).

The prototypical context-driven model is that proposed by Smith (1971). In this model, the representations which uniquely define printed words in memory are the abstract features (lines, curves, angles, etc.) which define the letters in those words, and there are presumed to be separate, "functionally equivalent feature lists" for letters appearing in different cases and fonts. When a printed word is encountered, features are extracted in all letter positions simultaneously, and word recognition occurs when a *criterial set* of features is successfully matched with its counterpart in memory. However, feature extraction is a selective process insofar as it is determined both by implicit knowledge of orthographic structure and by the ability to use linguistic context to predict words in the text ("The cat chased the —— ."). Thus, within this view, word recognition is largely a matter of confirming one's predictions and neither letter recognition nor phonological recoding (accessing word *names*) is entailed.

Empirical support for Smith's model is weak. The role of linguistic context is afforded some support by studies demonstrating that facility in word recognition can be affected by semantic congruence between the text and a target word (Morton, 1964; Perfetti & Roth, 1981; Stanovich, 1980; Tulving & Gold, 1963; Tulving, Mandler & Baumal, 1964). Yet, the role of context must be limited, because even highly skilled readers can, at best, predict only one out of every four words encountered in text (Gough, Alford, & Holley-Wilcox, 1981). Moreover, eye movement studies have shown conclusively that even highly skilled readers make very little use of prediction, since they fixate on virtually all of the words in a passage, except for short, high frequency functors such as *the* (Rayner & Pollatsek, 1989; Just & Carpenter, 1987).

It has also been shown that word identification among skilled readers is a rapidly executed *modular* process. A modular process, such as word recognition, is relatively *autonomous*, that is, it is "not controlled by higher level processes or supplemented by information from knowledge structures not contained in the module itself" (Stanovich, 1990, p. 82). Perfetti (1985, 1992) and Stanovich (1980, 1990) have, in fact, shown that most contextual effects are comprehension effects which take place after words have already been identified.

Smith's other claim, that familiarity with *orthographic redundancy* aids word recognition, has been validated many times over (e.g., Adams, 1979; Massaro, 1975; Smith, 1969). Moreover, it has been repeatedly demonstrated that skilled readers have little difficulty recognizing printed words appearing in different or even mixed cases and fonts, which is consistent with Smith's assumption that word recognition entails the use of functionally equivalent feature lists (Coltheart, 1981; Rayner, McConkie & Zola, 1980; Smith, Lott & Cronnell, 1969). However, these results can also be taken as support for the possibility that it is a word's letters that are the units of recognition, rather than the features which define those letters. Thus, Smith's model remains somewhat tenuous.

Stimulus-driven "bottom-up" models

A basic assumption of stimulus-driven models is that word recognition depends primarily on information contained in the stimulus, the actual printed word, and not on the linguistic context. A second assumption is that recognition takes place in discrete, hierarchically ordered and noninteractive stages. Information at one stage is *encoded* (transformed) for use at the next stage. Virtually all bottom-up models postulate a *sensory stage* in which visual features are extracted; a *recognition stage* in which a representation of the word is accessed; and an *interpretive stage* in which the word's meaning is accessed. The models differ, however, in their conceptualizations of how printed words are mentally represented and identified.

Whole word models

Whole word models of word recognition commonly assume that printed words are represented mentally as psychologically indivisible wholes and that a word is recognized by virtue of the unique patterns formed by its component letters, just as a face is recognized by its pattern of features. Johnson's (1977) *pattern unit* model is prototypical (see also Cattell, 1886; Theois & Muis, 1977). This model postulates that stimulus features are extracted from all letter positions in parallel, but the letters themselves are not perceived because their collective features are assigned a *unitary encoding*, during the sensory stage of processing. This mental representation is compared with the stimulus word, and, if they match, the word is recognized and its meaning is accessed. In cases where no match for a string of letters is found, then that string would be parsed using orthographic rules that assign encodings to lower level units. Thus, *xqz* would be encoded as individual letters and *snick* would be encoded as somewhat larger units, allowing for decoding of unfamiliar strings.

Support for the pattern unit model came from classic research suggesting that a word may be perceived more readily than its component letters (Cattell, 1886). Especially notable is the **word superiority effect** (Reicher, 1969)—a highly reliable phenomenon whereby a letter embedded in a word seen only briefly (wor*k*) can be verified ("Did the word contain a k or d?") more accurately than when it is embedded in a nonword (Qrk), or when seen alone. This, among other findings (Johnson, 1977), led to the speculation that a word has cohesive perceptual properties that transcend its letters. However, later studies (e.g., Mesrich, 1973; Johnson, 1981) showed that the word superiority effect occurred only under brief exposure and **backward masking** conditions (e.g., when the stimulus word is obliterated by noise patterns shortly after viewing), suggesting that it may not be a true perceptual effect, but, rather, a short term memory effect facilitated by one's ability to remember the name of the stimulus word. This, and other findings (see Vellutino, 1982), greatly weakened the pattern unit model and it has been all but discarded. The current view is that a word derives its cohesiveness, not from the visual patterns made by its letters, but from the higher level cognitive and linguistic information bonded to those letters.

Component letter models

Component letter models postulate that printed words are represented as uniquely ordered arrays of graphemes, and that all of a word's letters must be recognized if that word is to be recognized. For example, Gough (1972) suggests that feature extraction and letter recognition take place through *serial processing* (letter by letter), and word identification takes place through phonemic recoding of each letter in turn, using *grapheme-phoneme correspondence (GPC) rules* to access word names and meanings (Venezky, 1970). In contrast, Massaro (1975) suggests that feature extraction and letter recognition take place through *parallel processing*, and that one uses implicit knowledge of orthographic redundancy to facilitate perception of letters not fully processed (e.g., medial letters masked by adjacent letters). This *primary recognition* process becomes input to a *secondary recognition* process which accesses word meanings directly, rather than through phonological mediation.

The evidence for these models is mixed. Their common assumption that letter recognition is a prerequisite for word recognition, is supported by the studies cited earlier demonstrating that words can be readily recognized in different or mixed cases and fonts, and it is now generally agreed that letter recognition is a necessary condition for word recognition. However, the serial processing component of Gough's (1972) model is questioned by studies demonstrating that words are not readily recognized when their letters are presented in tandem (Kolers, 1970; Travers, 1973). These findings are more in keeping with Massaro's suggestion that a word's letters are processed in parallel, which is a widely accepted view.

The phonological recoding component of Gough's model is not so easily dispensed with (Gough, 1984). Although there is evidence that phonological code activation is a component of working memory that facilitates reading comprehension (see Daneman, 1991; and Perfetti, 1985, for reviews), whether or not phonological code activation occurs before or after a word's meaning is accessed is a matter of some debate, as we noted earlier. The prevailing view is that skilled readers access word meanings directly, but there is empirical support for each point of view.

Support for the direct access view comes from studies demonstrating that word meanings are accessed even when phonological coding is impaired (Barron & Baron, 1977; Kleiman, 1975). Also supportive of a direct access model is the fact that one can readily distinguish the meanings of *homophones* such as *new* and *knew* from the differences in their spellings (Baron, 1973). However, other studies have shown that homophony slows both semantic and lexical judgments ("Are *pear* and *pair* both fruits?" Van Orden, 1987; Van Orden, Johnston & Hale, 1988; "Is *brane* a word?" Rubenstein, Lewis & Rubenstein, 1971). Such findings, among others, (Perfetti, Bell & Delaney, 1988) have been taken as support for the contention that word identification necessarily entails phonological recoding. The common observation that skilled readers can decode *pseudowords* better than less skilled readers has also been cited as evidence for Gough's (1972) suggestion that GPC (grapheme-phoneme correspondence) rules are used to identify real words (Gough & Tunmer, 1986). Yet, real words tend to be identified more rapidly than pseudowords (Forster & Chambers, 1973; Perfetti & Hogaboam, 1975), which is more in keeping with a direct access view. Moreover, the fact that GPC rules fail with a large number of words (e.g., *have, put, bough, cough*) militates against any strong version of the phonological recoding theory, and some (e.g., Coltheart, 1978) have taken such inconsistency as evidence for the co-existence of both direct and phonologically mediated access mechanisms, as we will see below. Thus, the issue is controversial and remains open.

Syllabic units

Another word recognition model that postulates phonological recoding as a basic process is that of Spoehr and Smith (1973). In this model the units of recognition are not single letters but, rather, phonologically defined syllables called *Vocalic Center Groups (VCG)*. Following Hansen and Rogers (1965), the VCG is defined as a vowel or *vowel digraph* (e.g., *ou* or *ea*) flanked by consonants or consonant clusters. The word identification process begins with feature extraction and letter recognition (in parallel), followed by rule based parsing that tentatively isolates VCG units, which are phonologically recoded to recover the word's name. If this process fails, then the word is parsed again, according to the Vocalic Center Groups model, until it is identified (e.g., FATHER→FAT/HER→FA/THER).

The VCG model was given initial support by studies demonstrating that tachistoscopic recognition of target letters in words was greater when they appeared within syllabic boundaries than when they appeared across syllabic boundaries (Spoehr & Smith, 1973). However, in a later study, Spoehr (1978) found that such effects occurred only under brief exposure and backward masking conditions; this finding led her to abandon the idea that the VCG is a true perceptual unit. In addition, more recent studies (e.g., Prinzmetal, Treiman & Rho, 1988) have shown that, while skilled readers may be sensitive to both orthotactically defined (spelling based) syllables (VOD/KA is "legal;" VO/DKA and VODK/A are "illegal") and morphemically defined syllables (e.g., SUN/SET), they do not appear to be especially sensitive to phonologically defined syllables, which are often ambiguous (FA/THER and FATH/ER are both acceptable to many, Selkirk, 1980). Thus, Vocalic Center Groups theory is primarily of historical interest at this juncture.

Multilevel and parallel coding systems models

These models differ from those already discussed because each postulates more than one unit of recognition rather than a single unit, and each incorporates alternative vehicles for word identification.

LaBerge and Samuels' multilevel coding model

In the LaBerge and Samuels (1974) model, there are hierarchically ordered "codes" (representations) for features, letters, spelling patterns, and words.

Through a process called *perceptual learning* lower order codes are integrated and *unitized* (perceived as a unit) to form a new set of codes at each successive level. Perceptual learning entails focal attention, which is conceived as a limited cognitive

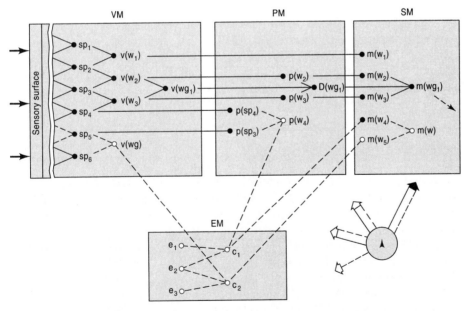

Figure 9.1

LaBerge & Samuels Model (1974)

e	Temporal-spatial event code
c	Episodic code
sp	Spelling pattern code
v(w)	Visual word code
v(wg)	Visual word group code
p(sp)	Phonological spelling pattern code
p(w)	Phonological word code
p(wg)	Phonological word group code

m(w)	Word meaning code
m(wg)	Word group meaning code
•	Code activated without attention
○	Code activated only with attention
A	Code momentarily activated by attention
◄--	Momentary focus of attention
——	Information flow without attention
---	Information flow only with attention

resource that cannot be allocated to two processes simultaneously. As one's ability to recognize unitized codes at a given level becomes *automatized*, attention is redeployed to the task of unitizing codes at the next level. The gradual emergence of both word and subword codes, and the integration of their visual and sound counterparts facilitate the use of both direct and phonologically mediated vehicles for word identification in developing readers, but skilled readers have fully integrated a vast inventory of both types of codes and can therefore allocate cognitive resources primarily to comprehension of connected text. Thus, for skilled readers, word identification typically occurs through direct visual access, but knowledge of letter-sound correspondences provides them with a mechanism for identifying unfamiliar letter strings.

In initial tests of their model, LaBerge and Samuels (1974) demonstrated that shifts of attention from familiar stimuli (e.g., b–d) to unfamiliar stimuli (ʌ Ϟ) exacted a cost in speed of processing on initial learning trials, but not on later trials. Since attentional shifts between two sets of familiar stimuli did *not* disrupt speed of processing, it was inferred that automatic processing consumes no attentional resources and may be defined by this criterion. (An alternative view, that automaticity is a continuum, is found in Logan, 1988, and Stanovich, 1991). LaBerge and Samuels' (1974) claim that lower level codes are gradually integrated into higher level codes is given some support in studies showing that disparities in speed of processing long versus short words are substantial in children in the lower grades, but not in children in the upper grades (see Samuels & Kamil, 1984, for a review).

Support for the existence of intermediate level codes comes from studies documenting that both letter clusters and syllables may function in word recognition (Adams, 1979; Greenberg & Vellutino, 1988; Petersen & LaBerge, 1977; Prinzmetal, et al., 1988; Spoehr & Smith, 1973; Taft, 1979). Thus, the model enjoys considerable empirical support.

Parallel coding systems models

The prototypical *parallel systems model* is Coltheart's (1978) *dual route* model. Discussed briefly in our section on development, the central assumption of this and related models (Carr & Pollatsek, 1985; Rayner & Pollatsek, 1989) is that there are separate coding systems that carry out recognition operations independently. Coltheart (1978) postulates two such systems, one that accesses lexical representations directly, using word specific associates, and another that accesses them indirectly, through the use of grapheme-phoneme correspondence (GPC) rules. Both of these systems are activated by a letter string, and depending on the nature of that string, one or the other system may bring about identification. Thus, highly familiar words would be identified through a direct visual route, whereas less familiar words and pseudowords would be identified through an indirect route using GPC rules. But, because the output codes of the GPC system must be *assembled* before identification can take place, it is the slower of the two processes.

Two different types of evidence have been cited in support of the dual route model. One type comes from studies of brain damaged patients, who have suffered what appears to be selective loss of either the direct visual or phonologically mediated access routes. One group of patients—called *deep dyslexics*—appear to be able to read most words, but have very limited ability to read pseudowords, make many semantic confusion errors (e.g., calling *cat—kitten* and *orchestra—symphony*), and have difficulty reading functors (e.g., *if, and, but*). This symptom pattern suggests that the direct route is intact in these patients, while the phonologically mediated route is impaired (Coltheart, Patterson, & Marshall, 1980). *Surface dyslexics*, by contrast, often decode pseudowords and regularly spelled words (e.g., *cat, fat*) more readily than they can decode irregularly spelled words (e.g., *epoch, ache*), and often *regularize* words with exceptional pronunciations (e.g., *have, put*), suggesting that they have lost word specific connections that allow them to use the direct access route (Patterson, Marshall, & Coltheart, 1985). Because the strengths and weaknesses observed in these acquired dyslexia patients are relative rather than absolute (performance is never totally deficient nor totally adequate), critics have suggested that their performance patterns on decoding and naming tasks may simply reflect different types and levels of impairment of a single, lexically based access mechanism, rather than selective impairment of one of two separate mechanisms (e.g., Humphrey & Evetts, 1985; Van Orden, Pennington & Stone, 1990).

A second type of evidence for the dual route model comes from naming tasks with skilled readers. It has been consistently found that skilled readers are able to name printed words faster than they decode (sound out) pseudowords and that they name high frequency words faster than low frequency words (e.g., Broadbent, 1967; Forster & Chambers, 1973; Perfetti & Hogaboam, 1975). This suggests that familiar words "use" the direct route, while less familiar words and pseudowords use the assembled route. It has also been consistently found that regular words are, in general, named faster than exception words (e.g., Baron & Strawson, 1976). But, whereas high frequency regular and exception words are both named with equal speed, low frequency, regular words are named faster than low frequency, exception words (Seidenberg, Waters, Barnes, & Tannenhaus, 1984; Waters & Seidenberg, 1985). Presumably the direct route always "wins the race" with the indirect route in the case of high frequency words. Because low frequency words are less familiar, the indirect route is better able to compete with the direct route, and this conflict affects the exception words more than the regular words.

This account may be oversimplified. Glushko (1979) found that a pseudoword such as *tave*, which is spelled similarly to the exception word *have*, takes longer to name than a pseudoword such as *feal*, whose real word "neighbors" all have regular pronunciations (e.g., *real, heal*). Glushko (1979) also found that regular words whose neighbors all have consistent pronunciations were named faster than regular words whose neighbors include words with inconsistent pronunciations. In addition, Seidenberg, et al. (1984) found that low frequency, regular/consistent words were named faster than low frequency regular/inconsistent words. Glushko (1979) and others (Humphreys & Evetts, 1985; Seidenberg, et al., 1984; Van Orden, et al., 1990) have interpreted these results as evidence for a single mechanism for lexical access (see also Barron, 1986) that identifies a word by "synthesizing patterns of activation" from other words with similar spellings (e.g., identifies *fat* by analogy with *cat* and *fan*). The implication is that this mechanism mimics the apparent rule-based properties said to be characteristic of the GPC mechanism. Thus, the issue is controversial and remains unresolved.

Activation or logogen models

Most of the models discussed thus far imply that a printed word acts as a stimulus that energizes or activates a code or set of codes representing that word in memory. However, none of these models has been explicit in describing the activation processes. The class of models we now illustrate is more explicit in doing so.

Morton's logogen model

Activation models are basically fashioned after a model of word recognition initially proposed by Morton (1969). Morton coined the term **logogen** (from the Greek word *logos*) to characterize an inferred *neural entity* that represents a printed word. Logogens function as threshold-type *detection devices* that incrementally register information derived from both sensory input and linguistic context. And, like neurons, they *fire* when a criterion threshold has been reached. When this occurs, the word is recognized and its meaning is accessed. In their *resting state* logogens have threshold values for each represented word that are determined by their frequency of occurrence in print. Thus, logogens representing high frequency words have lower thresholds of activation than do logogens representing lower frequency words. Linguistic context can also serve to lower or raise threshold values, depending on whether or not it contains information that is related to a word's meaning(s). Word recognition is believed to result from the interaction of stimulus and contextual information, and a word's meaning becomes available when a logogen is activated.

Support for Morton's (1969) model came largely from studies demonstrating that highly constraining contexts can facilitate word recognition, while incongruent contexts tend to impede recognition (Morton, 1964; Tulving & Gold, 1963; Tulving, Mandler & Baumal, 1964). However, except for some later work (e.g., Murrell & Morton, 1974) which suggests that logogens may be sensitive to morphemes rather than words (e.g., *walk/ing*), Morton, himself, provided limited documentation of his model.

Interactive-activation and connectionist models

Morton's model was pivotal in framing later models that provided greater specification of how logogens might work—the *interactive-activation model* of McClelland and Rumelhart (1981; see also Rumelhart & McClelland, 1982). In the latter model, word recognition is believed to result from the interaction of competing excitatory and inhibitory activations from interconnected logogen type detectors (*nodes*) corresponding with features, letters and words (see Figure 9.2). Each node is believed to

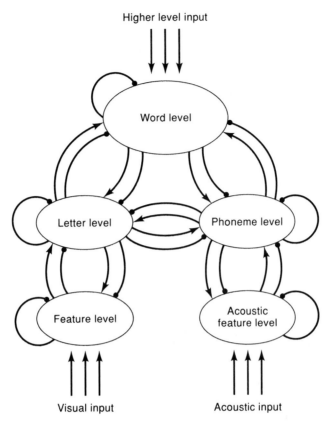

Figure 9.2

McClelland &
Rumelhart Model
(1981)

have a "resting level" threshold that depends on frequency of activation over time. The activation level of a given node is said to be determined in part by excitation from the stimulus word and in part by excitatory and inhibitory activations from neighboring words. The greater the overlap in spelling, the greater the activations stimulated by given neighbors. Linguistic context may also influence activation level. The momentary activation of a given node is said to have a real numerical value which changes over time, depending on the relative weights carried by excitatory and inhibitory activations. Thus, in mathematical terms, word recognition is determined by the algebraic summation of excitatory and inhibitory inputs which yield a net activation value that is a simple weighted average of these inputs. Because the excitatory activations prompted by a printed word stimulus are typically greater than the inhibitory activations prompted by neighboring words, the logogen for that word fires and the word is recognized.

The cardinal evidence for this *connectionist* model (the term reflecting its structural features) comes primarily from impressive computer simulations of some of the major word recognition phenomena documented in empirical research (McClelland & Rumelhart, 1981; Rumelhart & McClelland, 1982), the most notable being the word superiority effect discussed earlier, in which letters embedded in words are verified more accurately than those embedded in nonwords (Reicher, 1969). Moreover, the model rather handily accommodates Glushko's (1979) finding that pseudowords spelled like words with inconsistent pronunciations (e.g., *tave/have*) take longer to pronounce than pseudowords spelled like words with consistent pronunciations (*feal/real*). The underlying assumptions of the model are quite in keeping with Glushko's contention that words are identified by synthesizing patterns of activation from words with similar spellings.

But to complicate matters, a radically revised version of the interactive-activation model, recently proposed by Seidenberg and McClelland (1989), dispenses with word level nodes altogether, substituting a **parallel distributed processing (PDP)** format, whereby nodes for three letter spelling patterns are directly connected to nodes for the phoneme values of those spelling patterns (e.g., the word *heat* is represented -*he, hea, eat, at*-, the lines with spaces conforming with word boundaries). Thus, there is no mental lexicon, and no assumptions are made about the role of linguistic context in word identification. And, using processing parameters, similar to those outlined in McClelland and Rumelhart (1981), Seidenberg and McClelland (1989) were able to simulate an even broader range of word recognition phenomena: for example, the interaction between word frequency and regularity in word spellings, documented by Seidenberg, et al. (1984); the pseudoword and regular/exception word pronunciation effects documented by Glushko (1979); and so forth. Seidenberg and McClelland (1989) conclude that words are identified using a single nonlexical coding mechanism that makes use of distributed representations which encode the spelling-sound redundancies inherent in the orthography.

However, it should be noted that the corpus of words used in the simulations reported by McClelland and Rumelhart (1981) and Seidenberg and McClelland (1989) included only four-letter words; thus, their results may not readily be generalized to more complex words. Moreover, in a recent critique of the PDP model, Besner, Twilley, McCann, & Seergobin (1990) compared the Seidenberg and McClelland (1989) simulations with performance of skilled readers on tasks that were not reported by these investigators and found that the two data sets did not correspond as closely as they should have. For example, the model did not name pseudowords as well as skilled readers. Based on such findings, among others, Besner et al. (1990) concluded that the standard dual route model still provides a better account of most word recognition phenomena than does the PDP model. (See response to such criticisms in Seidenberg, 1992.)

Lexical search models

Whereas activation models postulate that printed words are identified by passive and automatic activation of letter and word detectors, *search models* postulate that word identification is the culmination of an active and ordered search for lexical addresses where information about given words is stored. Such a model was initially proposed by Forester (1976) and later extended by Taft (1979). In the current model, a word's lexical address is assumed to be located in an **orthographic access file**, in one of several **bins** containing representations of words with similar orthographic descriptions. Entries in each bin are ordered by frequency, with those representing high frequency words at the top of the bin and those representing low frequency words at the bottom of the bin. The bin containing a word's lexical address is located with the aid of an **access code**, which is defined as the first syllable in a stem morpheme. This unit—called the *Basic Orthographic Syllable Structure (BOSS)*—is isolated through left-to-right iterative parsing that maintains orthotactic and morphological integrity. In prefixed words, parsing commences after the prefix has been stripped away. Thus, the BOSS of *prefix* is *fix*, while the BOSS of *vodka* is *vod* (*vo/dka* and *vodk/a* are both illegal). Similarly, the BOSS of *sunset* is *sun* because the parsing process gives morphemes preeminent status. When the bin containing the lexical address of the stimulus word is located, all codes in the bin are matched with that word in order of their frequency. When the appropriate code is found, the word's lexical address is accessed and a full orthographic description of the stem morpheme becomes available. A post access "check" is made to compare this representation with the stimulus word, and, if they match, the word is identified and its meaning is accessed.

Support for the search model came initially from Forster and Chambers' (1973) observation that real words can be identified more rapidly than pseudowords, and that high frequency words can be identified more rapidly than low frequency words. However, such findings can also be explained by activation type models (McClelland & Rumelhart, 1981; Seidenberg & McClelland, 1989). Moreover, most of the research conducted to evaluate the search model has been devoted to validation of the access code, and such research provides only indirect support for the model. And while there is considerable support for the idea that skilled readers are sensitive to both orthotactically and morphologically defined units in complex words (orthotactic parsing—*vod/ka*; morphological parsing—*sun/set*; *walk/ing*; see Feldman, in press; Lima & Pollatsek, 1983; Murrell & Morton, 1974; Prinzmetal, et al., 1988; Taft, 1979; Taft & Forester, 1975, 1976), such findings do not constitute *prima facie* evidence for either access codes or search processes. In sum, the evidence for the BOSS unit is equivocal (Inhoff, 1989; Jordan, 1986; Lima & Pollatsek, 1983; Taft, 1979). Thus, whether words are identified through activation or search processes remains an open question (see Paap, Newsome, McDonald, & Schaneveldt, 1982, for a model that incorporates activation as well as verification and search processes).

Summary

In this chapter we have reviewed the history of writing, and we have discussed the kinds of complex abilities that humans have that make it possible for them to read written language. We have traced some of the accounts that describe children's acquisition of reading, and we have summarized some of the most prominent models of the reading process itself. Although humans have been a language-speaking species for tens of thousands of years, writing is a relatively recent phenomenon. Our earliest evidence of writing dates from as recently as the fourth millenium B.C. Literacy has, however, changed the human species dramatically by providing us with an objective means of considering our own language and thought and of connecting ourselves to other worlds of knowledge, across time and space.

Spoken language is the fountainhead, as the great linguist Edward Sapir noted, from which all other forms of language flow. And writing is no exception. Our writing is based upon an alphabetic principle: each written letter is meant to stand for a sound in the spoken word. This is the major principle that children must grasp. Once children have grasped this principle, they bring into play various complex skills as they move through the stages of literacy acquisition.

Study of the reading process involves, among other things, answering a number of questions about how printed words are recognized. Many of the questions that have motivated the study of the word recognition process remain unanswered, but we have, nevertheless, learned a great deal about how skilled readers recognize and identify printed words in addressing these questions. We know, for example, that words are not recognized on the basis of shape cues or supraletter patterns, that word recognition depends initially on letter recognition, and that a word's letters are recognized in parallel rather than through left to right serial processing. We also know that, while the skilled reader may use both stimulus and contextual information in identifying printed words, the weight given these two types of information appears to be asymmetric, insofar as skilled word identification has been shown to be an automatic, rapidly executed and modular process, regardless of whether words are identified in isolation or in sentence contexts.

There is, in addition, good reason to believe that skilled readers have internalized unitized representations of redundant spelling patterns that they can use to decode unfamiliar letter strings; they seem also to be sensitive to both orthotactic and morphological boundaries in identifying familiar strings. Whether or not such boundaries define access codes that mediate word identification, and whether identification takes place through activation as opposed to search processes, through direct or phonologically mediated access mechanisms or through both types of mechanisms operating independently, are among the questions that remain open.

References

Adams, M. J. (1979). Models of word recognition. *Cognitive Psychology, 11,* 133–176.

Adams, M. J. (1990). *Beginning to read: Thinking and learning about print.* Cambridge, MA: MIT Press.

Baron, J. (1973). Phonemic stage is not necessary for reading. *Quarterly Journal of Experimental Psychology, 25,* 241–246.

Baron, J., & Strawson, C. (1976). Orthographic and word-specific mechanisms in reading words aloud. *Journal of Experimental Psychology: Human perception and performance, 2,* 386–393.

Barron, R. W. (1986). Word recognition in early reading: A review of the direct and indirect access hypothesis. *Cognition, 24,* 93–119.

Barron, R. W. (1992). Proto-literacy, literacy and the acquisition of phonological awareness. *Learning and Individual Differences, 3,* 243–255.

Barron, R. W., & Baron, J. (1977). How children get meaning from printed words. *Child Development, 48,* 586–594.

Beck, I. L., Perfetti, C. A., & McKeown, M. G. (1982). Effects of long-term vocabulary instruction of lexical access and reading comprehension. *Journal of Educational Psychology, 74,* 506–521.

Bertelson, P. (1986). The onset of literacy: Liminal remarks. *Cognition, 24,* 1–30.

Bertelson, P., & De Gelder, B. (1989). Learning about reading from illiterates. In A. M. Galaburda (Ed.), *From neurons to reading* (pp. 1–23). Cambridge, MA: MIT Press.

Besner, D, Twilley, L., McCann, R. S., & Seergobin, K. (1990). On the association between connectionism and data: Are a few words necessary? *Psychological Review, 97,* 432–446.

Biemeller, A. (1970). The development of the use of graphic and contextual information as children learn to read. *Reading Research Quarterly, 6,* 75–96.

Bissex, G. L. (1980). *GNYS at work: A child learns to write and read.* Cambridge, MA: Harvard University Press.

Botstein, L. (1990). Damaged literacy: Illiteracies and American democracy. *Daedalus, 119,* 55–84.

Bower, G. H., & Hildgard, E. R. (1981). *Theories of learning.* Englewood Cliffs, NJ: Prentice-Hall.

Bower, G. H., & Minaire, H. (1974). On interfering with item versus order information in serial recall. *American Journal of Psychology, 87,* 557–564.

Bowers, P., & Wolf, M. (In press). Theoretical links among orthographic skills, naming speed, and reading. *Reading and Writing.*

Bowey, J. A., & Patel, R. K. (1988). Metalinguistic ability and early reading achievement. *Applied Psycholinguistics, 9,* 367–383.

Bradley, L., & Bryant, P. E. (1978). Difficulties in auditory organization as a possible cause of reading backwardness. *Nature, 271,* 746–747.

Bradley, L., & Bryant, P. E. (1983). Categorizing sounds and learning to read: A causal connection. *Nature, 301,* 419–421.

Bradley, L., & Bryant, P. E. (1985). *Rhyme and reason in reading and spelling* (IARLD Monographs, No. 1). Ann Arbor: University of Michigan Press.

Broadbent, D. E. (1967). The word frequency effect and response bias. *Psychological Review, 74,* 1–15.

Bryant, P. E. (1974). *Perception and understanding in young children.* New York: Basic Books.

Bryant, P. E., MacLean, M., & Bradley, L. L. (1990). Rhyme, language, and children's reading. *Applied Psycholinguistics, 11,* 237–252.

Carr, T. H., & Pollatsek, A. (1985). Recognizing printed words: A look at current models. In D. Besner, T. G. Waller, & G. E. MacKinnon (Eds.), *Reading Research: Advances in theory and Practice* (Vol. 5, pp. 1–82). Orlando: Academic Press.

Cattell, J. McK. (1886). The time it takes to see and name objects. *Mind, 11,* 63–65.

Chall, J. S. (1967). *Learning to read: The great debate.* New York: McGraw-Hill.

Chall, J. S. (1983). *Stages of reading development.* New York: McGraw-Hill.

Chomsky, C. (1972). Stages in language development and reading exposure. *Harvard Educational Review, 42,* 1–33.

Chomsky, N., & Halle, M. (1968). *The sound pattern of English.* New York: Harper & Row.

Coltheart, M. (1978). Lexical access in simple reading tasks. In G. Underwood (Ed.), *Strategies of information processing.* New York: Academic Press.

Coltheart, M (1981). Disorders of reading and their implication for models of reading. *Visible Language, 15*, 245–286.

Coltheart, M. (1982). The psycholinguistic analysis of acquired dyslexias: Some illustrations. *Philosophical Transactions of the Royal Society of London; 298*, 154–164.

Coltheart, M., Patterson, K., & Marshall, J. (Eds.). (1980). *Deep dyslexia*. London: Routledge & Kagan Paul.

Curtis, M. E. (1987). Vocabulary testing and vocabulary instruction. In M. G. McKeown & M. E. Curtis (Eds.), *The nature of vocabulary acquisition* (pp. 37–51). Hillsdale, NJ: Erlbaum.

Daneman, M. (1991). Individual differences in reading skills. In R. Barr, M. L. Kamil, P. B. Mosenthal, & P. D. Pearson (Eds.), *Handbook of reading research (Vol. II)*. New York: Longman.

Das, J. P., Kirby, J., & Jarman, R. F. (1975). Simultaneous and successive syntheses: An alternative model for cognitive abilities. *Psychological Bulletin, 82*, 99–114.

Ehri, L. C. (1985a). Effects of printed language acquisition on speech. In D. R. Olson, N. Torrance, & A. Hildyard (Eds.), *Literacy, language and learning: The nature and consequences of reading and writing* (pp. 333–367). New York: Cambridge University Press.

Ehri, L. C. (1985b). Sources of difficulty in learning to spell and read. In M. L. Wolvaich & D. Routh (Eds.), *Advances in development and behavioural pediatrics*. Greenwich, CT: Jai Press Inc.

Ehri, L. C. (1992). Reconceptualizing the development of sight word reading and its relationship to recording. In P. Gough, R. Treiman, & L. C. Ehri (Eds.), *Reading acquisition* (pp. 107–143). Hillsdale, NJ: Erlbaum.

Ehri, L. C., & Wilce, L. S. (1985). Movement into reading: Is the first stage of printed word learning visual or phonetic? *Reading Research Quarterly, 20*, 163–179.

Ellis, A. W. (1984). *Reading, writing and dyslexia*. London: Erlbaum.

Feldman, L. B. (in press.). The contribution of morphology to word recognition. *Psychological Review*.

Forster, K. I. (1976). Accessing the mental lexicon. In R. J. Wales & E. Walker (Eds.), *New approaches to language mechanisms* (pp. 255–287). Amsterdam: North Holland.

Forster, K. I., & Chambers, S. J. (1973). Lexical access and naming time. *Journal of Verbal Learning and Verbal Behavior, 12*, 627–635.

Frith, U. (1985). Beneath the surface of dyslexia. In K. Patterson, J. Marshall, & M. Coltheart (Eds.), *Surface dyslexia* (pp. 301–330). London: Lawrence Erlbaum.

Geschwind, N. (1974). *Selected papers on language and the brain*. Boston, MA: Reidel.

Gibson, E. J. (1969). *Principles of perceptual learning and development*. New York: Appleton, Century, Crofts.

Glushko, R. J. (1979). The organization and activation of orthographic knowledge in reading aloud. *Journal of Experimental Psychology: Human Perception and Performance, 5*, 674–691.

Goodman, K. S., & Goodman, Y. M. (1980). Learning about psycholinguistic processes by analyzing oral reading. In M. Wolf, M. K. McQuillan, & E. Radwin (Eds.), *Thought & language/Language & reading* (Harvard Educational Review Reprint series no. 14) (pp. 253–269). Cambridge, MA: Harvard Educational Review.

Goswami, U. C. (1985). *The role of analogy in early reading development*. Paper presented at the Society for Research in Child Development, Toronto, Ontario, Canada.

Gough, P. B. (1972). One second of reading. In J. F. Kavanagh & I.G. Mattingly (Eds.), *Language by ear and by eye: The relationship between speech and reading* (pp. 331–358). Cambridge, MA: MIT Press.

Gough, P. B. (1984). Word recognition. In P. D. Pearson, R. Barr, M. L. Kamil, & P. D. Mosenthal (Eds.), *Handbook of reading research* (Vol. 1, pp. 225–253). New York: Longman.

Gough, P. B., & Hillinger, M. L. (1980). Learning to read: An unnatural act. *Bulletin of the Orton Society, 30,* 179–196.

Gough, P. B., & Tunmer, W. E. (1986). Decoding, reading, and reading disability. *Remedial and Special Education, 7,* 6–10.

Gough, P. B., Alford, J. A., & Holley-Wilcox, P. (1981). Words and contexts. In O. J. L. Tzeng & H. Singer (Eds.), *Perception of print: Reading research in experimental psychology* (pp. 85–102). Hillsdale, NJ: Erlbaum.

Greenberg, S. N., & Vellutino, F. R. (1988). Evidence for processing constituent single and multilevel codes: Support for multilevel coding in word perception. *Memory and Cognition, 16,* 54–63.

Hansen, D., & Rogers, T. S. (1965). An exploration of psycholinguistic units in initial reading. In *Proceedings of the Symposium on the Psycholinguistic Nature of the Reading Process.* Detroit: Wayne State University.

Havelock, E. A. (1976). *Origins of western literacy.* Toronto, Ontario: The Ontario Institute for Studies in Education.

Healy, A. F. (1974). Separating item from order information in short-term memory. *Journal of Verbal Learning and Verbal Behavior, 13,* 644–655.

Houston, J. P. (1976). Item versus order information, proactive inhibition and serial recall. *American Journal of Psychology, 89,* 507–514.

Humphrey, G. W., & Evetts, L. J. (1985). Are there independent lexical and non-lexical routes in word processing? An evaluation of the dual-route theory in reading. *The Behavioral and Brain Sciences, 8,* 689–740.

Inhoff, A. W. (1989). Lexical access during eye fixations in reading: Are word access codes used to integrate lexical information across interword fixations? *Journal of Memory and Language, 28,* 444–461.

Johnson, D., & Mykelbust, H. (1984). *Learning disabilities,* (2nd Ed.) New York: Grune & Stratton.

Johnson, N. F. (1977). A pattern-unit model of word identification. In D. LaBerge & S. J. Samuels (Eds.), *Basic processes in reading: Perception and comprehension* (pp. 91–125). Hillsdale, NJ: Erlbaum.

Johnston, J. C. (1981). Understanding word perception: Clues from studying the word superiority effect. In O. J. L. Tzeng & H. Singer (Eds.), *Perception of print: Reading research in experimental psychology* (pp. 65–84). Hillsdale, NJ: Erlbaum.

Jordan, T. R. (1986). Testing the BOSS hypothesis: Evidence for position insensitive orthographic priming in the lexical decision task. *Memory and Cognition, 14,* 523–532.

Jorm, A. F., & Share, D. L. (1983). Phonological reading and acquisition. *Applied Psycholinguistics, 4,* 103–147.

Just, M. A., & Carpenter, P. A. (1987). *The psychology of reading and language comprehension.* Newton, MA: Allyn & Bacon.

Kameenui, E. J., Dixon, R. C., & Carmine, D. W. (1987). Issues in the design of vocabulary instruction. In M. G. McKeown & M. E. Curtis (Eds.), *The nature of vocabulary acquisition* (pp. 129–145). Hillsdale, NJ: Lawrence Erlbaum.

Kleiman, G. M. (1975). Speech recoding in reading. *Journal of Verbal Learning and Verbal Behavior,. 14,* 323–340.

Kolers, P. A. (1970). Three stages of reading, In H. Levin & J. P. Williams (Eds.), *Basic studies on reading* (pp. 90–118). New York: Basic Books.

Kolers, P. A. (1973). Some modes of representation. In P. Pliner, L. Krames, & T. Alloway (Eds.), *Communication and affect: Language and thought.* New York: Academic Press.

LaBerge, D., & Samuels, S. J. (1974). Toward a theory of automatic information processing in reading. *Cognitive Psychology, 6,* 293–323.

Liberman, I. Y., Liberman, A. M., Mattingly, I. G., & Shankweiler, D. (1980). Orthography and the beginning reader. In J. F. Kavanagh & R. L. Venezsky (Eds.), *Orthography, reading and dyslexia.* Baltimore, MD: University Park Press.

Liberman, I. Y., Shankweiler, D., Fischer, F. W., & Carter, B. (1974). Explicit syllable and phoneme segmentation in the young child. *Journal of Experimental Child Psychology, 18,* 201–212.

Lima, S. D., & Pollatsek, A. (1983). Lexical access via an orthographic code? The basic orthographic syllable structure (BOSS) reconsidered. *Journal of Verbal Learning and Verbal Behavior, 22,* 310–332.

Logan, G. D. (1988). Toward an instance theory of automatization. *Psychological Review, 95*(4), 492–527.

Luria, A. R. (1966). *Higher cortical functions in man.* New York: Basic Books.

Mann, V. A. (1986). Phonological awareness: The role of reading experience. *Cognition, 24,* 65–92.

Marsh, G., & Desberg, P. (1983). The development of strategies in the acquisition of symbolic skills. In D. A. Rogers & J. A. Sloboda (Eds.), *The acquisition of symbolic skills.* New York: Plenum Press.

Marshall, J. C., & Newcombe, F. (1973). Patterns of paralexia: A psycholinguistic approach. *Journal of Psycholinguistic Research, 2*(3), 175–199.

Massaro, D. W. (1975). *Understanding language: An information processing analysis of speech, perception, reading, and psycholinguistics.* New York: Academic Press.

McClelland, J. L., & Rumelhart, D. E. (1981). An interactive activation model of context effects in letter perception: Part 1. An account of basic findings. *Psychological Review, 88,* 375–405.

Mesrich, J. J. (1973). The word superiority effect in brief visual displays: Elimination by vocalization. *Perception and Psychophysics, 13,* 45–48.

Morton, J. (1964). The effects of context on the visual duration thresholds for words. *British Journal of Psychology, 55,* 165–180.

Morton, J. (1969). Interaction of information in word recognition. *Psychological Review, 76,* 165–178.

Murrell, C. A., & Morton, J. (1974). Word recognition and morphemic structure. *Journal of Experimental Psychology, 102,* 963–968.

Nicholson, T. (1991). Do children read words better in context or in lists? A classic study revisited. *Journal of Educational Psychology, 83,* (4), 444–450.

Olson, D. R. (1980). From utterance to text: The bias of language in speech and writing. In M. Wolf, M. K. McQuillan, & E. Radwin (Eds.), *Thought & language/Language & reading* (Harvard Educational Review Reprint series no. 14) (pp. 84–108). Cambridge, MA: Harvard Educational Review.

Olson, D. R. (1986). The cognitive consequences of literacy. *Canadian Psychology, 27*(2), 109–121.

Papp, K. R., Newsome, S., McDonald, J. E., & Schaneveldt, R. W. (1982). An activation-verification model for letter and word recognition: The word-superiority effect. *Psychological Review, 89,* 573–594.

Patterson, K. E., Marshall, J. C., & Coltheart, M. (Eds.). (1985). *Surface dyslexia.* London: Erlbaum.

Perfetti, C. A. (1985). *Reading ability.* New York: Oxford University Press.

Perfetti, C. A. (1992). The representation problem in reading acquisition. In P. Gough, L. Ehri, & R. Treiman (Eds.), *Reading acquisition* (pp. 145–174). Hillsdale, NJ: Erlbaum.

Perfetti, C. A., & Hogaboam, T. W. (1975). The relationship between single word decoding and reading comprehension skill. *Journal of Educational Psychology, 67,* 461–469.

Perfetti, C. A., & Roth, S. (1981). Same of the interactive processes in reading and their role in reading skill. In A. M. Lesgold & C. A. Perfetti (Eds.), *Interactive processes in reading* (pp. 269–297). Hillsdale, NJ: Erlbaum.

Perfetti, C. A., Beck, I., Bell, L. C., & Hughes, C. (1987). Phonemic knowledge and learning to read are reciprocal: A longitudinal study of first grade children. *Merrill Palmer Quarterly, 33,* 283–319.

Perfetti, C. A., Bell, L. C., & Delaney, S. M. (1988). Automatic (prelexical) phonetic activation in silent word reading: Evidence from backward masking. *Journal of Memory and Language, 27,* 59–70.

Petersen, R. J., & LaBerge, D. (1977). Contextual control of letter perception. *Memory and Cognition, 5,* 205–213.

Prinzmetal, W., Treiman, R., & Rho, S. H. (1988). How to see a reading unit. *Journal of Memory and Language, 25,* 461–475.

Rayner, K., & Pollatsek, A. (1989). *The psychology of reading.* Englewood Cliffs, NJ: Prentice Hall.

Rayner, K., McConkie, G. W., & Zola, D. (1980). Integrating information across fixations. *Cognitive Psychology, 12,* 206–226.

Read, C. (1981). Writing is not the inverse of reading for young children. In C. H. Frederiksen & J. F. Dominic (Eds.), *Writing: The nature, development and teaching of written communication.* Hillsdale, NJ: Erlbaum.

Read, C., Yun-Fei, Z., Hong-Yin, N., & Bao-Qing, D. (1986). The ability to manipulate speech sounds depends on knowing alphabetic writing. *Cognition, 24,* 31–44.

Reicher, G. (1969). Perceptual recognition as a function of meaningfulness of stimulus material. *Journal of Experimental Psychology, 81,* 275–280.

Roswell, F., & Natchez, G. (1971). *Reading disability: Diagnosis and treatment.* New York: Basic Books.

Rubenstein, H., Lewis, S. S., & Rubenstein, M. A. (1971). Evidence for phonemic recoding in visual word recognition. *Journal of Verbal Learning and Verbal Behavior, 10,* 645–657.

Rumelhart, D. E., & McClelland, J. L. (1982a). An interactive model of context effects in letter perception: Part 2. The contextual enhancement effect and some tests and extensions of the model. *Psychological Review, 89,* 60–94.

Rumelhart, D. E., & McClelland, J. L. (1982b). Interactive processing through spreading activation. In A. M. Lesgold & C. A. Perfetti (Eds.), *Interactive processes in reading* (pp. 37–60). Hillsdale, NJ: Erlbaum.

Samuels, S. J., & Kamil, M. J. (1984). Models of the reading process. In P. D. Pearson, R. Barr, M. L. Kamil, & P. Mosenthal (Eds.), *Handbook of reading research* (Vol. I, pp. 185–224). New York and London: Longman.

Schmandt-Besserat, D. (1991). The earliest precursor of writing. In W. S-Y. Wang (Ed.), *The emergence of language: Development and evolution* (pp. 31–45). New York: Freeman.

Seidenberg, M. (1992). Dyslexia in a computational model of word recognition in reading. In P. Gough, R. Treiman, & L. Ehri (Eds.), *Reading acquisition* (pp. 243–273). Hillsdale, NJ: Erlbaum.

Seidenberg, M. S., & McClelland, J. L. (1989). A distributed developmental model of word recognition and naming. *Psychological Review, 96,* 523–568.

Seidenberg, M. S., Waters, G. S. Barnes, M. A., & Tannenhaus, M. K. (1984). When does irregular spelling or pronunciation influence word recognition? *Journal of Verbal Learning and Verbal Behavior, 23*, 383–404.

Selkirk, E. (1980). *On prosodic structure and its relation to syntactic structure.* Bloomington, IN: Indiana University Linguistics Club.

Smith, F. (1969). The use of featural dependencies across letters in the visual identification of words. *Journal of Verbal Learning and Verbal Behavior, 8*, 215–218.

Smith, F. (1971). *Understanding reading: A psycholinguistic analysis of reading and learning to read.* New York: Holt, Rinehart & Winston.

Smith, F. (1980). Making sense of reading—And of reading instruction. In M. Wolf, M. K. McQuillan, & E. Radwin (Eds.), *Thought & language/Language & reading* (Harvard Educational Review Reprint series no. 14) (pp. 415–424). Cambridge, MA: Harvard Educational Review.

Smith, F., Lott, D., & Cronnel, B. (1969). The effect of type size and case alternation on word identification. *American Journal of Psychology, 82*, 248–253.

Snow, C. E. (1973). Literacy and language: Relationships during the preschool years. *Harvard Educational Review, 53*, 165–189.

Snowling, M. (1987). *Dyslexia.* Oxford: Basil Blackwell.

Snowling, M. (1990). *Dyslexia: A cognitive developmental perspective.* Oxford: Basil Blackwell.

Spoehr, K. T. (1978). Phonological encoding in visual word recognition. *Journal of Verbal Learning and Verbal Behavior, 17*, 127–141.

Spoehr, K. T., & Smith, E. E. (1973). The role of syllables in perceptual processing. *Cognitive Psychology, 5*, 71–89.

Stanovich, K. E. (1980). Toward an interactive-compensatory model of individual differences in the development of reading fluency. *Reading Research Quarterly, 16*, 32–71.

Stanovich, K. E. (1986). "Matthew effects" in reading: Some consequences of individual differences in the acquisition of literacy. *Reading Research Quarterly, 4*, 360–407.

Stanovich, K. E. (1990). Concepts in developmental theories of reading skill: Cognitive resources, automaticity, and modularity. *Developmental Review, 19*, 72–100.

Stanovich, K. E. (1991). Word recognition: Changing perspectives. In R. Barr, M. L. Kamil, P. Mosenthal, & P. D. Pearson (Eds.), *Handbook of reading research* (Vol. II, pp. 418–452). New York and London: Longman.

Stanovich, K. E. (1992). Speculations on the causes and consequences of individual differences in early reading acquisition. In P. Gough, L. Ehri, & R. Treiman (Eds.), *Reading acquisition* (pp. 307–342). Hillsdale, NJ: Erlbaum.

Stanovich, K. E., & West, R. F. (1989). Exposure to print and orthographic processing. *Reading Research Quarterly, 24*, 402–433.

Stevenson, H. W., Stigler, J. W., Tucker, G. W., Lee, S. Y., Hsu, C. C., & Ketanusa, S. (1982). Reading disabilities: The case of Chinese, Japanese, and English. *Child Development, 53*, 1164–1181.

Taft, M. (1979). Lexical access via an orthographic code: The Basic Orthographic Syllable Structure (BOSS). *Journal of Verbal Learning and Verbal Behavior, 18*, 21–39.

Taft, M., & Forster, K. I. (1975). Lexical storage and retrieval of prefixed words. *Journal of Verbal Learning and Verbal Behavior, 14*, 638–647.

Taft, M., & Forster, K. I. (1976). Lexical storage and retrieval of polymorphic and polysyllabic words. *Journal of Verbal Learning and Verbal Behavior, 15*, 607–620.

Theois, J., & Muise, J. G. (1977). The word identification process in reading. In N. J. Castellan, D. B. Pisoni, & G. R. Potts (Eds.), *Cognitive theory* (Vol. 2, pp. 289–321). Hillsdale, NJ: Erlbaum.

Travers, J. R. (1973). The effects of forced serial processing on identification of words and random letter strings. *Cognitive Psychology, 5*, 109–137.

Treiman, R. (1985). Onsets and rhymes as units of spoken syllables: Evidence from children. *Journal of Experimental Child Psychology, 39*, 161–181.

Tulving, E., & Gold, C. (1963). Stimulus information and contextual information as determinants of tachistoscopic recognition of words. *Journal of Experimental Psychology, 66*, 319–327.

Tulving, E., & Pearlstone, Z. (1966). Availability versus accessibility of information in memory for words. *Journal of Verbal Learning and Verbal Behavior, 5*, 381–391.

Tulving, E., Mandler, G., & Baumal, R. (1964). Interaction of two sources of information in tachistoscopic word recognition. *Canadian Journal of Psychology, 18*, 62–71.

Tzeng, O., & Wang, W. S-Y. (1984). Search for a common neurocognitive mechanism for language and movements. *American Journal of Physiology, 246*, 904–911.

Van Orden, G. C. (1987). A ROWS is a ROSE: Spelling, sound and reading. *Memory and Cognition, 15*, 181–198.

Van Orden, G. C., Johnston, J. C., & Hale, B. L. (1988). Word identification in reading proceeds from spelling to sound meaning. *Journal of Experimental Psychology: Learning, Memory and Cognition, 14*, 371–385.

Van Orden, G. C., Pennington, B. F., & Stone, G. O. (1990). Word identification in reading and the promise of subsymbolic psycholinguistics. *Psychological Review, 97*, 1–35.

Vellutino, F. R. (1982). Theoretical issues in the study of word recognition: The unit of perception controversy re-examined. In S. Rosenberg (Ed.), *Handbook of applied psycholinguistics (pp. 33–197)*. Hillsdale, NJ: Erlbaum.

Vellutino, F. R. (1991a). Dyslexia. In W. S-Y. Wang (Ed.), *The emergence of language: Development and evolution* (pp. 159–170). New York: Freeman.

Vellutino, F. (1991b). Introduction to three studies on reading acquisition: Convergent findings on theoretical foundations of code oriented vs. whole language approaches to reading instruction. *Journal of Educational Psychology, 83, (4)*, 437–443.

Vellutino, F. R., & Scanlon, D. M. (1987). Phonological coding, phonological awareness, and reading ability: Evidence from a longitudinal and experimental study. *Merrill Palmer Quarterly, 33*, 321–363.

Vellutino, F. R., Scanlon, D. M., & Tanzman, M. S. (1990). Differential sensitivity to the meaning and structural attributes of printed words in poor and normal readers. *Learning and Individual Differences, 2*, 19–43.

Vellutino, F. R., Scanlon, D. M., DeSetto, L., & Pruzek, R. M. (1981). Developmental trends in the salience of meaning versus structural attributes of written words. *Psychological Research, 43*, 131–153.

Venezky, R. L. (1970). *The structure of English orthography*. The Hague: Mouton.

Vygotsky, L. S. (1962). *Thought and language*. Cambridge, MA: MIT Press.

Walsh, D., Price, G., & Cunningham, M. (1988). The critical but transitory importance of letter naming. *Reading Research Quarterly, 23*, 108–122.

Wang, W. S-Y. (Ed.). (1991). *The emergence of language: Development and evolution*. New York: Freeman.

Waters, G. S., & Seidenberg, M. S. (1985). Spelling-sound effects in reading: Time course and decision criteria. *Memory and Cognition, 13*, 557–572.

Weber, R. M. (1970). The linguistic analysis of first-grade reading errors. *Reading Research Quarterly, 5*, 427–445.

Wolf, M. (1991a). Naming speed and reading: The contribution of the cognitive neurosciences. *Reading Research Quarterly, 26 (2)*, 123–141.

Wolf, M. (1991b). The word-retrieval deficit hypothesis and developmental dyslexia. *Learning and Individual Differences, 3,* 205–223.

Wolf, M., & Dickinson, D. (1985). From oral to written language: Transitions in the school years. In J. B. Gleason (Ed.), *The development of language.* Columbus, OH: Merrill.

Wolf, M., & Obregón, M. (1992). Early naming deficits, developmental dyslexia, and a specific-deficit hypothesis. *Brain and Language, 42,* 219–247.

Wolf, M., Bally, H., & Morris, R. (1986). Automaticity, retrieval processes, and reading: A longitudinal study in average and impaired readers. *Child Development, 57,* 988–1000.

Bilingualism and Second Language Acquisition

CATHERINE E. SNOW
Harvard Graduate School of Education

Introduction

For most of us living in North America, the topic of bilingualism or second language (SL) acquisition seems rather remote from issues of language processing or language use. Of course, many Americans study a foreign language in high school or at university, but they often discover when travelling to the country where that language is spoken or seeing a movie in that language that their proficiency is extremely limited. Since few North Americans consider themselves bilingual, it is perhaps hard to realize that being monolingual is actually atypical; most of the people in the world are, in fact, bilingual to some extent. Some of these are bilingual because they have grown up in societies which are officially or pervasively bilingual, in which the citizens must learn more than one language to survive (e.g., Quebec, Belgium, Switzerland). Some are bilingual because their own language is not the language used in their nation for schooling, for politics, or for economic exchange. For example, Zulu speakers in South Africa must learn English and Malayalam speakers in India must learn Hindi and English if they wish to get good jobs or read signs or go to school. Some are bilingual because they are immigrants to a country that does not use their traditional language, such as Spanish or Khmer speakers in the United States. Others are bilingual because colonization has imposed another language on them, for example, Quechua or Aymara speakers in Peru, Equador, and Bolivia. Some are bilingual because they are members of an educated elite and have benefitted from tutors and travel. Others are bilingual because they see economic or professional advantages to acquiring foreign languages, such as the Korean business executive studying English or the aspirant diplomat learning Arabic. And some people are bilingual because they grew up in households where two languages were used regularly; these we might think of as "native bilinguals."

Given the vast array of situations in which one might learn a second language, it is important to start out by defining what we mean by "second language learning" or "bilingualism." Identifying someone as "bilingual" is often taken to mean "perfectly bilingual." In fact, as we will see, the notion "perfect bilingual" is not really very useful, since very few bilinguals use both their languages equally for the same sort of task. For example, the Chicano boy living in California probably finds it easier to talk about school in English, and about visits to his grandparents in Spanish. It is said that the great French mathematician Pascal always did arithmetic in French but algebra in English, because he had studied first in French and then in English schools. For the purposes of this chapter, then, we will use the term "bilingual" to mean anyone who actually functions to whatever degree in more than one language. This would exclude English speakers who use foreign words only to impress other English speakers (as in *Bush, our soi-disant leader, makes up through connections what he lacks in machismo*), but would include English speakers using high school French to talk to taxi drivers or waiters in Paris.

Another term we should define is "second language acquisition." Does it differ from "foreign language learning?" What about third and fourth languages? What about two languages learned simultaneously? Broadly speaking, we are using the term "second language acquisition" here for cases in which a learner who already has some degree of control over one language system is introduced to a second (or third or fourth). We are interested in second language acquisition whether it occurs in a situation where the later learned language is widely used or not, including contexts of exposure that may emphasize or be limited to either oral or to literate uses. We use the term to include second language acquisition in **submersion** settings (one learner surrounded by native speakers), **immersion** settings (a group of learners taught through the medium of the second language), or formal foreign language classrooms. One of the interesting questions that arises is how different the process of studying a second language is from that of picking it up naturally. Thus, the phenomenon of second language acquisition is defined here as encompassing all the following sorts of cases: a Vietnamese-speaking 5-year-old in the U.S. who starts kindergarten in a bilingual program; the Sesotho-speaking South African 8-year-old who simultaneously learns conversational Xhosa from playing with neighbor children and literacy in English from exposure to it in school; the upper-class Peruvian 10-year-old who learns from a hired English governess and tutor; the American Ph.D. student who takes a course in "Reading German" to pass his university's language requirement; and the Anglophone Canadian civil servant who enrolls in an evening French course in order to keep her job. The phenomenon is meant to include cases of second language acquisition that result in stable bilingualism, those that result in only transient or very limited retention of the second language, and those that result in loss of the primary language and its replacement by the second language as the speaker's stronger language. However, if two languages are learned simultaneously from birth, we will call that *"native bilingualism"* rather than second language acquisition.

A good portion of the research on second language acquisition has been motivated by very practical questions: How can we improve foreign language teaching? How can we predict who will be a good foreign language learner? How can we improve academic achievement for children who start school unable to speak English? How can we decide if children should be in mainstream or English as a second language classes? Is it confusing or too difficult for children to grow up learning two languages simultaneously? Other lines of research, though, have been attempts to use the special characteristics of the bilingual speaker or the bilingual brain to test hypotheses about psycholinguistics. Do bilinguals take longer to process sentences because they know more words? Do they experience interference between their two language systems? Is language localized in bilinguals' brains in the same way as in monolinguals' brains? Is learning a third or a fourth language faster than a second? Is it possible to learn a second language as an adult and become a native-like speaker?

In this chapter, we will address these and other questions. First, we present a review of research on native bilinguals—children growing up exposed to two languages from birth. Then, we turn to a review of what we know about second language learners and the process of second language acquisition. Since thinking and research on second language acquisition has been done by several, rather separate groups of researchers whose work has not been integrated into a single view, we will distinguish four major lines of research on second language acquisition, and review the contributions of each separately.

Figure 10.1

Second language acquisition includes learning a language in a submersion setting.

Growing up bilingual

Traute Taeschner grew up in a family that had emigrated from Germany to Brazil. As a child, she spoke German with her parents and many of her parents' friends and their children in the sizable German immigrant community of Brazil, but of course spoke Portuguese at school and with other friends. When she grew up, she moved to Italy, where she married an Italian and started studying language development. Her own children, Lisa and Giulia, were perfect subjects for a study of native bilingualism, since they heard almost exclusively German from their mother and Italian from their father. Taeschner wrote a book about her children's language development called *The sun is feminine*; the title refers to her 3-year-old daughter Giulia's insistence on saying *la sole* (instead of the correct *il sole*), presumably because she knew that *sun* was feminine in German (*die Sonne*). While this example focuses on an error resulting from being bilingual, in fact Lisa and Giulia both became fluent, native-like speakers of both German and Italian, as is typical if a child's parents are consistent in using the two languages.

As one might expect, during the earliest stages of language development Lisa and Giulia did not fully distinguish their two languages. In fact, of Giulia's first 90 words, only seven Italian words had direct German equivalents: *scotta (heiss), grazie (danke), tutto-tutto (alle-alle), fatto (fertig), la (da), no (nei),* and *si (ja)*. Only in the second stage of language development, after about 18 months of age, did Giulia or

Lisa start systematically to acquire translation equivalents. As is common with bilingual children, they became quite insistent on knowing such equivalents, sometimes refusing to believe that proper trademark nouns like Tic Tac or Kleenex could not be translated. Lisa and Giulia both also produced utterances that used elements of both German and Italian; these are called **code-switches** and are often taken to be evidence that bilinguals speak neither language really well. In fact, though code-switched utterances sometimes occur because the speaker has forgotten or does not know a word in the language being spoken, children often correct their code-switches, indicating that they know both languages but have experienced a sort of bilingual slip of the tongue.

Identifying code-switches with failure to retrieve the desired lexical items in the speech of bilingual children is overly simple, though. In families where two languages are spoken, code-switching is fairly common, with words selected from the language that best expresses the intent. Mario, a boy who grew up mostly in the United States but with a Bolivian mother and an Italian father who spoke Spanish with him, was considered by his linguist father to be stronger in Spanish than in English until at least age seven or eight (Fantini, 1985). Nonetheless, he produced many sentences like the following:

> *Sabes mi school bus no tiene un stop sign.*
> *Hoy, yo era line leader en mi escuela.*
> *Ponemos cranberries y marshmallows y despues se pone el glitter y con glue.*

Clearly, Mario uses English words for experiences that are closely associated with English for him—his school, and American style foods. If an entire community is bilingual, such as many communities of Puerto Ricans living on the mainland, then code-switching as Mario does becomes a community norm—a way of identifying oneself as a member of this bilingual community. It is not surprising, then, that in Puerto Rican Spanish as spoken both on the mainland and on the island certain words of English origin have come to be considered the norm, such as *brown* (instead of *marron*), *super* (for *superintendent*), *la carpeta* (to mean *carpet*, not folder), *la boila* (*boiler*), *lonchar* (*to lunch*) and so forth (Zentella, 1981).

Children like Mario, Lisa, and Giulia who grow up with two languages often display a rather precocious understanding of language and how it works. They develop metalinguistic skills earlier than monolingual children, because they know that names for things and ways of expressing ideas are arbitrary and different in every language (Hakuta & Diaz, 1985; Reynolds, 1990). Do such children suffer any deficits from being bilingual? There is considerable worry among preschool and primary teachers, speech pathologists, and pediatricians that bilingual households produce language delay or contribute to language problems, but there is no evidence to support this. Children who are learning two languages may show vocabulary scores in each language that are slightly below normal during the preschool years—but that is simply because such tests are normed on monolingual children and do not take into account that bilinguals are learning almost twice as many words in the same time.

Mario, Giulia, and Lisa maintained their bilingualism at least through their school years. Keeping children bilingual is not easy, however, when they are living in a country that uses only one of their languages. Children, like adults, tend to lose languages they don't use often, a phenomenon called *language attrition*. Language attrition is possible even for well established first languages among adults who go many years without speaking or hearing their native tongues. For children, language attrition can occur even faster. Once they attend school and have many friends with whom they use the societal language, they may start to forget the less useful language, or even refuse to speak it. It usually requires visits from monolingual grandparents or spending time in the country where that language is spoken to ensure maintenance, let alone continued growth.

One of the lessons we can learn from native bilinguals is that the notion "bilingual" is a very relative one. Even for children like Mario, Giulia, and Lisa who can all use two languages extremely well, there are situations when one language is easier or more accessible than the other. It is very unlikely to be the case that they are equally good in all aspects of both languages (Grosjean, 1982). They might read better in one language, tell jokes or play games better in the other, discuss dinosaurs better in one and geography in the other. When Mario went to school, his English became stronger than his Spanish; then spending periods of time in Bolivia and Mexico strengthened his Spanish while his English receded temporarily. If even native bilinguals have fluctuations of skill in their native languages, perhaps we should not worry so much about second language learners' mistakes and difficulties, and focus instead on how effectively they can communicate in their second language.

Theories of second language acquisition

Five major groups of researchers have contributed to our understanding of second language acquisition. The first group were foreign language educators worried about their students' progress. The second were child language researchers who noticed that second language acquisition might be similar in interesting ways to first language acquisition. A third group were linguists who wanted to use second language acquisition to test notions about language universals. A fourth group were psycholinguists who were interested in language processing issues. A fifth group were sociolinguists and anthropologists interested in how language is used in various social settings. Because of differences in their backgrounds and training, these five groups of researchers have focused on different questions about second language acquisition, and have used different groups of second language learners in their research. It is important to keep these differences in mind when thinking about their various contributions.

In reviewing these five lines of research, we will keep returning to some major questions about second language learning and learners:

Is there an optimal age for starting second language acquisition?
How long does it take to learn a second language?
Are there optimal conditions for the acquisition of a second language?

What are the characteristics of very good or very poor second language
  learners?

To what extent is second language acquisition like first language acquisition, in
  terms of: a) stages or intermediate steps; b) underlying acquisition
  processes; c) predictive or facilitative factors?

Can learners function as efficiently and as competently in communicating,
  learning, reading, and talking in a second as in a first language?

To what extent is performance in a second language affected positively or
  negatively by the structure of the first language?

To what extent is performance in a first language facilitated or impeded by the
  acquisition of a second language?

Foreign language educators' contributions

The oldest tradition in second language research is one based strongly in foreign language teaching; this approach derives from an age-old interest in issues of pedagogical efficiency and effectiveness in foreign language training. The best methods for foreign language teaching have been discussed at least since the time of the Roman Empire, when Greek slaves were kept in upper-class homes to ensure that Roman children would acquire knowledge of Greek. During the Middle Ages, monastery schools struggled to teach future monks and priests enough Latin to be able to say their prayers and read the Vulgate Bible. Today, foreign language teachers still flock to conventions to learn about the latest methods for ensuring their students' success.

People who teach foreign languages tend to think about knowledge of a second language as what they teach rather than what students learn—the product of the curriculum, like knowledge of trigonometry or American history. Prototypical second language learners for this research tradition are students in language courses, acquiring a second language through formal study, and are typically adolescents or adults rather than younger learners. The major research activities are dictated by the problems those learners have. Foreign language speakers typically have noticeable accents. They also make many errors in grammar, in morphology, and in word choice. Foreign language learners may progress quite slowly; or they may seem to be learning at a reasonable pace, but then slow down or even stop before they achieve either error free or fluent use of the foreign language. Students often hate their foreign language classes, finding them boring (the drills, the vocabulary lists) or threatening (the dialogues, the conversation lessons).

In attempting to solve these problems, teachers keep trying new methods of teaching foreign languages. Popular teaching methods show regular patterns of alternation between what are called *grammar/translation methods* and *direct methods*. Grammar/translation methods involve teaching about the foreign language in the students' first language, with assignments that involve a lot of reading and translation of the foreign language but relatively little use of it in conversation. Direct methods (such as the audio-lingual method) may ban the use of the first language in the classroom; they emphasize direct aural/oral encounters with the second language, submersion in it, and avoidance of stating formal rules (see Coleman, 1929; Handschin, 1940 for an historical perspective). Nowadays, most foreign language teaching involves some mixture of these two extremes, but there is still considerable question about what the best methods are, and whether they are the same for all learners.

A dominant theme in foreign language teaching based research has been the value of contrastive analysis as a basis for teaching and as a predictor of aspects of learning. Contrastive analysis involves analyzing two languages to see where they are different, and then using the differences as the basis for predicting errors and for developing curriculum. The presumption of contrastive analysis is that language is a set of habits; the habits established in one's first language might work well in a second language (positive transfer), but they might also produce errors called *interference errors* resulting from negative transfer. Thus, for example, contrastive analysis would predict that Spanish speakers would have little trouble learning English plurals or progressive verb forms, because there are very similar forms in Spanish. The English possessive, on the other hand, is structured very differently from the Spanish possessive (*John's mother* vs. *la madre de Juan*). Contrastive analysis predicts that Spanish speakers will find it difficult to learn this English structure, suggesting that it should be taught and drilled extensively.

Foreign language teaching based research has identified many of the specific phenomena that continue to intrigue researchers. This research tradition has alerted us to the difficulty of perfect second language learning and to the likelihood of *fossilization* of nonnative features in the speech of even very advanced learners (Selinker, 1972). The nature of typical errors has been extensively probed by foreign

Figure 10.2

Formal instruction

language researchers (see Nemser, 1971; Hatch, 1983, for an overview). Typical errors and areas of difficulty for learners of English include the following:

1. Japanese and Chinese speakers have particular difficulty learning where they should use articles (*a* and *the*) in English (Thomas, 1989), presumably because there are no articles in their native languages, and because it is very hard even for native English speakers to explain the rules for article use.
2. Using *do* and getting the order of auxiliary verbs right in questions and negatives seems particularly hard for many groups of English learners: Spanish (cited in Hatch, 1983), German (Wode, 1978), and Chinese (Huang & Hatch, 1978; see additional cases documented in Gass & Selinker, 1983, and in the second section of Bailey, Long, & Peck, 1983). Errors like, "*Know you where the bus stop is?*" can be seen as direct interference from German or French, but also as related to the intrinsic difficulty of figuring out how and where to use *do* in English.
3. German and French speakers may have difficulty with the order of adverbials in English, producing sentences like, "*I go tomorrow to school,*" which mimic the order of these elements in their native languages ("*Ich gehe Morgen nach Schule;*" "*je vais demain à l'école*").
4. Hebrew speakers have difficulty acquiring the correct use of the English perfect and progressive forms, since Hebrew marks only tense (present, past), and makes no distinction between ongoing and punctual actions ("*I ate,*" vs. "*I was eating,*"), nor between past completed actions and past actions with continued relevance to the present ("*I was married eight years,*" vs. "*I have been married eight years*").

A major problem that confronts foreign language teachers is that there are enormous individual differences in speed and ultimate attainment of learners. Some students in foreign language classrooms seem to make great progress, whereas others never get beyond the limits of vocabulary lists and very predictable drills. In attempts to explain these differences, researchers have sought to develop measures of foreign language aptitude (Carroll, 1981), perhaps under the assumption that students with very low aptitude should be excluded from foreign language classrooms. Carroll's aptitude test reflects four factors that predict success in foreign language learning: associative memory, sound-symbol association, inductive ability, and grammatical sensitivity. One study of an exceptionally skilled foreign language learner—a young man who spoke four foreign languages fluently after only relatively brief study and exposure—revealed that he had extremely good memory for new symbol systems, Carroll's first aptitude component (Novoa, Fein, & Obler, 1988). However, it should also be pointed out that Carroll's Modern Language Aptitude Test is far from a perfect predictor of foreign language progress, and that it may work much better for students in foreign language classes than for those learning a language outside the classroom.

Predictions from the Modern Language Aptitude Test are greatly improved if one adds a measure of how much the learner wants to know the language in question. Motivation plays a particularly important role in second language acquisition, as was first discussed by Gardner and Lambert (1972). They related progress in learning

Figure 10.3

Some countries, such as
Canada, are officially
bilingual.

French to students' views of French speakers and French culture. In Quebec, where
Anglophones looked down on local French speakers, high school students had a
harder time learning French than in the United States, where French was associated
with the high culture of France rather than with the lower-status Quebecois. Gardner and Lambert suggested that U.S. students were benefitting from *integrative
motivation,* or the desire to identify with the culture of the language being learned.
While it is clear that integrative motivation can be a powerful help to the student
struggling with a second language, other motives can also work. *Instrumental motivation,* as when students sense that they needed to learn English in order to get a good
job, worked much better as a predictor of progress in the Philippines than did integrative motivation; in fact, Americans are quite unpopular in the Philippines, and if
learning English were entirely dependent on integrative motivation there would be
little chance that most students would make any progress. Fortunately, instrumental
motivation can be quite powerful.

The shortcomings of foreign language teaching based research derive from its
focus on learning as something that happens in classrooms. A second language is
defined as what is included in the curriculum, rather than as an abstract system of
knowledge. Progress in learning is defined as eliminating errors from one's speech.
This basic assumption of research in this tradition is undermined by current views

about the nature of language and language learning (see Chapters 1 and 8). We now know that any language system is extremely complex, that many aspects of the grammar have never been described and thus cannot be directly taught, that the knowledge acquired by a competent speaker goes far beyond the information given in the input, and that the active, creative role of the learner is more important than the role of the teacher in any successful language learning process. Although at some level foreign language teaching researchers acknowledge the active role of the learner and concede that foreign language classrooms at best provide knowledge that can be drawn upon in situations of real SL processing to generate proficiency in the SL, the research activities they carry out do not fully reflect these understandings. Furthermore, this research focuses more on the product than the process of acquisition, and does not cast much light on the nature of second language acquisition for nonformal learners. Nor does it attempt to approach issues such as the consequences of being bilingual for the learner.

Child language researchers' contributions

The research on child language acquisition reviewed in Chapter 8 presents a picture of the child as an active learner who at every stage of language acquisition generates hypotheses and tries to organize what she/he knows about language into a system. Language acquisition researchers love the errors that children make, because they reveal the child's hypotheses and rules. This basic notion of language acquisition as an active process was seen in the early 1970s to apply to second language learners as well. Whereas foreign language teachers cringe at students' errors, child language researchers say *"Errors are a sign of progress," "Learning involves reorganizing knowledge, not just storing it,"* and *"Language acquisition is a developmental process."* This different view of language learning caused a minor revolution in foreign language teaching, and in the kind of research done on second language learning.

A defining question for child language-based researchers is whether second language acquisition is a simple recapitulation of first language acquisition, and if not, why and how it is different (Ervin-Tripp, 1974). Child language researchers are trying to figure out if there is an innate language acquisition capacity, and if so, how it relates to the role of the learner's linguistic environment and specialized ways of using that environment. In the earliest research on language acquisition, three areas were identified as domains of study: the child's language acquisition device (LAD), the language acquisition social support system (LASS) available to the child, and the nature of the language system that emerges. The process could be summarized in a simple equation: LAD + LASS = Language. A persistent source of controversy among first language acquisition researchers has been the relative weight that should be assigned to LAD versus LASS, and whether the LAD is specialized for language or reflects general information processing and complex learning systems. First language researchers have extensively described the nature of language input to young children; understanding the role of language input in second language acquisition was seen to be just as important.

The prototypical second language learner for first language-based researchers is a young child moved to a second language setting, or an older learner engaged in untutored acquisition. If such learners display the same pattern of acquisition as first language learners, then it can be argued that the same processes of hypothesis testing and rule generation operate for both. Evidence offered in support of this position are of the following kinds:

a) the occurrence of "developmental errors" by second language speakers, for example errors which are explainable as overgeneralizations based on features of the target language, rather than interference from features of the native language. Thus, learners of English as a second language, like young children, produce forms such as *hided* or *foots*. Even more strikingly, second language learners avoid transfer of idiomatic forms and highly marked structures from their first language, even sometimes in cases where these are acceptable in SL (see Jordens, 1977; Kellerman, 1977). Thus, for example, a French speaker learning Spanish might produce *"Estoy hambre,"* rather than *"Tengo hambre,"* despite the fact that the structure in French *"J'ai faim,"* is the same as in Spanish.

b) Recapitulation of the same order of acquisition shown by first language learners. For example, Hakuta (1976) studied a Japanese girl who showed the same order as native English speakers in acquiring the 14 frequently used inflectional morphemes of English. English speakers learning Dutch acquired the rules governing allomorphic variation (Snow, Smith, & Hoefnagel-Höhle, 1980) and those governing word order (Snow, 1981) in much the same order as native Dutch speakers. Cancino, Rosansky, and Schumann (1974, 1975) studied Spanish speakers learning English, and found stages very like those of native English speakers for developing control over negation and question formation.

c) Similar acquisition for speakers of different language backgrounds. If speakers of languages as different as French and Thai show similar errors or similar orders of acquisition in English, this argues that the target language exerts a greater effect on acquisition than habits brought over from the native language. Dulay and Burt (1974) found that Chinese and Spanish speakers acquire English morphemes in much the same order, despite the fact that Spanish is very similar to English on morphological marking, whereas Chinese is quite different. Fuller and Gundel (1987) showed that speakers of Chinese, Japanese, and Korean, all topic-prominent languages, were no more likely to use topic-fronting rules in English than speakers of Arabic, Farsi, and Spanish, which are subject-prominent languages like English. These researchers have argued that the order of acquisition, though not necessarily the same as that of first language learners, reflects developmental processes governed by the way English works rather than interference effects from the learners' own first languages.

d) Identifiable strategies of acquisition that mimic those of young first language learners. Just as young first language learners often acquire some handy phrases in which to put new words, second language learners also use imitated chunks or "modular patterns" as a first strategy for communicating, then move on to analyzing syntactic structure in these chunks (Rescorla & Okuda, 1987; Wong Fillmore, 1976). Just as first language learners gradually increase the length of their utterances, so do young second language learners (Huang & Hatch, 1978).

Questions about the nature (Long, 1985; Snow & Hoefnagel-Höhle, 1982) and helpful qualities (Tomasello & Herron, 1988, 1989) of input to second language learners have become an important topic. It is clear that learners in a foreign language classroom have very different input from first language learners, and thus might be expected to show a different order of acquisition and maybe even different sorts of mistakes. But what about the child submerged in a second language classroom? What about the immigrant adult learning English from co-workers? Can we say anything about how their linguistic environment helps them learn?

A first point is that quantity of input is very important in determining speed of second language acquisition. Even classroom based language learners who seek opportunities to practice with native speakers learn much faster than those who don't (Seliger, 1977). The good second language learner also elicits particularly helpful input by trying to talk and receiving feedback from native speakers (Day, 1985). It is interesting to think about whether classroom contexts replicate optimal environments for language learning (Faerch & Kasper, 1985), and how they might be changed based on what we know about first language acquisition. Such issues of optimal input and natural order of acquisition are of interest to foreign language teachers as well. For example, Tomasello and Herron (1988) have shown that letting SL learners make overgeneralization errors and receive corrections produces better and longer lasting learning than preteaching the rule that would preempt the error. In effect, they found gains from letting teachers make the kinds of responses that mothers make to young children's errors (see also Krashen, 1985, for examples of foreign language teaching devices borrowed from mothers' behaviors with their children).

Because child language researchers have a basic interest in development, they have emphasized the consequences of second language learning for the learner—that young bilinguals and second language learners have advantages in certain types of tasks (Hakuta & Diaz, 1985; Reynolds, 1990), in particular metalinguistic and language analysis tasks. They have also emphasized the interdependence between performance on first language and on second language tasks. It seems to make sense that a child who was a fast and untroubled first language learner will have an easier time with a second language. Cummins (1979) has even argued that certain levels of achievement in a child's first language constitute a threshold for the easy addition of a second language. Others (Johnson, 1989; Malakoff, 1988; Snow, 1990) have suggested that if conditions of acquisition for a first and a second language are very different (e.g., one learned at home and the other at school), patterns of second language skill may not resemble or depend on primary language skills to any great extent.

Linguists' approaches to second language acquisition

Linguists tend to focus on the abilities displayed or errors produced by SL learners when they are relevant to testing hypotheses about the extrapolation of Universal Grammar to second language acquisition. A major starting point for linguists is that, at every stage of acquisition, the learner is operating with an organized system of knowledge. For second language learners, there are likely to be many such systems en route to full control of the target language grammar (if that is ever attained); each of these can be called an *interlanguage grammar* (Selinker, 1972). One question is whether these interlanguage grammars display the same constraints as first language learners' grammars, or whether they include "unnatural" or impossible sorts of rules or structures. If so, then presumably second language learning is not subject to Universal Grammar—perhaps because the learner is past some critical period, as Long (1990) argues (but see Snow, 1983, 1987; Snow & Hoefnagel-Höhle, 1978, for counterarguments).

There is no clear orthodox position among Universal Grammar adherents about its relevance to second language learning. There are a variety of views about how powerfully Universal Grammar operates in second language acquisition (see White, 1990; papers in Flynn & O'Neil, 1988). Given the close identification of Universal Grammar with an acquisition device (the LAD) that many believe becomes inaccessible after the critical period, it would be perfectly possible to argue that adult second language learners operate very differently from first language learners because of lack of access to Universal Grammar (Clahsen & Muysken, 1986). However, most linguists suggest that Universal Grammar may be at least partially available to the second language learner, though perhaps mediated by the first language in ways that may make it relatively inaccessible. Universal Grammar differentiates between two components of LAD—the principles, which are universal and should still be available to constrain language acquisition at any age, and the parameters, which constitute a set of options that may be more or less irreversibly set by exposure to a first language. Especially if the first language causes one to set a parameter in a "marked" or more inclusive way, the resetting of the parameter to the less marked or more neutral setting may be difficult. Examples of difficult-to-reset parameters for which evidence has been proffered through second language acquisition research include head direction, for example, whether heads precede (as in English) or follow (as in Japanese) the rest of the material in the structure. As a right branching or *head-first* language, English displays a structure in which prepositions come first in prepositional phrases (IN the bathtub), head nouns precede their relative clauses (THE BOY who is taking a bath), and matrix sentences normally precede their adverbial clauses (I SAW HIM when he jumped in). In Japanese, all these constituents are reversed. Flynn (1987) has shown that Japanese learners of English have persistent difficulty with imitating and correctly interpreting heavily right-branching structures, when compared to learners who speak Arabic, a language which matches English on head direction. Hyams (1986) has similarly argued that it should be easier for English speakers to learn to reset the agreement parameter to allow pro-drop (the omission of redundant, verb agreement marked subject pronouns) in Spanish (*veo el arbol*, instead of *yo veo el arbol*) than it is for Spanish speakers to reset their parameter to always supply the subject pronoun in English ("*Is a very nice day today, no?*").

The linguists' research on second language acquisition has contributed enormously to our understanding of the complexity of the grammatical knowledge that must be acquired, and of one route for first language influence on the process. Linguists are not interested, though, in many aspects of second language skill that seem very important to learners: vocabulary, socially useful expressions, conversational rules, and so forth. Linguists are also not interested in the learner's communicative effectiveness, nor in differences associated with motivation, aptitude, input, or instruction.

Psycholinguists' approaches to second language processing

One way to think about language acquisition is to consider it as a special sort of information processing (McLaughlin, Rossman, & McLeod, 1983) or psycholinguistic processing. Under this view, learning a language and understanding a language are not so very different from one another; both involve parsing an auditory stimulus and connecting that parsed string to a semantic representation. For skilled speakers of a language, as for learners, some strings are hard to parse, whether because they contain novel lexical items, acoustically unclear elements, or obscure referents. The major difference between the skilled speaker and the learner, in the view of the psycholinguist, is that the skilled speaker will more readily question or reject a string if interpretation proves difficult, whereas the learner is under greater pressure to try to incorporate all newly encountered structures into his/her system.

If learning a language is simply a matter of processing certain kinds of information efficiently, one might expect that learners who have already acquired several languages would be more skilled than monolingual learners. In fact, support for the notion of language learning as a processing skill at which one can get better with practice is supported by findings that "expert" (i.e., multilingual) language learners do much better than "novice" (monolingual) learners in acquiring a novel, artificial language (artificial languages are used in this sort of work to exclude any positive transfer from any of the languages known by the multilinguals; Nation & McLaughlin, 1986).

Psycholinguistic processing approaches to language acquisition acknowledge the likelihood of interference, but argue that interference from a first language to a second language operates at the level of processing tendencies, not habits (as the foreign language teacher might think), rules (as the child language researcher thinks), or parameters (as the linguist thinks). One psycholinguistic processing model extensively applied to SL research has been the **competition model** (Bates & MacWhinney, 1981; MacWhinney, 1987). The competition model proposes that sentence interpretation is governed by accumulated knowledge of the likelihood that certain cues indicate certain semantic roles. Thus, in English for example, the first noun in a sentence is very likely to indicate the actor: "The dog ate the bone." Thus, the hypothesis that first noun = actor has a very high probability for any speaker of

English, though it can be undermined by conflicting or competing cues, for example, that the first noun is not animate: "The bone ate the dog;" does not agree with the verb: "His parents above all loves the good boy;" or is pragmatically unlikely: "The patient cured the doctor." Competition theory suggests that the cue strengths from the first language are likely to be carried over into the early stages of second language processing, at least if the same cues are available in the second language. If the cue strengths of the first and second language match, this may operate in the learner's favor. However, quite often they do not match, even in closely related languages. English, Italian, and Dutch all have animacy, position, and agreement available as cues to the actor; but if these are in conflict with one another in the same sentence, then English speakers choose to rely on first position as the strongest cue. In Italian, animacy is much more important, and in Dutch agreement plays a much more dominant role (Gass, 1987; McDonald, 1987; Kilborn & Cooreman, 1987). Thus, one's acquisition of a second language can be impeded by the processing tendencies one imports from the native language, and even quite far into second language acquisition one might display a processing "accent." Further developments can go in many directions; some SL speakers manage to develop systems that mimic native speakers' systems closely, whereas others, particularly in social settings that permit a lot of code-switching, develop for use in both languages a merged system that represents a compromise between the systems of monolingual native speakers of both languages.

Psycholinguistic processing approaches to second language acquisition completely break down the distinction between comprehension and learning. Furthermore, under psycholinguistic processing approaches, learning a second language is just like learning one's first language except that one is starting with more information. The focus of psycholinguistic processing models is performance rather than competence, strategies rather than rules. Even native speakers of a language can show alternate patterns of preference for various cues (Harrington, 1987), suggesting that the notion "the native speaker" has somewhat less central status in psycholinguistic than in competence-based models, and thus that the distinction between first and second language speakers is also less sharp. There is no threshold of proficiency that defines a native speaker or a perfect bilingual, because acquisition is conceived of as continuous and likely in response to new information in any language.

Since processing speed and ease is a function of the amount of information available to be dealt with, it seems quite unsurprising within a psycholinguistic processing perspective that there can be processing costs to becoming bilingual. Bilinguals show slightly depressed reading speed, presumably because of their increased lexical retrieval times (Mägiste, 1979, 1987), and may well end up completely unable to separate their phonetic (Caramazza, Yeni-Komshian, Zurif, & Carbone, 1973; Mack, 1984) and syntactic judgment systems (Mack, 1984). On the other hand, such deficits are minor, and are evidently restricted to situations in which both languages are in relatively constant use. Psycholinguistic processing approaches have little difficulty in accounting for the widely reported ebb and flow of skill in language as a function of its use (see Grosjean, 1982, for examples), or even for significant amounts of attrition in one's first language (see Cohen & Weltens, 1989; Mägiste, 1987), since the accessibility of lexical items or syntactic structures in a language is clearly strongly affected by recent processing history.

Psycholinguistic processing approaches have little to say about learner factors that affect the speed or course of second language acquisition, focusing instead on the relation between the first and the second language in their reliance on various cues. Learning a second language is simply a matter of experiencing it and making attempts to comprehend it. There is no expectation of large individual differences in style or strategy of acquisition, unless input experiences differ widely. Psycholinguistic processing approaches reduce second language acquisition to a problem of input and processing efficiency, with little attention to the larger cultural and social context within which it occurs.

Sociocultural approaches to second language learning

When psycholinguists, developmental psychologists, and linguists think about second language acquisition, they emphasize the cognitive side of the picture—the problems faced by the learner acquiring a complex system that has more or less overlap with complex systems already acquired. Sociologists, social psychologists, anthropologists, and sociolinguists, on the other hand, think about the societal context of bilingualism. They point out that multilingualism is very common across the world and that more children are expected to grow up and learn two languages than not. They point out that language use is tied closely to personal identity, to cultural identification, to national or ethnic pride, to specific communicative tasks or situations, and to a set of attitudes and beliefs that have an impact on the course of second language acquisition. They point out that becoming too good a speaker of a second language can threaten the personal identity of the learner—that there can be reasons to remain less than perfectly bilingual if the second language is one that has some negative associations for the learner. At the same time, perfect control over accent or grammar may not relate to effectiveness in achieving communicative aims in the second language. One study showed that, among immigrants from Europe to the States during the period before the second world war, psychiatrists retained their German accents longer than those in other professions; we can only speculate that their professional credibility was actually enhanced by the maintenance of a foreign accent!

For those who approach second language acquisition from a sociocultural perspective, speaking two languages is simply an extension of what monolinguals do when exploiting the potential for variability within a language. Adjustments of vocabulary choice, grammar, and morphology to different addressees and situations is within the competence of all language users. Socially appropriate speakers of English may express anger to a colleague by saying, "shit," but to a child or a minister by saying "darn;" similarly a bilingual says "chair," to an English listener and, "silla," to a Spanish listener. Failure to make these sorts of adjustments might reflect feelings of hostility to the addressee, or a need to project a certain kind of personal and social identity for oneself. It need not be seen as a failure of "proficiency."

Many issues which seem intractable within the more cognitive and psycholinguistic approaches to second language acquisition are dealt with easily from the sociocultural perspective. Whereas the other approaches identify a linguistic norm, typically defined by the competence of the "native speaker," toward which the learner is clearly moving, sociocultural approaches recognize the social nature of language use and the impossibility of identifying better or worse varieties of any language. Around the world, for example, regional varieties of English are being established in countries like India and Nigeria; these are spoken in those countries only as second languages, and they have many nonstandard features (which we might consider errors, using British or American English as the standard). Nonetheless, these varieties are the appropriate targets of acquisition for speakers in those countries, who actively disprefer British, American, or Commonwealth varieties of English (Lowenberg, 1986).

Within sociocultural approaches, notions like language proficiency are replaced by notions like communicative effectiveness and social appropriateness. Whereas first language-based researchers struggle with the question of whether adult second language learners can become perfect bilinguals, sociocultural approaches emphasize the effective functioning in second languages of children and adults all over the world; since control over a first language includes a lot of variability in performance, it is not of central theoretical interest that such is also the case for second language users.

Sociocultural approaches are particularly helpful in understanding the social and cultural pressures affecting second language learners in situations where the social value attached to their first and their second language differs greatly. Why is it that children of immigrant families in the U.S. switch so rapidly to function better in English than in their parents' language? Simple psycholinguistic analyses cannot answer this question easily, but calculating the stigmatization associated with traditional languages and the value attached to speaking English as a marker of being an American can provide an answer. Why is it that in two-way bilingual programs, Spanish speakers learn English faster than English speakers learn Spanish? Perhaps even kindergarten-aged children are well aware of society's negative evaluation of Spanish speakers. Furthermore, if the Spanish speakers in those two-way programs learn English, they are very likely to lose Spanish (*subtractive bilingualism*), whereas the English speakers who learn Spanish will retain English (*additive bilingualism*)— a distinction which is only comprehensible with an understanding of the social context. How could a tiny Anglophone minority survive for generations in Quebec without learning any French? It seems impossible until the sociolinguistics of the relations between French and English speakers and the relative power and status of the two groups are considered. Why is it that Quechua-Spanish bilingual programs are on the decline in Peru, even though Quechua speaking children perform much better in them than in all Spanish classrooms? A culturally based analysis suggests that Quechua is not seen by Quechua speaking parents as an appropriate language for the school sphere (Hornberger, 1987, 1988). Understanding the patterns of language choice and language proficiency for an individual or a community requires understanding that language is a sociocultural phenomenon and not just a cognitive achievement.

Sociocultural approaches to second language acquisition de-emphasize the importance of grammatical or phonological correctness, but they open up an additional domain of complexity for the second language learner—the rules governing communicative effectiveness and social appropriateness. These rule systems are complex and as language specific as rules are for word order or morphology, though like grammar they have been described as having a universal "core" (Brown & Levinson, 1978). Cultural systems differ sufficiently that, though one can translate many words from one language to another with reasonable success, one can hardly ever translate "speech acts" directly without inviting miscommunication (Blum-Kulka, 1983). "We must have lunch sometime," is a friendly way of saying "good-bye" in American English, but its translation into French would be considered a sincere invitation (Wolfson, d'Amico-Reisner, & Huber, 1983); it is not surprising that French speakers think Americans are unfriendly and insincere, if they hear many such invitations that are never followed up on! In English it is appropriate to use indirect or polite forms with those serving you, so a boss might say, "Would you mind typing this?" to a secretary, and a customer in a restaurant says, "May I please see a menu?" In Spanish, "Bring me a menu," is perfectly appropriate; the Spanish speaker who translates that speech act (and its associated implications for social relationships) into English would be considered arrogant. It is not surprising, in light of differences like this, that highly developed bilinguals think of themselves as having different personalities in their different languages.

Sociocultural approaches to second language acquisition make clear that, in some sense, learning a second language means joining a second culture, not just acquiring a new system of grammar or a better accent. Speaking a new language means participating as a member of a certain group, engaging in a variety of novel social interactions, and establishing an enhanced or a changed personal identity.

Summary

In order to summarize what we know about second language acquisition from each of the five groups of researchers who have tackled the problem, let us return to our list of eight major questions and see how each question is answered by each of the lines of research.

Is there an optimal age for starting second language acquisition?

Foreign language teachers typically encounter adolescent and adult learners, so this question is not directly addressed by their research. However, evaluation of programs with preadolescent foreign language students (e.g., the FLES or Foreign Language in the Elementary School programs) reveal that younger children are considerably slower than high school-aged children or adults at learning languages through formal teaching. Child language researchers have pointed out that, contrary to what is generally believed, older learners also acquire second languages faster than younger ones in untutored settings (Snow 1983, 1987; Snow & Hoefnagel-Höhle, 1978), though older learners are also more likely to be subject to fossilization and persistent accents (Krashen, Long, & Scarcella, 1982), so their ultimate attainment may be lower. Linguists, because of their commitment to the notion of a biological substrate for language, are inclined to believe in the **critical period** hypothesis, which states that "normal" language acquisition must occur in (early) childhood. Neither the psycholinguists nor those taking sociocultural approaches to second language acquisition take much interest in the issue of an optimal age for learning; they see the process as gradual and incremental at all ages.

How long does it take to learn a second language?

Foreign language teachers point out that it takes more time to learn a very distant language, such as Chinese, than a closely related one like Spanish; taking language into account, becoming a proficient second language speaker takes two to four years of classroom exposure at the college level, plus a period of immersion to achieve full fluency. Child language researchers point out that it takes a child ten to twelve years to achieve full control over oral and literate uses of a first language; starting somewhat later means somewhat faster acquisition, but nonetheless it is quite normal for school-aged children to take as long as six or seven years to function like first language speakers, though some manage in only two or three years. Linguists have not paid much attention to this issue, and psycholinguists think of acquisition as something that continues throughout the learner's lifetime, though it slows down as fewer and fewer new structures are encountered. Sociolinguists do not have very clear criteria for deciding on native-like proficiency, so they do not consider this an interesting issue.

Are there optimal conditions for the acquisition of a second language?

Clearly, the foreign language teacher thinks that a well designed curriculum implemented by a native speaking teacher and supplemented by many opportunities for practice is the optimal condition. Child language researchers would emphasize the availability to the second language learner of the conditions that obtain for young first language learners: opportunities for conversations on topics of interest to the learner with native speakers who provide input adjusted to the learner's level, who provide conversational responses that build on learners' attempts, who are genuinely interested in communicating with the learner, and who have a positive affective relationship with the learner. Linguists are relatively uninterested in individual differences in speed of acquisition, and have not addressed this question. Psycholinguists would identify optimal conditions for learning with the opportunity to hear lots of sentences paired with information about meaning, perhaps with some manipulation of cue conflicts to sharpen learners' hypotheses. Finally, the sociocultural theorists would argue that conditions of social equality between members of the learner group and the target language speakers are optimal, and either mutual respect or perhaps personal intimacy between the learner and some native speaker interlocutors is desirable.

What are the characteristics of very good or very poor second language learners?

Foreign language teachers think good learners are like good students in any subject—those who work hard, are motivated, and score high on the Modern Language Aptitude Test. Child language researchers emphasize the learner's capacity to elicit input from native speakers—outgoing, talkative, uninhibited learners are probably better at this—and their willingness to generate and test hypotheses about the target language based on partial data. Linguists emphasize the sensitivity of the learner to information about the target language, and perhaps a gift for metalinguistic analysis as well. Psycholinguists would not predict large individual differences except those associated with efficiency of information processing. Sociocultural theorists would emphasize openness of the learner to other cultures, willingness to try on alternative social selves, and willingness to risk one's dignity in sincere communicative attempts.

To what extent is second language acquisition like first language acquisition, in terms of: a) stages or intermediate steps; b) underlying acquisition processes; c) predictive or facilitative factors?

The first language researchers and the psycholinguists come down most strongly on the affirmative in response to this question, assuming in both cases that the conditions of acquisition for the first and the second language are somewhat similar. Foreign language teachers emphasize the differences introduced by prior knowledge of a first language, whereas linguists emphasize as well the possibility that post critical period learning might be quite different from first language learning. Sociocultural theorists don't much care about this question, but would see both first and second language acquisition as strongly driven by communicative and social needs.

Can learners function as efficiently and as competently in communicating, learning, reading, and talking in a second as in a first language?

Foreign language teachers, child language researchers, and linguists agree that there is some small percentage of second language learners who become native-like, though these three groups would disagree on the reasons why most learners do not. Psycholinguists and sociocultural theorists downplay the notion of "perfect competence" for the native speaker, pointing out that even a native speaker may still be adjusting to the system as an adult; in this way, second language learners are not so different from first language learners.

To what extent is performance in a second language affected positively or negatively by the structure of the first language?

Foreign language teachers and linguists would be most prone to argue for a transfer effect from first to second language, though psycholinguists and sociocultural theorists also acknowledge such effects, in processing tendencies and communicative rules respectively. Child language theorists are the least likely to attribute a large role in second language acquisition to transfer.

To what extent is performance in a first language facilitated or impeded by the acquisition of a second language?

Neither linguists nor foreign language teachers confront the possibility that a first language might be affected by a second language—they attribute a different, special status to one's mother tongue. Child language researchers, on the other hand, often see cases of language attrition, and conversely see the positive effects of heightened metalinguistic skills in a first language from learning a second language. Psycholinguists have documented cases in which bilinguals achieve a merged processing system for their first and second languages, possibly with some negative consequences for speed of processing in the first language. Finally, sociocultural theorists acknowledge the possibility of first language attrition under conditions of low status, but also of the bilingual's enhanced understanding of communicative situations across both languages.

Clearly, many of the disagreements and differing conclusions by researchers from these varying groups reflect their interests in different aspects of the phenomenon of bilingualism and second language acquisition. Perhaps future research will be able to merge two or three of these perspectives, to ensure that full attention is paid to the role of the learner, the environment, and the broader social context in understanding what second language learners acquire and how they acquire it.

References

Bailey, K., Long, M., & Peck, S. (Eds.). (1983). *Second language acquisition studies*. Rowley, MA: Newbury House.

Bates, E., & MacWhinney, B. (1981). Second language acquisition from a functionalist perspective: Pragmatic, semantic, and perceptual strategies. In H. Winitz (Ed.), *Annals of the New York Academy of Science Conference on Native and Foreign Language Acquisition*. New York: New York Academy of Sciences.

Blum-Kulka, S. (1983). Interpreting and performing speech acts in a second language: A crosscultural study of Hebrew and English. In N. Wolfson & E. Judd (Eds.), *Sociolinguistics and language acquisition*. Rowley, MA: Newbury House.

Brown, P., & Levinson, S. (1978). Universals in language usage: Politeness phenomena. In E. Goody (Ed.), *Questions and politeness: Strategies in social interaction*. Cambridge, MA: Cambridge University Press.

Cancino, H., Rosansky, E., & Schumann, J. (1974). Testing hypotheses about second language acquisition: The copula and the negative in three subjects. *Working Papers in Bilingualism, 3*, 80–96.

Cancino, H., Rosansky, E., & Schumann, J. (1975). The acquisition of the English auxiliary by native Spanish speakers. *TESOL Quarterly, 9*, 421–430.

Carramazza, A., Yeni-Komshian, G., Zurif, E., & Carbone, E. (1973). The acquisition of a new phonological contrast: The case of stop consonants in French-English bilinguals. *Journal of the Acoustical Society of America, 54*, 421–428.

Carroll, J. (1981). Twenty-five years of research on foreign language aptitude. In K. Diller (Ed.), *Individual differences and universals in language learning aptitude*. Rowley, MA: Newbury House.

Clahsen, H., & Muysken, P. (1986). The availability of Universal Grammar to adult and child learners: A study of the acquisition of German word order. *Second Language Research, 2*, 93–119.

Clark, J. L. D., & Clifford, R. T. (1988). The FSI/ILR/ACTFL proficiency scales and testing techniques: Development, current status, and needed research. *Studies in Second Language Acquisition, 10*, 129–148.

Cohen, A., & Weltens, B. (Eds.). (1989). Language Attrition. Special issue of *Studies in Second Language Acquisition, 11*, 127–216.

Coleman, A. (1929). *The teaching of modern foreign languages in the United States*. New York: Macmillan.

Comrie, B. (1990). Second language acquisition and language universals research. *Studies in Second Language Acquisition, 12*, 209–218.

Cummins, J. (1979). Linguistic interdependence and the educational development of bilingual children. *Review of Educational Research, 49*, 222–251.

Day, R. (1985). The use of the target language in context and second language proficiency. In S. Gass & C. Madden (Eds.), *Input in second language acquisition*. Rowley, MA: Newbury House.

Dulay, H., & Burt, M. (1974). Errors and strategies in child second language acquisition. *TESOL Quarterly, 8*, 129–138.

Ervin-Tripp, S. (1974). Is second language learning like the first? *TESOL Quarterly, 8*, 111–127.

Faerch, C., & Kasper, G. (Eds.). (1985). Foreign language learning under classroom conditions. Special issue of *Studies in Second Language Acquisition, 7*, 131–248.

Fantini, A. (1985). *Language acquisition of a bilingual child: A sociolinguistic perspective (to age 10)*. San Diego, CA: College-Hill Press.

Flynn, S. (1987). *A parameter-setting model of L2 acquisition: Experimental studies in anaphora*. Dordrecht: Reidel.

Flynn, S., & O'Neil, W. (Eds.). (1988). *Linguistic theory in second language acquisition*. Dordrecht: Kluwer.

Fuller, J. W., & Gundel, J. K. (1987). Topic-prominence in interlanguage. *Language Learning, 37*, 1–18.

Gardner, R. C., & Lambert, W. (1972). *Attitudes and motivation in second-language learning*. Rowley, MA: Newbury House.

Gass, S. (1987). The resolution of conflicts among competing systems: A bidirectional perspective. *Applied Psycholinguistics, 4*, 329–350.

Grosjean, F. (1982). *Life with two languages: An introduction to bilingualism.* Cambridge, MA: Harvard University Press.

Hakuta, K. (1976). A case study of a Japanese child learning English as a second language. *Language Learning, 26,* 321–351.

Hakuta, K., & Diaz, R. (1985). The relationship between degree of bilingualism and cognitive ability: A critical discussion and some new longitudinal data. In K. E. Nelson (Ed.), *Children's Language* (Vol. 5). Hillsdale, NJ: Erlbaum.

Handschin, C. (1940). *Modern-language teaching.* Yonkers-on-Hudson: World Book.

Harrington, M. (1987). Processing transfer: Language specific processing strategies as a source of interlanguage variation. *Applied Psycholinguistics, 8,* 351–378.

Hatch, E. (1983). *Psycholinguistics: A second language perspective.* Rowley, MA: Newbury House.

Hornberger, N. (1987). Bilingual education success but policy failure. *Language in Society, 16,* 205–226.

Hornberger, N. (1988). *Bilingual education and language maintenance: A southern Peruvian Quechua case.* Dordrecht: Foris.

Huang, J., & Hatch, E. (1978). A Chinese child's acquisition of English. In E. Hatch (Ed.), *Second language acquisition.* Rowley, MA: Newbury House.

Hyams, N. (1986). *Language acquisition and the theory of parameters.* Dordrecht: Reidel.

Johnson, J. (1989). Factors related to cross-language transfer and metaphor interpretation in bilingual children. *Applied Psycholinguistics, 10,* 157–178.

Jordens, P. (1977). Rules, grammatical intuitions, and strategies in foreign language learning. *Interlanguage Studies Bulletin, 2*(2), 5–76.

Kellerman, E. (1977). Towards a characterization of the strategy of transfer in second language learning. *Interlanguage Studies Bulletin, 2*(1), 58–145.

Kilborn, K., & Cooreman, A. (1987). Sentence interpretation strategies in adult Dutch-English bilinguals. *Applied Psycholinguistics, 8,* 415–431.

Krashen, S. (1985). *The input hypothesis: Issues and implications.* London: Longman.

Krashen, S., Long, M., & Scarcella, R. (1982). Age, rate, and eventual attainment in second language acquisition. In S. Krashen, R. Scarcella, & M. Long (Eds.), *Child-adult differences in second language acquisition.* Rowley, MA: Newbury House.

Long, M. (1985). Input and second language acquisition theory. In S. Gass & C. Madden (Eds.), *Input in second language acquisition.* Rowley, MA: Newbury Press.

Long, M. (1990). Maturational constraints on language development. *Studies in Second Language Acquisition, 12,* 251–286.

Lowenberg, P. (1986). Nonnative varieties of English: Nativization, norms, and implications. *Studies in Second Language Acquisition, 8,* 1–18.

Mack, M. (1984). Early bilinguals: How monolingual-like are they? In M. Paradis & Y. LeBrun (Eds.), *Early bilingualism and child development.* Lisse: Swets & Zeitlinger.

MacWhinney, B. (1987). Applying the competition model to bilingualism. *Applied Psycholinguistics, 8,* 315–328.

Mägiste, E. (1979). The competing language systems of the multilingual: A developmental study of decoding and encoding processes. *Journal of Verbal Learning and Verbal Behavior, 18,* 79–89.

Mägiste, E. (1987). Further evidence for the optimal age hypothesis in second language learning. In J. Lantolf & A. LaBarca (Eds.), *Research in second language learning: Focus on the Classroom.* Norwood, NJ: Ablex.

Malakoff, M. (1988). The effect of language instruction on reasoning in bilingual children. *Applied Psycholinguistics, 9,* 17–38.

McDonald, J. L. (1987). Sentence interpretation in bilingual speakers of English and Dutch. *Applied Psycholinguistics, 8*, 379–414.

McLaughlin, B., Rossman, T., & McLeod, B. (1983). Second language learning: An information processing perspective. *Language Learning, 33*, 135–158.

Nation, R., & McLaughlin, B. (1986). Novices and experts: An information processing approach to the "good language learner" problem. *Applied Psycholinguistics, 7*, 41–56.

Novoa, L., Fein, D., & Obler, L. (1988). Talent in foreign languages: A case study. In L. Obler & D. Fein (Eds.), *The exceptional brain: Neuropsychology of talent and special abilities.* New York: Guilford.

Rescorla, L., & Okuda, S. (1987). Modular patterns in second language acquisition. *Applied Psycholinguistics, 8*, 281–308.

Reynolds, A. (1990). The cognitive consequences of bilingualism. In A. G. Reynolds (Ed.), *Bilingualism, multiculturalism, and second language learning: The McGill conference in honor of Wallace E. Lambert.* Hillsdale, NJ: Erlbaum.

Seliger, H. (1977). Does practice make perfect? A study of interaction patterns and L2 competence. *Language Learning, 27*, 263–278.

Selinker, L. (1972). Interlanguage. *International Review of Applied Linguistics, 10*, 219–231.

Snow, C. E. (1981). English speakers' acquisition of Dutch syntax. In H. Winitz (Ed.), *Native language and foreign language acquisition. Annals of the New York Academy of Sciences* (Vol. 379). New York: New York Academy of Sciences.

Snow, C. E. (1983). Age differences in second language acquisition: Research findings and folk psychology. In K. Bailey, M. Long, & S. Peck (Eds.), *Second language acquisition studies.* Rowley, MA: Newbury House.

Snow, C. E. (1987). Relevance of the notion of a critical period to language acquisition. In M. Bornstein (Ed.), *Sensitive periods in development: An interdisciplinary perspective.* Hillsdale, NJ: Erlbaum.

Snow, C. E. (1990). Diverse conversational contexts for the acquisition of various language skills. In J. Miller (Ed.), *Progress in research on child language disorders.* New York: Little, Brown & Co.

Snow, C. E., & Hoefnagel-Höhle, M. (1978). Critical period for language acquisition: Evidence from second language learning. *Child Development, 49*, 1263–1279.

Snow, C. E., & Hoefnagel-Höhle, M. (1982). School-age second language learners' access to simplified linguistic input. *Language Learning, 32*, 411–430.

Snow, C. E., Smith, N. S., & Hoefnagel-Höhle, M. (1980). The acquisition of some Dutch morphological rules. *Journal of Child Language, 7*, 539–553.

Stubbs, J., & Tucker, G. (1974). The close test as a measure of English proficiency. *The Modern Language Journal, 58*, 239–241.

Taeschner, T. (1983). *The sun is feminine: A study on language acquisition in bilingual children.* Berlin: Springer-Verlag.

Thomas, M. (1989). The acquisition of English articles by first- and second-language learners. *Applied Psycholinguistics, 10*, 335–357.

Tomasello, M., & Herron, C. (1988). Down the garden path: Inducing and correcting overgeneralization errors in the foreign language classroom. *Applied Psycholinguistics, 9*, 237–246.

Tomasello, M., & Herron, C. (1989). Feedback for language transfer errors: The garden path technique. *Studies in Second Language Acquisition, 11*, 385–396.

White, L. (1990). Second language acquisition and universal grammar. *Studies in Second Language Acquisition, 12*, 121–134.

Wode, H. (1978). The L1 versus L2 acquisition of English interrogatives. *Working Papers in Bilingualism, 15,* 37–57.

Wolfson, N., d'Amico-Reisner, L., & Huber, L. (1983). How to arrange for social commitments in American English: The invitation. In N. Wolfson & E. Judd (Eds.), *Sociolinguistics and language acquisition.* Rowley, MA: Newbury House.

Wong Fillmore, L. (1976). *The second time around: Cognitive and social strategies in second language acquisition.* Unpublished doctoral dissertation, Stanford University, Stanford.

Zentella, A. C. (1981). Language variety among Puerto Ricans. In C. A. Ferguson & S. B. Heath (Eds.), *Language in the U.S.A.* New York: Cambridge University Press.

Glossary

Acceptable. A sentence or utterance considered by native speakers of a language to be possible or permissible. Acceptable utterances may or may not be grammatical, as in the partial phrase, *"No, she isn't";* conversely, a sentence that may be grammatically correct may not seem acceptable to some speakers because of length or processing constraints, as in *The horse raced around the barn fell.*

Acoustics. The study of the physical properties of sound, such as intensity, frequency, and duration.

Action. In conversation, the level of speech acts, or conversational moves such as requests, refusals, or assertions made by means of speech or gestures.

Additive bilingualism. Learning a second language while retaining one's original language.

Address terms. Words used in direct address to identify addressee.

Adjacency pairs. Pairs of contingent moves across participants such that first calls for the second, e.g. question-answer.

Affix. A bound morpheme. Affixes can occur before a word stem, as in the prefix *-un;* they may occur after the word stem, as in the suffixes that signal the past tense, plural, or possession. In some languages, they appear within words (infixes).

Affricate. Sounds produced by an initial stop closure followed immediately by a gradual release of the air pressure. The articulatory gestures needed in the production of affricates are those for stops followed by a fricative. The sounds that begin and end the words *church* and *judge* are voiceless and voiced affricates, respectively.

Agnosia. [*G. no perception*] Loss of ability to properly interpret sensory stimuli.

Agrammatism. The absence of function words and word endings in some types of Broca's aphasia (*See also* **Broca's aphasia**).

Alexia without agraphia. (*See* **pure alexia**.)

Allophone. One of a phoneme's variant realizations. The phoneme /t/ has many possible realizations (aspirated, flapped, checked, etc.), depending upon surrounding phonetic context and position within a word or utterance.

Allophonic variation. The individual allophones in a phoneme category represent the allophonic variations permissible in that phoneme category.

Alphabetic phase. Penultimate stage of reading development, when the child begins a systematic learning and application of grapheme–phoneme rules. Followed by the **orthographic** (final) phase.

Alveolar. Refers to any consonant made with the tongue near or touching the alveolar ridge, which is behind the upper front teeth. In English the alveolar consonants are: [t], [d], [n], [s], [z], and [l].

Ambiguous. A word or sentence that has more than one meaning, as in *bill* or *Visiting relatives can be a nuisance.*

American Sign Language (ASL or **Ameslan).** A manual language used by many deaf Americans; one of the world's manual languages, characterized by its own phonology, morphology, lexicon, and grammar.

Anarthria. Loss of speech without loss of intellectual functioning.

Angular gyrus. [*Brodmann area 39*] An area in the parietal lobe that may be involved in word retrieval as well as reading and writing.

Anomia. A disturbance in naming due to brain damage.

Anosognosia. [*G. no disease knowledge*] Denial of illness, a behavior that may follow brain damage.

Anterior. A descriptor used in the distinctive features system of classifying speech sounds. Sounds produced at the front of the mouth, from the lips to the alveolar ridge are + anterior. All other places of articulation are − anterior.

Anticipation error.   Speech error in which a segment that will come later in the utterance inappropriately appears earlier than intended.

Aperiodic.   An event that does not occur at regular intervals; it is not cyclical. In acoustics, the turbulent noise associated with voiceless fricatives ([f], [θ], [s], [ʃ]) is aperiodic.

Aphasia.   [*G. no speech*] Language disturbance due to brain damage.

Apraxia of speech.   The loss of the ability to voluntarily position the articulators appropriately for speech, in spite of preserved muscle and sensory function.

Arcuate fasciculus.   A nerve tract connecting Broca's area and Wernicke's area (part of the superior longitudinal fasciculus).

Argument.   (a) Dispute; (b) assertion in the propositional structure of a dispute; (c) (in syntax) one of the complements of a verb, e.g. the subject or object.

Aspirated.   A sound produced with audible breath release, as in English initial voiceless stops (*pin, tin, kin*).

Assessment.   Judgment of value, e.g. "that's wonderful."

Association.   Cognitive process that underlies the ability to symbolize, or have one thing represent another. Each may prompt a reaction common to both.

Ataxia.   A breakdown in muscular coordination due to brain damage.

Attrition.   In language, the loss of language skill through disuse. For instance, a person who moves to a new language environment may lose his or her native language through lack of practice.

Automatic speech.   The retained ability in aphasia to produce overlearned materials.

Automaticity.   The potential of a process to be completed with great speed after long practice without allocating to it conscious attention. When a cognitive process becomes automatic, it does not require extra time or processing capacity.

Autonomous.   Not controlled by higher level processes or supplemented by information from knowledge structures not contained in the module (*see* **modular**.)

Axon.   The nerve fiber carrying impulses away from the nerve cell body.

Babbling.   Prespeech vocal behavior by infants, usually consisting of strings of syllables that the child either uses communicatively or in sound-play.

Backgrounding.   Using one part of text to provide information to help interpret another part, e.g. a "because" clause.

Backward masking.   Experimental condition in which the stimulus is obliterated by noise patterns timed to occur shortly after presentation.

Basal ganglia.   A mass of gray matter above and surrounding the diencephalon, mediating both motor and cognitive function.

Bilabial.   Sounds that are produced by bringing both lips together. The articulation of [p], [b] and [m] require these gestures; they are consequently described as bilabial.

Bilingual aphasia.   Language disturbance involving two languages following brain damage.

Borrowing.   Using a word or phrase from another language.

Bottom-up processing[1].   A listener's perceptual analysis of the physical sound pattern of speech "upward" from the level of the recognition of phonemes to eventual comprehension of sentence meaning.

Bottom-up processing[2].   A hypothesized mode of processing information. In speech perception, bottom-up processing follows this sequence: auditory analysis followed by phonetic analysis, then phonological, semantic, and syntactic levels of analysis.

Bound morpheme.   A morpheme that cannot stand alone as a word, as in prefixes such as *un-* and *re-*, and suffixes such as the plural, past tense, etc.

Brain stem.   A structure at the very base of the brain controlling vital functions such as respiration and heart beat.

Broca's aphasia.   Nonfluent, agrammatic language output due to brain damage.

Broca's area.   [*Brodmann areas 44 and 45*] An area of cortex originally defined by Broca as encompassing the third frontal gyrus.

Carotid artery.   A major arterial system supplying blood to the anterior two-thirds of the cerebrum.

Categorical perception.   A term used to describe a special pattern of results in identifying and discriminating speech stimuli that differ systematically along a phonetic continuum. In categorical perception, listeners are only able to discriminate between stimuli that are identified as members of two phoneme categories. This pattern of response is suggestive of perceptual discontinuity across a continuously varying physical dimension.

Caudal.   [*L. tail*] Toward the tail, posterior.

Caudate.   [*L. tail*] One of the structures making up the basal ganglia.

Central nervous system (CNS).   Those parts of the nervous system enclosed by the bony coverings of the skull and vertebral column.

Cerebral spinal fluid (CSF). A normally clear fluid produced in the ventricles and central canal of the spinal cord.

Cerebrovascular disease. Disease affecting the blood vessels of the brain that can cause death of neurons by depriving them of oxygen and glucose.

Characteristic features. Features of a stimulus that are typical, but not necessary for the stimulus to be included in a category (i.e. gray hair is typical of grandmothers, but grandmothers need not have gray hair).

Child-directed speech (CDS). The speech register used when addressing language-learning children, characterized by higher pitch, exaggerated intonation, special vocabulary, and shorter, repetitive, and paraphrased syntactic patterns.

Choreas. [*G. dance*] A class of hyperkinetic neuromotor disorders characterized by continual rapid, jerky movements.

Cingulate gyrus. [*L. belt*] An arch-shaped band of gray matter lying above the corpus callosum.

Citation form. Speech that is produced with clear and deliberate enunciation. Acoustic studies of speech have used samples of natural speech produced in citation form. This way of producing speech contrasts with underarticulation.

Classical conditioning. A form of learning, first described by Pavlov, in which previously neutral stimuli (such as words) that are repetitively paired with other stimuli eventually come to elicit responses to those stimuli.

Closed class words. Function words such as articles ("the," "a," "and"). They are called closed class words because it is unlikely that their ranks will expand.

Coarticulation. The influence of adjacent segments on the articulation of a given segment. It consists of overlapping speech motor gestures involving more than one point in the vocal tract.

Coda. The part of a story that follows the resolution of the plot.

Code-switching. Changing language within an utterance.

Codes. Abstract mental representations of the different attributes of the units of language; these include semantic, phonological, and syntactic grammatical codes.

Coherence graph. A network of connections expressing the relations among the propositions ("idea units") of an utterance.

Coherent. Composed of relevant turns that are thematically related.

Cohesive. Linguistically connected by devices like pronouns, conjunctions.

Commissure. A collection of nerve fibers connecting the two hemispheres of the brain.

Commissurotomy. The surgical cutting of a commissure; the cutting of the corpus callosum is sometimes referred to as "split-brain" operation.

Complex sentence. A sentence consisting of a main clause and one or more subordinate clauses.

Compound sentence. A sentence consisting of more than one main clause, or containing compound subjects, verbs, or objects.

Computerized transaxial tomography (CT scan). A form of X-ray imaging that can provide displays of sections of live as well as dead brains.

Conduction aphasia. A type of aphasia, first suggested by Wernicke, characterized by an inability to repeat (*see* **arcuate fasciculus**).

Confirmation checks. Questioning or repeating to identify misunderstanding.

Connectives. Joiners of clauses, conjunctions, discourse markers.

Connectionism. A position in cognitive science that uses the analogy of the network of neurons in the brain to explain cognitive processes.

Constituent. A linguistic unit that is part of a larger grammatical construction, such as a noun phrase or a verb phrase.

Content word. Nouns, verbs, and modifiers within a language are considered content words (*synonym: lexical*); words such as articles and auxiliary verbs are considered **function words** or **functors.**

Context. (1) Situation, participants, activities, setting of speech; (2) surrounding verbal text.

Contextualization. Cues that suggest background for interpretation.

Continuant. One of the components of sound production used in the distinctive feature system of classifying speech sounds. Sounds produced with continuous air flow are described as +continuant; those produced with a stoppage of air flow are described as −continuant.

Contralateral. Referring to the opposite side of the human body.

Conventional request. The desired act or object is not directly specified but is clear because of conventions familiar to both speaker and hearer. Questions such as *can you* are usually interpreted as requests rather than queries about ability.

Coordinate clause.   Clauses in same tense linked by and/but/so.

Copula.   A linking verb with virtually no independent meaning. In English, the only copular verb is *to be*, as in *The apple is red.*

Coronal.   A term used in the distinctive feature system of classifying speech sounds. Sounds produced by placing the tongue in contact with the palate are described as + coronal. Examples in English are [t], [d] and [n].

Corpus callosum.   [*L. calloused body*] The major commissure connecting the two hemispheres of the brain.

Corpus.   Body of data used for linguistic analysis. *Plural: corpora.*

Cortex.   [*L. bark*] The convoluted mass of gray matter covering the surface of the two cerebral hemispheres.

Cortical motor aphasia.   (*See* **Broca's aphasia**.)

Cortical sensory aphasia.   (*See* **Wernicke's aphasia**.)

Cranial nerves.   Nerves of the peripheral nervous system that exit directly from the cranium.

Craniometry.   Measurement of skulls and/or brains.

Cranium.   The skull.

Creole.   A **pidgin** that becomes the native language of a community, and is acquired by children growing up in that culture.

Critical period.   A span of time in development during which a particular behavior is best acquired.

Cross modal priming.   Refers to presentation of a priming word in one modality (e.g., spoken) and testing its effect on a related word presented in a different modality (e.g., visual presentation) (*see* **lexical priming**).

Cross-modal transfer.   The cognitive process by which information accessed through one sensory medium (e.g. sight) becomes available to other systems. Also called **intersensory integration.**

Cross-over stimulus.   A term used in categorical perception experiments. It is the stimulus on the continuum that marks the boundary between two phoneme categories.

Crossed aphasia.   An extremely rare form of aphasia resulting from damage to the right hemisphere in right-handed individuals.

Cytoarchitecture.   The organization of nerve cells, their morphology (shape), and layering.

Dative.   A sentence containing an indirect object relationship. In English, basic dative order is Subject–Verb–Direct Object–Indirect Object (as in *he baked a cake for Mary*); sentences that are ordered Subject–Verb–Indirect Object–Direct Object are usually more difficult to process and more difficult for children to acquire.

Decussation.   [*L. decem = Roman numeral X*] A crossing of nerve fibers from one side of the body to the other.

Deep dyslexia.   Reading disorder characterized by the ability to name most words, but not pseudowords, and by the production of many semantic errors.

Deep structure.   In transformational grammar, the underlying syntactic and semantic representation of a sentence.

Defining features.   Features of a stimulus that are considered to be necessary for the stimulus to be included within a given category (i.e. blood and having a heart are necessary features of animals).

Degeneracy (of input).   In child language acquisition, the term used by some linguists to characterize the fragmented, unsystematic, and sometimes ungrammatical utterances a child is exposed to; while seen as a problem for models of language development by nativists, the scope and impact of degeneracy is argued by other groups of child language researchers.

Dementia.   A gradual deterioration of intellectual abilities due to brain disease.

Dendrite.   [*L. tree*] Branch-like extensions from the nerve cell body upon which many synapses occur.

Derivational morphemes.   Affixes used in word formation. Derivational morphemes change the grammatical class of root forms (i.e., *happy→happiness*).

Derivational theory of complexity (DTC).   Early psychological attempt to link the derivation of sentences under Transformational Generative Grammar to the time taken to process such sentences.

Dialect.   A regional or socially conditioned variant of a language. Dialects may vary in their phonological, lexical, grammatical, and pragmatic conventions.

Diaschesis.   [*G. to split through*] Loss of function in an apparently normal area of the brain due to a lesion in another part of the brain.

Dichotic listening.   Simultaneous presentation of different sounds to each ear.

Diencephalon.   [*G. between brain*] The most centrally located part of the brain, a relay station for most sensations and motor functions.

Diminutive.   Affix signalling "little"; in English, diminutives such as *-ie* (*doggie*) are conventional in the Baby-talk (BT) or **Child-Directed Speech (CDS)** register.

Discontinuous.   A grammatical construction interrupted by the insertion of another constituent or phrase.

Discourse.   A spoken or written text of some length—monologue or dialogue.

Discourse markers. Words whose main function is to indicate relations between propositions, actions, or global text features, e.g. oh, well, but, because, so, ok.

Discourse operators. Same as discourse markers.

Discrimination. A perceptual task in which the subject has to indicate whether two stimuli are the same or different.

Discrimination peak. The highest level of accuracy in the discrimination of pairs of stimuli sampled from a continuum. In categorical perception the discrimination peak coincides with the phoneme boundary.

Disfluency. Break in the flow of spoken language. Disfluencies include pausal and hesitation phenomena, repetitions, retracings, etc. Also **dysfluency.**

Displacement. The ability of language to refer to events that are distant in space or time, or concepts not triggered by the immediate environment. One characteristic that distinguishes human language from animal communication systems.

Dispute. Dialogue in which disagreement continues three or more turns.

Dissociation. The separation of functions in the brain based on the effects of lesions.

Distinctive feature. A term developed by linguists to describe the components of speech sounds. In phonology, each phonetic segment is associated with a specific pattern of distinctive features. Each distinctive feature refers to a minimal contrastive unit that has a positive $(+)$ and a negative $(-)$ state. For example [p] is $+$ oral, $-$ continuant, $-$ voice, $+$ anterior.

Dorsal thalamus. [*G. bed chamber*] A major part of the diencephalon.

Dysarthria. [*G. disjointed*] A class of disturbances of speech sometimes following brain damage, in which articulation is impaired due to paralysis, loss of coordination, or spasticity of the muscles used in speaking.

Echolalia. Inappropriate repetition of part or all of an utterance.

Electrical stimulation of the brain (ESB). An experimental technique usually involving direct electrical stimulation of the cortex or other brain structures.

Ellipsis. Conversational deletion of noun or verb phrase. (*I will; the first*)

Encoded. In speech, the term is used to refer to coarticulated phonetic segments. Consonant–Vowel (CV) syllables that begin with a stop consonant are described as being highly encoded because the acoustic information for the consonant and the following vowel are merged together.

Encoding. Process of transforming information at one stage for use at the next stage.

Exchange system. System of moves in a speech event with turns.

Exchange. Speech error in which two segments reverse positions.

Exchanges. Series of moves in a dialogue.

Explicit request. Request that mentions desired act or desired object.

Expressive style. A speech style seen in some toddlers that is characterized by the use of many personal–social terms such as greetings and routines.

Extension. The items in the world to which a word applies.

External capsule. A band of outgoing (efferent) and incoming (afferent) nerve fibers surrounding the basal ganglia.

Feature view. The most popular view of conceptual meaning in which the concept is viewed as a composite of more primitive featural meanings.

Femoral artery. A major artery located in the thigh.

Feral child. A child raised in the wild, or isolated from human contact.

Filled pause. Nonsilent pause, filled by a vocalization such as *um, uh, well.*

Fine-tuning. Term used in describing changes made in the **Child-directed speech (CDS, babytalk, motherese)** register to accommodate the child's changing linguistic abilities.

Fissure. A deep valley in the cerebral cortex's landscape (*cf.* **sulcus**).

Fluency. Facility in the use of language, e.g., speaking or reading rapidly, effortlessly, and without error (*see* **automaticity**).

Foramen magnum. [*L. big hole*] A large hole at the base of the skull through which the brain and spinal cord interconnect.

Foregrounded. In the main clause.

Formant. A band of resonant frequencies. Resonant frequencies are determined by the shape of the oral cavity through which air flows during speech production. The first three bands of resonant frequencies (formants) are considered to be more important than the remaining formants in defining the identity of phonetic segments.

Formant transition. Change in resonant frequencies as a function of a change in the shape of the oral cavity. Formants change in their spectral composition as individuals produce two adjacent phonetic segments in a syllable.

Fractionation.   The concept that brain damage results in deficits to specific components of cognitive processing.

Framing move.   Move that sets up preparatory situation for request.

Free morpheme.   Morpheme that can stand alone as a word.

Freudian slip.   Speech error in which a word meaning the opposite of what was intended is chosen, or the speaker's ongoing thought process results in an inappropriate lexical selection.

Fricative.   Sound produced by creating a small constriction in the oral cavity and forcing air through it. This creates a turbulent (aperiodic) sound that is characteristic of fricatives. Some English fricatives are [v], [f], [s], [z]

Frontal eye field.   [*Brodmann area 8*] The area of frontal cortex related to conjugate eye movement.

Function word (functor).   Word that plays a purely grammatical function in sentence constructions, such as articles, auxiliary verbs, and conjunctions.

Functional neuroanatomy.   The relating of neuroanatomical structures to behavior.

Functionalist hypothesis.   The view that function rather than the physical nature of a stimulus determines in which hemisphere it is processed.

Fundamental frequency (F0).   The rate at which the vocal cords vibrate during phonation.

Garden path sentence.   A sentence whose structure is ambiguous to the point of being misleading or uninterpretable.

Gating.   A technique for studying word recognition in which listeners are asked to identify words based only on hearing varying amounts of the word onsets.

Generalization.   Production of a learned response in a new environment, as in the child's ability to form the plural of an unfamiliar word.

Generics.   Generalizations about how things normally are.

Genre.   Cultural type of text that has name, regular structural features.

Glial cells (glia).   [*G. glue*] One of the two basic types of cells that make up brain tissue (the other is the **neuron**).

Glide.   Speech sounds produced with little or no obstruction in the air flow through the oral cavity. The sounds [j] and [w] are glides. In articulating these sounds the tongue moves rapidly either away from or toward the adjacent vowel, hence the term glide.

Global aphasia.   The loss of virtually all language abilities due to the destruction of the perisylvian language area.

Global structure.   Major units of discourse, episodes, asides.

Globus pallidus.   [*L. pale globe*] One of the structures making up the basal ganglia.

Glottalized.   Made in the larynx, by closing or narrowing the glottis, the space between the vocal cords.

Glottis.   The location in the larynx where the vocal cords meet.

Government and Binding (GB).   A model of grammar descended from earlier Transformational Generative models. It proposes only one type of transformation (movement of elements), the specification of possible grammatical frames for lexical items and their mapping onto the syntax of sentences, and universal constraints on possible syntactic rules, among many other notions.

Grammatical.   Construction that conforms to the rules of the language. Ungrammatical constructions are conventionally preceded by asterisks in linguistics texts.

Grapheme.   The minimal contrastive unit in writing systems. In English, an alphabetic system, graphemes are letters.

Gray matter.   Masses of nerve cells as opposed to nerves.

Gyrus.   One of the hills of the cerebral cortex's landscape.

Habituals.   Verbs referring to recurrent events or acts.

Harmonics.   Even multiples of the **fundamental frequency (F0)**.

Hedge.   Qualifier or phrase reducing strength of assertion.

Hemidecorticate.   A patient who has had half of the cerebral cortex surgically removed.

Hemiplegia.   Paralysis confined to one side of the body.

Hemispherectomy.   Surgical removal of one cerebral hemisphere.

Hemispheric specialization.   (*See* **lateralization of function**.)

Heschl's gyrus.   [*Brodmann area 41*] The highest (most rostral) cortical area devoted to hearing.

Hesitation.   Category of spoken behaviors, including **filled pauses,** unfilled pauses, and other **disfluencies**.

Holistic view.   A view of conceptual meaning in which the concept is viewed as an unanalyzable whole rather than as a sum of parts.

Holophrase. Single word utterance used by children at the earliest stages of language acquisition that appears to carry the meaning or intent of a longer utterance, given its context.

Homo sapiens sapiens. [*L. man most wise*] Present-day human beings.

Homophones. Pairs of words that have different meanings but sound alike.

Huntington's chorea. An inherited hyperkinetic neuromuscular disease characterized by speech as well as cognitive disorders.

Hydrocephalus. [*G. water + head*] A disease characterized by excessive accumulation of cerebrospinal fluid in the brain.

Hyperkinesia. Characterized by too much movement.

Hypertrophy. Excessive growth of an organ.

Hypokinesia. Characterized by too little movement.

Ideational content. Thematic information, content of propositions.

Ideograms. Writing that consists of pictures that symbolize ideas or things, but not particular words for them.

Ideomotor apraxia. Inability to carry out individual limb or facial movements due to brain damage.

Immersion. Settings in which a group of learners are all taught a new language through the medium of the second language.

Implicit mediators. In associative learning, implicit mediators (or retrieval cues) link two associates in a component of memory called the **semantic network**.

Indirect request. (1) Request that does not refer to desired act; (2) Conventional request.

Inflection (inflectional affix). Morpheme that signals grammatical concepts such as plurality, past tense, possession, etc.

Innate. Inborn, as in the nativist belief that language is a biologically conditioned ability in humans.

Input language. (*See* **child-directed speech**.)

Intension. The meaning of a term (e.g. "chair" is an item of furniture that can be sat upon).

Interactive Models of Language Processing. The suggestion that knowledge gained at different levels of processing interacts freely in sentence processing as the sentence is being heard.

Interdental. Sounds produced with the tip of the tongue between the teeth. The initial sounds in *thin* and *then* are interdental.

Interlanguage grammar. For second language learners, one of many grammars they employ en route to full control of the target language grammar.

Internal capsule. A band of afferent and efferent nerve fibers in the area of the **diencephalon** and **basal ganglia**.

Intersensory integration. (*See* **cross-modal transfer**.)

Invariance. An attribute that is *not present* in speech sounds. If speech sounds were produced in exactly the same way in all contexts then they would be invariant. The complex effects of coarticulation result in the diversity characteristic of speech sounds.

Invariant dimensions. Distinguishing and unchanging attributes. For instance, the **phoneme** /p/ has some characteristics that remain constant (invariant) in all environments.

Invented spelling. Children's **linguistic guesswork** about how words are spelled, based in part on their phonological insights.

Ipsilateral. Referring to the same side of a structure such as the human body.

Irregular. Form that is an exception to a general rule of the language.

Isolation of the speech area. (*See* **mixed transcortical aphasia**.)

Jargon aphasia. A fluent form of aphasia that is largely unintelligible due to substitutions of inappropriate words.

Jargon agraphia. A fluent form of agraphia which renders the patient's writing largely unintelligible due to substitutions of inappropriate letters.

Key. Mood or style of discourse

Labiodental. Sounds produced by touching the front teeth to the lower lips. Articulatory gestures for [f] and [v] require the touching of the lip (labio-) with the teeth (-dental).

Language acquisition device (LAD). The innate mental mechanism that, according to linguistic theorists, makes language acquisition possible.

Larynx. Commonly called the "voice box," it is an anatomical structure that contains the vocal cords.

Lateral geniculate nucleus. A portion of the metathalamus involved in visual processing.

Lateralization of function. The observation that each cerebral hemisphere may control different types of behavior.

Lemma. Used in Levelt's model of speech production to refer to the semantic and syntactic properties of lexical items, as opposed to their phonological properties.

Lesion. An area of damage or pathological change.

Lexeme. An individual item in the **lexicon**.

Lexical decision[1].   A task in which subjects are asked to respond whether a stimulus is a legal word or a nonword (i.e., string of letters).

Lexical decision[2].   The speed (or accuracy) with which a person can decide whether or not a presented letter string forms a real word.

Lexical priming.   A means of testing whether the meaning of a word has been activated by testing the speed with which a related word can be recognized or distinguished as a real word versus a meaningless letter string.

Lexicon[1].   Greek word for "dictionary"; refers to all the words that a person knows.

Lexicon[2].   The vocabulary of a language.

Line.   In a typed or printed text, a single line, usually numbered.

Linguistic aphasiology.   The study of the breakdown of language structure due to brain damage.

Linguistic guesswork.   The basis for children's first understanding of meaning–print connections.

Liquid.   Speech sounds produced with some obstruction of the airstream in the oral cavity, but not enough to create friction noise. The sounds [l] and [r] are liquids.

Lobe.   A more or less distinct region of the brain.

Local system.   Turn by turn unplanned accommodations.

Logogen.   In Morton's model, a theoretical "scoreboard" for a word that keeps track of all incoming information to determine whether it will be accessed.

Logographic phase.   Early stage of reading acquisition in which highly familiar words are recognized visually, but novel or unknown words are inaccessible.

Logographs.   Somewhat abstract writing symbols that represent whole words and sounds, for instance, Egyptian hieroglyphs.

Logorrheia.   [*G. word flow*] excessive talkativeness due to brain damage.

Massa intermedia.   A bridge of gray matter connecting the two thalami.

Mean Length of Utterance (MLU).   Computation that measures the average length of utterances in a child's language sample in morphemes.

Medulla.   [*L. marrow*] A part of the **brain stem** containing motor nuclei for the control of speech (namely cranial nerves: IX, X, XI, and XII).

Meninges.   Layers of membrane wrapping and protecting the **central nervous system**.

Mental lexicon.   The memory store of words and their meanings.

Mental grammar.   Internalized knowledge of the rules of one's language.

Metalinguistic ability.   Ability to reflect on one's language use and knowledge.

Metathalamus.   The portion of the **diencephalon** containing the lateral and medial geniculate bodies involved in visual and auditory processing respectively.

Midbrain.   A portion of the brain stem containing nuclei involved in visual processing.

Mitigation.   Softening by vocal turn, hedges, address, politeness routines.

Mixed transcortical aphasia.   An aphasia characterized by retention of only the ability to repeat.

Modality-specific abilities.   Abilities that are limited to one sensory domain, e.g., to sight or to hearing.

Modularity[1].   The view that cognition and ultimately the brain is made up of a number of independent processing units.

Modularity[2].   (of mind or language). Presumes that the mind or language consists of a number of discrete subsystems, each with its own properties.

Modularity[3].   Modularity theorists are those who believe that input processes, such as word meaning activation, or syntactic analysis, occur automatically and independently without further mental activity.

Morpheme.   The smallest meaningful unit of language (e.g., "dogs" is composed of two morphemes: "dog" and "-s," which signifies plurality). A morpheme is the minimal grammatical unit. Morphemes consist of words and affixes.

Morphologically complex.   Word consisting of more than one morpheme; also multimorphemic.

Morphophonemic production rules.   Rules that help speakers arrive at correct pronunciations of **derived words**—words that have common root morphemes, but vary in form class, e.g., *decide, decision*.

Motherese (Babytalk).   Term used to describe the register used by adults when speaking to very young language learning children (*see also* **child-directed speech; input language**).

Motor strip.   [*Brodmann area 4*] The highest (most rostral) area devoted to motor functions.

Motor transcortical aphasia.   An aphasia comparable to that of Broca's aphasia, but with retained ability to repeat.

Motor homunculus.   The inverted motor figure fashioned by Penfield to represent the functions of the motor strip [*Brodmann area 4*] obtained by electrical stimulation.

Multiple sclerosis. A neuromotor and cognitive deficit produced by destruction of **myelin** in the brain.

Myasthenia gravis. A neuromuscular disease involving depletion of receptor sites for the neurotransmitter acetylcholine.

Myelin. A fatty covering of nerves produced by glial cells.

Narrative rounds. Series of stories on related themes by different speakers.

Narrative clauses. Propositions referring to two or more serial events.

Nasal. Speech sounds produced with air flow through the nasal passage. The sounds [m], [n] and [ŋ] are nasal consonants. In English no other sounds require air flow through the nasal passage, they are oral.

Nativism. In language acquisition, a theoretical approach emphasizing the innate, possibly genetic contribution to language development.

Natural kind terms. Terms like *animal, iron*, etc., that refer to inanimate and animate things found in nature, as opposed to artifacts that refer to person-made objects.

Negative evidence. Feedback from competent language users to children regarding ungrammatical or unacceptable constructions in the language. Nativists contend that children do not get such information and that this presents problems for certain accounts of the language acquisition process.

Negative politeness. Deference, avoiding intrusion or imposition.

Neologistic jargon. Speech characterized by use of nonexistent words in a language (*see* **jargon aphasia**).

Neurolinguistics. The study of the relationship between language structure and brain function.

Neurologist. A physician who specializes in nervous system disorders.

Neuron. A nerve cell consisting of a cell body (soma), dendrites, and one axon.

Neuropathology. The study of diseases of the nervous system.

Neurotransmitter. A chemical agent transmitting information from one neuron to another.

Nominal terms (or artifacts). Terms like "chair" and "table" that refer to person-made objects.

Notice. In child language, the intent to call attention to something, as in greetings.

Noun ellipsis. Noun omitted; demonstrative, possessive, numeral, or adjective remains.

Nucleus ambiguus. [*L. the ambiguous nucleus*] The brain stem nucleus for the cranial nerves controlling phonation (*namely, IX, X and XI*).

Object permanence. The ability of a child, developed in the latter part of the first year of life, to understand that objects continue to exist even when they are not visible to the child. Cognitive ability described in detail by Piaget.

Off-record. Conversational move in which intention is not explicit.

Olfaction. The sense of smell.

Oligodendroglia. A **glial cell** in the **central nervous system** involved in the process of myelination.

On-Line Processing. The comprehension of the words of a sentence as they are actually being heard. This is contrasted with off-line analyses of a sentence that occur later in memory.

Onset. Initial consonant of a syllable. The onset of "bat" is "b."

Open class words. Any word with "content" such as nouns, verbs, adjectives. They are called open class words because presumably we can think up new words to refer to things or properties (e.g., "mini-van" and "computer" are words that have arisen in the last century).

Open syllable. A syllable consisting of a consonant or consonant cluster followed only by a vowel.

Operant conditioning. Term used by Skinner to refer to the learning process in which behaviors that are followed by reinforcement occur more frequently, while those that are punished occur less frequently or are extinguished over time.

Optic chiasm. [*G. chi = Greek letter X*] The crossing of the optic tracts from the eye to the occipital lobe of the brain.

Optic tectum. [*L. roof*] A portion of the midbrain involved in visual processing.

Ordered recall. *see* **serial memory**.

Orthographic phase. Final stage of reading, characterized by the use of analogies, pronunciation rules dictated by context, and morphophonemic knowledge. Also called **fluent, orthographic reading**.

Orthotactic. Based on spelling.

Overextension. In child language, the use of a word to refer to an overly broad number of referents, as in *Daddy* for all men.

Overgeneralization. In child language, the application of a rule to exceptional cases, as in *goed for *went*.

Palatal. Sound produced with a raised tongue against the hard palate. This location is posterior to the alveolar ridge. English has two palatal frictives [ʃ] and [ʒ], where the constriction for producing the friction noise is made at the hard palate.

Parallel distributed processing (PDP). A computer-based model applied to grammatical development in children that compares development by analogical reasoning to the kinds of associative links that computers make.

Parallel processing. Carrying out several computations or cognitive tasks simultaneously.

Parallel transmission. More than one source of information available at the same time. In a stop-initial CV syllable (encoded consonant) the acoustic information about the consonant and the vowel is available at the same time and is transmitted in parallel to the listener.

Parallel search model. A theoretical model of word access that claims that items in the lexicon are activated simultaneously, or in parallel, in an attempt to find the correct lexical item.

Parameter. A principle of grammar that may be characterized by one of a finite number of values along which languages are free to vary. For example, the so-called pro-drop parameter distinguishes languages such as English and German, which do not permit omission of lexical subjects, from languages such as Spanish or Italian, which do.

Paraphasia. The substitution of incorrect sounds (literal paraphasia) or words (verbal paraphasia) for appropriate sounds and words in aphasia.

Paresis. Partial or incomplete paralysis.

Parkinson's disease. A hypokinetic neuromotor disturbance involving both speech and cognitive functions due to damage to the substantia nigra (a part of the **basal ganglia**).

Paroxysmal aphasia. A reversible form of aphasia caused by epilepsy.

Parsing. (Sentence parsing, linguistic parsing) The process by which a listener or reader assigns the words of a sentence to their appropriate linguistic categories so as to determine the syntactic structure of the sentence.

Participation structure. Turn-taking system; roles allowing speech.

Passive. In English, a sentence where the first noun phrase (normally the subject) is the logical object of the verb, while the second noun phrase is the logical subject, as in *The meal was prepared by skilled chefs.*

Perceptual learning. A type of processing that makes it possible to become increasingly efficient in searching for distinguishing attributes and attending selectively.

Periacqueductal gray. The gray neuronal cells surrounding the cerebral aqueduct in the midbrain.

Periodic. An event that is repeated regularly and cyclically. The vibration of the vocal folds during phonation is periodic.

Peripheral nervous system (PNS). Those parts of the nervous system that lie outside the skull and vertebral column.

Perisylvian area. The area of the cerebral cortex surrounding the Sylvian fissure (the principal language area in the dominant hemisphere).

Perseveration error. Speech error in which a segment early in an utterance reappears in an incorrect location later in the utterance. Also a naming error consisting of repetition of the previous response.

Personal encounters. Sociable or intimate exchange.

Pharynx. The throat cavity, made up of the nasopharynx, oropharynx, and laryngopharynx.

Phonation. The action of vocal cord vibration to generate sound

Phone. Physical realization of a phoneme.

Phoneme. The smallest unit of sound. E.g., /k/ and /ʃ/ are single phonemes. A phoneme is a minimally contrastive unit within the sound system of a language.

Phonemic restoration. A perceptual phenomenon in which a missing or distorted phoneme is "filled in" by the listener.

Phonological codes. (*See* **codes.**)

Phonology. The study of the sound systems of languages.

Phonotactics. Rules that govern sound sequences in a language.

Phrenology. A view developed by Gall that bumps on the skull might reveal hypertrophy of underlying neural areas of the brain subserving diverse human abilities.

Physical anthropology. The study of the fossil evidence for human evolution and any other physical as opposed to cultural aspect of human development.

Pictographs. Pictures used to represent an object or concept; this precursor to writing was created in the latter part of the fourth millennium B.C. by the ancient Sumerians.

Pidgin. Language variant formed when two mutually unintelligible communities attempt to develop a communicative system. Pidgins are characterized by some aspects of each contributing language, but show reduced grammatical and lexical complexity when compared to them. Over time, if a pidgin becomes the native language of a community, it becomes a **creole**.

Planum temporale. [*L. the temporal plane*] A region of the temporal lobe lying posterior to **Heschl's gyrus** that has been demonstrated to exhibit left/right asymmetries.

Plasticity. The presumed ability of undamaged parts of the brain to assume the functions of damaged areas.

Polarity question. Yes/no question.

Pons. [*L. bridge*] A portion of the brain stem containing motor nuclei for the control of speech (*namely, V and VII*).

Positive politeness. Rapport, camaraderie, flattery.

Positron emission tomography (PET). A neuroimaging technique that utilizes radioactive isotopes of various elements to measure changes in brain metabolism correlated with behavioral tests or neuropathology.

Pragmatic relations. Relations of speech to actors, actions, setting.

Pragmatics. The study of the use of language in social context to accomplish the speaker's conversational intent.

Pre-sequence. Moves before the main move, preparatory moves.

Preface markers. "Well" and other indicators of excuses, dispreferred.

Preference. Most rapid second turn in adjacency pair, without special markers

Pro-drop language. Language in which the subject may be optionally deleted from sentences; usually some information about the subject is conveyed by verbal inflections.

Programmed. Genetically or biologically predisposed (or "wired") to behave in certain ways, for instance to search for invariance in one's surroundings.

Propositional representation. The meaningful relationships between the objects, actions, and events in a sentence.

Propositions. Assertions made in clauses in sentences.

Prosody¹. The intonation contour, stress pattern, and tempo of an utterance.

Prosody². A general term that includes the melodic intonation pattern of a sentence, the pattern of stress received by each of the words, and the timing of the words in the utterance, such as where pauses are placed as a sentence is being spoken.

Protoliteracy period. The period when the precursors of written language are being laid, usually during the preschool years.

Prototype. The central figure of a category that shares many features with other members of the category and few features with members of other categories (e.g. a robin is a prototypical bird).

Pseudowords. Words that, according to word formation rules, are possible in the language, but that do not actually exist.

Psycholinguistics. The study of the cognitive and processing issues that underly language comprehension and use.

Pure word deafness. A type of agnosia involving the inability to interpret the speech sounds of one's native language.

Pure alexia. Impairment of reading ability alone due to brain damage.

Putamen. [*L. shell*] The most lateral structure in the **basal ganglia**.

Pyramidal tract. A major collection of motor nerve fibers controlling fine motor movements of the digits (fingers) and articulators.

Reaction time. A measure used in experiments to gauge how long a cognitive process takes, such as to respond whether a stimulus ("cat") is a member of a given category ("animals") or not.

Recasting. Adult response to a child's utterance in which the grammar is rephrased or corrected, although the message content is maintained.

Reciprocal causation. Relationship that exists in older impaired readers who early on developed problems in vocabulary knowledge as the result of delays in reading and then became further impeded in reading because they lacked vocabulary.

Recurrence. In child language, an intention that signals notice of, or request for more of something. It is usually signalled by the use of words such as *more, another, again*, etc.

Reference. The philosophical view that words stand for the objects to which they apply; they point to or *denote* those objects.

Referential style. In child language, an early language style characterized by relatively high frequency of naming behaviors.

Regional cerebral blood flow (rCBF). Changes in blood flow in the brain correlated with different behavioral tasks.

Register. Variant of a language used in certain social contexts or with particular classes of addressee, as in *babytalk* or *foreigner talk*.

Reply markers. Words used to index reply.

Representation abilities. Cognitive capacities that make it possible to store and access mental correlates of spoken or written language.

Resonance. The frequencies that are enhanced in a complex acoustic signal. The bands of resonant frequencies of speech sounds are called **formants**.

Retracing. Behavior seen when a speaker notes his/her speech error and "backtracks" to the beginning of the constituent to rephrase it.

Retrieval cues. (*See* **implicit mediators**.)

Rime. The latter part of a syllable as in the "at" in "bat."

Rostral. [*L. beak*] toward the beak, anterior.

Schwann cell. A **glial cell** in the **peripheral nervous system** involved in myelination.

Segmentation. Correct division of either spoken or written language into its constituent elements. The learner who believes that in English there is a fruit called "a napple" has made a *segmentation error.*

Selective attention. The ability to focus on the distinguishing attributes of things while ignoring irrelevant cues.

Semantic codes. (*See* **codes**.)

Semantic network. Mental organization of the lexicon whereby words and concepts that share some meaning are related both hierarchically and laterally.

Semantic priming. The tendency for a word to activate other words associated in meaning (e.g., table-chair), making those other words easier to recognize.

Semantic processing. Determining the meaning of an utterance.

Semantic relations. Relations in terms of word meanings.

Semantics. The study of meaning.

Semi-phonetic strategies. Early literacy skills, as children begin to apply some phonemic knowledge in both reading and spelling.

Sensory transcortical aphasia. An aphasia comparable to that of Wernicke's with retained ability to repeat.

Sensory stage. In bottom-up models of reading, early stage in which visual features are extracted.

Sentence processing. The process by which listeners or readers determine the structure of a sentence and gain access to its meaning.

Sequential transition markers. Global markers of side sequences, episodes.

Serial memory. A generalized ability to determine the order in which information was received.

Serial search model. A theoretical model of word access that claims items in the lexicon are searched serially, or one at a time, until the correct item is found.

Shadowing. A talk used in psycholinguistic research in which subjects are asked to listen to spoken passages and to repeat aloud what they are hearing word for word as it is being heard.

Side sequences. Going off main topic for asides, repairs.

Sign. Something that represents something else intrinsically, or by its very nature (e.g. smoke is a sign of fire).

Slip of the tongue (slip, spoonerism). Speech error in which sounds or words are mispronounced or rear-

ranged; they are useful in constructing models of the speech production process.

Sociolinguistics. Study of spoken language in terms of social features of speakers and of context.

Spectrogram. The visual display produced on a spectrograph.

Spectrograph. An instrument used in acoustic phonetics for speech analysis. It provides a visual representation of auditory stimuli, including speech, in which frequency is on the vertical axis, time is on the horizontal axis, and amplitude is indicated by the intensity of the markings on the display.

Spectrum. The full range of frequencies at different amplitudes in a signal.

Speech synthesis. Generation of speech sounds with the use of specialized machines, usually computers. Synthetic speech is different from natural speech, which is generated from the human vocal tract.

Spinal cord. Part of the **central nervous system** that controls all motor and sensory functions from the body and back of the head.

Spinal nerves. Nerves of the **peripheral nervous system** that exit directly from the vertebral column.

Spoonerism. (*see* **slip of the tongue**).

Standing behavior patterns. Regular expected actions for a role in a setting.

Statistical approximations. Word sequences that in themselves convey no meaning, but that maintain the mathematical regularities of the language.

Steady state. A term used in connection with vowels that are produced in a deliberate and elongated fashion. When the **formants** do not change in frequency over time, the signal is in steady state.

Stop consonant. A consonant produced with a period of stoppage of the air flow and then a sudden release of the impounded air. In English the stop consonants are [b], [p], [d], [t], [g] and [k].

Subcategorization constraint. Specification of the grammatical frames appropriate to a lexical item, as in the requirement that a transitive verb be followed by a noun phrase object.

Subcortical sensory aphasia. (*See* **pure word deafness**).

Subcortical motor aphasia. A type of nonfluent aphasia postulated by Lichtheim involving a disconnection of Broca's area from the motor strip.

Subglottal system. The lungs and associated muscles involved in speech production.

Submersion. Settings in which a second language learner is surrounded by native speakers.

Subtractive bilingualism. Bilingualism characterized by the loss of one's original language while learning a second language.

Sulcus. One of the valleys in the cerebral cortex's landscape.

Supplementary motor area. [*a portion of Brodmann area 6*] A medial area of frontal cortex intimately involved in movement initiation.

Surface dyslexia. Reading disorder characterized by the ability to decode pseudowords and regularly spelled words more readily than irregularly spelled real words.

Surface structure. (1) As opposed to Deep Structure in Standard Transformational Theory, the final stage in the derivation of a sentence, which most closely resembles the actual sentences we hear and say. (2) The specific words of a sentence that must be analyzed to determine the "deep structure," or meaning, of the sentence that underlies the surface structure.

Syllabary. Written system in which each symbol stands for a complete syllable in the language, rather than a single speech sound—e.g., the Japanese Kana, or the Devanagari syllabary used to write Sanskrit.

Syntactic/semantic codes. (*See* codes.)

Symbol. In semantics, something that represents or stands for something else arbitrarily (e.g. the word *cat* is a symbol for the concept "cat" in English; the word *chat* is a symbol for the same concept in French).

Synapse. [*G. connection*] The minute gap that separates output and input between neurons.

Syntactic autonomy. The proposal that syntactic analysis of a sentence can be carried out independently from the semantic analysis of the sentence where functional relationships are determined and the meaning of the utterance becomes available.

Syntagmatic. Reflecting a linearly ordered relationship between sentential constituents.

Syntax. The study of how words are combined to make grammatical sentences.

Tachistoscope (T-scope). A device used for rapid presentation of visual stimuli to the visual fields.

Tag question. Question appended to the end of a statement; used in English to request listener agreement with the speaker, as in *That's a nice dress, isn't it?*

Taxonomy. A way of classifying concepts into a category such that two members are related through nesting relationships (e.g. "bird" is nested within the category "animal") as opposed to a category in which members are related through theme (e.g. baseball and bat), color, etc.

Telegraphic speech. In child language, speech characterized by a general lack of function words and inflections, rather like a telegram.

Telencephalon. [*G. far brain*] The part of the brain that includes the **cerebral cortex, basal ganglia,** and limbic system.

Text. The language record of a spoken or written encounter.

Top-down processing[1]. The use of prior knowledge or linguistic expectations to facilitate word recognition and rapid sentence comprehension.

Top-down processing[2]. A hypothesized mode of processing information. In speech perception, top-down processing refers to the impact of higher levels (semantics and syntax) on perception of syllables and words. This mode of processing contrasts with **bottom-up processing**.

Trace theory. The presumption that, when linguistic elements are moved from one position to another as the words of a sentence are organized for production, a covert representation—or trace—of the word remains at its original position.

Transactional encounters. Task-oriented talk for a common impersonal goal.

Transcortical aphasia. Any type of aphasia characterized by the retained ability to repeat.

Transformational grammar. Grammar in which surface structure is derived from deep structure by the application of transformational rules.

Transparency. The ability to ascertain readily what linguistic functions have been lost due to brain damage.

Trauma. [*L. wound*] Injury to the skull and brain produced by external force.

Tumor. [*L. to swell*] An abnormal growth of brain tissue that may be cancerous (malignant).

Turn. The speech of one person continued until another takes the floor.

Unbounded states. Verb category describing nonvolitional states.

Underarticulation. Speech that is produced without full pronunciation of all segments. For example, relaxed conversational speech is underarticulated in comparison to speech that is clear and deliberate.

Universal grammar. Hypothetical set of restrictions governing the possible forms human languages may take.

Universal. Property assumed to characterize all human languages.

Unvoiced.   (*See* **voiceless**.)

Utterance.   A speaker's output, which may be less than a full sentence, as in exclamations, responses to questions (*I didn't*), warnings (*Don't*), etc.

Uvula.   Small fleshy mass that hangs from the back of the soft palate.

Ventricle.   [*L. belly*] A cavity in the brain that produces and contains cerebrospinal fluid.

Vocal folds.   Also known as vocal cords, they are two muscular, almond-shaped masses running from a single point inside the front of the thyroid cartilage ("Adam's apple") to the front ends of the arytenoid cartilage. The space between them is called the **glottis**. The vocal folds and the glottis are part of the **larynx**. The action of their vibration produces sound (**phonation**).

Vocal tract.   All the cavities above the **larynx**. These include the pharyngeal, oral, and nasal cavities.

Vocative.   Name used to identify the addressee (e.g., "Hey, lady!").

Voice-Onset-Time (VOT).   The interval of time between the release of air pressure in the production of word-initial stops and the onset of vocal cord vibration associated with the voicing of the following vowel. This duration is conventionally given positive values if release precedes voice onset and negative values if release follows voice onset.

Voiced.   Speech sounds that require vocal cord vibration in their production. Examples of voiced speech sounds are all the vowels and consonants such as [m], [b], and [z].

Voiceless.   Speech sounds that do not require vocal cord vibration in their production. Examples of voiceless speech sounds are [p], [t], and [s].

Wernicke's area.   [*a portion of Brodmann area 22*] An area of the temporal lobe defined by Wernicke as encompassing the posterior third of the first temporal gyrus.

Wernicke's aphasia.   Fluent, but largely meaningless language output due to brain damage.

White matter.   Nerves displaying a whitish appearance due to their **myelin** coating.

Word primitive.   The smallest form in which a word is stored in the lexicon. Some theorists argue word primitives are words themselves, other that words are built up out of morphemes, which are word primitives.

Word superiority effect.   Phenomenon whereby a letter embedded in a word seen only briefly (wor*k*) can be verified ("*Did the word contain a k or d*?") more accurately than when it is embedded in a nonword (Qr*k*).

Word-initial cohort.   The number of words in the language that share the same initial sounds.

Working memory.   A combined temporary memory and mental work space in which recent stimuli are briefly held, either for rehearsal and recall or for meaningful integration with other knowledge.

Wug.   Nonsense word and creature invented by Berko (1958) to test children's productive knowledge of plural forms.

Acknowledgments

—

PHOTOS

Chapter 1
Figure 1-1A. Baby crying. Credit: David M. Grossman. Figure 1-1B. Bee. Credit: © Jerry Berndt/Stock Boston. Figure 1-1C. Dog barking. Credit: © Ewing Galloway. Figure 1-1D. Caged bird. Credit: Kalman/The Image Works. Figure 1-1E. Child at dinner table, disappointed with food. Credit: Jerry Howard/Stock Boston. Figure 1-2. Ape using sign language. No credit line. Figure 1-5. Partially solved crossword puzzle. Credit: © Leslie Starobin/ The Picture Cube. Figure 1-7. Travelers asking police for directions. Credit: Lionel J-M Delevinge/Stock Boston.

Chapter 2
Figure 2-1. Statue of Broca. Credit: H. Roger Viollet. Figure 2-6. Saggital section of the human brain. Credit: © Fred Hossler/Visuals Unlimited.

Chapter 3
Figure 3-1. Instruments and F.S. Cooper painting on the pattern playback. Credit: Haskins Laboratories.

Chapter 6
Figure 6-1. Two young women in animated conversation. Credit: Katya Tripp. Figure 6-2. Several ethnic minority youths talking on an urban street corner storytelling on the street. Credit: Katya Tripp.

Chapter 7
Figure 7-1. William Spooner. Credit: The Bettmann Archive. Figure 7-2. The Wizard of Id. Credit: The creators syndicate.

Chapter 8
Figure 8-4a. Infant speech perception paradigm. James D. Wilson/Newsweek. Figure 8-5. Family with young child at dinner table. Credit: Karin Rosenthal/Stock Boston. Figure 8-6. Woman offering bottle to baby. Credit: Gabor Demjen/Stock Boston.

Chapter 9
Figure 9-1a. Various writing systems: hieroglyphics. Credit line: Hirmer Verlag Munchen. Figure 9-1b. Various writing systems: old phoenician alphabet. Credit line: The Bettmann Archive. Figure 9-1c. Various writing systems: Chinese picture writing. Credit line: Akos Szilvasi/Stock Boston. Figure 9-2. Warm shot of parent reading to a young child. Credit: Michael Heron/Woodfin Camp, 1985.

Chapter 10
Figure 10-1. Ethnically mixed preschoolers at play. Credit: Joanne Ciccarello. Figure 10-2. Teacher and student. Credit: Martha Stewart, 1991. Figure 10-3. Street scene showing street signs in French. Credit: Owen Franken/Stock Boston.

TABLES AND FIGURES

Chapter 2
Table 2.3. By permission of Academic Press. Credit: Whitaker, H. 1976, A Case of the isolation . . . Studies in neurolinguistics, 11. (p. 39, 40, 43). Table 2.5. By permission of Scientific American. Credit: Kimura, D. 1973. The asymmetry of the human brain. Scientific American. 223-70-78 (p. 78.)

Chapter 5
Figure 5.1. By permission of The Board of Trustees of the University of Illinois. Credit: G. A. Miller & J. A. Selfridge, Verbal context and the recall of meaningful material. *American Journal of Psychology*, 1950, 63: Figure 1, page 181, and five, 20-word lists as indicated from pages 184 and 185. Figure 5.4. By permission of the American Psychological Association. Credit: E. A. L. Stine, On-line processing of written text by younger and older adults. *Psychology and Aging*, 1990, 5: Figure 1, page 73. Figure 5.5. By permission of The Psychonomic Society, Inc. Credit: J. S. Sachs, Recognition memory for syntactic and semantic aspects of connected discourse. *Perception and Psychophysics, 2*: Figure 2, page 441. (1967). Figure 5.6. By permission of The Psychonomic Society, Inc. Credit: L. K. Tyler & J. Wessels, Is gating an on-line task? Evidence from naming latency data. *Perception and Psychophysics, 38*: Figure 1, page 220. (1985). Table 1.5. By permission of Cambridge University Press. Credit: R. Martin, Neuropsychological evidence on the role of short-term memory in sentence processing. In G. Vallar & T. Shallice (Eds.), *Neuropsychological Impairments of Short-Term Memory*. Cambridge: Cambridge University Press, 1990: Table 15.1, page 406.

Chapter 8
Figure 8.7. By permission of Erlbaum Publishers. Credit: Slobin, D. 1985. The Cross-Linguistic Study of Language Acquisition. J. & P. DeVilliers. Chapter 1, Table 1.5, p. 113. Figure 8.8. By permission of Harvard University Press. Credit: R. Brown. 1973. A First Language. Cambridge, MA: Harvard University Press. p. 54 (3 tables).

Index